# FleaMarket Trader

## Fifteenth Edition

### THOUSANDS OF ITEMS WITH CURRENT VALUES

## COLLECTOR BOOKS
*A Division of Schroeder Publishing Co. Inc.*

*Editorial Staff:*

Michael Drollinger, Donna Newnum, Loretta Suiters
*Cover Design:*
Beth Summers
*Layout:*
Mary Ann Hudson

Collector Books
P.O. Box 3009
Paducah, KY 42002-3009

www.collectorbooks.com

Copyright © 2006 Schroeder Publishing Company

The current values in this book should be used only as a guide. They are not intended to set prices, which vary from one section of the country to another. Auction prices as well as dealer prices vary greatly and are affected by condition and demand. Neither the editors nor the publisher assumes responsibility for any losses which might be incurred as a result of consulting this guide.

**Searching For A Publisher?**

We are always looking for people knowledgeable within their fields. If you feel there is a real need for a book on your collectible subject and have a large comprehensive collection, contact Collector Books.

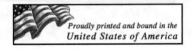

*Proudly printed and bound in the*
*United States of America*

# INTRODUCTION

The *Flea Market Trader* is a unique price guide, geared specifically for the convenience of the flea market shopper. Several categories have been included that are not often found in general price guides, while others on antiques not usually seen at flea markets have been omitted. The new categories will serve to introduce you to collectibles that are currently coming on, the best and often the only source for which is the market place. As all of us who religiously pursue the circuits are aware, flea markets are the most exciting places in the world to shop; but unless you're well informed on current values those 'really great' buys remain on the table. Like most pursuits in life, preparation has its own rewards; and it is our intention to provide you with the basic tool of education and awareness toward that end. But please bear in mind that the prices in this guide are meant to indicate only general values. Many factors determine actual selling prices; values vary from one region to another, dealers pay various wholesale prices for their wares, and your bargaining skill is important too.

We have organized our listings into general categories for easy use; if you have trouble locating an item, refer to the index. The values we have suggested reflect prices of items in mint condition. NM stands for minimal damage, VG indicates that the items will bring 40% to 60% of its mint price, and EX should be somewhere between the two. Glassware is assumed clear unless a color is noted. Only generally accepted abbreviations have been used.

Editors of
Schroeder Publishing Company

## ABBREVIATIONS

| | |
|---|---|
| dia — diameter | NRFB — never removed from box |
| ea — each | pc — piece |
| EX — excellent | pr — pair |
| gal — gallon | pt — pint |
| lb — pound | qt — quart |
| lg — large | sm — small |
| med — medium | sq — square |
| M — mint | VG — very good |
| MIB — mint in box | (+) — has been reproduced |

# Action Figures

The first line of action figures Hasbro developed in 1964 was GI Joe. It met with such huge success that Mego, Kenner, Mattel, and a host of other manufacturers soon began producing their own lines. Though GI Joe, Marx's Best of the West series, and several of Mego's figures were 12", others were 8" or 9" tall, and the most popular size in the last few years has been 3¾". Many lines came with accessory items such as vehicles, clothing, and guns. Original packaging (most now come on cards) is critical when it comes to evaluating your action figures, especially the more recent issues — they're seldom worth more than a few dollars if they've been played with. Values given MIB or MOC can be reduced by at least 60% when appraising a 'loose' figure in even the best condition. The market for action figures in general has become very soft over the past couple of years; there is very little interest in some of the lines that were once selling fairly well. We've tried to include those where trading is most active; some of these lines are beginning to show slight to moderate price increases.

Note: Some titles came in more than one size. MOC figures are the smaller standard size, while MIB figures are usually from 8" to 12" tall. Assume loose figures to be standard size unless noted otherwise. For more information refer to *Schroeder's Toys, Antique to Modern,* published by Collector Books.

See also GI Joe; Star Wars.

A-Team, accessory, Command Chopper & Enforcer Van, MIP............**25.00**

A-Team, accessory, Corvette (w/Face figure), Galoob, M....................**35.00**

A-Team, accessory, Off Road Attack Cycle, Galoob, MIP................**20.00**

A-Team, figure, Amy Allen, 6½", Galoob, MOC, from $28 to....................**32.00**

Action Jackson, accessory, Campmobile, Mego, MIB.....................**75.00**

Action Jackson, accessory, Jungle House, Mego, MIB.............**75.00**

Action Jackson, figure, Black, Mego, MIB, from $50 to................**60.00**

Action Jackson, figure, others, any MIB, from $25 to ..............**30.00**

**Action Jackson, outfit, Mego, MIP, any from $8.00 – 12.00.**

Alien, figure, Alien, 18", Kenner, MIB, from $400 to ...........**475.00**

Batman (Dark Knight), accessory, Joker Cycle, Kenner, MIB, from $20 to................................**25.00**

Batman (Dark Knight), figure, Night Glider, Kenner, MOC, from $30 to.........................**40.00**

Batman (Movie), figure, Batman (sq jaw), Toy Biz, MOC, from $20 to..**22.00**

Batman Crime Squad, accessory, Attack Jet, Kenner, MOC, from $12 to................**16.00**

Batman Forever, figure, Talking Riddler, Mego, MIP, from $18 to.........................22.00

Batman Returns, figure, Batman, 16", Kenner, MIB, from $60 to .......................65.00

Best of the West, figure, Bill Buck, Marx, MIB, from $400 to.....450.00

Best of the West, figure, Geronimo, Marx, MIB, from $125 to.......175.00

Best of the West, figure, Janice West, Marx, M, from $50 to.............75.00

Best of the West, figure, Johnny West, Marx, MIB, from $100 to.......................150.00

Best of the West, figure, Josie West, Marx, MIB, from $80 to .....110.00

Best of the West, figure, Princess Wildflower, Marx, MIB, from $150 to..............................175.00

Best of the West, horse, Comanche, Marx, MIB, from $100 to.......130.00

Big Jim, accessory, Boat & Buggy Set, Mattel, MIB, from $45 to.......................................55.00

Big Jim, accessory, Rescue Rig, Mattel, MIB, from $45 to............55.00

**Big Jim, figure, Baron Fangg, Mattel, MIB, from $40.00 to $60.00.**

Big Jim, figure, Big Jim, Mattel, MIB, from $65 to ...............85.00

Big Jim's PACK, accessory, Beast, Mattel, MIB, from $85 to.............110.00

Big Jim's PACK, figure, Torpedo Fist, Mattel, MIB, from $100 to.......................................150.00

Bionic Woman, accessory, Bubblin' Bath 'n Shower, Kenner, MIB, $50 to...............................75.00

**Bionic Woman, accessory, Designer Collection blue denim pantsuit, MOC, from $18.00 to $22.00.**

Bionic Woman, figure, Jaime Sommers, Kenner, MIB, from $125 to ..150.00

Bionic Woman, figure, Jaime Sommers (w/purse), Kenner, MIB, $160 to..............................180.00

Black Hole, figure, Humanoid, Mego, MOC, from $650 to ...............675.00

Black Hole, figure, STAR, Mego, MOC, from $275 to..........325.00

Buck Rogers, accessory, Land Rover, Mego, NMIB, from $30 to..50.00

Buck Rogers, figure, Dr Huer or Draco, Mego, MOC, ea from $18 to.........................................22.00

Buck Rogers, figure, Star Seeker, Mego, MOC, from $55 to.....75.00

Buck Rogers, figure, Tiger Man, 12", MIB, from $120 to .............130.00

Captain Action, accessory, Action Cave, Ideal, MIP, from $600 to..675.00

Captain Action, figure, Action Boy, Ideal, MIB, from $850 to .....**875.00**

Captain Action, figure, Ideal, loose (from Lone Ranger box), $200 to.......................................**230.00**

Captain Action, outfit, Batman, Ideal, M, from $175 to.....**225.00**

Captain Action, outfit, Buck Rogers (w/ring), Ideal, MIB, from $2,000 to.......................**2,500.00**

Captain Action, outfit, Flash Gordon, Ideal, M, from $175 to....**225.00**

Captain Action, outfit, Green Hornet (w/ring), Ideal, MIB, $6,000 to .**6,500.00**

Captain Action, outfit, Lone Ranger, Ideal, M, from $150 to....**175.00**

Captain Action, outfit, Steve Canyon, Ideal, M, from $200 to.....**225.00**

Captain Action, outfit, Superman, Ideal, M, from $150 to.....**175.00**

Captain Action, outfit, Tonto (w/ring), Ideal, MIB, from $900 to..**1,000.00**

CHiPs, accessory, motorcycle (for 3¾" figures), Mego, MIP, $25 to.........................................**35.00**

CHiPs, figure, Jon, 8", Mego, MOC ...**52.00**

Clash of the Titans, figure, Kraken, Mattel, rare, MOC, from $240 to.........................................**260.00**

Clash of the Titans, figure, Thallo, Mattel, MOC, from $40 to.............**45.00**

Dukes of Hazzard, figure, Bo, Mego, 8", MOC, from $28 to........**32.00**

Dukes of Hazzard, figure, Boss Hogg, Mego, 3¾", MOC, from $18 to.................................**22.00**

Dukes of Hazzard, figure, Boss Hogg, Mego, 8", MOC, from $38 to.........................................**42.00**

Dukes of Hazzard, figure, Coy or Vance, Mego, 3¾", MOC, ea $28 to.........................................**32.00**

Dukes of Hazzard, figure, Daisy, Mego, 3¾", MOC, from $25 to.....**28.00**

Dukes of Hazzard, figure, Daisy, Mego, 8", MOC, from $48 to........**52.00**

Dukes of Hazzard, figure, Luke, Mego, 3¾", MOC, from $18 to.....**22.00**

Dukes of Hazzard, figure, Luke, Mego, 8", MOC..................**32.00**

**Dukes of Hazard, figures, Boss Hogg, Mego, 8", M, from $24.00 to $28.00; Bo Duke, Mego, 8", M, from $15.00 to $18.00.**

Happy Days, accessory, Fonz's Garage, Mego, MIB, from $140 to.........................................**160.00**

Happy Days, accessory, Fonz's Jalopy or Motorcycle, Mego, MIB, ea..............................**85.00**

Indiana Jones, figure, Indiana, Kenner, 12", MIB, from $200 to....**275.00**

Indiana Jones (Adventures of), figure, Belloq, Kenner, MOC, from $45 to ....................**55.00**

Indiana Jones (Adventures of), figure, Sallah, Kenner, M, from $25 to..**35.00**

Indiana Jones (Adventures of), figure, Sallah, Kenner, MOC, from $90 to ..........................**100.00**

Indiana Jones (Adventures of), figure, Toht, Kenner, MOC, from $38 to...........................**42.00**

James Bond, figure, Bond, Gilbert, MIB, from $300 to ...........**350.00**

James Bond, figure, Bond (Pierce Brosnan), Mediacom, MIB ............**85.00**

James Bond, figure, Oddjob, Gilbert, 12", MIB, from $200 to ....**225.00**

**James Bond (Moonraker), figure, Bond, Mego, 12½", MIB, from $140.00 to $160.00.**

James Bond (Moonraker), figure, Jaws, Mego, MIB, from $475 to................................**525.00**

Legend of Lone Ranger, figure, Lone Ranger, Gabriel, MOC, from $24 to.................................**28.00**

Legend of Lone Ranger, horse, Scout, Gabriel, MOC, from $18 to.........................................**22.00**

Legend of Lone Ranger, horse, Silver, Gabriel, MOC, from $28 to.........................................**32.00**

Legend of Lone Ranger, horse, Smoke, Gabriel, MOC, from $24 to.........................................**26.00**

Lone Ranger Rides Again, accessory, Landslide, Gabriel, MIB, $25 to.........................................**30.00**

Lord of the Rings, figure, any, Toy Vault, MOC, ea from $8 to......**10.00**

M*A*S*H, accessory, Jeep (w/Hawkeye figure), Tri-Star, MIB, $25 to..**30.00**

M*A*S*H, figure, Hot Lips, Tri-Star, MOC, from $25 to..............**30.00**

M*A*S*H, figure, Klinger (in dress), Tri-Star, MOC, from $25 to.........................................**35.00**

Major Matt Mason, accessory, Rocket Launch, Mattel, MIB, from $70 to.........................................**80.00**

Major Matt Mason, accessory, Satellite Locker, Mattel, MIP, from $65 to................................**75.00**

Major Matt Mason, accessory, Space Probe, Mattel, MIB, from $70 to.........................................**80.00**

Major Matt Mason, accessory, Space Station, Mattel, MIB, from $250 to.......................................**300.00**

Major Matt Mason, figure, Callistro, Mattel, M, from $90 to ....**110.00**

Major Matt Mason, figure, Callistro, Mattel, MOC, from $200 to ...........................**225.00**

Major Matt Mason, figure, Jeff Long, Mattel, M, from $150 to................................**175.00**

Major Matt Mason, figure, Scorpio, Mattel, MOC, from $775 to.......................................**800.00**

Major Matt Mason, figure, Sgt Storm, MOC, from $350 to ..............**375.00**

Man From UNCLE, figure, Illya Kuryakin, Gilbert, MIB, from $325 to.............................**375.00**

Man From UNCLE, figure, Napoleon Solo, Gilbert, MIB, from $325 to ..**375.00**

Marvel Super Heroes, figure, Captain America, Toy Biz, MOC, $18 to..................................**22.00**

**Marvel Super Heroes, Secret Wars figure, Dr. Doom, MOC, from $18.00 to $22.00.**

Masters of the Universe, figure, Faker, Mattel, MOC, from $115 to......................................**125.00**

Masters of the Universe, figure, Grizzlor, Mattel, MOC, from $38 to..................................**42.00**

Masters of the Universe, figure, Man-E-Faces, Mattel, MOC, from $45 to.........................**55.00**

Masters of the Universe, figure, Modulok, Mattel, MOC, from $30 to..................................**35.00**

Masters of the Universe, figure, Prince Adam, Mattel, MOC, from $55 to.**65.00**

Masters of the Universe, figure, Rattlor, Mattel, MOC, from $30 to.**35.00**

Masters of the Universe, figure, Roboto, Mattel, MOC, from $30 to......................................**35.00**

Masters of the Universe, figure, Rokkon, Mattel, MOC, from $30 to......................................**35.00**

Masters of the Universe, figure, Zodac, Mattel, MOC, from $45 to......................................**55.00**

Micronauts, figure, Baron Karza, Mego, MIB, from $30 to......**35.00**

Micronauts, figure, Lobros, Mego, MOC, from $150 to..........**175.00**

One Million BC, accessory, Tribal Lair, Mego, MIB, from $150 to....................................**175.00**

One Million BC, creature, Hairy Rhino, Mego, MIB, from $225 to ...............................**275.00**

Planet of the Apes, accessory, Catapult & Wagon, MIB, from $125 to.**165.00**

Pocket Super Heroes, accessory, Batcave, Mego, MIB, from $275 to....................................**325.00**

Pocket Super Heroes, accessory, Spider-Machine, Mego, MIB, from $75 to..............................**125.00**

Pocket Super Heroes, figure, General Zod, Mego, MOC (red card), from $20 to........................**30.00**

Pocket Super Heroes, figure, Robin, Mego, MOC (red card), from $55 to......................................**65.00**

Power Lords, figure, any, MOC, ea from $20 to........................**30.00**

Six Million Dollar Man, figure, Oscar Goldman, Kenner, MIB, from $90 to......................**110.00**

Starsky & Hutch, accessory, car, Mego, MIB, from $150 to ................**175.00**

Super Heroes, figure, Aquaman, Mego, 8", M, from $55 to......**60.00**

Super Heroes, figure, Batgirl, Mego, 8", MOC, from $250 to ...............................**275.00**

Super Heroes, figure, Batman (removable mask), Mego, 8", MIB, from $500 to ...........**550.00**

Super Heroes, figure, Catwoman, Mego, 8", MIB, from $300 to ...............................**325.00**

Super Heroes, figure, Green Goblin, Mego, 8", MOC, from $850 to.....................900.00

Super Heroes, figure, Iron Man, Mego, 8", MOC, from $400 to .............................425.00

Super Heroes, figure, Mr Fantastic, Mego, 8", MOC, from $55 to................................65.00

Super Heroes, figure, Penguin, Mego, 8", MIB, from $145 to.............................165.00

Super Heroes, figure, Riddler, Mego, 8", MIB, from $200 to.............................225.00

Super Heroes, figure, Shazam, Mego, 8", M, from $55 to...................65.00

Super Heroes, figure, Spider-Man, Mego, 8", MIB, from $75 to ...........................100.00

Super Heroes, figure, Spider-Man, Mego, 12½", MIB, from $120 to......................................130.00

**Super Heroes, figure, Spider-Man, multi-jointed, marked D.C. Comics 1977 on head and 1978 Mego Corp. on back, 12¼", M, $60.00.**

Super Heroes, figure, Superman, Mego, 8", MIB (window box), from $150 to.....................175.00

Super Heroes, figure, Thing, Mego, 8", M, from $40 to................45.00

Super Heroes, figure, Thing, Mego, 8", MOC, from $55 to...65.00

Super Heroes, figure, Thor, Mego, 8", M, from $145 to.........165.00

Super Heroes, figure, Wonder Woman, Mego, 8", MIB, from $300 to............................325.00

Super Heroes, figure, Wondergirl, Mego, 8", MOC, from $350 to ...............................375.00

Super Powers, figure, Aquaman, Kenner, MOC, from $45 to............50.00

Super Powers, figure, Batman, Kenner, MOC, from $70 to..............................80.00

Super Powers, figure, Cyclotron, Kenner, M, from $38 to.....40.00

Super Powers, figure, Green Arrow, Kenner, MOC, from $45 to............................50.00

Super Powers, figure, Joker, Kenner, MOC, from $25 to...................35.00

Super Powers, figure, Mr Freeze, Kenner, MOC, from $60 to..............................70.00

Super Powers, figure, Red Tornado, Kenner, MOC, from $75 to.......................................80.00

Super Powers, figure, Shazam, Kenner, MOC, from $50 to ................60.00

Super Powers, figure, Superman, Kenner, MOC, from $32 to..38.00

Teen Titans, figure, Kid Flash, Mego, MOC, from $400 to...........425.00

Waltons, accessory, barn or country store, Mego, MIB, ea from $75 to.....................................100.00

Waltons, accessory, farmhouse (only), Mego, MIB, from $125 to .....................................175.00

Waltons, accessory, truck, Mego, MIB, from $65 to ..............75.00

Wizard of Oz, figure, Wizard, Mego, 8", MIB, from $245 to.........265.00

# Advertising Collectibles

As far back as the turn of the century, manufacturers used characters that identified with their products. They were always personable, endearing, amusing, and usually succeeded in achieving just the effect the producer had in mind, which was to make the product line more visual, more familiar, and therefore one the customer would more often than not choose over the competition. Magazine ads, display signs, product cartons, and TV provided just the right exposure for these ad characters. Elsie the Cow became so well known that at one point during a random survey, more people recognized her photo than one of the president!

There are scores of advertising characters, and many have been promoted on a grand scale. Today's collectors search for the dolls, banks, cookie jars, mugs, plates, and scores of other items modeled after or bearing the likenesses of their favorites, several of which are featured in our listings.

Condition plays a vital role in evaluating vintage advertising pieces. Our estimates are for items in at least near-mint condition, unless another condition code is present in the description. Try to be very objective when you assess wear and damage.

For more information we recommend *Antique and Collectible Advertising Memorabilia* by B.J. Summers. See also Breweriana; Bubble Bath Containers; Character and Promotional Glassware; Novelty Telephones; Pin-Back Buttons; Radios. See Clubs and Newsletters for information concerning *The Prize Insider* newsletter for Cracker Jack collectors and Peanut Pals, a club for collectors of Planters Peanuts.

Alka-Seltzer, thermometer, dial, metal/glass, 12" dia, EX+ .....**130.00**
American Steel Farm Fences, match holder, tin litho, 3½x5", VG .....**85.00**
Arden Ice Cream, porcelain sign, oval, 1959, 36x48" .....**425.00**

**Aunt Jemima and Uncle Mose salt and pepper shakers, plastic, F&F, 5", MIB with flyer dated 1957, $150.00 (EX no box, $75.00).**

Aunt Jemima, batter spoon, slotted alumimun, wirework handle, 1948, EX .....**30.00**
Aunt Jemima, Jr Chef Pancake Set, Argo Industries, 1949, EX .....**150.00**
Aunt Jemima, measuring cup, clear w/red pyro, Fire-King, 2-cup, EX .....**95.00**
Aunt Jemima, paperweight, etched glass, 1978 .....**45.00**
Aunt Jemima, recipe book, Cake Mix Miracles, 1950s, EX .....**35.00**

Aunt Jemima, recipe cards, from famous eating places, set of 16, VG ..................100.00

Big Boy, comic book, Adventures of Big Boy, #001..................250.00

Big Boy, decal, Big Boy for President ..................10.00

Big Boy, handbook, employee; 1956..................100.00

Big Boy, neon clock, Big Boy logo, working ..................100.00

Big Boy, playing cards, red, unopened..................25.00

Big Boy, yo-yo, wood, 1 side blue, other red, 1956..................35.00

Big Smith Work Clothes, clock/sign, light-up, electric, 22x20", EX..................135.00

Borden, book, Elsie's Funbook Cut-Out Toys & Games, 1940s, EX..................65.00

Borden, butter mold, Elsie or Beulah, ea..................28.00

Borden, creamer, Elsie's head on heavy china, no handle, Shenango, 2" ..................60.00

Borden, figurine, Elsie, PVC, 1993, 3½" ..................10.00

Borden, milk bottle, clear w/red lettering, ½-pt, M..................15.00

Borden, nightlight, Elsie head, rubber-type composition, 9", EX..................180.00

**Borden, paper sign, Elsie, multicolor, 9x27", EX, $125.00.**

Borden, push-button puppet, Elsie, wood, EX..................125.00

Borden, tablecloth, Elsie's family barbecue, print on white, 56" L, EX..................75.00

Bosco Chocolate, doll, Bosco the Clown, vinyl..................45.00

BP Clarke & Co, candy scoop, embossed glass, 7", VG .....175.00

Buster Brown, bank, molded plastic, atop ball, 1960s, 4" dia, EX..25.00

Buster Brown, comic book, 1959, EX..................25.00

Buster Brown, kite, 1940s..........40.00

Buster Brown, watch fob, BB Shoes, celluloid, 1930s..................125.00

Cadbury Chocolates, sign, tin, cocoa beans on red, 11¼x9", EX..110.00

Camel, ashtray, Joe and friend in car, cobalt glass, MIP........20.00

Camel, baseball cap, leather, purple crown w/black trim..............20.00

Camel, beach towel, Joe & the Hard Pack Band..................20.00

Camel, clock, neon (blue to pink), Joe playing saxophone, 15" dia, MIB ..................65.00

Camel, lighter, Zippo, 75th Birthday, MIB ..................28.00

Camel, plate, Joe playing pool, 14k gold rim, limited edition, MIB ..................35.00

Campbell's, doll, girl as cheerleader, 1967, vinyl, 8", EX ..........75.00

Campbell's, figurine, Downhill Racer, china, Leeber, 1999.........25.00

Campbell's, shirt, cotton w/red & white soup can..................10.00

Cap'n Crunch, Big Slick Gyro Car, blue plastic, 1972, MIP .....15.00

Cap'n Crunch, coloring book, Whitman, 1968, VG..................20.00

Cap'n Crunch, ring, plastic figure, M ..........100.00

Cap'n Crunch, wiggle figures, 3 different, 1969, EX, ea ..........50.00

Carhartt's Overalls & Gloves, poster, cloth back, worker, 58x40", VG ..........650.00

Castle Hall Twins Cigars, stork figure w/sign, chalk, 22", VG .550.00

Charlie Tuna, clock, wall; Charlie w/ fish friend, quartz, 8½" dia ..36.00

Charlie Tuna, pendant, Charlie on anchor ..........10.00

Cheetos, doll, Chester Cheetah, plush, 21", MIP ..........20.00

Colonel Sanders, bank, plastic figure, dated 1977, 7½" ..........12.50

Colonel Sanders, camera, figural, Japan premium, 3x4", MIB ..35.00

Colonel Sanders, coin, Visit the Colonel at Mardi Gras ..........10.00

Colonel Sanders, hand puppet, in white suit, plastic, 1960s, EX.....20.00

Colonel Sanders, mask, multicolored plastic, 1960s ..........38.00

Colonel Sanders, pin, lapel; Colonel's head, metal, EX ..........6.50

Colonel Sanders, poker chip, plastic, w/portrait, 1960s, M ..........17.50

Colonel Sanders, tie tac, gold-tone molded head w/diamond chip ........65.00

Cracker Jack, badge, ...Police on silver-tone metal star, 1931, 1¼" ..........55.00

Cracker Jack, circus figure, plastic, stands on base, Nosco, 1951-54 .3.00

Cracker Jack, decal, cartoon or nursery rhyme figure, marked, 1947-49 ..........12.00

Cracker Jack, Fortune Teller Game, spinner, tin & wood, marked, 1½" ..........90.00

Cracker Jack, hat, paper, Me for Cracker Jack, early ..........120.00

Cracker Jack, lunch box, embossed tin, 1970s, 4x7x9" ..........30.00

Cracker Jack, mirror, oval, Angelus (redhead or blond) on box.......89.00

Cream Dove Shortening/Peanut Butter, pocket mirror, boy w/can, EX ..........300.00

Dad's Root Beer, sign, tin, red/yellow/ black, 9x18", VG ..........110.00

Dairy Queen, ring, Mr Softee, premium, 1960s, VG+ ..........15.00

Del Monte, doll, Shoo Shoo Scarecrow, 1983, stuffed plush ..15.00

Energizer Batteries, squeeze light, Energizer Bunny figure, MIP..8.00

Eskimo Pie, doll, Eskimo Pie boy, stuffed cloth, 1970s, 15", EX..15.00

Eveready Batteries, display case, tin, 17x11x9¼", EX..........300.00

Florida Oranges, bank, Orange Bird, vinyl, 1974, MIP ..........40.00

Green Giant, dinnerware set, w/plate, cup, knife & fork, 1991, MIB ..........10.00

Green Giant, doll, Little Sprout, stuffed cloth, 1974, 10½" ..........15.00

Green Giant, fabric, Green Giant & Little Sprout, 48x45" ........20.00

Green Giant, flashlight, Little Sprout, MIB ..........45.00

Green Giant, jump rope, Little Sprout, MIB ..........20.00

Green Giant, lapel pin, Green Giant ..7.00

Green Giant, planter, Little Sprout, Benjamin Medwin, 1988, MIB.......35.00

Green Giant, spoon rest, Little Sprout, Benjamin Medwin, 1988, MIB ..........30.00

Hambone 5¢ Cigars, menu board, cardboard, 20¼x13", VG .....40.00

Hawaiian Punch, doll, Punchy, talking, Fun-4-All, 15", MIB ............**15.00**

Icee, bank, Icee bear w/drink in front of him, rubber, 7", EX ...............**30.00**

Jell-O, puppet, Mr Wiggles, red vinyl, 1966 ......................**150.00**

Jordache, doll, Jeans Man, Mego, 12", MIB ............................**30.00**

Kodak, doll, Colorkins, stuffed, ca 1980, 8" to 10", ea .............**20.00**

Kodak Film, sign, tin 2-sided diecut, multicolor on yellow, 14x18", VG ....................................**100.00**

Kool Cigarettes, figure, Dr Kool, chalk, 4½", VG ...................**95.00**

Levi's, rag doll, Knickerbocker, 1984, 24", EX ...................**120.00**

M&M, alarm clock, red figure in blue hat, dial in tummy, MIB........**50.00**

M&M, beanbag toys, peanut shape, golfer or witch, 6", ea.........**10.00**

M&M, clock, M&Ms Racing Team, quartz, battery-operated, MIB...................................**30.00**

M&M, dispenser, M&M shape, brown, 1991, sm...................**5.00**

M&M, dispenser, M&M shape, red, 1991, lg.............................**10.00**

M&M, dispenser, peanut shape, red, 1992, lg..............................**15.00**

M&M, dispenser, Rock 'n Roll Cafe, MIB .................................**45.00**

M&M, doll, M&M shape, plush, red, 12" .......................................**10.00**

M&M, doll, M&M shape, plush, 4½"..**5.00**

M&M, doll, M&M shape, plush, 8", EX..................................**50.00**

M&M, lamp, red figure w/spotlight atop blue & yellow figures, 20", MIB ...................................**40.00**

M&M, topper, green figure w/candy cane & Santa hat.................**10.00**

M&M, wind chimes, bag of M&Ms w/5 candies suspended below, 13"..**25.00**

Magic Chef, bank, molded vinyl, 1980s, 7", EX......................**20.00**

Meow Mix, figure, vinyl cat, EX.......**35.00**

Michelin, costume, Mr Bib, nylon & metal w/yellow sash, EX.....**900.00**

Michelin, cup, plastic, Mr Bib on side, EX...............................**5.00**

Michelin, pendant, Mr Bib figural, metal, 2", EX......................**15.00**

**Michelin, sign, Mr. Bib on motorbike, metal, double-sided, flanged, 19x18", VG+, $110.00.**

Mr Goodbar, pillow, candy bar shape, 4x6"..........................**8.00**

Old Crow, ashtray, Bakelite, 3½" dia....................................**25.00**

Old Crow, Bingo card, 100 proof, late 1940s, 6½x8¼" ....................**45.00**

Old Crow, bottle opener, plastic figure .....................................**35.00**

Old Crow, dice cup, Bakelite, black w/yellow lettering, felt-lined, M .....................................**100.00**

Old Crow, figure, painted plastic, 1950s, 4", EX.....................**30.00**

Oscar Mayer, bank, Weinermobile, plastic, 1988, 10" ...............**25.00**

Oshkosh B' Gosh Overalls, sign, porcelain, red/white/black, 10x30", VG ......................**130.00**

Pillsbury, bank, Poppin' Fresh, ceramic, mail-in premium, 1980s ...................................35.00

Pillsbury, canister, glass, clamp-on lid, from $18 to .................25.00

Pillsbury, decals, Poppin' Fresh, set of 18, MIP...........................18.00

Pillsbury, doll, Poppin' Fresh, plush, MIP......................................40.00

Pillsbury, figure, Popover Place, Danbury Mint, MIB ........100.00

Pillsbury, figure, Poppin' Fresh, vinyl, 1971, 7"...................15.00

Pillsbury, key chain, Poppin' Fresh figure, soft vinyl, MOC.........6.00

Pillsbury, puppet, Poppin' Fresh, vinyl & thin plastic, 1971, EX.....................................25.00

Pillsbury, timer, plastic, digital, 1992....................................10.00

Pillsbury, toaster cover, Poppin' Fresh w/cookie on blue w/lace, EX.....................................32.00

Planters, bank, Mr Peanut figure, clear plastic, 1950s-70s, EX, from $90 to......................150.00

Planters, baseball, image of Mr Peanut, EX..........................5.00

Planters, beach ball, yellow w/blue Mr Peanut, 1970s, 13½", EX.....................................10.00

Planters, cook booklet, Planter's Oil, 1948, EX............................25.00

Planters, doll, Mr Peanut, stuffed cloth, Chase Bag Co, 1967, 21", EX.....................................40.00

Planters, mug, Mr Peanut head, yellow plastic, 3¾".........40.00

Planters, mug, Mr Peanut head, tan plastic, M ...........................10.00

Planters, peanut butter maker, Picam, 1970s, 12", MIB.....50.00

**Planters, peanut container, shaped to resemble a peanut, 11", VG, $45.00.** (Photo courtesy B.J. Summers)

Planters, radio backpack, Munch 'N Go, 1991, EX, from $35 to ...................................40.00

Planters, standee, cardboard Mr Peanut figure, 12"..............10.00

Planters, tankard, metal pewter type, Wilton, 1983, 4¾".....10.00

Planters, toy train set, battery-operated, 1988, MIB................50.00

Planters, whistle, Mr Peanut figural, plastic, 2½", EX .................15.00

Player Tobacco, sign, cardboard, boxing scene, 19x14", VG.............110.00

Quick Meal Ranges, tip tray, chickens, 4½x3¼", VG ...............85.00

RCA, Nipper figure, crystal, Fenton, 4" .........................................60.00

RCA Victor, necktie, Nipper......20.00

RCA Victor, Nipper figure, rubber or plastic, 18", VG/EX..........150.00

RCA Victor, salt & pepper shakers, dog & phonograph, plastic, pr......................................45.00

RCA Victor, toy truck, RCA Television Service, Marx, 8½", MIB ..............................235.00

Reading Premium, clock, glass lens, 15" dia, VG......................155.00

Red Goose Shoes, card game, Cities, incomplete, w/box, VG....................................18.00

Reddy Kilowatt, apron, Reddy in garden w/She Loves Me, plastic, EX......................................30.00
Reddy Kilowatt, decal, 1960s, 12".......................................40.00
Reddy Kilowatt, earrings, brass w/red enamel, 1", EX, pr...............25.00
Reddy Kilowatt, mug, Reddy golfing, heavy china, Care Force, 1993, NM......................................40.00
Reddy Kilowatt, nodder figural, Wacky Wobbler, Funko, 7½", MIB......................................35.00

**Reddy Kilowatt, porcelain sign, red, white, and blue, 36x48", G, $230.00. (Photo courtesy B.J. Summers)**

Reddy Kilowatt, tape measure, chrome w/red image & name, EX......................................35.00
Reese's, doll, Reese's Bear, in Reese's T-shirt, 1989.........................10.00
Royal Marshmallows, glass container w/embossed letters, 12x10", EX......................................275.00
Royal Purple Grape Juice, tray, tin litho, elegant lady, 13", EX..385.00
Sinclair Oil, soap, Dino the Dinosaur figure, MIB........10.00
Smokey Bear, bank, ceramic figural, Japan, 1950s, 7".....................75.00
Smokey Bear, belt buckle, cast metal, 2½x1¾".....................18.00

Smokey Bear, blotter, I Will Be Careful, 1955, unused, EX..............8.00
Smokey Bear, bobbin' head, composition, Made in Japan, 6", EX.140.00
Smokey Bear, doll, Knickerbocker, complete w/all accessories, 17", EX......................................35.00
Smokey Bear, hand puppet, Ideal, 1969......................................35.00
Smokey Bear, mug, milk glass, Help Prevent & Smokey's head, 1960s......................................18.00
Smokey Bear, sheet, Smokey in forest w/friends, 1970s, twin size..15.00
Smokey Bear, thermos, w/original cap & lid, 1960s.................55.00
Squirrel Brand Peanuts, jar, clear glass w/paper label, tin lid, G....75.00
Stokeley's, tray, tin litho, yellow & black, 13¼x10½", VG........25.00
Texaco, sign, porcelain, star logo, multi-color on white, 15" dia, EX..500.00
Tony's Frozen Pizza, Mr Tony figure, vinyl, 8½", EX....................25.00
Tru-Pack Aspirin, cardboard display, easel-back, 8¾x12", VG .45.00

## Advertising Tins

Attractive packaging has always been a powerful marketing tool; today, those colorful tin containers that once held products ranging from cookies and dog food to motor oil and tobacco are popular collectibles.

For more information we recommend *Modern Collectible Tins* by Linda McPherson.

Baker's Cocoa, cardboard w/tin top, W Baker Co, 7x3¾x2½", EX.....15.00

Benjamin Franklin Brand Typewriter Ribbon, portrait, 2½" dia, EX...............................**25.00**

Benson & Hedges Virginia Rounds Cigarettes, 3¼x2¾", EX, from $10 to..............................**15.00**

Big Hit Coffee, Euclid Coffee Co, marked AC Co 68A, 4x5" dia, EX....................................**25.00**

Black Cat Cigarette Tobacco, cat on yellow, cylindrical, 4", EX..**20.00**

Cook's Cocoa, red, white & brown, sq, 6", EX............................**35.00**

De Parma Violet Talcum Powder, flowers on green ground, 4½x2½x1¼", EX..............**25.00**

**Dove Pumpkin Pie Spice, black and white on orange, 2x2½x1¼", EX, $20.00.** (Photo courtesy Fred Dodge)

Griffin ABC Black Wax Shoe Polish, 1x2½" dia, EX......................**5.00**

Hi-Plane Tobacco, red, white & blue, #701, 6½x5½" dia, EX....**125.00**

Honeymoon Cream Mints, blue & white, FH Leggett NY, 1¾x4x2¼", NM.................**20.00**

Kroger's Country Club Coffee, red & gold, 3½x5", EX, from $10 to.......................................**15.00**

Lady Churchill Cigars, gold lettering, 1930s, 3½x5¼x1¼", EX......**50.00**

McCormick's Bee Brand Cloves, black & red on cream, 3½x2¼x1"..**20.00**

McK & R Aspirin, brown, white & yellow, ¼x1¾x1¼", EX........**8.00**

Mennen Quinsana, black, cream & green, sq, 5x1½x1½", NM..**30.00**

Nescafé, Nestlé's Milk Products, red & yellow, 3¼x2½" dia, NM....................................**25.00**

No-Moth Reefer-Galler, red, white & black, 1950s, EX...............**18.00**

Porter's Laxative, cream & green, National Can, ⅜x1⅞x1½", EX...............................**12.00**

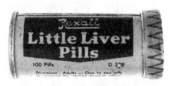

**Rexall Little Liver Pills, 1x1¾", EX, $15.00.** (Photo courtesy David Zimmerman)

Richmond Belle...Cut Plug, black, orange, yellow, 1x4½x3¼", EX....................................**15.00**

Rosemary Brand Sage, lady & flowers, Continental Can, 3x2x1", EX....................................**35.00**

Snowdrift Coconut, red paper label, oversize, 14¾x13", EX...**90.00**

Turret Cigarettes, 4-color on white, Imperial Tobacco, 1x5½x3"..**25.00**

Vantine's Rose Incense, Buddah, 4x1⅜x¼", EX ...................**15.00**

Watkins Pure Ground Mustard, portrait on red, 3¼x2x1¼", EX....................................**35.00**

Williams Talk La Tosca Rose, sample size, 3¼x1⅜x¾", EX...**55.00**

ZBT Baby Powder, babies on pink & blue, sq, 5⅛x1¾x1¾", EX...**22.00**

# Aluminum

From the late 1930s until early in the 1950s, kitchenwares and household items were often crafted of aluminum, usually with relief-molded fruit or flowers on a hammered background. Today many find that these diversified items make an attractive collection. Especially desirable are those examples marked with the manufacturer's backstamp or the designer's signature.

You've probably also seen the anodized (colored) aluminum pitchers, tumblers, sherbet holders, etc., that were popular in the late '50s, early '60s. Interest in these items has exploded, as prices on eBay sales attest. Be sure to check condition, though, as scratching and wear reduce values drastically. The more uncommon forms are especially collectible.

For more information refer to *Collectible Aluminum, An Identification and Value Guide* (Collector Books), by Everett Grist.

Unless noted otherwise, our values are for examples in mint to near-mint conditon.

Ashtray, Pine Cone, Wendell August Forge, 6" dia......................**25.00**
Basket, tulips, floral handle, Rodney Kent, 1930s, 5x7"..................**20.00**
Bowl, anodized, Bascal, 6", set of 8, EX......................................**26.00**
Bowl, Dogwood, fluted & crimped rim, Wendell August Forge, 2x7" dia ..............................**20.00**

Bowl, flat bottom, handles, Rodney Kent, 2⅝x8"......................**15.00**
Bowl, leaf shape, stem handle, Bruce Fox, 8¾x16¼"..........**55.00**
Bowl, Tulips, ear handles, serrated rim, Rodney Kent, 2x10" .....**35.00**
Box, cigarette; Bittersweet, Wendell August Forge, 1½x3x5".....**75.00**
Cake stand, band of shields, serrated edge, Wilson Metal, 8x12" ......**15.00**
Cake stand, pedestal foot, scalloped dome lid, 10x13" dia............**28.00**
Candleholders, triple; curved ribbon-like base, Bruce Box, 5¼", pr......................................**100.00**
Casserole, Apple, flower finial, Everlast, 5x9" ............................**8.00**
Casserole, Pyrex-type bowl w/Buenilum marked lid, 7½x11".**17.50**
Coaster, Capitol Building in Washington DC, Alpha Swiss, 4½" dia......................................**3.00**
Coasters, anodized pastel colors, duck scene, 3¼", set of 8..............**20.00**
Coasters, strong anodized colors, set of 8......................................**25.00**

**Coffee urn, Chrysanthemum, Continental Silver Co., $65.00; Coaster set, $25.00.**

Crumber & tray, leaf design, Everlast......................................**18.00**

Cups, anodized, Heller Hostess Ware, set of 8, MIP...........**45.00**

Cups, anodized, 5½", set of 6 ...........**30.00**

Dessert bowls, anodized, w/glass inserts, 3½", set of 8............**50.00**

Fish dish, Royal Hickman, EX details, 18¾x8⅛".............**85.00**

Ice bucket, flower intaglio, Everlast, 3x7" dia.............**20.00**

Ice bucket, hammered effect, black handles & finial, Kromex, 12x8" dia.............**10.00**

Ice bucket, red apple shape, anodized, 7"............**25.00**

Leaf dish, veins, turned-up edge, Buenilum, 6"............**10.00**

Measuring scoops, anodized, ½ cup, ⅓-cup & ¼-cup, set of 3 .....**20.00**

Mug, pink anodized, 3x3"...........**7.50**

Napkin rings, anodized, narrow, set of 8, MIB ............**28.00**

Pitcher, gold anodized, w/ice lip, unmarked............**28.00**

Pitcher, hammered effect, Buenilum, 8x6" dia .................**25.00**

Plate, Dogwood, Wendell August Forge, 9"............**18.00**

Plate, Intaglio, leaves along rim, EMPC/Everlast, 11¼" .......**17.00**

Popcorn set, anodized, 11" bowl w/4 5" individuals....................**30.00**

Refrigerator boxes, 5¼x4⅜", anodized, set of 4, various colors, from $40 to.........................**50.00**

Rolling pin, anodized, w/stand, EX .............**30.00**

Salad fork & spoon, unmarked, 12", pr ...........**45.00**

Salad set, Bascal, anodized, lg bowl & 8 footed individuals, EX+....**50.00**

Shot glasses, anodized, set of 6 on tray.......................**30.00**

Silent Butler, Rose, Everlast, 6" dia........................**10.00**

Spoon rest, green anodized, 3 rests....................**23.00**

Spoons, iced tea; anodized, 8", set of 6.............................**25.00**

Straw/stirrer, anodized, set of 12, from $25 to.........................**30.00**

Teakettle, blue anodized w/yellow lid, green Bakelite handle, 8¾"..**55.00**

Tray, Bamboo, 2-tier, bamboo finial, Everlast, 9x10" dia..............**15.00**

Tray, bar; rope & sea gulls, applied handles, Everlast, 15x9" ...**30.00**

Tray, bread; Apple Blossom, fluted sides, unmarked, 13x9".......**5.00**

Tray, cheese & cracker; Acorn & Leaf, Continental, 15" dia..............**15.00**

Tray, Dogwood, gold anodized, Arthur Armour, 5"............**10.00**

Tray, fish form, Bruce Fox, 22½x7"..**85.00**

Tray, horses, handles, Everlast, 12x16" .............**15.00**

Tray, Larkspur, Wendell August Forge, 13x20"....................**75.00**

Tray, lazy Suzan; on pedestal, Wilson Medal Prod..., 3x12"..............**25.00**

Tray, Pine Cone, twisted tab handles, Everlast, 14x6" ...................**22.00**

Tray, pineapple shape, leaf handle, Bruce Box, 13x6½" ...........**32.00**

Tray, purple anodized, 14" dia .....**15.00**

Tray, snack; fruit, lipped, self handles, 10x6" ..........................**2.00**

Tray, tulips on hammered ground, Everlasting Treasures, 16x11½" .....**15.00**

Tree ornaments, Christmas bells, anodized, 2x2", set of 5......**18.00**

Tree ornaments, twisted icicles, anodized, 15 in box .............**25.00**

Trivet, Acorn, serrated edge, Continental, 10" dia .................**12.00**

Trivet, Pine Cone, oval, Everlast Metal, 7½"..........................**29.00**

Tumblers, anodized, 5", w/matching 9" straws, set of 6 ......................**45.00**

Vase, anodized red with silver-tone foot, 6", $10.00.

Water set, anodized, Color Craft, 7½" pitcher, 8-5" tumblers, carrier.....................................**80.00**

# Anchor Hocking

From the 1930s until the 1970s Anchor Hocking (Lancaster, Ohio) produced a wide and varied assortment of glassware including kitchen items such as reamers, mixing bowls, and measuring cups in many lovely colors. Many patterns of dinnerware were made as well. Their Fire-King line was formulated to produce heat-proof glassware so durable that it was guaranteed for two years against breakage caused by heat. Colors included Jade-ite, Azur-ite, Turquoise, Sapphire blue, ivory, milk white (often decorated with fired-on patterns), Royal Ruby, and Forest Green. Collectors are beginning to reassemble sets, and for the most part, prices are relatively low, except for some of the rarer items. For more information, we recommend *Anchor Hocking's Fire-King & More, Third Edition,* by Gene and Cathy Florence (Collector Books).

Bubble, cup and saucer, Forest Green, $12.00. (Photo courtesy Gene and Cathy Florence)

Bubble, cup, crystal iridescent......**3.50**

Bubble, sugar bowl, Sapphire green ...............................**25.00**

Bubble, tidbit, ruby, 2-tier .......**67.50**

Charm, bowl, soup; Azur-ite, 6".....**15.00**

Charm, plate, salad; Forest Green, 6⅝" ......................................**18.00**

Charm, platter, Jade-ite, 11x8".....**55.00**

Charm, saucer, ivory, 5⅜"..........**5.00**

Early American Prescut, ashtray, crystal, 5"...........................**10.00**

Early American Prescut, bowl, gondola dish; crystal, #752, 9⅜".......**4.00**

Early American Prescut, cocktail shaker, crystal, 30-oz, 9"..**895.00**

Early American Prescut, pitcher, crystal, #7901, 60-oz..........**15.00**

Early American Prescut, plate, crystal, 11"...............................**12.00**

Early American Prescut, tray, hostess; crystal, #750, 6½x12"........**12.50**

Early American Prescut, vase, crystal, #742, 10".....................**12.50**

Early American Prescut, vase, crystal, footed, 5"..........................**695.00**

Forest Green, ashtray, sq, 3½".....**5.00**

Forest Green, batter bowl, w/ spout ..**28.00**

**19**

Forest Green, stem, iced tea; 14-oz..**14.00**
Forest Green, tumbler, fancy, 9-oz..**6.00**
Forest Green, vase, 9" .............**12.00**
Game Birds, bowl, vegetable; white
   w/decals, 8¼" .....................**60.00**
Game Birds, sugar bowl, white
   w/decals, w/lid...................**25.00**
Game Birds, tumbler, iced tea;
   white w/decals, 11-oz.........**12.00**
Gray Laurel, bowl, soup plate; 7⅝"..**7.00**
Gray Laurel, plate, salad; 7⅜"......**8.00**
Gray Laurel, sugar bowl, footed ......**5.00**
Harvest, bowl, dessert; white
   w/decals, 4⅝" ......................**5.00**
Harvest, plate, dinner; white
   w/decals, 10" ........................**6.00**
Jane Ray, bowl, dessert; Jade-ite,
   4⅞" ....................................**12.00**

**Jane Ray, dinner
plate, ivory, 9⅛",
$45.00; matching cup
and saucer, $30.00.**
(Photo courtesy Gene
and Cathy Florence)

Jane Ray, plate, dinner; Vitrock,
   9⅛" .....................................**20.00**
Jane Ray, plate, salad; Jade-ite, 7¾".**12.00**
Laurel, bowl, dessert; ivory, 4⅞"..**12.00**
Laurel, cup, ivory, 8-oz.............**10.00**
Laurel, plate, dinner; Peach Lustre,
   9⅛" ......................................**5.00**
Laurel, saucer, Peach Lustre,
   5⅜" ......................................**1.00**

Meadow Green, bowl, cereal; white
   w/decal, 8-oz, 4⅝" ...............**3.00**
Meadow Green, bowl, mixing; white
   w/decal, 1½-qt.....................**6.00**
Meadow Green, creamer, white
   w/decal, 2 styles, ea.............**3.00**
Meadow Green, loaf pan, white
   w/decal, 5x9" ......................**6.50**
Prescut (Oatmeal), cup, crystal......**2.00**
Prescut (Oatmeal), sherbet, crystal,
   5-oz .....................................**1.50**
Prescut (Oatmeal), tumbler, water;
   crystal, 9-oz..........................**2.00**
Prescut (Pineapple), butter dish,
   crystal, round.....................**15.00**
Prescut (Pineapple), pitcher, milk;
   white, 12-oz........................**10.00**
Prescut (Pineapple), syrup pitcher,
   crystal ...............................**12.00**
Primrose, bowl, dessert; white
   w/decal, 4⅝" ........................**3.50**
Primrose, casserole, white w/decal,
   knob cover, 1-qt .................**12.00**
Primrose, gravy/sauce boat, white
   w/decal .............................**250.00**
Primrose, platter, white w/decal,
   9x12" ..................................**15.00**
Rainbow, bowl, fruit; pastel, 6"......**25.00**
Rainbow, stem, pastel, 10-oz,
   7⅜" ....................................**10.00**
Rainbow, sugar bowl, primary col-
   ors, footed...........................**12.00**
Rainbow, tumbler, primary colors,
   straight sides, 12-oz, 4¾" .....**35.00**
Restaurant Ware, cup, demitasse;
   Jade-ite .............................**35.00**
Restaurant Ware, plate, luncheon;
   Jade-ite, G316, 8" .............**60.00**
Restaurant Ware, saucer, demi-
   tasse; Jade-ite...................**40.00**
Royal Ruby, beer bottle, 7-oz,
   8" ...................................**25.00**

**20**

Royal Ruby, creamer, footed ......**9.00**
Royal Ruby, pitcher, upright,
3-qt .................................**75.00**

**Royal Ruby, vase, 6⅜", $9.00. (Photo courtesy Gene and Cathy Florence)**

Royal Ruby, vase, 2 styles, 9"......**17.50**
Sandwich, bowl, cereal; Desert Gold,
6¾" ....................................**12.00**
Sandwich, bowl, ruby, scalloped,
8¼" ....................................**40.00**
Sandwich, pitcher, juice; pink,
6" .................................**350.00**
Sandwich, punch bowl, ivory,
9¾" ................................**15.00**
Sandwich, sugar bowl, crystal,
w/lid...................................**23.50**
Shell, bowl, cereal; Golden Shell,
6⅜" ...................................**10.00**
Shell, bowl, dessert; milk white,
4¾" .....................................**4.00**
Shell, creamer, Jade-ite, footed......**25.00**
Shell, plate, salad; Lustre Shell,
7¼" .....................................**3.50**
Shell, saucer, demitasse; Aurora
Shell, 4¾"...........................**20.00**
Swirl, bowl, fruit/dessert; Azur-ite,
4⅞" ....................................**12.00**
Swirl, bowl, soup plate; ivory,
7⅝" ...............................**10.00**
Swirl, bowl, vegetable; pink,
8¼" ...............................**30.00**
Swirl, cup, Jade-ite, 8-oz .........**40.00**
Swirl, cup, Lustre Pastel, 8-oz....**12.00**

Swirl, plate, salad; Rose-ite, 7⅜".....**100.00**
Swirl, platter, Sunrise, 12x9".....**18.00**
Swirl, sugar bowl, Golden 22k
Anniversary, open handles, foot-
ed .........................................**3.50**
Thousand Line, bowl, crystal, shal-
low, 7½"..............................**10.00**
Thousand Line, fork, crystal......**7.50**
Thousand Line, plate, salad; crys-
tal, 8"..................................**10.00**
Thousand Line, spoon, crystal.....**7.50**
Turquoise Blue, bowl, berry;
4½" ...............................**10.00**
Turquoise Blue, mug, 8-oz .......**10.00**
Turquoise Blue, plate, 10"........**30.00**

**Wheat, au gratin casserole, clear glass lid, 1½-quart, $14.00. (Photo courtesy Gene and Cathy Florence)**

Wheat, bowl, dessert; white w/decals,
4⅝" ......................................**3.50**
Wheat, mug, white w/decals......**50.00**
Wheat, platter, white w/decals,
9x12" .................................**14.00**
Wheat, tumbler, tea; white w/decals,
11-oz ...................................**8.00**

# Aprons

Vintage aprons evoke nostalgic memories — grandma in her kitchen, gentle heat radiating from the cookstove, a child tugging on her apron strings — and even if collectors can't relate to that scene personally, they still want to cherish and preserve those old aprons. Some are basic and functional, perhaps made of flour sack material, while others are embroidered and trimmed with lace or appliqués. Commercially made aprons are collectible as well, and those that retain their original tag command the higher prices. Remember, condition is critical, and as a general rule, those that are made by hand are preferred over machine- or commercially made aprons. Values are for examples in excellent condition unless noted otherwise.

Adult waist style, black and white organdy with rickrack trim, ca 1950s, from $9.00 to $15.00. (Photo courtesy La Ree Johnson Bruton)

Bib style, blue & white geometric pattern on clear plastic, ruffle, NM .....................................**85.00**
Bib style, dainty white w/crochet lace trim, ribbon ties .........**15.00**
Bib style, pale pink w/blue trim, 2 pockets ...............................**12.50**
Bib style, red checked gingham w/embroidery on white inset & collar, NM ..........................**35.00**
Bib style, scallops & rickrack trim, flower appliqués, 1950s.....**20.00**

Bib style, tulips print w/little girls & watering cans, 1950s.........**25.00**
Child's bib style, white plastic, nursery characters on clear.................................**75.00**
Child's waist style, crochet, coral & blue cotton, 1930s..............**15.00**
Child's waist style, white stitches w/blue stitches on pocket, 1930s ...................................**35.00**
Shoulder style, pink floral on white, 1930s ...................................**40.00**
Strapless, cotton elasticized top & waist, eyelet trim..............**14.00**
Waist style, black organdy w/red floral handkerchief pocket .....**15.00**
Waist style, blue checked cotton w/cherries print, pocket ....**15.00**
Waist style, Christmas motif, red, very fancy, 1940s-50s ........**13.00**
Waist style, crochet, red, white & blue, red pocket .................**24.00**
Waist style, Easter w/eggs & sm Spring flowers, 1950s........**15.00**
Waist style, floral chintz w/ grosgrain ribbon ruffle, 1950s ...................................**24.00**
Waist style, green gingham w/purple flowers, pocket, 1940s.........**45.00**
Waist style, lavender with rickrack, print pocket..........................**8.00**
Waist style, orange organdy w/ruffle trim, pocket........................**15.00**
Waist style, pleated cotton print, skirt length, 1950s.............**10.00**
Waist style, souvenir of New York City, silky rayon, 1950s....**24.00**
Waist style, white organdy w/red tulip pocket & trim............**10.00**
Waist style, white organdy w/ornate embroidered flowers, pocket, M ......................................**37.50**

# Ashtrays

Even though the general public seems to be down on smoking, ashtrays themselves are beginning to be noticed favorably by collectors, who perhaps view them as an 'endangered species'! Some of the more desirable examples are those with embossed or intaglio designs, applied decorations, added figures of animals or people, Art Deco stying, an interesting advertising message, and an easily recognizable manufacturer's mark.

Advertising, Aqua Velva, clear glass w/blue decal, 3¾" .................**7.00**

Advertising, Coor's Light, white ceramic w/gray transfer, 3⅞" dia.........................**7.00**

Advertising, Elgin Watches, ceramic, tan w/wine letters, 5⅜" dia..**14.00**

Advertising, Falstaff, pale amber glass, rings on bottom, 3½" .................**18.00**

Advertising, Glenmore Vodka, red glass w/white letters, 3 3" sides ...................................**18.00**

Advertising, Hershey's, heavy glass w/brown logo center, 4" dia.**9.00**

Advertising, Herva, alcohol-free drink, Germany, 4⅝".........**14.00**

Advertising, Lone Star, cream ceramic w/gold logo, old, 7½" ...........**10.50**

Advertising, Maxim Hotel/Casino, Las Vegas, amethyst glass, 3¾" ......................................**5.00**

Advertising, MGM Grand Hotel, white w/red lion & letters, 4½" dia.........................................**9.00**

Advertising, Moxie, copper, old, 5½" dia.....................................**60.00**

Advertising, Myer's Rum, True Jamaican Rum, brown ironstone, 7¾"..........................**29.00**

Advertising, Olympia Beer, black amethyst glass, stackable, 4⅛" dia........................................**9.50**

**Advertising, Pontiac, Indian leaning against tree, ceramic, two rests, 5¾", $110.00.** (Photo courtesy Nancy Wanvig)

Advertising, Reese Padlock, figural, cast aluminum, 3¾"..........**17.00**

Advertising, Resistol Hats, brown plastic hat, ad on brim, 4¾"....**25.00**

Advertising, Suntory Whiskey, brown ceramic, 3 rests, 4⅛" dia .....**10.00**

Advertising, White Horse Whiskey, horse's head, white ceramic, 4" ........................................**65.00**

Advertising, 7-Up, The International Drink, plastic, 5½" sq........**12.00**

Novelty, Big Mouth, devil's face, holes in eyes, 3¾" ..............**17.00**

Novelty, Big Mouth, elf, green hat, brown eyes, 4½".................**25.00**

Novelty, Big Mouth, frog, brown w/gold rests, Japan, 3¾" .....**9.00**

Novelty, Big Mouth, green fish, cigarette rest, Japan, 5"...........**18.00**

Novelty, Smoker, African face, vent in nose, Japan, 7⅝".............**45.00**

Souvenir, Massachusetts, Boston beans, 4¾"...........................**6.00**

Souvenir, Minnesota, Mayo Clinic, Rochester, 4¾" dia...............**4.00**

### Tire Ashtrays

Tire ashtrays were introduced around 1910 as advertising items. The very early all-glass or glass-and-metal types were replaced in the early 1920s by the more familiar rubber-tired varieties. Hundreds of different examples have been produced over the years. They are still distributed (by the larger tire companies only), but no longer display the detail or color of the pre-World War II tire ashtrays. Although the common ones bring modest prices, rare examples sometimes sell for several hundred dollars.

For more information we recommend *Tire Ashtray Collector's Guide* by Jeff McMcVey; he is listed in the Directory under Idaho.

Armstrong Rhino-Flex Tires, red & white pyro rhino on clear glass insert ................................. **55.00**

BF Goodrich, General Tire, uranium glass insert .......................... **55.00**

Dominion Royal Master, red rubber tire ...................................... **85.00**

Firestone, Century of Progress 1933, amber glass insert .............. **95.00**

Firestone, New York World's Fair 1939 souvenir .................... **50.00**

Firestone All Traction Field & Road F1512 Tractor, 1950s, 6½"..**45.00**

Firestone Deluxe Champion Gum Dipped, clear insert, 6"......**45.00**

Firestone Performance Racing, clear glass insert, 1940s..............**80.00**

General Ld250 Haf-Trac, clear insert, 7"............................**35.00**

Goodyear Eagle VR50 Corvette Performance, 1990s, 6" ...........**45.00**

Goodyear G3 All Weather, green glass insert.........................**60.00**

Goodyear Supertorque Tractor, glass insert, winged foot decal, 1950s ................................. **40.00**

**Red River Army Depot, $75.00. (Photo courtesy Jeff McVey)**

# Automobilia

Many are fascinated with vintage automobiles, but to own one of those 'classy chassis' is a luxury not all can afford! So instead they enjoy collecting related memorabilia such as advertising, owners' manuals, horns, emblems, and hood ornaments. The decade of the 1930s produced the items that are most in demand today, but the 1950s models have their own band of devoted fans as well as do the muscle cars of the 1960s.

Book, Austin-Helly 3000 MKS I & II Driver's Handbook, 1960s, 68-page .................................. **30.00**

Book, Automotive Giants of America, Forbe/Foster, 1st edition, 1926.................................. **10.00**

Book, Floyd Clymer's Catalog of 1914 Cars, c 1958, M.........**20.00**

Book, My Life & Work, Henry Ford, 1922, 1st edition, VG........**125.00**

Book, Shop Theory, Henry Ford Trade School, 1943, 268-page....................................**10.00**

Booklet, dealer's; Cadillac, Gentle Art of Motoring, 1948, 12-page, EX......................................**12.00**

Booklet, Horseless Carriage Days, HP Maxim, Dover Pub, paperback, 1962...........................**10.00**

Booklet, Keep On Rolling, American Automobile Association, 1943, 40-page................................**12.00**

Brochure, AMC, covers Ambassador, Hornet, etc, 1970, 46-page..**20.00**

Brochure, AMC, covers Pacer, Gremlet, Hornet, etc, 1977, 36-page....................................**14.00**

Brochure, Chevrolet Corvette, 1960, unfolds to 25½x10¼"..........**30.00**

Brochure, Chevrolet dealer's, 1946-47.........................................**15.00**

Brochure, Corvair, 1962, 12-page, 11x7".................................**25.00**

Brochure, DeSoto, 1953, unfolds to 24x19"...............................**22.00**

Brochure, Edsel, 1959 models shown, opens to 18¾x25"................**40.00**

Brochure, Ford, 1941 Ford on front, new 1941 models, 8½x11", EX........................................**65.00**

Brochure, Jeep Truck, 1947, 6-page, unfolds to 25½x11".............**30.00**

Brochure, Lincoln Continental Mark IV, 1972, 8-page, 10¼x13"..**15.00**

Brochure, Lincoln-Zephyr V 12, 1939, 3-page, 11x8½", VG..**50.00**

Brochure, Plymouth, 1956, unfolds to 34¾x9"...........................**28.00**

Calendar, Chevrolet Motor Cars, farm scene, 1920, 31x16", EX....................................**155.00**

Cap, radiator; Chevrolet, mid-1930s, 3x3¾" on top.....................**20.00**

Catalog, Hudson, cars on front cover, 1938, 11x6", EX.......**40.00**

Clock, Buick, cloisonné award in image of radiator, 4x5½", EX....................................**550.00**

**Clock, Cadillac, neon, black, white, and yellow, 18", EX, from $900.00 to $1,000.00.**

Clock, Cadillac Service, center logo, yellow case, glass lens, round................................**165.00**

Clock, Ford Genuine Parts, metal & glass, neon, octagon, 18", EX..**850.00**

Clock, Oldsmobile, electric light-up, Pam Clock Co, sq, 15½", VG.............................**475.00**

Clock, Oldsmobile Service, neon circle outside, 21x6", VG.............**600.00**

Emblem, BMW, 3-color enamel, 2 mounting studs on bk, 3½" dia....................................**30.00**

Emblem, body; Thunderbird, 1½x9¼"..............................**80.00**

Emblem, fender; Thunderbird, 1959, 1⅝"....................................**120.00**

Emblem, hood; Cadillac, all chrome, unknown year...................**30.00**

Emblem, radiator; Cadillac, 1920s,
2⅛" dia .............................**150.00**

Emblem, radiator; Chevrolet,
1920s ................................**60.00**

Emblem, radiator; Ford '60, year
unknown, w/bolts/clamps.....**60.00**

Emblem, radiator; Hudson '8,
clip/stud missing, 2½" .......**40.00**

Emblem, radiator; Studebaker,
white enameling, 2⅛"........**40.00**

**Emblem sign, Chevrolet, die-
cut, masonite, chain-hung,
1950s, 9½x21", EX, $350.00.**
(Photo courtesy B.J. Summers)

Jigsaw puzzle, Studebaker, products & services, men on wagon,
6x7", EX ...........................**300.00**

Latch, hood; Ford, 1930s ..........**40.00**

List, Chevrolet Master Parts, 1928,
269-page, 8½x11" ..............**60.00**

Manual, owner's; Buick Riviera,
1968, 58-page, 5¼x8¼" .....**20.00**

Manual, owner's; Cadillac, 1961,
w/original pouch, protection
plan, more ..........................**25.00**

Manual, owner's; Chrysler '58,
1926................................**80.00**

Manual, owner's; Chrysler Imperial,
1959................................**15.00**

Manual, owner's; Corvair, 1967 .....**30.00**

Manual, owner's; Dodge, 1946, 40-
page, 5⅞x8¾".....................**25.00**

Manual, owner's; Jaguar XK 150,
water damage, 1950s.........**20.00**

Manual, shop; Buick, 1953, 314-
page, 8½x11"......................**40.00**

Manual, shop; Chevrolet, 1941, 292-
page, 8¼x10¾"...................**40.00**

Manual, shop; Chevrolet Corvette,
1963, 478-page, 8¼x11" ....**60.00**

Manual, shop; Oldsmobile, 1942,
358-page............................**30.00**

Parts list, DeSoto Preliminary, Nov
1936, 102-page, 8½x11" ....**40.00**

Pen & pencil set, Chevrolet, The
Heartbeat of America, Parker,
EX....................................**25.00**

Photo, Packard '200' Club Sedan,
factory photo, 8x10"..........**24.00**

Pin-back button, A Ford Year, 1932
Ford, ¾" dia, EX ...............**25.00**

Postcard, Buick factory photo, post-
mark 1950 ...........................**7.00**

Postcard, Chevrolet, divided back,
1939 4-door car, 5½x3½",
NM.....................................**9.00**

Postcard, Packard photo, Genuine...
Photo-Matic...Chigago, 1949..**25.00**

Poster, Chevrolet, Guardian Mainte-
nance, paper, 44x17", EX..**105.00**

Promotional car, Chevrolet Pickup,
1972, 8¼", NM .................**150.00**

Promotional car, Edsel, 2-door
hardtop, friction drive, 1958,
from $150 to .................**195.00**

Sign, Corvette Sales & Service, metal,
1953, 18x12", VG.................**125.00**

Sign, General Motors in yellow on
blue embossed metal, 3¼x29",
EX....................................**95.00**

Sign, Jeep...Parts-Service, metal &
glass, 19x24", VG.............**275.00**

Sign, Pontiac Authorized Service,
Indian head, porcelain, 42" dia,
EX....................................**325.00**

Spoon, Ford Motor Company,
metal, logo on handle, 1930s,
EX....................................**15.00**

Stock certificate, Studebaker-Packard, 100 shares, 1957, cancelled ..................................**20.00**

Wrench, box-end; Indian Motorcycle, slightly bent..........................**45.00**

Wrench, hubcap; Hudson, 13", G..**15.00**

Wrench, open-end; Ford T-1917, 5¼"..**8.00**

## Autumn Leaf

Autumn Leaf dinnerware was a product of the Hall China Company, who produced this extensive line from 1933 until 1978 for exclusive distribution by the Jewell Tea Company. The Libbey Glass Company made co-ordinating pitchers, tumblers, and stemware. Metal, cloth, plastic, and paper items were also available. Today, though very rare pieces are expensive and a challenge to acquire, new collectors may easily reassemble an attractive, usable set at a reasonable price. Hall has produced special club pieces (for the NALCC) as well as some limited editions for an Ohio company, but these are well marked and easily identified as such. Refer to *The Collector's Encyclopedia of Hall China* by Margaret and Kenn Whitmyer (Collector Books) for more information.

See Clubs and Newsletters for information concerning the *Autumn Leaf* newsletter.

Baker, French, 2-pt, from $150 to .....................................**175.00**

Baker, French, 3-pt ..................**25.00**

Baker, oval, Fort Pitt, 12-oz individual..............................**225.00**

Bean pot, w/2 handles, 2¼-qt.....**250.00**

Bottle, Jim Beam, w/stand.....**130.00**

Bowl, cream soup; w/handles...**40.00**

Bowl, fruit; 5½", from $3 to........**6.00**

Bowl, soup; Melmac..................**20.00**

Bowl, vegetable; oval, Melmac, from $40 to................................**50.00**

Bread box, metal....................**800.00**

Butter dish, 1-lb, ruffled top, regular......................................**500.00**

Butter dish, ¼-lb, wings top, from $1,500 to ......................**2,000.00**

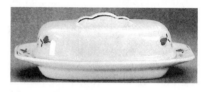

**Butter dish, ruffled top, ¼-pound, 8½" long, from $175.00 to $250.00.**

Canisters, sq, 4-pc set.............**350.00**

Clock, electric, from $400 to .....**550.00**

Clock, salesman's award ........**250.00**

Coffeepot, Rayed, 9-cup............**45.00**

Cookie jar, Tootsie, Rayed.....**310.00**

Creamer & sugar bowl, Nautilus..**125.00**

Cup, custard; Radiance, from $6 to..**10.00**

Flatware, silver plated, ea .......**35.00**

Fondue set, complete, from $200 to...**300.00**

Gravy boat, w/underplate (pickle dish)....................................**55.00**

Jug, batter; Sundial (bowl), rare ..**5,500.00**

Loaf pan, Mary Dunbar, from $90 to..**125.00**

Marmalade, 3-pc.....................**125.00**

Mug, conic, from $50 to ...........**65.00**

Plate, salad; Melmac, 7"..........**20.00**

Plate, 6", from $5 to...................**8.00**

Plate, 9"................................**12.00**

Saucer, regular, Ruffled D .........**2.50**

Shelf liner, paper, 108" roll......**50.00**

Syrup pitcher, club pc, 1995.....**95.00**

**Teapot, Newport, 1930s, from $200.00 to $275.00.**

Teapot, Rayed, long spout, 1935,
from $75 to..........................**95.00**
Tidbit tray, 3-tier....................**100.00**
Towel, tea; cotton, 16x33" ........**60.00**
Tray, glass, wood handle........**140.00**
Tray, metal, oval.....................**100.00**
Tumbler, Libbey, gold frost etched,
10-oz .................................**65.00**
Vase, bud; regular decal, 6".....**350.00**
Warmer, oval .........................**225.00**

# Avon

Originally founded in 1886 under the title California Perfume Company, the firm became officially known as Avon Products Inc. in 1939. Avon offers something for almost everyone such as cross collectibles including jewelry, Fostoria, Wedgwood, commerative plates, Ceramarte steins, and hundreds of other quality items. Among the most popular items are the Mrs. P.F.E. Albee figurines. Mrs. Albee was the first Avon lady, ringing doorbells and selling their products in the very early years of the company's history. The figurines are issued each year and awarded only to Avon's most successful representatives. Each are elegantly attired in magnificent period fashions. The workmanship is remarkable. Also sought are product samples, magazine ads, jewelry, awards, and catalogs. Their Cape Cod glassware has been sold in vast quantities since the '70s and is becoming a common sight at flea markets and antique malls. For more information we recommend *Bud Hastin's Avon Collector's Encyclopedia* by Bud Hastin. See also Cape Cod. For information concerning the National Association of Avon Collectors and the newsletter *Avon Times*, see Clubs and Newsletters. Values are for mint-condition examples unless noted otherwise. Mint-in-box items bring much higher prices than those without their original boxes.

**After shave, Tai Winds, in blue glass bottle in the shape of '64 Ford Mustang, empty, label on bottom, original box, $22.00.**
(Photo courtesy Monsen & Baer)

Bell, clear glass, Avon 100, President's Club Member, 1986, 6",
MIB ....................................**20.00**
Bottle, Aladdin's Lamp, green glass
w/gold lid, some contents.......**22.00**
Bottle, ballerina seated on sq base,
Zany, pink frosted glass, 1981........**12.00**

Bottle, car: Triumph TR3, green glass, Canadian, empty, 4¾" L ........................................**15.00**

Bottle, Fantastic-Cat Bubble Bath, pink, stylized, 15" ................**18.00**

Bottle, Hawaiian White Ginger Cologne Mist, 2-oz, MIB ......**26.00**

Bottle, Juke Box, Sweet Honesty, 5¼", NMIB ........................**15.00**

Bottle, lovebird, Regence, 1969, NMIB ..................................**10.00**

Bottle, mermaid, Skin So Soft, w/some contents, 10" .........**35.00**

Bottle, Occur, 4 tapered sides, beautiful lady on box, 1962, M (VG box)....................................**14.00**

Bottle, rainbow trout, green glass w/plastic head....................**18.00**

Bottle, Road Runner motorcycle, blue glass, plastic, 7½" L, MIB....................................**15.00**

Bottle, Small World, Oriental girl, MIB ....................................**18.00**

Bottle, soda-fountain drink w/straws, Pretty Peach, MIB ..............**12.00**

Bottle, Tabatha, black cat, Cotillion, 7", NMIB ............................**15.00**

Bottle, Tug-A-Brella, Moonwind, child w/umbrella, 11¾", MIB ....................................**15.00**

Box, President's Celebration, silver plated, embossed rose, 1974....................................**20.00**

Bracelet, 10k gold chain link w/topaz charm, Council Award, 2003, MIB ....................................**18.00**

Brooch, Elizabeth Taylor Equestrian Hearts in Tandem, 4x2⅞" ......**60.00**

Brooch, gingerbread man, solid perfume holder, full, 2", NM..**15.00**

Brooch, Siamese cat sitting, tail around feet, ceramic, 1¾"......**22.00**

Brooch, Victorian style w/black cabachon, Wishing, empty, 1½" L ........................................**14.00**

Coloring book, Introducing Small World, 11-page, unused, NM .......**22.00**

Figurine, Mrs Albee, in miniature, glass globe, from $8 to...........**15.00**

Figurine, Mrs Albee, 1973, 6½" .......**65.00**

Figurine, Mrs Albee, 1976, MIB......**60.00**

Figurine, Mrs Albee, 1978, 9½", from $45 to........................**60.00**

Figurine, Mrs Albee, 1979, 10", from $55 to................................**65.00**

Figurine, Mrs Albee, 1981, 9¾" ......**60.00**

Figurine, Mrs Albee, 1987, 10½", MIB ..................................**25.00**

Figurine, Mrs Albee, 1988, 11½" .......**60.00**

Figurine, Mrs Albee, 1991, 9", MIB..**45.00**

Figurine, Mrs Albee, 1992...........**55.00**

Figurine, Mrs Albee, 1993, 10", MIB...**55.00**

Figurine, Mrs Albee, 1996, 10½" .......**50.00**

Figurine, Mrs Albee, 1997, 10" .....**50.00**

Figurine, Mrs Albee, 1998, 10" ......**60.00**

Figurine, Mrs Albee, 2001, MIB ......**70.00**

Fluff Puff, puff & powder, pink plastic back & handle, MIB .....**45.00**

Going Avon Calling Award, rabbit in pink car, 1982, 5½x6x4" .......**15.00**

Lip pomade, ice cream-cone shape, Tutti-Frutti, 1970s, MIB .....**20.00**

Necklace, gold-tone w/1½" Easter Egg pendant, MIB .............**25.00**

Necklace & bracelet, cats alternate w/balls, gold-tone...............**30.00**

Pen, Team Leader, 1979, Cross, MIB ..................................**12.00**

Perfume compact, Hawaiian White Ginger, Honor Award, 1967, empty, NM ........................**30.00**

Pin, crystal heart, President's Sales Challenge Award, 1982, MIB ....................................**8.00**

Plate, Avon Rose Circle, gold trim, 2002, 8½", MIB .................12.50
Plate, Dashing Through the Snow, Christmas, Wedgwood, 9", MIB .................................12.00
Plate, Gentle Moments, swan mother, young, Enoch Wedgwood, 8½" .................................14.00
Playing cards, black horse backs, w/joker, E-2838 on Ace of Spades, MIB ......................20.00
Print, Avon Rose Circle Award, 1998, 9x11" (matted & framed)....25.00
Rollette, Miss Lollipop, 3½", MIB ................................25.00
Stein, Indians of the American Frontier, 1988, 8", MIB .....15.00
Stein, Wild Country, w/Alaskan moose, stoneware, 9½", MIB.............22.00
Sugar bowl, white w/gray trim, Sugar Bowl Award, 1960 ................22.50
Teacup & saucer, Honor Society Award, Queens, 1996..........15.00
Teacup & saucer, Mrs Albee Honor Society, 2003, 24k gold trim, MIB ................................25.00
Thermometer, Farmer's Almanac, tin, brown w/tan keyhole reserve, 9", EX...................10.00
Thimbles, stylish ladies (waist up), Mrs Albee award, w/wood rack, 8 for ..............................40.00
Trinket case, President's Tribute Award, 1999-2000, 12", MIB.........40.00
Trophy, Mrs Albee's face, President's Recognition Program, 1998.......15.00
Tumblers, Summer Fantasy Geranium, set of 6 on 12" metal tray, NM ...............................30.00
Vanity mirror, brush & comb, amber/black plastic w/cameo, EX.............................20.00

# Banks

After the Depression, everyone was aware that saving 'for a rainy day' would help during bad times. Children of the '40s, '50s, and '60s were given piggy banks in forms of favorite characters to reinforce the idea of saving. They were made to realize that by saving money they could buy that expensive bicycle or a toy they were particularly longing for.

Today on the flea market circuit, figural banks are popular collectibles, especially those that are character-related — advertising characters and Disney in particular.

Interest in glass banks has recently grown by leaps and bounds, and you'll be amazed at the prices some of the harder-to-find examples are bringing. Charlie Reynolds has written the glass bank 'bible,' called *Collector's Guide to Glass Banks*, which you'll want to read if you think you'd like to collect them. It's published by Collector Books. In our listings, the glass banks we've included will have punched factory slots or molded, raised slots. There are other types as well. Because of limited space, values listed below are mid range. Expect to pay as much as 50% more or less than our suggested prices.

Arkansas Razorback, white w/team logo, 7"...............................15.00
Bass drummer, drum on wheels, Save at Watkins on drum, 5½x6", NM ......................30.00

Blimp on base, white w/Miller Lite
Beer logo, 6x14", EX..........**10.00**
Cat, Feed Me on knee, white w/gold
collar, rhinestone details...**60.00**

**Cat with padlock,
marked Grantcrest
Japan, 7", from $40.00
to $45.00.** (Photo cour-
tesy Jim and Beverly
Mangus)

Court Jester w/dog, multicolored
w/gold trim, 11x8x5", EX .....**25.00**
Cow, black & white, 11x8x8",
EX...................................**25.00**
Egg w/chick in side, Shafford,
Japan, 5"............................**15.00**
Fisherman's basket, 4x2x2¼",
NM...................................**20.00**
Flower Power, VW Camper Van,
flower decor, MIB ..............**17.50**
Football player, boy in Green Bay
Packer uniform, 6½x5",
EX...................................**15.00**
Harley-Davidson Gas Tank, black
w/name on sides ................**30.00**
Hippie flower child, girl sitting cross-
legged, 1970s, 6x5½" ........**35.00**
House, Queens Silver Jubilee, 1977..**17.50**
Monkey, seated, glass eyes, Bradley
Exclusives, Japan, 8x4", EX .**17.50**

Pay phone, rotary style, black, 9x5",
EX.......................................**17.50**
Pig, black & white, 12x12x9".......**35.00**
Pig, pink w/floral decor, For My
Hope Chest on back, 1950s,
6x9x5", EX .........................**35.00**
Pig, seated, in suit & top hat,
w/money chest between feet,
6¼", NM .............................**15.00**
Pig, seated, white w/colored fea-
tures ..................................**55.00**
Pig, white w/closed eyes, 6½x9".......**40.00**
Pig, white w/clover decals, CHIC
Pottery, 1949, 6x10"..........**60.00**
Pig Policeman, brown uniform
w/black belt & accessories,
14½", EX .............................**17.50**
Police Call Box, blue, Tardis style,
6½x2½" ..............................**17.50**
Rhinoceros, hand carved, painted
w/gold trim, Publix Supermarkets,
MIB .....................................**25.00**
Sailor Boy, saluting, 8", EX......**17.50**
Sperm Bank, white w/brown trim,
1960s, 4½x8", EX................**17.50**
Swiss cheese wedge, Franklin Co, Made
in Korea, 3½x7", NMIB...........**17.50**

**Glass**

Barrel Bank, clear w/embossed
sides, 4½", NM...................**10.00**
Bunny, amber, 6"....................**160.00**
Globe on Bible, Christ for the World
My Peace I Give Unto You,
teal ....................................**20.00**
Hippopotamus, in suit w/glasses &
umbrella, 7¾" ....................**50.00**
House w/chimney, green, Wheaton,
6x4¾x3¼", NM....................**25.00**
Indian head w/buffalo on back,
round, clear, 6½", NM .......**15.00**

Liberty bell, A Penny Saved...Earned, clear, 4x4", NM ..................**25.00**

Lincoln, clear, Lincoln Food Inc, 10", NM ......................**12.00**

Log cabin, clear w/metal lid, EX ................................**25.00**

Pig, light blue, This Little Piggy Went to Market, 10½x19".............**55.00**

Pig, smoke w/Niagara Falls painted scene, 5x7", NM ..................**17.50**

Pig, smoky gray, 6x6½" ............**50.00**

Pig, white hobnail, 3⅛x5" ...........**30.00**

Save w/Pittsburg Paints, smiling sun on back, clear, 3¼" sq, NM..**20.00**

Snow Crest Bear, clear, metal lid, 7"..**17.50**

Uncle Sam bust, blue, Wheaton, 6½" .....................................**17.50**

## Plastic

Apple, wind-up, eyes open, worm comes & takes coin, 1970s..**30.00**

Basset hound, realistic paint, Union Products...Mass, 9x16x6", EX.......................................**24.00**

Carnation Milk truck, red & white, 1950s-early 1960s, 3x7", EX..**65.00**

Dog w/red felt sweater, hard red cap, Made in USA, 9½x6" .............**24.00**

Foremost Milk delivery van, pink & white, Como Plastics, 7" L, NM ...**25.00**

National League Bats (10) in red plastic holder w/league names on ea ...................................**30.00**

Pig, molded hard plastic, painted details, Hong Kong #7104, 10", NM ......................................**35.00**

Rocket Bank, red & yellow, State Bank Wellston MO, 10", EX..........**115.00**

Walt Disney World, princesses (4) surround castle w/pink roof ....................................**30.00**

## Character Related

Batman Returns (Movie), vinyl, 1991, 9", EX ......................**10.00**

Cecil's head (Beany & Cecil), molded plastic, NM ........................**35.00**

Daffy Duck, leaning against tree trunk, cast iron................**125.00**

Dopey (Snow White & 7 Dwarfs), porcelain, 1950s, 7", NM......**55.00**

Dr Dolittle w/monkey & dog at feet, plastic, NM ........................**50.00**

Elsie the Cow, metal, Master Crafters, w/key, 7"...........**200.00**

**Ernie in Train, marked Jim Henson Productions, Inc., Applause, 4", from $30.00 to $35.00. (Photo courtesy Jim and Beverly Mangus)**

Fred Flintstone standing next to safe, plastic, MIB...............**35.00**

Hopalong Cassidy bust, bronze-colored plastic, 1950s, MIB..**110.00**

Incredible Hulk, green plastic, black details, Renzi, 1978, NM...**35.00**

Jack Benny, TV Bank Safe, hard plastic, 1960s, 5x4", EX+............**80.00**

Linus (Peanuts) as baseball catcher, ceramic, rare, 7", NM ......**125.00**

Miss Piggy (Muppets), ceramic, Sigma, NM ......................**50.00**

Pebbles Flintstone, plastic, Transogram, 1960s, EX ...............**45.00**

Popeye, flesh-tone plastic w/multi-color details, Play Pal, 1972, NM .....................................**50.00**

Popeye Daily Dime Bank, tin litho, King Features, 1956, 2½" sq, EX.......................................**60.00**

Roy Rogers & Trigger, ceramic, 1950s, 7½", NM ...............**130.00**

Santa w/toy bag, holly in hand, spaghetti trim, ceramic, 1950s, Japan, 7", NM....................**22.50**

Speedy, Alka Seltzer mascot, rubber, 5¾", NM .............................**95.00**

Spider-Man, orange plastic, AJ Renzi Corp, 15⅜"...............**57.50**

Sylvester the cat, vinyl, Looney Tunes, EX ..........................**30.00**

Woodstock (Peanuts), plastic figure, 1972, 6", NM ......................**45.00**

Yoda (Star Wars), ceramic, Sigma, 7½", EX .............................**60.00**

# Barbie Dolls

Barbie doll was first introduced in 1959, and soon Mattel found themselves producing not only dolls but tiny garments, fashion accessories, houses, cars, horses, books, and games as well. Today's Barbie collectors want them all. Though the early Barbie dolls are very hard to find, there are many of her successors still around. The trend today is toward Barbie exclusives — Holiday Barbie dolls and Bob Mackie Barbie dolls are all very 'hot' items. So are special-event Barbie dolls.

When buying the older dolls, you'll need to do lots of studying and comparisons to learn to distinguish one Barbie doll from another, but this is the key to making sound buys and good investments. Remember, though, collectors are sticklers concerning condition; compared to a doll mint in box, they'll often give an additional 20% if that box has never been opened! As a general rule a mint-in-the-box doll is worth twice as much as one mint, no box. The same doll, played with and in only good condition, is worth half as much (or even less). If you want a good source for study, refer to one of these fine books: *Barbie Doll Fashion, Volumes I, II, and III*, by Sarah Sink Eames; *Collector's Encyclopedia of Barbie Doll Exclusives*, by J. Michael Augustyniak; *Collector's Encyclopedia of Barbie Doll Collector's Editions* by J. Michael Augustyniak; *Barbie, The First 30 Years*, by Stefanie Deutsch; *The Barbie Doll Years* by Patrick C. and Joyce L. Olds; and *Schroeder's Collectible Toys, Antique to Modern* (Collector Books).

Allan, 1964, painted red hair, straight legs, MIB ..........**100.00**

Allan, 1965, bendable legs, MIB ................................**300.00**

Barbie, #5, 1961, blond hair, MIB, from $375 to.....................**425.00**

Barbie, #5, 1961, red hair, original swimsuit, NM ..................**375.00**

Barbie, #6, blond hair, original swimsuit, EX ...................**250.00**

Barbie, #6, brunette hair, MIB..**425.00**

Barbie, American Airlines Stewardess, 1963, NRFB............................**700.00**

Barbie, American Girl, 1964, blond, brown or brunette hair, NRFB, ea....................................**1,500.00**

Barbie, Angel Lights, 1993, NRFB................................**100.00**

Barbie, Angel of Peace, 1999, Timeless Sentiments, NRFB ...**50.00**

Barbie, Arctic, 1996, Dolls of the World, NRFB .....................**25.00**

Barbie, Ballerina Barbie on Tour, 1976, NRFB .....................**125.00**

Barbie, Barbie Celebration, 1987, NRFB ................................**30.00**

Barbie, Bay Watch (Black or White), 1995, NRFB, ea ....................**20.00**

Barbie, Brazilian, 1989, Dolls of the World, NRFB .....................**75.00**

Barbie, Bubble-Cut, 1962, blond or brunette hair, MIB..........**250.00**

Barbie, Busy Talking Barbie, 1972, NRFB ...............................**200.00**

Barbie, Calvin Klein, 1996, Bloomingdales, NRFB .................**40.00**

Barbie, Celebration Cake Barbie (any), 1999, NRFB, ea.......**20.00**

Barbie, Children's Doctor, 2000, NRFB ................................**20.00**

Barbie, Cool Times, 1989, NRFB.**25.00**

Barbie, Deluxe Quick Curl, 1976, Jergens, NRFB ................**100.00**

Barbie, Dinner at Eight, 1964, NRFB ...............................**600.00**

Barbie, Dorothy (Wizard of Oz), 1994, Hollywood Legends Series, NRFB ...............................**350.00**

Barbie, Dramatic New Living, 1970, brunette hair, NRFB.......**250.00**

Barbie, Dutch, 1994, Dolls of the World, MIB .......................**35.00**

Barbie, Elizabethan, 1994, Great Eras, MIB...........................**50.00**

Barbie, Eskimo, 1982, Dolls of the World, NRFB ....................**65.00**

Barbie, Feelin' Groovy, 1987, NRFB..**175.00**

Barbie, Fountain Mermaid (Black or White), 1993, NRFB, ea ........**20.00**

Barbie, Glinda (Wizard of Oz), 2000, NRFB ................................**25.00**

Barbie, Holiday, 1988, NRFB, minimum value ......................**500.00**

Barbie, Holiday, 1991, NRFB...**200.00**

Barbie, Holiday, 1996, NRFB....**50.00**

Barbie, Indiana, 1998, University Barbie, NRFB ....................**15.00**

Barbie, Kellogg Quick Curl, 1974, Kellogg Co, NRFB .............**60.00**

Barbie, Knitting Pretty (royal blue), 1965, NRFB .....................**635.00**

Barbie, Lily, 1997, FAO Schwarz, NRFB ...............................**150.00**

Barbie, Malt Shop, 1993, Toys R Us, NRFB ...............................**30.00**

Barbie, Miss America, 1972, Kellogg Co, NRFB........................**175.00**

Barbie, My First Barbie, 1981, NRFB ................................**25.00**

Barbie, NASCAR 50th Anniversary, 1998, NRFB...........................**25.00**

Barbie, Neptune Fantasy, 1992, Bob Mackie, NRFB .................**500.00**

Barbie, Nutcracker, 1992, Musical Ballet Series, NRFB........**150.00**

Barbie, Paleontologist, 1997, Toys R Us, NRFB...........................**25.00**

Barbie, Peach Blossom, 1992, NRFB ................................**40.00**

Barbie, Pepsi Sensation, 1989, Toys R Us, NRFB ......................**75.00**

Barbie, Pilgrim, 1995, American Stories Collection, NRFB...........**20.00**

Barbie, Pink Sensation, 1990, Winn Dixie, NRFB ......................**25.00**

Barbie, Plum Royal, 1999, Runaway Collection, NRFB ..............**200.00**

Barbie, Polly Pockets, 1994, Hill's, NRFB ................................**30.00**

Barbie, Portrait in Blue, 1998, Wal-Mart, NRFB ..................**25.00**

Barbie, Queen of Hearts, 1994, Bob Mackie, NRFB ................**250.00**

Barbie, Ralph Lauren, 1997, Bloomingdale's, NRFB ...............**60.00**

Barbie, Rockettes, 1993, FAO Schwarz, NRFB ..............**120.00**

Barbie, Safari, 1998, Disney, NRFB ..............................**30.00**

Barbie, Songbird, 1996, NRFB ...**25.00**

Barbie, Sports Car, 1979, NRFB .**25.00**

Barbie, Swan Lake Ballerina, 1991, NRFB ............................**200.00**

**Barbie, Swirl Ponytail, blond, 1964, NRFB, $650.00.** (Photo courtesy McMasters Auctions)

Barbie, Ten Speeder, 1973, NRFB ..............................**30.00**

Barbie, Theatre Date, 1964, NRFB ...........................**660.00**

Barbie, Twirly Curls, 1983, MIB ..................................**45.00**

Barbie, Twist 'N Turn, 1966, blond hair, MIB ........................**600.00**

Barbie, Unicef, 1989, NRFB ....**20.00**

Barbie, Xavier, 1999, University Barbie, NRFB ...................**16.00**

Chris, 1967, blond hair, original outfit, NM ............................**125.00**

Christie, Fashion Photo, 1978, MIB ..**95.00**

Christie, Kissing, 1979, MIB ......**45.00**

Christie, Pink & Pretty, 1982, NRFB ...............................**45.00**

Christie, Pretty Reflections, 1979, NRFB ...............................**85.00**

Christie, Sunsational Malibu, 1982, NRFB ...............................**55.00**

Christie, Superstar, 1977, MIB .....**80.00**

**Christie, Talking, oxidized hair, nonworking, 1968, NMIB, $250.00.**

Francie, Busy, 1972, NRFB .....**425.00**

Ginger, Growing Up, 1977, MIB ......**100.00**

Ken, Arabian Knights, 1964, NRFB ..**425.00**

Ken, Busy, 1972, NRFB .........**150.00**

Ken, Crystal, 1984, NRFB .......**40.00**

Ken, Hawaiian, 1979, MIB ......**55.00**

Ken, King Arthur, 1964, NRFB ......**500.00**

Ken, Live Action, 1971, NRFB.......**150.00**

Ken, Party Time, 1977, NRFB ......**35.00**

Ken, Sun Charm, 1989, MIB......**25.00**

Ken, Superstar, 1977, MIB......**100.00**

Ken, Totally Hair, 1991, NRFB......**50.00**

Ken, Western, 1982, MIB.........**35.00**

Ken, 1962, painted blond hair, MIB .**125.00**

Midge, Cool Times, 1989, NRFB.......**30.00**

Midge, Earrings Magic, 1993, NRFB ..**30.00**

Midge, Ski Fun, 1991, Toys R Us, MIB ....................................**30.00**

Nikki, Animal Lovin', 1989, NRFB .**30.00**

PJ, Deluxe Quick Curl, 1976, MIB ..**65.00**

PJ, Free Moving, 1976, MIB ......**85.00**

PJ, Malibu, 1978, MIB .............**55.00**

Ricky, 1965, original outfit & shoes, NM ....................................**75.00**

Scott, Skipper's boyfriend, 1980, MIB ...................................**55.00**

Skipper, Growing Up, 1976, MIB .**100.00**

Skipper, Pepsi Spirit, 1989, NRFB ..**70.00**

Skipper, Totally Hair, 1991, NRFB ..**30.00**

Skipper, Western, 1982, NRFB ......**40.00**

Skooter, 1963, brunette hair, original swimsuit & bows, MIB.........**175.00**

Stacey, Twist 'N Turn, 1969, blond hair, NRFB ......................**500.00**

Steffie, Walk Lively, 1968, original outfit & scarf, NM ...........**175.00**

Teresa, All American, 1991, MIB ..**25.00**

Tutti, 1967, brunette hair, MIB.**165.00**

Whitney, Style Magic, 1989, NRFB ................................**35.00**

**Cases**

Barbie, Francie, Casey & Tutti, hard plastic, EX, from $50 to .....**75.00**

Barbie & Stacey, 1967, vinyl, NM, from $65 to.........................**75.00**

Barbie Goes Travelin', vinyl, rare, NM ..................................**100.00**

Circus Star Barbie, FAO Schwarz, 1995, NM ...........................**25.00**

Fashion Queen Barbie, 1963, red vinyl, w/mirror & wig stand, EX...**100.00**

**Clothing and Accessories**

Barbie, After Five, #934, 1962, NRFP ..............................**300.00**

Barbie, Busy Morning, #981, 1960, NRFP ..............................**325.00**

Barbie, Dog 'N Duds, #1613, NRFP ..............................**350.00**

Barbie, Fraternity Dance, #1638, NRFP ..............................**600.00**

Barbie, Jumpin' Jeans, Pak, 1964, NRFP ..............................**85.00**

Barbie, Make Mine Midi, #1861, 1969, NRFP ....................**300.00**

Barbie, Midi-Marvelous, #1870, 1969, NRFP ....................**160.00**

Barbie, My First Picnic, #5611, 1983, NRFP ......................**10.00**

Barbie, Plush Pony, #1873, 1969, NRFP ..............................**175.00**

Barbie, Scuba Do's, #1788, 1970, NRFP ................................**65.00**

Barbie, Skin Diver, #1608, 1964, NRFP ..............................**125.00**

Barbie, Sugar Plum Fairy, #9326, 1976, NRFP ......................**40.00**

Barbie, Trail Blazer, #1846, 1968, NRFP ..............................**250.00**

Barbie, Victorian Velvet, #3431, 1971, NRFP ....................**175.00**

Barbie, White Delight, #3799, 1982, NRFP ................................**15.00**

Barbie, Wild Things, #3439, 1971, NRFP ..............................**250.00**

Francie, Clam Diggers, #1258, 1966, NRFP ..............................**275.00**

Francie, Hip Knits, #1265, 1966, NRFP ..............................**225.00**

Francie, Slightly Summery Fashion Pak, 1968, NRFP.................**95.00**

Francie, Two for the Ball, #1232, MOC ..................................**225.00**

Francie & Casey, Victorian Wedding, #1233, 1969-70, MIB........**300.00**

Jazzie, Mini Dress, #3781 or #3783, 1989, NRFP, ea..................**10.00**

Julia, Brrr-Furr, #1752, 1969, NRFP ...............................**175.00**

Ken, Date With Barbie, #5824, 1983, NRFP .......................**10.00**

Ken, Pepsi Outfit, #7761, 1974, NRFP ..................................**40.00**

Ken, Summer Job, #1422, 1966, NRFP ................................**450.00**

Ken & Brad, Sun Fun Fashion Pak, 1971, MIP............................**75.00**

Skipper, All Over Felt, #3476, NRFP ...............................**150.00**

Skipper, Fun Time, #1920, 1965, NRFP ...............................**225.00**

Skipper, Popover, #1943, 1967, NRFP ...............................**175.00**

Skipper, Real Sporty, #1961, 1968, NRFP ...............................**200.00**

Skipper, Shoe Parade Fashion Pak, 1965, NRFP .......................**45.00**

Skipper, Tea Party, #1924, 1966, NRFP ...............................**325.00**

Stacey, Stripes Are Happening, #1544, 1968, NRFP ...........**75.00**

Tutti, Clowning Around, #3606, 1967, NRFP .....................**195.00**

Twiggy, Twiggy Turnouts, #1726, 1968, NRFP .....................**250.00**

Twiggy & Chris, Sea-Shore Shorties, #3614, 1968-69, MIP .......**150.00**

## Houses, Furnishings, and Vehicles

Action Sewing Center, 1972, MIB.**50.00**

Barbie & Ken Dune Buggy, pink, Irwin, 1970, MIB .............**250.00**

Barbie & Skipper School, 1965, rare, MIB ...................................**500.00**

Barbie Beautie Boutique, 1976, MIB..**40.00**

Barbie Cafe Today, 1971, MIB......**400.00**

Barbie Dream Dining Center, 1984, MIB ....................................**25.00**

Barbie Dream Luxury Bathtub, 1984, pink, MIB.................**20.00**

Barbie Glamour Home, 1985, MIB.**125.00**

Barbie Silver 'Vette, MIB.........**30.00**

Barbie Teen Dream Bedroom, MIB..**50.00**

Barbie Travelin' Trailer, MIB......**40.00**

Beach Bus, 1974, MIB..............**45.00**

California Dream Barbie Hot Dog Stand, 1988, NRFB ...........**50.00**

California Dream Beach Taxi, 1988, MIB ....................................**35.00**

Go-Together Chair, Ottoman & End Table, MIB ......................**100.00**

Go-Together Living Room, Barbie & Skipper, 1965, MIB ...........**50.00**

Jamie's Penthouse, Sears Exclusive, 1971, MIB .......................**475.00**

Ken's Classy Corvette, yellow, 1976, MIB ....................................**75.00**

Magical Mansion, 1989, MIB......**125.00**

Pink Sparkles Armoire, 1990, NRFB..**25.00**

Pink Sparkles Starlight Bed, 1990, MIB ....................................**30.00**

Snowmobile, Montgomery Ward, 1972, MIB ..........................**65.00**

Starlight Motorhome, 1994, MIB.**45.00**

Sunsailer, 1975, NRFB ............**55.00**

Surprise House, 1972, MIB ......**100.00**

Susy Goose Canopy Bed, 1962, MIB..**150.00**

Susy Goose Ken Wardrobe ...........**50.00**

Tutti Playhouse, 1966 ............**100.00**

Western Star Traveler Motorhome, 1982, MIB ..........................**50.00**

World of Barbie House, 1966, MIB ..................................**175.00**

1957 Belair Chevy, pink, 1990, 2nd edition, MIB.....................**125.00**

## Gift Sets

Army Barbie & Ken, 1993, Stars 'N Stripes, MIB ....................**60.00**

Barbie & Ken Campin' Out, 1983, MIB .....................................**75.00**

Barbie Loves Elvis, 1996, NRFB .**75.00**

Barbie's Olympic Ski Village, MIB .**75.00**

Birthday Fun at McDonald's, 1994, NRFB ................................**75.00**

Dolls of the World II, 1995, NRFB.**100.00**

Happy Birthday Barbie, 1985, NRFB ..................................**50.00**

Loving You Barbie, 1984, MIB .....**75.00**

Pretty Pairs Nan 'N Fran, 1970, NRFB ................................**250.00**

**Secret Hearts Barbie Deluxe Gift Set, Sam's Club, 1993, $24.00.** (Photo courtesy J. Michael Augustyniak)

Skipper Party Time, 1964, NRFB ..**500.00**

Superstar Barbie & Ken, 1978, MIB.**175.00**

Tutti & Todd Sundae Treat, 1966, NRFB ................................**500.00**

Wedding Party Midge, 1990, NRFB .**150.00**

**Miscellaneous**

Barbie & the Rockers, purse, vinyl, w/comb & cologne ..............**25.00**

Barbie Cutlery Set, Sears Exclusive, 1962, MIP...........................**50.00**

Barbie Ge-Tar, 1965 ...............**325.00**

Barbie Sew Magic Fashion Set, 1973-75, complete, MIB ..............**100.00**

Christie Quick Curl Beauty Center, Sears Exclusive, 1982, MIB .....................................**35.00**

Dictionary, blue vinyl w/Bubble-Cut Barbie graphics, 1963, VG....................................**35.00**

Nurse Kit, #1964, 1962, complete, NMIB ..............................**400.00**

Paper dolls, Barbie, Whitman #4601, 1963, uncut, M.......**85.00**

Picture Maker Designer Fashion Set, Mattel, 1969, NMIB.............**40.00**

Quick Curl Miss America Beauty Center, Sears Exclusive, 1975, MIB .....................................**75.00**

Sweet Sixteen Promotional Set, 1974....................................**70.00**

Tea set, Barbie 25th Anniversary, 1984, complete.................**150.00**

Wallet, black vinyl, Bubble-Cut Barbie in evening gown, 1982, VG.**20.00**

Yo-yo, plastic w/paper sticker, Spectra Star, MIP ......................**5.00**

# Bauer

The Bauer Company moved from Kentucky to California in 1909, producing crocks, gardenware, and vases until after the Depression when they introduced their first line of dinnerware. From 1932 until the early 1960s, they successfully marketed several lines of solid-color wares that are today very collectible. Some of their most popular lines are Ring, Plain Ware, and Monterey Modern.

Brusche Al Fresco, cup & saucer, Misty Gray, low .................**12.00**

Brusche Al Fresco, pitcher, Misty Gray, 2-pt............................**40.00**

Brusche Al Fresco, salt & pepper shakers, Coffee Brown, jumbo, pr........................................**30.00**

Cal-Art, flowerpot, Swirl, olive green, 6"............................**55.00**

Cal-Art, flowerpot, Swirl, yellow, 4"......................................**25.00**

Cal-Art, Spanish pot, speckled green, 4"..............................**20.00**

Contempo, cup & saucer, Spicy Green.................................**12.00**

Contempo, pitcher, Indio Brown, 1-pt.........................................**30.00**

Contempo, plate, dinner; Spicy Green, 10".............................**10.00**

Glass Pastel Kitchenware, baker, all colors, scarce, 11½x6½"......**45.00**

Glass Pastel Kitchenware, casserole, olive green, 1-qt.................**45.00**

Glass Pastel Kitchenware, custard cup, all colors.....................**10.00**

Glass Pastel Kitchenware, pitcher, any color, 1½-pt.................**25.00**

Hi-Fire, flower bowl, turquoise, deep, #211, 6"......................**45.00**

Hi-Fire, rose bowl, Monterey Blue, 4".......................................**5.00**

Hi-Fire, vase, black, Fred Johnson, #215, 7"............................**150.00**

**La Linda, blue cup, $20.00; and yellow saucer, $8.00.**
(Photo courtesy Jack Chipman)

Matt Carlton, bowl, orange red, sq, 2½x6"..............................**150.00**

Matt Carlton, vase, royal blue, embossed ribs, flared rim, 5¼"........**450.00**

Matt Carlton, vase, royal blue, twist handles, 9½".................**1,200.00**

Plain Ware, bowl, salad; 8¼"......**120.00**

Plain Ware, coffee server, w/lid, from $75 to......................**100.00**

Plain Ware, lamp base, 4½"......**450.00**

Plain Ware, pitcher, Dutch; orange-red, Carlton, 12", from $300 to......................................**350.00**

Plain Ware, sugar bowl..........**125.00**

Ring Ware, bowl, low salad; cobalt, 12"....................................**175.00**

Ring Ware, bowl, punch/salad; footed, 9"................................**500.00**

Ring Ware, cigarette jar.........**750.00**

Ring Ware, cup, punch; Chinese Yellow....................................**60.00**

Ring Ware, platter, oval, green, 9".....................................**100.00**

Ring Ware, salt & pepper shakers, burgundy, squat, pr...........**80.00**

Ring Ware, teapot, orange-red w/yellow lid, 6-cup.....................**95.00**

Speckled Kitchenware, bowl, mixing; white, #36...........................**25.00**

Speckled Kitchenware, bowl, salad; yellow, low, 7"....................**30.00**

Speckled Kitchenware, buffet server, brown...........................**45.00**

Speckled Kitchenware, candleholder, votive, brown................**15.00**

Speckled Kitchenware, casserole, pink, 2½-qt, w/lid...............**75.00**

Speckled Kitchenware, pitcher, pink, 1-pt...........................**35.00**

Speckled Kitchenware, pitcher, yellow, Brusche style, 1-pt..........................**35.00**

# Beanie Babies

Though everyone agrees Beanie Babies are on the downside of their highest peak, they're still a force to deal with, and you'll find Beanie Baby tables by the score in any large flea market field. New ones are being still being cranked out, thanks to collector demand — most of those are valued at $5.00 to $7.00 or less, but a few are a little higher. All of those we've listed here are retired; values reflect examples in mint condition.

Ally the Alligator, #4032 ..........**20.00**
Baldy the Eagle, #4074, from $5 to .**10.00**
Beak the Kiwi, #4211 ...............**10.00**
Bessie the Cow, #4009, brown .**15.00**
Blackie the Bear, #4011 ...........**10.00**
Blizzard the Tiger, #4163.........**10.00**
Bones the Dog, #4001, brown...**10.00**
Bongo the monkey, #4067, 2nd issue, tan tail, from $10 to.............**15.00**
Bronty the Brontosaurus, #4085, blue, minimum value ......**100.00**
Brownie the Bear, #4010, w/swing tag, minimum value ........**200.00**
Bubbles the Fish, #4078, yellow & black ...................................**10.00**
Bumble the Bee, #4045, minimum value.................................**50.00**
Caw the Crow, #4071, minimum value.................................**50.00**
Chilly the Polar Bear, #4012, minimum value ......................**200.00**
Chops the Lamb, #4019.............**20.00**
Coral the Fish, #4079, tie-dyed..**10.00**
Cubbie the Bear, #4010, brown..**15.00**
Curly the Bear, #4052, brown, from $5 to....................................**10.00**

Daisy the Cow, #4006, black & white ...................................**15.00**
Derby the Horse, #4008, 2nd issue, coarse mane & tail.............**10.00**
Digger the Crab, #4027, 1st issue, orange, minimum value......**50.00**
Digger the Crab, #4027, 2nd issue, red, minimum value..........**10.00**
Doodle the Rooster, #4171, tie-dyed....................................**10.00**
Flash the Dolphin, #4021, minimum value...................................**15.00**
Flashy the Peacock, #4339.......**10.00**
Flip the Cat, #4012, white........**10.00**
Floppity the Bunny, lavendar, from $7 to.....................................**9.00**
Flutter the Butterfly, #4043, minimum value...................................**50.00**
Garcia the Bear, #4051, tie-dyed, minimum value .................**20.00**
Glory the Bear, #4188, from $8 to .**10.00**

**Goldie the Goldfish, #4023, $10.00.** (Photo courtesy Amy Sullivan)

Grunt the Razorback Pig, #4092, red, minimum value..........**20.00**
Happy the Hippo, #4061, gray, minimum value .........................**50.00**
Happy the Hippo, #4061, 2nd issue, lavender, from $8 to.............**15.00**
Hippity the Bunny, #4119, mint green, from $7 to.................**9.00**
Holiday Teddy (1997), #4200, from $8 to...................................**10.00**

Holiday Teddy (1998), #4204 ...**10.00**
Holiday Teddy (1999), #4257 ...**10.00**
Holiday Teddy (2000), #4332 ...**10.00**
Holiday Teddy (2001), #4395 ...**10.00**
Holiday Teddy (2002), #4564 ...**10.00**
Hoot the Owl, #4073.................**10.00**
Hoppity the Bunny, #4117, pink, from $7 to.............................**9.00**
Humphrey the Camel, #4060, minimum value.......................**100.00**
Inch the Worm, #4044, felt antennae ................................**20.00**
Inch the Worm, #4044, yarn antennae, from $7 to...................**10.00**
Inky the Octopus, #4028, 3rd issue, pink, from $6 to .................**15.00**
Kiwi the Toucan, #4070, minimum value...................................**30.00**
Legs the Frog, #4020 .........**10.00**
Lefty the Donkey, #4087, gray..**20.00**
Libearty the Bear, #4057, minimum value..................................**50.00**
Lizzy the Lizard, #4033, tie-dyed, minimum value .................**50.00**
Lizzy the Lizard, #4033, 2nd issue, blue, from $10 to...............**20.00**
Lucky the Ladybug, #4040, 3rd issue, 11 spots, from $10 to .........**15.00**
Magic the Dragon, #4088, from $10 to........................................**20.00**

**Manny the Manatee, #4081, minimum value $20.00.** (Photo courtesy Amy Sullivan)

Millennium the Bear, #4226, from $10 to.................................**12.00**
Nectar the Hummingbird, #4361, from $10 to........................**20.00**
Nuts the Squirrel, #4114.........**10.00**
Patti the Platypus, #4025, 2nd issue, purple, from $10 to ...............**20.00**
Peanut the Elephant, #4062, light blue, from $7 to..................**15.00**
Peking the Panda Bear, #4013, minimum value.....................**100.00**
Pinchers the Lobster, #4026 .....**15.00**
Quackers the Duck, #4024, 2nd issue, w/wings, from $10 to ................................**20.00**
Quackers the Duck, #4024, 1st issue, no wings ...............**450.00**
Radar the Bat, #4091, black, minimum value.........................**30.00**
Rex the Tyrannosaurus, #4086, minimum value.....................**100.00**
Righty the Elephant, #4085, gray..**20.00**
Ringo the Raccoon, #4014, from $10 to.........................................**15.00**
Rover the Dog, #4101, red, from $10 to.........................................**15.00**
Sammy the Bear, #4215, tie-dyed....................................**10.00**
Seamore the Seal, #4029, white, minimum value .................**20.00**
Slither the Snake, #4031, minimum value...............................**200.00**
Snowball the Snowman, #4201, from $10 to...............................**12.00**
Snowgirl the Snowgirl, #4333, from $10 to.................................**12.00**
Spangle the Bear, #4245, blue face, from $10 to........................**20.00**
Sparky the Dalmatian, #4100, minimum value .........................**15.00**
Splash the Whale, #4022, minimum value...................................**15.00**

Spooky the Ghost, #4090, orange ribbon, minimum value.....**10.00**

Spot the Dog, #4000, with spot..**30.00**

Squealer the Pig, #4005 ...........**10.00**

Sting the Stingray, #4077, tie-dyed, minimum value .................**20.00**

Tabasco the Bull, #4002, red feet, minimum value .................**20.00**

Tank the Armadillo, #4031, no shell, 7 lines on back, minimum value...................................**40.00**

Teddy Bear, #4050, brown, new face, from $15 to.........................**30.00**

The Beginning Bear, #4267, w/silver stars ...................................**10.00**

The End Bear, #4265, black.....**10.00**

Trap the Mouse, #4042, minimum value................................**100.00**

Tusk the Walrus, #4076, minimum value...................................**20.00**

Valentino the Bear, #4058, white w/red heart..........................**10.00**

Velvet the Panther, #4064, minimum value..................................**10.00**

Web the Spider, #4041, black, minimum value .......................**100.00**

# The Beatles

Beatles memorabilia is becoming increasingly popular with those who grew up in the '60s. Almost any item that could be produced with their picture or logo was manufactured and sold by the thousands in department stores. Some have such a high collector value that they have been reproduced, so beware!

Assignment book, Select-O-Pack, 1964..................................**250.00**

Banner, Hallmark stamps promo, 3x18", VG+.........................**50.00**

Belt buckle, metal w/photo under plastic, EX...........................**40.00**

Binder, white vinyl, 3-ring, NM......**110.00**

Book, Lennon Remembers, hardback, 1971, NM..................**30.00**

Book, Letters to the..., 1964, EX..**25.00**

Brunch bag, blue vinyl w/zippered top, 8"...............................**460.00**

Calendar, portraits in doorway, 1964..................................**175.00**

Candy dish, Paul, pottery w/gilt edge, UK ..........................**150.00**

Card, Fan Club Member, 1964.....**39.00**

Clutch purse, cloth w/leather strap & allover pictures, NM..........**240.00**

Collector's stamps, 1964 Hallmark Edition, 5 for.....................**10.00**

Concert book, USA, 1964, 12x12"......**45.00**

Doll, John or George w/instrument, vinyl, Remco, 4", ea............**125.00**

Dolls, inflatable, NEMS, 1968, set of 4, EX................................**150.00**

**Drum, New Beat, with stand, sticks, etc., EX, $375.00.**

Eyeglasses case, John, facsimile signature, England.................**75.00**

Flasher rings, set of 4, EX........**80.00**

Halloween mask, John Lennon ......**125.00**

Handbag, white cloth w/brass handle, Dame, w/original tag, 1964..................................**600.00**

Harmonica, Hohner, M (NM box) ..**150.00**

Jigsaw puzzle, Sea of Monsters, Jaymar #5059, 100 pcs, EXIB..**100.00**

Magazine, Life, Paul & Linda on cover, 1971, NM.................**20.00**

Money clip, apple cutout, Apple Records...........................**275.00**

Paint by Number set, 1 portrait, US, 1964, MIB ....................**1,200.00**

Pins, Yellow Submarine, HP brass, 8 for ....................................**50.00**

Pop-up book, Yellow Submarine, NM ......................................**45.00**

Program, 1965, 6 pages, EX.....**60.00**

Record sleeve, Can't Buy Me Love, rare...................................**525.00**

Sheet music, I Want To Hold Your Hand, 1968........................**20.00**

Sunglasses, black plastic, Bachman Bros, 1964..........................**250.00**

Thermos, blue w/band image, 1965, EX..................................**275.00**

Thimble, Fenton, baked-on image, 1990s, EX..........................**15.00**

Tie-tac set, NEMS, 1964, MOC (watch for repros)..............**75.00**

Wallet, vinyl w/photo & all extras, by SPP, VG .....................**100.00**

# Beer Cans

Beer has been sold in cans since 1935, when the Continental Can Company developed a method of coating the inside of the can with plastic. The first style was the flat top that came with instructions on how to open it. Because most breweries were not equipped to fill a flat can, most went to the 'cone top,' but by the 1950s, even that was obsolete. Can openers were the order of the day until the 1960s, when tab-top cans came along. The heyday of beer can collecting was during the 1970s, but the number of collectors has since receded, leaving a huge supply of beer cans, most of which are worth no more than a few dollars each. The basic rule of thumb is to concentrate your collecting on cans made prior to 1970. Remember, condition is critical.

Values are based on cans in conditions as stated.

Cone top, Gold Crest 51, Memphis TN, EX...................................**90.00**

Cone top, Pickwick Ale, Haffenreffer, Boston MA, EX .......................**50.00**

Cone top, Royal Bru, Union, New Castle PA, VG.................**135.00**

Cone top, Sigraa, Reno NV, G+.......**40.00**

Cone top, Stock Ale, Croft Brewing, Lacrosse WI, G ....................**62.00**

Cone top, Sunshine Extra, Barbey's Reading PA, EX .................**135.00**

Cone top, Utica Club, West End, Utica NY, EX ...................**185.00**

**Crowntainer, Leinenkugel's Chippewa Pride Beer, Leinenkugels Brewing, Chippewa Falls, WI, 1950s, G, $50.00; Cone top, Fauerbach CB (Continental Beer) Fauerbach Brewing, Madison WI, 1950s, VG, $30.00; Cone top, Northern Beer, Northern Brewing, Superior, WI, 1950s, G+, $30.00.** (Photo courtesy Frank's Auctions)

Flat top, Acme Beer, Acme Brewing, San Francisco CA, EX.......**20.00**

Flat top, Alps Brau, Maier, Los Angeles, EX........................**60.00**

Flat top, Burger Ale, Burger, Cincinnati OH, EX.............**48.00**

Flat top, Fort Schuyler, Utica NY, EX.........................................**45.00**

Flat top, Goebel Beer, Goebel Brewing, Detroit MI, instructional, EX........................................**50.00**

Flat top, Golden Pilsner, Becker, Ogden UT, EX....................**45.00**

Flat top, Land of Lakes, Pilsen Brewing, Chicago IL, EX+..........**23.00**

Flat top, Old Craft, Oconto WI, EX.........................................**32.00**

Flat top, Old Tyme Beer, Maier Brewing, Los Angeles CA, G+..................................**20.00**

Flat top, Tempo Beer, Blatz Brewing, Milwaukee WI, G+ .............................**210.00**

Pull tab, Ballantine, Bock Ballantine, Newark NJ, EX...............................**65.00**

Pull tab, Drewerys Bock, Drewerys, South Bend IN, EX .................................**40.00**

Pull tab, Jax Draft, Jackson Brewing, New Orleans LA, EX .................................**45.00**

Zip tab, Blatz Pilsner, Blatz, Lawrence MI, J Spout, VG+ ............................**90.00**

Zip tab, Dakota, Bismark ND, NM ......................................**45.00**

Zip tab, E&B Special Beer, E&B Brewing, Detroit MI, EX+..**40.00**

Zip tab, Sebewaing Beer, Sebewaing Brewing, Sebewaing MI....**45.00**

# Birthday Angels

Here's a collection that's lots of fun, inexpensive, and takes relatively little space to display. They're not at all hard to find, but there are several series, so completing 12-month sets of them all can provide a bit of a challenge. Generally speaking, angels are priced by the following factors: 1) company — look for Lefton, Napco, Norcrest, and Enesco marks or labels (unmarked or unknown sets are of less value); 2) application of flowers, bows, gold trim, etc. (the more detail, the more valuable); 3) use of rhinestones, which will also increase price; 4) age; and 5) quality of the workmanship involved, detail, and accuracy of painting.

#1194, angel of the month series, white hair, 5", ea from $18 to........................................**20.00**

#1300, boy angels, wearing suit, white hair, 6", ea from $22 to........................................**25.00**

#1600, Pal Angel, month series of both boy & girl, 4", ea from $10 to........................................**15.00**

Japan, J-6726, June bride w/veil & rose bouquet, 1950s, 5¼"...**32.00**

Kelvin, C-230, holding flower of the month, 4½", ea...................**20.00**

Lefton, #0130, Kewpie, 4½", ea from $35 to...............................**40.00**

Lefton, #0556, boy of the month, 5½", ea from $25 to............**30.00**

Lefton, #0627, day of the week series, 3½", ea from $28 to.............**32.00**

Lefton, #1411, angel of the month, 4", ea from $28 to..............**32.00**

Lefton, #2600, birthstone on skirt, 3¼", ea from $25 to............**30.00**

Lefton, #5146, birthstone on skirt, 4½", ea from $22 to............**28.00**

Lefton, #6949, day of the week series in oval frame, 5", ea, from $28 to................................**32.00**

Lefton, AR-1987, w/ponytail, 4", ea from $18 to.........................**22.00**

**Napco, A1920, April angel boy with rabbit and basket, gold trim, 1956, 4¾", $60.00.**

Napco, A4307, angel of the month, sm, ea from $22 to.............**25.00**

Napco, S1291, day of the week, 'Belle,' ea from $22 to........**25.00**

Napco, S401-413, angel of the month, ea from $20 to.......**25.00**

Napco, X8371, Christmas boy playing accordion, 1950s, 3¾".**26.00**

Napco, X8371, Christmas girl playing violin, 1950s, 3¾" ........**26.00**

Norcrest, F-167, bell of the month, 2¾", ea from $8 to..............**12.00**

Norcrest, F-340, angel of the month, 5", ea from $20 to................**25.00**

Relco, 4¼", ea from $15 to........**18.00**

Relco, 6", ea from $18 to..........**22.00**

Ucagco, white hair, 5¾", from $12 to.......................................**15.00**

# Black Americana

This is a wide and varied field of collector interest. Advertising, toys, banks, sheet music, kitchenware items, movie items, and even the fine arts are areas that offer Black Americana buffs many opportunities to add to their collections. Caution! Because some pieces have become so valuable, reproductions abound. Watch for lots of new ceramic items, less detailed in both the modeling and the painting.

Ashtray, man sits on box & plays piano, cast iron, 1920s-30s, 2½"..**130.00**

Bank, boy by orange, painted ceramic, Souvenir of FL, 1940s, 5½".**75.00**

Book, Little Black Sambo, H Bannerman, Harter Pub, 1931, 13x9¼", EX .....................**175.00**

Book, Little Black Sambo, Saalfield, #2396, c 1942, EX ...............**125.00**

Book, Treasury of Steven Foster, 1st edition, hardcover, 1934, VG..**55.00**

Booklet, Porgy & Bess, S Goldwyn Motion Pictures, 1959, EX..**35.00**

Bottle, cowboy figural, lustre, Made in Japan, 1940s, 7½" ..............**125.00**

Candleholder, angel on tummy, Shafford Japan sticker, 1950s, 3", ea...................................**32.00**

Card, greeting; Why Fo' Am I Sendin' Dis?, boy fishing, 1940s, EX.....................................**15.00**

Cookie jar, Aunt Jemima, plastic, F&F ................................**650.00**

**Cookie jar, Mammy, F&F, plastic, 11½", EX, $450.00 or M, $650.00.**

Creamer & sugar bowl, native on elephant, lustreware, Japan, 1940s .................................**95.00**

Creamer & sugar bowl, Someone's in the Kitchen, colorful, Dept 56..**65.00**

Doll, Golliwog, stuffed knit yarn, 1950s-60s, 13", EX.............**40.00**

Drip jar, girl's head, exaggerated features, multicolor, Japan ............**50.00**

Fan, mother reading to 2 children printed on paper, 1930-50, EX ....................................**30.00**

Figure, boy & duck, painted ceramic, Japan, 1940s, 1⅞" ...............**65.00**

Figure, girl (well dressed) w/doll, bisque, Germany #27, 8½" ..**300.00**

Figure, Jungle Imp, native w/necklace & earrings, Nye #203, 4", EX............................................**65.00**

Figure, ministrel, pnt bisque, Made in Japan, 5" .......................**35.00**

Game, Bean-Em, caricatures of Mose, Sambo & Rastus, All Fair, 1931.......................**450.00**

Greeting card, caricature children, hinged jaw, Germany, 1930s, EX......................................**60.00**

Letter opener, sterling w/Sunny South character finial, 5¼" ......**165.00**

Little Brown Koko Has Fun, BS Hunt, American Colortype, 1945, EX............................**85.00**

**LP record, Ray Charles, The Genius Hits the Road, ABC Paramount, ca 1964, EX, from $45.00 to $55.00.** (Photo courtesy P.J. Gibbs)

Magazine, Life, He Had a Dream, Coretta Scott King cover, 1959, NM ....................................**45.00**

Menu, Coon Chicken Inn, die-cut cardboard head of bellhop, NM................................**80.00**

Mug, man w/exaggerated eyes, arm handle, Stern, 1930s-40s, 5½"......**150.00**

Noise maker, tin litho of caricature man, Made in USA, 1950s, NM.......**45.00**

Paper plate, Aunt Jemima Days Are Here Again.., 9¼"..................**30.00**

Pillow, Mammy w/child transfer, Play You's Er Squirrel Chile, 17x20" .............................**100.00**

Place mat, Aunt Jemima...at Disneyland, paper, 1955, 13¾x9¾"..**45.00**

Plaque, All God's Children, girl's head in fence, Holcombe, 1988, EX....................................**50.00**

Plaque, exaggerated native's head, ceramic, Italy, 1930s, 6½"..**65.00**

Poster, Le Roy Jones (activist), black/tan, EH Cobb, 1967, 22x17" .............................**200.00**

Poster, Smash the State, black & white, 1969-71, 16⅝x11⅜", NM ................................**125.00**

Print, Wash Day, lady observed by boy, black & white half-tone, Tarbel................................**70.00**

Record, Blue Tail Fly, 1953, 78 rpm, w/original 10¼" picture sleeve ..**29.00**

Record, Blue-Tailed Flay, banjo player caricature sleeve, 78-rpm, EX.............................**30.00**

Record, Brave Little Sambo, 1950s, 78 rpm, in picture sleeve...**55.00**

Sack, Aunt Jemima Hominy Grits, heavy paper, 1960s-70s, 11½x5½" ...........................**22.00**

Shakers, children sitting in basket, ceramic, Japan, 1940s, 3-pc .......**90.00**

Sheet music, Cotton Fluff, child w/cotton balls, 1936, EX......**30.00**

Stamp, Benjamin Banneker, Feb 1980, 2⅝x1".........................**5.00**

Stamp, Booker T Washington, April 1940, uncancelled, 1¼x1"..**15.00**

Syrup pitcher, Aunt Jemima, F&F, 5½" ....................................**70.00**

Tablecloth, caricatures on printed cotton, yellow edge, 1950s, 51" sq .....................................**225.00**

Tea towel, boy eating watermelon printed on white, 1950s, unused, 27" .......................**45.00**

Tea towel, printed cotton, man w/banjo & boy at cabin, 1940s, 29x16" ..............................**57.00**

Teapot, boy on elephant, bamboo handle, Japan, 1940s, 5¼"..**215.00**

Teapot, Mammy figure, Japan, 1980s, 7"..............................**75.00**

Trivet/platter, Mammy's head, painted & glazed redware, Japan, 8".........................**75.00**

Vase, lady native's head, pottery, black w/gold trim, 1960s, 6", EX......................................**30.00**

View Master & Reel, Little Black Sambo, 1948, EX ..............**85.00**

# Black Cats

This line of fancy felines was marketed mainly by the Shafford (importing) Company, although black cat lovers accept similarly modeled, shiny glazed kitties of other importing firms into their collections as well. Because eBay offers an over supply of mid-century collectibles, the value structure for these cats has widened, with prices for common items showing a marked decline. At the same time, items that are truely rare, such as the triangle spice set and the wireware cat face spice set have shot upwards. Values that follow are for examples in mint (or nearly mint) paint, an important consideration in determining a fair market price. Shafford items are often minus their white whiskers and eyebrows, and this type of loss should be reflected in your evaluation. An item in poor paint may be worth even less than half of given estimates. Note: Unless 'Shafford' is included in the descriptions, values are for cats that were imported by other companies.

Bank, seated, coin slot in top of head, Shafford, from $200 to ......**225.00**

Cigarette lighter, Shafford, 5½", from $175 to.....................**190.00**

Condiment set, 2 joined heads, J&M bows, spoons, Shafford, 4" ......................................**135.00**

Cookie jar, head form, Shafford.**100.00**

Creamer, Shafford, from $25 to..**35.00**

Decanter, long cat w/red fish in mouth as stopper...............**75.00**

Decanter set, upright, yellow eyes, 6 plain wines.........................**35.00**

Grease jar, sm head, Shafford, from $150 to..............................**175.00**

Ice bucket, cylinder w/embossed yellow-eyed cat, 2 sizes, ea................**60.00**

Mug, cat's head above rim, Shafford, standard, 3½", from $50 to..**60.00**

Mug, cat's head below rim, Shafford, scarce, 3½" ......................**200.00**

Mug, Shafford, hard to find, 4", from $65 to..................................**75.00**

Pincushion, cushion on back, tongue measure..............................**25.00**

Planter, upright, Shafford, from $35 to........................................**45.00**

Shakers, range; upright, Shafford, 5", pr....................................**35.00**

Shakers, round-bodied 'teapot' cats, Shafford, pr.........................**75.00**

Spice set, 6 sq shakers on wood frame, Shafford, from $175 to........**225.00**

Spice set, 9 pcs in wood frame, yellow eyes, Wales, from $95 to...**110.00**

Sugar bowl, Shafford, from $25 to.**35.00**

Teapot, ball-shaped body, head lid, Shafford, sm, 4-4½", ea .....**25.00**

Teapot, ball-shaped body, head lid, Shafford, 7", from $60 to......**75.00**

Tray, flat face, wicker handle, Shafford, scarce, from $75 to.**100.00**

Utensil: strainer, dipper or funnel, wood handles, Shafford, ea..**150.00**

Wall pocket, 'teapot' cat, Shafford, minimum value ...............**150.00**

Wine, embossed face, green eyes, Shafford, sm.....................**50.00**

# Blade Banks

In 1903 the safety razor was invented, making it easier for men to shave at home. But the old, used razor blades were troublesome, because for the next twenty-two years, nobody knew what to do with them. In 1925 the first patent was filed for a razor blade bank, a container designed to hold old blades until it became full, in which event it was to be thrown away. Most razor blade banks are 3" or 4" tall, similar to a coin bank with a slot in the top but no outlet in the bottom to remove the old blades. These banks were produced from 1925 to 1950. Some were issued by men's toiletry companies and were often filled with shaving soap or cream. Many were made of tin and printed with an advertising message. An assortment of blade banks made from a variety of materials — ceramic, wood, plastic, or metal — could also be purchased at five-and-dime stores.

For information on blade banks as well as many other types of interesting figural items from the same era, we recommend *Collectibles for the Kitchen, Bath & Beyond* (featuring napkin dolls, egg timers, string holders, children's whistle cups, baby feeder dishes, pie birds, and laundry sprinkler bottles) by Ellen Bercovici, Bobbie Zucker Bryson, and Deborah Gillham. (Available through Antique Trader Books.)

Barber bust w/handlebar mustache, coat & tie, from $50 to .....**70.00**
Barber chair, sm, from $100 to ......**125.00**
Barber head, different colors on collar, Cleminson, from $25 to ....**35.00**
Barber holding pole, Occupied Japan, 4", from $50 to .......**60.00**
Barber pole, red & white stripes, Royal Copley sticker, 6½" ...............**30.00**
Barber pole w/face, red & white, from $30 to .........................**40.00**
Bell, white w/man shaving, California Cleminsons, 3½".....................**25.00**
Dandy Dans, plastic w/brush holders, from $25 to .........................**35.00**
Friar Tuck, Razor Blade Holder (on back), Goebel ...................**300.00**
Frog, green, For used Blades, from $60 to.................................**70.00**

**Gay Blade, marked Cleminson, 4", from $25.00 to $35.00.** (Photo courtesy Jack Chipman)

Grinding stone, For Dull Ones, from $80 to...............................**100.00**

Indian head, porcelain, Japan, 4"..**25.00**
Listerine donkey, from $20 to ......**30.00**
Listerine elephant, from $25 to.......**35.00**
Listerine frog, from $15 to .......**25.00**
Looie, right- or left-hand version, from $85 to.......................**110.00**
Man shaving, mushroom shape, Cleminson, from $25 to .....**35.00**
Razor Bum, from $85 to .........**100.00**
Safe, green, Blade Safe on front, from $40 to.........................**60.00**
Shaving brush, wide style w/decal, from $45 to.........................**65.00**
Tony the Barber, Ceramic Art Studios, from $85 to ................**95.00**

# Blair Dinnerware

American dinnerware has been a popular field of collecting for several years, and the uniquely styled lines of Blair are very appealing, though not often seen except in the Midwest (and it's there that prices are the strongest). Blair was located in Ozark, Missouri, manufacturing dinnerware from the mid-1940s until the early 1950s. Gay Plaid, recognized by its squared-off shapes and brush-stroke design (in lime, green, brown, and dark green on white), is the pattern you'll find most often. Several other lines were made as well. You'll be able to recognize all of them easily enough, since most pieces (except for the smaller items) are marked.

Beer mug, Gay Plaid ...............**55.00**
Bowl, cereal; Gay Plaid ............**10.00**
Bowl, dessert; Leaves ...............**12.00**

Creamer, Gay Plaid .................**25.00**

**Cup and saucer, Brick, from $25.00 to $35.00.**

Cup & saucer, Leaves ...............**12.00**
Pitcher, Gay Plaid, ice lip .........**80.00**
Pitcher, Leaves, ice lip .............**85.00**
Plate, dinner; Gay Plaid ...........**15.00**
Plate, dinner; Leaves ................**15.00**
Plate, salad; Bamboo .................**8.00**
Plate, salad; Gay Plaid ...............**8.00**
Platter, Brick, 10" sq ................**18.00**
Sugar bowl, Gay Plaid, w/lid ......**25.00**
Tumbler, Leaves .......................**15.00**
Tumbler, Spiced Pear ...............**25.00**

# Blue Garland

This lovely line of dinnerware was offered as premiums through grocery store chains during the decades of the '60s and '70s. It has delicate garlands of tiny blue flowers on a white background trimmed in platinum. Rims are scalloped and handles are gracefully curved. Though the 'Haviland' backstamp might suggest otherwise, this china has no connection with the famous Haviland company of Limoges. 'Johann Haviland' (as contained in the mark) was actually the founding company that later became Philip Rosenthal & Co., the German manufacturer who produced chinaware for export to the USA from the mid-1930s until as late as the 1980s.

This line may also be found with the Thailand Johann Haviland backstamp, a later issue. Our values are for the line with the Bavarian mark; expect to pay at least 30% less for the Thailand issue.

Bell, 5½x3¼", from $50 to ........**70.00**
Bowl, fruit; 5⅛", from $2.50 to ......**3.00**
Bowl, oval, 11¼", from $50 to .....**60.00**
Bowl, soup; 7½", from $10 to .....**14.00**
Bowl, vegetable; oval, 10½" L, from $60 to .................................**70.00**
Bowl, vegetable; round, w/lid, from $70 to .................................**80.00**
Butter dish, ¼-lb, from $75 to ........**85.00**
Butter pat/coaster, 3½" .............**5.00**
Candlesticks, 1-light, 4", pr from $40 to ...................................**50.00**
Casserole/soup tureen, w/lid, 11" L..**50.00**
Clock plate, from $40 to ...........**50.00**
Coaster, 3¾" .............................**8.00**
Creamer, marked Thailand, 9-oz, 4¼" .....................................**13.00**
Creamer, 9-oz, 4¼" ...................**20.00**
Cup & saucer, flat, from $8 to ......**12.00**
Fondue pot, w/lid, from $50 to ......**65.00**
Nut dish, footed w/handles .......**30.00**
Plate, bread & butter, 6¼" .........**3.00**
Plate, dinner; 10" .....................**12.00**
Plate, salad; 7¾" .........................**9.00**
Platter, serving; oval, 12⅞" ......**35.00**
Skillet, metal, w/lid, 8½", from $35 to .......................................**45.00**
Teapot, marked Thailand, 4-cup.**35.00**
Tray, tidbit; 2-tiered .................**40.00**
Tray, tidbit; 3-tiered .................**50.00**

# Blue Ridge

Some of the most attractive American dinnerware made in the twentieth century is Blue Ridge, produced by Southern Potteries of Erwin, Tennessee, from the late 1930s until 1956. More than four hundred patterns were hand painted on eight basic shapes. Elaborate or appealing lines are represented by the high end of our range; use the lower side to evaluate simple patterns. The Quimper-like peasant-decorated line is one of the most treasured and should be priced at double the amounts recommended for the higher-end patterns.

Ashtray, advertising, round, from $60 to..................................**70.00**
Ashtray, individual...................**24.00**
Basket, aluminum edge, 7", from $25 to..................................**30.00**
Bonbon, divided, center handle, China, from $85 to.............**95.00**
Bowl, cereal/soup; Premium, 6", from $25 to........................**30.00**
Bowl, hot cereal .......................**25.00**
Box, cigarette; sq .....................**90.00**
Box, Mallard Duck, from $650 to..**700.00**
Butter dish................................**45.00**
Butter dish, Woodcrest, from $45 to..**50.00**
Butter pat/coaster, from $25 to ......**30.00**
Cake lifter ................................**35.00**
Cake tray, Maple Leaf, China, from $50 to................................**65.00**
Celery, Skyline, from $30 to.....**40.00**
Child's feeding dish, divided, from $150 to..............................**175.00**
Cigarette box, sq, from $85 to........**90.00**
Coffeepot, ovoid, from $150 to .....**175.00**

Creamer, demi; China, from $75 to..**85.00**
Creamer, Fifties shape.............**20.00**
Cup & saucer, Holiday, from $60 to........................................**75.00**
Demitasse pot, earthenware, from $125 to.............................**175.00**
Egg cup, Premium, from $50 to..**60.00**
Egg dish, deviled; from $60 to ..**75.00**
Gravy boat, from $15 to............**20.00**
Jug, character; Indian, from $600 to........................................**700.00**
Lamp from pitcher, teapot, etc, from $70 to................................**80.00**
Marmite, Charm House, w/lid, from $170 to.............................**200.00**
Pitcher, Alice, earthenware, 6¼", from $150 to.....................**200.00**

**Pitcher, Fruit Basket, Alice shape, china, 6¼", from $150.00 to $175.00.**

Plate, dinner; Premium, 9¼", from $25 to..................................**35.00**
Ramekin, w/lid, 7½", from $35 to..**45.00**
Relish, T-hdl, from $65 to.........**75.00**
Salt & pepper shakers, Apple, 1¼", pr from $50 to ...................**55.00**
Sconce, wall; from $70 to..........**75.00**
Sugar bowl, Colonial, eared, from $15 to................................**20.00**
Teapot, ball shape, Premium, from $200 to.............................**250.00**
Tidbit, 3-tier, from $40 to.........**50.00**
Toast, lid only, Premium & Peasant, from $200 to.....................**250.00**

Tray, from waffle set, 9½x13½",
from $100 to.....................**125.00**
Vase, handles, China, from $95 to.**100.00**

# Blue Willow

Inspired by the lovely blue and white Chinese exports, the Willow pattern has been made by many English, American, and Japanese firms from 1950 until the present. Many variations of the pattern have been noted — mauve, black, green, and multicolor Willow ware can be found in limited amounts. The design has been applied to tinware, linens, glassware, and paper goods, all of which are treasured by today's collectors. Refer to *Gaston's Blue Willow, 3rd Edition*, by Mary Frank Gaston (Collector Books) for more information. See also Royal China. See Clubs and Newsletters for information concerning *The Willow Review* newsletter.

Ashtray, Japan, sq, 7½" ...........**55.00**
Bank, 3 stacked pigs, Japan, 7".......**75.00**
Bowl, flat soup; Eagle, 8" .........**12.50**
Bowl, Maestricht, 2¾x9⅞" .....**120.00**
Bowl, vegetable; Wood's Ware, 10" ..**40.00**
Bowl & pitcher, Wedgwood .....**1,200.00**
Canisters, tin, sq, unmarked, set of 4........................................**500.00**
Casserole, Empress, w/lid, Homer Laughlin...........................**75.00**
Creamer, Japan ........................**10.00**
Creamer, red, Royal China ......**15.00**
Cup, chili; Japan, 3½x4" ..........**50.00**
Cup, chili; w/liner plate, Japan......**75.00**
Cup, demi; Homer Laughlin......**25.00**

Dish, child's, Ridgeway, w/lid, 5" ....................................**175.00**
Egg cup, double, 4¼" ...............**30.00**
Horseradish dish, Doulton, 5½" ......**65.00**
Jug, milk; Homer Laughlin ......**150.00**

**Kerosene lamp with reflector, Japan, 8", $150.00. (Photo courtesy Mary Frank Gas-**

Leaf dish, unmarked English, 6" L .....................................**175.00**
Mug, unmarked Japan, 3½".....**15.00**
Pitcher, milk; Homer Laughlin, 5" .....................................**45.00**
Pitcher, milk; tankard form, Allerton's, 7", EX .....................**125.00**
Plate, dessert/bread & butter; Japan...................................**5.00**
Plate, dinner; Imperial, 9¾".....**27.00**
Plate, dinner; Liner & Carter, 9½".**24.00**
Plate, salad; red, Wallace China......**8.00**
Platter, Allerton's, 16x12"......**275.00**
Salt box, wall-mount, wooden lid, unmarked Japan, 5"........**110.00**
Sugar bowl, w/lid, Japan..........**15.00**
Teapot, Allerton's, 6", NM.....**225.00**
Tumbler, juice; glass, Jeannette, 3½" ....................................**12.00**
Tumbler, water; glass, Jeannette, 5½" ....................................**12.00**

# Bookends

Bookends have come into their own as a separate category of collectibles. They are so diversified in styling, it's easy to find some that appeal to you, no matter what your personal tastes and preferences. Metal examples seem to be most popular, especially those with the mark of their manufacturer, and can still be had at reasonable prices. Glass and ceramic bookends by noted makers, however, may be more costly — for example, those made by Roseville or Cambridge, which have a crossover collector appeal.

Louis Kuritzky and Charles de Costa have written an informative book titled *Collector's Encyclopedia of Bookends* (Collector Books); Louis Kuritzky is listed in the Directory under Florida. See Clubs and Newsletters for information concerning the Bookend Collectors Club.

African Elephant, trunk up, cast iron, ca 1920, 5½"...........**125.00**

Angelus Call to Prayer, gray metal, K&O, ca 1925...................**125.00**

Blacksmith, arm raised at anvil, cast iron, Littco, ca 1925, 5"...**175.00**

Cavalier, head & shoulders, bronze clad, Hertzel, ca 1928, 5½"..**125.00**

Covered Wagon, in relief, cast iron, WH Howell, ca 1926, 4½"..**65.00**

End of the Trail, gray metal, Ronson, ca 1930, 6"................**110.00**

Frisky Airdales, gray metal, Ronson, ca 1925, 4¼"....................**110.00**

Hall's Bookcase, Bakelite, SW Hall, c 1928, 5¾".......................**135.00**

Holy Mother & Child, cast iron, Sneed Ironworks, 1924, 4¾"..........**90.00**

I'se Comin, child on knees, gray metal, ca 1923, 5¼".........**175.00**

Indian Brave (in relief), CI, att Judd, ca 1926, 5".............**175.00**

Knight Errant, on charger, bronze, ca 1935, 6¼".......................**95.00**

Lady Godiva, clear glass, Haley, ca 1940, 6"............................**135.00**

Lindy, bust portrait, cast iron, Verona, ca 1928, 6"..........**110.00**

Man Reading, chalk on stone base, marked JBH/RUHL, ca 1932, 4½"....................................**125.00**

Masonic Emblem, cast iron, Judd, ca 1928, 5¼".........................**100.00**

Nude on Sphinx, bronze clad, Armor Bronze, ca 1925, 6".............**175.00**

Oak Leaf, gray metal, PM Craftsman, ca 1965, 6½"........................**45.00**

Peacock Splendor, tail wide, bronze, ca 1930, 5¾".....................**175.00**

Pierrot Plays, on stepped base, gray metal, ca 1925..................**175.00**

Pontiac (emblem), aluminum, Bruce Fox, 1983............................**50.00**

Proud Penguin, gray metal, Frankart, ca 1930, 7"......**300.00**

**Sailboats, multicolor shiny glazes on ceramic, Japan label, 4¾", from $25.00 to $35.00 for the pair.** (Photo courtesy Carole Bess White)

Scottie on Fence, bronze, ca 1928, 6"......................................**175.00**

Sir Francis Drack, gray metal, JB (Jennings Bros), ca 1925, 3"..**50.00**
Think Figuratively, gray metal, Ronson, ca 1935, 6" .........**100.00**
Wait Here, enameled gray metal & celluloid, marble base, 1926 ....**275.00**

## Bottles

Bottles have been used as containers for commercial products since the late 1800s. Specimens from as early as 1845 may still be occasionally found today (watch for a rough pontil to indicate this early production date). Some of the most collectible are bitters bottles, used for 'medicine' that was mostly alcohol, a ploy to avoid paying the stiff tax levied on liquor sales. Spirit flasks from the 1800s were blown in the mold and were often designed to convey a historic, political, or symbolic message. Refer to *Bottle Pricing Guide* by Hugh Cleveland (Collector Books) for more information.

### Dairy Bottles

The storage and distribution of fluid milk in glass bottles became commonplace around the turn of the century. They were replaced by paper and plastic containers in the mid-1950s. Perhaps 5% of all US dairies are still using some glass, and glass bottles are still widely used in Mexico and some Canadian provinces.

Milk packaging and distribution plants hauled trailer loads of glass bottles to dumping grounds during the conversion to the throw-away cartons now in general use. Because of this practice, milk bottles and jars are scarce today. Most collectors search for bottles from hometown dairies; some have completed a fifty-state collection in the three popular sizes.

Bottles from 1900 to 1920 had the name of the dairy, town, and state embossed in the glass. Nearly all of the bottles produced after this period had the copy painted and then pyro-glazed onto the surface of the bottle. This enabled the dairyman to use colors and pictures of his dairy farm or cows on the bottles. Collectors have been fortunate that there have been no serious attempts at this point to reproduce a particularly rare bottle!

Alamito Dairy, Omaha Nebraska, covered wagon pyro, cream top, 1-qt .................**110.00**
Anderston Bros & Trojan warrior, blue pyro, round, 10-oz ........**8.00**
Borden's, ruby red w/white letters, squat, 1-qt ....................**1,750.00**
Buena Vista Farms, Pulaski VA, red pyro, 1-qt .........................**240.00**
Carnation, RD Thompson Dairy, Eugene OR, red pyro, cream top, 1-qt ...........................**365.00**
Ferer's Dairy Products, Pocatella ID, red pyro, 1937, 1-qt ...........**160.00**
Fountain Dairy Farm, JC Charvat, Hopewell VA, red pyro, 1-pt..**215.00**
Kane Dairy, Kane PA, orange pyro, 1-qt .........................**90.00**

KY American Dairy, Hilo, embossed words, Hawaiian, 1-pt.....**315.00**

Mt Desert Island Dairies, Barharbout ME, red pyro, 1-qt..**235.00**

Nashville Pure Milk Co, amber w/white pyro, 1-qt............**160.00**

Neumann Milk Co, Mars Hill IN, clear w/embossed letters, 1-qt.....**160.00**

Onatru Farm, Ridgefield CT, goat on back, black pyro, 1-qt..........**100.00**

Thomas Bros Dairy, Frankfort IN, clear w/embossed letters, 1-qt.**135.00**

Waldron's Dairy, Califon NJ, red pyro, round, 1-pt................**15.00**

## Soda Bottles With Applied Color Labels

This is a specialized area of advertising collectibles that holds the interest of bottle collectors as well as those who search for soda pop items; both fields attract a good number of followers, so the market for these bottles is fairly strong right now. See also Coca-Cola; Soda Pop.

Birdsboro Lemon Soda, green w/red & white label of bird, 7-oz.**16.00**

Black Kow, brown w/lg 3-color label w/cow in center.....................**8.00**

Bright Belt Beverage, 2-color label.....................................**50.00**

Bubble Up, green w/red & white label, king size.....................**9.00**

College Club, dark green w/red & white label, 6-oz.................**10.00**

Dodger Beverage, clear w/2 color label on body & neck, 9-oz..............**8.00**

Donald Duck, clear w/blue & white Donald Duck label.............**12.50**

Dr Pepper, commemorative for 1994 OK rodeo, man on bronco label, 8-oz......................................**8.00**

Grapette Soda, clear w/white label, 1939, 6-oz............................**8.00**

Huberty's Quality Beverages, 2-color label, 10-oz.........................**10.00**

IBC Rootbeer, brown w/red & white label, 16-oz.........................**10.00**

Jones Beverages, clear w/black & white label, excavated, 10-oz, G........................................**12.00**

Kist Soda, pale green w/white label, 7-oz......................................**12.00**

**Milde's Soda, clear with yellow label, unopened, 10 ounce, $18.00. (Photo courtesy B.J. Summers)**

NuGrape, clear w/logo label, straight sides, 10-oz.............**5.00**

O-So Grape, clear w/1-color label: Rich in Dextrose..., 1950s, 6-oz.**12.00**

Orange Crush, amber w/embossed ribs, diamond logo w/Crushy, 1950s.................................**12.00**

Orange Crush, dark amber w/diamond-shaped label, 7½".............**10.00**

Pepsi Cola, clear w/multicolor label & shoulder ribbon, 12-oz..**65.00**

Queen-O, 2-color label on body & at neck, 7-oz.........................**12.00**

Roundup, clear w/brown & white label of rider on rearing horse...**35.00**

Sep's, dark green w/black & white label, 24-oz...........................**10.00**

Ski, green w/multicolor label, 1979, 16-oz......................................**9.50**

Springtime Anytime, clear w/black & yellow label showing 2 birds, 7-oz......................................**15.00**

Whistle, green w/musical notes label, 10-oz...........................**10.00**

7-Up, green w/red & white label, 10-oz...........................................**5.00**

**7-Up commemorative, green with red and white label saluting Indiana University, 16 ounce, $8.00.**

## Miscellaneous

Barber, emerald green, embossed ribs & white enameling, 7½"...**60.00**

Cologne, monument figural, milk glass, smooth base, 12"......**100.00**

Cologne, purple amethyst, 12-sided w/sloped shoulders, smooth base, 5"..............................**160.00**

Cornucopia/Urn flask, GIII-4, yellow-olive amber, pontil scar, 1-pt...**140.00**

Double Eagle flask, GII-40, bluish aqua, pontil scar, haze, 1-pt.....**160.00**

Double Eagle flask, GII-92, deep aqua, smooth base, common, 1-pt......................................**110.00**

Dr Anderson Cin O, bluish aqua, pontil scar, flared lip, 4⅞"..**60.00**

Hawthorne back bar, clear w/white enamel lettering, smooth base, 11"....................................**160.00**

John Ogden's Mineral Water Pittsburgh O, blue aqua, iron pontil, 7⅝"....................................**170.00**

Kohl & Beans Mineral...PA, medium blue-green, iron pontil, 7½"....................................**130.00**

Medicine or utility, pale green, flared lip, pontil scar, ca 1800, 5"......................................**50.00**

Missisquoi A Spring, dark emerald green, smooth base, qt.....**130.00**

Pistol figural, medium yellow amber, metal screw cap, 9½"........**50.00**

Rumford Chemical Works, medium yellowish olive green, 8-sided, 8¾"....................................**180.00**

Star Kidney & Liver Bitters, medium amber, smooth base, 8¾".**110.00**

Umbrella ink, blue-green, 8-sided, pontil scar, rolled lip, 2½".**130.00**

Warner's Safe Nervine...NY, medium amber, smooth base, 7½"..**140.00**

# Boyd Crystal Art Glass

Since it was established in 1978, this small glasshouse located in Cambridge, Ohio, has bought molds from other companies as they went out of business, and they have designed many of their own as well. They may produce several limited runs of a particular shape in a number of the lovely colors of glass they themselves formulate, none of which are ever reissued. Of course, all of the glass is handmade, and each piece is marked with their 'B-in-diamond' logo. Most of the pieces we've listed are those you're more apt to find at flea markets, but some of the rarer items may be worth a great deal more. See Clubs and Newsletters for information concerning a Boyd's Crystal Art Glass newsletter.

Airplane, Blue Flame Carnival......**25.00**
Airplane, Olympic Blue............**25.00**
Angel, Cobalt Blue....................**25.00**
Bunny on Nest, Classic Black Slag..**40.00**
Bunny Salt, Confetti.................**40.00**
Cat Slipper, Pink & Blue Slag......**20.00**
Chuckles the Clown, Rubena ......**60.00**
Chuckles the Clown, Vaseline.....**45.00**
Duke (Scottie), Vaseline...........**30.00**
Fuzzy the Teddy Bear, Plum .....**25.00**
Hen Covered Dish, Confetti, 3" .....**45.00**
Hen Covered Dish, Cranberry, 3".......**22.50**
Hen Covered Dish, Rubena, 5" .....**35.00**
Hen on Nest, Ivory Blush, 3".........**20.**
Hen on Nest, Primrose, 3".......**27.50**
Hen on Nest, Salmon, 5" .........**27.50**

**Hen on Nest Covered Salt, purple, 2x2½", $26.50.**

JB Scotty, Mint Green.............**65.00**

JB Scotty, Touch of Pink .........**35.00**
Jennifer the Doll, Vaseline.......**22.50**
Joey the Horse, Budding Pink......**70.00**
Joey the Horse, Delphinium ......**35.00**
Joey the Horse, Light Rose ......**45.00**
Little Joe, Baby Blue................**22.50**
Louise Doll, Rubina .................**30.00**
Lucky the Unicorn, Spring Beauty..**25.00**
Owl, Blackberry Carnival ........**32.50**
Owl Bell, Blue Slag..................**20.00**
Owl Bell, Pink Carnival ...........**22.50**
Owl Bell, Purple Slag ..............**22.50**
Owl Bell, Vaseline ...................**35.00**
Patrick the Balloon Bear, Vaseline..**30.00**
Pooch, Joh's Surprise...............**15.00**
Scottie Salt, Cotton..................**30.00**
Skate Boot, Cobalt Slag...........**85.00**
Skate Boot, Crown Tuscan Carnival ..**60.00**
Skate Boot, Golden Delight......**35.00**
Skate Boot, Ice Blue ................**85.00**
Skate Boot, Violet Slate ...........**65.00**
Tommy the Tiger, Cobalt .........**40.00**
Turkey Covered Dish, Aloe, 5" .....**40.00**
Turkey Covered Dish, Aruba Slag, 5"..**40.00**
Turkey Covered Dish, Cherry Red, 5"..**37.50**
Turkey Covered Dish, Vaseline Carnival, 5" .............................**40.00**

## Breweriana

Beer can collectors and antique advertising buffs alike enjoy looking for beer-related memorabilia such as tap knobs, beer trays, coasters, signs, and such. While the smaller items of a more recent vintage are quite affordable, signs and trays from defunct breweries often bring three-digit prices. Condition is important in evaluating early advertising items of any type.

Ashtray, City Club Beer, clear glass w/black painted center, sq...**45.00**

Ashtray, Hamm's Bear & bear in white on blue, metal..........**35.00**

Ashtray, Lone Star Beer, For the Big Country, red on clear, glass..**25.00**

Beer tray, Anheuser-Bush, lg A w/eagle, oval, 1960s repro, 15" L, EX ..................................**35.00**

Beer tray, Beverwyck, Albany NY, Join the...Parade on green, 13", VG ......................................**68.00**

Beer tray, Dick's, Quincy IL, letters on red, white & blue, 12", VG ......................................**50.00**

Beer tray, Dixie 45, New Orleans, blue letters on yellow & red, 13", EX ..............................**48.00**

Beer tray, Great Falls Select in red banner on yellow, Canco, 13", NM ....................................**50.00**

Beer tray, Iron City, letters, red, white & black, CA C0 71-A, 12", EX......................................**38.00**

Beer tray, Narragansett Lager & Ale Beer, comic art ............**80.00**

Beer tray, Old Tap Ale/Old Tap Bohemian, man lifting glass, 12", EX ..............................**75.00**

Beer tray, Original Pabst Blue Ribbon, comic bartender on red, 13" ..**42.00**

Beer tray, Wayne Brewing Co, Mad Anthony Wayne Block House, 13", NM ..............................**60.00**

Beer tray, Yuengling, Pottsville PA, bottle/glass on red, raised rim..**50.00**

Bottle, Ballentine's Canadian Malt Ale, glass w/early paper label, qt ..**55.00**

Charger, Falstaff, medieval man at table w/friends, 24" dia, EX..**175.00**

Clock, Du Bois Budweiser, electric, light-up, 15" dia, EX........**325.00**

Clock, Fort Pitt, metal body, glass front, Telechron, 15" dia, EX ...**155.00**

Coaster, Bass & Co, Light Export...on Draught, porcelain, 5" dia, EX..**45.00**

Coaster, Genesee 12 Horse Ale, 2-sided w/verse on reverse, 4¼" dia....................................**35.00**

Coaster, Yuengling Beer-Ale-Porter, 1940s, 4" dia, EX..................**18.00**

Lighter, Blatz Beer, bottle shape w/label, KEM Co, 1950s, 2¾"..**40.00**

Lighter, Duke Beer, Duquesne Brewing Co, can shape, 5½" ....**15.00**

Opener, Pabst Blue Ribbon Beer, bottle shape, metal, 4".....**110.00**

Pin-back button, Bunker Hill Brewery, Oh Be Jolly, Owl Musty, EX.......................................**75.00**

Pin-back button, Old Dutch Beer, bar scene, 1¼", NM ..........**75.00**

Playing cards, Grain Belt Beer, complete w/jokers, EXIB............**25.00**

Playing cards, Mertz Beer, waiter w/glass & bottle of Mertz on tray.....................................**40.00**

Print, Duquesne Pilsner, Finest Beer in Town, Otto, 1934, 29x32", EX ......................**140.00**

Print, Eagle Liqueur Distilleries, nude on company sign, 20x25", EX....................................**625.00**

Sign, Augustine Beer, painted tin, nicely aged, 20x13¾", G..**45.00**

Sign, Berghoff Beer, tin on cardboard, bird dogs in snow, 21x13", EX..**120.00**

Sign, Budweiser Beer, cash register light, 10¼x8¼", EX............**45.00**

Sign, Goebel Bantam Beer, rooster cardboard diecut, 9x11", EX.....**30.00**

Sign, Hamm's, lighted waterfall, panoramic, motion, 1965, 12½x40x4" ....................**1,540.00**

Sign, Jacob Ruppert Beer & Ale, metal, Famous for..., 1940s, 24x12", G..............................**85.00**

Sign, Miller High Life, neon, new, EX......................................**145.00**

Sign, Ranier Ale & Beer, embossed metal diecut, 1940s, 13x8⅜", NM ..................................**135.00**

Sign, Silver Spring Brewery, fireman w/glass, paper litho, 16" dia, VG ...............................**70.00**

Statue, Blatz at Local Prices, skater, VG ....................................**100.00**

**Statue, Blatz at Local Prices, skater, EX, $135.00. (Photo courtesy B.J. Summers)**

Statue, Blatz Beer, baseball players, 1950s, 16x19x9"................**235.00**

Statue, Heileman Brewing, cavalier hoisting stein, cast metal, 8" ........................................**90.00**

Statue, Iron City Beer, 4 figures at bar, white chalkware, 1958, 10"...**45.00**

Statue, Simon Pure Beer, bust of man points to sign, 7½x8x3½" ..**175.00**

Statue/bell, Sterling, lady figural, heavy painted metal, 15x5", NM....**115.00**

Tap handle, Bud Light, phone shape w/Bud Light I Said on top.**50.00**

Tap handle, Coors Light, wolf's head w/white hard hat, 1980s....**45.00**

Tap handle, DAB Imported German Beer, EX..............................**30.00**

Tap handle, Guiness-Extra Cold in white letters on blue w/black base ....................................**60.00**

Tap handle, Heineken Beer, wooden, G..........................................**10.00**

Tap handle, Murphy's Irish Stout..**55.00**

Tap handle, Pabst Breweries, worn red letters on white ball, ca 1933....................................**110.00**

Tip tray, Bartholomy Ale, pretty lady on metal, 4¼" dia, VG..........**140.00**

Tip tray, Bixel's Ale..., Brantford, Ontario, star/triangle, G.....**750.00**

Tip tray, Drink...Dick Bros Quincy Beer on black & gold, 4½", VG ....................................**135.00**

Tip tray, Feigenpan, PON in red circle, raised rim, 4⅜", NM ..............**25.00**

Tip tray, Goebel's Malt Extract, girl at chalkboard, 4½", EX...**145.00**

Tip tray, Hannis Whiskey, black & gold w/red triangle logo, 4¼", EX......................................**45.00**

Tip tray, Krueger Ambassador, Newark NJ, red, white & black on gold, EX..........................**15.00**

Tip tray, Lewis 66 Whiskey, girl in plumed hat, 4" dia, EX......**100.00**

Tip tray, Old Stegmaier Brewing Co, hand w/3 bottles, 4¼", EX..**115.00**

Tray, Hamm's Beer, Preferred Stock, metal, 1950s, 13" dia, EX...**40.00**

Tray, Harry Mitchell's Quality Lager Beer, 3-color, 13", EX.........**90.00**

Tray, National Beer, National Brewing Co, elk's head, 4¼" dia, VG+..**50.00**

Tray, Valley Forge Beer Aged in..., maid w/tray, 13¼x10½", EX..**60.00**

Tray, Yuengling Premium Beer, red & black on white, 12", NM..**65.00**

Wall plaque, Grain Belt Beer, fish shape, chalkware, 13", EX....................**175.00**

Wooden crate, Moosehead Beer w/logo on sides, slide-in lid, EX..**550.00**

# Breyer Horses

Breyer collecting has grown in popularity over the past several years. Though horses dominate the market, cattle and other farm animals, dogs, cats, and wildlife have also been produced, all with exacting details and lifelike coloration. They've been made since the early 1950s in both glossy and matt finishes. (Earlier models were glossy, but from 1968 until the 1990s when both glossy and semigloss colors were revived for special runs, matt colors were preferred.) Breyer also manufactures dolls, tack, and accessories such as barns for their animals.

For more information we recommend *Schroeder's Collectible Toys, Antique to Modern* (Collector Books), and *Breyer Animal Collector's Guide* by Felicia Browell.

Adios (#50), buckskin w/black points, Traditional, 1978................**232.00**

Andalusian (#5606), buckskin w/black points, Stablemate, 2003......................................**6.00**

Big Ben (#483), chestnut w/star & stripe, Traditional, 1997-current ....................................**31.00**

Black Stallion (#3030), red bay w/black points, Classic, 1990-93.........**12.00**

Cody (#471), chestnut w/dark mane & tail, Traditional, 2001..**40.00**

El Pastor (#61), bay w/black points, solid face, Traditional, 1987..................................**124.00**

Foundation Stallion (#64), black, no markings, Traditional, 1977-87.......................................**26.00**

Grazing Foal (#151), black w/bald face, Traditional, 1964-70...............**32.00**

Jet Run (3035JR), light chestnut w/dark mane & tail, Classic, 1987...................................**16.00**

Jumping Horse (#300), bay w/black mane & tail, Traditional, 1965-88.......................................**27.00**

Lonesome Glory (#572), bay pinto w/black points, Traditional, 2001...................................**575.00**

Man O' War (#602), red chestnut w/dark mane & tail, Classic, 1975-90..............................**17.00**

**Might Tango (A Pony for Keeps), light dapple gray with gray points, Classic scale, 1990-91, $14.00.**

Morgan (#48), black w/bald face, front socks, Traditional, 1965-87.......................................**38.00**

Morgan Stallion (#9005), seal brown w/black points, 1984-88 .....**8.00**

Native Dancer (#5023), bay w/vague right socks, JC Penny, 1995..**5.00**

Nursing Foal (#3155FO), bay w/black points, Traditional, QVC, 2001.........................**17.00**

Pluto (#475), Lipizzaner Stallion, Traditional, Spiegel, 1993........**166.00**

Quarter Horse Mare (#3045MA), chestnut w/black points, JC Penney, 1991......................**15.00**

Racehorse (#36), chestnut w/bald face, Traditional, 1956-67..**71.00**

Saddlebred (#5002), dapple gray w/darker points, Stablemate, 1975-76..............................**33.00**

Sham the Godolphin Arabian (#410), red bay w/black, Traditional, 1995........................**32.00**

Shire (#95), shaded bay w/ black points, Traditional, 1998-99...............................................**28.00**

Strapless (#583), dark bay w/tiny star, Traditional, 2003......**35.00**

Terrang (#605), palomino w/white mane & tail, Classic, 1997........**13.00**

Thoroughbred Mare (#5026), black, Saddle Club/ Stablemate, 1994-95..............................................**5.00**

Western Horse (#57), palomino, complete w/saddle, Traditional, 1995...................................**26.00**

# Bubble Bath Containers

Figural bubble bath containers were popular in the 1960s and have become highly collectible today. The Colgate-Palmolive Company produced the widest variety called Soakies. Purex's Bubble Club characters were also popular. Most Soaky bottles came with detachable heads made of brittle plastic which cracked easily. Purex bottles were made of a softer plastic but lost their paint easier. Condition affects price considerably.

The interest collectors displayed in the old bottles prompted many to notice foreign-made products. Some of the same characters have been licensed by companies in Canada, Italy, the UK, Germany and Japan, and the bottles they've designed have excellent detail. They're usually a little larger than domestic bottles, and though fairly recent, are often reminiscent of those made in the US during the 1960s.

For more information, we recommend *Schroeder's Collectible Toys, Antique to Modern*, published by Collector Books.

Anastasia, Kid Care, 1997, NM......**8.00**

Atom Ant, Purex, 1965, NM.....**70.00**

Augie Doggie, Purex, orange w/green shirt, original tag, EX....................................**45.00**

Baba Looey, Roclar, 1977, NM......**15.00**

Bamm-Bamm, Purex, black or green suspenders, NM, ea...............**35.00**

Batman, Colgate-Palmolive, 1966, NM, from $75 to ................**90.00**

Bear, Tubby Time, 1960s, NM.....**35.00**

Betty Bubbles, Lander, 1960s, NM ....................................**15.00**

Bozo the Clown, Step Riley, cap head, EX.............................**30.00**

Broom Hilda, Lander, 1977, EX......**30.00**

Bullwinkle, Fuller Brush, 1970s, NM ....................................**60.00**

Care Bear, AGC, 1984, NM......**10.00**

Cinderella, Colgate-Palmolive, moveable arms, 1960s, NM....................**30.00**

Darth Vader, Omni, 1981, NM .....**20.00**
Dino & Pebbles, Cosrich, 1994, NM ......................................**15.00**
Dum Dum, Purex, white w/pink accents, 1964, rare, NM .....**100.00**
Elmo, Kid Care, 1997, NM .......**10.00**
ET, Avon, 1984, NM .................**15.00**
Fozzie Bear, Muppet Treasure Island, Calgon, 1996, NM ..................**10.00**

**Frankenstein, Soaky, Colgate-Palmolive, NM, from $100.00 to $125.00.**

Genie (Aladdin), Cosrich, NM......**5.00**
Gumby, M&L Creative Packaging, 1987, NM ...........................**30.00**
Huckleberry Hound, Secol, blue w/yellow bow tie, 1960s, rare, EX.....................................**100.00**
Hunchback of Notre Dame in robe w/sceptor, Kid Care, NM.....**5.00**
Jasmine (Aladdin), w/bird or mirror, Cosrich, original tag, NM, ea......................................**6.00**
Lippy the Lion, purple vest, Purex, 1962, rare, EX....................**35.00**
Little Orphan Annie, Lander, 1977, NM .....................................**25.00**
Magilla Gorilla, Purex, 1960s, NM ....................................**60.00**
Mickey Mouse, Avon, 1969, MIB................................**30.00**

Miss Piggy, Muppet Treasure Island, Calgon, 1996..........**10.00**
Mr Robottle, Avon, 1971, MIB ..**20.00**
Mummy, Colgate-Palmolive, 1960s, NM, from $100 to .............**125.00**
Pebbles & Dino, Cosrich, Pebbles on Dino's back, NM .................**6.00**
Pluto, Colgate-Palmolive, 1960s, orange w/cap head, NM.....**20.00**
Popeye, Colgate-Palmolive, 1977, blue w/white accents, NM..**35.00**

**Punkin' Puss, Purex, 1966, VG, $30.00.**

Raggedy Ann, Lander, 1960s, NM...................................**50.00**
Rainbow Brite, Hallmark, 1995, NM ...................................**10.00**
Robocop, Cosway, 1990, NM ....**15.00**
Schroeder, Avon, 1970, MIB ....**25.00**
Simba, Kid Care, NM ................**6.00**
Snoopy as Flying Ace, Avon, 1969, MIB ...................................**20.00**
Snoopy as Joe Cool, Minnetonka, 1996, NM ...........................**10.00**
Snow White, Colgate-Palmolive, moveable arms, 1960s, NM..............................**35.00**
Splash Down Space Capsule, Avon, 1970, MIB .........................**20.00**

**Superman, Avon, 1978, MIB, $35.00.**

Superman, Colgate-Palmolive, 1965, EX......................................**50.00**

Tazmanian Devil in Inner Tube, Kid Care, 1992, EX......................**8.00**

Tex Hex (Brave Starr), Ducair Bioescence, w/tag, NM ......**15.00**

Thumper, Colgate-Palmolive, 1960s, EX......................................**25.00**

Tic Toc Tiger, orange w/yellow hands & hat, Avon, NM ....**15.00**

Tommy (Rugrats), Kid Care, 1977, NM.......................................**8.00**

Touchè Turtle standing, Purex, NM..**40.00**

Wendy the Witch, Colgate-Palmolive, 1960s, NM.................**30.00**

Whitey the Whale, Avon, 1959, EX..**15.00**

Winsome Witch, Purex, 1965, rare, NM ....................................**30.00**

Woodsey Owl, Lander, early 1970s, EX......................................**35.00**

Yogi Bear, brown, Milvern (Purex), rare, NM ..........................**50.00**

# Cake Toppers

The first cake toppers appeared on wedding cakes in the 1880s and were made almost entirely of sugar. The early 1900s saw toppers carved from wood and affixed to ornate plaster pedestal bases and backgrounds. A few single-mold toppers were even made from poured lead. From the 1920s to the 1950s bisque, porcelain, and chalkware figures reigned supreme. The faces and features on many of these were very realistic and lifelike. The beautiful Art Deco era was also in evidence.

Celluloid kewpie types made a brief appearance from the late 1930s to the 1940s. These were quite fragile because the celluloid they were made of could be easily dented and cracked. The true Rose O'Neill kewpie look-alike also appeared for awhile during this period. During and after World War II and into the Korean Conflict of the 1950s, groom figures in military dress appeared. Only a limited amount was ever produced; they are quite rare. From the 1950s into the 1970s, plastics were used almost exclusively. Toppers took on a vacant, assembly-line appearance with no specific attention to detail or fashion.

In the 1970s, bisque returned and plastic disappeared. Toppers were again more lifelike. For the most part, they remain that way today. Wedding cakes now often display elegant and elaborate toppers such as those made by Royal Doulton and Lladro.

Toppers should not be confused with the bride and groom doll sets of the same earlier periods. While some smaller dolls could and did serve as toppers, they were usually too unbalanced to stay upright on a cake. The true topper consisted of a small bride and groom anchored to (or a part of) a round flat base which made it extremely stable for resting on a soft, frosted cake surface. Cake toppers never did double duty as play items.

Cinderella's Silver Coach, light up, Lefton, 8", EX ................**410.00**
Elvis w/Bride & Groom, light up, 6½x3½", EX ....................................**190.00**
Kewpie couple, bisque & molded plaster base .....................**100.00**
Marine dress uniform on groom, bisque, 4½" ........................**40.00**
Mickey & Minnie Mouse, WDP/ Wedgwood, 5½", MIB........**65.00**
Military couple, flowers, leaves, 48-star flag..............................**60.00**
Sailor uniform on groom, all plaster, 4½" ....................................**40.00**

**World War II military couple, all plaster, 48-star flag, 6", $45.00.** (Photo courtesy Jeannie Greenfield)

1900s couple, carved wood figures on plaster stand................**50.00**

1920s couple, all bisque, bride in dropped-waist gown, 4".....**50.00**
1920s couple, single mold, poured lead....................................**45.00**
1940s couple, carved basalt figures, 1-pc....................................**20.00**
1940s couple, plaster & chalkware w/lily-of-the-valley flowers.....**40.00**
1940s couple, plaster/chalkware combination .......................**25.00**
1950s (early) couple, chalkware.....**20.00**

# California Potteries

In recent years, pottery designed by many of the artists who worked in their own small studios in California during the 1940s through the 1960s has become highly sought after. Values continue to be impressive, though slightly compromised by the influence of the Internet. Among the more popular studios are Kay Finch, Florence Ceramics, Brayton, Howard Pierce, and Sascha Brastoff; but Matthew Adams, Marc Bellair, and deLee are attracting their share of attention as well, and there are others.

It's a fascinating field, one covered very well in Jack Chipman's *Collector's Encyclopedia of California Pottery* and *California Pottery Scrapbook*, both published by Collector Books. Mike Nickel and Cynthia Horvath have written *Kay Finch Ceramics, Her Enchanted World* (Schiffer), a must for collectors interested in Kay Finch ceramics; and to learn more about Florence ceramics, you'll want to read *The*

*Complete Book of Florence Ceramics: A Labor of Love,* written by Margaret Wehrspaun and Sue and Jerry Kline. They are listed in the Directory under Tennessee. See also Bauer; Cookie Jars; Franciscan; Metlox.

## Adams, Matthew

Ashtray, Husky dog, 13x10" ....**65.00**
Bowl, polar bear on green, free-form, 7½" L.................................**50.00**
Creamer, seal, #144, 5x5¼" .....**20.00**
Jar, Eskimo on ice blue, 6".......**30.00**
Pitcher, walrus, 11½", pitcher +6 4½" mugs .........................**255.00**
Platter, house, 12" ....................**45.00**
Tile, walrus on blue, 10x8½" .....**75.00**

**Trivet, polar bear, 6", $40.00.**

Tumbler, cabin .........................**20.00**
Vase, iceberg on gray, 7" .........**50.00**
Vase, reindeer, 4½" .................**45.00**

## Bellaire, Marc

Ashtray, Beachcomber, free-form, 13¾x6¾" ...........................**65.00**
Bowl, Hawaiian, 3 figures on mottled pink, 15x8".......................**125.00**
Bowl, Jamaica, man w/guitar, free-form, w/lid, 1½x11" ...........**80.00**

Bowl, sea horse, 4 lobes, pyramid base, 5½x5½".....................**70.00**
Box, brown w/fruit decoration on lid, 2x4½x3½" ..........................**75.00**
Dish, Leaf, taupe background, 5x5"..**30.00**
Figurine, Mardi Gras, masked dancer, standing, 24" ......**700.00**
Figurine, terrier, Chauncey, #144, chocolate brown, 5½" ........**35.00**

## Brastoff, Sascha

Bowl, marbleized dark green, 3-footed, 2½x5¾", from $50 to..............**70.00**
Box, Rooftops on gray, w/lid, V-21, 2x5x8" ...............................**50.00**
Figurine, cat seated, frosted green resin, 10¼".......................**150.00**
Pitcher, diamond design on turquoise, marked #068, 10".....................**50.00**

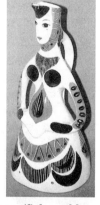

**Pitcher, 13", from $450.00 to $500.00.**

Plate, ocean waves w/fish on blue, signed Brastoff '57, 10⅞"..**215.00**
Plate, Plum Dancer on gray & black, 11¾" ....................................**50.00**
Plate, stylized fish on cream, 15"......**70.00**
Vase, Rooftops on black, slanted rim, oval, 6" ......................**60.00**
Vase, Star Steed, on cream, 7¾x1¾x5" ..........................**60.00**

## Brayton Laguna

Candleholders, Blackamoor, seated, 4¾", pr ...............................**125.00**

Figurine, baby fawn, Disney sticker, 1930s, 6", from $90 to.........**120.00**

Figurine, cat w/1 paw raised, 3½", from $25 to.........................**35.00**

Figurine, dice player, Black boy w/yellow hat, belt & boots, EX .....................................**55.00**

Figurine, fox, red, seated, head turned, 4", from $200 to.....**250.00**

Figurine, lady in lavender, basket in 1 hand, hat in other, 8½" ..............................**60.00**

Figurine, Olga, Russian girl, Childhood series .........................**60.00**

**Figurine, Pat with doll at back, 7", $100.00.**

Figurine, Pluto, sniffing, Disney, 3x6" .....................................**85.00**

Figurine, Sambo, Black boy, 7¾" .**140.00**

Figurine, vendor w/cart, 9x11½"..**35.00**

Figurine, 3 men in bar, Gay Nineties series, 8½x7½", EX+ ..**110.00**

Figurines, Peruvian Dancers, 9¼", 9", pr, from $350 to .........**400.00**

Figurines, Zizi & Fifi, maroon & green, pr...........................**495.00**

Planter, Red Flambè, panels w/scrolls, 3x3¼x5"..............**35.00**

Teapot, brown w/white & yellow flowers, green leaves, 6½"...........**45.00**

Vase, sea horse w/vase on back, 8½" .....................................**95.00**

## Brock of California

Candleholder, California Farmhouse, rooster, footed, 2¼x6½", ea........................................**17.50**

Casserole, California Farmhouse, w/lid, 4x5¾" dia.................**45.00**

Coffeepot, California Farmhouse, 10" ......................................**30.00**

Jam jar, California Farmhouse, milk-can shape, notched lid, 4¾" .....................................**20.00**

Pitcher, California Farmhouse, 7½" .....................................**25.00**

Server, California Farmhouse, 2-part, 11" .............................**20.00**

Shakers, California Farmhouse, milk-can shape, 3", pr .......**25.00**

Sugar packet caddy, California Farmhouse, 3x3" dia .........**17.50**

## Cleminson Pottery

Ashtray, You're the Big Wheel, 8" .**15.00**

Bowl, white w/brown flowers, Gram's in blue-grey, w/lid, 2½x4" ...............................**27.00**

Creamer, rooster figure, 5½".....**48.00**

Cup, child's; clown head, hat is lid..**80.00**

Cup, jumbo; My Old Man, man sleeping in chair................**20.00**

Cup, Morning After/Never Again, comic face w/ice-bag lid.....**20.00**

Gravy boat, Distlefink, bird figure, 5¾x6" ................................**35.00**

Pie bird, rooster figural, white w/green, yellow & pink .....**50.00**

Pitcher, watering can shape, white w/floral decoration, 5" .......**35.00**

Range set, Cherry, 5" grease jar & 6" salt & pepper shakers, 3-pc..**30.00**

Ring holder, dog figure, tail up, peach & white, 3" ..............**27.00**

Salt & pepper shakers, bowling-pin shape, 5⅝", pr....................**40.00**

String holder, heart shape w/ verse..................................**45.00**

String holder, winking man's head, wearing hat, 1930s, 5½x5½"..**80.00**

String holder, You'll Always Have a Pull With Me, heart shape..**45.00**

Wall pocket, black kettle w/heart & verse...................................**30.00**

Wall pocket, coffee grinder, Time Out For Coffee...................**40.00**

Wall pocket, coffeepot, w/verse, 8½" .....................................**35.00**

Wall pocket, pitcher & bowl, w/verse, 8x7".......................**35.00**

## DeForest of California

Ashtray, brown w/orange highlights, S-shaped center, 10¾x8¾" ..**20.00**

Covered dish, peanut w/squirrel finial....................................**20.00**

Jam jar, comical face, Jam on yellow hat lid, 4¼" ........................**30.00**

Mug, onion face, 4", set of 4, EX......**70.00**

Mustard server, Chinaman's head w/hat as lid, 4½x3¾".........**35.00**

Pitcher, pig face, pink w/black highlights, 7½x7½"..................**125.00**

Relish dish, comic face w/Relish on lid, 1956 .............................**35.00**

Salt & pepper shakers, pig's head, pr........................................**25.00**

Spoon rest, boy & girl faces form 2 rests ..................................**50.00**

## deLee

Bank, Money Bunny, pink & white w/blue purse, 9"................**95.00**

Figurine, Amigo, donkey, white w/black features, marked '39, 5" ........................................**37.50**

Figurine, Annabelle, pink, 8" .....**49.00**

Figurine, bull, seated, flowers in mouth, 4¼" ........................**25.00**

Figurine, June, seated w/open book, 4" ........................................**85.00**

Figurine, Sadie & Cy, pigs, 3", 2½", pr........................................**60.00**

Figurine, Siamese cat, white w/brown markings, lying down, 1⅝" ....................................**25.00**

**Figurine, Siamese cat, white with brown markings, blue eyes, 1950s, 12", $60.00.**

Figurine, Siamese cat, white w/brown markings, seated, 3¼".........**25.00**

Flower holder, boy w/puppy under left arm, 7"..........................**35.00**

Planter, boy in top hat & vest stands before planter, 7½" ...............**35.00**

Planter, Hattie, pink roses on bodice & along hem, #40, 7½" ..............**35.00**

Planter, Linda, opening in hat crown, 7½" ..........................**50.00**

Planter, Lizzie, tipping hat, planter behind & to the right, 9" ...**35.00**

Planter, Maria, green & purple flowers, 1940s, 6¾" ..................**20.00**

Planter, Sahara Sue, opening in saddle, 5" ...........................**85.00**

Salt & pepper shakers, Sniffy & Snuffy, skunks, 3¾", pr.....**25.00**

Toothbrush holder, skunk, seated w/opening at tail, 4" ..........**40.00**

### Finch, Kay

Ashtray, swan, #4958, 4½" ......**35.00**

Bank, pig, Winkie, #185, 3¾x5".....**150.00**

Candlesticks, turkey figural, #5794, 3¾", pr ..............................**175.00**

Cup, Missouri Mule, natural colors, 4¼" .....................................**125.00**

Figurine, baby bunny, #5303, 3½"..**125.00**

Figurine, bull, #6211, 6¼" .....**300.00**

Figurine, camel, #464, 4½x5½" ......**395.00**

Figurine, Dog Show Westie, #4833 ...............................**400.00**

Figurine, Happy Monkey, #49093, 11" ....................................**700.00**

**Figurine, hippopotamus, bow at neck, $250.00 to $275.00.**

Figurine, Mama Quail, #5984, 7"..**425.00**

Figurine, Tootsie, owl, #189, 3¾"..**35.00**

Figurine, turkey, #5843, 4½".....**100.00**

Plaque, Baby Fish, 2¼x3"........**60.00**

Stein, attached poodle, #5488......**450.00**

Toby mug, Santa w/hat lid, 5½"......**150.00**

Tureen, Turkey, #5361, platinum & gray, 9", w/ladle...............**300.00**

Wall pockets, Girl & Boy, #5501, 10", ea ..............................**350.00**

### Florence Ceramics

Note: The amount of applied decoration — lace, flowers, etc. — has a great deal of influence on values. Our ranges reflect this factor.

Amelia, 8¼" ...........................**275.00**

Baby, flower holder, from $75 to ................................**100.00**

Carmen, rare, 12½", from $2,750 to ..................................**3,000.00**

Charles, 8¾" ..........................**325.00**

Diane.....................................**450.00**

Edward, 7" .............................**450.00**

Judy, 9", from $450 to ...........**500.00**

Kiu, 11" ..................................**250.00**

Madonna, 10½", from $500 to.....**550.00**

Nita, 8"...................................**550.00**

Peter, rare, 9¼", from $500 to..**550.00**

Rhett, beige w/green trim, 9", from $325 to ...........................**375.00**

Sue, 6", from $60 to .................**70.00**

Summer, 6¼", from $400 to...**450.00**

Vivian, lamp, 10", from $550 to.**650.00**

Vivian, 10", from $350 to ......**400.00**

### Josef

Basket Pet series, bisque finish, 6 in series, Japan, 3½", ea.........**15.00**

Birthstone Doll of Month, January-December, Japan, common, 3½", ea ...............................**15.00**

Character Cat series, Cleo, Honey, etc, Japan, 4", ea ...............**30.00**

Christmas Mouse, various poses, Japan, 2¼", ea ....................**10.00**

Crystal Wing Greeting Angels, various greetings, CA, 4", ea ..**55.00**

Days of the Week, 7 in series, 3½", ea........................................**55.00**

Doll of the Month, tilted head, January-December, 3¼", ea ........**45.00**

Lullaby & Good Night, series of 2, 3¾", ea ...............................**55.00**

Morning Noon Night series, 9 girls, 3 boys, 5½", ea....................**55.00**

Taffy, made in various colors, 4½", ea........................................**45.00**

Wee Ching or Wee Ling, Oriental boy or girl, 5", ea ...............**40.00**

### Kaye of Hollywood

Figurine, lady in bonnet carrying basket, Kaye #3121, 10¼", EX .**45.00**

Figurine/flower holder, girl w/basket on ea hip, #3125, 9½" ...........**30.00**

Flower holder, Colonial man stands before vase, #3147, 9½".....**35.00**

Flower holder, girl w/hands to chin, holder ea side of waist, 9".**45.00**

Wall pocket, lady w/full skirt, #201....................................**25.00**

Wall pocket, Oriental lady w/ornate headdress w/flowers, #345, 7" ........................................**55.00**

### Keeler, Brad

Bowl, lettuce leaves w/red lobster ea side as handle, #856, 15"..**145.00**

Charger, fish decoration w/2 fishing lures, #141, 11"................**150.00**

**Dish, red lobster between two green leaves, #872, 12x7", $75.00.**

Figurine, cardinal, male, #19, 9½"....................................**55.00**

Figurine, chicken, #936, 4½"....**35.00**

Figurine, cocker spaniel puppy, white w/black, #748, 4½" ...**50.00**

Figurine, exotic bird, #703, 13½"...............................**150.00**

Figurine, female pheasant on branch, #21, 6½"...............**80.00**

Figurine, quail, 6x3¾".............**35.00**

Figurine, Siamese cat, seated, #798, 7"......................................**65.00**

Salt & pepper shaker, red-pepper shape, foil label, 1¼", pr ...**20.00**

### Pierce, Howard

Bank, turtle, black w/green shell, ink stamp, 3x8", from $150 to .....................................**175.00**

Figurine, bison, unmarked, 9", from $150 to .............................**175.00**

Figurine, dinosaur, brown ink stamp, 1991, 5½x4½", from $80 to .....................................**100.00**

Figurine, pelican, black ink stamp, 7½x4½", from $75 to .........**85.00**

Figurine, stylized bird, gold leaf, unmarked, 2½x5½", $35 to.........................................**55.00**

Whistle, bird, black ink stamp, 2¾x2", from $100 to ........**125.00**

## Schoop, Hedi

Ashtray, butterfly form, gold trim, 11x9" .................................**22.00**

Figurine, rooster, browns, greens & cream, 13" ........................**125.00**

**Flower holder, girl with large basket and flowers, 9½", from $70.00 to $80.00.**

Flower holder, lady dancing w/hands at side, dress spread out, 9½".............................**110.00**

Plaque, Irish setter profile on sq, Art Creations, 7⅜" ............**50.00**

Tray, black poodle w/flowers & leaves in hair & on collar, 7⅜"x7⅜" ..............................**70.00**

Vase, rolled petal, teal w/gold trim, #477, 15" ...........................**45.00**

## Twin Winton

Bank, foo dog, TW-422, 8"......**125.00**

Bank, owl, TW-420, 8"..............**65.00**

Bank, poodle, TW-419, 8".........**65.00**

Bank, teddy Bear, TW-409, 8" .....**40.00**

Candy jar, angel, 8"..................**40.00**

Figurine, blind mouse, #208,¾" .....**10.00**

Figurine, boy skier, 7".............**175.00**

Figurine, chipmunk in top hat, 3"..**40.00**

Figurine, elf in shoe, 6" ..........**120.00**

Figurine, elf on turtle, 5" .........**75.00**

Figurine, girl playing w/teddy bear, 4" ......................................**35.00**

Figurine, mare, recumbent, #317, 1" ........................................**10.00**

Figurine, squirrel w/folded paws, 2½x4" ...............................**30.00**

Garlic holder, garlic bread, 4½" .**40.00**

Ladies of the Mountain, stein, 8".**70.00**

Men of the Mountain, mug, #H-102, 5" ........................................**25.00**

**Men of the Mountain, pitcher, 7½", from $65.00 to $75.00.**

Mug, Bamboo Line, w/rope & spur handle, 4".............................**40.00**

Mug, Bamboo Line, 6" ..............**20.00**

Mug, elephant, trunk handle, 3½x5" ...............................**125.00**

Mug, squirrel handle, 5" ........**100.00**

Planter, bamboo, 12" ...............**45.00**

Planter, fisherman's basket, 6" ...................................**60.00**

Planter, Merry Xmas, 2-pc, 4x15" ...................................**40.00**

Planter, pipe, 5"........................**50.00**

Plate, Santa's face, 7"...............**30.00**

Plate, Santa's Face, 14"...........**50.00**

Salt & pepper shakers, garlic w/face, 3", pr ...................................**40.00**

Salt & pepper shakers, man &
woman, 4", pr .....................**30.00**
Soap boat, Donald Duck, 5¾x6¾x5"...**125.00**
Stein, Bamboo Line, 8".............**35.00**
Teapot, rooster, 10" ................**175.00**
Toothpick dispenser, pig w/front
quarters down, 5" ..............**60.00**

## Wallace China

Bowl, Boots & Saddle, oval, 9½" ..**200.00**
Bowl, mixing; Longhorn, lg......**295.00**
Creamer, Chuck Wagon, 2-oz,
2½" ...................................**95.00**
Cup & saucer, El Rancho, from $45
to .......................................**65.00**
Cup & saucer, Rodeo, from $50
to .....................................**70.00**
Plate, dinner; Boots & Saddle, 10½",
from $120 to .....................**140.00**
Plate, dinner; Longhorn, 10½" .....**125.00**
Plate, dinner; Rodeo, 10¾".....**110.00**
Plate, dinner; Ye Olde Mill,
10⅝" ..............................**20.00**
Plate, Pioneer Trails, 7¼" ........**65.00**
Plate, salad; El Rancho, 8¼" ......**45.00**
Platter, Chuck Wagon, oval,
13x9" ..............................**110.00**
Salt & pepper shakers, Rodeo, over-
sz, 4⅞", pr .......................**140.00**
Teapot, Dahlia .......................**100.00**

## Weil Ware

Bowl, serving; Malay Blossom, 4-
compartment, sq, 10½" .....**50.00**
Bowl, serving; Yellow Rose, sq,
3x7¾" ...............................**25.00**
Candleholders, Bamboo, sq base,
2¼x4", pr...........................**22.50**
Candy dish, Ming Tree, w/lid, footed,
5½x5½" ...........................**27.50**

Creamer & sugar bowl, Bamboo,
w/lid ..................................**25.00**
Flower holder, Dutch girl w/yellow
basket, #3041, 7¼" ...........**40.00**
Flower holder, lady w/accordion,
#4062, 9⅞" .......................**130.00**

**Flower holder, lady with
vase behind, from $75.00
to $80.00; figurine, from
$75.00 to $80.00.**

Plate, Bamboo, 7¾" ..................**10.00**
Plate, Malay Blossom, sq, 9¾" ..**17.50**
Platter, Bamboo, 9¼x7" ...........**14.00**
Platter, Bamboo, 13" ...............**20.00**
Tidbit, Malay Blossom, 3-tiered,
5¾", 8", 9¾" ......................**60.00**
Vase, leaf shape, aqua, #701, 9½x5¾" .**25.00**
Vase, Ming Tree, #907 ............**20.00**
Vase, Ming Tree, #925, 5½x6" ..**35.00**
Wall pocket, Salmon Bamboo,
#2106, 5⅞" .......................**35.00**

## Will-George

Bird figurine, blue jay, wings
spread, 4x4" .....................**45.00**
Bird figurine, flamingo, head down
feeding, wings closed, 6¼"..**100.00**
Bird figurine, pheasant, round base,
16" L................................**165.00**
Cup & saucer, purple onion design ..**35.00**

Figurine, elephant, green w/gold
  trim, 6x9"..........................**175.00**
Figurine, Oriental girl w/pot on pole
  over shoulder, 8½"..............**85.00**
Flower frog, cardinal on tree trunk,
  7"........................................**40.00**
Goblet, wine; rooster stem, 5" ...**30.00**
Tray, flamingo pond, green w/pink
  interior, 9¼x14¾"..............**60.00**
Tumbler, rooster, formed by tall tail
  feathers, 4½"......................**60.00**

## Winfield

Bowl, Bamboo, 3x9¼"...............**60.00**
Bowl, Passion Flower, divided,
  2½x8x13" ...........................**15.00**
Casserole, Dragon Flower, w/lid,
  6x9x14" .............................**25.00**
Pitcher, Dragon Flower, high lip,
  7¾" .....................................**40.00**
Plate, Pussy Willow, 10" ..........**20.00**
Platter, Bamboo, sq, 14½", from $35
  to ........................................**40.00**
Tidbit, Passion Flower, 2-tier, 7½" &
  10¼" tiers...........................**30.00**

## Yona

Cookie jar, clown, Emmett Kelly-
  like face, 1950s, 8½x7"......**55.00**
Figurine, angel w/dog, Be Kind to
  Animals, 5" ........................**20.00**
Figurine/vase, cowgirl playing
  banjo, Yona #12, 11½".......**50.00**
Ice bucket, Country Club, red &
  white stripes, 6x6".............**40.00**

# California Raisins

In the fall of 1986, the California Raisins made their first commer-
cials for television. In 1987 the PVC
figurines were introduced. Initially
there were four: a singer, two conga
dancers, and a saxophone player. At
this time, Hardee's issued similar
but smaller figures. Later that year
Blue Surfboard (horizontal), and
three Bendees (which are about 5½"
tall with flat pancake-style bodies)
were issued for retail sale.

In 1988 twenty-one Raisins were
made for sale in retail stores and in
some cases used for promotional
efforts in grocery stores: Blue Surfboard (vertical), Red Guitar, Lady
Dancer, Blue/Green Sunglasses, Guy
Winking, Candy Cane, Santa Raisin,
Bass Player, Drummer, Tambourine
Lady (there were two styles), Lady
Valentine, Male Valentine, Boy
Singer, Girl Singer, Hip Guitar Player, Sax Player with Beret, and four
Graduates. The Graduates are identical in design to the original four
characters released in 1987 but stand
on yellow pedestals and are attired in
blue graduation caps and yellow tassels. Bass Player and Drummer were
initially distributed in grocery stores
along with an application to join the
California Raisin Fan Club located in
Fresno, California. Later that year
Hardee's issued six more: Blue Guitar, Trumpet Player, Roller Skater,
Skateboard, Boom Box, and Yellow
Surfboard. As was true with the 1987
line, the Hardee's characters were
generally smaller than those produced for retail sales.

Eight more made their debut in
1989: Male in Beach Chair, Green

Trunks with Surfboard, Hula Skirt, Girl Sitting on Sand, Piano Player, 'AC,' Mom, and Michael Raisin. During that year the Raisins starred in two movies: *Meet the Raisins* and *The California Raisins — Sold Out*, and were joined in figurine production by five movie characters (their fruit and vegetable friends): Rudy Bagaman, Lick Broccoli, Banana White, Leonard Limabean, and Cecil Thyme.

The latest release of Raisins came in 1991 when Hardee's issued four more — Anita Break, Alotta Style, Buster, and Benny. All Raisins issued for retail sales and promotions in 1987 and 1988, including Hardee's issues for those years, are dated with the year of production (usually on the bottom of one foot). Of those Raisins released for retail sale in 1989, only the Beach Scene characters are dated, and they are actually dated 1988. Hardee's Raisins, issued in 1991, are also undated. On Friday, November 22, 1911, the California Raisins were enshrined in the Smithsonian Institution to the tune of *I Heard It Through the Grapevine*. We recommend *Schroeder's Collectible Toys, Antique to Modern*, for more information.

Prices are down from their peak of a few years ago — hard hit, as many things have been, by the economy as well as eBay. Our prices reflect this downturn.

Beach Theme Edition, Boy w/Surfboard, brown base, 1988 ...**20.00**

Beach Theme Edition, Female w/Boom Box, purple glasses, 1988.....**20.00**

Beach Theme Edition, Male in Beach Chair, orange sunglasses, 1988................**20.00**

Christmas Issue, candy cane or red hat, 1988, ea ........................**7.50**

Graduate Key Chain, Sax Player, 1988................**85.00**

Hardee's 1st Promotion, Sax Player, gold sax, no hat, 1987 ........**3.00**

Hardee's 2nd Promotion, FF Strings, blue guitar, 1988, sm, $1 to ....................**3.00**

Hardee's 2nd Promotion, Trumpy Trunote w/Trumpet, 1988, sm, $1 to ....................**3.00**

Hardee's 2nd Promotion, Waves Weaver II, w/yellow surfboard, 1988, sm, $1 to....................**2.00**

Meet the Raisins 1st Edition, AC, 'Gimme 5' pose, 1989........**225.00**

Meet the Raisins 1st Edition, piano player, blue piano, green sneakers, 1989 ............................**35.00**

Meet the Raisins 1st Promotion, Banana White, yellow dress, 1989................**20.00**

Meet the Raisins 2nd Edition, AC in 'Gimme-5' pose, 1989........**225.00**

Meet the Raisins 2nd Edition, Cecil Thyme (carrot), 1989......**250.00**

Meet the Raisins 2nd Edition, Lenny Limabean, purple suit, 1989 ................................**175.00**

Post Raisin Bran Issue, Graduate, yellow base, 1988, from $45 to ....................**65.00**

Post Raisin Bran Issue, Graduate Singer, yellow base, 1988, $45 to ....................**65.00**

Post Raisin Bran Issue, Hands, left points up, right is down, 1987......................................**2.00**

Post Raisin Bran Issue, Male Singer, right hand in fist, 1987......................................**2.00**

Post Raisin Bran Issue, Saxophone, inside of sax painted red, 1987......................................**2.00**

**Second Commercial Issue/Calrab, Bass Player, gray shoes, 1988, M, $8.00.**

Special Edition, Michael Raisin, 1989......................................**15.00**

Special Lover's Edition, Valentine, boy holding heart, 1988 ......**8.00**

Special Lover's Edition, Valentine, girl holding heart, 1988 ......**8.00**

Unknown Production, Male on Blue Surfboard, 1988.................**35.00**

1st Commercial Issue, Guitar Player, red guitar, 1988.....................**8.00**

1st Commercial Issue, Male Singer, microphone in left hand, 1988......................................**6.00**

1st Commercial Issue, Winky, hitchhiker winking, 1988...**5.00**

1st Key Chains, Hands, pointing up w/thumbs touching head, 19878..................................**5.00**

1st Key Chains, Male in Sunglasses, finger on face, 1987 ..............**5.00**

1st Key Chains, Sax Player, gold sax, no hat, 1987 .................**5.00**

2nd Commercial Issue, Bass Player, gray slippers, 1988..............**8.00**

2nd Commercial Issue, Drummer, 1988..................................**10.00**

2nd Commercial Issue, Ms Delicious, female tambourine player, 1988 ..............................**15.00**

2nd Key Chains, Hip Band Guitarist (Hendrix), headband/guitar, 1988..................................**65.00**

3rd Commercial Issue, Sax Player, black beret, blue eyelids, 1988..................................**15.00**

# Cameras

Whether buying a camera for personal use, adding to a collection, or for resale, use caution. Complex usable late-model cameras are difficult to check out at sales, and you should be familiar with the camera model or have confidence in the seller's claims before purchasing one for your personal use. If you are just beginning a camera collection, there are a multitude of different types and models and special features to select from in building your collection; you should have on hand some of the available guide books listing various models and types. Camera collecting can be a very enjoyable hobby and can be done within your particular funding ability.

Buying for resale can be a very profitable experience if you are careful in your selection and have made arrangements with buyers who have made their requirements known to you. Generally, buying low-cost, mass-produced cameras is not advisable; you may have a difficult time finding a buyer for such cameras. Of these low-cost types, only those that are mint or new in the original box have any appreciable appeal to collectors. Very old cameras are not necessarily valuable — it all depends on availability. The major criterion is quality; prices offered for mint-condition cameras may be double or triple those of average-wear items. You can expect to find that foreign-made cameras are preferred by most buyers because of the general perception that their lenses and shutters are superior. The German- and Japanese-made cameras dominate the 'classic' camera market. Polaroid cameras and movie cameras have yet to gain a significant collector's market.

The cameras listed here represent only a very small cross section of thousands of cameras available. Values are given for examples with average wear and in good working order; they represent average retail prices with limited guarantees. It is very important to note that purchase prices at flea markets, garage sales, or estate sales would have to be far less for them to be profitable to a resaler who has the significant expense of servicing the camera, testing it, and guaranteeing it to a user or a collector.

Agfa, Billy, early 1930s ............**15.00**

Agfa, Isolette ............................**20.00**
Agfa, Optima, 1960s, from $15 to ....................................**35.00**
Ansco, Cadet ............................**5.00**
Ansco, Memar, 1954-58 ...........**20.00**
Ansco, Speedex, Standard, 1950......**15.00**
Argoflex, Seventy-five, twin-lens reflex, 1949-58 .....................**7.00**
Argus C4, 2.8 lens w/flash .......**30.00**
Asahiflex I, 1st Japanese single-lens reflex ...............................**500.00**
Bell & Howell Dial-35 ..............**40.00**
Bosley B2 ................................**20.00**
Burke & James, Cub, 1914 ......**20.00**
Canon AE-1, from $40 to..........**80.00**
Canon F-1 ..............................**225.00**
Canon III................................**250.00**
Canon P, 1958-61, from $250 to....................................**350.00**
Canon S-II, Seiki-Kogaku, 1946-47, from $600 to ....................**800.00**
Canon TL, from $40 to ............**60.00**
Canon VT, 1956-57, from $250 to ....................................**300.00**
Ciroflex, twin-lens reflex, 1940s, from $20 to........................**30.00**
Contessa 35, 1950-55, from $100 to....................................**150.00**

**Coronet 3D, Binocular viewfinder, 1954, from $65.00 to $75.00.** (Photo courtesy C.E. Cataldo)

Eastman Folding Brownie Six-20.....................................**12.00**

Eastman Kodak Hawkeye, plastic ......................................**8.00**

Eastman Kodak No 1 Folding Pocket camera ..........................**20.00**

Eastman Kodak Pony 135........**10.00**

Eastman Kodak Retina IIa......**80.00**

Eastman Kodak Retina IIIc, from $125 to .............................**180.00**

Eastman Kodak 35...................**20.00**

Edinex, by Wirgen....................**30.00**

Exakta VX, 1951, from $75 to......**85.00**

Fujica AX-3..............................**80.00**

Fujica ST-701 ..........................**60.00**

Hasselblad 1000F, 1952-57, from $350 to .............................**550.00**

Kodak No 2 Folding Pocket Brownie, 1904-07 ..............................**25.00**

Konica FS-1 .............................**60.00**

Kowa H, 1963-67 .....................**25.00**

Leica IID, 1932-38, from $250 to ................................**400.00**

Mamiya-Sekor 500TL, 1966 ....**20.00**

Mercury Model II, CX, 1945 ....**35.00**

Minolta SR-7..............................**50.00**

Minolta SRT-202, from $50 to......**90.00**

Minolta XD-11, 1977, from $110 to.....................................**160.00**

Minox B, spy camera..............**125.00**

Nikon FG .................................**100.00**

Nikon S2 Rangefinder, 1954-58, from $700 to .................**1,000.00**

Nikon EM, from $45 to.............**65.00**

Olympus OM-10, from $40 to.....**60.00**

Pax M3, 1957 ..........................**30.00**

Pentax ME, from $50 to...........**75.00**

Petri-7, 1961 ............................**20.00**

Polaroid SX-70..........................**35.00**

Prakita FX, 1952-57.................**30.00**

Realist Stereo, 3.5 lens ..........**100.00**

Ricoh Singlex, 1965, from $50 to..**80.00**

Rollei 35, miniature, Singapore, from $100 to ...................**175.00**

Rolleiflex Automat, 1937 model ..**125.00**

Rolleiflex 3.5E ........................**300.00**

Spartus Press Flash, 1939-50.....**10.00**

Tessina, miniature, from $300 to ................................**500.00**

Topcon Super D, 1963-74.......**125.00**

Tower 45, Sears, w/Nikkor lens..**200.00**

**Universal Mercury II 35 millimeter, half frame, 1945, $50.00.** (Photo courtesy C.E. Cataldo)

Univex-A, Univ Camera Co, 1933 .................................**25.00**

Voigtlander Bessa, w/rangefinder, 1936 ................................**140.00**

Voigtlander Vitessa L, 1954, from $150 to .............................**200.00**

Voigtlander Vito II, 1950 .........**40.00**

Yashica Electro-35, 1966 .........**25.00**

Yashicamat 124G, twin-lens reflex, from $125 to ...................**200.00**

Zeiss Ikon Juwell, 1927-39 ....**500.00**

Zeiss Ikon Super Ikonta B, 1937-56 ......................................**150.00**

# Candlewick

Candlewick was one of the all-time bestselling lines of The Imperial Glass Company of Bellaire, Ohio. It was produced from 1936 until the company closed in 1982. More than 741 items were made over the years; and though many are still easy to find today, some (such as the desk calendar, the chip and dip set, and the dresser set) are a challenge to collect. Candlewick is easily identified by its beaded stems, handles, and rims characteristic of the tufted needlework of our pioneer women for which it was named. For a complete listing of the Candlewick line, we recommend *Elegant Glassware of the Depression Era* by Gene and Cathy Florence (Collector Books).

Ashtray, eagle, #1776/1, 6½" ...**55.00**
Ashtray, round, #400/19, 2¾" ....**9.00**
Basket, #400/73/0, handled, 11"..**275.00**
Bowl, cream soup; #400/50, 5" ..**45.00**
Bowl, deep, handles, #400/113A, 10" ....................................**155.00**
Bowl, float; #400/101, 1½x13"...**65.00**
Bowl, heart w/hand, #400/73H, 9" ......................................**175.00**
Bowl, lily; 4-footed, #400/741, 7" ......................................**75.00**
Bowl, pickle/celery; #400/58, 8½"..**20.00**
Bowl, relish; 2-part, #400/268, 8" ......................................**20.00**
Bowl, relish; 3-compartment, #400/256, 10½" .................**30.00**
Bowl, round, #400/92B, 12"......**45.00**
Bowl, salad; #400/75B, 10½"....**40.00**
Bowl, sauce; deep, #400/243, 5½" ....................................**40.00**
Bowl, sq, #400/232, 6" ...........**135.00**
Cake stand, low foot, #400/67D, 10" ......................................**60.00**
Candleholder, flower, #400/40C, 5", ea......................................**35.00**
Candleholder, 3-toed, #400/207, 4½", ea......................................**100.00**
Cigarette box, #400/134, w/lid......**35.00**
Coaster, #400/78, 4" .................**10.00**
Compote, 3-bead stem, #400/220, 5" ......................................**85.00**

Cruet, oil; bead base, #400/166, 6-oz....................................**75.00**

**Cup and saucer, after dinner; $22.00. (Photo courtesy Gene and Cathy Florence)**

Cup, coffee; #400/37....................**7.50**
Fork & spoon set, #400/75 .......**40.00**
Ice tub, #400/168, 7"...............**250.00**
Jar tower, #400/655, 3 sections..**495.00**
Mirror, round, standing, 4½" ...**135.00**
Pitcher, #400/419, plain, 40-oz...**50.00**
Pitcher, low foot, #400/19, 16-oz..**250.00**
Plate, salad; oval, #400/38, 9" ....**45.00**
Plate, torte; #400/17D, 14".......**50.00**
Plate, triangular, #400/266, 7½" ..**95.00**
Salt spoon, #400/616, 3"...........**11.00**
Stem, brandy; #3800 ...............**60.00**
Stem, cocktail; #400/190, 4-oz ...**22.00**
Sugar bowl, domed foot, #400/18..**135.00**
Tumbler, footed, #3400, 10-oz...**20.00**
Tumbler, parfait; #400/18, 7-oz.**85.00**
Vase, bud; footed, #400/187, 7"..**310.00**
Vase, flat, crimped edge, #400/143C, 8" ......................................**95.00**

# Cape Cod by Avon

Though now discontinued, the Avon company sold this dark ruby red glassware through their catalogs since the '70s, and there seems to be a good supply of it around today. In addition to the place settings (there are plates in three sizes, soup and dessert bowls, a cup and saucer, tumblers in two sizes, three different goblets, a mug, and a wine glass), there are many lovely accessory items as well. Among them you'll find a cake plate, a pitcher, a platter, a hurricane-type candle lamp, a butter dish, napkin rings, and a pie plate server. Note: Mint-in-box items are worth about 20% more than the same piece with no box.

Bell, hostess; marked Christmas 1979, 6½" ................................**22.50**

Bell, hostess; unmarked, 1979-80, 6½" .....................................**18.50**

Bowl, dessert; 1978-90, 6½".....**12.50**

Bowl, rimmed soup; 1991, 7½"..**24.50**

Bowl, vegetable; unmarked, 1986-90, 8¾" ................................**30.00**

Box, trinket; heart form, w/lid, 1989-90, 4" .................................**19.50**

Butter dish, w/lid, 1983-84, ¼-lb, 7" L .........................................**24.50**

Cake knife, red plastic handle, wedged blade, Sheffield, 1981-84, 8" ...................................**18.00**

Candleholder, hurricane type w/clear chimney, 1985, ea...............**40.00**

Candlestick, 1975-80, 8¾", ea...**12.50**

Candlestick, 1983-84, 2½", ea....**9.00**

Candy dish, 1987-90, 3½x6" dia.**19.50**

Christmas ornament, 6-sided, marked Christmas 1990, 3¼" ....................................**12.50**

Cruet, oil; w/stopper, 1975-80, 5-oz ..**12.50**

Cup & saucer, 15th Anniversary, marked 1975-1990 on cup, 7-oz...................................**24.50**

Cup & saucer, 1990-93, 7-oz ....**19.50**

Decanter, w/stopper, 1977-80, 16-oz, 10½" ..................................**18.00**

Goblet, claret; 1992, 5-oz, 5¼" ..**14.00**

Goblet, saucer champagne; 1991, 8-oz, 5¼"................................**15.00**

Goblet, water; 1976-90, 9-oz ......**9.50**

Goblet, wine; 1977-80, 3-oz, 4½"..**2.50**

Mug, pedestal foot, 1982-84, 5-oz, 5"..**12.00**

Napkin ring, 1989-90, 1¾".........**9.50**

Pie/plate server, 1992-93, 10¾" dia......................................**38.50**

Pitcher, water; footed, 1984-84, 60-oz ........................................**49.50**

Plate, bread & butter; 1992-93, 5½" ....................................**10.00**

Plate, cake; pedestal foot, 1991, 3½x10¾" dia.....................**50.00**

Plate, dessert; 1980-90, 7½" ......**8.00**

Plate, dinner; 1982-90, 11" ......**30.00**

Platter, oval, 1986, 13".............**59.50**

Salt & pepper shakers, marked May 1978, ea..............................**9.50**

Sauce boat, footed, 1988, 8" .....**29.50**

**Sugar bowl, $9.50; Salt and pepper shakers, $15.00 for the pair; Creamer, $9.50.**

Tidbit tray, 2-tiered (7" & 10" plates), 1987, 9¾".............**56.50**

Tumbler, straight sides, footed, 1988, 8-oz, 3½" .................**12.00**

Tumbler, straight sides, 1990, 12-oz, 5½" ....................................**14.00**

Vase, footed, 1985, 8" .............**24.00**

# Carnival Chalkware

Chalkware statues of Kewpies,

glamour girls, assorted dogs, horses, etc., were given to winners of carnival games from about 1910 until the 1950s. Today's collectors especially value those representing well-known personalities such as Disney characters and comic book heroes. Refer to *The Carnival Chalk Prize* by Tom Morris for more information. Mr. Morris is in the Directory under Oregon.

Apache Babe, unmarked, ca 1936, 15" ......................................**65.00**
Boy & Dog, marked Pals, ca 1935-45, 10x9" ................................**35.00**
Call Me Papa, 1935-45, 14" ......**15.00**
Cat sitting & looking into fishbowl, ca 1940-50, 9½" .................**75.00**
Clown standing w/hands in pockets, ca 1940-50, 9½" .................**45.00**
Colonial lady standing w/dog, 1935-45, 11¼" .............................**17.50**
Donald Duck, 1934-50, 14" ......**70.00**
Elephant rearing & wild, ca 1930-45, 9¾" ...............................**45.00**
Gorilla standing beating chest, 1940s, 6¼" ..........................**15.00**
Hula girl playing ukulele, ca 1935-45, 12¾" ...........................**150.00**
Jockey on horse jumping barrier, ca 1935-45, 9¼" ......................**45.00**
Lone Ranger, 16" ......................**85.00**
Maggie & Jiggs, marked Armistice, KFS, 1925-40, 11½" ........**285.00**
Mexican taking siesta, ashtray, marked 1936, 6½" .............**45.00**
Oriental lady, bust, ca 1930-40, 5½"..**65.00**
Pancho, 1940s, 11½" ................**25.00**
Pinocchio standing w/arms down to side, 1940-50, 11½" ..........**95.00**
Porky Pig, 1940-50, 11"............**65.00**
Shirley Temple standing in short skirt, bows on dress/in hair, 16½" ................................**320.00**

Snow White standing w/hands clasped, 1930s, 13½" ........**95.00**

**Sugar, marked Jenkins, 1948, 13", $120.00.**

Uncle Sam rolling up his sleeve, ca 1935-45, 15" .....................**125.00**
Westward Ho Cowboy, 1945-50, 10"......................................**25.00**
Wimpy eating hamburger (You Bring the Ducks), marked 1929, 13" ...................................**190.00**

## Cat-Tail Dinnerware

Cattail was a dinnerware pattern popular during the late 1920s until sometime in the 1940s. So popular, in fact, that ovenware, glassware, tinware, and even a kitchen table was made to coordinate with it. The dinnerware was made primarily by Universal potteries of Cambridge, Ohio, though a catalog from Hall China Co., circa 1927, shows a three-piece coffee service, and there may have been other pieces made by Hall as well. Cattail was sold for years by Sears Roebuck and Company, and some items bear a mark with their name.

The pattern is unmistakable — a cluster of red cattails (usually six but sometimes only one or two) with black stems on creamy white. Shapes certainly vary; Universal used a minimum of three of their standard mold designs — Camwood, Old Holland, Laurella — and there were possibly others. Some pieces are marked 'Wheelock' on the bottom. Wheelock was a department store in Peoria, Illinois.

If you are trying to decorate a '40s vintage kitchen, no other design could afford you more to work with. To see many of the pieces that are available and to learn more about the line, read *The Collector's Encyclopedia of American Dinnerware* by Jo Cunningham (Collector Books).

Bowl, footed, 9½" ...................... **20.00**
Bowl, mixing; 6" ........................ **17.50**
Bowl, mixing; 7" ........................ **20.00**
Bowl, mixing; 8" ........................ **23.00**
Bowl, salad ................................ **25.00**
Bowl, soup; flat rim, 7¼" .......... **15.00**
Bowl, soup; tab handles, 8" ...... **17.50**
Bowl, straight sides, 6¼" ......... **12.00**
Bowl, vegetable; oval, 9" .......... **27.50**
Bowl, w/lid, part of ice box set, 4" .. **12.00**
Bowl, w/lid, part of ice box set, 6" .. **18.50**
Butter dish, 1-lb ...................... **30.00**
Cake cover & tray, tinware ...... **35.00**
Canister set, tin, 4-pc .............. **60.00**

**Casserole, with lid, 8½" diameter, $30.00.**

Coffeepot, electric ................... **150.00**
Coffeepot, 3-pc .......................... **70.00**
Cookie jar, barrel shape, Universal USA, 6¾" ......................... **150.00**
Cookie jar, from $75 to ........... **100.00**
Creamer ...................................... **9.00**
Cup & saucer, from $6 to ......... **10.00**
Custard cup ................................ **9.00**
Jug, canteen; ceramic-topped cork stopper ............................... **38.00**
Jug, 1-qt, 6" .............................. **25.00**
Pickle dish/gravy boat liner, 9¼x5¼" .. **20.00**
Pie plate .................................... **30.00**
Pie server, hole in handle for hanging, marked ..................... **175.00**
Pitcher, glass, w/ice lip, from $75 to .. **125.00**
Pitcher, milk/utility ................. **22.50**
Plate, chop ................................ **35.00**
Plate, dinner; Laurella shape, from $15 to ................................ **20.00**
Plate, luncheon; 9" ................... **35.00**
Plate, salad/dessert; rnd ........... **6.50**
Plate, sq, 7¼" ............................. **7.00**
Plate, 6¼" .................................... **5.50**
Platter, oval, tab handles, 13⅜" ..... **30.00**
Platter, oval, 11½", from $15 to ..... **20.00**
Platter, oval, 14¾" .................... **55.00**
Platter, round, tab handles, 11" ..... **30.00**
Range shakers, 4: Pepper & Salt (2¾"), Flour & Sugar (4), milk, from $70 to ..................... **85.00**
Salad set (fork, spoon & bowl), from $50 to ................................ **60.00**
Scales, metal ............................ **37.00**
Stack set, 3-pc w/lids, from $35 to .. **40.00**
Sugar bowl, w/lid, from $20 to ..... **25.00**
Syrup, red top .......................... **70.00**
Teapot, 4-cup ............................ **35.00**
Teapot, 6-cup ............................ **50.00**
Tray, for batter set ................... **75.00**
Tumbler, juice; glass ............... **30.00**
Tumbler, water; glass ............. **35.00**

Waste can, step-on, tinware.....**35.00**

# Ceramic Arts Studio

Whether you're a collector of American pottery or not, chances are you'll like the distinctive styling of the figurines, salt and pepper shakers, and other novelty items made by the Ceramic Arts Studio of Madison, Wisconsin, from about 1938 until approximately 1952. They're not especially hard to find — a trip to any good flea market will usually produce at least one good buy from among their vast array of products. They're easily spotted, once you've seen a few examples; but if you're not sure, check for the trademark — most are marked.

See the Directory for information concerning the CAS Collector's Association, listed under Clubs and Newsletters.

Bank, Paisley Pig, 3".............**150.00**
Blade bank, Tony the Barber, 4¾", from $75 to ......................**100.00**
Bowl, Bonita, paisley shape, 3¾" L........................................**75.00**
Bowl, Space, aqua, round/stylized, 5¼".....................................**80.00**
Candleholder, Triad Girl, left or right, from $80 to ...........**110.00**
Candleholders, Bedtime Boy & Girl, 4¾", pr from $150 to .........**190.00**
Figurine, Annie (baby elephant) & Benny, 3¼", 3¾", pr, $115 to......................................**160.00**
Figurine, Bali-Hai, standing, 8"..**135.00**

Figurine, Balinese Dance Man, 9½".................................**165.00**
Figurine, Bear Mother & Cub, realistic, 3¼", 2¼", pr, $320 to......................................**380.00**
Figurine, Blessing Angel, hand down, 5¾".........................**100.00**
Figurine, Bright Eyes cat, 3", from $30 to ...............................**40.00**
Figurine, bunny, 1¾" ...............**50.00**
Figurine, Chinese Boy & Girl, 3", pr......................................**65.00**
Figurine, cockatoo, female, tail up, 5".....................................**110.00**
Figurine, Colonial Man, 6½"....**65.00**
Figurine, Daisy, donkey, 4¾", from $85 to ...............................**110.00**
Figurine, Dem, donkey, 4½" ...**125.00**
Figurine, Fifi & Fufu poodles, 3", 2½", pr from $180 to .......**240.00**
Figurine, frog, singing, 2" ........**45.00**
Figurine, Gingham Dog, 2¾" ...**45.00**
Figurine, Hans, Dance Boy, 5½" ..**70.00**

**Figurines, Harem Trio, sultan & two harem girls, from $320.00 to $395.00.**

Figurine, Isaac & Rebekah, 10", pr, from $140 to ....................**200.00**
Figurine, lamb w/bow, 4" .........**65.00**
Figurine, Lightning & Thunder stallions, 5¾", pr from $300 to......................................**350.00**
Figurine, Little Jack Horner, #2, 4" ......................................**80.00**

Figurine, lovebirds, 1-pc, 2¾" ...**45.00**

**Figurines, Lover Boy and Willing, $135.00 for the pair.**

Figurine, Madonna w/golden halo, 9½", from $350 to ............**450.00**

Figurine, Mary, 6¼" .................**49.00**

Figurine, Minnehaha .............**125.00**

Figurine, Mop-Pi & Smi-Li, pr..**65.00**

Figurine, Our Lady of Fatima, 9", from $260 to ....................**285.00**

Figurine, pekingese, 3" ............**95.00**

Figurine, Pioneer Sam & Suzie, 5½", 5", pr from $80 to ..............**100.00**

Figurine, Polish Boy & Girl, 6½", pr..**120.00**

Figurine, Praise Angel, hand up, 6"..**135.00**

Figurine, Rhumba Man & Woman, 7¼", 7", pr from $80 to ....**120.00**

Figurine, Santa Claus, 2¼"......**145.00**

Figurine, Saucy Squirrel w/jacket, 2¼", from $175 to ............**200.00**

Figurine, spring colt, 3½" ......**125.00**

Figurine, Spring Sue, 5", from $125 to ......................................**150.00**

Figurine, St Francis w/extended arms, 7", from $175 to.....**225.00**

Figurine, Swan Lake Man, 7" .....**250.00**

Figurine, tortoise w/hat, crawling, 2½" L................................**125.00**

Figurine, Wee Chinese boy & girl, 3", pr ..................................**45.00**

Figurine, zebra, 5" .................**125.00**

Head vase, African Man, 8" ...**325.00**

Head vase, Barbie, blond, 7"....**175.00**

Head vase, Becky, 5¼", from $100 to ......................................**125.00**

Head vase, Mei-Ling, 5".........**150.00**

Metal accessory, arched window for religious figure, 6½", $125 to......**150.00**

Metal accessory, diamond shape, 15x13", from $45 to ...........**55.00**

Metal accessory, ladder for Jack, rare, 13", from $125 to ....**150.00**

Metal accessory, musical score, 14x12", from $85 to .........**100.00**

Metal accessory, parakeet cage, 13", from $125 to ....................**150.00**

Metal accessory, rainbow arch w/shelf, black, 13½x19", $100 to ......................................**120.00**

Metal accessory, sofa, for Maurice & Michelle, from $250 to .....**275.00**

Metal accessory, star for angel, flat back, from $65 to...............**75.00**

Miniature, pitcher, Adam & Eve, 3" ........................................**60.00**

Miniature, pitcher, Pine Cone, 3¾" ......................................**65.00**

Plaque, Goosey Gander, scarce, 4½", from $140 to ....................**160.00**

Plaque, Greg & Grace, 9½", 9", pr..**145.00**

Plaque, Hamlet & Ophelia, 8", pr from $360 to ....................**440.00**

Plaque, Lotus, lantern woman, 9" ......................................**125.00**

Plaque, Shadow Dancers A & B, 7", pr......................................**185.00**

Plaque, Zor & Zorina, 9", pr ...**145.00**

Salt & pepper shakers, Blackamoor, 4¾", pr from $140 to .......**160.00**

Salt & pepper shakers, covered wagon & oxen, ea 3" L, pr, $100 to..**135.00**

Salt & pepper shakers, fish on tail, pr......................................**125.00**

Salt & pepper shakers, horse's head, pr .........................................**95.00**

Salt & pepper shakers, kangaroo mother & joey, snugglers, pr from $130 to ....................**170.00**

Salt & pepper shakers, Paul Bunyan & evergreen, pr from $200 to ..**225.00**

Salt & pepper shakers, Sabu & elephant, 2¾", 5", pr .............**285.00**

Salt & pepper shakers, Sooty & Taffy, Scottie dogs, pr .......**65.00**

Shelf sitter, Banjo Girl, 4", from $80 to .......................................**100.00**

Shelf sitter, boy w/dog, 5¼" .....**65.00**

Shelf sitter, canaries singing/sleeping, 5", pr from $300 to ...**350.00**

Shelf sitter, Collie mother, 5" ...**95.00**

Shelf sitter, Dutch Boy & Girl, 4½", pr from $50 to....................**70.00**

Shelf sitter, En Pos & En Repos, 4½", pr .............................**195.00**

Shelf sitter, Harmonica Boy, 4" ..**75.00**

Shelf sitter, Nip & Tuck, 4¼", 4", pr.........................................**60.00**

Shelf sitter, Sun-Li & Su-Lin, chubby, 5½", pr..........................**65.00**

Shelf sitter, Tuffy & Fluffy cats, 7", pr from $120 to.................**160.00**

Teapot, applied swan, open, miniature....................................**65.00**

Tray, Pixie Girl kneeling, 4½", from $125 to .............................**150.00**

Vase, Flying Ducks, round, 2" ..**95.00**

# Character and Promotional Glassware

Once routinely given away by fast-food restaurants and soft-drink companies, these glasses have become very collectible; and though they're being snapped up by avid collectors everywhere, you'll still find there are bargains to be had. The more expensive are those with Disney or Walter Lantz cartoon characters, super-heroes, sports greats, or personalities from Star Trek or the old movies. For more information refer to *The Collector's Guide to Cartoon and Promotional Drinking Glasses* by John Hervey (L-W Book Sales and *McDonald's Drinkware* by Michael J. Kelly (Collector Books). See Clubs and Newsletters for information on *Collector Glass News*.

Al Capp, 1975, flat bottom, Joe Btsfplk, from $35 to .................**50.00**

Al Capp, 1975, footed, Joe Btsfplk, from $40 to.........................**60.00**

Archies, Welch's, 1971 & 1973, many variations in ea series, ea....**5.00**

Beverly Hillbillies, CBS promotion, 1963, rare .........................**200.00**

Bozo the Clown, Capital Records, 1965, Bozo on 3 sides only .**10.00**

California Raisins, Applause, 1989, juice, 12-oz, 16-oz, ea from $4 to .........................................**6.00**

California Raisins, Applause, 1989, 32-oz, from $6 to..................**8.00**

Children's Classics, Libbey Glass Co, The Wizard of Oz, from $25 to .......................................**30.00**

Cinderella, Disney/Libbey, 1950s-60s, set of 8......................**120.00**

Dick Tracy, Domino's Pizza, from $75 to ..............................**100.00**

Dick Tracy, 1940s, frosted, 8 different characters, 3" or 5", ea.......................................**75.00**

Disney's All-Star Parade, 1939, 10 different, ea from $25 to ...**50.00**

Donald Duck, Donald Duck Cola, 1960s-70s, from $10 to......**15.00**

ET, Pepsi/MCA Home Video, 1988, 6 different, ea from $15 to ....**25.00**

ET, Pizza Hut, 1982, footed, 4 different, ea from $2 to ................**4.00**

Ghostbusters II, Sunoco/Canada, 1989, 6 different, ea from $3 to ..........................................**5.00**

Goonies, Godfather's Pizza/Warner Bros, 1985, 4 different, ea from $3 to .....................................**5.00**

Great Muppet Caper, McDonald's, 1981, 4 different, 6", ea.......**2.00**

Happy Days, Dr Pepper/Pizza Hut, 1977, any character, ea from $6 to ..........................................**10.00**

Hopalong Cassidy, milk glass w/red & black graphics, 3 different, ea.......................................**25.00**

Hopalong Cassidy's Western Series, ea from $25 to....................**30.00**

James Bond 007, 1985, 4 different, ea from $10 to....................**15.00**

Jungle Book, Disney/Canada, 1966, 6 different, numbered, 5", ea..**65.00**

Jungle Book, Disney/Pepsi, 1970s, Mowgli, unmarked, from $15 to .......................................**20.00**

Jungle Book, Disney/Pepsi, 1970s, Rama, unmarked, from $25 to .......................................**35.00**

Little Mermaid, 1991, 3 different sizes, ea from $6 to............**10.00**

Mickey Mouse Club, 4 different, filmstrip bands top/bottom, ea from $10 to.........................**20.00**

Mister Magoo, Polomar Jelly, many variations & styles, ea, from $25 to ...............................**35.00**

Pac-Man, Arby's Collector Series, 1980, rocks glass, from $2 to ..**4.00**

PAT Ward, Pepsi, late 1970s, static pose, Boris & Natasha, 6"..**20.00**

PAT Ward, Pepsi, late 1970s, static pose, Bullwinkle, 5", from $15 to .......................................**20.00**

PAT Ward, Pepsi, late 1970s, static pose, Dudley Do-Right, 5", from $10 to ...............................**15.00**

PAT Ward, Pepsi, late 1970s, static pose, Rocky, 5", from $15 to.......................................**20.00**

PAT Ward, Pepsi, late 1970s, static pose, Snidley Whiplash, 5", from $8 to .................................**10.00**

Peanuts Characters, milk glass mug, Snoopy in various poses, from $2 to...........................**4.00**

Peanuts Characters, Smuckers, 1994, 3 different, ea from $2 to ....**4.00**

Pinocchio, Dairy Promo/Libbey, 1938-40, 12 different, ea from $15 to ...............................**25.00**

Pocahontas, Burger King, 1995, 4 different, MIB, ea................**3.00**

Popeye, Coca-Cola, 1975, Kollect-A-Set, any character, ea from $3 to .......................................**5.00**

Roy Rogers Restaurant, 1883-1983 logo, from $3 to...................**5.00**

Sleeping Beauty, American, late 1950s, 6 different, ea from $8 to .......................................**15.00**

Sleeping Beauty, Canadian, late 1950s, 12 different, ea from $10 to .......................................**15.00**

Smurfs, Hardee's, 1982 (8 different)/ 1983 (6 different), ea from $1 to .......................................**3.00**

Star Trek, Dr Pepper, 1976, 4 different, ea from $15 to ...........**20.00**

Star Trek, Dr Pepper, 1978, 4 different, ea from $25 to ...........**30.00**

Star Trek: The Motion Picture, Coca-Cola, 1980, 3 different, ea from $10 to..........................**15.00**
Sunday Funnies, 1976, Broom Hilda, from $90 to...........**125.00**
Super Heroes, Marvel/7 Eleven, 1977, footed, Amazing Spider-Man, from $25 to...............**30.00**
Super Heroes, Marvel/7 Eleven, 1977, footed, Incredible Hulk, from $10 to.........................**15.00**
Walter Lantz, Pepsi, 1970s, Chilly Willy or Wally Walrus, ea from $25 to.................................**45.00**
Walter Lantz, Pepsi, 1970s, Cuddles, from $40 to................**60.00**
Walter Lantz, Pepsi, 1970s, Space Mouse, from $150 to........**200.00**
Walter Lantz, Pepsi, 1970s, Woody Woodpecker, from $7 to ....**15.00**
Walter Lantz, Pepsi, 1970s-80s, Buzz Buzzard/Space Mouse, from $15 to.........................**20.00**
Warner Bros, Pepsi, 1976, Interaction, ea from $8 to.............**15.00**

**Warner Bros., Pepsi, 1976, Interaction, Pepe Le Pew and Daffy Duck, from $5.00 to $10.00.**

Warner Bros, Six Flags, 1991, clear, Yosemite Sam, from $10 to.......................................**15.00**
Warner Bros, Welch's, 1976-77, 8 different, names at bottom, ea from $5 to............................**7.00**

Warner Bros, 1995, Taz's Root Beer/Serious Suds, clear glass mug...**7.00**
Wild West Series, Coca-Cola, Buffalo Bill, Calamity Jane, ea from $10 to .......................................**15.00**
Winnie the Pooh, Sears/WDP, 1970s, 4 different, ea from $7 to ...**10.00**
Wizard of Oz, Swift's, 1950s-60s, fluted bottom, Glinda, from $15 to .......................................**25.00**
Wizard of Oz, Swift's, 1950s-60s, fluted bottom, Wicked Witch, from $35 to.........................**50.00**
Ziggy, Number Series, 1-8, ea, from $4 to ...................................**8.00**

# Character Collectibles

One of the most active areas of collecting today is the field of character collectibles. Flea markets usually yield some of the more common items. Toys, books, lunch boxes, children's dishes, and games of all types are for the most part quite readily found. Disney characters, television personalities, and comic book heroes are among the most sought after.

For more information, refer to *Schroeder's Collectible Toys, Antique to Modern*; *Cartoon Toys & Collectibles* by David Longest; *Star Wars Super Collector's Wish Book* by Geoffery T. Carlton; *G-Men and FBI Toys and Collectibles* by Harry and Jody Whitworth; and *The World of Raggedy Ann Collectibles* by Kim Avery. All are published by Collector Books.

See also Advertising; Banks; Bubble Bath Containers; California Raisins; Character and Promotional

Glassware; Children's Books; Cookie Jars; Games; Garfield; Kliban Cat; Lunch Boxes; Novelty Telephones; Peanuts; Puzzles; Radios; Star Wars.

A-Team, Signal Light, 1983, MOC ................................**35.00**

Addams Family, bank, Lurch, ceramic, Korea, 1970s, 8", NM .................................**200.00**

Addams Family, doll, Morticia, stuffed cloth, 27", NM .......**50.00**

Annie (Movie), doll, Annie, Knickerbocker, 6", MIB .................**45.00**

Archies, doll, Archie, stuffed cloth, 1960s, 18", MIP .................**75.00**

Archies, stencil set, 1983, MOC .....**18.00**

Aristocats, Colorforms, 1960s, MIB ....................................**50.00**

Atom Ant, Play Fun Set, Whitman, 1966, NMIB ......................**50.00**

Bambi, push-button puppet, Kohner, Disney, 1960s, EX ..................**40.00**

Banana Splits, guitar, Snorky Elephant, 1960s, 10", EX..........**25.00**

Banana Splits, Kut-Up-Kit, Larami, 1973, MOC (sealed) ..............**20.00**

Banana Splits, tambourine, plastic & cardboard, 1973, MIP.........**35.00**

Batman, coin set, Transogram, 1966, MIP (sealed) ............**35.00**

Batman, Colorforms Cartoon Kit, 1966, EXIB .......................**40.00**

Batman, doll, cloth costume, Toy & Novelty Co, 1966, 16", NM .............................**175.00**

Batman, makeup kit, Joker, 1989, MIP .....................................**15.00**

Batman, Paint-By-Number Set, Hasbro, 1973, NMIB .........**30.00**

Batman, pencil box, gun shape, 1966, unused, MOC.........**175.00**

Batman, Sparkle Paints, Kenner, 1966, EXIB ........................**75.00**

Batman, Stamp & Print Set, AHI, 1966, MOC.......................**100.00**

Batman, wristwatch, batwings keep time on round face, 1966, NMIB ..............................**850.00**

Beany & Cecil, Beany-Copter, Mattel, 1961, NMOC ...............**75.00**

Ben Casey, doctor kit, Transogram, EX ......................................**35.00**

Betty Boop, figure, Bimbo, wood & composition, jointed, 7", EX .............................**330.00**

Betty Boop, tambourine, lithographed tin, 1930s, 6" dia, EX ....**150.00**

Bewitched, doll, Samantha, red gown & hat, Ideal, 1965, 11½", NM ...................................**300.00**

Bionic Woman, Styling Boutique, Kenner, 1977, MIB............**50.00**

Bionic Woman, wallet, pink or blue w/image, Fabergé, 1976, MIP..**20.00**

Bozo the Clown, wristwatch, image & name in red, vinyl band, 1960s, EX...........................**50.00**

Brady Bunch, banjo, Larami, 1973, 15", MIP.............................**65.00**

Brady Bunch, Fishin' Fun Set, Larami, 1973, MOC .................**30.00**

Buck Rogers, gum wrapper, 1979, 5x6", VG+...........................**10.00**

Buck Rogers, Strato-Kite, Aero-Kite Co, 1946, EXIP ...............**100.00**

Bugs Bunny, wall clock, w/carrot, plastic case, S Thomas, 10" dia, NM .....................................**85.00**

Buzz Lightyear, yo-yo, Disney, NM..**5.00**

Captain America, Flashmite, Jane X, 1976, MOC ...................**75.00**

Captain Hook, figure, plastic, Disney, 8", NM+.....................**25.00**

Captain Kangaroo, Colorforms, GIB.....................................**20.00**

Captain Planet, ring, Light & Sound, 1991, MOC.............**25.00**

Charlie McCarthy, figure, composition, 12", EX ....................**150.00**

CHiPs, bicycle siren, 1977, EX .**25.00**

Daisy Duck, wristwatch, US Time, 1948, EXIB ......................**300.00**

Davy Crockett, binoculars, plastic, Harrison, MIB.................**175.00**

Davy Crockett, napkins, Beach Prod, 1950s, 30 5" sq, MIP...........**40.00**

Davy Crockett, play horse, Pied Piper Toys, MIB ..............**125.00**

Dennis the Menace, Mischief Kit, Hasbro, 1955, NMIB.........**50.00**

Dennis the Menace, paint set, Pressman, 1950s, EXIB .............**50.00**

Dennis the Menace, Tiddly Winks, Whitman, 1960s, EX+.......**45.00**

Dick Tracy (Movie), doll, Tracy, Applause, 1990s, 14", M....**45.00**

Donald Duck, figure, as pirate, ceramic, WDP, 1970s, 3½", EX......**30.00**

Donald Duck, figure, rubber w/squeaker, Sieberling, 6", EX+ .................................**125.00**

Dr Dolittle, doll, talker, Mattel, 1969, 24", MIB, from $125 to .....................................**150.00**

Dr Seuss, doll, Gowdy the Dowdy Grackle, MIB ..................**275.00**

Dracula, doll, cloth outfit, Lincoln Toys, 1975, 8", NM..........**375.00**

Dumbo, figure, squeeze rubber, Dell, Disney, 1950s, 5", EX+ .................................**25.00**

Evel Knievel, wristwatch, vinyl band, Bradley, 1976, EX ..............**150.00**

Fat Albert, doll, vinyl w/cloth outfit, Remco, 1985, lg, NRFB.......**50.00**

Fat Albert, figure, vinyl, 1973, 3", VG .....................................**10.00**

Felix the Cat, figure, wood, Schoenhut, 8", EX ......................**225.00**

Felix the Cat, pencil box, School Companion, 1939, empty, EX.....**75.00**

Felix the Cat, Pencil Color-By-Number, Hasbro, MIP (sealed).**75.00**

Flash Gordon, Road-Stars Spaceship, die-cast metal, 1975, MOC..**30.00**

Flash Gordon, table cover, paper, 1978, 54x88", MIP.............**25.00**

Flintstones, Colorforms, 1972, NMIB .................................**30.00**

**Flintstones, Dino and Pebbles bank, from $35.00 to $40.00.**

Flintstones, doll, Barney, vinyl, Knickerbocker, 1960s, 10", EX ......**85.00**

Flintstones, doll, Betty, vinyl, Knickerbocker, 1960s, 10", EX........**100.00**

Flintstones, doll, Fred, vinyl, Knickerbocker, 1960s, 10", EX+.......**75.00**

Flintstones, doll, Wilma, vinyl, Knickerbocker, 1960s, 10", EX.........**100.00**

Flower, figure, beanbag type, Disney, 6", EX ..........................**8.00**

Fury, picture slide (7), 1962, VG+ ...................................**10.00**

Gene Autry, flashlight, Cowboy Lariat, EXIB.........................**100.00**

Grease, gum wrapper, 1978, 5x6", VG+ ...................................**10.00**

Green Hornet, Ed-U Cards, 1966, NMIB ................................**75.00**

Green Hornet, figure, bendable, Lakeside Toys, 1966, 6", MOC..**175.00**

Green Hornet, flicker rings, any of 6, 1966, EX, ea...................**25.00**

Gremlins, Colorforms Play Set, 1984, unused, MIB.............**35.00**

Gumby & Pokey, figure, Gumby, seated, wind-up, 1966, 4", NM ..**25.00**

Gumby & Pokey, stick horse, Pokey, VG ......................................**65.00**

Hanna-Barbera, doll, Yogi Bear, Knickerbocker, 1959, 10", EX ......................................**75.00**

Hanna-Barbera, doll, Yogi Bear, stuffed, 50", EX ...............**200.00**

Hanna-Barbera, Yogi Bear, Ge-Tar, Mattel, 1960, EX ...............**25.00**

Hanna-Barbera, figure, Birdman, vinyl, Japan, 11", NM .....**250.00**

Hanna-Barbera, figure, Quick Draw McGraw, ceramic, EX ..........**55.00**

Hanna-Barbera, guitar, Yogi Bear Ge-Tar, Mattel, 1960s, EX........**75.00**

Hanna-Barbera, magic slate, Pixie & Dixie, Melmac, 1960, 8", EX..**20.00**

Hanna-Barbera, plate, Jellystone Park, Melmac, 1960s, 8", NM ......................................**20.00**

Happy Days, Flip-A-Knot, National Marketing, 1977, MIP.......**20.00**

Happy Days, Miracle Bubble Shooter, Imperial, 1981, MOC..**15.00**

Happy Days, mug, Fonzie, thermo plastic, 1976, EX ...............**15.00**

Happy Days, wallet, Larami, 1981, MIP .....................................**20.00**

Heckle & Jeckle, film, 8mm, 1962, EXIB ................................**35.00**

Heckle & Jeckle, pinball game, 7½", EX ......................................**15.00**

Hector Heathcote, Colorforms, 1964, EXIB ................................**40.00**

Honey West, doll, Honey West, Gilbert, 1965, rare, 11½", MIB................................**400.00**

Honey West, Pet Set, Gilbert, unused, MIB.....................**85.00**

Hopalong Cassidy, doll, rubber/cloth, w/gun & holster, 1950s, 21", NM..........................**300.00**

Hopalong Cassidy, nightlight, glass gun in holster, Aladdin, 1950s, NM ..................................**350.00**

Hopalong Cassidy, stationery folio, w/paper & envelopes, complete, VG+ ....................................**50.00**

Howdy Doody, bubble pipe, Howdy, Lido, 1950s, 4", EX ..........**175.00**

Howdy Doody, doll, Howdy, talker, Ideal, 24", EXIB .............**350.00**

Incredible Hulk, Flip-It, Tillotson, 1977, MOC........................**50.00**

James Bond, 007, ID tags, 1984, MOC...................................**25.00**

Jetsons, Colorforms, 1960s, EXIB ..**75.00**

Jetsons, doll, Astro, plush, Nanco, 1989, 10", NM....................**10.00**

Jiminy Cricket, mask, painted & molded gauze, Fishback/WDP, 1940, EX ...........................**50.00**

Joan Palooka, doll, Ideal, 1952, 14", EX ....................................**135.00**

Josie & the Pussycats, chalkboard, 1970s, M ...........................**75.00**

Josie & the Pussycats, vanity set, Larami, 1973, MOC ..........**30.00**

Kayo, figure, jointed & painted wood, Jaymar, 1938, M ...............**125.00**

King Kong, Colorforms Panoramic Play Set, 1976, EXIB ........**25.00**

Knight Rider, Colorforms, Adventure Set, 1982, MIB.....................**35.00**

Kojak, doll, Excel Toy Corp, 1976, 8", MOC ............................**150.00**

Krusher, figure, expandable, Mattel, 1970s, 13½", EX.................**65.00**

Land of the Giants, Colorforms, 1968, NMIB ........................**60.00**

Land of the Lost, Give-A-Show Projector, Kenner, 1975, EXIB......**35.00**

Land of the Lost, magic slate, Whitman, 1975, unused, M .........**40.00**

Land of the Lost, Safari Shooter gun, Larami, 1975, MIP....**45.00**

Land of the Lost, Spark Shooter, Larami, 1975, MIP............**30.00**

Lash LaRue, wristwatch, MIB..**50.00**

Laugh-In, Button Kit, Schlatter, 1968, EXIB ........................**20.00**

Little Lulu, charm bracelet, Larami, 1973, MOC...........................**15.00**

Little Mermaid, purse, vinyl, 6" dia, NM+ ...................................**15.00**

Lone Ranger, horseshoe set, rubber, Gardner, NMIB .................**85.00**

Lone Ranger, ring-toss, diecut cardboard, Rosebud Art, MIB..**250.00**

Looney Toons, Bugs Bunny Cartoon Kit, Colorforms, EXIB.....**100.00**

Looney Tunes, bank, Daffy Duck figure, Applause, 1980s, EX+..**25.00**

Looney Tunes, doll, Foghorn Leghorn, plush, recent, NM ...................................**35.00**

Looney Tunes, squeak toy, Porky Pig, Sun Rubber, NM........**75.00**

Love Boat, Barber Shop, Fleetwood, 1979, MOC (sealed)...........**30.00**

Love Boat, In Port Set, Fleetwood, 1979, MOC (sealed)...........**30.00**

Luney Toons, doll, Bugs as baseball player, 1950s, rare, NM.**350.00**

Magilla Gorilla, doll, plush, Ideal, 1960s, 18½", NM+...........**100.00**

Man From UNCLE, Secret Weapon Set, Ideal, 1965, NMIB ...**400.00**

Man From UNCLE, Thrush Buster Car, EXIB ........................**285.00**

Marvel Super Heroes, Colorforms, 1983, MIB ..........................**30.00**

Mary Poppins, figure, bendable, Gund, Disney, 12", EX+ ....**60.00**

Mary Poppins, pencil case, vinyl w/zipper, Disney, 1960s, EX+ ...................................**15.00**

Maverick, Eras-O-Picture Book, Hasbro, 1958, complete, EX ......**40.00**

Mickey Mouse, bank, ceramic, head only, Disney, 6", EX+ .........**50.00**

Mickey Mouse, bubble-flowing figure, rubber, Tootsietoy, 1993, 5", MIP.................................**8.50**

Mickey Mouse, egg cup, porcelain, figural w/painted details, 1930s, 3" .....................................**125.00**

Mickey Mouse, figure, talker, Hasbro, Disney, 1970s, 8", NM+ ......**50.00**

Mighty Mouse, Basketball Game, 1973, MOC.........................**25.00**

Minnie Mouse, alarm clock, image on face, Bradley/WDP, 1970s-80s, EXIB...........................**65.00**

Moon Mullins, figure, bisque, 1930s, 7½", G ..............................**125.00**

Mork & Mindy, Magic Transfer Set, 1979, MIP .........................**15.00**

Mother Goose, jack-in-the-box, Mattel, 1971, EX+ ....................**25.00**

Mr Magoo, doll, Ideal, 1970, 12", EXIB ................................**50.00**

Mr T, transfer set, 1984, MIB (sealed)..............................**50.00**

Munsters, doll, Baby Herman, Ideal, 1965, NM ..........................**65.00**

Munsters, Koach Toy w/Motor Noise, plastic, AMT, EX+IB.....**1,100.00**

My Favorite Martian, Magic Tricks Set, Gilbert, 1964, NMIB..**175.00**

New Zoo Review, mobile, musical, 1975, MIB ..........................**25.00**

Pac Man, bulletin board, cork, 1980, 17x23", MIB (sealed)..........**35.00**

Pac Man, tray, metal, 1980, 12x17", VG+ ....................................**15.00**

Partridge Family, bulletin board, 1970s, 18x24", NM ..........**100.00**

Partridge Family, doll, Laurie, Remco, 1973, 19", MIB ....**325.00**

Peanuts, Colorforms Happy Birthday Snoopy (Pop-Up), MIB.......**35.00**

Peanuts, doll, Snoopy, rag-type, Ideal, 7", MIP .....................**25.00**

Peanuts, doll, Woodstock as Santa, plush, Applause, 9", MIP ...**20.00**

Peanuts, hairbrush, Charlie Brown, vinyl, 1971, 6", VG+ ...........**10.00**

Peter Potamus, movie, Stars on Mars, 8mm, black & white, NMIB..**25.00**

Phantom, dagger set, Larami, 1970s, EXIB.....................**125.00**

Phantom, Squirt Camera, Larami, 1976, EXIB ......................**125.00**

Pink Panther, Cartoonarama, 1970, EXIB ..................................**60.00**

Pinocchio, bank, vinyl, head only, Play Pal, Disney, 1970s, 10", NM+ ..................................**25.00**

Pixie & Dixie, magic slate, Melmac, Hanna-Barbera, EX ..........**20.00**

Planet of the Apes, Colorforms Play Set, 1967, EXIB .................**60.00**

Pluto, hand puppet, cloth & vinyl, Gund, Disney, 1950s, EX....**25.00**

Pogo, figure, Pogo, vinyl, Walt Kelly, 1969, 4", VG+.....................**15.00**

Pokemon, wristwatch, black plastic band, General Mills premium, MIP ....................................**12.00**

Popeye, Beach Boat, 1980, MOC.................................**50.00**

**Popeye, Bifbat paddle, red print on wood, 11", EX, $10.00.**

Popeye, Bubble Pipe Set, box only, 1936, 5x7", NM .................**65.00**

Popeye, Colorforms Popeye the Weatherman, 1959, NMIB....................**20.00**

Popeye, doll, Brutus, vinyl w/cloth outfit, w/original tag, 13", M..**25.00**

Popeye, doll, Olive Oyl, vinyl & cloth, 11", MIP..................**30.00**

Popeye, doll, Popeye, plush, 1994, 13", EX ...............................**10.00**

Popeye, figure, Jeep, composition, jointed, KFS, 1933, 13", G+..**750.00**

Roger Rabbit, figure, Applause, Disney, 17", NM+....................**50.00**

Roy Rogers, Crayon Set, Standard Toykraft #940, 1950s, VGIB..**75.00**

Roy Rogers, fountain pen, name on plastic barrel, 1950s, 5", VG..**50.00**

Roy Rogers, Trick Lasso, Classy Products, 1950s, complete, EXIP....................................**75.00**

Superman, horseshoe set, Super Swim Inc, 1950s, EXIB .....**100.00**

Superman, Krypton Rocket Set, Parks Plastic, 1950s, NMIB.............................**150.00**

Superman, Kryptonite Rock, DC Comics, 1977, NMIB .........**30.00**

Superman, playsuit, Ben Cooper/ Superman Inc, NMIB......**150.00**

Superman, wallet, Superman in flight, Croyden, 1950s, EXIB....**175.00**

Superman, wristwatch, Dabbs, NM ...................................**100.00**

Superman Jr, doll, squeeze vinyl, 1978, 7", EX.......................**25.00**

Tarzan, flasher ring, Vari-Vue, 1960s, EX+..........................**20.00**

Three Stooges, Colorforms, 1959, NMIB ...............................**120.00**

Three Stooges, dolls, any character, Presents, 1988, 14", M, ea..**65.00**

Three Stooges, picture slide (7), 1961, VG+...........................**10.00**

Thumper, figure, beanbag type, Disney, 8", EX ...........................**8.00**

Tom & Jerry, jack-in-the-box, Mattel, 1965, EX......................**45.00**

Tom & Jerry, Mattel Music Maker, lithographed tin, 1960s, NM..**75.00**

Toonerville Trolley, figure, Skipper, bisque, Japan, 1920s, 3", EX..**125.00**

Toonerville Trolley, trolley, bisque, 3½", 1920s, EX+................**250.00**

Ultimate Warrior, kite, WWF/Spectra, 1990, 4½-ft, MIB........................**15.00**

Universal Monsters, valentines, pack of 30, 1991, MIP .......**15.00**

V (TV Series), Bop Bag, vinyl, 1970s, MIB ........................**30.00**

Welcome Back Kotter, Colorforms Set, 1976, MIB...................**20.00**

Winky Dink, paint set, Standard Toykraft, 1950s, EXIB ......**85.00**

Wizard of Oz, doll, any character, Ideal, 1984-85, 9", MIB, ea................**50.00**

Wizard of Oz, doll, any character, Largo, 1989, 14", MIB, ea.....**45.00**

Wizard of Oz, picture slide (7), 1961, VG+...................................**10.00**

Wizard of Oz, place mat, vinyl, 1989, 12x16", EX .........................**15.00**

Wonder Woman, Color-A-Deck Card Game, MOC .......................**50.00**

Wonder Woman, Flashmite, Jane X, 1976, MOC.........................**75.00**

Woody Woodpecker, figure, NASCAR beany, 1999, 10", M ...............**20.00**

Woody Woodpecker, mug, porcelain, 1983, 16-oz, MIB ...............**20.00**

**Yogi Bear, camera, 1960s, MIB with instruction brochure, $65.00.**

Zorro, bolo tie, metal & plastic, portrait on red, NM ................**50.00**

Zorro, hand puppet, vinyl & cloth, felt hat, Gund/WDP, 1950s, EX+..**75.00**

Zorro, tote bag, red vinyl, EX.....**275.00**

Zorro, wristwatch, black face, US Time/WDP, 1950s, NM in EX hat box ..............................**125.00**

# Cherished Teddies

First appearing on dealers' shelves in the spring of 1992, Cherished Teddies found instant collector appeal. They were designed by artist Priscilla Hillman and produced in the Orient for the Enesco company. Besides the figurines, the line includes waterballs, frames, plaques, and bells.

#103942, ...Friends Are Bear Essentials, 1996 .........................**25.00**

#155438, A Mother's Heart Is Full of Love, 1997...........................**45.00**

#202398, You're the Jewel of My Heart, 1998........................**30.00**

#203491, I'm Your Bathing Beauty..**17.00**

#217914, Grandma....................**25.00**

#219118, Heading Into the Holidays with Deer Friends.................**30.00**

#354112, You Bring Out the Devil in Me, 1998 .............................**17.50**

#534099, You're a Good Friend That Sticks Like Honey, 1999 ...**17.50**

#534110, You Make Me Smile From Ear to Ear, 1999.................**17.50**

#534129, I've Got a Notion To Give You a Potion, 1999 ............**30.00**

#542644, Wishing for a Future As Bright As the Stars...........**15.00**

#589969, I've Packed My Trunk & I'm Ready To Go, 1999......**20.00**

#661740, ...We're Kindred Spirits, 2000..**30.00**

#731870, I Scored a Strike When I Met You .............................**16.00**

#786705, A Sprinkling of Fairy Dust Will Make You Feel Better..**25.00**

#910651, Friendship Blossoms with Love, 1992...........................**75.00**

#911402, Love Bears All Things..**25.00**

**#950521, Jeremy, Friends Like You Are Precious and True, 1991, MIB, $25.00.**

#950742, The Spirit of Friendship Warms the Heart, 1993 ....**40.00**

#951129, A Season Filled With Sweetness, 1992.................**18.00**

# Children's Books

Books were popular gifts for children in the latter 1800s; many were beautifully illustrated, some by notable artists such as Frances Brundage and Maxfield Parrish. From this century tales of Tarzan by Burroughs are very collectible, as are those familiar childhood series books — for example, The Bobbsey Twins and Nancy Drew. For more information we recommend *Boys' & Girls' Book Series,* by Diane McClure Jones and Rosemary Jones (Collector Books).

### Big Little Books

Probably everyone who is now sixty to seventy years of age owned a few Big Little Books as a child. Today these thick hand-sized adventures bring prices from $10.00 to $75.00 and upwards. The first was published in 1933 by Whitman Publishing Company. Dick Tracy was the featured character. Kids of the early '50s preferred the format of the comic book, and the Big Little Books were gradually phased out. Stories about super heroes and Disney characters bring the highest prices, especially those with an early copyright.

Ace Drummond, Whitman #1177, 1935, EX ...........................**18.00**

Adventures of Huckleberry Finn, Whitman #1422, NM........**40.00**

Arizona Kid on the Bandit Trail, Whitman #1192, EX.........**20.00**

Billy the Kid, Whitman #773, 1935, EX .....................................**35.00**

Blondie & Dagwood in Hot Water, Whitman #1410, NM.........**40.00**

Bonanza, Bubble Gum Kid, Whitman #2002, 1967, EX.....................**12.00**

Buck Rogers in City of Floating Globes, Cocomalt Premium, EX.......**150.00**

Bugs Bunny All Pictures Comics, Whitman #1435, 1944, EX..**30.00**

Dick Tracy & Tiger Lily Gang, Whitman #1460, 1949, VG..........**35.00**

Donald Duck in Volcano Valley, Whitman #1457, 1949, NM .........**95.00**

Ellery Queen the Master Detective, Whitman #1472, 1942, NM ..**60.00**

Flash Gordon in Ice World of Mongo, Whitman #1443, 1942, EX..**45.00**

Frankenstein Jr, Whitman, 1968, NM .....................................**10.00**

Freckles & the Lost Diamond Mine, Whitman #1164, EX ............**35.00**

Goofy in Giant Trouble, Whitman, 1968, NM ...........................**10.00**

Houdini's Big Little Book of Magic, Whitman #715, 1927, 1933, NM .....................................**60.00**

Hugh O'Brien TV's Wyatt Earp, 1958, VG ...........................**10.00**

Jungle Jim & the Vampire Woman, Whitman #1139, NM.........**75.00**

Li'l Abner in New York, Whitman #1198, 1936, EX ................**60.00**

Lone Ranger & the Secret Killer, Whitman #1431, EX..........**45.00**

Mutt & Jeff, Whitman #1113, NM..**75.00**

Popeye & Queen Olive Oyl, Whitman #1458, EX+ ................**40.00**

Roy Rogers & the Deadly Treasure, Whitman #1437, VG .........**25.00**

Sir Lancelot, Whitman #1649, NM .....................................**15.00**

Smilin' Jack & the Stratosphere Ascent, Whitman #1152, 1937, EX .....................................**35.00**

Smokey Stover, Whitman #1413, 1942, EX ...........................**35.00**

Tarzan & the Golden Lion, Whitman #1448, NM.................**75.00**

Tarzan in Land of Giant Apes, Whitman #1467, 1949, EX...........**45.00**

The Tarzan Twins, first edition, rare, NM, from $115.00 to $125.00.

Tom Mix & Tony Jr in Terror Trail, Whitman #762, 1934, NM.**70.00**

Two-Gun Montana, Whitman #1104, VG .....................................**20.00**

Zip Sanders King of the Speedway, Whitman #1465, EX..........**20.00**

## Little Golden Books

Little Golden Books (a registered trademark of Western Publishing Company Inc.), introduced in October of 1942, were an overnight success. First published with a blue paper spine, the later spines were of gold foil. Parents and grandparents born in the '40s, '50s, and '60s are now trying to find the titles they had as children. From 1942 to the early 1970s, the books were numbered from 1 to 600, while books published later had no numerical order. Depending on where you find the book, prices can vary from 25¢

to $30.00 plus. The most expensive are those with dust jackets from the early '40s or books with paper dolls and activities. The three primary series of books are the Regular (1 – 600), Disney (1 – 140), and Activity (1 – 52).

Television's influence became apparent in the '50s with stories like the Lone Ranger, Howdy Doody, Hopalong Cassidy, Gene Autry, and Rootie Kazootie. The '60s brought us Yogi Bear, Huckleberry Hound, Magilla Gorilla, and Quick Draw McGraw, to name but a few. Condition is very important when purchasing a book. You normally don't want to purchase a book with large tears, crayon or ink marks, or missing pages.

As with any collectible book, a first edition is always going to bring the higher price. To determine what edition you have on the 25¢ and 29¢ cover price books, look on the title page or the last page of the book. If it is not on the title page, there will be a code of 1/(a letter of the alphabet) on the bottom right corner of the last page. A is for first edition, Z would refer to the twenty-sixth printing.

There isn't an easy way of determining the condition of a book. What is 'good' to one might be 'fair' to another. A played-with book in average condition is generally worth only half as much as one in mint, like-new condition. To find out more about Little Golden Books, we recommend *Collecting Little Golden Books* (published by Books Americana) by Steve Santi.

A Day in the Jungle, #18, 1st edition, 1943, VG ............................**30.00**

Animal Quiz, #396, A edition, 1960, VG ........................................**5.00**

Bugs Timmy, #50, A edition, 1948, G+.............................................**25.00**

Chicken Little, #413, A edition, 1960, NM+ ...........................**8.00**

Cinderella's Friends, #D17, A edition, 1950, NM+ .........................**18.00**

Day at the Playground, #119, A edition, 1951, EX....................**25.00**

Donald Duck & Santa Claus, #D27, A edition, 1952, EX.................**25.00**

Donald Duck's Adventure, #D14, 1950, A edition, VG+........**20.00**

Gunsmoke, #320, A edition, 1958, VG ......................................**18.00**

Helicopters, #357, A edition, 1959, NM+ ....................................**10.00**

Howdy Doody's Circus, #99, A edition, 1950, EX ...........................**20.00**

Jack & the Beanstalk, #281, A edition, 1957, NM+ .........................**10.00**

Little Red Hen, #6, M edition, 1952, VG ......................................**20.00**

National Velvet, #431, A edition, 1961, NM+ .........................**15.00**

Old Yeller, #D65, A edition, 1957, VG ......................................**15.00**

Quick Draw McGraw, #398, A edition, 1960, VG ...........................**15.00**

Raggedy Ann & Fido, #585, 1st edition, 1972, NM+................**10.00**

Rin-Tin-Tin, #276, A edition, 1956, NM+ ....................................**18.00**

Roy Rogers & the Mountain Lion, #231, A edition, 1955, NM+..**25.00**

Sleeping Beauty, #D61, 1957, A edition, EX............................**18.00**

Snow White & the Seven Dwarfs, #D4, A edition, 1948, VG.....**15.00**

Story of Jesus, #27, F edition, 1949, NM+ .................................**20.00**

Three Little Kittens, #1, Q edition, 1948, NM ..........................**18.00**

Up in the Attic, #53, A edition, 1948, NM ...................................**20.00**

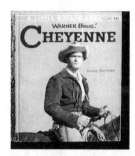

**Warner Bros. Cheyenne, TV Series first edition, 1953, VG+, $25.00.**

Whistling Wizard, #132, A edition, 1953, VG ...........................**15.00**

Yogi Bear, #395, A edition, 1960, VG ....................................**15.00**

Zorro, #D68, D edition, 1965, NM+ ................................**15.00**

## Series

Everyone remembers a special series of books they grew up with: The Hardy Boys, Nancy Drew Mysteries, Tarzan — there were countless others. And though these are becoming very collectible today, there were many editions of each, and most are very easy to find. As a result, common titles are sometimes worth very little. Generally the last few in any series will be the most difficult to locate, since fewer were printed than the earlier stories which were likely to have been reprinted many times. As is true of any type of book, first editions or the earliest printing will have more collector value. For further reading see *Boys' & Girls' Book Series,* by Diane McClure Jones and Rosemary Jones (Collector Books).

Amelia Bedelia, Peggy Parish, Harper & Row, hardcover w/jacket..............................**20.00**

**Borrowers Afloat, Mary Norton, Harcourt, Brace & World, first edition, hardcover with dust jacket, $75.00 ($20.00 without dust jacket). (Photo courtesy Diane McClure Jones and Rosemary Jones)**

Cherry Ames, H Wells or J Tatham, Grossett, plain cover w/jacket..**30.00**

Desmond the Dog, H Best, Viking, hardcover (no jacket).........**10.00**

Donna Parker, M Martin, Whitman, hardcover, 1957-64...............**15.00**

Famous Five, E Blyton, Hodder & Stoughton, hardcover, later printing.............................**10.00**

Just-So Stories, R Kipling, Rand McNally Elf Book, 1955-56......**8.00**

Little Bear, EH Minarik, Harper Row, Sendak illustrations, 1st edition .............................**150.00**

Lyle the Crocodile, Waber, Houghton Mifflin, hardcover w/jacket...............................**25.00**

Meg, HB Walker, Whitman, pictorial hardcover...........................**15.00**

Patience, L Hill, Burke, 1951-55, hardcover w/jacket.............**15.00**

Power Boys, Mel Lyle, Whitman, pictorial hardcover.............**10.00**

Thomas the Tank Engine, Awdry, Kay & Ward, London, hardcover w/jacket..............................**20.00**

Tom Swift Jr Adventures, Appleton II, Grossett & Dunlop, yellow spine..................................**15.00**

## Whitman Tell-A-Tale Books

Though the Whitman Company produced a wide variety of children's books, the ones most popular with today's collectors (besides the Big Little Books which are dealt with earlier in this category) are the Tell-A-Tales. They were published in a variety of series, several of which centered around radio, TV, and comic strips.

Alphabet Rhymes, #2400-2, 1956, EX ........................................**8.00**

Amy's Long Night, Carber, 1970, EX..**10.00**

Bible Stories, #828, 1947, EX ....**8.00**

Big Little Kitty, #2515, 1953, VG..**10.00**

Cinderella, #2552, 1959, EX ....**10.00**

Circus Alphabet, #2531, 1974, EX..**5.00**

Circus Alphabet, 1954, EX.......**15.00**

Ernie the Cave King, #2604, 1975, EX ........................................**5.00**

Frisker, #2426, 1956, EX ...........**5.00**

Hooray for Lassie, 1964, EX......**10.00**

Lassie & the Kittens, 1956, EX......**15.00**

**Lazy Fox and Red Hen, illustrated by Suzanne, copyright 1952, EX, $10.00.**

Little Black Sambo, 1959, EX......**50.00**

Little Miss Muffet, #2464-33, 1958, EX ........................................**5.00**

Magilla Gorilla, 1965, EX ........**12.00**

Pete's Dragon, #248-3, 1977, EX......**5.00**

Three Bears, #2592, 1968, EX .....**5.00**

Tweety, #2481, 1953, EX .........**10.00**

## Wonder Books

Though the first were a little larger, the Wonder Books printed since 1948 have all measured 6½" x 8". They've been distributed by Random House, Grosset Dunlap, and Wonder Books Inc. They're becoming very collectible, especially those based on favorite TV and cartoon characters. Steve Santi's book *Collecting Little Golden Books* includes a section on Wonder Books as well.

A Horse for Johnny, #754, 1952, EX..**5.00**

ABC & Counting Rhymes, #823, EX+ ........................................**5.00**

Billy & His Steam Roller, #537, 1951, EX ................................**5.00**

Counting Book, #692, 1957, EX .....**8.00**

Famous Fairy Tales, #505, 1949, EX...**10.00**

Henry in Lollipop Land, #664, 1953, EX .....................................**25.00**

I Can Do Anything...Almost, #822, 1963, EX .............................**5.00**

Little Audrey & the Moon Lady, #759, 1977, EX ..................**10.00**

Luno the Soaring Stallion, #831, 1964, EX ............................**15.00**

Muppets Suprise Party, #794, 1955, EX+ ....................................**15.00**

Pony Engine, #626, 1957, EX ....**8.00**

**Popeye, #667, 1950s, EX, $15.00.**

Romper Room, 1957, EX ..........**10.00**

Soupy Sales & the Talking Turtle, #860, 1965, EX ...................**10.00**

Trick on Deputy Dawg, 1964, NM ..**6.00**

What's for Breakfast?, #846, 1950, VG .....................................**10.00**

Who Likes Dinner?, #598, 1953, EX+ ....................................**10.00**

## Miscellaneous

A Penny for Candy, Jr Elf, 1946, VG+ ....................................**10.00**

Beany & Cecil Captured for the Zoo, 1954, EX+ ............................**5.00**

Dennis the Menace, Holt, 1952, 1st edition, EX+ ........................**15.00**

Donald Duck & His Friends, Disney/Heath, 1939, NM ..........**50.00**

Gene Autry in Golden Ladder Gang, 1950, EX ............................**20.00**

Gene Autry in Redwood Pirate, 1946, EX ............................**20.00**

Hansel & Gretel, Elf, 1960, EX .....**10.00**

Here They Are, Disney/Heath, 1940, NM+ ...................................**50.00**

Little Red Wagon, Jr Elf, 1949, VG+ ....................................**10.00**

Magilla Gorilla Takes a Banana Holiday, 1965, EX+ .............**6.00**

**Merlin's Mistake, Robert Newman, 1970 Atheneum, hardcover, first edition, with dust jacket, $25.00.** (Photo courtesy Diane McClure Jones and Rosemary Jones)

Mickey Never Fails, Disney/ Heath, 1939, NM+ .........................**55.00**

Mighty Mouse, McGraw Hill, 1964, NM .....................................**20.00**

My Toys, Jr Elf, 1955, EX........**10.00**

Perri, Big Golden Book, 1939, M ...............................**22.00**

Peter's Treasure, by Clara Judson, 1945, EX ...........................**10.00**

Popeye's How To Draw Cartoons, 1939, EX+ ..........................**40.00**

Quick Draw McGraw, Tip Top, VG+ ....................................**20.00**

Raggedy Ann Scratch & Sniff, 1976, EX ......................................**25.00**

Roy Rogers in Sundown Valley, 1950, EX ...........................**20.00**

School Days in Disneyville, Disney/ Heath, 1939, NM .................**50.00**

Shirley Temple, by J Neatty, Saal- field, 1935, EX ...................**40.00**

Tarzan, Golden, 1964, lg size, NM ...**10.00**

Terry & the Pirates, Big Big Book, 1938, EX ..........................**250.00**

Tom Swift & His Jetmarine, Gros- set & Dunlap, 1954, NM..**10.00**

Tom Terrific!, Pines #4, 1958, NM ...................................**20.00**

Tony the Tramp, by Horatio Alger Jr, ca 1915, VG..................**20.00**

Tuffy the Tugboat, Tip Top, 1947, VG ......................................**10.00**

Valley of the Dinosaurs, T Rand, 1975, NM+ ..........................**8.00**

Welcome to Upsy Downsy Land, Mattel, 1969, NM .............**30.00**

Wild Bill Hickok & Joey, Elf, 1954, VG+ ....................................**20.00**

# Christmas

No other holiday season is cele- brated to such an extravagant extent as Christmas, and vintage decora- tions provide a warmth and charm that none from today can match. Ornaments from before 1870 were imported from Dresden, Germany. They were usually made of card- board and sparkled with tinsel trim.

Later, blown glass ornaments were made there in literally thousands of shapes such as fruits and vegetables, clowns, Santas, angels, and animals. Kugles, heavy glass balls (though you'll sometimes find fruit and veg- etable forms as well) were made from about 1820 to late in the centu- ry in sizes up to 14". Early Santa fig- ures are treasured, especially those in robes other than red. Figural bulbs from the '20s and '30s are pop- ular, those that are character related in particular. Refer to *Pictorial Guide to Christmas Ornaments & Collectibles* by George Johnson and *Collector's Encyclopedia of Electric Christmas Lighting* by Cindy Chipps and Greg Olson, both published by Collector Books, for more informa- tion.

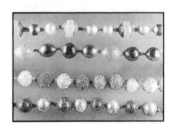

**Beads: Painted, from $4.00 to $6.00 per foot; Oblong col- ored glass, from $9.00 to $10.00 per foot; Wire- wrapped unsilvered, from $10.00 to $12.00 per foot; Wire-wrapped silvered, from $10.00 to $12.00 per foot.** (Photo courtesy George Johnson)

Bubble light, tulip form, Paramount, ca 1959-72, from $4 to.........**6.00**

Bulb, ball covered w/holly, milk glass, Japan, ca 1950, 1¾" ...............**15.00**

Bulb, bird in birdcage, milk glass, Japan, ca 1935-55, 2" ........**15.00**

Bulb, bubble-light single replacement, Noma, 1960, mini, MIB ....................................**15.00**

Bulb, candy cane, milk glass w/red stripes, 2¾", from $50 to .....**60.00**

Bulb, clown head, milk glass, round, ca 1950, 1¾", from $50 to..**60.00**

Bulb, frog, milk glass, egg shaped, Japan, ca 1950, 1½" ........**110.00**

Bulb, jack-o'-lantern, milk glass, double-sided, Japan, 1¼" ..........**50.00**

Bulb, owl-headed girl, frosted glass, 2½", from $75 to ................**90.00**

Bulb, pelican, milk glass, ca 1950, 2¼", from $30 to .................**40.00**

Bulb, puppy on ball, milk glass, Japan, 2¼", from $25 to ......**35.00**

Bulb, Snowman w/umbrella, milk glass, Japan, 1950s, 2½"...**12.00**

Candelabrum, 9 candle lights, greens & poinsettia, Glolite #110, 1940..........................**85.00**

Candle tree, Cheer-O-Lite Tree, Noma #615, 1936, 10" .....**100.00**

Candle tree, Glolite Corp #18/2, ca 1949, 18" ...........................**50.00**

Candle tree, revolves, Glolite Corp, ca 1955, 14"........................**50.00**

Candles, 8 mini socket candles on base, Royal Electric #782, ca 1954....................................**65.00**

Candy container, apple, embossed multicolor cardboard, 2¾", from $70 to ...............................**90.00**

Candy container, pine cone, painted paper w/red ribbon, ca 1948, 7"..........................................**45.00**

Candy container, Santa, pressed cardboard, stapled seams, 1950s, 9" ..........................**175.00**

Candy container, slipper, Dresden-like w/netting, 7¼", from $75 to .....................................**100.00**

Candy container, violin, cardboard w/litho body, 3", from $90 to ...............................**110.00**

Chain, beads in molded shapes, Japan, priced per foot, MIP, $3 to ..........................................**4.00**

Decoration, angel standing, white plastic, Bradford, 1955, 3¼"...**12.00**

Decoration, geometric shape w/jewels, hard plastic, ca 1965, 3", from $1 to .....................................**1.50**

Decoration, Santa, vinyl w/flocking, 4½", from $3 to ....................**4.00**

Figure, angel, ceramic, holds 1-socket candle, Japan, 1960, 9"......................................**15.00**

Figure, Santa, plastic, lights up, Raylite #61, ca 1949, 7".....**40.00**

Figure, Santa on platform, plastic, lights up, Levinson, 1955, 9"......................................**75.00**

Figure, stag, compo w/cast lead antlers, Germany, 3¼", from $25 to ................................**35.00**

Lamp, motion; Santa & Reindeer, LA Goodman, 1955, 11" ..........**900.00**

Lamp, Santa revolves, conical shape, Econolite, ca 1950, 25" ...............................**400.00**

Lamp, TV; rotating Christmas scene, Hong Kong, 1965, 9".........**225.00**

Lantern, snowman (glass) in metal frame, Hong Kong, ca 1960, MIB ................................**100.00**

Lighting set, Goodlight Electric G14 Lamp Set, 7-socket, 1955, MIB ..................................**25.00**

Lighting set, Leo Pollock Corp #257, 25-socket, ca 1950, MIB ....**35.00**

Lighting set, Star Lights, Raylite #710, ca 1938, MIB ...........**75.00**

Lighting set, Twinkle Lite, Festive #500B, 20-socket, ca 1950, MIB .................................**15.00**

Lighting set, Twinkle-Glo, Glolite Corp, 15-socket, 1955, MIB.................................**45.00**

Menorah candelabrum, 9-socket, white & w/blue flames, Taiwan, ca 1965...............................**25.00**

Ornament, angel bust, blown glass, Germany, 1980s, 4", from $15 to .......................................**20.00**

Ornament, baby buggy, 3-D cast tin, 3", from $100 to ...............**125.00**

Ornament, basket of fruit, mold blown, Germany, 1980s, 2", from $20 to.........................**25.00**

Ornament, clown on drum, blown glass, Germany, 1980s, 1½", from $40 to.........................**50.00**

Ornament, cornucopia, embossed foil w/multicolor decor, 1940s, 9¼" .......................................**12.00**

Ornament, flamingo, blown glass, Germany, 3", from $20 to ............**25.00**

Ornament, flower basket, free-blown, Germany, 1950s-80s, 2-3", from $30 to ....................**40.00**

Ornament, girl holding puppy (Madeline's Puppy), Radko, 1992, 4" .............................**35.00**

Ornament, icicle, mold blown, tubes w/embossed lines, 6", from $5 to .......................................**10.00**

Ornament, man in the Moon (Type III), blown, 1950s, 3", from $80 to .......................................**100.00**

Ornament, orange, blown, unsilvered, Germany, 1991, 1¾", $20 from to...............................**30.00**

Ornament, Santa w/hands behind back, celluloid, 7", from $75 to.....................................**100.00**

Ornament, tree w/decorations, blown glass, Germany, 1970s, 3", from $30 to ...................**35.00**

**Rope: foil type by DoubleGlo, 1950s, 10' in original packaging, from $10.00 to $15.00; Celophane Christmas Garland, ca 1950, in original packaging, from $6.00 to $10.00.** (Photo courtesy George Johnson)

Tree stand, cast iron, 8 mini base sockets, Noma #170, ca 1928, 14" .....................................**45.00**

Tree stand, metal w/6 points, 6-socket, USA, ca 1940, 16" dia .................................**60.00**

Tree stand, plastic, 8-sided, 1 light socket, Good-Lite, 1955, 13½" ......**40.00**

Tree topper, angel, compo w/cardboard wings, USA, 1930s-40s, 9".............................**25.00**

Tree topper, Blinking Pixie, Thomas Co #169, ca 1965 ...................**10.00**

Tree topper, star, chenille covered, 1-socket, Japan, ca 1930 .....**25.00**

Tree topper, star, gold & silver foil, National Tinsel, 9", MIB.....**8.00**

Tree topper, Star of Bethlehem, 5-light, Noma #120, ca 1928, MIB ................................**100.00**

Wall hanger, Rudolph on rooftop, plastic, lights up, Burwood, 1950s...............................**300.00**

Wall hanger, star, chenille-covered w/10 mini sockets, USA, 1930s, 12"......................................**50.00**

Wall hanging, Merry Christmas, Raylite Electric Corp #471, 1959, 23" W........................**20.00**

Wall hanging, Star of Bethleham, Vinylite, Noma #460, 1959, 29"......................................**29.00**

Wreath, glass beads, 2 candle lights in center, Japan, ca 1930..**45.00**

Wreath, silver foil leaves, 9 sockets, Noma Electric #1109, 1960..**65.00**

## Cigarette Lighters

Pocket lighters were invented sometime after 1908 and were at their peak from about 1925 to the 1930s. Dunhill, Zippo, Colibri, Ronson, Dupont, and Evans are some of the major manufacturers. An early Dunhill Unique model if found in its original box would be valued at hundreds of dollars. Quality metal and metal-plated lighters were made from the 1950s to about 1960. Around that time disposable lighters never needing a flint were introduced, causing a decline in sales of figurals, novelties, and high-quality lighters.

What makes a lighter collectible? — novelty of design, type of mechanism (flint and fuel, flint and gas, battery, etc.), and manufacturer (and whether or not the company is still in business). For further information we recommend *The Big Book of Cigarette Lighters,* by James Flanagan.

Advertising, Bosch, spark plug shape, 1975, 3¼x⅞"..........**40.00**

Advertising, Tivola Beer, tube style, late 1940s, 3x⅜"................**45.00**

Colibri, chromium butane, mid-1970s, 2½x⅞".....................**45.00**

Crown, gold-tone case, musical, ca 1984, 2⅝............................**45.00**

DRP/Germany, chromium & leather table lighter, 1950s, 3¼"...**65.00**

Evans, chromium lift arm pocket lighter, early 1920s, 2⅛x1½".............................**50.00**

Evans, cowboy boot form, table lighter, ca 1948, 5x5"........**60.00**

Germany, electric drill form, butane pocket lighter, 2x3".............**25.00**

Germany, megaphone form, butane pocket lighter, 2⅞x2".........**25.00**

Germany, wrench form, butane pocket lighter, 2⅞x1¼".....**25.00**

**Give-A-Gift Inc., ceramic and brass candle table lighter, spare flint in flame, mid-1960s, 6¼x3¼", from $20.00 to $40.00. (Photo courtesy James Flanagan)**

Japan, blow dryer form, butane key-ring lighter, ca 1990, 2x2⅛"................................**15.00**

Japan, camera form, butane, 1980s, 1¾x2½"............................**15.00**

Negbaur, golf clubs & bag form, brass, ca 1939, 5x1½"......**100.00**

New Method, twin bullet form, painted metal, early 1930s, 2¼x1⅛" ............................**35.00**

Occupied Japan, belt buckle form, chrome, late 1940s, 1¼x1⅞" ..........................**200.00**

Occupied Japan, football form, chrome, late 1940s, 2¾x2¾" ...........**175.00**

Occupied Japan, horse's head form, chrome, 1940s, 3⅛x3".......**100.00**

Occupied Japan, pistol form, chrome w/plastic grips, ca 1949, 2x2¾" ................................**60.00**

**Ronson, Cupid table lighter, three gold cherubs on black enamel, ca 1956, 2¼x1¾", from $35.00 to $50.00.** (Photo courtesy James Flanagan)

Ronson, De-Light, pocket lighter, ca 1928, 2⅝x1½" .....................**75.00**

Ronson, Gem, pocket lighter, ca 1937, 2x1¼" .......................**30.00**

Ronson, Sport, chromium & leather in gift box, ca 1956, 2x1¾"..**60.00**

Ronson, Standard, chromium pocket lighter, ca 1935, 2x1⅝" .......**70.00**

Ronson, Vara Flame, chromium butane pocket lighter, 1960s, 2¾x1" ................................**40.00**

Swank, television form, table lighter, early 1960s, 2¾x3⅞" ........**50.00**

# Clothes Sprinkler Bottles

From the time we first had irons, clothes were sprinkled with water before ironing for the best results. During the 1930s and until the 1950s when the steam iron became a home staple, some of us merely took sprinkler tops and stuck them into old glass bottles to accomplish this task, while the more imaginative bought and enjoyed bottles made in figural shapes. The most popular, of course, were the Chinese men marked 'Sprinkle Plenty.' Some bottles were made by American Bisque, Cleminson of California, and other famous figural pottery makers. Many were made in Japan for the export market.

Cat, marble eyes, ceramic, American Bisque ..............................**400.00**

Cat, variety of designs & colors, handmade ceramic, from $75 to ......................................**125.00**

Chinese man, arms to chest, yellow top, green bottom, Cardinal (?)..**60.00**

Chinese man, towel over arm, ceramic, from $300 to......**350.00**

Chinese man w/removable head, ceramic, from $250 to......**400.00**

Clothespin, hand decorated, ceramic, from $250 to................**400.00**

Clothespin, red, yellow & green plastic, from $20 to...........**40.00**

Dearie Is Weary, ceramic, Enesco, from $350 to ....................**500.00**

Dutch boy, green & white, ceramic..............................**275.00**

Elephant, pink & gray, ceramic, from $65 to..................................**85.00**

Fireman ...............................**3,000.00**

Iron, blue flowers, ceramic, from $100 to ..............................**150.00**

Iron, green, plastic, from $35 to .....**75.00**

Iron, green ivy, ceramic ..........**60.00**

**Iron, lady ironing, ceramic, $75.00.** (Photo courtesy Ellen Bercovici)

Iron, man & woman farmer, ceramic, from $200 to................**275.00**

Iron, souvenir of Wonder Cave, ceramic............................**300.00**

Mammy, ceramic....................**400.00**

Mary Maid, all colors, plastic, Reliance, from $20 to ........**35.00**

Myrtle, ceramic, Pfaltzgraff, from $250 to ............................**300.00**

Poodle, gray, pink or white, ceramic, ea from $200 to................**300.00**

# Coca-Cola

Introduced in 1886, Coca-Cola advertising has literally saturated our lives with a never-ending variety of items. Some of the earlier calendars and trays have been known to bring prices well into the four figures. Because of these heady prices and extreme collector demand for good Coke items, reproductions are everywhere, so beware! In addition to reproductions,

'fantasy' items have also been made, the difference being that a 'fantasy' never existed as an original. Don't be deceived. Belt buckles are 'fantasies.' So are glass doorknobs with an etched trademark, bottle-shaped knives, pocketknives, and there are others.

When the company celebrated its 100th anniversary in 1986, many 'centennial' items were issued. They all carry the '100th Anniversary' logo. Many of them are collectible in their own right, and some are already high priced.

If you'd really like to study this subject, we recommend these books: *Goldstein's Coca-Cola Collectibles* by Sheldon Goldstein; *Collectors's Guide to Coca-Cola Items, Vols I* and *II,* by Al Wilson; *Petretti's Coca-Cola Collectibles Price Guide* by Allan Petretti; and *B.J. Summers' Guide to Coca-Cola* by B.J. Summers.

Ashtray, tin, High in Energy, Low in Calories, 4 rests, 1950s, EX ..**30.00**

**Bank, metal Coca-Cola truck, Advertising Dept. on side, recent, NMIB, $35.00.** (Photo courtesy B.J. Summers)

Belt, vinyl, Drink Coca-Cola blocks, white, 1960, EX ................**20.00**

Blotter, I Think It's Swell, girl, 1942, EX ....................................**35.00**

Book, Wonderful World of Coca-Cola, NM...........................**85.00**

Bottle, aqua, block print embossed on base, 6½-oz, EX ............**35.00**

Bottle carrier, aluminum, 6-pack, wire handle, 1950s, NM...**175.00**

Bottle carrier, cardboard, triangular, 1950s ..........................**65.00**

Bottle hanger, Ice Cold Coca-Cola King Size, red, white, green.**15.00**

Calendar, 1925, VG...............**425.00**

Calendar, 1945, EX+..............**375.00**

Calendar, 1952, Coke Adds Zest, full pad, EX ............................**150.00**

Calendar, 1959, Santa w/bottles of Coke, complete, 22x12", VG..**85.00**

Calendar, 1964, Things Go Better..., lady on couch/man w/bottle, EX..**75.00**

Calendar, 1972, Lillian Nordica, cloth, VG ............................**10.00**

Clock, Drink CC, bottle/yellow dot, Pam, 1950s, 15" dia, EX+..**200.00**

Clock, light-up countertop, Serve Yourself, 1940s-50s, EX...**750.00**

Coaster, metal, Hilda Clark artwork, EX ..............................**8.00**

Coaster, metal, Santa, white .....**8.00**

Coin changer, Have a Coke, red/chrome, 12x15x4", VG.....**425.00**

Cuff links, bottle form, gold, marked 1/10, 10k, ¾", NM, pr .......**50.00**

**Cuff links, gold finish, Enjoy Coca-Cola on glass shape, 1970s, EX, $65.00.**
(Photo courtesy B.J. Summers)

Doll, Buddy Lee as delivery man, 1950s, replica uniform, NM..............................**290.00**

Fan, Quality Carries On, bottle in hand, 1950, EX.................**65.00**

Festoon, Howdy Pardner/Pause... Refresh, 3-pc, 1950s, EX+...........**2,250.00**

Festoon, nautical, 9-pc, 1930s, EX+ ...............................**4,700.00**

Ice bucket, waxed cardboard, striped swag around top, EX+................................**50.00**

**Kerchief, The Cola Clan, Silhouette Girl, red and white, 1970s Coca-Cola Collectors' Banquet piece, EX, $35.00.** (Photo courtesy B.J. Summers)

Lighter, bottle shape, 1950s, M.....**30.00**

Lighter, musical, 1960s, EX .....**200.00**

Miniature, plastic case w/12 bottles, red on yellow, 1950s, EX+......**180.00**

Opener, metal, flat, 1950s, EX.....**35.00**

Pin-back button, Member Hi-Fi Club, multicolor, 1950s, EX.**20.00**

Playing cards, Drink Coca-Cola, party scene, 1960, M (sealed)..**100.00**

Postcard, Bobby Allison race car, 1973, EX ...........................**15.00**

Radio, cooler design, upright, 1980s, EX ......................................**75.00**

Scarf, silk, 30x30".....................**40.00**

Sign, button, porcelain, Coca-Cola over bottle in red, 24", EX..............**375.00**

Sign, cardboard, girl at refrigerator, 1940s, 36x20", EX..............**450.00**

Sign, cardboard, Planning Hospitality, hand at 6-pack, 16x27", EX ..**375.00**

Sign, cardboard, Real Holidays..., 1970s, 36", EX ..................**35.00**

Sign, cardboard, Santa's Helpers, w/2 bottles, 1960s, 32x66", EX..**125.00**

Sign, cardboard carton insert, Coke Is a Natural, EX................**15.00**

Sign, cardboard lithograph, circus performers, framed, 1936, 27x18" .............................**275.00**

Sign, cardboard standup, military girl w/bottle, 1943, 17", EX.......**425.00**

**Sign, masonite and metal, clock face, 1960s, 64", G, $225.00. (Photo courtesy B.J. Summers)**

Sign, neon, Coke w/Ice, 3-color, 1980s, EX.........................**400.00**

Sign, porcelain, bottle on yellow disc, 15" dia, VG..............**175.00**

Sign, porcelain button, Drink Coca-Cola, 24", NM ..................**525.00**

Sign, tin flange, Drink Coca-Cola, 1941, 21x24", EX.............**400.00**

Sign, wood, Battleship, K Displays, 8½x25", EX.....................**650.00**

Thermometer, metal, Enjoy Coca-Cola, white on red, EX......**110.00**

Tip tray, 1910, NM+............**1,400.00**

Tray, 1941, Ice Skater, 10½x13¼", NM .................................**450.00**

Tray, 1942, Roadster, 10½x13¼", NM+ ................................**500.00**

Tray, 1950s, Girl w/Wind in Hair, solid background, 10½x13¼", NM ..................................**225.00**

Tray, 1955, Menu Girl, 10½x13¼" NM ....................................**65.00**

Tray, 1957, Rooster, 10½x13", NM ..................................**175.00**

Tray, 1957, Umbrella Girl, 10½x13¼", NM...............**375.00**

Tray, 1961, Pansy Garden, 10½x13¼", NM.................**30.00**

Tumbler, clear bell, Enjoy Coca-Cola, 1970s .........................**8.00**

Tumbler, flared, frosted, 5¢ arrow logo, EX+..........................**500.00**

# Coin Glass

Coin Glass was originally produced in crystal, ruby, blue, emerald green, olive green, and amber. Lancaster Colony bought the Fostoria Company in the mid-1980s and reproduced this line in crystal, green, blue, amber, and red. Except for the red and crystal, the colors are 'off' enough to be pretty obvious, but the red is so close it's impossible to determine old from new. Here are some (probably not all) of the items made after that time: bowl, 8" diameter; bowl, 9" oval; candlesticks, 4½"; candy jar with lid, 6¼"; cigarette box with lid, 5¾" x 4½"; creamer and sugar bowl; footed comport; decanter, 10¼"; jelly; nappy with handle, 5¼"; footed salver, 6½"; footed urn with lid, 12¾"; and wedding bowl, 8¼". Know your dealer!

Emerald green is most desired by collectors. You may also find some crystal pieces with gold-decorated coins. These will be valued at about double the price of plain crystal if the gold is not worn. (When the gold is worn or faded, value is minimal.) Numbers included in our descriptions were company-assigned stock numbers that collectors use as a means to distinguish variations in stems and shapes. For further information we recommend *Collectible Glassware from the 40s, 50s & 60s*, by Gene and Cathy Florence (Collector Books).

Ashtray, amber, #1372/124, 10" .....**30.00**
Ashtray, blue, #1372/123, 5" .....**25.00**

**Ashtray, blue, four rests, $50.00.** (Photo courtesy Gene and Cathy Florence)

Ashtray, crystal, round, #1372/114, 7½" .....................................**25.00**
Ashtray, green, center coin, #1372/119, 7½" .................**35.00**
Ashtray, green, oblong, #1372/115 ....................................**25.00**
Bowl, amber, footed, w/lid, #1372/212, 8½" .....................................**30.00**
Bowl, blue, footed, w/lid, #1372/199, 8½" .....................................**90.00**
Bowl, crystal, round, #1372/179, 8"..**25.00**
Bowl, green, footed, #1372/199, 8½"..**125.00**
Bowl, olive, round, #1372/179, 8"..**25.00**
Bowl, ruby, oval, #1372/189, 9"......**50.00**

Bowl, wedding; green, w/lid, #1372/162 ........................**150.00**
Candleholders, ruby, #1372/326, 8", pr......................................**125.00**
Candy box, amber, #1372/354, 4⅛"..**30.00**
Candy box, crystal, #1372/354, w/lid, 4⅛" ....................................**30.00**
Cigarette box, blue, #1372/374, 5¾x4¼" ..............................**80.00**
Cigarette box, green, #1372/374, 5¾x4½" ............................**115.00**
Cigarette holder w/ashtray lid, crystal, #1372/372 ....................**45.00**
Cigarette urn, blue, footed, #1372/381, 3⅜" .................**45.00**
Condiment set, amber, #1372/737, tray+2 shakers+cruet......**225.00**
Condiment tray, olive, #1372/738, 9⅝" ....................................**75.00**
Creamer, blue, #1372/680 ........**16.00**
Cruet, blue, #1372/531, 7-oz.....**165.00**
Cruet, olive, #1372-531, 7-oz......**80.00**
Decanter, amber, #1372/400, 1-pt, 10¼" ................................**125.00**
Jelly, amber, #1372-448 ...........**17.50**
Jelly compote, blue or ruby, #1372/448............................................**25.00**
Lamp, coach; blue, electric, #1372/321, 13½" ..........................**23.50**
Lamp, courting; amber, #1372/310, oil, handled, 9¾"..............**110.00**
Lamp, courting; blue, #1372-310, 9¾" ....................................**190.00**
Lamp, patio; crystal, #1372/466, electric, 16⅝" ...................**135.00**
Lamp chimney, courting; blue, #1372-292 ..........................**65.00**
Nappy, crystal, #1372/495, 4½".....**22.00**
Nappy, green, w/handle, #1372/ 499, 5⅜" ....................................**40.00**
Pitcher, green, #1372/453, 32-oz, 6¼" ....................................**195.00**

Punch bowl base, crystal, #1372/602 ...................................**165.00**

Punch cup, crystal, #1372/615 .....**35.00**

Salt & pepper shakers, olive, #1372/652, w/chrome tops, 3¼", pr.........................................**30.00**

Stem, sherbet; olive, #1372/7, 9-oz, 5¼" ......................................**45.00**

Stem, sherbet; ruby, #1372/7, 9-oz, 5¼" ......................................**70.00**

Stem, wine; ruby, #1372/652, 5-oz, 4" ......................................**100.00**

Tumbler, iced tea; ruby, #1372/58, 14-oz, 5¼" ..........................**75.00**

Tumbler, iced tea/highball; crystal, #1372/64, 12-oz, 5⅛" ..........**37.50**

Tumbler, juice/old fashioned; crystal, #1372/81, 9-oz, 3⅝" ...........**30.00**

Urn, olive, footed, w/lid, #1372/829, 12¾" ...................................**80.00**

Vase, bud; blue, #1372-799, 8" .....**40.00**

Vase, bud; green, #1372/799, 8"......**60.00**

Vase, crystal, footed, #1372/818, 10" ..**45.00**

# Coloring Books

Throughout the 1950s and even into the 1970s, coloring and activity books were produced by the thousands. Whitman, Saalfield, and Watkins-Strathmore were some of the largest publishers. The most popular were those that pictured well-known TV, movie, and comic book characters, and these are the ones that are bringing top dollar today. Condition is also an important worth-accessing factor. Compared to a coloring book that was never used, one that's only partially colored is worth from 50% to 70% less. Unless noted otherwise, our values are for near-mint to mint-condition examples.

Alice in Wonderland, Playmore, 1975...................................**15.00**

Archies Coloring & Activity Fun, Whitman, 1969, NM..........**15.00**

Batman, Whitman #1002, 1967, NM...**30.00**

Ben-Hur, Lowe #2851, 1959, some coloring, NM......................**40.00**

Black Hole, Whitman, 1979...........**15.00**

Bongo, Disney, 1948, some coloring, EX+ ....................................**25.00**

Buck Rogers Coloring & Activity Book, 1979 .........................**20.00**

**Bugs Bunny and Porky Pig Paint Book, Whitman, 1946, EX, $25.00.** (Photo courtesy David Longest)

Car 54 Where Are You?, Whitman, 1962, some coloring, NM.....**40.00**

Casper, 1973, 13x11", NM .......**18.00**

Cheyenne, Whitman, 1950s, some coloring, EX ......................**20.00**

Chitty-Chitty Bang Bang, 1968, NM ....................................**28.00**

Disneyland, Golden Books #1136-20, 1983...................................**10.00**

Dr Kildare, Saafield, 1963, some coloring, EX............................**15.00**

Dukes of Hazzard, 1981 ...........**10.00**

Felix the Cat, Saafield, 1956, NM..**50.00**

First Ladies' Gowns, 1983 .........**25.00**

Flash Gordon, A McWilliams/King Features #217525 ..............**75.00**

Gilligan's Island, Whitman, 1965, sea gulls on cover, NM ......**50.00**

Heidi, 1954, some coloring, EX ..**18.00**

Hopalong Cassidy, Whitman, Authorized Edition, 1951 ...............**75.00**

Huckleberry Hound, Western Printing #1883-2, 1962, EX .........**15.00**

Jack & the Beanstalk, 1960s, some coloring, NM ......................**10.00**

Kiddie Dreams, 1965, some coloring, EX ......................................**10.00**

Land of the Lost Coloring & Activity Book, Whitman #1271, 1975..**25.00**

Little Lulu, #1663, some coloring, G.............................................**10.00**

Millie the Lovable Monster, Artcraft, 1963, some coloring, EX....**25.00**

Miss America, 1990 .................**15.00**

Mrs Beasley, Whitman #1648, 1975...................................**25.00**

Nancy & Sluggo, 1955, some coloring, EX ..............................**35.00**

Nancy & the Professor, 1971, NM ...................................**20.00**

New Zoo Revue, Artcraft #5484, 1973...................................**30.00**

New Zoo Revue, Saafield #CO544, 1973...................................**30.00**

Partridge Family, Saafield #3839, 1971...................................**30.00**

Partridge Family Pictures To Color, Artcraft, 1970 ....................**30.00**

Patty Duke, Whitman #1122 or #1141, 1964-66, ea.............**30.00**

Pluto, 1971, some coloring, EX..**15.00**

Popeye, 1964, steering ship, some coloring, EX ......................**20.00**

Prince Valiant, Saalfield, 1957, some coloring, rare, EX.....**30.00**

Puss 'N Boots, 1970s ................**15.00**

Rescuers, Golden #1224-03, 1977..................................**10.00**

Rin-Tin-Tin, Whitman, 1956, some coloring, EX+ .....................**25.00**

Rita Hayworth, Merrill, 1942, some coloring, EX .......................**55.00**

Road Runner, Whitman, 1968, NM ...................................**20.00**

Rocketeer, Golden #2968, 1991, NM....................................**5.00**

**Roy Rogers Paint Book, Whitman, 1944, NM, $50.00** (Photo courtesy David Longest)

Shirley Temple's My Book To Color, Saafield #1768, 1937, EX..**50.00**

Sigmund the Sea Monsters, Saalfield #C1853, 1974......................**30.00**

Spider-Man Seeing Double, 1976, some coloring, EX..............**15.00**

Steve Canyon, Saalfield, 1952, oversized, NM..........................**50.00**

Superman, Whitman #1005, NM ...................................**15.00**

Terry & the Pirates, Saalfield, 1946, NM ...................................**50.00**

Three Stooges, Lowe #2965, 1962, some coloring, EX.............**65.00**

Tom & Jerry, Whitman, 1968, some coloring, EX+ ....................**15.00**

Waltons, Whitman #1028, 1975, NM ....................................**20.00**

Welcome Back Kotter, Whitman #1081, 1977.........................**20.00**

Wild Bill Hickock, 1958, some coloring, VG..............................**20.00**

# Comic Books

Factors that make a comic book valuable are condition, content, and rarity, not necessarily age. In fact, comics printed between 1950 and the late 1970s are most in demand by collectors who prefer those they had as children to the earlier comics. Issues where the hero is first introduced are treasured. While some may go for hundreds, even thousands of dollars, many are worth very little; so if you plan to collect, you'll need a good comic book price guide such as *Overstreet's* to assess your holdings. Condition is extremely important. Compared to a book in excellent condition, a mint issue might be worth six to eight times as much, while one in only good condition should be priced at less than half the price of the excellent example. For more information see *Schroeder's Collectible Toys, Antique to Modern* (Collector Books).

Adventures of Big Boy, #181, 1972, VG+ ....................................**10.00**

Aquaman, #23, 1965, VG .........**25.00**

Aquaman, #30, 1966, VG .........**20.00**

Batman, #104, 1956, G.............**35.00**

Batman, #143, 1961, VG+........**25.00**

Batman, #171, 1965, VG..........**60.00**

Batman, #188, 1966, VG..........**15.00**

Buffalo Bill Jr, #742, 1956, EX .....**25.00**

Buster Brown, #39, 1955, VG .......**15.00**

**Captain Easy, 1939, VG, $47.50.**

Chan Clan, #1, 1973, EX..........**20.00**

Colt .45, #9, 1961, VG+ ............**25.00**

Daffy Duck, #14, 1958, VG+ ....**10.00**

Date With Judy, #3, 1948, VG .....**20.00**

Donald Duck, #56, 1957, VG+ .....**10.00**

E-Man, #1, 1973, EX ................**15.00**

Fight Comics, #30, 1944, G .........**15.00**

Fox & the Crow, #18, 1954, VG ......**15.00**

Funny Folks, #8, 1948, VG ......**20.00**

Get Smart, #7, 1967, VG+........**20.00**

Great Grape Ape, #1, 1976, VG .....**10.00**

Gunslinger, #1220, 1961, VG+.....**35.00**

Hanna-Barbera Laff-a-Lympics, #3, 1978, EX ............................**10.00**

Hot Rod Racers, #75, 1965, VG.....**15.00**

Inch High Private Eye, #14, 1974, VG .....................................**10.00**

Jesse James, #22, 1955, VG+ .....**15.00**

Kid Cowboy, #05, 1951, VG .....**15.00**

Laff-a-Lympics, #13, 1979, EX......**10.00**

Life With Archie, #2, 1964, VG+.....**10.00**

Lomax NYPD, #1, 1975, VG+ .......**15.00**

Magilla Gorilla, #4, 1971, VG+ ......**15.00**

Magnus Robot Fighter, #23, 1968, EX ......................................**10.00**

Mandrake the Magician, #5, 1967, VG+ ...................................**10.00**

Monkees, #04, 1967, EX...........**35.00**

Navy Action, #18, 1957, VG.....**10.00**

Occult Files of Dr Spektor, #1, 1973, EX ......................................**20.00**

Outlaw Kid, #1, 1970, VG+......**10.00**

Planet of the Apes, #9, 1976, VG+ ..**10.00**

Raiders of the Lost Ark, #1, 1981, VG+ ...................................**10.00**

Reptisaurus the Terrible, #3, 1962, VG+ ...................................**15.00**

Roy Rogers, #25, 1950, VG+ ....**25.00**

**Roy Rogers, Dell #84, Vol. 1, 1954, M, $65.00.**

Sleeping Beauty, #564, 1954, VG+ ................................**15.00**

Spartacus, #1139, 1960, EX.....**35.00**

Spooky, #38, 1971, VG+ ...........**10.00**

Star Wars, #16, 1978, EX.........**10.00**

Taffy, #7 (Dane Clark issue), 1947, VG ......................................**15.00**

Teen Titans, #50, 1977, NM ....**25.00**

Tom Mix, #34, 1950, VG+ ........**25.00**

Treasure Chest, #20, Vol 17, 1962, VG+ ...................................**35.00**

Uncle Scrooge, #109, 1956, VG+ .....**15.00**

Weird Science, #1, 1990, VG+ .....**10.00**

Wild Wild West, #2, 1966, EX .....**45.00**

Wyatt Earp, #07, 1959, VG+ ......**25.00**

Zane Grey, #30, 1956, EX ........**25.00**

2001: A Space Odyssey, #1, 1976, VG..**15.00**

# Compacts

Prior to World War I, the use of cosmetics was frowned upon. It was not until after the war when women became liberated and entered the work force that makeup became acceptable. A compact became a necessity as a portable container for cosmetics and usually contained a puff and mirror. They were made in many different styles, shapes, and motifs and from every type of natural and manmade material. The fine jewelry houses made compacts in all of the precious metals — some studded with precious stones. The most sought-after compacts today are those made of plastic, Art Deco styles, figurals, and any that incorporate gadgets. Compacts that are combined with other accessories are also very desirable.

See Clubs and Newsletters for information concerning the *Powder Puff.*

Basket, brass-colored metal, swing handle, metal interior, K&K, 2⅛" ...................................**100.00**

Bolster, silver-tone w/carrying chain, Winnie Winkle, 1920s, 1¾" ...................................**275.00**

Book, gold-tone, embossed grid pattern, polished border, Coty, 1940s ...............................**60.00**

Bracelet, round gold-tone w/ stretch band, compact, ⅞" ............**250.00**

Carryall, clutch, white enamel w/black polka-dots, 4¼"....................**300.00**

Carryall, oblong, silver w/engraved design, w/chain, Germany......**200.00**

Clamshell, brushed leather, set-in lipstick, slip-in pockets, 1970s ..**72.00**

Clamshell, gold-tone w/blue stone thumbpiece, Givenchy.....**150.00**

**Columbia Fifth Avenue, gold-tone filigree lid plate, faux gemstone bijou, damask puff with logo, glued-in beveled mirror, 2⅝", from $65.00 to $85.00.** (Photo courtesy Laura M. Mueller)

Cornucopia, gold-tone w/embossed leaves; mirror, sifter, puff; 2x4½" ..............................**425.00**

Damascene, black matt w/gilt Egyptian scene inlay.......**100.00**

Envelope, gold-tone, Coty, 1940s ..**80.00**

Fan shape, gold-tone w/yellow enameling, Wadsworth, 1940s...**100.00**

Fur w/coin-purse snap closure, Argentina...........................**85.00**

Harlequin mask, polished gold-tone, E Arden, 3x1⅝" ...............**150.00**

Heart, gold-tone w/gazelles on etched rays, Superb, 2⅞" .................**50.00**

Horseshoe, blue leather (no design) ..**60.00**

Octagon, silver-tone/black, dancers/ saxophonist, Pat #, 2x2" .....**200.00**

Oval, mother-of-pearl w/faux sapphires & rhinestones, K&K, 1930s-40s ..........................**75.00**

Owl shape, gold-tone w/faux emerald & diamond eyes, Italy, 2¾x2" ...............................**400.00**

Pendant, Sphinx enameling, fitted interior, chain, 1⅜" dia.....**125.00**

Pendant, sterling w/black onyx lid, silver cartouch, 3x1½" dia .....**300.00**

Pocket-watch style, mother-of-pearl, Volupte, 1940s-50s...............**75.00**

**Rex Fifth Avenue, gold-tone with blue plastic domed lid plate, hand-painted lily, puff with logo, 3¾", from $75.00 to $100.00.** (Photo courtesy Laura M. Mueller)

Roulette wheel (spins) on brass lid, Majestic ...........................**150.00**

Round, cloisonné scene on gold-tone, Schildkraut, 2½" ..............**60.00**

Round, cork w/abstract enameling on gold-tone lid, 3" dia ......**65.00**

Round, gold-tone & cloisonné w/2 peacocks on white, Schildkraut..**50.00**

Round, gold-tone basketweave, original pouch, Ritz, 3"............**50.00**

Round, gold-tone coin w/Roman profile/eagle reliefs, Elgin, 3" ..**75.00**

Round, orange Bakelite, mirror, cord, 2 lipsticks tubes, tassels, 2" ....................................**750.00**

Round, Silver Queen, resembles gold ball, De Corday, 2" ...........**40.00**

Round, silver-tone w/3-tone Deco design, Estee Lauder, 4" ..**225.00**

Round, white metal w/red anchor & blue rope decor, Volupte, 2½" ...**70.00**

Scalloped, gold-tone w/allover stylized design, Kigu, 3½".......**80.00**

Square, British flag w/gold-tone emblem, Evans, 2¼"........**125.00**

Square, clear Lucite, insert photo behind removeable mirror, 3¼" ....**80.00**

Square, gold-tone w/heart & flowers in oval, 2 part, Marathon..**80.00**

Square, gold-tone w/painted tropical scene on encased Lucite lid..**60.00**

Square, silver-tone, Nouveau relief, perfume combo, mirror, 2x2" ....**200.00**

Suitcase, brown lizard w/2 carrying handles, zippered ............**150.00**

Vanity, flapjack, cloisonné floral motif, La Mode ..................**70.00**

Vanity, floral on lavender, mirror & compartments, 2x1½"........**50.00**

Vanity, oblong, rhinestone floral decor, 2¾" ........................**150.00**

Vanity, oval, salmon Bakelite w/painted flowers & rhinestones, 3"..........................**300.00**

Vanity book, floral design on tan leather, Mondaine, 3"........**80.00**

Vanity case, leather textured blue silvered w/lid, chain, 1940s ....**90.00**

Vanity case/watch, black enamel horseshoe shape, Timepact.........**175.00**

Vanity cigarette case, brushed gold-tone w/enamel, 3x5".........**165.00**

Vanity pouch, gilt-mesh white cloisonné, Evans, late 1930s..**100.00**

# Cookbooks

Cookbook collecting can be traced back to the turn of the century. Good food and recipes on how to prepare it are timeless. Cookbooks fall into many subclassifications with emphasis on various aspects of cooking. Some specialize in regional or ethnic food; during the World Wars, conservation and cost-cutting measures were popular themes. Because this field is so varied, you may want to decide what field is most interesting and specialize. Hardcover or softcover, Betty Crocker or Julia Childs, Pillsbury or Gold Medal — the choice is yours!

Cookbooks featuring specific food items are plentiful. Some are diecut to represent the product — for instance, a pickle or a slice of bread. Some feature a famous personality, perhaps from a radio show sponsored by the food company. Appliance companies often published their own cookbooks, and these appeal to advertising buffs and cookbook collectors alike, especially if they illustrate pe-1970s kitchen appliances.

Perhaps no single event in the 1950s attracted more favorable attention for the Pillsbury Flour Company than the first Pillsbury Bake-Off in 1949. Early in the year, company officials took the proposal to their advertising agency. Together they came up with a plan that would become an American institution.

For more information, we recommend *Collector's Guide to Cookbooks* by Frank Daniels, published by Collector Books.

When no condition is noted, our values are for examples in near-mint condition.

Acme Spices & How To Use Them, American Stores Co, 1939, softcover ................................... **40.00**

Alice's Restaurant Cookbook, w/record, 1969, 4th printing, 148 pages ........................... **35.00**

Bananas & How To Serve Them, Fruit Dispatch Co, 1940, softcover, G .............................. **20.00**

Best of Byerly's, 1985 1st edition, 4th printing, hardcover ..... **28.00**

Better Homes & Gardens Barbecue, 1965, hardcover .................... **35.00**

Better Homes & Gardens Meals in Minutes, 1963, hardcover, 10x7¼" .............................. **12.00**

Better Homes & Gardens So Good w/Fruit, 1967, hardcover, 160 pages ................................... **15.00**

Bettina's Best Salads..., Weaver & LeCron, 1923, hardcover, 203 pages ................................... **30.00**

Betty Crocker Outdoor Cookbook, 1967, 1st edition, hardcover..**37.50**

Betty Crocker's Cookbook, foods in pie shape on red cover, 1972 ...... **75.00**

Betty Crocker's Dinner in a Dish, 1965, 1st edition, hardcover ...... **25.00**

Betty Crocker's New Good & Easy, 1962, 1st edition, spiral hardback .................................... **35.00**

Betty Crocker's Pasta Cookbook, 1995, hardcover, 192 pages ................ **16.00**

Betty Crocker's Picture Cookbook, 1950 1st edition, w/ dust jacket ......... **40.00**

Betty Crocker Your Share, red/white/blue cover, 1943, 8x5½" ............................... **34.00**

Bisquick Cookbook, 1964, 1st edition, hardcover .................. **28.00**

Blueberry Hill Menu Cookbook, Masterson, 1963, 373 pages ...... **18.00**

Borden's Magic Recipes, 1932, softcover, 35 pages, 9¾x7¾"...**20.00**

Campbell's Soup Main Dishes, 1974, hardcover, 134 pages.......... **12.50**

Cast Iron Cook Book, Hester Nitty Gritty, 1969, softcover, 213 pages ................................. **10.00**

**Come to the Kitchen Cook Book, Mary and Vincent Price, first edition, 1951, 212 pages, $25.00.**

Cooking w/Mickey Vol II, Disney, 1987, spiral hardback ........................ **26.00**

Dogpatch USA Cookbook, Malone & Lankford, 1971 printing, softcover .................................. **20.00**

Early American Recipes, H Frost, Phillips, 1953, hardcover.....**35.00**

Fannie Farmer Cookbook, FM Farmer, revised 11th edition, VG ...................................... **27.50**

Fine Old Dixie Recipes, Culinary Arts Press, 1939, 1st edition ............................. **38.00**

First Ladies Cookbook, Parents' Magazine, 1969, revised edition ...............................**35.00**

**First Ladies Cook Book, 1969, $18.00. (Photo courtesy Colonel Bob Allen).**

Fleischmann's Recipes, 1914, softcover, 47 pages, 7x5⅞" ......**20.00**

Frugal Gourmet, Jeff Smith, Morrow & Co, 1984, hardcover w/dust jacket ......................**12.50**

Galloping Gourmet TV Cookbook, G Kerr on cover, 1960s, 126 pages ...................................**10.00**

General Electric New Art of Modern Cooking, 1937, spiral paperback ..........................**27.50**

Good Housekeeping Cookbook, 1930, 2nd printing, hardcover, 256 pages ...................................**25.00**

Good Housekeeping International, 1964 World's Fair edition, hardcover...................................**25.00**

Gourmet & Gormand Cookbook, Justin Wilson, 1984, autographed copy ......................................**30.00**

Great American Favorite Brand name, International Ltd, 1993, hardback ............................**32.00**

Home Cooking w/a French Accent, Michael, 1983, 1st edition, hardcover...................................**50.00**

Japanese Country Cookbook, Rudzinsky, Russ & Nelson, 1959, paperback ................**15.00**

Jell-O Easy Homemade Desserts, 1979, 1st edition, spiral ....**10.00**

Jell-O Recipes for Delicious Ice Cream, 1936, 15 pages......**27.50**

Joy of Cooking, Rombauer, 1946 edition, hardcover, 884 pages ..**35.00**

Julia Child Mastering Art of French Cooking, Vols I & II, 1961/ 1970...................................**35.00**

Kids in the Kitchen, Pampered Chef, 1998, softcover, 96 pages ...................................**20.00**

Kitchen-Klatter Cookbook, Prairie Press, 3rd edition, plastic spiral......................................**25.00**

Knox On-Camera Recipes, 1962, soft cover, 48 pages ..................**20.00**

Knox Sparkling Gelatin Recipes, 1943, softcover, 40 pages.....**15.00**

Kraft 75 Years of Good Food Ideas, vinyl-covered 3-ring binder.................................**30.00**

Little House Cookbook, Walker, Harper Collins, 1995 reissue, hardcover...........................**20.00**

Magic Chef New Magic of Microwave Cookbook, 1978, hardcover, 256 pages.........**12.50**

Mansion on Turtle Creek Cookbook, Fearing, 1st edition, 281 pages ...................................**20.00**

Mrs Beeton's Everyday Cookery, Ward Lock, 1963, VG w/dust jacket..................................**24.00**

My First Cookbook, Imperial Sugar, 1959, 35 pages, 6x9", VG ..**25.00**

Nancy Drew Cookbook, c Keene, Grosset & Dunlap, 1978, hardcover, VG ............................**28.00**

New York Times Natural Foods, Hewit, 1971, 1st edition, hardcover ..................................**15.00**

Northwestern Yeast...Making Bread at Home, 1939 World's Fair cover ..................................**26.00**

Peanuts Cookbook, Scholastic Book Services, 1970, softcover, VG ......................................**25.00**

Pillsbury Family Cookbook, 1963 1st edition, hardcover binder ..**25.00**

Pillsbury Kitchens' Family Cookbook, c 1979, 3rd printing, ring binder ................................**55.00**

**Pillsbury's 2nd Grand National, 1951, $200.00.**

Polly-O Parrot Cooking w/Cheese, 1977 1st edition, softcover, 80 pages ..................................**30.00**

Royal Baking Powder, 1929, softcover, 49 pages, 9x5" ..............**12.50**

Soul Food Cookbook, Nitty Gritty Book, softcover, 1969 1st edition, EX ......................................**60.00**

Southern Heirloom Cooking, McQueen/ Haydel, Good Books, 2001, softcover ..................................**18.00**

Southern Heritage Cookie Jar Cookbook, Oxmoor House, 1985, hardcover ..........................**27.50**

Sunkist Orange Recipes, CA Fruit Growers, 1940, softcover, 31 pages ..................................**45.00**

Sunset Cookbook of Soups & Stews, 1972, softcover, 96 pages ..**24.00**

Towns, Trails & Special Times, Marlboro Country Cookbook, w/dust jacket, NM .............**48.00**

Treasury of Great Recipes, V Price, 1965 1st edition, hardback ..**25.00**

Wesson & Snowdrift Everyday Recipes, 1932, softcover, 29 pages ....................................**5.00**

Woman's Home Companion Cook Book, PF Collier & Son, 1942-43, VG ..............................**65.00**

## Cookie Cutters and Shapers

Cookie cutters have come into their own in recent years as worthy kitchen collectibles. Prices on many have risen astronomically, but a practiced eye can still sort out a good bargain. Advertising cutters and product premiums, especially in plastic, can still be found without too much effort. Aluminum cutters with painted wooden handles are usually worth several dollars each if in good condition. Red and green are the usual handle colors, but other colors are more highly prized by many. Hallmark plastic cookie cutters, especially those with painted backs, are always worth considering, if in good condition.

Be wary of modern tin cutters being sold for antique. Many present-day tinsmiths chemically antique their cutters, especially those done in a primitive style. These are often sold by others as 'very old.' Look closely, because most tinsmiths today sign and date these cutters.

American flag, red plastic, Tupperware, EXIB .........................**25.00**
Baker Man, tin, flat back, ca 1930, 5x3" ....................................**25.00**
Betsy McCall, aluminum, McCall Publishing, 1971, 8" ..........**38.50**
Card suits, aluminum, ea 2½", set of 4.............................................**6.00**

**Cartoon Set, Lowe's Inc., Tom, Jerry, and four others, red plastic, 1956, $20.00 for the set.** (Photo courtesy Rosemary Henry)

Chick, tin, flat back, soldered loop handle, 1930s, 2½x2½" .....**13.00**
Cookie Monster, yellow plastic, 5" ........................................**8.00**
Crow, tin, flat back, 5¾x2⅝" .....**95.00**
Cupid, red plastic, Amscan-Harrison... Hong Kong, 4x3" ....................**8.00**
Donald Duck, red plastic, Loma Plastics, 3¾", EXOC..........**25.00**
Duck, red plastic, Domar Life-Like, Grant Mfg, 4", M (EX card).......**10.00**
Dumbo the Elephant, red plastic, Hallmark, 1977, 4", MIP .....**20.00**

Formay Shortening, rabbit, aluminum, 6"..........................................**25.00**
Gingerbread man, red plastic, Betty Crocker, 3⅞" ......................**15.00**
Girl Scout emblem, aluminum, marked, Drip-O-Lator.......**22.50**
Girl Scout Trefoil, aluminum, 2½x2½", EX ......................**12.00**
Gumby, green plastic, Domino Sugar, MIP ........................**25.00**
Heart & hand, tin, flat back, 3¼x3¼" ............................**385.00**
Heart w/sm heart inside, ceramic, Brown Bag Cookie Art Co, 1992, EX ......................................**18.00**
Hobby horse, tin, flat back, 4¼x3¼" .**15.00**
International Harvester, tin, logo in mold, 3" dia.........................**13.50**
Iowa Hawkeyes, yellow plastic, team emblem .....................**15.00**

**Jack Frost Sugar Elf, white plastic, $2.00.** (Photo courtesy Rosemary Henry)

Linus (Peanuts), red plastic, Hallmark, 1971, 5" ...................**30.00**
Pillsbury Dough Boy, white plastic .........................................**5.00**
Porky Pig, red plastic, 5"............**5.00**
Rabbit, tin-plated aluminum, Formay Shortening, from $20 to ....**25.00**
Raggedy Ann, tin, flat back w/handle, 5" ................................**35.00**

Robin Hood Flour, Robin Hood shape, green plastic, 4" .....**27.50**

Santa & Rudolph, red plastic, marked HRM, pr ...............**15.00**

Santa head, red plastic, Aunt Chicks, 5x3" ........................**8.00**

Santa w/gift bag, tin, flat back, 6½x4" ................................**35.00**

Scottie dog, red plastic, marked HRM, 3¾" ..........................**12.00**

Sesame Street, yellow plastic, Wilson, set of 4, MIP ...............**18.50**

Snoopy's Valentine, heart shape w/Snoopy, plastic, 5" .........**20.00**

Snowman, aluminum, 5" ............**8.00**

**Snowman or Gingerbread Boy, metal, 8", MIB, $8.00.**

Swan's Down, heart, aluminum, flat back, 2½x2¾" .....................**15.00**

Troll, w/decorating tube & instructions, Mirror Aluminum, 1966, NMIB ................................**75.00**

Twelve Days of Christmas, red plastic, Chilton, 1978, NM ................**10.00**

Witch on broomstick, copper-colored aluminum, 5¼" ..................**17.00**

WWF Wrestlers, blue plastic, 1992, MIP .....................................**15.00**

X&O, red plastic, Hallmark, 1983, 3", pr ..................................**10.00**

# Cookie Jars

McCoy, Metlox, Twin Winton, Robinson Ransbottom, Brush, and American Bisque were among the largest producers of cookie jars in the country. Many firms made them to a lesser extent. Figural jars are the most common (and the most valuable), made in an endless variety of subjects. Early jars from the 1920s and 1930s were often decorated in 'cold paint' over the glaze. This type of color is easily removed — take care that you use very gentle cleaning methods. A damp cloth and a light touch is the safest approach.

For further information we recommend *Collector's Encyclopedia of Metlox Potteries* by Carl Gibbs, *The Ultimate Collector's Encyclopedia of Cookie Jars* by Joyce and Fred Roerig, and *An Illustrated Value Guide to Cookie Jars* by Ermagene Westfall (all published by Collector Books). Values are for jars in mint condition unless otherwise noted. Beware of modern reproductions!

A Little Company, Indian Couple, 1991 ................................**150.00**

Abingdon, Hobby Horse, 3602 ......**175.00**

**Abingdon, Miss Muffet, #622, $225.00.**

Abingdon, Mother Goose, #695 .....**275.00**

Abingdon, Old Lady, decor, #471, minimum value ............... **250.00**

Abingdon, Three Bears, #696, from $90 to .............................. **100.00**

Abingdon, Wigwam, #665 ...... **200.00**

American Bisque, Milk Can, bell in lid, mk USA ....................... **60.00**

American Bisque, Teakettle, black, USA mark .......................... **35.00**

Applause, Sylvester Head w/Tweety ..**95.00**

Brush, Clown Bust, #W49 ...... **275.00**

Brush, Dog & Basket ............. **225.00**

Brush, Fish, #W52 (+) ............ **425.00**

Brush, Hen on Basket, unmarked.**125.00**

Brush, Old Clock, #W10 ......... **125.00**

Brush, Puppy Police (+) ......... **525.00**

Brush, Stylized Owl ............... **325.00**

Brush, Treasure Chest, #W28 ..... **150.00**

Brush-McCoy, Cinderella Pumpkin, #W32 ................................... **225.00**

Brush-McCoy, Dog & Basket...... **225.00**

Brush-McCoy, Granny, pink apron, blue dots on skirt ............... **300.00**

Brush-McCoy, Happy Bunny, white, #W25 ............................... **200.00**

Brush-McCoy, Night Owl ....... **125.00**

Brush-McCoy, Squirrel on Log, #W26 ............................... **100.00**

Brush-McCoy, Treasure Chest, #W28 ............................... **150.00**

California Originals, Cookie Bakery, green roof, #863, from $35 to ....................................... **45.00**

California Originals, Fire Truck, #841 ................................ **225.00**

California Originals, Yellow Cab, unmarked ........................ **175.00**

DeForest of California, Henny (Dandee Hen), from $200 to ................................. **225.00**

DeForest of California, King, 1957, minimum value ............... **450.00**

DeForest of California, Rabbit in Hat, brown w/multicolor details ............................... **50.00**

**Doranne of California, Cat, green, $35.00.**

Doranne of California, Doctor, CJ-130 .................................... **200.00**

Doranne of California, Hippo..**100.00**

Doranne of California, School Bus, #120, from $100 to .......... **125.00**

Enesco, Bear, Signature Store exclusive, 1993, from $75 to........**95.00**

Enesco, Clown's Head, #E-5835, from $125 to .................... **150.00**

Enesco, Frostie the Snowman, Warner/Chapppel Music, 1994, $50 to ................................. **60.00**

Enesco, Lucy & Me Bear, Armstrong, from $125 to..................... **150.00**

Enesco, Mary's Moo Moo, 1993, from $40 to .............................. **50.00**

Enesco, Owl, 1997, 8¼", from $20 to ....................................... **30.00**

Enesco, Pinocchio Head, WDP .**210.00**

Enesco, Poodles & Butterflies, on white, 9" ........................... **230.00**

Fitz & Floyd, Adam & Eve Apple Tree, 1987, minimum value ..**300.00**

Fitz & Floyd, owl, from $40 to ..**50.00**

Gilner, Mother Goose, blue bonnet, yellow apron, #G-720 ....**300.00**

Japan, Chipmunk, #2863 ........**30.00**

Maurice of California, Gigantic Clown, #JA 10 .................**225.00**

McCoy, Bobby Baker ...............**65.00**

**McCoy, Chipmunk, $125.00.**

McCoy, Coalby Cat .................**300.00**

McCoy, Cookie Boy .................**225.00**

McCoy, Cookie Cabin ...............**80.00**

McCoy, Cookie Safe .................**65.00**

McCoy, Drum, red ....................**90.00**

McCoy, Dutch Treat Barn ........**50.00**

McCoy, Elephant ....................**150.00**

McCoy, Friendship 7 .............**200.00**

McCoy, Granny .......................**120.00**

McCoy, Hocus Rabbit ...............**45.00**

McCoy, Ice Cream Cone ...........**45.00**

McCoy, Kangaroo, blue ..........**300.00**

McCoy, Lemon ..........................**75.00**

McCoy, Modern..........................**65.00**

McCoy, Monk ............................**50.00**

McCoy, Orange .........................**55.00**

McCoy, Pineapple .....................**80.00**

McCoy, Puppy, w/sign ..............**85.00**

McCoy, Raggedy Ann .............**110.00**

McCoy, Sad Clown....................**85.00**

McCoy, Teapot, 1972 ................**60.00**

McCoy, Tomato..........................**60.00**

McCoy, Traffic Light ................**50.00**

McCoy, Windmill ....................**100.00**

McCoy, Yosemite Sam, cylinder.......**125.00**

Metlox, Bucky Beaver, from $125 to...**150.00**

Metlox, Dutch Boy, from $375 to ....................................**400.00**

Metlox, Gingham Dog, blue, from $175 to .............................**200.00**

Metlox, Lucy Goose, from $125 to ....................................**150.00**

Metlox, Merry Go Round, any color, from $250 to ...................**275.00**

Metlox, Rag Doll, boy, 1¾-qt, from $200 to .............................**225.00**

Metlox, Topsy, yellow polka dots, from $375 to ....................**400.00**

Pantry Parade, Apple, red gloss, unmarked .........................**25.00**

Regal China, Cat, from $340 to......**385.00**

Regal China, Churn Boy, unmarked .**375.00**

Regal China, Dutch Girl, from $600 to ....................................**655.00**

Regal China, Hobby Horse, from $250 to .............................**270.00**

Regal China, Quaker Oats.....**115.00**

**Regal China, Toby Cookies, unmarked, from $600.00 to $650.00. (Photo courtesy Joyce Roerig)**

Regal China, Tulip, from $200 to..**225.00**

Robinson Ransbottom, Bud, Army man, brown, 1942-43, 12", from $150 to ............................**175.00**

Robinson Ransbottom, Log w/ Squirrel, from $250 to ...............**300.00**

Shawnee, Fruit Basket, #84, 8", from
$225 to ..............................**250.00**
Shawnee, Great Northern Girl, #1026,
from $475 to ....................**500.00**
Shawnee, Little Chef, yellow, marked
USA, from $175 to ........**200.00**
Shawnee, Sailor Boy, cold paint,
marked USA, from $150 to..**200.00**

**Shawnee, Smiley the Pig, blue neckerchief, black feet, marked USA, from $180.00 to $200.00. (Photo courtesy Fred and Joyce Roerig)**

Shawnee, Smiley the Pig, shamrock,
marked USA, from $400 to..**450.00**
Sierra Vista, ABC Bear..........**125.00**
Sierra Vista, Dog on Drum ......**50.00**
Sierra Vista, Train ...................**75.00**
Treasure Craft, Cookieville......**45.00**
Treasure Craft, Dopey (Snow White),
Disney, from $100 to......**125.00**
Treasure Craft, Rocking Horse, c
Made in USA .....................**45.00**
Twin Winton, Baker, TW-67, 11x7"..**400.00**
Twin Winton, Chipmunk, TW-45,
10x10" ................................**75.00**
Twin Winton, Fire Engine, TW-56,
7x12" .................................**85.00**
Twin Winton, Shaggy Pup, TW-40,
11x8" ................................**300.00**

# Coppercraft Guild

Sold during the 1960s and 1970s through the home party plan, these decorative items are once again finding favor with the buying public. The Coppercraft Guild of Taunton, Massachusetts, made a wonderful variety of wall plaques, bowls, pitchers, trays, etc. Not all were made of copper, some were of molded plastic. Glass, cloth, mirror, and brass accents added to the texture. When uncompromised by chemical damage or abuse, the finish they used on their copper items has proven remarkably enduring. Collectors are beginning to take notice, but prices are still remarkably low. If you enjoy the look, now is the time to begin your collection.

Bowl, Revere, 4x8¾" dia ..........**18.00**
Bread plate, embossed decor, rolled
rim, 12x6½" .......................**15.00**
Butter dish, satin glass bottom
w/copper lid, stick size ......**15.00**
Candleholder, cup-like base w/center holder, 2x4¾" ...............**10.00**
Chocolate pot, stick handle, 8¼"..**25.00**
Compote, 7x4⅛"........................**20.00**
Cup, handleless, 2¾x3¼", set of 8..**30.00**
Fork & spoon, copper & silver plate,
12¼, 12", pr .......................**18.00**
Hurricane lamp, copper, glass &
wood, 9½"...........................**25.00**
Ice bucket, w/liner, lion's head handles, 8" ...............................**40.00**
Napkin holder, embossed wheat,
4⅜x7x1⅞" .........................**15.00**
Napkin rings, round w/floral etching, set of 12, MIB .............**25.00**

Planter, hanging 3" ball form on curving stand ..................... **15.00**

Plate, Colonial hearth scene, 10½" dia ...................................... **15.00**

Stein, 5x3¼" ............................. **10.00**

Teapot, w/cast-iron stand & copper burner ............................... **20.00**

Tray, detailed etching w/scalloped edges, 1x9¾x6" .................... **8.00**

Tray, hammered, 12¾" dia ...... **15.00**

Tray, leaf shape w/raised strawberries & leaves, 1x9x10¾" ....... **8.00**

Wall hanging, Last Supper, 10x20¾" ............................ **22.50**

Wall hanging, pheasant in tree, 6x6" in wooden frame, 8½x8½". **10.00**

Wall hanging, sailing ship, antiqued finish, 1962, 21" .................. **70.00**

Wall hanging, 2 owls in tree in relief, 11½x9½" .................. **12.00**

# Cracker Jack

The name Cracker Jack was first used in 1896. The trademark as well as the slogan 'The more you eat, the more you want' were registered at that time. Prizes first appeared in Cracker Jack boxes in 1912. Prior to then, prizes or gifts could be ordered through catalogs. In 1910 coupons that could be redeemed for many gifts were inserted in the boxes.

The Cracker Jack boy and his dog Bingo came on the scene in 1916 and have remained one of the world's most well-known trademarks. Prizes themselves came in a variety of materials, from paper and tin to pot metal and plastic. The beauty of Cracker Jack prizes is that they depict what was happening in the world at the time they were made.

To learn more about the subject, you'll want to read *Cracker Jack Toys, The Complete Unofficial Guide for Collectors*, and *Cracker Jack Advertising Collectibles,* both by Larry White, who is listed in the Directory under Massachusetts.

Note: Words in capital letters actually appear on the prize.

A-MAZE PUZZLE, plastic/paper, dexterity game, about 1" sq ........... **5.00**

ANIMATED JUNGLE BOOK, paper, pop-up book ............ **85.00**

Aviation wings, metal, CRACKER JACK AIR CORPS ............ **65.00**

BIKE STICKER, paper, series ID 1380, any ............................ **3.00**

Blotter, Cracker Jack question mark box, yellow, 7¾x3¾" ........ **185.00**

Book, Uncle Sam Song Book, Cracker Jack, 1911, ea ................ **35.00**

Bookmark, plastic, set #40, any of 14 ........................................ **3.50**

BREAKFAST SET, agateware in matchbox .......................... **27.50**

BUTTON CLIP-ON, plastic, series 1375, any ............................ **8.50**

Canister, commemorative, white w/red scroll, 1980s, ea ......... **8.00**

Canister, tin, Cracker Jack Candy Corn Crisp, 10-oz ............... **75.00**

Ceramic figure, JAPAN, 2-3", various, some paint, ea ............. **9.50**

Clamshell w/water flowers inside, about 1½" ........................... **25.00**

CRACKER JACK BANK, metal, book shape ...................... **300.00**

CRACKER JACK RIDDLES, paper book w/jester on cover........**15.50**

Dirigible, metal w/celluloid 'blimp' charm................................**75.00**

GOOFY ZOO, paper, wheeled zoo animal poses.....................**35.00**

Hoe, metal w/wood handle, about 6" L............................................**9.50**

HOLD UP TO LIGHT, plastic, astronaut, egg, etc, ea.......**15.00**

JIG-SAW PUZZLE, paper, 6 sections, boy fishing, etc, ea.....**8.50**

NURSURY RHYMES & RIDDLES, paper, booklet...................**125.00**

Pencil holder, paper, 2x4"........**78.00**

PUT...TAKE, metal spinner, about 1½"......................................**27.00**

RING TOSS, game, paper, Makatoy..**24.00**

Sailboat, plastic, put-together ...**55.00**

**Scales, metal, $75.00; Tray, plastic, $11.00; Outline figure, plastic, $8.00; Standup boy on scooter, metal, $27.00; Lobster game, paper, $35.00; Koala bear, pastic, $8.00.** (Photo courtesy Larry White)

Serving tray, plastic, 5 fishes, thick, Canadian ...........................**10.00**

Sign, Santa & prizes, multicolored cardboard, Cracker Jack, early, lg ......................................**265.00**

TAG ALONGS, plastic, SERIES #72, any of 15 ......................**5.00**

TRANSFER FUN, paper, B SERIES 35, any of 20 ......................**7.50**

Whistle, metal, airplane shape w/eagle design ...................**45.00**

WORDS OF WISDOM, paper, book, about 3x5"........................**275.00**

Zodiac coin, plastic, 1 of 12 ........**5.00**

# Crackle Glass

Most of the crackle glass you see on the market today was made from about 1930 until the 1970s. At the height of its popularity, almost five hundred glasshouses produced it; today it is still being made by Blenko, and a few pieces are coming in from Taiwan and China. It's hard to date, since many pieces were made for years. Some colors, such as red, amberina, cobalt, and cranberry, were more expensive to produce; so today these are scarce and therefore more expensive. Smoke gray was made for only a short time, and you can expect to pay a premium for that color as well. For more information we recommend *Crackle Glass From Around the World* by Stan and Arlene Weitman (Collector Books).

**Basket, blue, Kanawha, 1957 – 87, 3¾", from $55.00 to $85.00.** (Photo courtesy Stan and Arlene

Creamer, blue, drop-over handle, unknown maker, 3⅛".......**40.00**

Cruet, amberina, pulled-back handle, 2-bubble stopper, Rainbow, 7".................................**100.00**

Cruet, ruby, pulled-back handle, 2-bubble stopper, Rainbow, 6¼".....**85.00**

Decanter, amberina, mushroom stopper, Rainbow, 1940-60s, 7¾".................................**105.00**

Decanter, sea green, slim neck, Blenko, 1960s, 13¼".......**125.00**

Decanter, tangerine, ruffled rim, Brischoff, 1942-63, 12"....**125.00**

Mug, amber, drop-over handle, unknown maker, 1950s-60s, 6¼".................................**30.00**

Pitcher, charcoal, clear drop-over handle, waisted, Blenko, 1960s, 10"...............................**125.00**

Pitcher, dark amber, drop-over handle, pear shape, Pilgrim, 1949-69, 4".................................**40.00**

Pitcher, green, pulled-back handle, slim neck, Kanawha, 1950s, 6¼"...**50.00**

Pitcher, green, pulled-back handle, Williamsburg, w/label, 4¾"..**60.00**

Pitcher, light amethyst, pulled-back handle, Pilgrim, 1949-69, 4½".................................**55.00**

Pitcher, olive green, wide mouth, drop-over handle, Blenko, 5¾".................................**55.00**

Pitcher, ruby, clear drop-over handle, waisted, Pilgrim, 3¾".........**45.00**

Pitcher, tangerine, drop-over handle, waisted, Pilgrim, 1940s+, 3½".................................**45.00**

Pitcher, tangerine, pulled-back handle, Pilgrim, 1949-69, 4".....**45.00**

Pitcher, topaz, clear ribbed handle, trumpet neck, Pilgrim, 3¾"..**50.00**

Tumbler, topaz, slim, unknown maker, 6¾".......................**50.00**

Vase, amberina (tangerine), waisted, Blenko, 1961, 7"...........**85.00**

Vase, amethyst, double-neck, Blenko, 1940s-50s, 4"........**85.00**

Vase, amethyst, 3-ruffle top, trumpet neck, unknown maker, 4"..**85.00**

Vase, crystal w/blue rosettes, Blenko, 1940s-50s, 7"......**110.00**

Vase, crystal w/cobalt rim-to-base handles, Blenko, 1946, 8"..**135.00**

Vase, crystal w/sea green leaves, Blenko, 1940s-50s, 7"......**110.00**

Vase, dark amber, 3-scallop rim, Blenko, 1950s, 7¼"..........**145.00**

Vase, Jonquil, footed, crimped rim, Blenko, 1950s, 7¼"..........**145.00**

Vase, olive green, cylindrical, Blenko, 1940s-50s, 10"....**110.00**

Vase, sea green, crystal drop-over angular handles, Blenko, 7½".................................**100.00**

Vase, smoke gray, flared cylinder, unknown maker, 5½"........**70.00**

Vase, tangerine, applied rigaree at neck, scalloped rim, Pilgrim, 4½".................................**75.00**

Vase, topaz, pinched rim, unknown maker, 5"..........................**45.00**

Wine bottle, fish figural, topaz w/green eyes, unknown maker, 15".................................**100.00**

# Czechoslovakian Glass

Czechoslovakia was established as a country in 1918. It was an area rich in the natural resources needed to produce both pottery and glassware. Wonderful cut and pressed scent bottles were made in a variety of colors with unbelievably well-detailed intaglio stoppers. Vases in vivid hues were decorated with contrasting applications or enamel work. See Clubs and Newsletters for information concerning the *Czechoslovakian Collectors Guild International.*

Atomizer, green w/embossed Deco lady & flowers, fan shape, 4½" .................................**100.00**

Bowl, crystal w/Deco floral & yellow stripes, 4¼" .......................**90.00**

Bowl, mottled autumn colors, amber cased, footed, 4⅛" ..............**175.00**

Bowl, red w/black trim, cased, 3", from $30 to........................**40.00**

Box, trinket; amethyst, painted decor, gold-tone closure, 2x1½" .....**50.00**

Candlesticks, pink w/applied green ornaments, 8", pr .............**130.00**

Candy basket, black w/silver mica, blue lined, black handle, 8"..**350.00**

Candy basket, green varicolored w/red overlay, green handle, 8½" .................................**275.00**

Candy basket, pink w/plum stripes, pink handle, 8" ................**200.00**

Candy jar, green w/dark blue ornaments & finial, 6"............**275.00**

Champagne glass, cranberry w/crystal stem, 6", from $40 to...**50.00**

Decanter, orange cased w/silver exotic bird on branch, 12"............**135.00**

Perfume, black crystal/frosted Deco design, simple crystal top, 6½" ...................................**165.00**

Perfume, blue w/geometric cuttings, blue faceted stopper, 5"...**220.00**

**Perfume, clear crystal with frosted Art Deco floral design, green crystal stopper, 4⅜", $185.00. (Photo courtesy Monsen & Baer)**

Perfume, crystal w/geometric cuttings, nude w/jug intaglio stopper, 6"...............................**350.00**

Perfume, crystal w/overall cuttings, 4-footed, faceted stopper, 6⅜" ...................................**110.00**

Perfume, green w/cross-hatching, crystal roses & trellis stopper, 6" .......................................**145.00**

Perfume, metal clad w/goddess cameo & blue stones, 2"................**175.00**

Perfume, smoke, roses intaglio, frosted rose intaglio stopper, 10" ..**15.00**

Perfume, smoky topaz w/embossed nude, floral top, Ingrid, 5⅜"...............................**1,045.00**

Perfume, star shape, crystal stopper w/cut rays, dauber, 5⅜" ...................................**220.00**

Perfume, yellow cut crown form, ornate cut yellow stopper, 6¼"...................................**25.00**

Perfume lamp, enameled florals,
4".....................................**350.00**

Pitcher, orange w/white applied
handle, cobalt threads at rim,
6"......................................**70.00**

Powder box, red w/coralene design,
3½", from $40 to................**45.00**

Shade, mottled colors, globular,
cased, 5¾"........................**150.00**

Vase, blue lustre, chalice form,
5⅞"...................................**750.00**

Vase, bud; multicolor mottle, cased,
8½"....................................**65.00**

Vase, cobalt, trumpet neck, 7"..**100.00**

Vase, cream w/mottled red & yellow
base, fluted rim, 9", from $60
to.......................................**65.00**

Vase, multicolor canes on black, red
band, stemmed foot, 6".....**200.00**

Vase, multicolor mottle, slim neck,
8¼"....................................**85.00**

Vase, pink w/embossed swirls, 3
cobalt handles, 7⅞".........**200.00**

Vase, red & yellow w/clear feet,
cased, sq sides, 13¼", from $60
to.......................................**65.00**

Vase, varicolored swirls, cased, classic form, 8"......................**125.00**

Vase, white opal, graduated balls
form handles, 8⅝"..........**275.00**

Vase, yellow cased w/black serpentine
decor, shouldered, 7¼"......**110.00**

Wine, red cased w/black stem & foot,
silver trim, 7½".................**65.00**

# Dakin

From about 1968 through the
late 1970s, the R. Dakin Company
produced a line of hollow vinyl
advertising and comic characters
licensed by companies such as
Warner Brothers, Hanna-Barbera,
and the Disney corporation. Some
figures had molded-on clothing; others had felt clothes and accessory
items. Inspiration for characters
came from TV cartoon shows, comic
strips, or special advertising promotions. Dakins were offered in different types of packaging. Those in
colorful 'Cartoon Theatre' boxes
command higher prices than those
that came in clear plastic bags.
Plush figures were also produced,
but the examples we've listed below
are the most collectible. Assume all
to be complete with clothes, accessories, and original tags unless otherwise noted. For further
information and more listings we
recommend *Schroeder's Collectible
Toys, Antique to Modern* (Collector
Books).

Bambi, Disney, 1960s, MIP.....**35.00**

Bamm-Bamm, Hanna-Barbera,
w/club, 1970, EX...............**30.00**

Benji, 1978, plush, EX.............**10.00**

Bugs Bunny, Warner Bros, 1978,
MIP (Fun Farm bag).........**20.00**

Daffy Duck, Warner Bros, 1968,
EX.....................................**30.00**

Deputy Dawg, Terrytoons, 1977,
EX.....................................**50.00**

Dream Pets, Bull Dog, cloth,
EX.....................................**10.00**

Dream Pets, Midnight Mouse, cloth,
original tag, EX.................**15.00**

Dumbo, Disney, 1960s, cloth collar,
MIB....................................**25.00**

Elmer Fudd in tuxedo, Warner Bros,
1968, EX............................**30.00**

Foghorn Leghorn, Warner Bros, 1970, EX+ ..........................**75.00**

Fred Flintstone (Movie), 1993, 12", MIB ....................................**15.00**

Goofy Gram, Dog, Congratulations Dumm-Dumm, EX ............**25.00**

Goofy Gram, Tiger, To a Great Guy, EX .......................................**25.00**

Huckleberry Hound, Hanna-Barbera, 1970, EX+.................**60.00**

Lion in Cage, bank, 1971, EX.....**25.00**

Mickey Mouse, Disney, cloth clothes, EX ......................................**20.00**

Monkey on a Barrel, bank, 1971, EX ......................................**25.00**

Opus, 1982, cloth, w/tag, EX.....**20.00**

Pepe Le Pew, Warner Bros, 1971, EX .......................................**55.00**

Pinocchio, Disney, 1960s, EX.....**20.00**

Porky Pig, Warner Bros, 1968, EX.....................................**30.00**

Road Runner, Warner Bros, 1968, EX .......................................**30.00**

Scooby Doo, Hanna-Barbera, 1980, EX .......................................**75.00**

Second Banana, Warner Bros, 1970, EX .......................................**35.00**

Snagglepuss, 1971, Hanna-Barbera, EX ....................................**100.00**

Speedy Gonzales, Warner Bros..**35.00**

Sylvester, Warner Bros, 1968, EX ..............................**20.00**

**Sylvester, Warner Bros., 1976, MIB (Cartoon theatre box), $40.00.**

Tazmanian Devil, Warner Bros, 1978, rare, NM ................**300.00**

Wile E Coyote, Warner Bros, 1968, MIB ....................................**30.00**

Yosemite Sam, Warner Bros, 1968, MIB ....................................**40.00**

## Decanters

The James Beam Distilling Company produced its first ceramic whiskey decanter in 1953 and remained the only major producer of these decanters throughout the decade. By the late 1960s, other companies such as Ezra Brooks, Lionstone, and Cyrus Noble were also becoming involved in their production. Today these fancy liquor containers are attracting many collectors.

Beam, Animal Series, Koala Bear, Australia, gray, 1973 ........**15.00**

Beam, Automotive Series, '57 Bel Air Convertible, black, 1990...............................**80.00**

Beam, Automotive Series, '59 Cadillac, pink convertible, 1991.......**60.00**

Beam, Automotive Series, '78 Corvette Pace Car, black & silver, 1987 .................................**250.00**

Beam, Birds Series, Bluejay, 1969..**9.00**

Beam, Casey Jones Series, Box Car, green, 1990 ........................**30.00**

Beam, Convention Series, Denver, #1, 1971..............................**10.00**

Beam, Executive Series, Presidential, 1968............................**11.00**

Beam, JB Turner Train Series, Log Car, 1984 ..........................**75.00**

Beam, Sports Series, Boxing, Rocky Marciano, 1973.................**37.00**

Beam, States Series, Wyoming, 1965....................................**47.00**

Brooks, Animals & Birds Series, Owl #1, Old EZ, 1977.......**25.00**

Brooks, Automotive Series, Indy Car, STP #40, 1983...........**80.00**

Brooks, Indian Series, Cigar Store Indian, 1968.........................**8.00**

Brooks, Organizations Series, Conquistadors, 1971................**10.00**

Brooks, People Series, Farmer, Iowa, 1977.........................**27.00**

Brooks, Sports Mascots Series, Trojan Horse, 1974.................**22.00**

Cyrus Noble, Assayer, mini, 1974................................**16.00**

Cyrus Noble, Assayer, 1972.....**114.00**

Cyrus Noble, Moose & Calf, #1, 1976....................................**95.00**

Double Springs, Automotive, Cale Yarborough Race Car, 1974..**78.00**

Double Springs, Bicentennial Series, Iowa, 1976.........................**52.00**

Famous First, Automotive & Transportation Series, Ferrari, red, 1983....................................**76.00**

Famous First, Bell, Alpine, black, 1970....................................**18.00**

Famous First, Warrior Series, Garibaldi, 1979..................**28.00**

Garnier, Birds Series, Cardinal, 1969....................................**15.00**

Grenadier, Automotive Series, Pontiac Trans Am, 1979..............**50.00**

Grenadier, Soldiers Series, Foreign Generals, Count Pulaski, 1978......**55.00**

Hoffman, Aesop's Fables Series, Shepherd's Boy, 1978........**22.00**

Hoffman, Animals Series, Mare & Colt, 1979..........................**44.00**

Hoffman, Automotive Series, Distillery Truck, 2000ML, 1981........**58.00**

**Hoffman, Birds Series, Bicentennial Eagle, musical base, 1977, $39.00.**

Hoffman, Duck Decoys series, Blue Bill (pr), mini, 1978............**14.00**

Hoffman, Mr Lucky Series #2, Dancer, 1974.....................**35.00**

Jack Daniels, Maxwell House, 1976..**21.00**

Kontinental, John Lennon Bust, silver or gold, 1981................**42.00**

Lionstone, Bird Series, Mallard w/Base, 1981.....................**40.00**

Lionstone, Circus Series, Barker, 1973, mini..........................**25.00**

Lionstone, Firefighter Series, Fireman #6, fire hydrant, 1981..**95.00**

Lionstone, Safari Series, Zebras, 1977, mini..........................**20.00**

McCormick, Bicentennial Series, John Hancock, 1975..........**25.00**

McCormick, Bird Series, Wood Duck, 1980.........................**33.00**

McCormick, Confederate Series, Robert E Lee, 1976............**55.00**

McCormick, Entertainer Series, Hank Williams Jr, 1980...............**95.00**

McCormick, Shrine Series, Dune Buggy, 1976.......................**38.00**

Old Commonwealth, Coal Miners Series, Cole Miner #1, 1980, mini...................................**27.00**

Old Commonwealth, Dogs of Ireland, 1980 ...........................**18.00**

Old Commonwealth, Hunter Series, Waterfowler #1, 1978......**56.00**

Old Fitzgerald, Memphis, 1969.....**15.00**

Old Fitzgerald, WV Forest Festival, 1973.....................................**30.00**

Pacesetter, Corvet-Stingrays Series, dark blue, 1975...................**29.00**

Ski Country, Animals - Grand Slam Series, Dall Sheep, 1980.....**175.00**

Ski Country, Animals Series, Palomino, 1976, mini........**41.00**

Ski Country, Animals Series, Raccoon, 1975 ...........................**55.00**

Ski Country, Birds Series, White Falcon, 1977, mini..............**49.00**

**Ski Country, Bird Series, Wood Duck, banded, 1982, miniature, $95.00.**

Ski Country, Circus Series, Tom Thumb, 1974.......................**33.00**

Ski Country, Indians Series, Warrior w/Lance, 1975.............**26.00**

Wild Turkey, Habitat Series, Habitat #1, 1988.......................**110.00**

Wild Turkey, Series #1, Strutting, #8, 1978..............................**42.00**

Wild Turkey, Series #2, Lore, #4, 1982................................**46.00**

Wild Turkey, Series #3, Turkey Fighting, #3, 1983 ...........**145.00**

Wild Turkey, Series #4, Turkey & Eagle, #1, 1984 .................**88.00**

Wild Turkey, Series #4, Turkey & Skunk, #9, 1986.................**99.00**

# Degenhart

Elizabeth Degenhart and her husband John produced glassware in their studio at Cambridge, Ohio, from 1947 until John died in 1964. Elizabeth restructured the company and hired Zack Boyd who had previously worked for the Cambridge Glass Company, to help her formulate almost 150 unique and original colors which they used to press small-scale bird and animal figures, boxes, wines, covered dishes, and toothpick holders. Degenhart glass is marked with a 'D in heart' trademark. After her death and at her request, this mark was removed from the molds, some of which were bequeathed to the Degenhart museum. The remaining molds were acquired by Boyd, who added his own logo to them and continued to press glassware very similar to Mrs. Degenhart's.

Bird Salt, Vaseline ...................**20.00**

Bow Slipper, Crown Tuscan ....**20.00**

Bow Slipper, Milk Blue............**20.00**

Candy Dish, w/lid, Tomato ......**50.00**

Child's Stork & Peacock Mug, Heliotrope ..........................**30.00**

Heart Jewel Box, Opal .............**25.00**

Hen Covered Dish, Bloody Mary, 2" .......................................**45.00**

Hen Covered Dish, Honey Amber, 2" .................................**20.00**
Hen Covered Dish, Milk Blue, 2" .................................**20.00**
Hen Covered Dish, Pink Carnival, 2" .................................**35.00**
Hen Covered Dish, Ruby, 5" ....**90.00**
Hen Covered Dish, Toffee Slag, 3" .................................**30.00**
Kat Slipper, Opal ....................**15.00**
Owl, Amethyst, dark ................**20.00**
Owl, Caramel, dark ..................**75.00**
Owl, Crystal .............................**12.00**
Owl, Delft Blue .........................**40.00**
Owl, Peach Blo .........................**20.00**
Owl, Periwinkle ........................**40.00**
Owl, Persimmon .......................**20.00**
Owl, Rose Marie .......................**20.00**
Owl, Vaseline ............................**20.00**
Pooch, Caramel Slag, 3" ..........**20.00**
Portrait Plate, Vaseline ...........**30.00**
Salt, Daisy & Button, Vaseline ..**12.00**
Skate Boot (Roller Skate), Crown Tuscan ..............................**50.00**
Skate Boot (Roller Skate), Sapphire ..**25.00**
Turkey Covered Dish, Vaseline, 5" .................................**35.00**

# Department 56 Inc.

In 1976 this company introduced their original line of six handcrafted ceramic buildings. The Original Snow Village quickly won the hearts of young and old alike, and the light that sparkled from their windows added charm and warmth to Christmas celebrations everywhere. Accessories followed, and the line was expanded. Over the years, new villages have been devel-oped — the Dickens Series, New England, Alpine, Christmas in the City, and Bethlehem. Offerings in the '90s included the North Pole, Disney Parks, and Seasons Bay. Their popular Snowbabies assortment was introduced in 1986, and today they're collectible as well.

Bartholomew the Baker, Merry Makers Series, #9361-0, MIB ...**75.00**
Desert Oasis, Little Town of Bethlehem, #59901, 5 pcs, MIB ...**70.00**
Elvis Presley's Graceland, Snow Village, #55041, MIB ..........**100.00**
Floral Gardens, Dickens Village, #58551, MIB .....................**65.00**

**General Store, New England Village, MIB, $100.00.**

Harley-Davidson Manufacturing Plant, Snow Village, #54948, 3-pcs, MIB ............................**75.00**
Heritage Village Express HO Scale Train & Track Set, #5980-3, MIB .................................**190.00**
Katie McCabe's Restaurant, Christmas in the City, #59208, MIB .................................**70.00**
Kite of Spring, The; Seasons Bay, #53608, MIB ...................**240.00**

Lucky's Pony Rides, North Pole Series, #56776, MIB..........**90.00**

M&M Candy Factory, North Pole Series, #56773, MIB..........**75.00**

Mission Style House, Snow Village, #DP55332, MIB..................**70.00**

Mulberry Court, #58345, MIB ..**75.00**

Old Globe Theatre, Dickens Village, #58501, MIB ......................**75.00**

Old North Church, Heritage Village, MIB ....................................**95.00**

Peppermint House, Snow Village, #55350, 5 pcs, MIB............**65.00**

Pillsbury Doughboy Bake Shop, Snow Village, #55342, MIB...........**70.00**

Polar Power Company, North Pole Series, #56749, MIB..........**75.00**

Red Owl Grocery Store, Snow Village, #55178, MIB .............**70.00**

Rockefeller Plaza Skating Rink, musical, #52504, MIB .....**120.00**

Rocky's 56 Filling Station, Snow Village, #55305, 3 pcs, MIB...**75.00**

Seaside Inn, Seaside Bay, #53449, MIB ..................................**125.00**

Snowbaby, Eloise on Polar Bear Express, girl w/baby on polar bear, MIB..........................**36.00**

Snowbaby, Gift...from Madeline, girl w/gift by baby & polar bear, MIB ....................................**32.00**

Snowbaby, Winter Tales of the Snowbabies, baby on snowball, MIB ....................................**40.00**

Snowbaby, 4 carrying evergreen tree, 4¾ x 8½ x 5", MIB ....**30.00**

Tavern in the Park Restaurant, Christmas in the City, #58928, MIB ..**70.00**

Victoria Station, train station, Dickens Village, #5574-3, MIB ..**95.00**

Village Town Hall, Snow Village, #55044, MIB ......................**75.00**

# Depression Glass

Depression glass, named for the era when it sold through dime stores or was given away as premiums, can be found in such varied colors as amber, green, pink, blue, red, yellow, white, and crystal. Mass produced by many different companies in hundreds of patterns, Depression glass is one of the most sought-after collectibles in the United States today. For more information, refer to *Pocket Guide to Depression Glass & More*; *Collector's Encyclopedia of Depression Glass; Elegant Glassware of the Depression Era;* and *Treasures of Very Rare Depression Glass;* all are by Gene and Cathy Florence (Collector Books). See also Anchor Hocking/Fire-King. See Clubs and Newsletters for information concerning the National Depression Glass Association.

Adam, ashtray, pink, 4½"......**30.00**

Adam, butter dish, pink, w/lid.....**110.00**

Adam, tumbler, green, 4½"......**30.00**

American Pioneer, bowl, crystal or pink, w/lid, 9¼" ...............**125.00**

American Pioneer, cup, crystal, pink or green.............................**12.00**

American Pioneer, sugar bowl, green, 3½".........................**22.00**

American Sweetheart, bowl, cereal; cremax, 6" ..........................**16.00**

American Sweetheart, plate, dinner; pink, 9¾"............................**42.50**

American Sweetheart, tidbit, pink or monax, 2-tier, 8" & 12"..........**60.00**

Aunt Polly, bowl, berry; green or iridescent, 4¾".........................**7.00**

Aunt Polly, creamer, blue ........**55.00**
Aunt Polly, vase, blue, footed, 6½"..**60.00**
Aurora, plate, cobalt or pink, 6½"..**12.50**
Aurora, saucer, cobalt or pink.....**4.00**
Aurora, tumbler, cobalt or pink, 10-
    oz, 4¾".................................**27.50**
Avocado, bowl, relish; crystal, foot-
    ed, 6" .....................................**9.00**
Avocado, pitcher, pink, 64-oz .....**1,000.00**
Avocado, sherbet, green ...........**65.00**
Beaded Block, bowl, jelly; blue,
    stemmed, 4½" ....................**42.00**
Beaded Block, bowl, lily; red, round,
    4½" ......................................**495.00**
Beaded Block, creamer, crystal,
    pink, green or amber.........**22.00**
Block Optic, bowl, salad; green,
    7¼" .....................................**195.00**
Block Optic, plate, luncheon; yellow,
    9" .........................................**50.00**
Block Optic, tumbler, pink, 3-oz,
    2⅝" .....................................**30.00**
Cameo, bowl, sauce; crystal w/plat-
    inum, 4¼" ...........................**7.00**
Cameo, goblet, wine; pink, 4".....**250.00**
Cameo, vase, green, 8" .............**60.00**
Cherry Blossom, bowl, berry; pink,
    4¾" .....................................**18.00**
Cherry Blossom, mug, pink, 7-oz ......**450.00**
Cherry Blossom, plate, grill; green,
    10" .....................................**125.00**
Chinex Classic, bowl, cereal; Brown-
    stone or plain ivory, 5¾" .....**5.50**
Chinex Classic, creamer, w/decal.**10.00**
Chinex Classic, sugar bowl, castle
    decal ....................................**20.00**
Circle, bowl, green, 5¼" ...........**25.00**
Circle, creamer, pink................**25.00**
Circle, tumbler, juice; green, 4-oz,
    3½" .....................................**9.00**
Cloverleaf, bowl, dessert; pink,
    green or yellow, 4".............**40.00**

Cloverleaf, cup, pink or green ......**9.00**
Cloverleaf, salt & pepper shakers,
    black, pr..........................**100.00**
Colonial, bowl, berry; pink, 3¾"..**65.00**
Colonial, bowl, berry; pink or green,
    4½" .....................................**20.00**
Colonial, platter, crystal, oval, 12"..**20.00**
Colonial Block, bowl, pink or green,
    4" ........................................**11.00**
Colonial Block, creamer, white..**8.00**
Colonial Block, goblet, crystal .....**6.00**
Colonial Fluted, bowl, cereal; green,
    6" ........................................**18.00**
Colonial Fluted, plate, sherbet;
    green, 6"..............................**4.00**
Colonial Fluted, saucer, green ....**2.00**
Columbia, bowl, crystal, ruffled
    edge, 10½"..........................**25.00**
Columbia, butter dish, crystal.....**20.00**
Columbia, cup, pink .................**25.00**
Coronation, bowl, berry; pink or Royal
    Ruby, w/handles, 4¼"...............**8.00**
Coronation, cup, pink................**5.50**

**Coronation, pitcher, pink,
68-ounce, 7¾", $595.00.**
(Photo courtesy Gene and
Cathy Florence)

Coronation, sherbet, green ......**85.00**
Cremax, creamer, cremax..........**4.50**
Cremax, plate, bread & butter; blue
    w/castle decal, 6¼" ..............**6.00**
Cremax, saucer, cremax.............**1.00**
Cube, bowl, salad; pink, 6½" .....**14.00**

Cube, pitcher, green, 45-oz, 8¾"......**250.00**

Cube, tumbler, pink, 9-oz, 4" ...**80.00**

Diamond Quilted, bowl, cream soup; pink or green, 4¾"................**15.00**

Diamond Quilted, cup, blue or black...................................**17.50**

Diamond Quilted, whiskey, pink or green, 1½-oz........................**10.00**

Diana, ashtray, crystal, 3½" ......**2.50**

Diana, coaster, pink, 3½"...........**8.00**

Diana, plate, sandwich; amber, 11¾" ...................................**10.00**

Dogwood, bowl, cereal; pink, 5½" ....................................**33.00**

Dogwood, plate, luncheon; green, 8" ........................................**10.00**

Dogwood, tumbler, pink, molded band ...................................**25.00**

Doric, bowl, cream soup; green, 5"..**450.00**

Doric, pitcher, Delphite, flat, 32-oz, 5½" .................................**1,500.00**

Doric, plate, grill; pink or green, 9"..**25.00**

Doric & Pansy, bowl, berry; green or ultramarine, 4½"................**25.00**

Doric & Pansy, plate, dinner; pink or crystal, 9" .......................**20.00**

Doric & Pansy, tumbler, green or ultramarine, 10-oz, 4¼".....**595.00**

English Hobnail, bonbon, pink or green, w/handles, 6½".......**25.00**

English Hobnail, bowl, turquoise or Ice Blue, rolled edge, 11".....**80.00**

English Hobnail, marmalade, turquoise or Ice Blue, w/lid.................**85.00**

English Hobnail, vase, straw jar; pink or green, 10"............**125.00**

Floral & Diamond Band, bowl, berry; pink, 4½".................**10.00**

Floral & Diamond Band, tumbler, iced tea; green, 5"..............**50.00**

Florentine No 1, ashtray, green, 5½" ....................................**22.00**

**Florentine No. 1, butter dish, green, $125.00.**

Florentine No 1, plate, sherbet; yellow or pink, 6"......................**7.00**

Florentine No 1, sugar bowl, cobalt, ruffled ...............................**70.00**

Florentine No 2, bowl, yellow, shallow, 7½" ...........................**100.00**

Florentine No 2, coaster, green, 3¼" ....................................**13.00**

Florentine No 2, plate, salad; green or pink, 8½" ........................**8.50**

Flower Garden w/Butterflies, candlesticks, amber or crystal, 4", pr.......................................**42.50**

Flower Garden w/Butterflies, cup, pink, green or blue-green.....**75.00**

Flower Garden w/Butterflies, vase, black, w/handles, 6½" .......**225.00**

Flower Garden w/Butterflies, vase, blue or canary, 10½".........**235.00**

Fortune, bowl, pink or crystal, rolled edge, 5¼"...........................**22.00**

Fortune, plate, sherbet; pink or crystal, 6"....................................**8.00**

Fortune, saucer, pink or crystal......**5.00**

Fruits, pitcher, green, flat bottom, 7"......................................**100.00**

Fruits, sherbet, green or pink .....**12.00**

Fruits, tumbler, green, 12-oz, 5".**175.00**

Georgian, bowl, vegetable; green, oval, 9" ...............................**60.00**

Georgian, hot plate, green, center design, 5" ..........................**80.00**

Georgian, platter, green, closed handles, 11½" ...........................**65.00**

Hex Optic, bowl, mixing; pink or green, 9" .............................**28.00**

Hex Optic, plate, luncheon; pink or green, 8" ...............................**5.50**

Hex Optic, whiskey, pink or green, 1-oz, 2" ...................................**9.00**

Hobnail, bowl, cereal; crystal, 5½" ..**4.00**

Hobnail, plate, sherbet; pink, 6" .....**5.00**

Hobnail, tumbler, juice; crystal, 5-oz..**4.00**

Homespun, coaster/ashtray, pink or crystal ...................................**6.50**

Homespun, cup, pink or crystal .....**13.00**

Homespun, sherbet, pink or crystal, low, flat .............................**18.00**

Indiana Custard, plate, salad; French Ivory, 7½" ...............**16.00**

Indiana Custard, platter, French Ivory, oval, 11½" ................**35.00**

Indiana Custard, sugar bowl, French Ivory, w/lid............**35.00**

Iris, bowl, soup; crystal, 7½" .....**155.00**

Iris, creamer, crystal or iridescent, footed ...................................**12.00**

Iris, creamer, transparent green or pink, footed......................**150.00**

Iris, vase, crystal, 9" .................**30.00**

Jubilee, bowl, fruit; pink, flat, 11½"..**195.00**

Jubilee, tumbler, juice; yellow, footed, 6-oz, 5" ..........................**95.00**

Jubilee, vase, pink, 12" ..........**250.00**

Laced Edge, basket bowl, opalescent..**225.00**

Laced Edge, creamer, opalescent.**38.00**

Laced Edge, platter, opalescent, 13"..**185.00**

Lake Como, plate, salad; 7¼" .....**20.00**

Lake Como, salt & pepper shakers, pr........................................**45.00**

Largo, bowl, amber or crystal, crimped, 7½"......................**22.50**

Largo, comport, blue or red, double spout, pedestal .................**75.00**

Largo, tray, relish; amber or crystal, 5-part, 14" ..........................**40.00**

Laurel, bowl, jade or decorated rims, 3-legged, 6" ........................**28.00**

Laurel, bowl, white opal or French Ivory, 11" ..........................**40.00**

Laurel, platter, Poudre Blue, oval, 10¾" ...................................**60.00**

Lincoln Inn, bonbon, cobalt blue or red, oval, w/handles ..........**16.00**

Lincoln Inn, nut dish, green, footed .**12.00**

Lincoln Inn, salt & pepper shakers, black, pr............................**300.00**

Lorain, bowl, cereal; crystal, 6"..**50.00**

Lorain, platter, yellow, 11½".....**45.00**

**Lorain, sugar bowl and creamer, yellow, $60.00 for the pair.**

Madrid, butter dish, amber .....**70.00**

Madrid, pitcher, pink, sq, 60-oz, 8"..**35.00**

Madrid, plate, dinner; blue, 10½" ...................................**75.00**

Manhattan, bowl, salad; crystal, 9"..**30.00**

Manhattan, cup, crystal...........**15.00**

Manhattan, cup, pink.............**275.00**

Mayfair (Federal), creamer, crystal, footed ...............................**10.50**

Mayfair (Federal), plate, grill; amber, 9½"........................**17.50**

Mayfair (Federal), saucer, amber or green ...................................**4.00**

Mayfair (Open Rose), celery dish, pink, 10"............................**50.00**

Mayfair (Open Rose), plate, grill; yellow, w/handles, 11½"..........**125.00**

Mayfair (Open Rose), tumbler, water; blue, 9-oz, 4¼"......**115.00**

Miss America, bowl, berry; green, 4½" ....................................**15.00**

**Miss America, candy dish, pink, 11½", $165.00.**

Miss America, goblet, wine; crystal, 3-oz, 3¾" ...........................**20.00**

Miss America, goblet, wine; Royal Ruby, 3-oz, 3¾"................**325.00**

Moderntone, bowl, soup; cobalt, 7½" ....................................**165.00**

Moderntone, plate, salad; amethyst, 6¾" ......................................**10.00**

Moondrops, bowl, pickle; blue or red, 7½" ......................................**35.00**

Moondrops, goblet, wine; Ice Blue, 4-oz, 4" ....................................**12.00**

Moondrops, vase, blue or red, rocket style, 9¼" ..........................**295.00**

Mt Pleasant, leaf dish, amethyst, black or cobalt, 8"..............**15.00**

Mt Pleasant, mint dish, pink or green, center handle, 6"......**16.00**

Mt Pleasant, tumbler, amethyst, black or cobalt, footed .......**28.00**

Mt Vernon, butter tub, crystal, 5" .**15.00**

Mt Vernon, plate, torte; crystal, 13¼" ....................................**27.00**

New Century, goblet, cocktail; green or crystal, 3¼-oz ...............**33.00**

New Century, tumbler, green or crystal, 5-oz, 3½" ...............**18.00**

**New Century, tumbler, green, footed, 9-ounce, 4⅞", $25.00.** (Photo courtesy Gene and Cathy Florence)

Newport, creamer, cobalt.........**16.00**

Newport, sherbet, cobalt or amethyst...........................**15.00**

No 610 Pyramid, bowl, master berry; crystal, 8½".............**30.00**

No 610 Pyramid, tumbler, green, footed, 11-oz......................**90.00**

No 612 Horseshoe, pitcher, green, 64-oz, 8½" ......................**335.00**

No 612 Horseshoe, plate, luncheon; green, 10⅜"......................**135.00**

No 616 Vernon, cup, green or yellow ..**16.00**

No 616 Vernon, saucer, crystal .....**2.00**

No 618 Pineapple & Floral, creamer, crystal, diamond shape .........**9.00**

No 618 Pineapple & Floral, sherbet, amber or red, footed.............**18.00**

Normandie, bowl, berry; amber or pink, 5"...............................**10.00**

Normandie, plate, dinner; amber, 11" ......................................**33.00**

Old Cafe, olive dish, crystal or pink, oblong, 6" ..........................**10.00**

Old Cafe, vase, Royal Ruby, 7¼" ..**55.00**

Old Colony, bowl, pink, plain, 7¾" ..............................**30.00**

Old Colony, comport, pink, footed, w/lid, 7" ..............................**65.00**

Old Colony, plate, grill; pink, 10½" ..**25.00**

Orchid, cake stand, red, black, cobalt or blue, sq, 2" ........**150.00**

Orchid, green, vase, 10" .........**135.00**

Ovide, creamer, black.................**6.50**

Ovide, plate, luncheon; decorated white, 8"..............................**14.00**

**Oyster and Pearl, candleholder, pink, 3½", $20.00; relish dish, pink, oblong, 10¼", $18.00; bowl, pink, with handles, 6½", $20.00.** (Photo courtesy Gene and Cathy Florence)

Parrot, bowl, soup; green, 7" .....**55.00**

Parrot, plate, dinner; green, 9"......**60.00**

Parrot, sugar bowl, amber, w/lid ..**600.00**

Patrician, bowl, cereal; amber, crystal or pink, 6".....................**25.00**

Patrician, pitcher, green, applied handle, 75-oz, 8¼"..........**175.00**

Patrician, plate, dinner; pink or green, 10½"......................**45.00**

Patrick, candlesticks, pink, pr.....**195.00**

Patrick, tray, yellow, w/handles, 11"....................................**60.00**

Peacock & Wild Rose, bowl, all colors, flat, 8½" ....................**135.00**

Peacock & Wild Rose, ice bucket, all colors, 6" ..........................**225.00**

Peacock & Wild Rose, plate, all colors, 8" ................................**25.00**

Peacock Reverse, cup, any color......**150.00**

Peacock Reverse, vase, any color, 10" ....................................**250.00**

Petalware, cup, crystal...............**3.00**

Petalware, plate, salver; pink, 11" ..**15.00**

Pillar Optic, mug, crystal, 12-oz......**12.00**

Pillar Optic, pretzel jar, amber, green or pink, 130-oz.......**150.00**

Primo, bowl, yellow or green, 7¾" ..**45.00**

Primo, plate, yellow or green, 7½"..**15.00**

Princess, ashtray, green, 4½".....**80.00**

Princess, plate, sandwich; topaz or apricot, w/handles, 10¼".....**195.00**

Princess, vase, pink, 8" ............**60.00**

Queen Mary, comport, pink, 5¾"..**25.00**

Queen Mary, creamer, crystal, footed........................................**25.00**

Queen Mary, vase, crystal, #441, 6½" ....................................**12.00**

Radiance, bowl, pickle; Ice Blue or red, 7".................................**35.00**

Radiance, creamer, amber .......**15.00**

Radiance, lamp, amber, 12" .....**65.00**

Ribbon, bowl, berry; green, 4".....**38.00**

Ribbon, plate, sherbet; green, 6¼"..**3.00**

Ring, bowl, soup; crystal, 7".....**10.00**

Ring, plate, sandwich; crystal, 11¼"..**7.00**

Ring, tumbler, crystal, 4-oz, 3" .....**4.00**

Rock Crystal, bowl, relish; crystal, 2-part, 11½"......................**38.00**

Rock Crystal, pitcher, red, w/lid, lg, 9"....................................**895.00**

Rock Crystal, vase, crystal, footed, 11" ....................................**85.00**

Rose Cameo, bowl, berry; green, 4½" ..**16.00**

Rose Cameo, plate, salad; green, 7"..**15.00**

Rosemary, bowl, cream soup; green, 5" ......................................**33.00**

Rosemary, platter, amber, oval, 12"..**16.00**

Roulette, bowl, fruit; crystal, 9"......**9.50**

Roulette, plate, sandwich; pink or green, 12".............................**7.50**

Round Robin, bowl, berry; green, 4".........................................**12.00**

Round Robin, sherbet, iridescent..**10.00**

Roxana, bowl, cereal; yellow, 6"..**22.00**

Roxana, plate, sherbet; yellow, 6".........................................**10.00**

Royal Lace, bowl, vegetable; crystal, oval, 11".............................**28.00**

**Royal Lace, butter dish, clear, $80.00.**

Royal Lace, pitcher, pink, straight sides, 48-oz ......................**100.00**

Royal Lace, saucer, green ........**10.00**

S Pattern, plate, dinner; yellow, amber or crystal w/trims, 9¼".....**10.00**

S Pattern, tumbler, crystal, 12-oz, 5"..**12.00**

Sandwich, goblet, amber or crystal, 9-oz.....................................**13.00**

Sandwich, plate, bread & butter; amber or crystal, 7".............**4.00**

Sharon, cake plate, amber, footed, 11½"...................................**27.50**

Sharon, cup, green....................**20.00**

Sharon, tumbler, pink, footed, 15-oz, 6½"...........................................**55.00**

Ships, cocktail mixer, blue & white, w/stirrer.............................**33.00**

Ships, plate, salad; blue & white, 8".........................................**30.00**

Sierra, creamer, pink ...............**22.50**

Sierra, platter, green, oval, 11".....**80.00**

Spiral, bowl, mixing; green, 7".....**15.00**

Spiral, saucer, green .................**2.00**

Starlight, plate, luncheon; crystal or white, 8½"............................**5.00**

Starlight, plate, sandwich; pink, 13".......................................**18.00**

Strawberry, olive dish, crystal or iridescent, w/handles, 5".........**9.00**

Strawberry, sugar bowl, pink or green, w/lid.......................**120.00**

Sunburst, bowl, crystal, 10¾".....**27.50**

Sunburst, tumbler, crystal, flat, 9-oz, 4"...................................**35.00**

Sunflower, ashtray, pink, center design only, 5" .....................**9.00**

Sunflower, saucer, green..........**10.00**

Swirl, plate, sandwich; pink, 12½" ...............................**22.00**

Tea Room, bowl, finger; green or pink ...................................**70.00**

Tea Room, salt & pepper shakers, pink, pr .............................**75.00**

Tea Room, vase, green, straight, 11" ....................................**160.00**

Thistle, bowl, fruit; pink, lg, 10¼"...**550.00**

Thistle, plate, grill; green, 10¼"..**30.00**

Tulip, bowl, amethyst or blue, oval, oblong, 13¼" ....................**115.00**

Tulip, ice tub, crystal or green, 3x4⅞" ...............................**65.00**

Twisted Optic, basket, blue or canary yellow, 10" .............**95.00**

Twisted Optic, plate, salad; pink, green or amber, 7"...............**4.00**

Twisted Optic, sugar bowl, green, pink or amber .....................**7.00**

US Swirl, creamer, green or pink..**20.00**

US Swirl, sherbet, pink, 3¼" .....**5.00**

Victory, bonbon, blue, 7"..........**20.00**

Victory, bowl, console; black, amber, pink or green, 12" .................**35.00**

Victory, saucer, blue..................**8.00**

Vitrock, bowl, vegetable; white, 9½" ...................................**15.00**

Vitrock, saucer, white ................**2.50**

Waterford, cup, pink ................**15.00**

Waterford, plate, dinner; crystal, 9⅝" ...................................**12.00**

Windsor, ashtray, crystal, 5¾".....**13.50**

Windsor, plate, chop; green, 13⅝"..**42.00**

Windsor, tumbler, pink, 5-oz, 3¼" ...................................**22.00**

# Desert Storm

On August 2, 1990, Saddam Hussien invaded Kuwait, taking control of that small nation in less than four hours and capturing nearly a fourth of the world's oil supply. Saudia Arabia seemed to be his next goal. After a plea for protection by the Saudis, President George H.W. Bush set a January 15, 1991, deadline for the removal of Iraqi soldiers from Kuwait. January 16 saw the bombing of Baghdad and other military targets, followed by SCUD missile attacks. The brief but bloody war ended in March 1991, with Iraqi soldiers leaving Kuwait and US combat forces returning home.

Many Desert-Storm related items were created as remembrances of this brief time in history. Topps published a series of Desert Storm trading cards, and Mattel got in on the action with Barbie and Ken in Desert Storm uniforms. Many other items were issued as well. Actual battle-related items are extremely scarce, but highly coveted by collectors.

Book, Desert Storm Air War, RF Dorr, 128 pages, 1991, 8x9", NM ...................................**22.50**

Boots, GI issue, Cordura/suede leather, Panama soles, 10", EX, pr........................................**40.00**

Bracelet, Military ID; red aluminum, 1991, EX ..............**25.00**

Buckle, commemorative, USS America CV-66, gold & silver, 2½ x 3½"..**36.00**

Coin, Desert Storm Veteran Challenge, MIP .........................**35.00**

Coin, Victory & Honor, 4 service branches represented, silver, MIP ....................................**60.00**

Helmet, Kevlar; PASGT w/tan & camo covers, EX ................**75.00**

Kercheif, Victory, Freedom, Home, eagle, 1991, 21x21"..............**5.00**

Knife, commando; commemorative, silver handle, engraved blade, 11" ...................................**100.00**

Knife, pilot's; w/sheath, EX......**30.00**

Knife, US M-3 Fighting; w/M-10 sheath, 11¾", EX+.............**80.00**

Lighter, Operation Desert Storm, Zippo, MIB.........................**30.00**

Magazine, Desert Storm: A Commemorative Salute, 1991, NM ....**60.00**

Mask, marked US Mask, Chemical-Biological-Field-M17A2, EX w/bag/case.........................**25.00**

Medal, US Army Desert Storm Liberation of Kuwait, MIB .........**40.00**

Medal, US Army Freedom; 1991, made in Italy, MIB............**40.00**

Patch, Elmer Fudd, Be Vewy Vewy Quiet, We're Hunting I-Wackis, NM ....................................**20.00**

Patch, USAF 1st Fighter Wing, Southern Watch, embroidery, 4 x 4½" .................................**37.50**

**Patch, 159th Desert Storm Dustoff 159th Medical Company, Joe Camel, 4" diameter, M, $25.00.**

Patch, 806th BMW Provisional bomb wing, velcro back, NM......**60.00**

Pin-back button, I Support Our Troops, Desert Storm/flag, 1", NM .....................................**5.00**

Service plaque, First Day cover, medals, flag, wood frame, 11x13".............................**30.00**

Train set, K-Line US Army, 9000 locomotive+cars+helcopter+ missle, MIB .....................**125.00**

Wristwatch, aviator dial, Seiko Automato, tough blue band, MIB ...................................**70.00**

# Dollhouse Furnishings

Collecting antique dollhouses and building new ones is a popular hobby with many today, and all who collect houses delight in furnishing them right down to the vase on the table and the scarf on the piano! Flea markets are a good source of dollhouse furnishings, especially those from the 1940s through the 1960s made by Strombecker, Tootsietoy, Renwal, or the Petite Princess line by Ideal. For an expanded listing, see *Schroeder's Collectible Toys, Antique to Modern*.

**Baby's room, baby, crib, dresser, and rocking horse, Fisher-Price #257, 1978 – 84, from $10.00 to**

Barbecue grill, Fisher-Price, #272, 1983-84, MOC.......................**4.50**

Bathtub, painted cast iron, ivory, Arcade..............................**125.00**

Broom, any color, Irwin..............**5.00**

Buffet, walnut, Nancy Forbes.....**3.00**

Bunk bed, blue or pink, Best .....**5.00**

Carriage, blanket insert, blue w/pink wheels, Renwal .....**30.00**

Chair, hostess dining; Ideal Petite Princess................................**8.00**

Chair, kitchen; any color, Plasco.....**2.00**

Chaise, ivory w/bright pink, Marx Little Hostess ....................**12.00**

Chest, 4-drawer, light brown, Blue Box ......................................**4.00**

Clothes washer, white, front load, Ideal ...................................**22.00**

Cradle, doll insert, blue, stenciled, Renwal...............................**25.00**

Dustpan, red, Superior, ¾" scale......**8.00**

Floor lamp, soft plastic, yellow, Marx, ¾" scale ....................**6.00**

Garbage can, yellow w/red decal, Renwal...............................**8.00**

Hair dryer, blue, Sounds Like Home.................................**5.00**

Hearthplace, Regency #4422-2, Ideal Petite Princess, complete....**4.00**

Hutch, aqua or red, Allied/Pyro ......**4.00**
Lowboy, red, Marx Little Hostess ..**12.00**
Nightstand, light green or pink, Strombecker, ¾" scale.........**6.00**
Piano bench, brown, Reliable ....**4.00**
Planter, bathroom, no towels, Tomy-Smaller Homes...................**10.00**
Refrigerator, yellow, Irwin Interior Decorator ............................**5.00**
Rocker, bedroom; blue, Tootsietoy .**12.00**
Rocker, yellow w/green or yellow w/red, Acme/Thomas, ea .....**4.00**

**Royal Dressing table and stool, Petite Princess, Ideal #4417-2, ca 1960s, NM in EX box, from $20.00 to $25.00.**

Secretary, dark marbleized maroon, Ideal, complete.....................**40.00**
Server, brown, opening door, Renwal ...........................................**8.00**
Sink, bathroom, ivory, Jaydon ....**10.00**
Sofa, sm middle section, rose, Ideal Young Decorator................**12.00**
Stove, ivory w/red door (opens), Renwal......................................**18.00**
Table, coffee; brown or dark marbleized maroon, Ideal........**10.00**
Table, kitchen; white w/red marbleized top, Fisher-Price .....**3.00**
Table, patio; blue w/ivory legs; Plasco, sm ....................................**4.00**
Tea cart, dark brown, Tootsietoy ..**22.00**

Telephone, Fantasy #4432-1, Ideal Petite Princess.....................**8.00**
Toilet, Tomy-Smaller Homes .....**10.00**
Vacuum cleaner, no bag, blue w/red or yellow, no bag, Ideal............**20.00**
Vanity, ivory w/blue, good mirror, Ideal ...................................**18.00**

# Dolls

Doll collecting is no doubt one of the most active fields today. Antique as well as modern dolls are treasured, and limited edition or artists' dolls often bring prices in excess of several hundred dollars. Investment potential is considered excellent in all areas. Dolls have been made from many materials — early to middle nineteenth-century dolls were carved of wood, poured in wax, and molded in bisque or china. Primitive cloth dolls were sewn at home for the enjoyment of little girls when fancier dolls were unavailable. In this century from 1925 to about 1945, composition was used. Made of a mixture of sawdust, clay, fiber, and a binding agent, it was tough and durable. Modern dolls are usually made of vinyl or molded plastic.

Learn to check your intended purchases for damage which could jeopardize your investment. In the listings values relate to condition codes given within the description or the subcategory narrative. Compared to near-mint dolls, played-with, soiled dolls are worth from 50% to 75% less, depending on wear. Many are worthless.

We recommend *Small Dolls of the 40s & 50s* by Carol Stover, and *Collector's Encyclopedia of American Compostion Dolls* by Ursula R. Mertz, published by Collector Books. See also Action Figures; Advertising Collectibles; Character Collectibles; Holly Hobbie and Friends; Strawberry Shortcake Collectibles. See Clubs and Newsletters for information on *Doll Castle News* Magazine.

## American Character

In business by 1918, this company made both composition and plastic dolls, all of excellent quality. Many collectors count them among the most desirable American dolls ever made. The company closed in 1968, and all of their molds were sold to other companies. The hard plastic dolls of the 1950s are much in demand today. See also Betsy McCall.

For more information, we recommend *American Character Dolls* by Judith Izen (Collector Books).

Baby, hard plastic head/vinyl body, re-dressed, 12", EX............**60.00**
Bessie the Bashful Bride, w/tag, MIB.................................**225.00**
Bottletot, compo/cloth, crier, sleep eyes, open mouth, 1926, 13", EX .....................................**250.00**
Elise, cloth, orange yarn hair, Christmas dress, 1950s, 15", EX .....................................**260.00**
Maggie Make Up, vinyl, grow hair, bendable legs, 1965-66, 11", M.........**75.00**
Sally Says, plastic & vinyl, talker, 1965, 19", M......................**70.00**

Sweet Sue Sophisticate, vinyl head, Sunday Best, 1953-61, 19", M......**350.00**
Tiny Tears, hard plastic & vinyl, 1950-62, 8", M....................**75.00**
Tressy, Black; vinyl, high-heels, 1960s, 11", M, minimum value ...............................**300.00**

## Annalee

Annalee Davis Thorndike made her first commercially sold dolls in the late 1950s. They're characterized by their painted felt faces and the meticulous workmanship involved in their manufacture. Most are made entirely of felt, though Santas and rabbits may have flannel bodies. All are constructed around a wire framework that allows them to be positioned in imaginative poses. Depending on rarity, appeal, and condition, some of the older dolls have increased in value more than ten times their original price. Dolls from the 1950s carried a long white red-embroidered tag with no date. The same tag was in use from 1959 until 1964, but there was a copyright date in the upper right-hand corner. In 1970 the company changed its tag to a white satiny tag with a date preceded by a copyright symbol in the upper right-hand corner. In 1975 they made another change to a long white cotton strip with a copyright date. In 1982 the white tag was folded over, making it shorter. Many people mistake the copyright date as the date the doll was made — not so! It wasn't until 1986 that they finally began to date the tags with the year of manufacture, making it much easier for collectors to identify their dolls. Besides the red-lettered white Annalee tags, numerous others were used in the 1990s, but all reflect the year the doll was actually made.

For more information, refer to *Teddy Bears, Annalee's, and Steiff Animals,* by Margaret Fox Mandel, and *Garage Sale and Flea Market Annual.* Both are published by Collector Books. Values are given for dolls in clean, near-mint condition.

Bear on sled, 1988, 10".............**50.00**
Cat w/valentine, 1985, 18".......**75.00**
Clown, 1980, 10".......................**45.00**
Dracula Kid, 1994, 7"..............**30.00**
Frog Bride & Groom, 1981, 10",
   pr.....................................**100.00**

**Gnome, 1976, 8",**
**$125.00. (Photo courtesy Jane Holt)**

Gnome, 1980, 18"......................**80.00**
Hockey Kid, 1995, 7"................**30.00**
Mouse w/metal mailbox, 1970,
   7".......................................**50.00**
Santa's Helper, 1993, 10".........**35.00**
Spring Fairy, 1990, 10"............**30.00**
Tiger Kid, 1998, 7" ...................**25.00**
Windsurfer Mouse, Annalee birth
   date on sail, 1982, 7".......**125.00**

## Betsy McCall

Tiny 8" Betsy McCall was manufactured by the American Character Doll Company from 1957 until 1963. She was made from fine quality hard plastic with a bisque-like finish and had hand-painted features. Betsy came with four hair colors — tosca, blond, red, and brown. She has blue sleep eyes, molded lashes, a winsome smile, and a fully jointed body with bendable knees. On her back is an identification circle which reads © McCall Corp. The basic doll could be purchased for $2.25 and wore a sheer chemise, white taffeta panties, nylon socks, and Maryjane-style shoes.

There were two different materials used for tiny Betsy's hair. The first was soft mohair sewn onto mesh. Later the rubber skullcap was rooted with saran which was more suitable for washing and combing.

Betsy McCall had an extensive wardrobe with nearly one hundred outfits, each of which could be purchased separately. They were made from wonderful fabrics such as velvet, felt, taffeta, and even real mink fur. Each ensemble came with the appropriate footware and was priced under $3.00. Since none of Betsy's clothing is tagged, it is often difficult to identify other than by its square snap closures (although these were used by other companies as well).

Betsy McCall is a highly collectible doll today but is still fairly easy to find at doll shows. The prices remain reasonable for this beautiful clothes horse and her many accessories, some of which we've included below. For further information we recommend *Betsy McCall, A Collector's Guide* by Marci Van Ausdall. See Clubs and Newsletters for information concerning the Betsy McCall's Fan Club.

**Betsy McCall, vinyl head, hard plastic Tony Walker body, 1952 – 54, 14", MIB, $400.00.** (Photo courtesy McMasters Doll Auctions)

Doll, American Character, hard plastic, 1957, 8", M..........**350.00**

Doll, American Character, vinyl, rooted hair, jointed, 1961, 22", NM ..................................**250.00**

Doll, Horsman, vinyl & hard plastic, sleep eyes, 1961, 12½", G ......................................**25.00**

Doll, Uneeda, vinyl, rooted hair, sleep eyes, slim, 1964, 11½", NM ..................................**95.00**

Linda McCall, American Character, vinyl, rooted hair, 1959, 36", G........................................**50.00**

**Celebrities**

Dolls that represent movie or TV personalities, fictional characters, or famous sports figures are very popular collectibles and can usually be found for well under $100.00. Mego, Horsman, Ideal, and Mattel are among the largest producers. Condition is vital. To price a doll in mint condition but without the box, deduct about 65% from the value of one mint-in-the-box. Dolls in only good or poorer condition drop at a very rapid pace. For an expanded listing, see *Schroeder's Collectible Toys, Antique to Modern,* and *Collector's Guide to Celebrity Dolls* by David Spurgeon.

Andy Gibb, Ideal, 1979, MIB ...**85.00**

Boy George, LNJ, 1984, 11½", rare, M (EX box)..........................**80.00**

Cher, swimsuit, Mego, 1981, 12", MIB.**50.00**

Eleanor Roosevelt, Effanbee, 1985, 14", MIB............................**125.00**

Elly May/Donna Douglas, Exclusive Premier, 1997, 9", MIB .....**30.00**

Farrah Fawcett, white jumpsuit, blond hair, Mego, 1975, EX..**25.00**

Jimmy Osmond, Mattel, 1978, 10", EX ......................................**45.00**

Muhammad Ali, Hasbro, 1997, 12", MIB ..................................**45.00**

**Patty Duke, as teenager, Horsman, all original, 11", M, from $100.00 to $125.00.** (Photo courtesy Cindy Sabulis)

Selena, Arm Enterprise, 1996, 11½",
MIB ......................................**85.00**
Vinnie Barbarino/John Travolta,
Mattel, 1976, 9½", MOC ...**75.00**
Willie Nelson, stuffed cloth, Catena
Int Inc, 1989, 16", M .........**65.00**

## Eegee

The Goldberger company made
these dolls, Eegee (E.G.) being the
initials of the company's founder.
Dolls marked 'Made in China' were
made in 1986.

Annette, vinyl, teen-type fashion, rooted hair, 1963, 11½", EX.........**55.00**
Baby Care, vinyl, drinks & wets, 1959,
18", M w/nursery set................**45.00**
Ballerina, vinyl & hard plastic,
1964, 31", M.....................**100.00**
Granny Clampett, gray rooted hair,
14", VG..............................**20.00**
Karena Ballerina, vinyl & hard plastic, fully jointed, 1958, 21",
M .......................................**45.00**

L'il Sister, 9½", MIB, from
$35.00 to $45.00. (Photo
courtesy Cindy Sabulis)

Shelly, Tammy type w/grow hair,
1964, 12", M......................**18.00**
Tandy Talks, vinyl & hard plastic,
pull-string talker, 1961, 20",
M .......................................**55.00**

## Effanbee

This company has been in business since 1910, continually producing
high quality dolls, some of all composition, some composition and cloth, and
a few in plastic and vinyl. In excellent
condition, some of the older dolls often
bring $300.00 and up.

Baby Lisa Grows Up, plastic & vinyl
toddler, 1983, NM w/trunk,
wardrobe.........................**150.00**

Candy Ann, vinyl,
sleep eyes, wig, all
original, 1954, 20",
$300.00. (Photo cour-
tesy Barbara DeFeo
and Carol Stover)

Gumdrop, vinyl, jointed toddler,
sleep eyes, all original, 16",
NM ...................................**35.00**
Pat-o-Pat, compo & cloth, clapping
mechanism, 1925+, 13", VG..**50.00**
Patsy Joan, compo, 1931, all original, 16", EX.....................**550.00**

Patsy Lou, compo, open/close eyes, all original, 22", EX.........**675.00**

Sister, compo & cloth, painted eyes, yarn hair, re-dressed, 12", EX.**175.00**

Sweetie Pie, compo, caracul wig, bent limbs, re-dressed, 1939, 20", VG..............................**85.00**

### Fisher-Price

Since the mid-1970s, this well-known American toy company has been making a variety of dolls. Many have vinyl heads, rooted hair, and cloth bodies. Most are marked and dated.

Audrey, #203, 1974-76, 13", EX ..**35.00**

Honey, #208, 1977-80, NRFB ..**60.00**

Joey, #206, 1975-76, 13", EX ...**35.00**

Miss Piggy, Dress-Up Muppet, #890, 1981-84, EX ......................**12.00**

My Friend Mandy, #211, 1979-81, EX .....................................**30.00**

Natalie, #202, 1974-76 .............**50.00**

**Natalie, vinyl head, stuffed body, known as a lapsitter, 1973, 14", MIB, from $50.00 to $75.00. (Photo courtesy Cindy Sabulis)**

### Horsman

During the 1930s, this company produced composition dolls of the highest quality. Today many of their dolls are vinyl. Hard plastic dolls marked '170' are also Horsmans.

Angelove, plastic & vinyl, made for Hallmark, 1974, 12", MIB..**25.00**

Baby Tweaks, vinyl & cloth, 1967, 20", EX ..............................**15.00**

Betty Jo, vinyl & hard plastic, 16", MIB ....................................**30.00**

Cinderella, vinyl & hard plastic, painted eyes, 1965, 11½", MIB ....................................**30.00**

Floppy, vinyl head, foam body & legs, 1958, 18", EX..............**8.00**

**Lullaby Baby, music box and speaker in tummy, re-dressed, working, 12", EX, from $20.00 to $25.00. (Photo courtesy Cindy Sabulis)**

Poor Pitiful Pearl, marked on neck, Horsman 1963, 1963, 11", EX .....................................**40.00**

Tynie Baby, vinyl, 1950s, 15", MIB .................................**110.00**

## Ideal

For more than eighty years, this company produced quality dolls that were easily affordable by the average American family. Their 'Shirley Temple' and 'Toni' dolls were highly successful. They're also the company who made 'Miss Revlon,' 'Betsy Wetsy,' and 'Tiny Tears.' For more information see *Collector's Guide to Ideal Dolls* by Judith Izen. See also Dolls, Shirley Temple and Tammy.

Baby Coos, vinyl & hard plastic, painted hair, 1948-53, 16", NM..**100.00**
Bizzie Lizzie, vinyl, rooted hair, power pack, 18", M............**50.00**
Bonnie Play Pal, vinyl, rooted blond hair, 1959, 24", EX...........**275.00**
Cinderella, compo, flirty eyes, wig, 1939-39, 13", EX.............**325.00**
Clown Flexy, compo & wood, 1938-42, 13½", EX....................**225.00**
Cover Girl, Dana, Black, poseable, jointed hands, 12½", M.....**50.00**
Dennis the Menace, printed cloth, blond hair, 1976, 7", M......**15.00**
Kissy Baby, vinyl, bib, all original, 1963-64, 22", NM............**240.00**

**Pebbles and Bamm-Bamm, both missing some accessories, 12", from $35.00 to $45.00 each.**
(Photo courtesy Cindy Sabulis)

Tammy, vinyl & plastic, 1961+, 12", M.....................................**110.00**

## Jem

The glamorous life of Jem mesmerized little girls who watched her Saturday morning cartoons, and she was a natural as a fashion doll. In 1985 Hasbro introduced the Jem line of 12" dolls representing her, the rock stars from Jem's musical group, the Holograms, and other members of the cast, including Rio, the only boy, who was Jem's road manager and Jerrica's boyfriend. Production was discontinued in 1987. Each doll was poseable, jointed at the waist, heads, and wrists, so that they could be positioned at will with their musical instruments and other accessory items. Their clothing, their makeup, and their hairdos were wonderfully exotic, and their faces were beautifully molded. More information on Jem dolls may be found in *Dolls of the 1960s and 1970s, Volumes I* and *II,* by Cindy Sabulis (Collector Books).

Accessory, Backstager, M........**25.00**
Accessory, Star Stage, M.........**30.00**
Doll, Aja, 2nd issue, original outfit, M......................................**90.00**
Doll, Clash, original outfit, M..**40.00**
Doll, Jem/Jerrica, star earrings, original outfit, M...............**35.00**
Doll, Jetta, original outfit, M.....**40.00**
Doll, Pizzaz, 1st issue, original outfit, M ...................................**50.00**
Doll, Stormer, original outfit, M ....**45.00**
Doll, Video, original outfit, M ......**45.00**

Outfit, Designing Woman, MIP......**35.00**
Outfit, Moroccan Magic, MIP......**75.00**
Outfit, We're Off & Running, MIP..**35.00**

## Kenner

This company's dolls range from the 12" jointed teenage glamour dolls to the tiny 3" 'Mini-Kins' with the snap-on changeable clothing and synthetic 'hair' ponytails. (Value for the latter: doll only, $8.00; doll with one outfit, $15.00; complete set, $70.00.)

Blythe, over-lg plastic head, small vinyl body, eyes change color, 11", M ...........................**600.00**
Crumpet, battery-op/pull-string, serves tea, 1971, complete, 18", M ....................................**45.00**
Dana, black fashion model, 1978, #47000, 12½", MIB, from $100 to....................................**125.00**
Darci, black fashion model, 1978, 12½", MIB, from $75 to .....**100.00**
Dusty, sports fashion doll, swivel waist, 1974, re-dressed, 11½", EX....................................**15.00**
Gabbigale, repeats what you say, #16, General Mills, 16", MIB.......**50.00**
Madcap Molly, plastic wind-up, w/shopping cart, skis, etc., 12", MIB................................**80.00**

## Liddle Kiddles

Produced by Mattel between 1966 and 1971, Liddle Kiddle dolls and accessories were designed to suggest the typical 'little kid' in the typical neighborhood. These dolls can be found in sizes ranging from ¾" to 4", all with poseable bodies and rooted hair that can be restyled. Later, two more series were designed that represented storybook and nursery rhyme characters. The animal kingdom was represented by the Animiddles and Zoolery Jewelry Kiddles. There was even a set of extraterrestrials. And lastly, in 1979 Sweet Treets dolls were marketed.

Items mint on card or mint in box are worth about 50% more than one in mint condition but with none of the original packaging. Based on mint value, deduct 50% for dolls that are dressed but lack accessories. For further information we recommend *Dolls of the 1960s and 1970s, Volumes I* and *II,* by Cindy Sabulis; and *Schroeder's Collectible Toys, Antique to Modern.* All are published by Collector Books.

Annabell Autodiddle, #3770, MIP..**75.00**
Aqua Funny Bunny, #3532, MIP..**65.00**
Frosty Mint Kone, #3653, complete, M ......................................**50.00**
Heart Ring Kiddle, #3744, MIP..**50.00**
Kiddles Sweet Shop, #3807, NRFB ..............................**300.00**
Lois Locket, #3541, complete, M ......................................**65.00**
Lolli-Mint, #3658, MIP.............**75.00**
Luscious Lime, #3733, glitter version, complete, M...............**75.00**
Sizzly Friddle, #3513, complete, M ......................................**75.00**
Snap-Happy Furniture, #5171, MIP ......................................**30.00**
Windy Fliddle, #3514, complete, M ......................................**75.00**

## Madame Alexander

Founded in 1923, Beatrice Alexander began her company by producing an Alice in Wonderland doll which was all cloth with an oil-painted face. By the 1950s there were over six hundred employees making dolls of various materials. The company is still producing lovely dolls today. For further information, we recommend *Collector's Encyclopedia of Madame Alexander Dolls, 1948 – 1965, Madame Alexander Store Exclusives & Limited Editions,* and *Madame Alexander Collector's Dolls Price Guide,* all by Linda Crowsey. All are published by Collector Books.

Anatolia, straight legs, #524, 1987 only, 8" ...............................**65.00**
Christening Baby, cloth & vinyl, 1951-54, 11-13" ..................**15.00**
Clarabell Clown, 1951-53, 19"..**350.00**
Hyacinth, vinyl toddler, blue dress & bonnet, 1953 only, 9"...**150.00**
Indian, hard plastic, bend-knee walker, Wendy Ann, #775, 1965, 8" ............................**125.00**
Lucinda, plastic & vinyl, Janie, 1969-70, 12", minimum value ...**525.00**
Maid of Honor, composition, Wendy Ann, 1940-44, 18", minimum value ...............................**700.00**
Morocco, hard plastic, bend-knee, Wendy Ann, #762, 1968-70, 8" .........................................**90.00**
Rozy, plastic & vinyl, Janie, #1130, 1969 only, 12" ..................**375.00**
Timmy Toddler, plastic & vinyl, 1960-61, 23" .....................**150.00**

Winnie Walker, hard plastic, Cissy, 1953 only, 15" ..................**325.00**
Yolanda, Brenda Star, 1965 only, 12", minimum value........**375.00**

## Mattel

Though most famous, of course, for Barbie and her friends, the Mattel company also made celebrity dolls, Liddle Kiddles, Chatty Cathy, talking dolls, lots of action figures (the Major Matt Mason line and She-Ra, Princess of Power, for example), and in more recent years, 'Baby Tenderlove' and 'P.J. Sparkles.' See also Barbie; Dolls, Liddle Kiddles.

To learn more about Mattel dolls, consult *Talking Toys of the 20th Century* by Kathy and Don Lewis. They are listed in the Directory under California.

Baby Beans, vinyl, bean-bag body, 1971-75, 12", M..................**70.00**
Baby Go Bye-Bye & Her Bumpety Buggy, battery-operated, 1970, 11", M...............................**100.00**
Baby Play-a-lot, poseable, pull string/switch, 172-73, 16" .**22.00**
Baby Small Talk, vinyl, says 8 phrases, 1958-59, 10¾", M..**55.00**
Baby Tender Love, newborn, plastic skin, all original, 13", M ...**65.00**
Drowsy, vinyl/cloth, pull-string talker, 1965-74, 15½", M.......**175.00**
Teachy Keen, vinyl & cloth, talker, Sears, 1955-70, 16", M ......**30.00**
Tippee Toes, battery-operated, rides accessory, 1968-70, 17", M .......................................**80.00**

## Nancy Ann Storybook

Nancy Ann Abbott was a multi-faceted, multitalented Californian who seemed to excel at whatever was her passion at the moment. Eventually she settled on designing costumes for dolls. This burgeoned into a full-fledged and very successful doll company which she founded in 1937. Early on, her 5" dolls were imported from Japan; but very soon she was making her own dolls, the first of which had jointed legs, while those made in the early '40s had legs molded as part of the body (frozen). But it was their costumes that made the dolls so popular. Many series were designed around various themes — storybook characters; the flower series; Around the World Dolls of every ethnic persuasion; the American girls; sports and family series; and dolls representing seasons, days of the week, and the months of the year. Ms. Abbott died in 1964, and within a year the company closed.

To learn more about this extensive line, we recommend *Encyclopedia of Bisque Nancy Ann Storybook Dolls* by Elaine M. Pardee and Jackie Robertson (Collector Books).

Around the World Series, English Flower Girl, bisque, MIB ....**400.00**
Audrey Ann, toddler, Nancy Ann Storybook 12, 6", EX .......**250.00**
Baby Sue Sue, vinyl, nude, 1960s, EX ......................................**35.00**
Debbie, hard plastic, school dress, name on wrist tag, 10", EX............**100.00**

Little Miss Nancy Ann, in day dress, 1959, 8½", MIB..................**50.00**
Lori Ann, vinyl, 1950s, 7½", MIB, minimum value ...............**175.00**
Margie Ann Series, Margie Ann, EX ......................................**60.00**
Muffie, hard plastic, wig, sleep eyes, non-walker, 1953, 8", EX.....**75.00**

**Thursday's Child Has Far To Go, jointed legs, #183, $135.00.** (Photo courtesy Elaine M. Pardee and Jackie Robertson)

## Raggedy Ann and Andy

Designed by Johnny Gruelle in 1915, Raggedy Ann was named by combining two James Whitcomb Riley poem titles, *The Raggedy Man* and *Orphan Annie*. The early cloth dolls he made were dated and had painted-on features. Though these dolls are practically nonexistent, they're easily identified by the mark, 'Patented Sept. 7, 1915.' P.F. Volland made these dolls from 1920 to 1934; theirs were very similar in appearance to the originals. The Mollye Doll Outfitters were the first to print the now-familiar red heart on her chest, and they added a black outline around her nose. These dolls carry the handwritten inscription

'Raggedy Ann and Andy Doll/ Manufactured by Mollye Doll Outfitters.' Georgene Averill made them ca 1938 to 1950, sewing their label into the seam of the dolls. Knickerbocker dolls (1963 to 1982) also carry a company label. The Applause Toy Company made these dolls for two years in the early 1980s, and they were finally taken over by Hasbro, the current producer, in 1983.

Besides the dolls, scores of other Raggedy Ann and Andy items have been marketed, including books, radios, games, clocks, bedspreads, and clothing. For more information see *The World of Raggedy Ann Collectibles* by Kim Avery.

Applause, 1981-83, 8", NM ......**15.00**
Applause, 1981-83, 17", NM ....**50.00**
Bobbs-Merrill, ventroliquist's, hard plastic/foam body, 1974, 30", NM ...................................**175.00**
Georgene Novelties, 1950s, 18", NM, ea.......................................**300.00**
Georgene Novelties, 1960-63, 15", NM, ea ...........................**110.00**

**Knickerbocker, scarce orange wig variation, made in Japan, 15", from $55.00 to $65.00.** (Photo courtesy Kim Avery)

Knickerbocker, 1960s, 15", NM, ea..**350.00**

Knickerbocker, 1970s, 12", NM, ea.........................................**45.00**
Knickerbocker, 1980s, 24", NM, ea.........................................**55.00**

## Remco

The plastic and vinyl dolls made by Remco during the 1960s and 1970s are gaining popularity with collectors today. Many have mechanical features that were activated either by a button on their back or batteries. The Littlechap Family of dolls (1964), Dr. John, his wife Lisa, and their two children, Judy and Libby, came with clothing and fashion accessories of the highest quality. Children found the family less interesting than the more glamorous fashion dolls on the market at that time, and as a result, production was limited. These dolls in excellent condition are valued at about $15.00 to $20.00 each, while their outfits range from about $30.00 (loose and complete) to a minimum of $50.00 (MIB).

Baby Grow a Tooth, vinyl & hard plastic, battery-operated, 1968, MIB ...................................**20.00**
Baby Stroll A Long, 1966, 15", MIB ...................................**15.00**
Dave Clark Five, vinyl & rigid plastic, 1964, set of 5, EX................**50.00**
Grandpa Munster, vinyl & plastic, #1821, 1964, 4¾", EX........**65.00**
Heidi, all vinyl, push-button waver, 1967, 5½", M in case...........**67.00**
Jumpsy, vinyl & hard plastic, molded-on shoes & socks, 1970, 14", EX ......................................**5.00**

Libby Littlechap, 1963+, 10½", EX ..**35.00**

Mimi, vinyl & hard plastic, battery-operated singer, 1973, 19", MIB ..**75.00**

Uncle Fester of Addams Family, 1964, 4½", EX ....................**15.00**

Winking Heidi, Pocketbook Doll, 5½", MIB, from $45.00 to $55.00. (Photo courtesy Cindy Sabulis)

## Shirley Temple

The public's fascination with Shirley was more than enough reason for toy companies to literally deluge the market with merchandise of all types decorated with her likeness. Dolls were a big part of that market, and the earlier composition dolls in excellent condition are often priced at a minimum of $600.00 on today's market. Many were made by the Ideal Company, who in the 1950s also issued a line of dolls made of vinyl.

For more information see *The Complete Guide to Shirley Temple Dolls and Collectibles* by Tonya Bervaldi-Camaratta (Collector Books).

Compo, 18", Ideal, incomplete, VG...**250.00**

Vinyl, flirty eyes, 1958-61, Ideal, ST/15, 15", EX .................**400.00**

Vinyl, sleep eyes, wig, with slip and undies, Ideal, ST/12, 12", MIB, from $425.00 to $450.00. (Photo courtesy Judith Izen)

Vinyl, 1972, Montgomery Ward reissue, 17", NM in plain box .......**225.00**

## Tammy

In 1962 the Ideal Novelty & Toy Company introduced their teenage Tammy doll. Slightly pudgy and not quite as sophisticated as some of the teen fashion dolls on the market at the time, Tammy's innocent charm captivated consumers. Her extensive wardrobe and numerous accessories added to her popularity with children. Tammy had everything including a car, a house, and a catamaran. In addition, a large number of companies obtained licenses to issue products using the 'Tammy' name. Everything from paper dolls to nurse's kits were made with Tammy's image on them. Tammy's success was not confined to the United States. She was also successful in Canada and in several European countries. Doll values listed here are for mint-in-box examples. (Loose dolls are generally about half mint-in-box value as they are relatively common.)

Accessory Pak, electric skillet & frying pan w/lids, NRFP ...............**50.00**
Accessory Pak, tennis racket, score book & sneakers, #9188-8, NRFP ..**15.00**
Doll, Bud, MIB, minimum value..**600.00**
Doll, Glamour Misty the Miss Clairol Doll, MIB.............**150.00**
Doll, Patti, MIB .....................**200.00**
Doll, Pepper, MIB....................**65.00**
Doll, Pos'n Ted, MIB .............**100.00**

**Doll, Tammy, top braid, straight-leg variation, Ideal, 12", from $25.00 to $40.00 for doll only; from $30.00 to $45.00 for blouse and pedal pushers sold as 'switchables.' (Photo courtesy Cindy Sabulis)**

Doll, Tammy, MIB....................**85.00**
Doll, Tammy's Dad, MIB .........**65.00**
Doll, Tammy's Mom, MIB........**75.00**

## Vogue

This is the company that made the 'Ginny' doll famous. She was first made in composition during the late 1940s, and if you could find her in mint condition, she'd bring about $450.00 on today's market. (Played with and in relatively sad condition, she's still worth about $90.00.) Ginnys from the 1950s were made of rigid vinyl. The last Ginny came out in 1969. Tonka bought the rights in 1973, but the dolls they produced sold poorly. After a series of other owners, Dakin purchased the rights in 1986 and began producing a vinyl doll that resembled the 1950-style Ginny very closely. For more information, we recommend *Collector's Encyclopedia of Vogue Dolls* by Judith Izen and Carol Stover (Collector Books).

Baby Too Dear, vinyl, open mouth w/2 teeth, 1963-65, NM............**350.00**
Fairy Godmother, Meyer's Collectibles, 1986, M ...........................**210.00**
Ginny, black, hard plastic, 1953-54, all original, 8", EX, minimum value ...............................**600.00**
Jill, all original, complete, EX .....**100.00**
Li'l Imp, hard plastic, orange wig, freckles, 1960, 8", NM.....**400.00**

## Doorstops

Doorstops, once called door porters, were popular from the Civil War period until after 1930. They were used to prop the doors open during the hot summer months so that the cooler air could circulate. Though some were made of brass, wood, and chalk, cast iron was by far the most preferred material, usually molded in amusing figurals — dogs, flower baskets, frogs, etc. Hubley was one of the largest producers. Beware of reproductions! All of the examples in the listing that follows are made of cast iron and are priced relative to the conditon code in the description. See Clubs and Newsletters for information concerning the Doorstop Collectors of America.

Bathing Beauties, 2 under umbrella, Fish, Hubley, 10⅞x 5¼", VG+..**770.00**

Boston Terrier, stands w/head to left, Hubley, 10x10", EX .**110.00**

Bulldog, head slightly turned, Hubley, 4⅝ x 5½", NM ..........**660.00**

Cape Cod, ocean-side cottage, Hubley, 5½ x 7¾", M ..............**245.00**

Colonial Pilgrim, 2-sided, pointing left, 8¾ x5⅜", NM ..........**410.00**

Cottage w/flowers along walls & doorway, Hubley, 5¾ x 7½", EX ..**135.00**

Dancing Girl, holds skirt wide, joyous look, 9", VG ...............**110.00**

**Fisch Footman, worn paint, G-, $240.00.**

Flower Basket, Hubley #475, 7¼ x 7", M .................................**385.00**

Fox Terrier, stands w/head to right, 8", EX ...............................**190.00**

Fruit (assorted) in basket, Albany, 10⅛x7½", M ....................**355.00**

Geese (3 facing left), Fred Everett, Hubley, 8x8", EX ............**660.00**

Highland Lighthouse, keeper's home beside, 9 x 7¾", M ..........**4,125.00**

Jack (child's game pc), red pnt, 4¾", NM ...................................**250.00**

Lighthouse Atop Cliffs, gold w/red & green, 7½", EX ................**650.00**

Little Miss Muffet, on tuffet, 7¾", EX ....................................**155.00**

Major Domo, CJO #1240, 8⅜x5⅛", EX+ ...................................**110.00**

Man Walking w/Cane, wedge-style stopper, #1256, 7⅜", NM..**2,750.00**

Modernistic Dog, Deco style, Hubley, 11x4¾", EX ...............**440.00**

Old Woman, w/flowers & umbrella, Bradley & Hubbard, 11x7", EX..**65.00**

Pansy Bowl, realistic, Hubley, 7 x 6½", NM ...........................**330.00**

Parrot in Ring, heavy base, Bradley & Hubley 428B, 13¾", M..**250.00**

Pirate Girl, drawn sword, 13¾", NM..**165.00**

Poppies in Clay Pot, Hubley #330, 7x6", NM ..........................**300.00**

Red Riding Hood, wolf at side, Nuydea, 7½ x 9½", M ..........**3,850.00**

Russian Wolfhound, hole in collar for chain leash, 7¾ x12", EX ..**360.00**

Senorita, hand on hip, 2nd w/flower basket, 11¼ x 7", NM .....**660.00**

Sunbonnet Girl, profile facing right, 8¾", M ..............................**165.00**

Woman w/Hat, dramatic pose, 6⅜x4⅛", M ..........................**85.00**

Yawning Child, 1931 M-L-C Group NYC, 9x5", EX ..................**55.00**

Zinnias, Hubley #267, 7¼x 7", M ..**275.00**

# Dragon Ware

Dragon ware is fairly accessible and still being made today. The new Dragon ware is distinguishable by the lack of detail in the dragon, which will appear flat.

Colors are primary, referring to background color, not the color of the dragon. New pieces are shinier than old. New colors include green, lavender, yellow, pink, blue, pearlized, and orange as well as the classic blue/black. Many cups have lithophanes in the bottom. Nude lithophanes are found but are scarce. New pieces may have lithophanes; but again, these tend to be without detail and flat.

Items listed below are unmarked unless noted otherwise. Ranges are given for pieces that are currently being produced. Be sure to examine unmarked items well; in particular, look for good detail. Newer pieces lack the quality of workmanship evident in earlier items and should not command the prices of the older ware. Use the low end to evaluate any item you feel may be new.

Ashtray, blue, ¾", from $7.50 to ......**12.50**
Ashtray, gray w/gold, ball form, Made in Japan, 2¼ x 4", from $40 to ................................**55.00**
Casserole, black w/gold handle, w/lid, Made in Japan, 9", from $75 to ...............................**125.00**
Cup & saucer, coffee; blue, Dianan, from $25 to.........................**45.00**
Cup & saucer, demitasse; orange cloud, Made in Occupied Japan, from $20 to........................**25.00**

Dutch shoe, gray, from $20 to .....**30.00**
Ice bucket, black, rattan handle, M-over-wreath mark, 8", from $75 to ......................................**125.00**
Pitcher, yellow, Made in Japan, miniature, 2⅞", from $15 to............**25.00**
Planter, gray, hanging, Hand Painted Japan, 6", from $75 to..........**125.00**
Planter, orange, w/frog, Made in Japan, 5½", from $30 to .......**75.00**
Plate, blue cloud, 7¼", from $20 to .**25.00**
Saki set, blue cloud, Orient China Japan, from $50 to ............**75.00**
Saki set, white, whistling, Hand Painted Japan, 5-pc, from $75 to ......................................**125.00**
Salt & pepper shakers, black, pr in boat-shaped holder, from $35 to..**45.00**
Salt & pepper shakers, gray, unmarked, pr from $20 to.....................**25.00**
Table lighter, black, from $50 to.....**75.00**
Tea set, demitasse; white pearl, Japan, 17-pc, from $75 to..**125.00**
Tea set, gray, gold trim, 1940s-50s, 7½", pot, creamer & sugar bowl..**65.00**
Teapot, green cloud, 8x3", from $35 to ......................................**50.00**
Tidbit tray, gray, Nippon, 9 x 6½", from $100 to ...................**175.00**
Vase, aqua, Deco style, Made in Japan, 10¼", from $100 to ..........**175.00**
Vase, gray, yellow or orange, 4¼", set of 3 from $30 to............**60.00**

**Vase, moriage Golden Gate Bridge on back, 5", from $25.00 to $50.00.**

Vase, orange, 4", from $20 to......**50.00**
Wall pocket, blue/orange lustre, Japan flower mark, 7", from $25 to .......................................**50.00**
Wall pocket, orange, Made in Japan, 9", from $50 to ...................**75.00**

# Egg Timers

The origin of the figural egg timer appears to be Germany, circa 1920s or 1930s, with Japan following their lead in the 1940s. Some American companies may have begun producing figural timers at about the same time, but evidence is scarce in terms of pottery marks or company logos.

Figural timers can be found in a wide range of storybook characters (Oliver Twist), animals (pigs, ducks, rabbits), career and vocational uniformed people (chef, London Bobby, housemaid), or people in native costume.

All types of timers were a fairly uniform height of 3" to 4". If a figural timer no longer has its sand tube, it can be recognized by the hole which usually goes through the back of the figure or the stub of a hand. Most timers were made of ceramic (china or bisque), but a few are of cast iron and carved wood. They can be detailed or quite plain. Listings below are for timers with their sand tubes completely intact.

Bellhop on phone, Japan, 3" ....**50.00**
Black chef standing w/frying pan, chalkware, Japan............**125.00**

Bobby policeman, black outfit, Germany ................................**125.00**
Bobby policeman, blue outfit, Japan..**95.00**
Boy skiing, Germany, 3" ........**125.00**
Boy w/black cloak & cane, Germany, 3¾" ....................................**125.00**

Boy with red tie, Germany, from $75.00 to $100.00.

Bunny rabbit, floppy ears, timer in mouth, Japan ....................**60.00**
Cat standing by base of grandfather clock, Germany, 4¾".........**125.00**
Chef holding lg orange egg, 3¼".....**95.00**
Chicken, wings hold tube, Germany, 2¾" ....................................**125.00**

Chimney Sweep, Germany, $75.00; Maid, German, timer in left hand, $70.00. (Photo courtesy Jeannie Greenfield)

Geisha, Germany, 4½" ..........**125.00**
Goebel, double roosters, various colors, Germany, 4"..............**125.00**

Kitten w/ball of yarn, chalkware .....**50.00**
Mrs Santa Claus, timer sits on bag
next to her .........................**75.00**
Musician boy playing guitar, Ger-
many, 3½" .........................**195.00**
Sailboat, lustre, Germany......**100.00**
Sea gull, lustre, Germany........**65.00**
Windmill w/dog on base, Japan, 3¾"...**75.00**

# 8-Track Tapes and Players

What CDs are to this genera-
tion, 8-tracks were to the youth of
the '60s and '70s. Not only the tapes
themselves but the players as well
are now collectible. Just watch for
signs of aging and wear. Condition
is extremely important.

Case, Tempo, Hagerstown Leather Goods
#5138, holds 24, sealed, M ........**25.00**
Player, Fisher ER-8110, NMIB .....**90.00**
Player, Motorola Model RV400, for
automobile, MIB..............**120.00**
Player/recorder, Akai GXR-82-D,
EX ....................................**190.00**
Player/recorder, Pioneer Model H-
R99, EX............................**150.00**
Tape, AC/DC, Back in Black, EX .....**20.00**
Tape, Aerosmith, Toys in the Attic,
EX ....................................**50.00**
Tape, Bad Finger, Straight Up, EX.**15.00**
Tape, Black Ivory, Don't Turn
Around, sealed, M ............**50.00**
Tape, Black Sabbath, Paranoid, EX..**35.00**
Tape, Brownsville Station, Yeah,
1973, sealed, M..................**15.00**
Tape, Creedence Clearwater Revival,
Pendulum, 1970, EX.............**15.00**
Tape, David Bowie, Diamond Dogs,
1974, EX ..........................**13.00**

Tape, Doobie Brothers, What Were
Once Vices Are Now Habits,
sealed, M............................**17.50**
Tape, Doors, 13, 1970, EX........**15.00**
Tape, double; KISS, Alive II, Casablanca
7076, sealed, M.....................**25.00**
Tape, double; Paul McCartney,
Wings Over America, 1976,
sealed, M............................**30.00**
Tape, Eagles, On the Border, EX.....**15.00**
Tape, Guess Who, Power in the
Music, 1975, sealed, M......**20.00**
Tape, Jackson 5, Boogie, Motown,
1974, sealed, M................**150.00**
Tape, Jim Croce, Photographs &
Memories: His Greatest Hits,
EX ....................................**20.00**
Tape, Kinks, Muswell Hillbillies, EX..**15.00**
Tape, KISS, Love Gun, sealed, M.**13.50**
Tape, Lou Reed, Transformer, EX
w/sleeve..............................**17.50**
Tape, New Riders of the Purple Sage,
Powerglide, sealed, M ........**135.00**
Tape, Pat Travers, Heat in the Street,
Polydir, 1978, sealed, M......**25.00**
Tape, Pink Floyd, Animals, Colum-
bia, 1977, EX ....................**25.00**

**Tape, Pretenders,
1980, EX, $12.00.**

Tape, Santana's Greatest Hits, Columbia
33050, 1974, EX ..................**45.00**

Tape, Steve Miller Band, The Joker, EX ......................................**45.00**

Tape, Three Dog Night, Coming Down Your Way, EX .........**25.00**

Tape, Van Morrison, Wavelength, sealed, M...........................**13.50**

Tape, ZZ Top, Tres Hombres, w/sleeve, EX ......................**35.00**

# Elegant Glass

To quote Gene Florence, Elegant glassware 'refers mostly to hand-worked, acid-etched glassware that was sold by better department and jewelry stores during the Depression era through the 1950s, differentiating it from dime store and give-away glass that has become known as Depression glass.' Cambridge, Duncan & Miller, Fostoria, Heisey, Imperial, Morgantown, New Martinsville, Paden City, Tiffin, U.S. Glass, and Westmoreland were major producers. For further information we recommend *Elegant Glassware of the Depression Era,* by Gene and Cathy Florence (Collector Books).

## Cambridge

Apple Blossom, bowl, cereal; crystal, 6" ........................................**35.00**

Apple Blossom, comport, fruit cocktail; yellow or amber, 4" .....**28.00**

Apple Blossom, pitcher, pink or green, #3130, 64-oz .........**350.00**

Apple Blossom, platter, crystal, 11½" ....................................**55.00**

Candlelight, bonbon, crystal, footed, w/handles, #3900/130, 10" ..**40.00**

Candlelight, stem, wine; crystal, #3776, 3½-oz......................**65.00**

Candlelight, vase, keyhole; crystal, footed, #1238, 12" ............**150.00**

Caprice, bowl, crystal, crimped, 4-footed, #61, 12½" ...............**40.00**

Caprice, cigarette box, blue or pink, w/lid, #208, 4½ x 3½"..........**75.00**

Caprice, vase, ball; crystal, #237, 4½" .....................................**75.00**

Chantilly, creamer, crystal ......**18.00**

Chantilly, saucer, crystal...........**4.00**

Chantilly, syrup, crystal ........**225.00**

Cleo, bowl, blue, oval, 11½" ......**125.00**

Cleo, mayonnaise, pink, green, yellow or amber, footed..........**45.00**

Cleo, tumbler, blue, footed, #3077, 5-oz ........................................**60.00**

Daffodil, celery, crystal, #248, 11" ..**65.00**

Daffodil, plate, crystal, #1174.....**30.00**

Daffodil, salt & pepper shakers, crystal, squat, #360, pr .....**65.00**

Decagon, bowl, cereal; pastel colors, belled, 6" ............................**10.00**

Decagon, ice bucket, blue.........**75.00**

Decagon, salt cellar, pastel colors, footed, 1½" .........................**25.00**

Diane, bottle, bitters; crystal.....**175.00**

Diane, cabinet flask, crystal .....**295.00**

Diane, pitcher, crystal, Doulton.....**350.00**

Diane, vase, globe; crystal, 5" .....**75.00**

Elaine, candlestick, crystal, 5" ...**35.00**

Elaine, plate, salad; crystal, 8"......**22.00**

Elaine, stem, wine; crystal, #3104, 3-oz....................................**150.00**

Gloria, bowl, cranberry; green, pink or yellow, 3½" ....................**75.00**

Gloria, icer, crystal, w/ice insert.......**65.00**

Gloria, vase, crystal, squarish top, 10" .....................................**150.00**

Marjorie, comport, crystal, #4004, 5" ........................................**35.00**

Marjorie, stem, cocktail; crystal, #3750, 3½-oz......................**25.00**

Marjorie, tumbler, whiskey; crystal, #7606, 1½-oz......................**25.00**

Mt Vernon, ashtray, amber or crystal, #68, 4"..........................**12.00**

Mt Vernon, mug, stein; amber or crystal, #84, 14-oz .............**30.00**

Number 520, bottle, oil; Peach Blo or green, #193..................**175.00**

Number 520, butter dish, Peach Blo or green, w/lid..................**195.00**

Number 520, saucer, Peach Blo or green, #933 ..........................**7.00**

Number 704, bowl, soup; all colors, 8½"......................................**30.00**

Number 704, celery tray, all colors, #652, 11" ............................**45.00**

Number 704, plate, all colors, 8".....**15.00**

Portia, bowl, crystal, flared, 4-footed, 10" ................................**50.00**

Portia, mayonnaise, crystal, w/liner & ladle ...............................**65.00**

Portia, vase, flower; crystal, 13".......**150.00**

Rosalie, bowl, blue, pink or green, 11"......................................**75.00**

Rosalie, platter, amber or crystal, 15" ....................................**100.00**

Rosalie, relish, blue, pink or green, 2-part, 11"..........................**50.00**

Rose Point, bell, dinner; crystal, #3121 .............................**150.00**

Rose Point, bowl, crystal, #1398, 13"....................................**150.00**

Rose Point, cheese dish, w/lid, #980, 5"....................................**625.00**

Tally Ho, cheese & cracker, amber or crystal, 17½" .................**70.00**

Tally Ho, goblet, cordial; Carmen or Royal ...................................**50.00**

Tally Ho, plate, finger bowl; Forest Green ...............................**12.50**

**Tally Ho, stem, luncheon; red with crystal foot, 10 ounce, $22.00; tumbler, red with crystal foot, 12 ounce, $20.00.** (Photo courtesy Gene and Cathy Florence)

Valencia, bowl, crystal, #1402/82, 10" ....................................**45.00**

Valencia, relish, crystal, 3-compartment, #1402/91, 8".............**60.00**

Valencia, tumbler, crystal, footed, #3500, 16-oz......................**30.00**

Wildflower, butter dish, crystal, #3900/52, ¼-lb .................**225.00**

Wildflower, plate, crescent salad; crystal .............................**185.00**

## Duncan and Miller

**Canterbury, mayonnaise, crystal, three-piece set, $45.00.**

Canterbury No 115, bowl, fruit nappy, crystal......................**8.00**

Canterbury No 115, candleholder, crystal, low, 3", ea .............**12.50**

Canterbury No 115, salt & pepper shakers, crystal, pr............**22.50**

Canterbury No 115, top hat, crystal, 3" ........................................**18.00**

Caribbean, bowl, salad; crystal, 9"..**30.00**

Caribbean, ice bucket, blue, w/handles, 6½" ...........................**195.00**

Caribbean, plate, torte; blue, 16"..**110.00**

First Love, candle, crystal, #115, 3½" .....................................**25.00**

First Love, nappy, crystal, w/handles, #111, 1¾ x6"..............**22.00**

First Love, tray, celery; #91, 11".....**40.00**

Lily of the Valley, ashtray, crystal, 3" ........................................**25.00**

Lily of the Valley, mayonnaise liner, crystal ...............................**15.00**

Lily of the Valley, plate, crystal, 9"...**45.00**

Nautical, candy jar, blue, w/lid.....**550.00**

Nautical, comport, opalescent, 7"..**595.00**

Nautical, creamer, crystal .......**15.00**

Sandwich, basket, crystal, w/loop handle, 11½"....................**250.00**

Sandwich, butter dish, crystal, w/lid, ¼ lb .....................................**60.00**

Sandwich, relish, crystal, 3-part, 12".**45.00**

Tear Drop, comport, crystal, footed, 4¾" .....................................**12.00**

Tear Drop, plate, lazy Susan; crystal, 18"...............................**75.00**

Tear Drop, sugar bowl, crystal, 6-oz..**6.00**

Terrace, cheese stand, crystal or amber, 3 x 5¼"...................**25.00**

Terrace, plate, cracker; cobalt or red, w/ring, w/handles, 11" .......**110.00**

## Fostoria

For more information we recommend *The Fostoria Value Guide* by Milbra Long & Emily Seate, published by Collector Books.

American, bowl, crystal, cupped, 4½ x 7" .....................................**55.00**

American, bowl, rose; crystal, 5"..**30.00**

**American, candlestick, crystal, two-light, bell base, 6½", $120.00. (Photo courtesy Gene and Cathy Florence)**

American, tray, crystal, rectangular, 2½ x 5" ...............................**80.00**

Brocade, bonbon, crystal, #2375..**30.00**

Brocade, comport, blue, twist stem, #2327, 7" ...........................**75.00**

Brocade, vase, crystal, scalloped rim, #4105, 6" ....................**65.00**

Colony, bowl, crystal, oval, 10½"..**60.00**

Colony, lamp, electric; crystal ..**175.00**

Colony, vase, cornucopia; crystal, 9" ........................................**85.00**

Fairfax, bowl, soup; rose, blue, orchid, 7"............................**60.00**

Fairfax, nut cup, amber, blown..**22.00**

Fairfax, platter, green or topaz, oval, 12" ............................**45.00**

Fuchsia, cup, crystal, #2440 ....**20.00**

Fuchsia, plate, dinner; crystal, #2440, 9" ...........................**67.50**

Fuchsia, stem, cordial; Wisteria, #6004, ¾-oz......................**175.00**

Hermitage, ashtray, crystal, #2449..**3.00**

Hermitage, mug, azure, footed, #2449, 9-oz........................**15.00**

Hermitage, vase, Wisteria, footed, 6"......................................**22.00**

June, creamer, crystal, footed .....**15.00**

June, whipped cream pail, topaz ................................**195.00**

Kashmir, bowl, fruit; yellow or green, 5"..............................**13.00**

Kashmir, plate, dinner; blue, 10"..**70.00**

Kashmir, stem, wine; blue, 2½-oz ................................**60.00**

Lafayette, bowl, cereal; crystal or amber, 6"............................**20.00**

Lafayette, bowl, relish; Wisteria, 3-part, 7½"........................**110.00**

Lafayette, platter, rose, green or topaz, 12" ..........................**52.50**

Navarre, bell, dinner; crystal .....**75.00**

Navarre, bowl, crystal, flared, #2496, 12" ..........................**75.00**

Navarre, pickle, crystal, #2440, 8½"......................................**32.50**

New Garland, bowl, baker; amber or topaz, 10" ..........................**35.00**

New Garland, platter, rose, 1 2"........................................**45.00**

New Garland, vase, rose, 8".....**85.00**

Rogene, almond, crystal, footed, #4095...................................**8.00**

Rogene, plate, crystal, 8"..........**15.00**

Rogene, plate, salad; crystal, #2283, 7" ......................................**10.00**

Royal, bowl, baker; amber or green, oval, #2350, 9" ...................**45.00**

Royal, candy dish, amber or green, w/lid, 3-part, #2331 ..........**85.00**

Royal, plate, chop; amber or green, #2350, 15" ..........................**60.00**

Seville, creamer, amber, footed, #2350½..............................**12.50**

Seville, plate, luncheon; green, #2350, 8½" ..........................**6.50**

Seville, urn, amber, #2292, 8" .....**75.00**

Sun Ray, decanter, crystal, w/stopper, 18-oz ..........................**75.00**

Sun Ray, pitcher, crystal, w/ice lip, 64-oz................................**115.00**

Sun Ray, vase, sweet pea; crystal..**75.00**

Trojan, bowl, soup; rose, #2375, 7".....................................**125.00**

**Trojan, ice bucket, topaz, #2375, $990.00. (Photo courtesy Gene and Cathy Florence)**

Trojan, sauce boat, topaz, #2375 ...............................**105.00**

Trojan, saucer, rose, #2375........**8.00**

Versailles, bowl, soup; pink or green, #2375, 7"...............**110.00**

Versailles, comport, blue, #2375, 7½" ....................................**95.00**

Versailles, vase, yellow, #2417, 8" ................................**225.00**

Vesper, candlestick, green, #2394, 3"........................................**23.00**

Vesper, egg cup, amber, #2350..**45.00**

Vesper, stem, water goblet; blue, #5093................................**55.00**

## Heisey

For more information, we recommend *Heisey Glass, 1896 – 1957*, by Neila & Tom Bredehoft, published by Collector Books.

Charter Oak, bowl, finger; crystal, #3362....................................**10.00**

**Charter Oak, cup and saucer, #1231 Yeoman, Flamingo, $25.00.** (Photo courtesy Gene and Cathy Florence)

Charter Oak, pitcher, Flamingo, flat, #3362.........................**160.00**

Charter Oak, tumbler, Moongleam, flat, #3362, 12 oz. .................**25.00**

Chintz, bowl, mint; crystal, footed, 6" .........................................**20.00**

Chintz, grapefruit, Sahara, footed, Duquesne, #3389...............**60.00**

Chintz, stem, sherbet; crystal, #3389, 5-oz..........................**10.00**

Crystolite, ashtray, crystal, 4½" sq.........................................**10.00**

Crystolite, cigarette holder, crystal, oval.....................................**25.00**

Crystolite, plate, sandwich; crystal, 12" .........................................**45.00**

Ipswich, bowl, finger; crystal, w/underplate .....................**40.00**

Ipswich, candy jar, pink, w/lid, ½-lb..**325.00**

Ipswich, pitcher, green, ½-gal.....**750.00**

Lariat, bowl, nappy; crystal, 7".....**20.00**

Lariat, creamer, crystal ...........**20.00**

Lariat, plate, cookie; crystal, 11".....**35.00**

Minuet, bowl, salad dressing; crystal, 7"...................................**40.00**

Minuet, cup, crystal .................**30.00**

Minuet, vase, crystal, #4192, 10"..**110.00**

New Era, bowl, floral; crystal, 11"...**35.00**

New Era, stem, claret; crystal, 4-oz..**18.00**

New Era, sugar bowl, crystal.....**37.50**

Octagon, bowl, jelly; crystal, #1229, 5½" .....................................**15.00**

Octagon, bowl, vegetable; Flamingo, 9" .......................................**32.00**

Octagon, tray, celery; Sahara, 9"..**20.00**

Old Colony, comport, Sahara, footed, oval, 7" ...............................**80.00**

Old Colony, pitcher, Sahara, #3390, 3-pt...................................**230.00**

Old Colony, vase, Sahara, footed, 9"...**150.00**

Old Sandwich, beer mug, crystal, 14-oz...................................**55.00**

Old Sandwich, cup, Flamingo......**40.00**

Old Sandwich, parfait, Moongleam, 8-oz...................................**38.00**

Pleat & Panel, bowl, chow chow; crystal, 4"..............................**6.00**

Pleat & Panel, pitcher, Flamingo, 3-pt .....................................**140.00**

Pleat & Panel, vase, Moongleam, 8" .......................................**100.00**

Provincial, ashtray, crystal, 3" sq....................................**12.50**

Provincial, bowl, nappy; Limelight Green, 5½" .........................**40.00**

Provincial, stem, crystal, 10-oz..**20.00**

Queen Ann, bonbon, crystal, 6"..**30.00**

Queen Ann, comport, crystal, 6" sq....................................**40.00**

Queen Ann, platter, crystal, 14"..**30.00**

Ridgeleigh, bowl, floral; crystal, 10" .......................................**45.00**

Ridgeleigh, plate, salver; crystal, 14" .......................................**50.00**

Ridgeleigh, stem, oyster cocktail; crystal, blown, 4-oz...........**30.00**

Saturn, bowl, baked apple; crystal..**25.00**

Saturn, bowl, whipped cream; Zircon or Limelight, 5".........**150.00**

Saturn, plate, crystal, 6" ............**5.00**

Stanhope, bowl, salad; crystal, 11"..**90.00**

Stanhope, plate, crystal, 7"......**20.00**

Stanhope, vase, ball; crystal, 7" ..**100.00**

Twist, bowl, floral; crystal, 9".....**25.00**

Twist, claret, Flamingo, 4-oz ...**30.00**

Twist, tumbler, soda; Marigold, footed, 5-oz ..............................**36.00**

Victorian, bowl, rose; crystal .....**90.00**

Victorian, plate, sandwich; crystal, 13" .....................................**90.00**

Victorian, vase, crystal, footed, 6"..**100.00**

## Imperial

Cape Cod, bowl, crystal, #160/7F, 8¾" ....................................**30.00**

Cape Cod, bowl, crystal, #160/75B, 12" .....................................**40.00**

Cape Cod, candleholder, crystal, Aladdin style, #160/90, 4", ea.....................................**150.00**

Cape Cod, creamer, crystal, #160/30..**8.00**

Cape Cod, egg cup, crystal, #160/225.....................................**32.50**

**Cape Cod, epergne, crystal, #160/196, 12", $265.00.**

Cape Cod, fork, crystal, #160/701 ..**12.00**

Cape Cod, ladle, punch; crystal.....**25.00**

Cape Cod, plate, butter; crystal, #160/34, 4½" ........................**8.00**

Cape Cod, puff box, crystal, w/lid, #1601................................**50.00**

Cape Cod, salt spoon, crystal, #1600..**8.00**

Cape Cod, sugar bowl, crystal, footed, #160/31.........................**15.00**

Cape Cod, tumbler, crystal, #160, 16-oz.................................**35.00**

Cape Cod, vase, crystal, #160/22, 6¼"...**35.00**

Cape Cod, vase, crystal, footed, #160/21, 11½" ....................**70.00**

## Morgantown

**Golf Ball, candlestick, Spanish Red with clear foot, $175.00.**
(Photo courtesy Gene and Cathy Florence)

Golf Ball, creamer, green or red ..**175.00**

Golf Ball, pilsner, green or red, 11-oz, 9⅛"..............................**175.00**

Golf Ball, stem, water; green or red, 9-oz, 6¾" ............................**50.00**

Queen Louise, bowl, finger; crystal w/pink, footed .................**225.00**

Queen Louise, stem, cocktail; crystal w/pink, 3-oz .....................**375.00**

Queen Louise, stem, water; crystal w/pink, 9-oz .....................**400.00**

Sunrise Medallion, cup, crystal ..**40.00**

Sunrise Medallion, pitcher, blue ..**595.00**

Sunrise Medallion, vase, pink or green, bulbous bottom, 10" ........**350.00**

Tinkerbell, bowl, finger; azure or
green, footed .....................**100.00**
Tinkerbell, stem, goblet; azure or
green, 9-oz ........................**150.00**
Tinkerbell, stem, wine; azure or
green, 2½-oz ....................**135.00**

## New Martinsville

Janice, basket, crystal, 9 x 6½".....**75.00**
Janice, ice tub, blue or red, footed,
6" .....................................**265.00**

**Janice, salad plate, red,
#4579, 8½", $17.50. (Photo cour-
tesy Gene and Cathy Florence)**

Janice, saucer, blue or red .........**4.50**
Meadow Wreath, bowl, crystal,
crimped, flat, 13" ...............**50.00**
Meadow Wreath, bowl, crystal,
flared, flat, 10" ...................**35.00**
Meadow Wreath, vase, crystal,
flared, #42/26, 10" .............**50.00**

## Paden City

Black Forest, batter jug, crystal ..**250.00**
Black Forest, bowl, console; amber,
11" .....................................**95.00**
Black Forest, ice bucket, black...**225.00**
Black Forest, plate, luncheon; green
or pink, 8" ..........................**40.00**
Gazebo, cake stand, crystal .....**65.00**
Gazebo, creamer, crystal..........**22.50**

Gazebo, mayonnaise liner, blue..**225.00**
Gazebo, vase, blue, 10¼"........**195.00**

## Tiffin

Cadena, bowl, cream soup; crystal ..**25.00**
Cadena, plate, pink or yellow, 6"..**12.00**
Cadena, sugar bowl, crystal.....**20.00**
Cherokee Rose, bowl, finger; crystal,
5" .......................................**30.00**
Cherokee Rose, stem, sherry; crys-
tal, 2-oz .............................**35.00**
Cherokee Rose, vase, crystal, flared,
12" ...................................**135.00**
Classic, cheese & cracker set,
crystal ..............................**100.00**
Classic, pitcher, pink, 61-oz .....**495.00**
Classic, vase, bud; crystal ........**27.50**
Flanders, celery, crystal, 11"......**40.00**
Flanders, plate, dinner; pink,
10¼"................................**125.00**
Flanders, tumbler, yellow, footed,
10-oz, 4¾" .........................**30.00**
Fontaine, cup, amber, green or pink,
#8869..................................**60.00**
Fontaine, plate, Twilight, #8818, 10"..**145.00**
Fontaine, stem, water; amber, green
or pink, #033.....................**55.00**
Fuchsia, bitters bottle, crystal ..**450.00**
Fuchsia, nut dish, crystal, 6¼" ..**40.00**
Fuchsia, tumbler, juice; crystal, flat,
4¾" ...................................**35.00**
Julia, creamer, amber .............**35.00**
Julia, stem cocktail; amber ......**25.00**
Julia, tumbler, tea; amber, footed ..**30.00**
June Night, bowl, salad; crystal,
deep, 10" ...........................**70.00**
June Night, stem, wine; crystal, 3
½-oz...................................**27.50**
June Night, table bell, crystal ..**85.00**
Jungle Assortment, bowl, center-
piece; #320 ........................**55.00**

Jungle Assortment, night cap set, #6712 ..............................**100.00**

Jungle Assortment, vase, wall; #320...**75.00**

Psyche, bonbon, crystal w/green stem ...................................**65.00**

Psyche, stem, claret; crystal w/green stem ...................................**65.00**

Psyche, vase, bud; crystal w/green stem ...............................**125.00**

# Elvis Presley Memorabilia

The king of rock 'n roll, the greatest entertainer of all time (and not many would disagree with that), Elvis remains just as popular today as he was in the height of his career. Over the past few years, values for Elvis collectibles have skyrocketed. The early items marked 'Elvis Presley Enterprises' bearing a 1956 or 1957 date are the most valuable. Paper goods such as magazines, menus from Las Vegas hotels, ticket stubs, etc., make up a large part of any Elvis collection and are much less expensive. His 45s were sold in abundance, so unless you find an original Sun label, a colored vinyl or a promotional cut, or EPs in wonderful condition, don't pay much! The picture sleeves are usually worth much more than the record itself! Albums are very collectible, and even though you see some stiff prices on them at antique malls, there's not many you can't buy for well under $25.00 at any Elvis convention.

Remember, the early mark is 'Elvis Presley Enterprises'; the 'Box-car' mark was used from 1974 to 1977, and the 'Boxcar/Factors' mark from then until 1981. In 1982 the trademark reverted back to Graceland.

For more information, we recommend *Elvis Collectibles* and *Best of Elvis Collectibles* by Rosalind Cranor (Overmountain Press): see the Directory under Virginia for ordering information. Also available: *Elvis Presley Memorabilia* by Sean O'Neal (Schiffer).

Calendar, RCA, heavy stock, 1963, NM .....................................**55.00**

Cigarette lighters, 25th Anniversary of Death, Zippo, set of 4, MIB..**75.00**

Cookie jar, 1968 Comeback, Vandor, MIB .....................................**75.00**

Decanter, McCormick, 1978, Elvis Bust, no music box, 750 ml ......**75.00**

**Decanter, McCormick, 1978, Elvis '77, plays 'Love Me Tender,' 750 ml, from $120.00 to $125.00.**

Decanter, McCormick, 1979, Elvis '55, plays Loving You, 750 ml ....................................**150.00**

Decanter, McCormick, 1981, Aloha Elvis, plays Blue Hawaii, 750 ml ....................................**150.00**

Decanter, McCormick, 1983, Elvis Gold Mini, plays My Way, 50 ml, from $125 to ..............**150.00**

Decanter, McCormick, 1983, Sgt Elvis, plays GI Blues, 750 ml....**295.00**

Decanter, McCormick, 1984, Sgt Elvis Mini, plays GI Blues, 50 ml ......................................**95.00**

Doll, '68 Comeback, Hasbro, 1993, MIB ...................................**30.00**

Doll, gold suit, made by Gemmy, EPE, plays Blue Christmas, 19", MIB ...................................**65.00**

Doll, Phoenix Elvis, vinyl, World Doll Co, 21", MIB ..............**90.00**

Doll, white jumpsuit, Timeless Treasures, Mattel, NRFB.............**75.00**

Figurine, green-gold metallic glaze, Zsolnay, 15½", from $300 to .....................................**350.00**

Figurine, in white jumpsuit, Continental Studios, 1976, 13½", EX .....................................**18.00**

**Frisbee, Elvis The King of Rock 'N Roll, blue on yellow, M, $20.00.** (Photo courtesy Lee Garmon)

Guitar, toy; Rock 'N Roll & Elvis' image, Selcol, 1960s, 20", NMIB ..............................**650.00**

Handkerchief, w/guitar on white, 1956 ...............................**500.00**

Lobby card, Jailhouse Rock, 1956, 11x14", VG+.......................**75.00**

Lobby card, King Creole, 1958, 11x14", EX .........................**80.00**

Lobby card, Wild in the Country, 1961, 11x17", EX ...............**55.00**

Menu, Las Vegas Hilton, Summer Festival Menu '75, EX.....**465.00**

Music box, baby grand piano, plays Final Curtain, ca 1980, 6".**28.00**

Ornament, w/guitar, brass-plated, Hallmark, 1992, M (EX box)..**9.00**

Overnight bag, pink w/images overall, EPE, 1956, EX .........**135.00**

Photo folio tour book, 1957, 12 pages, 8x10", NM ...........**175.00**

Pinback, Don't Be Cruel, red, white & blue, ⅞" .........................**30.00**

Plate, '68 Comeback Special, Delphi, 1990, MIB .......................**30.00**

Plate, Heartbreak Hotel, Delphi, 1992, MIB .........................**35.00**

Postage stamps, full sheet of 29¢ stamps (40 total) ...............**55.00**

Postcard, close-up color portrait, early, Germany, NM ........**14.00**

Profile plaque, Clay Art, 10", from $150 to .............................**175.00**

Record, For LP Fans Only, Victor 1990, 1959, EX ................**130.00**

Salt & pepper shakers, blue suede shoes, Vandor, pr, MIB .....**25.00**

Sheet music, Hound Dog.........**55.00**

Song book, included w/the Love Me Tender guitar by Emenee, NM ..**80.00**

Suitcase, black & white photos overall, brown leather trim, 17x21", NM .....................................**70.00**

Ticket, Alabama & Mississippi Fair & Dairy Show, 1956, EX.........**80.00**

Ticket, Indiana State University, September 16, 1977, NM...........**30.00**

Ticket, Kemper Arena, Kansas City MO, June 18, 1977, unused..**135.00**
Tour book, Jail House Rock tour, 1956, 12 pages, 8x10", NM ...........**160.00**
Wallet, cream, red or turquoise vinyl, EPE, 1956, EX, from $575 to ......................................**600.00**

# Enesco

Enesco is an importing company based in Elk Grove, Illinois. They're distributors of ceramic novelties made for them in Japan. There are several lines styled around a particular character or group, and with the emphasis collectors currently place on figurals, they're finding these especially fascinating. During the 1960s, they sold a line of novelties originally called 'Mother-in-the Kitchen.' Today's collectors refer to them as 'Kitchen Prayer Ladies.' Ranging from large items such as canisters and cookie jars to toothpick holders and small picture frames, the line was fairly extensive. Some of the pieces are very hard to find, and those with blue dresses are much scarcer than those in pink. Where we've given ranges, pink is represented by the lower end, blue by the high side. If you find a white piece with blue trim, add another 10% to 20% to the high end.

Another Enesco line that has become very collectible is called 'Kitchen Independence.' It features George Washington with the Declaration of Independence scroll held at his side, and Betsy Ross wearing a blue dress and holding a large flag.

Both lines are pictured in *The Ultimate Collector's Encyclopedia of Cookie Jars* by Joyce and Fred Roerig. See also Cookie Jars.

Air freshener, Kitchen Prayer Lady.**90.00**
Bank, Dear God Kids (girl), 1982, from $40 to........................**50.00**
Bank, Guinness toucan, 8½ x 5½", MIB .....................................**85.00**
Bank, turtle, winking, 6¾ x 4½ x 4"...**50.00**
Bell, Kitchen Prayer Lady .......**75.00**

**Candy containers, Dear God Kids, 1983, from $40.00 to $50.00 each.**
(Photo courtesy Fred and Joyce Roerig)

Candy tin, Roly Poly, Cara Goldberg, 1983, 7 x 5½".....................**210.00**
Cookie jar, Kitchen Prayer Lady..**175.00**
Figurine, A Shoulder To Lean On, Friends of the Feather, 1999, NM .....................................**65.00**
Figurine, Allyris the Mermaid, Coral Kingdom, #533068, 1993....**50.00**
Figurine, bear wearing 5 of Hearts, Lucy & Me .........................**45.00**
Figurine, Bringing Home the Gifts, man carrying presents, #E-64005.................................**65.00**
Figurine, cheerleader bear, Lucy & Me, from $45 to ................**60.00**

Figurine, Ear, Nose & Throat Specialist, paper tag, 7½", NM..**65.00**

Figurine, Eggbert, chick emerging from egg w/boxing gloves on, 1989....................................**10.00**

Figurine, Eggbert Eggstractor, dentist, 1989, MIB ..................**20.00**

Figurine, Human Bean, flute player, 1981, 4½", from $10 to ............**15.00**

Figurine, mermaid w/treasure chest, fish, coral & jewels, 1994, 5"..**90.00**

Figurine, Miss Martha's Clean Clothes for Dolly, 1991......**60.00**

Figurine, Sisters & Best Friends, girls in washtub, #137111, MIB ....................................**45.00**

Figurines, Bar Hounds, dogs on bar stools drinking, 6", set of 6..**275.00**

Hors d'oeuvres holder, Snappy the Snail, 7 x 5½" ....................**65.00**

Jam jar, Winkin' Kitty, w/spoon & notched lid, 5½"..................**40.00**

Music box, Dream Keeper, animated, #562491, 9", MIB.......**210.00**

Music box, Eiffel Tower, animated, plays I Love Paris, 17¼", MIB..**110.00**

Music box, Majestic Ferris Wheel, animated, 16x10x11" ......**170.00**

Music box, mice playing on cash register, animated, 1991, from $150 to ............................**160.00**

Napkin holder, Kitchen Prayer Lady ....................................**20.00**

Nightlight, elephant figural, 1990, 4½ x 6" ..............................**30.00**

Ornament, Coca-Cola's Trunk Full of Treasures, M (EX box) ..**35.00**

Planter, Kitchen Prayer Lady....**90.00**

Ring holder, Kitchen Prayer Lady, from $65 to..........................**75.00**

Salt & pepper shakers, Kitchen Prayer Lady, pr ................**15.00**

Salt & pepper shakers, Siamese cats, #E3340, 4¼", NM, pr..**65.00**

Spoon rest, Kitchen Prayer Lady..**40.00**

String holder, Kitchen Prayer Lady ..**100.00**

Teapot, Kitchen Prayer Lady ..**85.00**

Teapot, Snappy the Snail, 7x8"..**55.00**

Teapot, Winkin' Kitty, 5¼" ......**90.00**

Vase, bud; Kitchen Prayer Lady ..**125.00**

Wall hanging, sea horse family: mom, dad & 2 babies, EX..**75.00**

# Ertl Banks

The Ertl company was founded in the mid-'40s by Fred Ertl, Sr., and until the early 1980s, they produced mainly farm tractors. In 1981 they made their first bank, the 1913 Model T Parcel Post Mail Service #9647; since then they've produced thousands of models with the logos of countless companies. The size of each run is dictated by the client and can vary from a few hundred up to several thousand. Some clients will later add a serial number to the vehicle; this is not done by Ertl. Other numbers that appear on the base of each bank are a four-number dating code (the first three indicate the day of the year up to 365, and the fourth number is the last digit of the year, '5' for 1995, for instance). The stock number is shown only on the box, never on the bank, so be sure to keep them in their original boxes. For more information, see *Schroeder's Collectible Toys, Antique to Modern* (Collector Books).

Ace Hardware, 1918 Ford Runabout Delivery Truck, M (EX box)..**270.00**

Ace Hardware, 1955 Chevrolet Cameo Pickup Truck, 1994, MIB ....................................**30.00**

Anheuser-Busch, Trolley Car, #2214, MIB ........................**40.00**

Bloomsburg Fair Association, 1931 Hawkeye Stake Truck, MIB..**55.00**

Boar's Head, 1925 Kenworth Truck, MIB ....................................**40.00**

Brinks Armored Truck, MIB......**55.00**

Budweiser, 1913 Ford Model T Truck, #1315, MIB ............**65.00**

Budweiser, 1931 Hawkeye Crate Truck, MIB ........................**45.00**

Budweiser, 1954 GMC Series 950 Tractor Trailer, MIB.......**115.00**

Budweiser, 8-Hitch Clydesdale Wagon, M (wood & plastic case).....**70.00**

**Campbell's Soup Harvest of Good Foods Produce Truck, #F603, 1987, MIB, $30.00.**

Champlin Oil, 1930 Diamond T Tanker, MIB ......................**55.00**

Dallas Cowboys, 1913 Ford Model T Delivery Van, MIB ............**90.00**

Denver & Ephrata PA Phone Co, 1932 Ford Panel Delivery, #9300, MIB ......................**35.00**

Eastwood Tanker Truck, 1930 Diamond 2½-ton model, MIB..**60.00**

Farmer's Almanac, 1913 Ford Model-T, 1991, 3¼ x 6", NM................**20.00**

Gulf Oil, 1925 Kenworth Wrecker, MIB ..................................**60.00**

Harley-Davidson, Horse & Wagon, MIB ..................................**125.00**

Jack Daniels, 1931 Hawkeye Crate Truck, #0151, MIB............**35.00**

Jim Beam, 1955 Chevy Cameo Pickup, MIB..............................**45.00**

John Deere, 1926 Mack Delivery Truck, MIB ........................**40.00**

Miller's Lite Beer, 1918 Ford Runabout Barrel Truck, MIB..**45.00**

Moorman Mfg Co, 1905 Ford Delivery Truck, M (EX box).......**60.00**

New Holland, 1912 Ford Open Front Panel Truck, Christmas 1993, MIB ..................................**30.00**

Philips 66, Horse & Tanker Wagon, #2095, MIB ......................**120.00**

Sohio Oil, 1926 Mack Tanker Truck, #9269, MIB ......................**80.00**

State Farm, 1926 Seagrave Fire Truck, MIB ........................**75.00**

Sun Oil, 1931 International Tanker Truck, MIB ........................**45.00**

Sunoco Oil, 1926 Mack Tanker Truck, #9795, blue & silver, MIB ...**85.00**

Sunray Oil, 1930 Diamond T Tanker Truck, MIB ........................**45.00**

Texaco, Wings of; Texaco Eaglet, glider, MIP........................**50.00**

Texaco, Wings of; 1827 Ford Tri-Motored Monoplane, MIB.**45.00**

Texaco, Wings of; 1929 Lockheed Air Express, #3801, MIB.......**100.00**

Texaco, Wings of; 1930 Travel Air Model R Mystery Ship, airplane, MIB ......................**220.00**

Texaco, 1905 Ford, #3277, MIB..**50.00**

Texaco, 1913 Model T Van, #2128, MIB ..............................**1,070.00**

Texaco, 1918 Ford Runabout, MIB..**45.00**

Texaco, 1925 Kenworth Stake Truck, #9385, MIB ............**60.00**

Texaco, 1926 Mack Bulldog Tanker, NM ...................................**150.00**

Texaco, 1927 Graham Panel Delivery Truck, #21320P, MIB .**70.00**

True Value, 1913 Ford Model T-Delivery Truck, M (NM box)......**105.00**

True Value, 1932 Ford Panel Delivery Truck, MIB...................**55.00**

True Value, 1948 Chevy Panel Delivery Truck, MIB.........**45.00**

Trustworthy, 1917 Ford Model T-Van, #9260, MIB .............**110.00**

University of Iowa, 1923 Chevy ½-Ton Truck, MIB.................**50.00**

University of KY, 1912 Ford Model T Delivery Van, MIB.........**95.00**

University of KY, 1930 Ford Roadster, MIB............................**65.00**

University of KY, 1951 Ford Pickup, MIB ...................................**45.00**

Wix Filters, 1957 Chevy Drag Car & Trailer, MIB ......................**70.00**

Wix Filters, 1959 El Camino w/1957 Chevy Drag Car w/Trailer, MIB ...................................**50.00**

# Fenton

The Fenton Art Glass Company, organized in 1906 in Martin's Ferry, Ohio, is noted for their fine art glass. Over one hundred thirty patterns of carnival glass were made in their earlier years, but even their newer glass is considered collectible. Only since 1970 have some of the pieces carried a molded-in logo; before then paper labels were used. For more information we recommend *Fenton Art Glass, 1907 to 1939*; *Fenton Art Glass Patterns, 1939 to 1980*; *Fenton*

*Art Glass Colors and Hand-Decorated Patterns*; and *Fenton Art Glass Hobnail Pattern,* all by Margaret and Kenn Whitmyer. Two of Fenton's later lines, Hobnail and Silver Crest, are shown in Gene and Cathy Florence's book called *Collectible Glassware from the 40s, 50s, and 60s.* All are published by Collector Books. See also Glass Animals; Glass, Porcelain, and Pottery Shoes. For information on Fenton Art Glass Collectors of America, see Clubs and Newsletters.

Apple Blossom, ashtray, 1960-61, from $35 to.........................**45.00**

Apple Blossom, basket, #7336, 1960-61, 6½" .............................**150.00**

Aqua Crest, bowl, double-crimped, #192, 1942-43, 10½", from $65 to.......................................**70.00**

Aqua Crest, plate, #7219, 1942-43, 6½" ......................................**15.00**

Aqua Crest, vase, tulip; triangular, #1924, 1942-43, 5", from $30 to.......................................**32.00**

Black Crest, tidbit tray, 2-tier, #7294, 1970s ....................**150.00**

Blue Crest, hurricane lamp, #7398, 1953-55............................**325.00**

Blue Ridge, basket, French opal spirals, #1923, ca 1939, 6", from $150 to............................**160.00**

Cactus, basket, topaz opal, 1959-60, 7", from $140 to ...............**160.00**

Cactus, creamer & sugar bowl, milk glass, w/lid, 1959-61, from $38 to.......................................**47.00**

Cactus, vase, milk glass, 1959-61, 9", from $10 to ...................**12.00**

Coin Dot, candleholder, blue opal, #1524, 1947-58, ea from $85 to...........**95.00**

Coin Dot, candleholder, French opal, #1524, 1947-54, ea..............**155.00**

Coin Dot, creamer, French opal, #33, 1948-49, from $45 to..............**55.00**

Coin Dot, jug, cranberry, crimped, 1947-52, 70-oz, from $295 to..**325.00**

Coin Dot, vase, blue opal, #189, 1947-52, 10", from $175 to..............**190.00**

Crystal Crest, basket, cone shape, #36, 1942, 8", from $145 to..............**165.00**

Crystal Crest, bowl, double-crimped, #1523, 13½"......................**110.00**

Daisy & Button, basket, Colonial Green, oval, 1965-73, from $10 to..........................................**12.00**

Daisy & Button, bootee, blue pastel, 1954-55, from $30 to............**35.00**

Daisy & Button, bowl, turquoise, cupped, 1955-56, 7", from $35 to..........................................**40.00**

Daisy & Button, candleholder, milk glass, 2-light, 1953-63, ea $18 to..........................................**20.00**

Daisy & Button, leaf ashtray, Colonial Amber, 1968-80, from $8 to..........................................**10.00**

Daisy & Button, vase, fan; green pastel, footed, 1954-56, 9", from $50 to..................................**60.00**

Diamond Lace, cake plate, blue opal, #1948-A, 1949-51, 11", $70 to..**90.00**

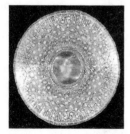

**Diamond Lace, cake plate, French opal with Aqua Crest, #1948, 1949 – 50, 14", from $100.00 to $125.00.** (Photo courtesy Margaret and Kenn Whitmyer)

Diamond Lace, comport, French opal w/Aqua Crest, #1948, from $100 to..............................**125.00**

Diamond Lace, vase, French opal, double-crimped, #1948, 6½", from $30 to........................**35.00**

Diamond Optic, bottle, ruby overlay, #192, 1942-49, 5½", from $55 to................................**65.00**

Diamond Optic, jug, Mulberry, #1353, 1942, 70-oz..........**450.00**

Diamond Optic, tumbler, ruby overlay, #1353, 1942-49, 10-oz, from $25 to................................**27.00**

Diamond Optic, vase, tulip; Mulberry, #192, 1942, 6"......................**70.00**

Emerald Crest, bonbon, double-crimped, #36, 1949-56, 5½", from $24 to........................**28.00**

Emerald Crest, bottle, oil; #680, 1950-55, from $185 to......**200.00**

Emerald Crest, sherbet, footed, #680/#7226, 1949-56.........**27.50**

**Emerald Crest, tulip vase, #711, 1949 – 52, 6", from $50.00 to $60.00.** (Photo courtesy Margaret and Kenn Whitmyer)

Emerald Snowcrest, vase, #4516, 1950-54, 8½", from $75 to..............**85.00**

Gold Crest, candleholder, 1963-65, ea from $35 to....................**40.00**

Gold Crest, tidbit, 2-tier, 1963-65, from $65 to........................**85.00**

Hobnail, banana bowl, topaz opal, 1959-60, from $195 to......**225.00**

Hobnail, basket, Colonial Amber, 1967-80+, from $25 to .......**35.00**

Hobnail, bell, French opal, 1978-81, 6", from $35 to ..................**45.00**

Hobnail, bonbon, green pastel, double-crimped, 1954-56, 6", from $12 to..................................**14.00**

Hobnail, bottle, cologne; topaz opal, 1941-44, from $140 to .......**150.00**

Hobnail, bowl, blue opal, double-crimped, 1941-55, 9"..........**40.00**

Hobnail, bowl, cranberry, oval, flared, 1940-44, 7", from $60 to.........................................**70.00**

Hobnail, bowl, milk glass, sq, 1954-61, 9", from $50 to...............**60.00**

Hobnail, cake plate, blue opal, footed, 1941-44, 12", from $125 to ..**145.00**

Hobnail, candy/butter bowl, Colonial Blue, 1970-80, from $20 to..**30.00**

Hobnail, comport, milk glass w/holly, double-crimped, 1973-74, 6"..**35.00**

Hobnail, creamer & sugar bowl, milk glass, w/lid, 1960-80+, from $20 to.........................**25.00**

**Hobnail, creamer and sugar bowl, rose pastel, #3906, 1954 – 57, from $25.00 to $35.00. (Photo courtesy Margaret and Kenn Whitmyer)**

Hobnail, decanter, cranberry opal, w/handle, 1941-50, from $500 to.........................................**600.00**

Hobnail, fairy light, custard, 1972-78, from $25 to...................**35.00**

Hobnail, jam & jelly, French opal, 1955-56, from $100 to......**115.00**

Hobnail, kettle, blue pastel, 1954-55, from $20 to....................**25.00**

Hobnail, nappy, green opal, double-crimped, 1940-41, 6", from $22 to.........................................**27.00**

Hobnail, relish, milk glass, chrome handle, 1970-80+, from $22 to.........................................**25.00**

Hobnail, slipper, blue marble, 1970-74, from $20 to...................**22.00**

Hobnail, syrup jug, Wild Rose, 1961-63, 12-oz, from $40 to ...........**50.00**

Hobnail, vase, Apple Green overlay, 1961-62, 11", from $90 to ...................................**100.00**

Hobnail, vase, fan; milk glass w/bluebells, 1973-71, 8½", from $85 to.................................**95.00**

Hobnail, vase, lime green opal, double-crimped, 1952-53, 6", from $80 to.................................**90.00**

Hobnail, vase, peach blow, double-crimped, 1952-56, 6", from $45 to.........................................**55.00**

Hobnail, vase, powder blue overlay, 1961-61, 11", from $90 to..**110.00**

Ivory Crest, vase, crimped, #186, 1940-42, 8½" .....................**35.00**

Laced Edge, bowl, banana; turquoise opaque, #9024, 1955-56......................................**52.50**

Laced Edge, plate, rose pastel #9018, 1954-55, 8" .............**18.00**

Peach Crest, basket, #201, 1940-47, 10" ....................................**155.00**

Peach Crest, bowl, double-crimped, #1522, 1940-70, 10", from $75 to.........................................**85.00**

Peach Crest, vase, tulip; #711, 1949-67, 6", from $40 to ...............**45.00**

Rose Crest, creamer, 1947-48, #1924, from $50 to.............**60.00**

Rose Crest, jug, 1946-48, #192-A, 9",
from $125 to......................**150.00**

Silver Crest, basket, Apple Blossom
decor, 1969-71, sm, from $65
to.........................................**75.00**

Silver Crest, plate, #680, 1948-60,
12", from $40 to .................**50.00**

Silver Crest, vase, double-crimped, #36,
1943-67, 4½", from $14 to .**16.00**

Silver Crest w/Spanish Lace, candy
box, 1965-80, from $65 to..**75.00**

Silver Rose, bowl, 1956-58, 7", from
$35 to..................................**45.00**

Spiral Optic, bowl, cranberry, crimped,
#1522, 1938-40, 10"........**100.00**

Spiral Optic, candy box, blue opal,
1979-80, from $75 to..........**85.00**

**Spiral Optic, pitcher,
blue opal, #3164, 1979
– 80, 44 ounce, from
$100.00 to $135.00.**
(Photo courtesy Margaret
and Kenn Whitmyer)

Spiral Optic, pitcher, cranberry, #187,
1938-40, from $400 to........**500.00**

Spiral Optic, top hat, green opal,
#1923, 1939, 6", from $60 to..**70.00**

Spiral Optic, vase, cameo opal, 1979-
80, 6½", from $30 to...............**35.00**

Violets in the Snow on Spanish
Lace, bell, 1974-80+, from $50
to.........................................**60.00**

# Fiesta

Since it was discontinued by
Homer Laughlin in 1973, Fiesta has
become one of the most popular collectibles on the market. Values have
continued to climb until some of the
more hard-to-find items now sell for
several hundred dollars each. In 1986
HLC reintroduced a line of new Fiesta. To date these colors have been
used: cobalt (darker than the original), rose (a strong pink), black, white,
apricot (very pale), yellow (a light
creamy tone), turquoise, sea mist (a
light mint green), lilac, persimmon,
periwinkle (country blue), sapphire
blue (very close to the original cobalt),
chartreuse (brighter), gray, juniper
(teal), cinnabar (maroon), sunflower
(yellow), plum (dark bluish-purple),
shamrock (similar to the coveted
medium green), tangerine, scarlet,
and peacock. There is a strong secondary market for limited edition and discontinued pieces and colors of the
post-86 Fiesta as well. When old
molds were used, the mark will be the
same, if it is a molded-in mark such as
on pitchers, sugar bowls, etc. The ink
stamp differs from the old — now all
the letters are upper case.

'Original colors' in the listings indicates values for three of the original six
colors — light green, turquoise, and yellow. The listing that follows is incomplete due to space restrictions; refer to
*The Collector's Encyclopedia of Fiesta*
by Sharon and Bob Huxford (Collector
Books) for more information. See also
Clubs and Newsletters for information
on *Fiesta Collector's Quarterly.*

Ashtray, yellow, light green or turquoise, from $35 to ......**50.00**

Bowl, covered onion soup; cobalt or ivory, from $600 to .........**675.00**

Bowl, cream soup; '50s colors, from $60 to.................................**75.00**

Bowl, dessert; red, cobalt or ivory, 6", from $40 to ...................**50.00**

Bowl, fruit; '50s colors, 5½", from $35 to.................................**40.00**

Bowl, fruit; red, cobalt or ivory, 4¾", from $25 to........................**30.00**

Bowl, individual salad; red, turquoise or yellow, 7½", from $80 to...**100.00**

Bowl, nappy; red, cobalt or ivory, 8½", from $45 to ................**50.00**

Bowl, salad; footed, yellow or light green, from $275 to .........**375.00**

Candleholders, bulb; yellow or light green, pr from $80 to .........**110.00**

Casserole, French; yellow, from $250 to.............................**300.00**

Coffeepot, light green or turquoise, from $180 to.....................**220.00**

Compote, sweets; red, cobalt, ivory or turquoise, from $125 to........**135.00**

Creamer, '50s colors, from $25 to..**30.00**

Creamer, red, cobalt or ivory, from $25 to.................................**30.00**

**Creamer, red, individual, $325.00+; Sugar bowl, yellow, individual with lid, from $125.00 to $175.00; Figure-8 tray, turquoise, from $350.00 to $400.00.**

Cup, demitasse; '50s colors, from $325 to.............................**400.00**

Cup, demitasse; yellow, light green or turquoise, from $70 to...**80.00**

Egg cup, red, cobalt or ivory, from $60 to.................................**70.00**

Marmalade, red, cobalt, ivory or turquoise, from $275 to .....**300.00**

Mixing bowl, #1, red, cobalt, ivory or turquoise, from $275 to .....**300.00**

Mixing bowl, #2, red, cobalt, ivory or turquoise, from $125 to .....**150.00**

Mixing bowl, #3, red, cobalt, ivory or turquoise, from $125 to .....**150.00**

Mixing bowl, #4, red, cobalt, ivory or turquoise, from $150 to.....**185.00**

Mug, Tom & Jerry, ivory w/gold letters, from $55 to ................**65.00**

Pitcher, disc juice; yellow, from $45 to.........................................**50.00**

**Pitcher, ice; cobalt, from $135.00 to $145.00.**

Pitcher, jug, 2-pint; light green or turquoise, from $70 to .......**80.00**

Plate, '50s colors, 6", from $7 to........**10.00**

Plate, '50s colors, 10", from $45 to ...................................**50.00**

Plate, calendar; 1954 or 1955, 10", from $45 to.........................**55.00**

Plate, chop; light green or turquoise, 13", from $40 to .....................**50.00**

Plate, compartment; red, cobalt or ivory, 10½", from $40 to .....**45.00**

Plate, deep; '50s colors, from $50 to .......................................**55.00**

Plate, red, cobalt or ivory, 10", from $35 to...............................**40.00**

Plate, yellow, light green or turquoise, 9", from $10 to .......................**15.00**

Platter, red, cobalt or ivory, from $50 to..................................**55.00**

Relish tray base, yellow or light green, from $80 to ...........**100.00**

Relish tray side insert, red, cobalt, ivory or turquoise, from $50 to .....................................**60.00**

Saucer, original colors, from $2 to ........................................**3.00**

Sugar bowl, yellow, individual, from $125 to..............................**175.00**

Syrup, yellow or light green, from $375 to..............................**400.00**

Teacup, light green or turquoise, from $15 to.........................**20.00**

Teapot, red, cobalt, ivory or turquoise, lg, from $300 to.....................**350.00**

Teapot, yellow, light green or turquoise, medium, from $150 to.......................................**200.00**

Tray, utility; red, cobalt, ivory or turquoise, from $45 to.......**50.00**

Vase, bud; yellow or light green, from $75 to.......................**115.00**

Vase, red, cobalt, ivory or turquoise, from $650 to.......................**800.00**

### Kitchen Kraft

Bowl, mixing; 10".....................**110.00**

Cake plate ...............................**35.00**

Cake server, from $150 to ......**175.00**

Casserole, individual, from $150 to .....................................**160.00**

Casserole, 7½"...........................**75.00**

Covered jar, sm, from $300 to......**325.00**

Fork, from $150 to ..................**160.00**

Pie plate, 9"..............................**40.00**

Platter, from $60 to ..................**75.00**

Spoon, from $150 to...............**200.00**

**Stacking refrigerator lid, from $90.00 to $110.00; Stacking refrigerator units, excluding ivory, from $50.00 to $60.00 each.**

### Post 86 Line

Bowl, bouillon; lilac, 6¾", from $40 to.......................................**50.00**

Bowl, mixing; chartreuse, 44-oz, from $25 to......................**30.00**

Bowl, pasta; apricot, 12", from $15 to.......................................**20.00**

Bowl, vegetable; sapphire, lg, 39-oz, from $60 to.........................**70.00**

Candle bowl, chartreuse.........**235.00**

Candlestick, pyramid; lilac, ea from $275 to.............................**300.00**

Carafe, chartreuse, from $65 to......**80.00**

Coffee server, lilac, 36-oz, from $150 to.......................................**160.00**

Cup & saucer, AD; sapphire, from $22 to.................................**28.00**

Mug, lilac, 10-oz, from $35 to......**40.00**

Pitcher, disc; apricot, lg, from $45 to..**60.00**

Place setting, sapphire, 5-pc, from
$150 to..............................**180.00**
Plate, dinner; chartreuse, 10½",
from $22 to........................**28.00**
Plate, salad; apricot, 7", from $8
to......................................**12.00**
Platter, lilac, #8, 11⅝", from $60
to......................................**75.00**
Skillet, apricot, from $22 to .....**28.00**
Steak knife set, apricot, from $15
to......................................**20.00**
Sugar caddy, lilac, from $45 to......**50.00**
Teapot, chartreuse, 2-cup, from $30
to......................................**40.00**
Tray, round serving; sapphire, 11",
from $50 to.........................**65.00**
Vase, Millennium, chartreuse, from
$125 to..............................**150.00**

# Fishbowl Ornaments

Mermaids, divers, and all sorts of
castles have been devised to add interest to fishbowls and aquariums, and
today they're starting to attract the
interest of collectors. Many were made
in Japan and imported decades ago to
be sold in 5-&-10¢ stores along with the
millions of other figural novelties that
flooded the market after the war. The
condition of the glaze is very important;
for more information we recommend
*Collector's Encyclopedia of Made in
Japan Ceramics* by Carole Bess White
(Collector Books). Unless noted otherwise, the examples in the listing that
follows were produced in Japan.

Bathing beauty on shell, cinnamon
& white lustre, red Japan mark,
3" ......................................**50.00**

Bathing beauty on turtle, red, tan &
green on white, 2½"..........**25.00**
Boy riding dolphin on wave, multicolored matt glazes, 3¾" .........**25.00**
Castle, multicolored, black Japan
mark, 2¼", from $18 to......**25.00**
Castle, multicolored, black Japan
mark, 3¾", from $22 to......**30.00**
Castle, multicolored glossy glazes, no
mark, 4½", from $20 to...........**32.00**
Castle w/arch, multicolored, 2½" or
3½", ea................................**20.00**
Colonade w/palm tree, green, blue &
white, 3¾x4" ......................**20.00**
Coral, shiny orange w/shadow of black
sea diver, red mark, 3½" ......**23.00**
Diver, orange, black mark, 3¼",
from $15 to.........................**25.00**
Diver, white, black Japan mark,
4¾", from $15 to ................**25.00**
Doorway, stone entry w/open aqua
wood-look door, 2"..............**15.00**
Fish, multicolored, black mark, 2½",
from $15 to.........................**25.00**
Fish riding waves, 2 white fish on
cobalt waves, 3½x3" ..........**22.00**
Lighthouse, orange, yellow & brown,
2x2½" ................................**16.00**
Lighthouse, tan, black, brown &
green, 6½x4" ......................**26.00**
Mermaid, painted bisque, black Japan
mark, 4¾", from $45 to.........**65.00**
Mermaid on sea horse, white, green &
orange glossy glazes, 3¼".....**25.00**
Mermaid on snail, 4", from $45 to..**65.00**
Mermaid on 2 seashells, multicolored matt glazes, 3½", from $30
to......................................**40.00**
Nude on starfish, painted bisque,
4½", from $75 to ..............**125.00**
Pagoda, triple roof, blue, green &
maroon, 5½x3¾"................**20.00**

Sign on tree trunk, No Fishing, brown, black & white, 2½x4" ................................**12.00**

Torii gate, multicolored glossy glazes, 3¾" ........................**22.00**

**Turtle, black Japan mark, 4", from $12.00 to $18.00.** (Photo courtesy Carole Bess White)

# Fisher-Price

Since about 1930 the Fisher-Price Company has produced distinctive wooden toys covered with brightly colored lithographed paper. Plastic parts were first added in 1949. The most valuable Fisher-Price toys are those modeled after well-known Disney characters and have the Disney logo. A little edge wear and some paint dulling are normal for these well-loved toys and to be expected; our prices are for toys in very good played-with condition. Mint-in-box examples are extremely scarce and worth from 50% to 60% more.

Our advisor for this category is Brad Cassity. For further information we recommend *A Pictorial Guide to the More Popular Toys, Fisher-Price Toys, 1931 – 1990*, by Gary Combs and Brad Cassity; *Fisher-Price, A Historical Rarity Value Guide*, by John J. Murray and Bruce R. Fox (Books Americana); and *Schroeder's Collectible Toys, Antique to Modern* (Collector Books). See also Dolls, Fisher-Price. See Clubs and Newsletters for information on the Fisher-Price Collectors Club.

#5 Bunny Cart, 1948-49 ...........**50.00**
#51 Ducky Cart, 1950 ...............**50.00**
#99 Play Family A-Frame, 1974-76 ..**50.00**
#102 Drummer Bear, 1931 .......**700.00**
#112 Picture Disk Camera, 1968-71, w/5 picture discs ................**25.00**
#124 Roller Chime, 1961-62 & Easter 1963 ...............................**25.00**
#131 Toy Wagon, 1951-54 .......**225.00**
#140 Coaster Boy, 1941 ..........**700.00**
#150 Barky Buddy, 1934-35 .....**600.00**
#151 Happy Hippo, 1962-63 .......**85.00**
#160 Donald & Donna Duck, 1937 ..**700.00**
#164 Chubby Cub, 1969-72 ........**15.00**
#171 Pull-Along Plane, 1981-88 .......**5.00**
#172 Roly Raccoon, 1980-82 .......**5.00**
#189 Looky Chug-Chug, 1958-60 ..**75.00**
#190 Molly Moo-Moo, 1956 & Easter 1957 ................................**200.00**
#194 Push Pullet, 1971-71 .......**15.00**
#215 Fisher Price Choo-Choo, 1955-57, engine & 3 cars ...............**85.00**
#301 Shovel Digger, 1975-77 ........**25.00**
#303 Bunny Push Cart, 1957 .......**75.00**
#310 Adventure People Sea Explorer, 1975-80 .........................**20.00**
#313 Roller Grader, 1977 .........**20.00**

#320 Husky Race Car Rig, 1979-82 ..................................**25.00**

**#321, Husky Firefighters, 1978-80, MIB, $45.00.** (Photo courtesy Brad Cassity)

#327 Husky Load Master Dump, 1984 ...................................**20.00**
#345 Boat Rig, 1981-84 ............**10.00**
#360 Adventure People Alpha Recon, 1982-84...................**10.00**
#375 Adventure People Sky Surfer, 1978 ...................................**25.00**
#400 Donald Duck Drum Major, 1946-48............................**275.00**
#415 Super Jet, 1952 & Easter 1953 .................................**200.00**
#423 Jumping Jack Scarecrow, Æ1979 .................................**5.00**
#445 Nosey Pup, 1956-58 & Easter 1959 ...................................**75.00**
#460 Movie Viewer, 1973-85, crank handle ...............................**2.00**
#466 Busy Bunny Cart, 1941-44......................................**75.00**
#472 Jungle Giraffe, 1956 .......**225.00**
#478 Pudgy Pig, 1962-64 & Easter 1965 ...................................**45.00**
#499 Kitty Bell, 1950-51 ........**125.00**
#502 Action Bunny Cart, 1949.........**200.00**
#512 Bunny Drummer, 1942 ........**225.00**
#533 Thumper Bunny, 1942........**500.00**

**#559, Basic Hardboard Puzzle, horse, 1974 – 75, MIB, $15.00.** (Photo courtesy Brad Cassity)

#563 Basic Hardwood Puzzle, Weather, 1975 ...................**10.00**
#615 Tow Truck, 1960-61 & Easter 1962...................................**65.00**
#616 Chuggy Pop-Up, 1955-56..**75.00**
#630 Fire Truck, 1959-62.........**45.00**
#642 Bob-Along Bear, 1979-84..**10.00**
#642 Dinky Engine, 1959, black litho ...................................**60.00**
#659 Puzzle Puppy, 1976-81........**5.00**
#667 Picnic Basket, 1975-79.......**20.00**
#695 Lady Bug, 1982-84............**5.00**
#703 Bunny Engine, 1954-56.......**100.00**
#715 Ducky Flip Flap, 1964-65 ........**50.00**
#719 Cuddly Cub, 1973-77 .........**5.00**
#724 Jolly Jalopy, 1965 ............**10.00**
#734 Teddy Zilo, 1964, no coat ..**55.00**
#749 Egg Truck, 1947.............**225.00**
#755 Jumbo Rolo, 1951-52 .......**225.00**
#757 Snappy-Quacky, 1950........**225.00**
#761 Play Family Nursery Set, 1973...................................**10.00**
#767 Pocket Radio, 1977-78, I'd Like To Teach the World To Sing...**15.00**
#777 Squeaky the Clown, 1958-59..**225.00**
#786 Perky Penguin, 1973-75.......**15.00**
#810 Timber Toter, 1957 & Easter 1958 ...................................**85.00**

#902 Junior Circus, 1963-70 ...**225.00**

#928 Play Family Fire Station, 1980-82..............................**50.00**

**#938, Play Family Sesame Street House, 1975 – 76, M, $75.00.** (Photo courtesy Brad Cassity)

#945 Offshore Cargo Base, 1978-79........................................**65.00**

#997 Play Family Village, 1973-77........................................**50.00**

#2500 Little People School, 1988-89........................................**20.00**

#2501 Little People Farm, 1986-89 ........................................**15.00**

#4551 Pontiac Firebird, 1985......**20.00**

#4580 Power Tow, 1985-86 ......**20.00**

# Fishing Collectibles

Very much in evidence at flea markets these days, old fishing gear has become very collectible. Early twentieth-century plugs were almost entirely carved from wood, sprayed with several layers of enamel, and finished off with glass eyes. Molded plastics were of a later origin. Some of the more collectible manufacturers are James Heddon, Shakespeare, Rhodes, and Pflueger. Rods, reels, old advertising calendars, and company catalogs are also worth your attention. For more information we recommend *19th-Century Fishing Lures* by Arlan Carter; *Fishing Lure Collectibles, Volume One,* by Dudley Murphy and Rick Edmisten; *Fishing Lure Collectibles, Volume Two,* by Dudley and Deanie Murphy; *Collector's Encyclopedia of Creek Chub Lures and Collectibles* by Harold E. Smith, MD; *Modern Fishing Lure Collectibles, Volumes 1 – 4,* by Russell E. Lewis; *Field Guide to Fishing Lures* by Russell E. Lewis; *Spring-Loaded Fish Hooks, Traps & Lures* by William Blauser & Timothy Mierzqa; and *Captain John's Fishing Tackle Price Guide* by John Kolbeck. All are published by Collector Books.

## Lures

Values are for lures in good average condition. Mint-in-the-box examples are worth about twice as much.

Baby Crab Wiggler #1900, 2 double hooks, 1916, 3⅛"................**50.00**

Creek Chub, Beetle #3800, 2 trebles, 1931-54, 2½" ....................**130.00**

Creek Chub, Fin Tail Shiner #2100, 2 trebles, 1930, 4" ...................**60.00**

Creek Chub, Polywiggle #1700, single hook, 1924, 1¾"...........**60.00**

Creek Chub, Wigglefish #2400, 1925-57, 74-77, 3½"...........**50.00**

Heddon, Crazy Crawler, 2 trebles, wings, 1940, 2½"................**30.00**

Heddon, Dowagiac Minnow #210, 2 double hooks, 1920, 3½"......**30.00**

Heddon, Giant Vamp #7550, 3 trebles, ca 1939, 5⅝" ..............**45.00**

Heddon, Laguna Rung L-10, 2 trebles, 1939, 2½"..................**75.00**

Heddon, Meadow Mouse #F4000, leather ears, 1955, 2¾" .....**20.00**

Heddon, Top Sonic #300, purple, lg treble, 1967, 1⅞"................**10.00**

Keeling, Long Tom, 3 trebles, 1923, 4" ........................................**60.00**

Paw Paw, Frog, shaped wooden body, 1940, 1⅜".................**45.00**

Paw Paw, Lippy Joe, 2 trebles, 1949, 2⅜" .......................................**20.00**

Paw Paw, Old Wounded Minnow #2500, 2 trebles, 1940s, 3½"..**24.00**

Paw Paw, Spoon Belly Wobbler, 3 trebles/spoon, 1940, 5⅝".........**240.00**

Paw Paw Midget #7100, 2 trebles, 1960, 1⅝", from $9 to .......**12.00**

Pflueger, Frisky Minnow #61000, 2 trebles, 1952, 1¼".............**25.00**

Pflueger, Zam #4800, plated, 1941, 2⅛" ....................................**25.00**

Shakespeare, Egyptian Wobbler #6636, 3 trebles, 1940, 5".....**75.00**

Shakespeare, Grumpy #6602, 2 trebles, 1941, 1¾"...................**12.00**

Shakespeare, Slim Jim #52, 3 trebles, 1930, 4½"................**100.00**

South Bend, King Andy #975, nickel plated, 1951-53, 4⅝" ............**40.00**

South Bend, Pike-Oreno #957, yellow, 2 trebles, 1928, 4½".....**45.00**

South Bend, Tex-Oreno Sinker #995, 2 trebles, 1938-39, 2¾" ....................................**90.00**

Super Duper #509, South Bend, polished, 1 treble, 1953-64, 2¼"..**5.00**

Wilson, Sizzler, 2 singles, 1915, 2¼" ....................................**100.00**

## Reels

BF Meek #4, non-reflective, 1883-1893, 2¼" dia, NM........**2,750.00**

C-1907 Pflueger Wildside, side winder, maple, 1907-09, 5½", EX................................**440.00**

Edsell's Casting...Sept 1901, combination handle, VG ...........**135.00**

Hardy Bros...C-1885 Birmingham Trout, brass, 2⅜", NM.....**500.00**

Julis Vom Hofe...Size 4, hard rubber plates, handle, 2⅛", EX ......**250.00**

Nottingham, brass/walnut w/Slater latch, bone handle, 3½", VG......**135.00**

**Pflueger (Bulldog logo) Supreme, Level Wind Free Spool Anti-Back Lash, Pat. June 15, 1908, and other patents, Silverline Model No. 1573, NM with papers, $330.00.** (Photo courtesy Lang's Sporting Collectibles, Inc.)

Salmon/salt water; Billy Pate high quality spool type, 3½", EX....................................**275.00**

Trout, Leonard Mills, raised pillar, crank handle, 3" dia, VG .....**660.00**

## Miscellaneous

Creel, split willow, leather pouch front, original green, VG.................**550.00**

Decoy, painted wood w/tin fins & glass eyes, Chub Buchman, 12", EX....................................**350.00**

Decoy, wooden catfish w/tin fins, glass eyes, wire whiskers, 13", EX................................**290.00**

Eel trap, woven splint, 26½", EX........**145.00**
Landing net, maple/tiger maple handle, metal frame w/hoop net, 82", EX ...............................**58.00**
Spear, eel; wrought iron, 6 barbed tines, mk IT Frantz, 59½", EX..........**175.00**

# Flashlights

The flashlight was invented in 1898 and has been produced by the Eveready Company for these past ninety-six years. Eveready dominated the flashlight market for most of this period, but more than one hundred twenty-five other U.S. flashlight companies have come and gone, providing competition along the way. Add to that number over thirty-five known foreign flashlight manufacturers, and you end up with over one thousand different models of flashlights to collect. They come in a wide variety of styles, shapes, and sizes. The flashlight field includes tubular, lanterns, figural, novelty, litho, etc. At present, over forty-five different categories of flashlights have been identified as collectible. For further information we recommend consulting the Flashlight Collectors of America, see Clubs and Newsletters.

Bright Star #1949, 8", M (NM box) ..**15.00**
Bright Star Dentalite, EX ........**40.00**
Brownie #11-401, Girl Scouts, 1960s, 6¼", EXIB...............**50.00**
Collins' No Battery, #E37931, crank style, 1924, EX.................**320.00**
Daimon Field Flashlight, German, red, green & blue filters, EX.....**75.00**

Delta, Power King, 12 volt, EX......**30.00**
Diamond Spotlight, chrome w/red lens on back end, NM (torn box)..**45.00**
Eveready, Daylo, EX ...............**30.00**
Eveready #1654, Candle Flashlight, EX..............................**15.00**
Eveready #59, black & yellow plastic, NMIB ..........................**17.50**
Eveready Big Jim #101, Sealed Beam, EX..........................**15.00**
Eveready Masterlight, chrome w/painted rings, EX..........**12.00**
Philips Type #7424, hand-powered, squeeze trigger, Holland, EX..**35.00**
Ray-O-Vac #Z22R, set of 6 on store display, 1940s-50s, 7½", EX.........**175.00**
Ray-O-Vac Hunter Lantern, 1960s, M (EX box) ........................**55.00**
Ray-O-Vac Sportsman, leather strap, 19", EX....................**70.00**
Winchester #1511, 6¾", EX......**15.00**

**Winchester, solid copper, 8", VG, $35.00.**

Winchester Solid 22k-Copper, #1818, 8", EX ....................**50.00**

# Flower Frogs

Nearly every pottery company and glasshouse in America produced their share of figural flower 'frogs,' and many were imported from Japan as well. They were probably most popular from about 1910 through the 1940s, coinciding not only with the heyday of American glass and ceramics, but with the gracious, much less hectic style of living the times allowed. Way before a silk flower or styrofoam block was ever dreamed of, there were fresh cut flowers on many a dining room sideboard or table, arranged in shallow console bowls with matching frogs such as we've described in the following listings. For further information see *Collector's Encyclopedia of Made in Japan Ceramics* by Carole Bess White (Collector Books). See also specific pottery and glass companies.

Bird, multicolor ceramic, Made in Japan, many styles, up to 6", from $20 to.........................**25.00**
Bird in flight, lime green, Camark, 5" on 3x4" base..................**25.00**

**Bird on stump, majolica style, multicolor, Japan mark, 6½", from $28.00 to $35.00.** (Photo courtesy Carole Bess White)

Black amethyst glass, 2½x4"......**35.00**
Black glass, 4¼" dia.................**48.00**
Clear glass w/3 tiny feet, ¾x2½" dia.......................................**12.50**
Disk, green monochrome w/8 holes, Weller...............................**50.00**
Disk, Jade-ite green stoneware, fluted, wire center, 1930, 2x3½" ...............................**62.00**

Frog, heavy metal w/worn green pnt, 5 flower holes, 3x3"....**60.00**
Golden Retriever, 3 holes in base, natural colors, Japan, 3x3¼x2" ....**45.00**
Green Depression glass, 5" dia, NM .....................................**25.00**
Hummingbird on stump, multicolored matt, Germany, 6⅝" .............**75.00**
Junque Boat, metal, 2½x6½", EX.**42.00**
Lovebirds, multicolored lustre, Noritake mark, 7¼" ................**250.00**
Monkeys, Hear No..., etc, lustreware, Mitsu-Boshi Japan, 4⅞" .....**55.00**
Nude lady, black gloss, Camark, 9" .....................................**125.00**
Nude lady, pastels on white ceramic, Germany, 1930s, 7½"......**245.00**
Nude lady, white ceramic, Made in Western Germany, 1940s-50s, 6" .....................................**175.00**
Nude lady w/arms folded, white ceramic, marked 10077 IV, 6"....................................**145.00**
Nude on polar bear, white, Germany, 7x4¼" ...................**295.00**
Parrot on stump, multicolored, Czechoslovakia, 5".............**28.00**
Parrots in tree, multicolored ceramic, unmarked, 5" ................**49.00**
Ruby glass, domed top, 8 holes, Fenton, 1¾x3" ........................**135.00**
Sea gull, clear, 9 holes in base, Cambridge, 9½x6".....................**75.00**
Turtle, honeycomb back, metal, 5x3x1"...............................**40.00**
Turtle form, turquoise, Van Briggle, 5" dia, NM.......................**125.00**
Turtle on log looks down on sm green frog, multicolored paint, Japan, 4"...........................**70.00**
Water lily, silver-plated metal, Leonard, 3x7", 3-pc set......**22.00**

White metal w/brown enameling, 15 holes, Made in Japan, 4" ......................................**20.00**

# '40s, '50s, and '60s Glassware

With scarcity of the older Depression glassware items that used to be found in every garage sale or flea market, glass collectors have refocused their interests and altered buying habits to include equally interesting glassware from more recent years, often choosing patterns that bring back warm childhood memories. For an expanded listing and more information, see *Collectible Glassware from the '40s, '50s, and '60s,* by Gene and Cathy Florence (Collector Books). See also Anchor Hocking.

## Cambridge

Cascade, ashtray, crystal, 4½" .....**6.00**
Cascade, bowl, relish; crystal, 6½" ..**13.00**

**Cascade, candlestick, green, #4000/67, $35.00.** (Photo courtesy Gene and Cathy Florence)

Cascade, compote, crystal, 5½" .....**17.50**
Cascade, plate, bread & butter; crystal, 6½" ................................**5.50**

Cascade, sugar bowl, yellow or green...**20.00**
Cascade, tumbler, flat, crystal, 5-oz..**10.00**
Cascade, vase, green, 9½" ........**75.00**
Square, ashtray, crystal, 3½".....**8.00**
Square, bonbon, crystal, 8" ......**24.00**
Square, bowl, dessert; crystal, 4½"..**12.00**
Square, bowl, punch; crystal .....**75.00**
Square, celery bowl, 11" ...........**25.00**
Square, creamer, crystal, individual .**10.00**
Square, plate, salad; crystal, 7"..**12.00**
Square, saucer, tea; crystal........**5.00**
Square, stem, cordial, crystal .....**25.00**
Square, vase, crystal, 6" ...........**22.50**

## Federal Glass Co.

Golden Glory, bowl, soup; white w/gold decor, 6⅜".................**9.00**
Golden Glory, mug, white w/gold decor...................................**15.00**
Golden Glory, platter, oval, white w/gold decor, 12".................**12.00**
Golden Glory, sugar bowl, white w/gold decor .........................**4.00**
Heritage, bowl, berry; blue or green, 8½" ...................................**295.00**
Heritage, creamer, footed, crystal..............................**25.00**
Heritage, plate, luncheon; crystal, 8" .....................................**700.00**
Heritage, saucer, crystal ...........**2.00**
Park Avenue, ashtray, crystal, sq, 3½" .....................................**5.00**

**Park Avenue, ashtray, crystal, 4½", from $7.00 to $8.00.** (Photo courtesy Gene and Cathy Florence)

Park Avenue, bowl, dessert; yellow, 5" ..........................................**7.00**

Park Avenue, tumbler, juice; yellow, 4½-oz, 3½"............................**7.00**

Pioneer, bowl, crystal, 10½".....**18.00**

Pioneer, nappy, pink, shallow, 5⅜"..**12.00**

Pioneer, plate, crystal, 12" .......**12.50**

Pioneer, plate, pink/sprayed colors, 8" ..........................................**12.00**

Star, bowl, cereal; crystal, 5⅜".....**6.00**

Star, butter dish, crystal ..........**95.00**

Star, plate, salad; yellow, 6³⁄₁₆" ....**6.00**

Star, tumbler, iced tea; yellow, 12-oz, 5⅛" ...............................**18.00**

## Fostoria

Buttercup, ashtray, crystal, individual, 2⅝"..............................**27.50**

Buttercup, bottle, salad dressing; crystal ..............................**295.00**

Buttercup, candlesticks, crystal, 6", pr ..**32.50**

Buttercup, plate, crystal, 7½" .....**12.00**

Buttercup, relish, crystal, 2-part, 6½x5" ................................**25.00**

Buttercup, salt shaker, crystal, 2⅝", ea.............................**35.00**

Buttercup, syrup, crystal, Sani-cut...**325.00**

Camellia, bowl, fruit; crystal, 5"......**16.00**

Camellia, bowl, salad; crystal, 8½".**40.00**

Camellia, compote, crystal, 4⅜"......**25.00**

**Camellia, plate, dinner; crystal, 9½", $30.00. (Photo courtesy Gene and Cathy Florence)**

Camellia, plate, salad; crystal, 7½"..**10.00**

Camellia, platter, crystal, 12" .....**47.50**

Camellia, saucer, crystal............**4.00**

Camellia, sugar bowl, crystal, footed, 4"...................................**14.00**

Camellia, vase, bud; crystal, 6".....**35.00**

Century, ashtray, crystal, 2¾"......**10.00**

Century, bowl, lily pond; crystal, 9"..**30.00**

Century, candlestick, crystal, 4½", ea........................................**17.50**

Century, compote, crystal, 4⅜".....**20.00**

Century, creamer, crystal, 4¼".......**9.00**

Century, ice bucket, crystal .....**65.00**

Century, pitcher, crystal, 16-oz, 6⅛"..**60.00**

Century, plate, salad; crystal, 7½"..**8.00**

Century, platter, crystal, 12".....**47.50**

Century, saucer, crystal .............**3.50**

Century, tray, muffin; crystal, w/handles, 9½"...................**30.00**

Century, vase, crystal, oval, 8½" ......**67.50**

Chintz, bell, dinner; crystal......**125.00**

Chintz, bowl, fruit; crystal, #2496, 5" ........................................**33.00**

Chintz, mayonnaise, crystal, 3-pc; #2496½..............................**55.00**

Chintz, plate, cracker; crystal, #2496, 11" ............................**40.00**

Chintz, plate, luncheon; crystal, #2496, 8½" .........................**19.00**

Chintz, platter, crystal, #2496, 12"..**110.00**

Chintz, relish, crystal, 5-part, #2419.................................**40.00**

Chintz, stem, cocktail, crystal, #6026, 4-oz, 5"....................**22.00**

Corsage, bowl, finger; crystal, #869.................................**32.00**

Corsage, bowl, flared, crystal, #2496, 12" ..........................**60.00**

Corsage, plate, crystal, #2337, 9½"..**37.50**

Corsage, relish, crystal, 5-part, #2419.................................**60.00**

Corsage, saucer, crystal, #2440......**5.00**

Corsage, stem, claret, crystal, #6014, 4-oz, 7⅞"................**35.00**

Corsage, vase, bud; crystal, #5092, 8".......................................**65.00**

Heather, bowl, cereal; crystal, 6"..**28.00**

Heather, cup, crystal, footed, 6-oz..**17.00**

Heather, plate, torte; crystal, 14"..**65.00**

Heather, sugar bowl, crystal, individual..................................**15.00**

Heather, vase, oval, crystal, 8½"......**85.00**

Holly, ashtray, crystal, individual, 2⅝".....................................**22.00**

Holly, plate, dessert; crystal, 6"......**5.00**

Holly, plate, torte; crystal, 16".....**85.00**

Holly, vase, crystal, 9½".........**125.00**

Horizon, bowl, fruit; cinnamon, crystal or spruce, 4½".................**7.00**

Horizon, coaster, cinnamon, crystal or spruce............................**10.00**

Horizon, plate, salad; cinnamon, crystal or spruce, 7".............**8.00**

Horizon, saucer, cinnamon, crystal or spruce...............................**2.00**

Horizon, sugar bowl, cinnamon, crystal or spruce, 3⅛"........**12.00**

Jamestown, bowl, dessert; amber or brown, 4½"...........................**8.50**

Jamestown, celery, amethyst, crystal or green, 9¼"................**32.50**

**Jamestown, salver, green, 7x10", $250.00.** (Photo courtesy Gene and Cathy Florence)

Jamestown, stem, wine; blue, pink or ruby, 4-oz, 4⁵⁄₁₆"............**24.00**

Jamestown, tumbler, amber or brown, 12-oz, 5⅛"................**9.00**

Lido, bowl, finger; crystal.........**25.00**

Lido, ice bucket, crystal............**85.00**

Lido, plate, crystal, 6".................**6.00**

Lido, plate, torte; crystal, 14".....**55.00**

Lido, shaker, crystal, 2¾".........**30.00**

Lido, tidbit, 3-footed, flat, crystal, 8¼"...................................**20.00**

Lido, vase, crystal, 5"...............**75.00**

Mayflower, bowl, finger; crystal.....**27.50**

Mayflower, bowl, w/handles, crystal, 11".......................................**60.00**

Mayflower, compote, crystal, 5½"..**30.00**

Mayflower, plate, crystal, 8½".....**15.00**

Mayflower, salt & pepper shakers, crystal, pr..........................**75.00**

Mayflower, vase, crystal, 8"......**115.00**

Meadow Rose, bowl, bonbon; crystal, 3-footed, 7⅜".....................**27.50**

Meadow Rose, celery, crystal, 11"..**37.50**

Meadow Rose, cup, crystal.......**20.00**

Meadow Rose, ice bucket, crystal, 4⅜" high..........................**100.00**

Meadow Rose, plate, bread & butter; crystal, 6"...........................**11.00**

Meadow Rose, plate, cracker; crystal, 11"................................**30.00**

Meadow Rose, tumbler, tea; footed, crystal, 13-oz, 5⅞".............**28.00**

Meadow Rose, vase, crystal, footed, 10".....................................**165.00**

Navarre, bell, dinner; blue or pink...................................**95.00**

Navarre, candlestick, crystal, 4", ea...**25.00**

Navarre, cup, crystal...............**20.00**

Navarre, sauce dish, crystal, 6½x5¼"..............................**80.00**

Navarre, stem, claret; blue or pink, 4½-oz, 6"...........................**85.00**

Navarre, stem, magnum; blue or pink, 16-oz, 7¼" ...............**195.00**

Navarre, vase, crystal, footed, 10"..**250.00**

Romance, bowl, baked apple; crystal, 6" ..................................**22.00**

Romance, candlestick, crystal, 4", ea..**20.00**

Romance, mayonnaise, crystal, 5"..**25.00**

Romance, pitcher, crystal, footed, 53-oz, 8⅛" ........................**335.00**

Romance, plate, torte; crystal, 16"..**100.00**

Romance, saucer, crystal............**5.00**

Romance, tumbler, crystal, footed, 12-oz, 6" ..............................**28.00**

Romance, vase, crystal, 10" .....**100.00**

Seascape, bowl, pansy; opalescent, 4½" ......................................**35.00**

Seascape, creamer, opalescent, 3⅜"..**25.00**

Seascape, plate, buffet; opalescent, 14" ......................................**80.00**

Seascape, tray, oval, opalescent, footed, 7½" ........................**55.00**

Wistar, bowl, fruit; white, 13"......**27.50**

Wistar, bowl, salad; crystal, 10"......**25.00**

Wistar, creamer, crystal, footed, 4" .**10.00**

Wistar, tumbler, white, 12-oz .....**17.00**

## Hazel Atlas

Capri, ashtray, blue, triangular, 3¼"..**6.00**

Capri, bowl, blue, swirled, 4¾" .....**6.00**

Capri, bowl, blue, 3x9⅛" ..........**25.00**

Capri, plate, blue, sq, 8" .............**8.00**

Capri, stem, water; blue, 5½".......**9.00**

Capri, vase, blue, ruffled, 8½"......**35.00**

Colonial Couple, bowl, Platonite w/trim, 5" ...........................**15.00**

Colonial Couple, plate, dessert; Platonite w/trim......................**10.00**

Colonial Couple, tumbler, flat, Platonite w/trim, 8-oz .............**20.00**

Moderntone Platonite, bowl, berry; white or w/stripes, rimmed, 5" ......**3.00**

Moderntone Platonite, bowl, cream soup; pastel colors, 4¾".........**6.50**

Moderntone Platonite, bowl, Deco/red or Blue Willow, rimmed, 8"..**45.00**

Moderntone Platonite, mug, white or w/stripes, 8-oz, 4" ............**9.00**

Moderntone Platonite, plate, sherbet; pastel colors, 6¾"..........**4.00**

Moderntone Platonite, platter, Deco/red or Blue Willow, oval, 11"........**40.00**

Moderntone Platonite, tumbler, white or w/stripes, footed cone .....**6.00**

Moroccan Amethyst, ashtray, round, 3¼" ......................................**5.50**

Moroccan Amethyst, cocktail shaker w/lid..................................**30.00**

Moroccan Amethyst, ice bucket, 6"..**38.00**

Moroccan Amethyst, vase, ruffled, 8½" ......................................**35.00**

Newport, bowl, berry; white, 4¾"..**3.50**

Newport, creamer, fired-on colors...**7.50**

Newport, platter, fired-on colors, oval, 11¾"............................**22.00**

Newport, sherbet, white.............**3.50**

Ovide, ashtray, fired-on colors, sq ....................................**4.00**

Ovide, creamer, fired-on colors .....**4.00**

Ovide, plate, luncheon; Art Deco, 8"...**50.00**

Ovide, sugar bowl, open, white w/trims ................................**4.50**

Ripple, bowl, berry; all colors, shallow, 5"................................**12.50**

Ripple, creamer, all colors..........**7.50**

Ripple, saucer, all colors, 5⅝".......**1.00**

Ripple, tidbit, all colors, 3-tier......**35.00**

Ripple, tumbler, all colors, 20-oz, 6¼" ......................................**10.00**

## Heisey

Cabochon, bowl, cereal; crystal, #1951, 7" .............................**6.00**

Cabochon, bowl, gardenia; crystal, #1951, 13" ..........................**18.00**

Cabochon, candy dish, w/lid, crystal, #1951, 6¼" ........................**38.00**

Cabochon, plate, salad; crystal, #1951, 8" ............................**6.00**

Cabochon, stemware, blown, crystal, #6092, 6-oz ..........................**4.00**

Cabochon, sugar bowl, crystal, w/lid, #1951 ..................................**18.00**

Cabochon, tumbler, crystal, pressed, #1951, 5-oz ..........................**7.00**

Cabochon, vase, crystal, flared, #1951, 3½" ......................**24.00**

Lodestar, ashtray, Dawn..........**85.00**

Lodestar, creamer, Dawn.........**50.00**

Lodestar, tumbler, juice; Dawn, 6-oz ....................................**40.00**

New Era, bowl, flower; crystal, 11"..**45.00**

New Era, pilsner, crystal, 12-oz .....**32.50**

New Era, tray, celery; crystal, 13"..**30.00**

Orchid, bowl, gardenia; crystal, 13"..**70.00**

Orchid, plate, dinner; crystal, 10½" ..**150.00**

Plantation, ashtray, crystal, 3½"......**35.00**

Plantation, comport, crystal, 5" ......**60.00**

Plantation, plate, punch bowl liner, crystal, 18" ......................**145.00**

Plantation, vase, crystal, flared, footed, 9" ..........................**375.00**

**Plantation #1567, candleblock, crystal, 3", $110.00. (Photo courtesy Gene and Cathy Florence)**

Rose, cigarette holder, crystal, #4035................................**125.00**

Rose, pitcher, crystal, #4164, 73-oz..**575.00**

Rose, stem, wine, crystal, #5072, 3-oz ......................................**95.00**

Rose, vase, crystal, #4198, 10" ......**245.00**

## Imperial

Crocheted Crystal, basket, 6"......**30.00**

Crocheted Crystal, bowl, console; 12" ....................................**35.00**

**Crocheted Crystal, bowl, crystal, Laced Edge #78C, 2x6", $20.00. (Photo courtesy Gene and Cathy Florence)**

Crocheted Crystal, creamer, flat......**35.00**

Crocheted Crystal, lamp, hurricane; 11" ....................................**75.00**

Crocheted Crystal, plate, salad; 8" ..**7.50**

Crocheted Crystal, plate, 14" .....**25.00**

Crocheted Crystal, punch bowl, 14" ....................................**65.00**

Crocheted Crystal, stem, sherbet; 6-oz, 5"..................................**35.00**

## Indiana Glass Co

Christmas Candy, bowl, crystal, 5¾"..**4.50**

Christmas Candy, cup, teal......**30.00**

Christmas Candy, plate, dinner; crystal, 9⅝" ........................**11.00**

Christmas Candy, sugar bowl, teal ..**30.00**

Constellation, basket, centerpiece; crystal, 11" ..........................**30.00**

Constellation, bowl, punch; flat, crystal ................................**35.00**

Constellation, creamer, crystal .....**10.00**

Constellation, platter, crystal, oval..**22.50**

**Daisy, cup and saucer, amber, $6.50.** (Photo courtesy Gene and Cathy Florence)

Daisy, bowl, berry; red or amber, 4½" ......................................**9.00**

Daisy, bowl, cereal; green, 6".....**14.00**

Daisy, bowl, vegetable; crystal, oval, 10" ....................................**10.00**

Daisy, plate, grill; red or amber, 10⅜" ...................................**10.00**

Daisy, platter, green, 10¾" ........**8.50**

Daisy, tumbler, crystal, footed, 12-oz ..................................**20.00**

Diamond Point, ashtray, crystal w/ruby, 5½" ..........................**5.00**

Diamond Point, candleholder, crystal w/ruby, footed.................**7.50**

Diamond Point, creamer, crystal w/ruby, footed .....................**4.00**

Diamond Point, vase, crystal w/ruby, footed ....................**12.00**

Orange Blossom, bowl, dessert; milk white, 5½" ...........................**5.00**

Orange Blossom, cup, milk white .....**4.00**

Orange Blossom, plate, luncheon; milk white, 8⅞"....................**8.00**

Pretzel, bowl, berry; crystal, 9⅜"......**16.00**

Pretzel, pitcher, crystal, 39-oz ......**495.00**

Pretzel, plate, dinner; crystal, 9⅜"..**10.00**

Pretzel, sugar bowl, crystal........**4.50**

Sandwich, basket, amber or crystal, 10" H ..................................**30.00**

Sandwich, bowl, teal blue, hexagonal, 6" .................................**14.00**

Sandwich, creamer, red............**45.00**

Sandwich, goblet, red, 9-oz.......**45.00**

Sandwich, pitcher, amber or crystal, 68-oz .................................**25.00**

Sandwich, sherbet, teal blue, 3¼"......**12.00**

**Sandwich #170, candleholder, crystal, 3½",  $15.00.** (Photo courtesy Gene and Cathy Florence)

### Jeannette

Camellia, bowl, fruit; crystal, 5"......**16.00**

Camellia, bowl, salad; crystal, 8½"..**40.00**

Camellia, plate, torte; crystal, 14" ..**60.00**

Camellia, vase, bud; crystal, 6" ......**35.00**

Dewdrop, bowl, crystal, 4¾".......**5.00**

Dewdrop, creamer, crystal .........**8.00**

Dewdrop, pitcher, crystal, flat.....**50.00**

Dewdrop, plate, crystal, 11½" .....**17.50**

Dewdrop, punch bowl base, crystal ..**10.00**

Dewdrop, tumbler, iced tea; crystal, 12-oz, 6"..............................**30.00**

Floragold, ashtray/coaster, iridescent, 4" ................................**5.50**

Floragold, comport, plain top, iridescent, rare, 5¼" .............**1,100.00**

Floragold, platter, iridescent, 11¼"..**25.00**

Floragold, sugar bowl, iridescent .....**6.50**

Floragold, vase, iridescent .....**450.00**
Harp, cake stand, crystal, 9" .....**28.00**
Harp, coaster, crystal .................**4.50**
Harp, plate, crystal, 7" .............**14.00**
Holiday, bowl, soup; pink, 7¾".....**60.00**

**Holiday, pink: Tumbler, flat, 10 ounce; 4", $22.50; Oval vegetable bowl, 9½", $28.00; Cup and saucer, $12.00.** (Photo courtesy Gene and Cathy Florence)

Holiday, pitcher, milk; crystal, 16-oz, 4¾" ...............................**15.00**
Holiday, platter, iridescent, oval, 11⅜" ...................................**12.50**
Holiday, tumbler, pink, footed, 6" ......................................**165.00**
Iris, bowl, cereal; crystal, 5"....**110.00**
Iris, butter dish, iridescent ......**45.00**
Iris, creamer, green or pink, footed ..............................**150.00**
Iris, goblet, crystal, 8-oz, 5½".....**24.00**
Iris, plate, sherbet; iridescent, 5½" ...................................**11.00**
Iris, vase, green or pink, 9" ......**225.00**
National, ashtray, crystal, sm....**3.00**
National, lazy Suzan, crystal....**45.00**
National, punch set, crystal, 15-pc..**90.00**
National, vase, crystal, 9" ........**20.00**
Shell Pink, ashtray, butterfly shape ................................**25.00**
Shell Pink, cake stand, 10" ......**45.00**
Shell Pink, punch bowl, 7½-qt..**125.00**
Shell Pink, vase, 7"..................**35.00**

## US Glass

King's Crown/Thumbprint, bowl, divided mayonnaise; ruby flashed, 5" .........................**70.00**
King's Crown/Thumbprint, cheese stand, ruby flashed............**35.00**
King's Crown/Thumbprint, pitcher, ruby flashed....................**215.00**

**King's Crown/Thumbprint, plate, dinner; ruby flashed, 10", $40.00.**

King's Crown/Thumbprint, stem, oyster cocktail, ruby flashed, 4-oz ......................................**14.00**

## Viking

Prelude, bowl, crystal, crimped, 8"...**35.00**
Prelude, bowl, crystal, shallow, 10"..**35.00**
Prelude, candlestick, crystal, 4", ea ..**17.50**
Prelude, cup, crystal.................**25.00**
Prelude, pitcher, crystal, 78-oz......**265.00**
Prelude, plate, crystal, 18".......**85.00**
Prelude, sugar bowl, crystal.....**12.50**
Prelude, vase, crystal, footed, 11"..**75.00**

# Franciscan

When most people think of the Franciscan name, their Apple or Desert Rose patterns come to mind immediately, and without a doubt these are the most collectible of the hundreds of lines produced by Gladding McBean. Located in Los Angeles, they produced quality dinnerware under the trade name Franciscan from the mid-1930s until 1984, when they were bought out by a company from England. Many marks were used; most included the Franciscan name. An 'F' in a square with 'Made in USA' below it dates from 1938, and a double-line script F was used later. Some of this dinnerware is still being produced in England, so be sure to look for the USA mark. For an expanded listing, see *Schroeder's Antiques Price Guide* (Collector Books).

Apple, bowl, batter; minimum value .................................**450.00**
Apple, bowl, cereal; 6" ..............**12.00**
Apple, casserole, stick handle & lid, individual ...........................**65.00**
Apple, coaster ...........................**65.00**
Apple, plate, 9½" ......................**22.00**
Apple, plate, 10½" .....................**20.00**
Apple, shaker & pepper mill, wooden top, pr .........................**395.00**
Apple, teapot ............................**105.00**
Apple, vase, bud .......................**85.00**
Apple, ½-apple baker, from $125 to..**195.00**
Coronado, bowl, fruit; from $6 to ......**12.00**
Coronado, butter dish, from $25 to ..**35.00**
Coronado, creamer, from $8 to ......**12.00**
Coronado, jam jar, w/lid, from $45 to ..**60.00**
Desert Rose, ashtray, ind .........**12.00**
Desert Rose, coffeepot ..............**75.00**
Desert Rose, gravy boat............**25.00**
Desert Rose, mug, 7-oz .............**25.00**
Desert Rose, pitcher, syrup ......**75.00**
Desert Rose, plate, 10½" ..........**18.00**

Desert Rose, soup ladle ............**75.00**
Desert Rose, tea canister .......**225.00**
El Patio, bowl, fruit ..................**12.00**
El Patio, cup & saucer, jumbo .....**32.00**
El Patio, plate, 6½" .....................**8.00**
El Patio, platter, oval, 15½" .....**45.00**
El Patio, teapot .........................**75.00**
Forget-Me-Not, candy dish, oval ...**225.00**
Forget-Me-Not, lamp, hurricane..**325.00**
Ivy, bowl, mixing; med ...........**200.00**
Ivy, candleholders, pr.............**115.00**
Ivy, napkin ring ........................**60.00**
Ivy, pitcher, jug.......................**230.00**
Meadow Rose, ashtray, sq......**195.00**
Meadow Rose, casserole, 1½-qt .....**75.00**
Meadow Rose, goblet, footed.....**225.00**
Meadow Rose, plate, TV.........**150.00**
Meadow Rose, tea canister.....**225.00**
Poppy, plate, chop; 12" .............**75.00**
Poppy, platter, oval, 10" ...........**30.00**
Starburst, bonbon ....................**22.00**
Starburst, bowl, salad; individual ..**25.00**
Starburst, casserole, lg...........**100.00**
Starburst, jug, water; 10".........**90.00**
Starburst, mug, tall .................**95.00**
Starburst, pitcher, water; 10" .....**85.00**
Starburst, plate, 11" .................**45.00**
Starburst, vinegar cruet...........**75.00**

**Starburst, three-part relish, $35.00; large oval ashtray, $50.00.**

# Frankoma

Since 1933 the Frankoma Pottery Company has been producing dinnerware, novelty items, vases, etc. In 1965 they became the first American company to produce a line of collector plates. The body of the ware prior to 1954 was a honey tan that collectors refer to as 'Ada clay.' A brick red clay (called 'Sapulpa') was used from then on, and this and the colors of the glazes help determine the period of production.

For more information refer to *Frankoma and Other Oklahoma Potteries* by Phyllis and Tom Bess (Schiffer), and *Frankoma Pottery, Value Guide and More*, by Susan N. Cox. See Clubs and Newsletters for information on the Frankoma Family Collectors Association.

Ashtray, Teardrop, Desert Gold, 13" ................................**10.00**

Ashtray, 4-leaf clover, brown satin, 6" ......................................**20.00**

Bowl, Dogwood, Prairie Green, shallow, 8½x13", from $25 to ..**30.00**

Bowl, mint; Prairie Green, Beauceant Okla 34 City mark .............**250.00**

Candleholders, Dogwood, Prairie Green, pr from $25 to ........**30.00**

Canteen, Thunderbird, turquoise, Ada Clay, #59, from $75 to .**85.00**

Casserole, Aztec, Sapula clay, #7W, 10" ......................................**40.00**

Christmas card, 1953, from $90 to ..**110.00**

Christmas card, 1958-60 ..........**65.00**

Christmas card, 1976-82, ea.......**25.00**

Earrings, pr from $20 to...........**35.00**

Leaf dish, Prairie Green, #227, lg ......................................**40.00**

Mug, Elephant, 1969, from $40 to ...................................**60.00**

Mug, Mayan-Aztec, Prairie Green, 16-oz ...................................**22.50**

Mug, Plainsman, Prairie Green or dark brown satin, 12-oz, ea.............**15.00**

Pitcher, batter; Desert Gold, Ada clay, #553, miniature, from $15 to........................................**20.00**

Pitcher, Flame Red, #8, 7¼" .....**115.00**

Plaque, Indian Head, #132, 4⅛x2¼"..**60.00**

Plate, Christmas; She Loved & Cared, White Sand, 1974, from $20 to................................**25.00**

Plate, dinner; Wagon Wheel, Prairie Green, 10" .........................**22.00**

Plate, Wildlife, 1977-79, ea from $55 to........................................**85.00**

Platter, Plainsman, Prairie Green, 17" ....................................**70.00**

Salt & pepper shakers, Wagon Wheel, Desert Gold, Ada clay, pr from $22 to ....................**25.00**

Sculpture, Bucking Bronco, Ivory, ca 1942, 5¾" ........................**300.00**

Sculpture, Fan Dancer, Woodland Moss, pre-1970, from $350 to......................................**400.00**

Sculpture, Greyhound, Flame Orange, Ada clay, 2½x3"................**120.00**

**Sculpture, Indian Bowl Maker, Prairie Green, Sapulpa clay, 6", $90.00 (if marked 'Taylor,' $2,500.00 to $3,000.00.)**

Sculpture, Miniature Walking Elephant, White Sand, #169, 1¾"....**110.00**

Sculpture, Ponytail Girl, Prairie Green, 10" ..........................**80.00**

Sculpture, Trojan Horse, Desert Gold, Ada clay, 2½x3", from $175 to..............................**185.00**

Teacup, Plainsman, Prairie Green, 5-oz, from $10 to ................**12.00**

Teapot, ovoid, ca 1934-35, mini, 2", from $125 to.....................**150.00**

Tumbler, Plainsman, Terra Cotta, glazed inside only, 12-oz, from $7 to......................................**8.00**

Vase, bud; Snail, Flame, Sapula clay, #31, from $30 to ........**40.00**

Vase, Cattle Brand, from $10 to......**15.00**

Vase, collector; V-05, 1973, 13"......**85.00**

Vase, collector; V-14, from $75 to..**80.00**

Vase, Red Bud, Ada clay, #43, 8"..**85.00**

Vase, Tall Cornucopia, #56, Ada clay, 7"...............................**50.00**

Vase, Tall Ram's Head, #74, 9¼", from $100 to.....................**150.00**

Wall pocket, Phoebe, Prairie Green, Ada clay, #730, 7½" .............**150.00**

Wall pocket, Wagon Wheel, 7" .....**50.00**

# Fruit Jars

Some of the earliest glass jars used for food preservation were blown, and corks were used for seals. During the nineteenth century, hundreds of manufacturers designed over 4,000 styles of fruit jars. Lids were held in place either by a wax seal, wire bail, or the later screw-on band. Jars were usually made in aqua or clear, though other colors were also used. Amber jars are popular with collectors, milk glass jars are rare, and cobalt and black glass jars often bring $3,000.00 and up, if they can be found! Condition, age, scarcity, and unusual features are also to be considered when evaluating old fruit jars.

Acme (on shield w/stars & stripes), qt ..........................................**2.00**

Atlas, green, green lid, pt.........**18.00**

Atlas HA Mason, qt .....................**1.00**

Ball (leaning ls) Perfect Mason, bl, qt ........................................**12.00**

Ball (undropped a) Perfect Mason, soft sq, 6-rib, ½-gal..............**5.00**

Ball Freezer Jar, 16-oz ...............**2.00**

Ball Ideal, sq, pt..........................**3.00**

Ball Improved (dropped a), pt ......**9.00**

Ball Perfect Mason, blue, 40-oz......**25.00**

Ball Perfect Mason, Made in USA, blue, 8 ribs, qt....................**25.00**

Ball Sure Seal, blue, pt...............**3.00**

Canadian Jewel, Made in Canada, qt ...........................................**4.00**

Clark's Peerless, aqua, pt...........**6.00**

Corona Jar, Made in Canada, pt......**3.00**

Crown Crown (ring crown), aqua, ½-gal......................................**17.00**

Daisy FE Ward & Co (in circle), aqua, qt ..............................**15.00**

Drey Improved Ever Seal Pat 1920, pt ............................................**5.00**

Electrollix, zinc lid, pt ................**3.00**

Eureka (script), base: Eureka jar Co..., light green, qt...........**25.00**

Gem, aqua, midget ..................**50.00**

Gilberds (star) Jar, aqua, qt .....**350.00**

Hazel Preserve Jar, ½-pt..........**40.00**

Improved Crown Crown, aqua, qt..**12.00**

Ivanhoe (base), qt ......................**4.00**

Kerr Bicentennial, cobalt, bell, pontiled ..................................**190.00**

Knox (K in keystone) Mason, regular zinc lid, qt......................**2.00**

Lockport Mason, aqua, qt.........**20.00**

Mason's (keystone) Patent Nov 30th 1858, aqua, qt.....................**12.00**

Mason's Patent, aqua, ½-gal.....**10.00**

Mason's Patent Nov 30th 1858, aqua, midget......................**35.00**

Mason's 13 Patent Nov 30th 1858, aqua, qt..............................**60.00**

Mason's 24 (underlined) Patent Nov 30th 1858, aqua, qt..............**30.00**

Mason Star Jar, qt......................**1.00**

Perfect Seal Wide Mouth Adjustable, pt......................**6.00**

Presto Supreme Mason, pt.........**1.00**

Putnam (on base), aqua, 7⅜".....**75.00**

Safe Seal (in circle), blue, pt......**5.00**

Superior AG Co (in circle), aqua, pt..**12.00**

**The Marion Jar Mason's Patent Nov 30th 1858, medium bluish green, period zinc lid, pint, $50.00; Mason, medium amber, zinc lid, ca 1915 – 25, pint, $55.00. (Photo courtesy Pacific Glassworks Auctions)**

TM Lightning, aqua, pt..............**4.00**

Trade Mark 'The Smiley' Self Sealer, qt.........................................**6.00**

Trademark Banner Warranted, blue, pt.................................**7.00**

Victory (in shield) on milk glass lid, twin side clamps, pt.............**8.00**

Wears Jar (in circle), pt..............**9.00**

# Games

The ideal collectible game is one that combines playability (i.e., good strategy, interaction, surprise, etc.) with interesting graphics and unique components. Especially desirable are the very old games from the nineteenth and early twentieth centuries as well as those relating to early or popular TV shows and movies. As always, value depends on rarity and condition of the box and playing pieces. For a greatly expanded list and more information, see *Schroeder's Collectible Toys, Antique to Modern* (Collector Books).

A-Team, 1984, EXIB................**25.00**

Addams Family, Ideal, 1965, VGIB..**35.00**

Adventures of Robin Hood, Betty-B, 1956, EXIB........................**65.00**

Alien, Kenner, 1979, EXIB.......**50.00**

Amazing Chan & the Chan Clan, Whitman, 1973, NMIB......**20.00**

Archies, Whitman, 1969, NMIB......**40.00**

Arrest & Trial, Transogram, 1963, EXIB................................**30.00**

Babes in Toyland, Whitman, 1961, EXIB................................**20.00**

Bargain Hunter, Milton Bradley, 1981, NMIB......................**20.00**

Barney Miller, Parker Bros, 1977, NMIB................................**20.00**

Bat Masterson, Lowell, 1958, NMIB..**75.00**

Beat the Clock, Milton Bradley, 1960s, NMIB......................**15.00**

Bermuda Triangle, 1976, EXIB.....**25.00**

Big Game (Pinball), Marx, 1950s, NM.................................**60.00**

Black Beauty, Transogram, 1957, EXIB................................**25.00**

Blondie, Parker Bros, 1970s, NMIB ..**15.00**

Bozo Ed-U Cards, 1972, EXIB .....**15.00**

Bug-A-Boo, Whitman, 1968, NMIB..**25.00**

Bullwinkle's Hide 'N' Seek Games, Milton Bradley, 1961, EXIB ..**50.00**

Can't Stop, Parker Bros, 1980, NMIB ...............................**15.00**

Captain Caveman Card Game, 1979, MIB ..........................**10.00**

Careers, Parker Bros, 1965, NMIB..**20.00**

Challenge the Chief, Ideal, 1973, NMIB ................................**25.00**

CHiPs, Ideal, 1981, MIB ..........**25.00**

Chopper Strike, Milton Bradley, 1976, VGIB ........................**10.00**

Cinderella, Parker Bros, 1964, EXIB....................................**50.00**

Clue, Parker Bros, 1972, NMIB ......**10.00**

Containment, Shamus Gamus, 1979, EXIB........................**15.00**

Crazy Clock, Ideal, 1964, NMIB .....**50.00**

Dark Crystal Game, Milton Bradley, 1982, NMIB ......................**25.00**

Davy Crockett Ed-U Cards, 1955, EXIB....................................**30.00**

Detectives, Transogram, 1961, NMIB ................................**50.00**

Dick Tracy, SelRight, 1961, NMIB..**40.00**

**Dick Van Dyke Game, Standard Toykraft, 1964, MIB, $75.00. (Photo courtesy Rick Polizzi)**

Dogfight, Milton Bradley, 1962, EXIB....................................**40.00**

Dr Kildare, Ideal, 1962, NMIB .....**30.00**

Dukes of Hazzard, Ideal, 1981, EXIB ..**25.00**

Emergency, Milton Bradley, 1973, NMIB ................................**20.00**

Eye Guess, 1966, EXIB ............**20.00**

Flintstones, Milton Bradley, 1971, NMIB ................................**20.00**

Flipper Flips, Mattel, 1965, NMIB..**40.00**

Games People Play, Alpsco, 1967, NMIB ................................**25.00**

Get in That Tub, Hasbro, 1974, unused, NMIB ...................**50.00**

Godzilla, Mattel, 1978, EXIB.....**40.00**

Gomer Pyle, Transogram, 1964, EXIB....................................**50.00**

Gumby & Pokey Playful Trails, 1968, NMIB ......................**25.00**

Hangman, Milton Bradley, 1976, NMIB ................................**15.00**

High Gear, Mattel, 1953, NMIB..**40.00**

Hoopla, Ideal, 1966, NMIB ......**60.00**

Hoppity Hooper, Milton Bradley, 1964, NMIB ......................**75.00**

I Spy, Ideal, 1965, NMIB .........**75.00**

James Bond 007 Tarot Game, 1973, NMIB ................................**75.00**

Jeopardy, Milton Bradley, 1964, EXIB....................................**30.00**

Jeopardy, Milton Bradley, 1972, 10th edition, NMIB ...........**15.00**

Jetson's Fun Pad, Milton Bradley, 1963, NMIB ......................**80.00**

Joker's Wild, Milton Bradley, 1973, NMIB ................................**15.00**

Jungle Book, Parker Bros, 1966, NMIB ................................**45.00**

Land of the Lost, Milton Bradley, 1975, NMIB ......................**30.00**

Let's Drive, 1969, VGIB ...........**20.00**

Lone Ranger, Milton Bradley, 1966, NMIB ................................**35.00**

Mad's Spy vs Spy, Milton Bradley, 1986, NMIB ......................**40.00**

Man From UNCLE Card Game, 1965, 1965, NM .................**35.00**

Match Game, 1963, EXIB ........**50.00**

McHale's Navy, Transogram, 1962, NMIB ..............................**50.00**

Melvin the Moon Man, Remco, 1959, NMIB ..............................**65.00**

Merry Milkman, Hasbro, 1955, EXIB..................................**40.00**

Miami Vice, Pepper Lane, 1984, EXIB..................................**25.00**

Mighty Mouse, Parker Bros, 1964, NMIB ..............................**65.00**

Mission Impossible, Ideal, 1966, EXIB..................................**75.00**

Monkees Game, Transogram, 1968, EXIB..................................**50.00**

Ms Pac Man Board Game, 1982, EXIB..................................**25.00**

Mystery Date, Milton Bradley, 1965, NMIB ..............................**100.00**

Newlywed Game, Hasbro, 1969, NMIB ..............................**20.00**

**Napoleon Solo The Man From U.N.C.L.E. Game, Ideal, 1965, NMIB, $50.00.** (Photo courtesy American Pie Collectibles)

Nurses, Ideal, 1963, NMIB ......**40.00**

Partridge Family, Milton Bradley, 1971, NMIB ......................**35.00**

Peter Gunn, Parker Bros, 1969, NMIB ..............................**40.00**

Philip Marlow, Transogram, 1960, EXIB..................................**25.00**

Planet of the Apes, Milton Bradley, 1974, EXIB........................**25.00**

Poky the Clown Target Game, Wyandotte, 1950s, EXIB ...............**75.00**

Popeye Ring Toss, Transogram, EXIB................................**165.00**

Prince Valiant, Transogram, 1955, EXIB..................................**45.00**

Raise the Titanic, Hoyle, 1987, EXIB..................................**20.00**

Rebel, Ideal, 1961, NMIB.........**75.00**

Road Runner Game, Milton Bradley, 1968, NMIB .......................**10.00**

Rondevous, Create, 1965, NMIB .....**25.00**

Ruff & Ready Spelling Game, Exclusive Plaything, 1958, EXIB ......**30.00**

Secret Agent, Milton Bradley, 1966, EXIB..................................**25.00**

Smack-A-Roo Game Set, Mattel, 1964, EXIB........................**40.00**

Smokey Bear, Milton Bradley, 1968, unused, NMIB ...................**75.00**

Snoopy Card Game, Ideal, 1965, NMIB ..............................**25.00**

Spy Detector, Mattel, 1960, NMIB ..**75.00**

Star Trek Board Game, 1975, EXIB..**50.00**

Submarine Search, Milton Bradley, 1973, EXIB........................**40.00**

Superstition, Milton Bradley, 1977, NMIB ..............................**20.00**

That Girl, Remco, 1969, EXIB .....**70.00**

Tip It, 1965, VGIB ...................**20.00**

Tom & Jerry, Milton Bradley, 1977, EXIB..................................**35.00**

Voodoo, Schaper, 1967, EXIB .....**25.00**

Wink Tennis, Transogram, 1956, NMIB ..............................**15.00**

Wonder Woman, Hasbro, 1973, NMIB ..............................**50.00**

Wyatt Earp, Transogram, 1958, EXIB..................................**50.00**

10-4 Good Buddy, 1976, EXIB......**25.00**

# Garfield

America's favorite grumpy cat, Garfield has his own band of devotees who are able to find a good variety of merchandise modeled after his likeness. Garfield was created in 1976 by Jim Davis. He underwent many changes by the time he debuted in newspaper in 1978. By 1980 his first book was released, followed quickly in 1981 by a line of collectibles by Dakin and Enesco. The stuffed plush animals and ceramic figures were a huge success. There have been thousands of items made since, with many that are hard to find being produced in Germany, the Netherlands, England, and other European countries. Banks, displays, PVCs, and figurines are the most desirable items of import from these countries.

Alarm clock, Garfield sleeping on moon, 2 lg black bells for alarms ....**20.00**

**Alarm clock, smiling face plastic case, Sunbeam, 6½", NM, $20.00.**

Band-Aids, Garfield Bandages on box, 25 sterile ¾" strips, MIB ...............**12.00**

Bank, ceramic, piggy bank shape, Paws, MIB .........................**45.00**
Bank, Feed the Kitty, Enesco, 1980, 5¾x6" .................................**18.00**
Comforter, double sided, twin size, EX......................................**25.00**
Cookie jar, coming out of chimney, Enesco, 1981, 5", NM ........**80.00**
Doll, Big Bad Wolf, plush, Furry Tales tag, MIB ...................**55.00**
Doll, Jack in the Beanstalk, plush, NM ....................................**55.00**
Figurine, Let's Get Fiscal, w/Odie, Enesco, 1976, M (original tag)..**50.00**
Figurine, Sitting Pretty, in chair w/popcorn, drink & remote, 1978...................................**20.00**
Figurine, snorkling, PVC, 3" L......**12.00**
Fish tank, figure w/clear stomach tank, red rocks inside, electric, EX......................................**55.00**
Ornament, in pajamas & Christmas hat, w/stocking w/teddy bear, 1994...................................**15.00**
Teapot, figural holding fish (spout), ceramic, 6" .........................**25.00**
Toothbrush holder, figurine w/hole in back, Enesco, 1981 ...............**45.00**
Wacky Wobbler, orange plastic, MIB...**60.00**
Wall light, head & front feet, porcelain w/metal base, EX........**110.00**

# Gas Station Collectibles

From the invention of the automobile came the need for gas service stations, who sought to attract customers through a wide variety of advertising methods. Gas and oil companies issued thermometers, signs, calendars, clocks, banks, and scores of other items emblazoned with their logos and catchy slogans. Though a rather specialized area, gas station collectibles encompass a wide variety of items that appeal to automobilia and advertising collectors as well. For further information we recommend *Value Guide to Gas Station Memorabilia* by B.J. Summers and Wayne Priddy (Collector Collector Books).

Badge, Shell, metal, logo w/red cloisonné Shell name, 2x2", EX.............**450.00**

Blotter, Goodrich Tires, cardboard, winter scene, 1950s, 6½", VG .....................................**12.00**

Calendar, Mobiloil, Magnolia Trail, ocean scene, 1933, EX......**95.00**

Calendar, Sinclair, lady w/jump rope, Moran, 1946, 33½x16", NM ..................................**165.00**

Clock, Cadillac Service, center logo, yellow plastic, round, EX..**175.00**

Clock, Firestone Tires Batteries, wood & glass, spark plug on face, EX............................**225.00**

Clock, GMC Trucks Sales Service, metal & glass, neon, G .....**800.00**

Clock, Leak-Proof Piston Rings, lights up, Telechron, 15" dia, NM ..................................**495.00**

Clock, Mobil Service, Pegasus logo, metal frame/glass lens, round, EX....................................**195.00**

Clock, Monroe Clock Absorbers, lights up, G ..................**2,115.00**

Clock, Oilzum Motor Oil, man in center, plastic/metal, sq, 16", EX....................................**175.00**

Clock, Quaker State Motor Oil, Ask For..., plastic, sq, 16", VG..**80.00**

Clock, Sinclair, metal & glass, Dino logo, lights up, 1950s, EX..**500.00**

Display, Firestone Battery Cables, tin, name above hooks, 8x20", VG .....................................**45.00**

Gas globe, Atlantic Ethyl, metal frame, glass inserts, 16½", EX ...**650.00**

Gas globe, Capitol Kerosene Oil Co, glass frame & insert, 13½", EX..**600.00**

Gas globe, Esso, glass frame & insert, 13½", EX ..............**325.00**

Gas globe, Kendall Deluxe, Capcolite body w/red paint, 13½", EX..**350.00**

Gas globe, Red Indian Gasoline, Indian chief, glass body, 13½", VG ...................................**725.00**

**Globe, Red Indian Gasoline, screw-on glass body, 13½", EX, $1,300.00.** (Photo courtesy B.J. Summers and Wayne Priddy)

License plate reflecter, D-X, Dura Products, metal, 5½x4", VG..**25.00**

Map rack, Atlantic Maps, metal, black, white & red, 36x8½", EX....**110.00**

Patch, Citgo, cloth, for sleeve, sq, 2⅜", EX ..............................**10.00**

Patch, Gulf, cloth, for sleeve, 2½x2¼", G.........................**12.00**

Road map, Sunoco, Michigan, older model car under logo, from $15 to..**18.00**

Sign, AC Oil Filters, tin, yellow/black/white, ca 1941, 8¾x18", EX ........................**50.00**

Sign, Armstrong Rhino-Flex Tires, metal, yellow & black, 29x12", EX...................................**125.00**

Sign, Cities Service Kold Pruf, cardboard diecut, 2-sided, 18x12", NM ...................................**275.00**

Sign, Esso Credit Cards Honored, porcelain, 2-sided, 14x18", EX...**80.00**

Sign, Golden-Tip Gasoline, metal arrow, blue & yellow, 48" long, VG .....................................**600.00**

Sign, Marathon Products, runner, tin, teal/gold/black/white, round, VG.......................**675.00**

Sign, Niehoff Automobile Products, metal/glass, lights up, 11" dia, VG .....................................**75.00**

Sign, Phillips 66, Ethyl logo, porcelain, 2-sided, 30" dia, EX..**350.00**

Sign, price; Gulf, w/attachment arm, logo at top, VG, from $225 to.......................................**275.00**

Sign, Quaker State Motor Oil, framed metal, 2-sided, 30x28", EX...................................**110.00**

Sign, Service Entrance, porcelain arrow, blue & white, 10x24¼", EX...................................**200.00**

Sign, Texaco, No Smoking, porcelain, multicolor, 4x23", VG ...........**110.00**

Sign, We Recommend D-X, porcelain, red, white & black, 2-sided, VG...........................**165.00**

Statue, Firestone man, molded rubber, 5¾x3", EX...................**50.00**

Thermometer, Mobilgas, Friendly service, porcelain, 34½x4¼", EX ..**250.00**

Tin container, Atlantic Motor Oil, red plane, blue chevron, qt, VG+..**25.00**

Tin container, Bellube Grease, oil derrick & bell on red, 10-oz, G...**35.00**

Tin container, Grand Champion... Motor Oil, race scene, 2-gallon, EX....................................**145.00**

Tin container, Mobilgrease #4, Saxony, 100-lb, VG, from $35 to........................................**55.00**

Tin container, Pep Boys' Pure as Gold Cup Grease, 1-lb, 4¼" dia, EX....................................**185.00**

# Gay Fad

Here's another new area of collecting that's just now taking off. The company started out on a very small scale in the late 1930s, but before long, business was booming! Their first products were hand-decorated kitchenwares, but it's their frosted tumblers, trays, pitchers, and decanters that are being sought out today. In addition to souvenir items and lines with a holiday theme, they made glassware to coordinate with Royal China's popular dinnerware, Currier and Ives. They're also known for their 'bentware' — quirky cocktail glasses with stems that were actually bent. Look for an interlocking 'G' and 'F' or the name 'Gay Fad,' the latter mark indicating pieces from the late 1950s to the early 1960s. Gay Fad is mentioned in *Hazel-Atlas Glass Identification and Value Guide*, by Gene and Cathy Florence. See also Anchor Hocking.

Ashtray, Trout Flies, clear .........**8.00**

Batter bowl, Fruits, milk white, signed w/F (Federal Glass), handled..**55.00**

Bent tray, classic design, paper label, 2 sq trays in metal frame....**22.00**

Bent tray, Phoenix Bird, clear, signed Gay Fad, 13¾" dia .................**17.00**

Bent tray, Stylized Cats, clear, signed Gay Fad, 11½" dia ................**26.00**

Beverage set, Magnolia, clear, 86-oz pitcher & 6 13-oz tumblers ..**75.00**

Bowl, chile; Fruits, 2¼x5" ........**12.00**

Bowl, splash-proof; Fruits, Fire-King, 4¼x6½" .....................**55.00**

Cansiter set, Red Rose, red lids, white interior, 3-pc ............**60.00**

Casserole, Apple, w/lid, Fire-King, Ivory, 1-qt ..........................**65.00**

Casserole, Fruits, w/lid, Fire-King, 1-qt ....................................**35.00**

Cocktail shaker, full-figure ballerina, frosted, 28-oz, 9" ..........**35.00**

Cruet set, Oil & Vinegar, Cherry, clear....................................**14.00**

Goblet, Bow Pete, Hoffman Beer, 16-oz .........................................**15.00**

Ice tub, Gay '90s, frosted .........**21.00**

Loaf pan, Apple, Fire-King, Ivory..**35.00**

Mug, Fruits, stackable, Fire-King, 3" .........................................**12.00**

Mug, Notre Dame, frosted, 16-oz..**15.00**

Pitcher, Currier & Ives, blue & white, frosted, 86-oz ..........**70.00**

Pitcher, juice; Ada Orange, frosted, 36-oz ...................................**18.00**

Pitcher, Rosemaling (tulips), white inside, 32-oz .......................**28.00**

Plate, Fruits, lace edge, Hazel Atlas, 8½" ....................................**17.50**

Range set, Rooster, frosted w/red metal lids, 8-oz, 4-pc........**120.00**

Refrigerator container, Distlefink on white, Fire-King, w/lid, 4x8"..**50.00**

Salt & pepper shakers, Fruits, 3½", pr, MIB ...............................**50.00**

Stem, bent cocktail, Beau Brummel, clear, signed Gay Fad, 3½-oz..**10.00**

Tom & Jerry set, Christmas bells, milk white, marked GF, bowl & 6 cups .................................**70.00**

Tumbler, Christmas Greetings From Gay Fad, frosted, 4-oz............**17.00**

Tumbler, Hors D'oeuvres, clear, 14-oz ........................................**10.00**

Tumbler, Ohio Presidents, frosted, 12-oz, set of 8 .....................**60.00**

Tumbler, Oregon state map on pink picket fence, clear, marked GF ..**8.00**

Tumbler, Say When, frosted, 4-oz..**8.00**

Tumbler, Zombie, giraffe, frosted, marked GF, 14-oz ..............**14.00**

Tumblers, Dickens Christmas Carol characters, frosted, 12-oz, set of 8.........................................**40.00**

Tumblers, Ohio Presidents, frosted, 12-oz, set of 8 .....................**55.00**

Vanity set, butterflies in meadow, pink inside, 5-pc ...............**60.00**

Vase, Red Poppy, clear, footed, 10"...**24.00**

**Waffle set, Little Black Sambo on frosted glass, 48 ounce waffle batter jug and 11½" syrup jug, $275.00 for the pair.**

Wine set, Grapes, decanter & 4 2½-oz stemmed wines, clear, 5-pc..**40.00**

# Geisha Girl China

More than sixty-five different patterns of tea services were exported from Japan around the turn of the century, each depicting geishas going about the everyday activities of Japanese life. Mt. Fuji is often featured in the background. Geisha Girl Porcelain is a generic term collectors use to identify them all. Many of our lines contain reference to the color of the rim bands, which many collectors use to tentatively date the ware.

Ashtray, Temple A, spade shape, multicolor............................**25.00**

Biscuit jar, Baskets of Mums, melon ribbed, 3-footed, red w/gold..**50.00**

Bowl, berry; Fan A, cobalt/brick red/gold, scalloped, marked......................**22.00**

Bowl, carp, red w/gold, 6".........**15.00**

Bowl, Cherry Blossoms, red-orange edge, 7½"............................**30.00**

Bowl, salad; Garden Bench A, 9-lobed, red, 7¼" ...................**25.00**

Butter pat, Fan A, red, 4¼"........**8.00**

**Dresser tray, Blind Man's Bluff, cobalt background, $70.00.** (Photo courtesy Elyce Litts)

Cocoa pot, Pillar Print, red-brown w/gold, cylindrical..............**55.00**

Egg cup, double, Child Reaching for Butterfly, red w/gold ...........**13.00**

Lemonade set, Bellflower, brown w/trim, pitcher+5 mugs .....**125.00**

Mint dish, Gardening, 4-lobed, cobalt w/gold ......................**13.00**

Mint dish, Seamstress, floriate shape, handles, Japan mark, 5¼x4" .................................**14.00**

Plate, Fan w/Fan Dance reserves, red-orange, toy size, 4½" ...........**15.00**

Plate, Wait for Me, floriate shape, red-orange w/gold buds, 8¾".......**26.00**

Puff box, Field Laborers, red w/gold..**20.00**

Salt & pepper shakers, Dressing, red, pr.................................**12.00**

Sauce dish, meeting B, dark apple green ................................**12.00**

Tea set, Visitor to the Court, cobalt w/gold, Ozan mark, 3-pc....**65.00**

Teacup & saucer, Blue Hoo......**14.00**

Teacup & saucer, Cloud B, red-orange w/yellow .................**14.00**

Teacup & saucer, Writing B, blue w/gold ...............................**15.00**

Toothpick holder, Circle Dance, cylindrical, red...................**15.00**

Tray, dresser; Garden Bench D, hand-painted green & red w/gold ...............................**55.00**

Vase, bud; Watching the Carp, red-orange, 4½" ........................**18.00**

Vase, Cloud A, cobalt w/gold-drip neck & rim, 5½" .................**30.00**

# GI Joe

Introduced by Hasbro in 1964, 12" GI Joe dolls were offered in four basic packages: Action Soldier, Action Sailor, Action Marine, and

Action Pilot. A Black figure was included in the line, and there were representatives of many nations as well. Talking dolls followed a few years later, and scores of accessory items such as vehicles, guns, uniforms, etc., were made to go with them all. Even though the line was discontinued in 1976, it was evident the market was still there, and kids were clamoring for more. So in 1982, Hasbro brought out the 'little' 3¾" GI Joe figures, each with his own descriptive name. Sales were unprecedented. The small figures are easy to find, but most of them are 'loose' and played with. Collectors prefer old store stock still in the original packaging; such examples are worth from two to four times more than those without the package, sometimes even more.

For more information we recommend *Schroeder's Collectible Toys, Antique to Modern*, published by Collector Books.

## 12" Figures and Accessories

Accessory, armored suit, Demolition, EX.......................................**15.00**
Accessory, binoculars, red w/string, 1960s, EX...........................**14.00**
Accessory, boots, Flying Space Adventure, yellow, EX.......**32.00**
Accessory, combat field jacket, 1964, MOC................................**700.00**
Accessory, entrenching tool, Australian, EX.........................**10.00**
Accessory, fatigue pants, Action Marine #7715, camo, M (NM card)................................**400.00**

Accessory, flag, Army or USAF, EX, ea.........................................**35.00**
Accessory, head gear, Landing Signal Officer, 1960s, EX..............**60.00**
Accessory, helmet, British, EX..**18.00**
Accessory, jackhammer, EX+..**275.00**
Accessory, pup tent, Marine, EX .**25.00**
Accessory, radio, Airbourne MP, black, marked Hong Kong, G+ ..**245.00**
Accessory, scuba suit, MIP (sealed)..**580.00**
Accessory, sleeping bag, #7515, MOC................................**185.00**
Accessory, uniform, State Trooper, w/accessories, NM ...........**100.00**
Figure, Action Marine, #7700, EXIB................................**350.00**

Figure, Action Marine, #7700, MIB, $400.00.

Figure, Action Nurse, #8060, MIB (sealed)........................**5,000.00**
Figure, Action Pilot, #7800, M (EX box)....................................**400.00**
Figure, Action Sailor, #7600, NM (EX box) ...........................**300.00**
Figure, Action Sailor, Landing Signal Officer, NM................**200.00**
Figure, Action Soldier, #7800, MIB, from $275 to.....................**375.00**

Figure, Action Soldier, Green Beret, EX......................................**115.00**

Figure, Action Soldier, Ski Patrol, EX......................................**315.00**

Figure, Action Soldier, West Point Cadet, NM.........................**325.00**

Figure, Action Team Adventurer (Black), #7404, NMIB, from $250 to.............................**300.00**

Figure, Action Team Commander (Talking), #7400, EX.......**195.00**

Figure, Adventure Team Adventurer, Aerial Recon, EX................**175.00**

Figure, Adventure Team Bullet Man, #8026, NM, from $250 to......................................**275.00**

Figure, Adventure Team Man of Action, Photo Recon, EX....**98.00**

Figure, Adventure Team of Action, #7500, VGIB .....................**200.00**

Figure, Australian Desert Jeep Driver, EX .............................**165.00**

Figure, British Commando, #8104, EX, from $275 to..............**350.00**

Figure, German Soldier, near complete, EX ..........................**150.00**

Figure, German Stormtrooper, near complete, EX....................**150.00**

Vehicle, Amphibian Duck, M, from $150 to.............................**180.00**

Vehicle, Combat Jeep Set, #7000, EX (EX box) .....................**265.00**

Vehicle, German Staff Car, Action Man Task Force, M (VG+ box)....**275.00**

Vehicle, Iron Knight Tank, M.**135.00**

Vehicle, Panther Jet, EX........**400.00**

Vehicle, Space Capsule, VG+ ....**55.00**

## 3¾" Figures and Accessories

Accessory, Ammo Dump Unit, 1985, EXIP..................................**20.00**

Accessory, Crimson Attack Tank, 1985, MIB ........................**325.00**

Accessory, Dreadnok Attack Jeep, EX......................................**150.00**

Accessory, Equilizer, 1989, NMIB.**165.00**

Accessory, Hovercraft, 1984, mail-in, MIP......................................**40.00**

Accessory, LCV Recon Sled, 1983, EX..........................................**5.00**

Accessory, Mobile Missle System, EX........................................**45.00**

Accessory, Q-Force Battle Gear, Action Force, MIP................**5.00**

Figure, Ace, 1983, EX...............**15.00**

Figure, AVAC, 1985, NM+.......**35.00**

Figure, Bazooka, 1985, EX.......**11.00**

Figure, Beach Head, 1986, NM.....**20.00**

Figure, Blocker, 1987, MOC.....**15.00**

Figure, Budo, 1988, EX............**12.00**

Figure, Buzzer, 1985, MOC......**35.00**

Figure, Clutch, 1984, tan, NM.......**27.00**

Figure, Crazylegs, 1987, MOC ......**18.50**

Figure, Croc Master, 1987, NM.......**13.50**

**Figure, Deep Six, 1989, MOC, $22.00.**

Figure, Destro, 1983, MOC ......**35.00**

Figure, Dr Mindbender, 1986, MOC ..**35.00**

Figure, Drop-Zone, 1990, MOC......**25.00**

Figure, Falcon, 1987, NM ........**33.00**

Figure, Fridge, 1986, mail-in, NM ..**20.00**

Figure, Hardball, 1988, NM.....**12.00**
Figure, Jinx, 1987, MOC..........**52.50**
Figure, Low-Light, 1986, NM.....**25.00**
Figure, Maverick, 1987, NM.....**10.00**
Figure, Nunchuk, 1992, MOC.....**11.50**
Figure, Recoil, 1989, EX...........**10.00**
Figure, Red Dog, 1987, NM........**8.00**
Figure, Ryu, 1993, MOC..........**12.50**
Figure, Sci-Fi, 1986, MOC.......**25.00**
Figure, Slip Stream, 1986, EX.......**7.00**
Figure, Snake Eyes, 1985, NM.....**75.00**
Figure, Spirit, 1984, MOC........**15.00**
Figure, Taurus, 1987, NM........**10.00**
Figure, Thunder, 1984, NM.....**17.50**
Figure, Torch, 1985, EX...........**15.00**

**Figure, Voltar, MOC,
$30.00.**

Figure, Wet Suit, 1986, NM.....**23.00**
Figure, Zartan, 1984, NM........**30.00**

# Glass Animals and Birds

Nearly every glasshouse of note has at some point over the years produced these beautiful models, some of which double for vases, bookends, and flower frogs. Many were made during the 1930s through the 1950s and 1960s, and these are the most collectible. But you'll also be seeing brand new examples, and you need to study to know the difference. A good reference to help you sort them all out is *Glass Animals, Including Animal & Figural Related Items,* by Dick and Pat Spencer (Collector Books). See also Fenton.

Airedale, caramel slag, Imperial..**100.00**
Airedale, crystal, Heisey.....**1,400.00**
Bird, orange, #1311, Viking, 10".....**40.00**
Bird in flight, Amber Marigold, wings out, Westmoreland, 5" W....**45.00**
Bird of Paradise, crystal, Duncan & Miller..............................**650.00**
Bunny, light blue, Fenton........**20.00**
Butterfly, crystal, Westmoreland, 4½"....................................**40.00**
Camel, crystal, LE Smith.........**50.00**
Cardinal, Green Mist, Westmoreland ...................................**22.00**
Cat, Sassy Suzie, black satin w/painted decoration, #9448, Tiffin, 11".........................**175.00**
Chanticleer, black, Fostoria, 10¾"..**500.00**

**Chanticleer, crystal, Fostoria, 1950 – 58, 10¾", from $200.00 to $250.00.** (Photo courtesy Pat and Dick Spencer)

Colt, amber, balking, Imperial.....**120.00**

Colt, cobalt, kicking, Heisey ......**2,000.00**
Cygnet, caramel slag, Imperial ......**35.00**
Dog, orange, Viking .................**50.00**
Donkey, Ultra Blue, Imperial.....**55.00**
Dragon swan, crystal, Paden City, 9¾" L ...............................**250.00**
Duck, ruby, round, footed, Viking, 5" ..**40.00**
Flower frog, Bashful Charlotte, green, Cambridge, 11½" ................**350.00**
Flower frog, Rose Lady, green, Cambridge, 8½" ......................**225.00**
Flower holder, Blue Jay, crystal, Cambridge ......................**150.00**
Flying mare, crystal, Heisey ......**4,000.00**

Gazelle, ultra blue clear, made for Mirror Images, by Imperial, marked ALIG, 11", from $150.00 to $200.00. (Photo courtesy Pat and Dick Spencer)

Giraffe, Rosalene, Fenton, issued for Heisey ...............................**80.00**
Goldfish, crystal, vertical, Fostoria..**150.00**
Heron, crystal, Cambridge, lg, 12"..**150.00**
Horse, crystal, rearing, Paden City....................................**325.00**
Mopey dog, crystal, Federal, 3½"..**10.00**
Owl, milk glass, Imperial.........**35.00**
Pelican, crystal, Paden City......**650.00**
Penguin, crystal, Viking, 7" .....**25.00**
Pig, amberina, Westmoreland .....**85.00**
Piglet, crystal, standing, New Martinsville ..........................**175.00**
Plug horse, cobalt, Heisey......**1,200.00**

Police dog, ruby, Viking for Mirror Images...............................**100.00**
Pony, black, Paden City, 12" .....**350.00**
Rabbit, mama, crystal, New Martinsville ..........................**350.00**

**Ringneck Pheasant, crystal, hollow base, American Glassware Co., (K.R. Haley Glassware Co. mold), ca. 1947, 11½" long, from $40.00 to $50.00.** (Photo courtesy Pat and Dick Spencer)

Robin, red, Westmoreland, 5⅛" .....**27.50**
Rooster, amber, Heisey, 5⅜"......**2,500.00**
Rooster, amber, Imperial .......**400.00**
Rooster, Chanticleer, blue, Paden City, 9½" .........................**300.00**
Seal, topaz, Fostoria, 3⅞".........**75.00**
Sparrow, crystal, Heisey ........**100.00**
Swan, ebony, Cambridge, 10½" ......**300.00**
Swan, emerald, Cambridge, 3" ......**55.00**
Swan, milk glass w/decoration, LE Smith, 8½" .........................**35.00**
Swordfish, blue opalescent, Duncan & Miller, rare..................**500.00**
Tiger, crystal frost, head down, New Martinsville, 7¼" .............**200.00**
Trout, crystal, LG Wright ......**150.00**
Turkey, green, Cambridge, w/lid...**550.00**
Wren, Pink Mist, 2½" ..............**25.00**

# Glass, Porcelain, and Pottery Shoes

While many miniature shoes

were made simply as whimsies, you'll also find thimble holders, perfumes, inkwells, salts, candy containers, and bottles made to resemble shoes of many types. See also Degenhart

## Glass

Baby shoe, clear frosted, hollow sole, laces flat, 1930s, 3⅛" ............**50.00**
Boot, Daisy & Button top, amber, foot simulated alligator, 2½" ......**25.00**
Boot, green cut to crystal, 7¾x 5½" ..**85.00**
Boot, green w/embossed western motif, applied handle, 1950s, 10x7" ..................................**45.00**
Boot, multicolor spatter w/mica, applied crystal decor, 5½"..**125.00**
Boot, purple slag, rolled cuff, EX details................................**85.00**
Boot, Texas; cobalt, Imperial, 1974, 2⅝x2⅝", from $45 to ......**55.00**
Bootie, crystal w/cut decor, paperweight, Waterford, ca 1986, 4⅛" ....................................**85.00**

**Martini boot, clear with green textured decoration and gold, ca 1950, 10x8", $35.00.** (Photo courtesy Earlene Wheatley)

Sandal, Daisy & Button, amethyst, 1⅜x4½" ..............................**85.00**
Santa boot, cobalt, ca 1930, 2¾x2½", from $15 to........................**20.00**
Shoe, Daisy & Button, milk glass, ca 1930, 2⅛x4⅞" ....................**30.00**
Shoe, heavy crystal w/Cuban heel, beading at vamp, 1930s ....**40.00**
Slipper, blue & white millefiori w/crystal ruffle & heel, 5⅛" ......................**95.00**
Slipper, diamond pattern, blue, lg bow, sm heel, 2½x5⅛" .......**75.00**
Slipper, high-cut, Cane pattern, blue, mesh sole, US Glass, 4¾" ...**75.00**
Slipper, man's, dark amber, used as pipe holder, 1930s, 5"..........**40.00**
Slipper, pink & green latticinio ribbons, paper Murano label, 2x6"..**85.00**
Slipper, Salt Lake City Utah lettered in gold, gold trim, from $65 to.................................**75.00**

## Porcelain and Pottery

Baby shoes, white w/painted laces, Block Pottery Co, unjoined pr ....**65.00**
Baby shoes (2 joined), lg bows, blue, McCoy mark, 1948..............**45.00**
Bootie, flower decals, 6 open eyelets, Austria, 1930, 4x2" .............**125.00**
Brogan, blue & white w/colonial scene, Old Foley..., 1960s, 5¼"....**45.00**
Shoe, gray lustre w/applied pink rose & flowers, Germany, 1935, 3½" ....................................**55.00**
Shoe, variegated blue, green & tan, Made in Holland, 1960 ........**65.00**
Slipper, country roses on white, English, ca 1950, 3x4⅛" ............**30.00**
Slipper, Daisy & Button, milk glass w/decal, Heirloom of Tomorrow, 2" ......................................**35.00**

Slipper, Dutch style, couple/flowers/gold trim, Limoges, 1968, 3½" .....................................**40.00**

Slipper, Dutch style, Delft windmill & flowers, ca 1960, 6¼" ......**25.00**

Slipper, white lustre w/orange stripe, Czechoslovakia, 1920s, 6" ........................................**45.00**

Slippers, applied & painted flowers w/gold, miniature, 2½", pr..**45.00**

Slippers, ballerina; red, joined at heel, marked Germany, ca 1950, 9" ........................................**35.00**

Goblet, pilsner; 11-oz..................**9.00**
Goblet, sherbet; 6½-oz................**5.00**
Goblet, water; 9-oz......................**7.50**
Ice tub, in metal 3-footed frame .....**20.00**
Pitcher, 5¼", w/metal frame......**16.50**
Salad dressing set, includes 3 bowls (4") & brass-finished caddy..**19.50**
Tumbler, beverage; 12½-oz ........**8.50**
Tumbler, cooler; 14-oz ...............**9.50**
Tumbler, jigger; 2-oz...................**7.00**
Tumbler, juice; 6-oz ...................**5.00**
Tumbler, old-fashioned; 9-oz......**6.00**
Tumbler, shot glass, 2-oz............**6.50**
Tumbler, water; 10-oz ...............**8.50**

# Golden Foliage

If you can remember when this glassware came packed in boxes of laundry soap, you're telling your age. Along with 'white' margarine, Golden Foliage was a product of the 1950s. It was made by the Libbey Glass Company, and the line was rather limited; as far as we know, we've listed the entire assortment here. The glassware features a satin band with various leaves and gold trim. (It also came in silver.)

**Creamer and sugar bowl, $15.00 for the set.**

Goblet, cocktail; 4-oz...................**6.00**
Goblet, cordial; 1-oz ...................**8.50**

# Graniteware

Graniteware is actually a base metal with a coating of enamel. It was first made in the 1870s, but graniteware of sorts was made well into the 1950s. In fact, some of what you'll find today is brand new. But new pieces are much lighter in weight than the old ones. Look for seamed construction, metal handles, and graniteware lids on such things as tea- and coffeepots. All these are indicators of age. Colors are another, and swirled pieces — cobalt blue and white, green and white, brown and white, and red and white — are generally older, harder to find, and therefore more expensive. For a comprehensive look at this popular collectible, we recommend *The Collector's Encyclopedia of Graniteware* by Helen Greguire (Collector Books).

Baking pan, red & white lg swirl, cobalt trim, oval, 15¼", VG.............**3,650.00**

Biscuit sheet, brown & white mottle, 24-cup, Onyx Enamel..., 24-cup....................................**650.00**

Bowl, soup/cereal; solid yellow w/white interior, black trim, 2⅝x6" ..............................**25.00**

Bowl, water; violet shading to light lavender, Thistle Ware, sm, NM ....**225.00**

Butter dish, white w/cobalt trim, seamless, L&G Mfg Co, 4¾x8⅞"..**275.00**

Chamber pot, blue & white lg swirl w/black trim, Azure...label, w/lid.................................**275.00**

**Chamber pot, blue and white speckled, 8" diameter, G, $150.00.**

Coffee basket, solid light gray, stemmed, 4¾x2⅜" dia .......**45.00**

Coffee biggin, red & white medium mottle, red trim, 4-pc, 9¼"..**600.00**

Coffeepot, blue & white wavy mottle, black trim, seamed, 9¼"....................................**425.00**

Coffeepot, lavender & white lg mottle, metal bands, 8½x5¾".....**395.00**

Coffeepot, red & white lg swirl, black trim, seamed, 9½x5¼"....**245.00**

Colander, dark green & white lg swirl w/cobalt, footed, deep ....**425.00**

Custard cup, cream w/green trim, 2¼x3⅜" .............................**55.00**

Dustpan, solid red, 13⅜x10½" .....**265.00**

Egg pan, solid red, 7-eye, 1⅛x9⅞" dia......................................**90.00**

Flask, coffee; cobalt & light blue w/white flecks, seamless, 4½" ..................................**495.00**

Funnel, percolator; cobalt & white lg swirl, 7⅝x4¼" ..................**675.00**

Kettle, cream w/green trim, 16 ribs, w/lid, 6x7⅜" ........................**40.00**

Measure, lavender-blue & white lg swirl, graduated shape, 1-cup...**435.00**

Milk can, blue & white lg swirl, black trim, seamed, 8¾x5⅛" ......**850.00**

Milk can, brown & white lg swirl, black trim, seamless, 9½" .**950.00**

Milk can, cobalt & white lg swirl, white interior, black trim, 9"..........**825.00**

Mold, solid yellow w/white interior, ring type, 2¼x8⅛" .............**50.00**

Muffin pan, redipped brown & white mottle, 8-cup, 14" L ..........**250.00**

Mug, camp/mush; blue & white wavy mottle, black trim, 4⅜x6"..**175.00**

Mug, red & white lg swirl, cobalt trim, seamless, 3⅛x3¼" ...**895.00**

Pie plate, red & white lg mottle, white interior, cobalt trim, 9¾" ...**595.00**

Pitcher, molasses, solid white, dark blue handle/trim, 5½x3½".**145.00**

Plate, light blue & white medium swirl, ¾x10" ......................**75.00**

Potty, gray lg mottle, EL-AN-GE...label, 3¾x6½"..........**145.00**

**Pudding mold, gray mottle, melon shape, 4x7¾", EX, $60.00.**

Pudding pan, lg gray mottle, La Fayette Quality...label, 5¼"..**50.00**

Scoop, gray lg mottle, rolled seamed edges, 8½" .........................**375.00**

Scoop, solid white, 2¾x9¼" ......**95.00**

Teakettle, dark gray relish, aluminum whistle, 4⅝" ........**130.00**

Teapot, blue & white lg mottle, white interior, black handle/trim, 8" ......................................**240.00**

Teapot, white w/flowers, metal trim & mounts, 9¾x5⅝" ..........**375.00**

# Griswold

Cast-iron cooking ware was used extensively in the nineteenth century, and even today lots of folks think no other type of cookware can measure up. But whether they buy it to use or are strictly collectors, Griswold is the name they hold in highest regard. During the latter part of the nineteenth century, the Griswold company began to manufacture the finest cast-iron kitchenware items available at that time. Soon after they became established, they introduced a line of lightweight, cast-aluminum ware that revolutionized the industry. The company enjoyed many prosperous years until its closing in the late 1950s. You'll recognize most items by the marks, which generally will include the Griswold name; for instance, 'Seldon Griswold' and 'Griswold Mfg. Co.' But don't overlook the 'Erie' mark, which the company used as well. See Clubs and Newsletters for information on the Griswold and Cast Iron Cookware Association.

Ashtray, #770, sq, from $20 to ......**30.00**

Breadstick pan, #21, from $125 to ...................................**175.00**

Bundt cake pan, PIN 935, from $800 to........................................**900.00**

Cake mold, Lamb, #866, from $75 to......................................**100.00**

Cake mold, Santa, from $400 to .................................**500.00**

Corn/wheatstick pan, #272, no feet, from $125 to....................**175.00**

Cornstick pan, #283, from $125 to...................................**175.00**

Dutch oven, #6, Erie trademark, round bottom, from $200 to .................................**250.00**

Dutch oven, #9, Erie trademark, round bottom, from $50 to...**75.00**

Dutch oven cover, #8, hinged, from $25 to.................................**35.00**

Gem pan, #1, EPU trademark, PIN 940, from $200 to.............**250.00**

Gem pan, #6, full writing, from $250 to........................................**350.00**

Gem pan, #9, Brownie Cake Pan, PIN 947, from $125 to .............**150.00**

Gem pan, #12, marked NO 12, sq corners, from $175 to........**225.00**

Gem pan, #14, Turk Head, PIN 641, from $600 to.....................**700.00**

Gem pan, #15, French roll, fully marked, from $125 to......**150.00**

Gem pan, #18, popover, wide handle, 6 cups, from $50 to .............**75.00**

Gem pan, #24, breadstick, PIN 957, from $400 to.....................**450.00**

Gem pan, #50, heart & star, from $1,000 to .......................**1,500.00**

Gem pan, #2700, wheatstick, from $275 to............................**325.00**

Griddle, #10, handled, slant/EPU trademark, from $50 to .....**75.00**

Griddle, #16, bailed, Erie trademark, from $75 to............**100.00**

Heat regulator, #300, raised markings on 1 side, from $125 to........................................**175.00**

Iron, The Erie Fluter, detachable handle, PINs 297 & 298, from $200 to..............................**250.00**

Kettle, #7, low, Erie trademark, from $50 to.........................**75.00**

Loaf pan, #877, from $250 to...**350.00**

Muffin pan, #273, cornstick, 7 cups, from $15 to.........................**25.00**

Paperweight, pup, marked #30 Griswold Pup, from $200 to ....................................**300.00**

Pitcher, bailed, aluminum, from $225 to.............................**275.00**

Skillet, #2, block trademark, heat ring, from $1,800 to......**2,200.00**

Skillet, #2, slant/EPU trademark, heat ring, from $375 to ....**425.00**

Skillet, #2, slant/Erie trademark, from $350 to.....................**400.00**

Skillet, #3, Slant/Erie trademark, from $30 to.........................**40.00**

Skillet, #3, sm trademark, hinged, from $25 to.........................**45.00**

Skillet, #3, Square Fry, PIN 2103 (+), from $75 to ................**125.00**

Skillet, #4, block trademark, heat ring, from $375 to............**425.00**

Skillet, #4, slant/Erie trademark, nickel plated, from $40 to ..**60.00**

Skillet, #5, block trademark, heat ring, from $375 to............**425.00**

Skillet, #5, Victor, from $350 to....................................**450.00**

Skillet, #7, Victor, fully marked, from $35 to.........................**45.00**

Skillet, #8, sm trademark, extra deep, w/hinge, from $35 to............**45.00**

Skillet, #11, block trademark, from $125 to..............................**175.00**

Skillet, #13, block trademark, from $1,500 to ......................**2,000.00**

Skillet, #15, oval, w/lid, from $750 to......................................**900.00**

Skillet, sq utility; PIN 768, from $25 to......................................**50.00**

Skillet lid, #3, high smooth, from $150 to..............................**200.00**

Skillet lid, #14, low dome, raised writing, from $425 to.......**525.00**

Teakettle, #8, spider trademark top, from $400 to.....................**500.00**

Trivet, Grapes, PIN 1729, lg & decorative, from $10 to.............**20.00**

Trivet, Old Lace (coffeepot), PIN 1739, lg, from $75 to........**125.00**

Wafer iron, w/side-handle base, from $300 to.............................**400.00**

Waffle iron, #9, aluminum, side-handle base, ball hinge, from $30 to.................................**50.00**

Waffle iron, #19, heart & star, low bailed base, from $250 to........................................**300.00**

**Tea-sized cornstick pan #262, with original box, $75.00.**

# Guardian Ware

The Guardian Service company

was in business from 1935 until 1955. They produced a very successful line of hammered aluminum that's just as popular today as it ever was. Sold through the home party plan, special hostess gifts were offered as incentives. Until 1940 metal lids were used, but during the war when the government restricted the supply of available aluminum, glass lids were introduced.

Be sure to judge condition when evaluating Guardian Service. Wear, baked-on grease, scratches, and obvious signs of use devaluate its worth. Our prices range from pieces in average to exceptional condition. To be graded exceptional, the interior of the pan must have no pitting, and the surface must be bright and clean. An item with a metal lid is worth 25% more than the same piece with a glass lid.

Ashtray, glass, w/knight & stars logo, hostess gift, from $10 to .....................................**15.00**

Beverage urn (coffeepot), glass lid, w/screen & dipper, 15" ......**50.00**

Can of cleaner, unopened.........**15.00**

Cookbook, Guardian Service or Pressure Cooker, from $20 to .....................................**35.00**

Dome cooker, 1-qt, glass lid, w/handles, 6¾" dia, from $35 to..**50.00**

Fryer, breakfast; glass lid, 10", from $35 to...............................**50.00**

Fryer, chicken; glass lid, 12", from $60 to...............................**80.00**

Gravy boat, w/undertray, from $30 to........................................**45.00**

Griddle/tray, w/handles, 12½" cooking area, 17" L, from $20 to.....**30.00**

Handle, clamp-on style, from $15 to.........................................**20.00**

Ice bucket, glass lid, liner & tongs, 9", from $45 to ...................**65.00**

**Kettle oven, glass lid, bail handle, with rack, 8x12" diameter, from $100.00 to $125.00.** (Photo courtesy Marilyn Jewell)

Kettle oven, glass lid, w/rack, 6-qt, 11" dia, from $125 to .......**140.00**

Pressure cooker, minimum value.**100.00**

Roaster, turkey; glass lid, w/rack, 16½" L, from $125 to .......**150.00**

Steak servers, well & tree bottom, oval, set of 4, EX................**60.00**

Tray, serving; hammered center, w/handles, 13" dia, from $20 to........................................**30.00**

Trivet, for Economy Trio set, 11¾" dia, from $35 to..................**45.00**

Tureen, bottom; glass lid, from $40 to........................................**65.00**

Tureen, casserole; glass lid, from $65 to...............................**90.00**

Tureen, top; glass lid, from $30 to .....................................**45.00**

# Gurley Candles

Santas, choir boys, turkeys, and angels are among the figural candles made by this company from the 1940s until as late as the 1960s, possibly even longer. They range in size from 2½" to nearly 9", and they're marked 'Gurley' on the bottom. Because they were so appealing, people were reluctant to burn them and instead stored them away and used them again and again. You can still find them today, especially at flea markets and garage sales. Tavern candles (they're marked as well) were made by a company owned by Gurley; they're also collectible.

Christmas, angel, marked Gurley, 5" .........................................**7.00**
Christmas, Black caroler man w/red clothes, 3" .............................**9.50**
Christmas, caroler man w/red clothes, 7" ............................**8.50**
Christmas, choir boy or girl, 2¾", ea .........................................**3.50**
Christmas, grotto w/shepherd & sheep .....................................**14.50**
Christmas, reindeer, marked Tavern, 3½" ...............................**2.50**
Christmas, Santa, 6¼" .............**12.00**
Christmas, snowman running w/red hat, 3" ....................................**7.50**
Christmas, white church w/choir boy inside, 6" ............................**14.50**
Christmas, 3" deer standing in front of candle, 5" ...........................**7.50**
Easter, duck, yellow w/purple bow, 5" .........................................**9.50**
Easter, pink egg w/bunny inside, 3" .........................................**10.00**

Easter, pink winking rabbit w/carrot, 3¼" ...............................**6.00**
Easter, white lily w/blue lip & green candle, 3" ............................**4.50**
Halloween, black owl on orange stump, 3½" ..........................**10.00**
Halloween, ghost, white, 5" ......**20.00**
Halloween, pumpkin-faced scarecrow, 5" ...............................**12.00**
Halloween, witch, black, 8" ......**22.50**

**Halloween, witch, red dress and black cape, 5", $8.00.** (Photo courtesy Melissa Katcher)

Other Occasions, birthday boy, marked Tavern, 3" ...............**5.00**
Other Occasions, Eskimo & igloo, marked Tavern, 2-pc .........**12.50**
Thanksgiving, acorns & leaves, 3½" .....................................**5.00**
Thanksgiving, Indian boy & girl, brown & green clothes, 5", pr .................................**30.00**
Thanksgiving, turkey, 2½" .........**2.50**

# Hagen-Renaker

This California company has been producing quality ceramics since the mid-1940s — mostly detailed, lifelike figurines of animals, though they've made other decorative items as well. Their

Designers Workshop line was primarily horses, larger than most of their other figures. Their portrayal of Disney charcters is superb. Other lines collectors seek are their Millesan Drews Pixies, Rock Wall Plaques and Trays (decorated with primitive animals similar to cave drawings), Black Bisque animals, and Little Horribles (qrotesque miniature figures). In the late 1980s, they introduced Stoneware and Specialty lines, larger than the miniatures but smaller than the Designer Workshop line. They continue to make the Specialties yet today.

Designer's Workshop figurine, Betty, squirrel w/acorn, 1960-66, 3¼" .............................**40.00**

Designer's Workshop figurine, Bing, English bulldog, 1954-72, 1¾x3"..**60.00**

Designer's Workshop figurine, Dandy, Hereford calf, 3x4¼".........**55.00**

Designer's Workshop figurine, Gypsy, pointer dog, 1954-55, 2½x5" ..............................**135.00**

Designer's Workshop figurine, Harry, donkey foal, 1956, 3¾x3" ..**60.00**

Designer's Workshop figurine, piglet, brown, 1970 only, 2x3"...**270.00**

Designer's Workshop figurine, pony, head up, chestnut, 1982-84, 7" ......................................**200.00**

Designer's Workshop figurine, Tabbie, sitting w/hat, 1956, 4" .....**75.00**

Disney miniature, Chip & Dale chipmunks, 1956, 1¼", ea ............**85.00**

Disney miniature, Ruffles from Lady & the Tramp, 1955-59, ⅝".**40.00**

Disney miniature, Tinkerbell kneeling, 1957-60, 1¾" ..............**300.00**

Disney miniature, Wendy from Peter Pan, 1957-60, 2".....**350.00**

**Designer's Workshop, Arab family in rose gray: Amir (stallion), $700.00; Zila (foal), $350.00; and Zara (mare), $900.00. Adults are 9" tall.** (Photo courtesy Ed and Sheri Alcorn)

Little Horribles, Bongo Player, 1959, 1½" ..........................**150.00**

Miniature, bison, 1994-98, 1⅞"......**12.00**

Miniature, cat in purple jacket w/piece of pie, A-302, 1956, 1¾"...**120.00**

Miniature, circus horse w/head up, blue harness, 1980s, 2⅜"......**70.00**

Miniature, cobra in basket, 1992-93, 3⅛" .....................................**35.00**

Miniature, horse rearing, white, A-234, 1958, 3½" .................**125.00**

Miniature, moose, 1950s, 2¼" .....**50.00**

Miniature, pelican flying w/wire, A-810, 1982, 4" ......................**30.00**

Miniature, penguin, 1948 (early), 2¼" .....................................**60.00**

Miniature, raccoon baby, 1983-89, ⅞" .........................................**8.00**

Specialty figurine, baby elephant, gray, #3269, 1¾x3" ...........**35.00**

Specialty figurine, doves in bower, 1992-93, 2x3½" .................**40.00**

Specialty figurine, iguana on rock, 1992-95, 2¼" ......................**45.00**

Specialty figurine, tiger, recumbent, A-2029, 1991-94, 1½".................**40.00**

Wall plaque, butterfly facing right, faux AZ flagstone, 1959-70, 14" .....................................**75.00**

Wall plaque, mosaic rooster on wood board, 1959, rare, 12x18"..**350.00**

# Hall

Most famous for their extensive lines of teapots and colorful dinnerwares, the Hall China Company still operates in East Liverpool, Ohio, where they were established in 1903. Refer to *The Collector's Encyclopedia of Hall China* by Margaret and Kenn Whitmyer (Collector Books) for more information. See Clubs and Newsletters for information on the Hall China Collector's Club. For listings of Hall's most popular dinnerware line, see Autumn Leaf.

Acacia, marmite, w/lid..............**40.00**
Arizona, bowl, cereal; Tomorrow's Classic, 6"............................**9.00**
Arizona, vinegar bottle, Tomorrow's Classic...............................**70.00**
Autumn Flowers, bean pot, New England, #4......................**160.00**
Beauty, custard........................**21.00**
Blue Blossom, ball jug, #3......**135.00**
Blue Blossom, teapot, Hook Cover...**300.00**
Blue Bouquet, cake plate .........**42.50**
Blue Bouquet, soup tureen.....**305.00**
Blue Garden, custard, Thick Rim ..**22.00**
Blue Garden, water bottle, Zephyr..**565.00**
Blue Willow, casserole, 5" ........**80.00**
Bouquet, butter dish, Tomorrow's Classic..............................**200.00**
Bouquet, platter, Tomorrow's Classic, 15" ................................**32.50**
Bouquet, vase, Tomorrow's Classic ..**90.00**
Buckingham, bowl, celery; oval, Tomorrow's Classic............**23.00**

Buckingham, candlestick, Tomorrow's Classic, 8", ea ......................**42.50**
Cactus, casserole, Five Band.....**50.00**
Cactus, creamer, Viking...........**32.50**
Cameo Rose, bowl, fruit; E-style, 5¼" ......................................**6.00**

**Cameo Rose, flat soup, 8", from $12.00 to $14.00.** (Photo courtesy Margaret and Kenn Whitmyer)

Cameo Rose, plate, E-style, 8" ......**9.00**
Caprice, egg cup, Tomorrow's Classic ........................................**46.00**
Caprice, platter, Tomorrow's Classic, 17" ................................**36.00**
Christmas Tree & Holly, cookie jar, Zeisel, E-style .................**325.00**
Christmas Tree & Holly, tidbit, 2-tier, E-style ......................**115.00**
Crocus, bowl, fruit; D-style, 5½" ......**9.50**
Crocus, custard ........................**30.00**
Crocus, plate, D-style, 8¼".......**11.00**
Dawn, bowl, fruit; Tomorrow's Classic, 5¾" ................................**7.50**
Dawn, marmite, w/lid, Tomorrow's Classic ...............................**33.50**
Eggshell, bowl, salad; Dot, 15½" ......**50.00**
Eggshell, teapot, Rutherford, Swag....**300.00**
Fantasy, coffeepot, Tomorrow's Classic, 6-cup .....................**90.00**
Fantasy, vinegar bottle, Tomorrow's Classic ...............................**70.00**

Fern, jug, Century ..................**30.00**

Fern, ladle, Century ................**20.00**

Five Band, cookie jar, red or cobalt.**135.00**

Five Band, syrup, colors other than red or cobalt ......................**65.00**

Flair, ashtray, Tomorrow's Classic .....**9.00**

Flair, onion soup, Tomorrow's Classic, w/lid .............................**40.00**

Flare-Ware, bowl, Gold Lace, 7¾"..**7.50**

Flare-Ware, casserole, Heather Rose, 3-qt ...........................**25.00**

French Flower, creamer, Bellevue..**22.50**

French Flower, teapot, Parade.**135.00**

Frost Flowers, casserole, Tomorrow's Classic, 2-qt ......................**50.00**

Frost Flowers, coffeepot, Tomorrow's Classic, 6-cup....................**100.00**

Game Bird, plate, E-style, 10"...**70.00**

Garden of Eden, bowl, fruit; Century, 5¾" ......................................**6.50**

Garden of Eden, ladle, Century...**19.00**

Gold Label, baker, French........**16.00**

Golden Glo, casserole, hen on nest....................................**45.00**

Golden Glo, mug, #343 .............**11.00**

Golden Oak, creamer, modern ..**11.00**

Golden Oak, gravy boat, D-style..**16.50**

Harlequin, saucer, Tomorrow's Classic .........................................**2.00**

Harlequin, teapot, Thorley, Tomorrow's Classic ...................**275.00**

Heather Rose, creamer, E-style ...**9.00**

Heather Rose, teapot, London, E-style..................................**22.50**

Holiday, cup, AD; Tomorrow's Classic ....................................**25.00**

Holiday, plate, Tomorrow's Classic, 8" ........................................**8.50**

Homewood, plate, D-style, 9"...**11.00**

Homewood, teapot, New York ..**165.00**

Lyric, bowl, open baker; Tomorrow's Classic, 11-oz .....................**21.00**

Lyric, egg cup, Tomorrow's Classic..**52.50**

Medallion, casserole, Lettuce....**32.50**

Medallion, drip jar, ivory .........**18.00**

Medallion, teapot, Chinese Red, 64-oz ......................................**200.00**

Mulberry, candlestick, Tomorrow's Classic, 4½", ea..................**30.00**

Mulberry, sugar bowl, w/lid, Tomorrow's Classic ......................**21.00**

Mums, baker, French ..............**35.00**

Mums, pretzel jar ..................**225.00**

No 488, casserole, Radiance.....**42.50**

No 488, jug, Medallion .............**95.00**

Orange Poppy, bowl, Radiance, 9"..**32.50**

Orange Poppy, custard, Radiance ..**8.00**

Orange Poppy, teapot, Boston...**225.00**

Pastel Morning Glory, ball jug, #3 or #4, ea................................**190.00**

Pastel Morning Glory, pie baker..**45.00**

Peach Blossom, bowl, fruit; Tomorrow's Classic, footed, lg...**37.50**

Peach Blossom, ladle, Tomorrow's Classic ...............................**20.00**

Pine Cone, casserole, Tomorrow's Classic, 1¼-qt ...................**33.00**

Pine Cone, cup, Tomorrow's Classic..**4.00**

Pine Cone, tidbit, 3-tier, Tomorrow's Classic ...............................**60.00**

Radiance, bowl, red or cobalt, #3, 6" ........................................**15.00**

Radiance, stack set, ivory........**36.00**

Red Poppy, coffeepot, Daniel....**20.00**

Red Poppy, salt & pepper shakers, Teardrop, pr......................**40.00**

Ribbed, bean pot, Chinese Red..**135.00**

Ribbed, ramekin, Russet, 6-oz ...**8.00**

Sear's Arlington, bowl, soup; flat, E-style, 8"................................**9.00**

Sear's Arlington, platter, oval, E-style, 15½" .........................**22.50**

Sear's Fairfax, gravy boat, w/underplate, E-style....................**24.00**

Sear's Monticello, bowl, cereal; E-style, 6¼".............................**8.00**
Sear's Monticello, plate, E-style, 10"..**10.00**
Sear's Mount Vernon, creamer.....**8.50**
Sear's Richmond/Brown-Eyed Susan, bowl, vegetable; round, 9".**20.00**
Serenade, bowl, Radiance, 9"......**20.00**
Serenade, plate, D-style, 9"......**10.00**
Silhouette, bowl, Medallion, 8½"..**20.00**
Silhouette, cup, St Denis..........**32.50**

**Silhouette, teapot, Medallion, from $60.00 to $80.00. (Photo courtesy Margaret and Kenn Whitmyer)**

Springtime, ball jug, D-style, #3..**50.00**
Springtime, cake plate .............**15.00**
Springtime, teapot, French......**80.00**
Sundial, batter jug, red or cobalt.**190.00**
Sundial, cookie jar, Art Glaze colors..**210.00**
Sunglow, casserole, Century .....**60.00**
Sunglow, plate, Century, 10¼"......**13.00**
Tulip, bowl, Thick Rim, 7½".....**22.00**
Tulip, saucer, St Denis..............**8.50**
Wildfire, bowl, D-style, oval.....**25.00**
Wildfire, sugar bowl, Sani-Grid..**27.50**
Yellow Rose, drip jar, Radiance,w/lid..**37.50**
Yellow Rose, saucer, D-style ......**2.00**
Yellow Rose, teapot, New York..**175.00**

# Hallmark

Since 1973 the Hallmark Com-
pany has made Christmas ornaments, some of which are today worth many times their original price. Our suggested values reflect the worth of those in mint condition and in their original boxes.

Across the Miles, QX3044, 1992.......**15.00**
Amanda Doll, QX4321, 1984 ......**36.00**
Angel, QX1396, 1978..............**100.00**
Annunciation, QX2167, 1983.....**35.00**
Arctic Tenor, QX4721, 1988.....**15.00**
Baby's 1st Christmas, QX2111, 1976................................**160.00**
Baker Elf, QX4912, 1985..........**35.00**
Barbie, 40th Anniversary, QXI8049, 1999................................**26.00**
Big on Gardening, QX5842, 1993..**12.00**
Brass Bell, QX4606, 1982 ........**32.00**
Calico Mouse, QX1376, 1978......**185.00**
Caroling Owl, QX4117, 1983 ......**45.00**
Carousel Zebra, QX515, 1989......**20.00**
Charmers, QX1351, 1975 .........**60.00**
Christmas Morning, QX5997, 1995.**18.00**
Cool Decade #2, QX6992, 2001......**18.00**
Cozy Goose, QX4966, 1990.......**15.00**
Disney, Cinderella, QXD4045, 1997 ..**28.00**
Disney, QX8055, 1981 ..............**37.00**
Doc Holiday, QX4677, 1987 .....**45.00**
Elvis, QX5624, 1992 .................**20.00**
Feliz Navidad, QX4161, 1988 .....**35.00**
Football, Joe Namath, QX16182, 1997................................**15.00**
Frisbee Puppy, QX4444, 1984......**55.00**
Garfield, QX2303, 1990............**23.00**
Godchild, QX6035, 1981...........**39.00**
Goodcheer Blimp, QLX7046, 1987 ..**60.00**
Ice Fairy, QX4315, 1981.........**130.00**
Katybeth, QLX7102, 1985........**45.00**
Manger Scene, XHD1022, 1973 ......**45.00**
Mary Hamilton, QX2194, 1980.......**25.00**
Mop Top Wendy, QX6353, 1998.....**25.00**

Nurse Gentle, QX5973, 1994......**20.00**
Peanuts, QX1622, 1977.........**105.00**

**Rocking Horse, Collector's Series, 1988, from $75.00 to $85.00.**

Snowball & Tuxedo #2, QX8033, 2002....................................**22.00**
Snowgoose, QX1071, 1974........**50.00**
Teacher, QX2139, 1979 ............**25.00**
Tonka-Dump Truck, QX6321, 1996..**30.00**
Toyland Tower, QLX7129, 1991..**45.00**
Winnie the Pooh, QX5454, 1996..**32.00**
Winter Suprise 3, QX4277, 1991..**35.00**
Wizard of Oz, The Great Oz, QLX7361, 2000....................................**44.00**
Yarn & Fabric Angel, QX1641, 1980..**17.00**
12 Days of Christmas #11, QX3183, 1994....................................**15.00**
50 Years Together, QX4006, 1986..**20.00**

# Halloween

Halloween items are fast becoming the most popular holiday-related collectibles on the market today. Although originally linked to pagan rituals and superstitions, Halloween has long since evolved into a fun-filled event; and the masks, noisemakers, and jack-o'-lanterns of earlier years are great fun to look for.

Pamela E. Apkarian-Russell (the Halloween Queen), has written several books on the subject: *Collectible Halloween; Salem Witchcraft and Souvenirs; More Halloween Collectibles; Halloween: Decorations and Games; Anthropomorphic Beings of Halloween;* and *The Tastes and Smells of Halloween.* She is listed in the Directory under New Hampshire. See Clubs and Newsletters for information concerning *The Trick or Treat Trader.*

Balancing toy, pumpkin man, celluloid, EX .............................**250.00**
Candy container, pumpkin-head man w/accordion, plastic, 1950s, 5", EX .................................**55.00**
Candy container, scarecrow on wheeled cart, pouch on back, plastic, 6" .........................**145.00**
Cookie cutters, Trick or Treat, tin, 1954, set of 6, EXIB...........**25.00**
Costume, Aquaman, Ben Cooper, 1967, NMIB .....................**125.00**
Costume, Captain America, Ben Cooper, 1966, M (NM box) ...............**210.00**
Costume, CHiPs, any character, Ben Cooper, 1978, MIB, ea .........**25.00**
Costume, Dr Solar, Collegeville, 1966, EXIB........................**40.00**
Costume, Jimmy Osmond, Collegeville, 1977, MIB...........**20.00**
Costume, Spider-Man, Ben Cooper, 1965, EXIB........................**45.00**
Figure, devil, embossed cardboard diecut, from $95 to...........**150.00**
Figure, house, egg shape, celluloid, M .....................................**400.00**
Figure, owl on tree, celluloid, M..**200.00**

Figure, pumpkin-face pirate, celluloid, M .............................**400.00**

Figure, witch, plain, celluloid, M..**175.00**

Figure, witch in auto, celluloid, M..................................**450.00**

Figure, witch on rocketship, hard plastic, EX.......................**100.00**

Figure, witch pulling cart w/ghost, celluloid, M ......................**400.00**

Figure, witch sitting on pumpkin, celluloid, M ......................**350.00**

Jack-o'-lantern, composition w/original insert, 3½" .................**250.00**

Jack-o'-lantern, molded cardboard w/original insert, 3"...........**95.00**

Jack-o'-lantern, pressed cardboard pulp w/original face, 4"......**95.00**

**Lantern, cat, black and orange with wire handle, 8x6", $75.00.**

Lantern, skeleton head, milk glass in black frame, 1950s, 7½", EX.....................................**55.00**

Lantern (ghost, skull, devil, witch, etc), molded cardboard, 3-4" ..**300.00**

Lantern (skull, devil, witch, ect), composition, 3", minimum value ...**375.00**

Noisemaker, bell type, cats/bats/etc on litho tin, wooden handle, EX.....................................**25.00**

Noisemaker, cat (3-D) on wood rachet, composition, German .......**95.00**

Noisemaker, clicker, litho tin....**35.00**

Noisemaker, devil (3-D) on wood rachet, composition, German .......**95.00**

Noisemaker, frying pan paddle, litho tin, German, 5" L...............**75.00**

Noisemaker, horn, witches, bats, etc on litho tin, USA, 10½", EX ...**35.00**

Noisemaker, veggie (3-D) horn (w/painted face), composition, German ...........................**125.00**

Noisemaker, witch (3-D) on wood rachet, composition, German .......**95.00**

Pennant, Salem Witch Museum, orange on black felt, 1950s, EX+...................................**40.00**

Sparkler, jack-o'-lantern, litho tin, Chein, 4¾x2⅜", EX (VG box)..**300.00**

Tambourine, black cat face, litho tin, T Cohn, 1940s, EX.............**95.00**

Tambourine, litho tin, Ohio Art, 1930s, 6" dia......................**75.00**

Tambourine, masquerade party scene, litho tin, Kerchof, 1950s, 6", NM ...............................**85.00**

Trick or Treat bag, Green Hornet & Kato, Vernors Soda ad, plastic, EX.....................................**55.00**

# Handkerchiefs

Lovely to behold, handkerchiefs remain as feminine keepsakes of a time past. Largely replaced by disposable tissues of more modern times, handkerchiefs found today are often those that had special meaning, keepsakes of special occasions, or souvenirs. Many collectible handkerchiefs were never meant for everyday use, but intended to be a feminine addition to the lady's total ensemble. Made in a wide variety of styles and tucked away in grandmother's dresser, handkerchiefs are now being brought out and displayed for their dainty loveliness and fine craftsmanship. For further information we recommend *Handkerchiefs, A Collector's Guide, Vol. 1* and *Vol. 2*, by Helene Guarnaccia and Barbara Guggenheim (Collector Books).

**Cotton, appliques or embroidery, some with lace trim, dating from the 1920s through the 1950s, each from $5.00 to $12.00.** (Photo courtesy La Ree Johnson Bruton)

Cotton, blue w/pink/blue/white variegated tatting along edge, 12x12" ...............................**20.00**

Cotton, blue w/printed flowers & ribbons, ca 1930-40, 10x10"....**15.00**

Cotton, blue w/printed yellow & white daisies, 16x16".........**18.00**

Cotton, pastel blue w/pale blue monogram, lg ......................**8.00**

Cotton, pink w/boldly printed multicolor flowers, 15x15"..........**16.00**

Cotton, pink w/embroidered violets, Made in Switzerland label, 13x13" ...............................**10.00**

Cotton, purple w/white appliquè roses in corners, 13x13" ....**10.00**

Cotton, white w/machine-embroidered violets in ea corner, scalloped.................................**15.00**

Cotton, white w/printed animals depicting various professions, 9x9" .....................................**22.00**

Cotton, white w/printed cats & flowers along blue border, 9x9"..**14.00**

Cotton, white w/printed Christmas theme, holly border, 13x13"..**24.00**

Cotton, white w/printed donkeys along flower border, scalloped, 9x9" .....................................**16.00**

Cotton, white w/printed ducks & flowers along green border, 9x9"..**14.00**

Cotton, white w/printed floral wreath in center, blue crochet edge .....................................**18.00**

Cotton, white w/printed orchids & ribbons, scalloped, 15½x16"..**12.50**

Cotton, white w/printed pig playing bango & 2 dancing ducklings, 9x9" .....................................**15.00**

Cotton, white w/printed Southern belle in corner, tulips border, 1930s ................................**10.00**

Cotton, white w/red & white hairpin lace trim, 12x12"...............**10.00**

Cotton, white w/simple pink crochet roses & trim in corners ...**8.00**

Lawn w/wide lace border & fine embroidery, white, 9½x10"..**12.50**

Linen, white w/embroidered flowers & monogram, drawn & cutwork, sm .........................................**6.00**

Linen, white w/machine-embroidered flower sprays, 1960s, 16x15½" ............................**12.00**

Linen, white w/tatted lace inset & edge, 11½".........................**19.00**

Linen, white w/wide drawn-work edge, 10"...........................**10.00**

Linen, white w/wide Madeira lace border, 11¼x11¼"..............**48.00**

Silk, cream w/embroidered flowers, initial & edging..................**10.00**

Silk, white w/pastel embroidered flowers at corners, scalloped edge ....................................**18.00**

Silk, white w/poodles print in black, white, turquoise & pink, 1950s....**25.00**

Silk, white w/printed wild violets on checkerboard, 1940s, 16".......**10.00**

Souvenir, coronation; King George V & Queen Mary portraits ............**38.00**

Wedding, white cotton w/ornate floral lace border, Desco sticker, 11" ....................................**30.00**

# Harker

One of the oldest potteries in the East Liverpool, Ohio, area, the Harker company produced many lines of dinnerware from the late 1920s until it closed around 1970.

Alpine, bowl, vegetable; round, 8¾" ....................................**25.00**

Alpine, salt & pepper shakers, pr..**20.00**

Amy, bowl, 4½x9", from $22 to..**28.00**

Amy, creamer, 6-oz, 2⅜"..........**20.00**

Amy, plate, salad; 7⅜"................**6.00**

Batter jug, Calico Tulip, 7", NM, from $65.00 to $75.00.

Black-Eyed Susan, plate, bread & butter; 6⅜" ...........................**4.00**

Black-Eyed Susan, saucer..........**2.00**

**Bowl, batter; Deco Dahlia, marked Hotoven, 9⅝" dia., from $40.00 to $50.00.**

Bouquet, plate, luncheon; 9¼"......**7.00**

Bouquet, platter, serving; oval, 12"..**30.00**

Cameo Rose, creamer & sugar bowl, Gem shape .........................**20.00**

Cameo Rose, tidbit, center handle ..**20.00**

Chesterton, ashtray, sm, 4⅝".....**6.50**

Chesterton, gravy boat, w/underplate ...................................**35.00**

Chesterton, plate, salad; 7⅜".....**7.00**

Chesterton, sugar bowl, w/lid......**20.00**

Cock O'Morn, bowl, vegetable; round, 8¾"...........................**22.00**

Cock O'Morn, salt & pepper shakers, pr ................................**18.00**

Colonial Lady, bowl, cereal; 6⅛".....**8.00**

Colonial Lady, pie plate, 9¼" ........**40.00**

Colonial Lady (Embossed Platinum), bowl, rimmed soup; 8" .........**8.00**

Coronet, bowl, vegetable; round, 8⅞" ....................................**22.00**

Coronet, casserole, w/lid, round, 2-qt, 9" ....................................**45.00**

Dogwood (Tan), platter, serving; oval, 13⅜"..........................**25.00**

Dogwood (Tan), saucer ...............**2.00**

Everglades, plate, dinner; 10¼" .....**9.00**

Everglades, platter, serving; oval, 13⅜" ...................................**25.00**

Godey, bowl, vegetable; round, 8⅞"..**25.00**
Godey, cake stand, metal pedestal...**32.00**
Ivy, cup & saucer ..................**12.00**
Ivy, nightlight ........................**24.00**
Ivy Wreath, bowl, coupe soup; from
   $12 to..............................**14.00**
Ivy Wreath, plate, dinner; 10", from
   $13 to..............................**16.00**
Ivy Wreath, platter, 12", from $16
   to.....................................**20.00**
Lemon Tree, bowl, fruit; 5⅛" .....**6.00**
Lemon Tree, platter, serving; oval,
   13⅛" ................................**30.00**
Magnolia, plate, dinner; 10¼" .....**14.00**
Magnolia, sugar bowl, w/lid .....**20.00**
Mallow, pie baker, 9¾" .............**36.00**
Mallow, salt & pepper shakers, sky-
   scraper shape, 4½", pr, $16 to ..**20.00**
Modern Tulip, bowl, cereal; 6⅛" ......**7.00**
Modern Tulip, casserole, w/lid, 8⅝" ..**36.00**
Modern Tulip, spoon, 8½", from $18
   to.....................................**22.00**
Pate Sur Pate, creamer, 5¾", from
   $12 to..............................**15.00**
Pate Sur Pate, salt & pepper shak-
   ers, pr from $12 to .............**15.00**
Petit Point, bowl, mixing; 2⅞x5⅞",
   from $20 to.......................**25.00**
Petit Point, rolling pin, from $150
   to.....................................**165.00**
Rocaille, creamer ....................**15.00**
Rocaille, plate, bread & butter; 6¼" ..**5.00**
Rosebud, salt & pepper shakers, pr .**18.00**
Rosebud, saucer ........................**3.50**
Sea Fare, bowl, fruit; 5¼"...........**6.00**
Sea Fare, creamer....................**15.00**
Silhouette, bowl, serving; 3x8½"..**18.00**
Silhouette, plate, bread; 6¼", from
   $6 to.....................................**8.00**
Souvenir plate, First State Bank,
   Columbus TX, 9", from $20
   to.....................................**25.00**

Springtime, bowl, vegetable; divid-
   ed, oval, 10"........................**22.00**
Springtime, gravy boat.............**20.00**
Springtime, plate, salad; 8¼".....**4.50**
Sweetheart, bowl, rimmed soup;
   8⅜" ......................................**8.00**
Sweetheart, bowl, vegetable; round,
   10¼" .................................**22.00**
Sweetheart Rose, bowl, fruit; 5⅜"..**9.00**
Teal Rose, bowl, cereal; 6¼".......**8.00**
Teal Rose, saucer ........................**3.00**
Violets, creamer.....................**16.00**
Violets, plate, bread & butter; 6⅜"..**4.00**

# Hartland

    Hartland Plastics Inc. of Hart-
land, Wisconsin, produced a line of
Western and Historic Horsemen and
Standing Gunfighter figures during
the 1950s, which are now very collectible. Using a material called vir-
gin acetate, they molded such
well-known characters as Annie
Oakley, Bret Maverick, Matt Dillon,
and many others, which they painted with highest attention to detail.
In addition to these, they made a
line of sports greats as well as one
featuring religious figures.

Gunfighter, Bat Masterson, stand-
   ing, standing, NMIB........**500.00**
Gunfighter, Bret Maverick, stand-
   ing, NMIB ......................**600.00**
Gunfighter, Clay Holister, standing,
   NM....................................**150.00**
Gunfighter, Dan Troop, standing,
   NM ..................................**600.00**
Gunfighter, Jim Hardy, standing,
   NM................................**150.00**

Gunfighter, Paladin, standing, NM..**400.00**
Gunfighter, Wyatt Earp, standing, NM.....................................**150.00**
Horseman, Bill Longley, NM ..**600.00**
Horseman, Buffalo Bill, NM .......**300.00**
Horseman, Cactus Pete, NM ......**150.00**
Horseman, Cheyenne, w/tag, NM.**190.00**
Horseman, Commanche Kid, NM .**150.00**
Horseman, Dale Evans, purple, NM .....................................**250.00**
Horseman, General Robert E Lee, NMIB ..............................**175.00**
Horseman, Jim Hardy, NMIB......**300.00**
Horseman, Lone Ranger, rearing, NMIB ..............................**300.00**
Horseman, Rebel, NMIB.....**1,200.00**
Horseman, Roy Rogers, walking, NMIB ..............................**300.00**
Horseman, Tonto, semi-rearing, rare, NM .........................**650.00**
Sports, Babe Ruth, 1960s, NM, from $125 to..............................**175.00**
Sports, Dick Groat, 25th Anniversary, MIB .....................................**45.00**
Sports, Eddie Matthews, 1960s, NM..**125.00**
Sports, Hank Aaron, 1960s, EX..**190.00**
Sports, Harmon Killebrew, 25th Anniversary, MIB..............**35.00**
Sports, Lou Gerhrig, 1990s, NMIB .**95.00**
Sports, Mickey Mantle, 1960s, NM ................................**200.00**
Sports, Nellie Fox, 1960s, EX, from $150 to..............................**175.00**
Sports, Roger Maris, 1960s, NM, minimum value ..............**300.00**
Sports, Ted Williams, 1960s, EX.**200.00**
Sports, Washington Redskins, 1960s, EX........................**310.00**
Sports, Willie Mays, 25th Anniversary, MIB............................**35.00**
Sports, Yogi Berra, w/mask, NM, from $175 to.....................**250.00**

# Hawaiian Shirts

Vintage shirts made in Hawaii are just one of many retro fads finding favor on today's market. Those with the tag of a top designer can bring hefty prices — the more colorful, the better. Shirts of this type were made in the states as well. Look for grapics that shout 'Hawaii!' Fabrics are typically cotton, rayon, or polyester (poly in our lines).

Aloha Tike, floral bands, red, white, black, cotton, unused, 1960s..**40.00**
Andrade, batik geometric print on cotton, 1960s.....................**35.00**
Hawaiian Togs, hibiscus print, fuchsia on tan & white, cotton ..**17.50**
Kai Nani, pineapples, vines & flowers, cotton blend, 1960s ...**28.00**
Kai Nani Tiki Aloha, flowers & abstracts, 4-color barkcloth cotton.....**40.00**
Keone Sportware, stylized flowers, blue, green, white, mango, poly..**22.00**
Keoni, surfers, swirls, borders in green tones, cotton ............**60.00**
Liberty House Ialani, blue, green & white abstract print, cotton..**22.50**
Malihini Hawaai, yellow & orange print, 1970s......................**15.00**

**Original by Hale Hawaii, featuring Rainbow Falls at Hilo, rayon, ca 1950s, EX, $175.00.** (Photo courtesy pilaliilii)

219

Papeete Tahiti, Tapa print, brown floral, cotton, 1960s ..........**40.00**

Richard Douglas, wide blue hibiscus border on white barkcloth, 1960s ....................................**75.00**

Sir Clifford, palms & named islands, multicolor on white poly....**20.00**

Tropicana Orange Juice promo, palms on yellow, ca 1980.................**25.00**

Twenty Six Red, hibiscus, palms, etc, rayon, 1970s................**20.00**

Ui Maikia, hibiscus leis on teal cotton ......................................**35.00**

Unknown Hawaiian maker, floral, green & neon colors, 1970s ..**25.00**

# Head Vases

Many of them Japanese imports, head vases were made primarily for the florist trade. They were styled as children, teenagers, clowns, and famous people. There are heads of religious figures, Blacks, Orientals, and even some animals. One of the most common types are ladies wearing pearl earrings and necklaces. Refer to *Collecting Head Vases* by David Barron (Collector Books) for more information. See Clubs and Newsletters for information concerning the *Head Hunter's Newsletter*.

Angel child praying in blue, blond hair, Lefton label, #7341, 7" ...**160.00**

Baby, blond hair, sideways bonnet, Enesco, 5".............................**55.00**

Baby, brown hair, blanket over head, holds kitten, unmarked, 6" ......................................**65.00**

Baby girl w/kitten, bow in hair, Enesco, 5½".........................**55.00**

Child in ruffled bonnet, blond hair, pink bow/trim, art mark label, 6" ......................................**100.00**

Clown, white w/red nose, mouth & cheeks, hat, Inarco EE6730, 5½" ....................................**80.00**

Girl, blond, flowered hat, holds fan, winking, unmarked, 6" ....**95.00**

Girl, blond updo w/hat, both hands up, Enesco, 3".....................**45.00**

Girl holds gift, hat w/daisies, gold trim, Japan, 5½" ................**55.00**

Girl w/umbrella, blond in aqua plaid, 3½"+umbrella........**250.00**

**Ladies in hats, Lefton #2900 and #4228, 8", $85.00 each.**

Lady, Art Deco, white w/brown hair, yellow hat, pearls, unmarked, 7½" ....................................**110.00**

Lady, blond, green bodice w/flowers, pearls, Ardco label, 6".........**210.00**

Lady, blond, hat, sleeveless bodice, hands to face, Lefton #2900, 6"....................................**125.00**

Lady, blond, pearls, green bodice, Napcoware #C7294, 7½" .........**320.00**

Lady, blond, thick lashes, pearls, Inarco, E-1062, 6½".........**260.00**

Lady, blond, thick lashes, pearls, 2-ruffle collar, Napcoware #C5939, 6".........................**215.00**

Lady, blond hair, green bodice, leaf pin, pearls, Napco C7472, 6"..**200.00**

Lady, blond in black top hat, hand up, unmarked, 6", +original flowers.............................**210.00**

Lady, blond in flat-brim hat, hand to face, Lefton #2359, 7½".......**325.00**

Lady, blond up-do, pearls, white bodice, #3855, 4½"...........**170.00**

Lady, blond w/bow, pearl earrings, thick lashes, Lefton #3515, 8"....................................**315.00**

Lady, blond w/hand to neck, black bodice, pearls, Ardco, 7½".....**325.00**

Lady, blond w/pearls, scalloped bodice, thick lashes, Enesco, 6" ....................................**215.00**

Lady, brown up-do w/flower, gloved hands, pearls, unmarked, 7"..**125.00**

Lady, frosted hair, green hat, pearls, Napcoware #C7498, 10½" ................................**875.00**

Lady, hooded head, gold & white daisies w/pearls, Vcagco, 5½" ....................................**155.00**

Lady, white w/gold trim, Glamour Girl, 6½"............................**45.00**

Man, white scarf over black hair, 1 gold ear, Royal Copley, 7¾"..**65.00**

Newborn on pillow, white w/blue trim, Hull 92-USA, 5¾".....**72.50**

Pirate, Royal Copley, 8½".........**45.00**

Teen girl, blond hair, brown bodice, Inarco #E5624, 5½"...........**135.00**

Teen girl, blond ponytail, brown top hat, hand up, unmarked, 6½" ....................................**85.00**

Teen girl, brown curls, green bonnet w/bow, unmarked, 5¼".........**75.00**

Teen girl, white scarf over blond hair, thick lashes, Vcagco, 6" ....................................**85.00**

**Teenage girl, Inarco E-6210, 7", $400.00.** (Photo courtesy David Barron)

Uncle Sam, allover green, unmarked, 6½" ....................................**45.00**

# Holly Hobbie and Friends

About 1970 a young homemaker and mother, Holly Hobbie, approached the American Greeting Company with some charming country-styled drawings of children. Since that time over four hundred items have been made with almost all being marked HH, H. Hobbie, or Holly Hobbie.

Apron, Holiday Wishes..., red quilted waist, child size...................**25.00**

Cake tin, American Greetings, 1975, 17x9", EX ..........................**15.00**

Cake topper, Holly w/cat & 11 in front, porcelain, 1983, 5½", NM ....................................**45.00**

Camera, uses Kodak film, Vanity Fair, 1978, unopened, MIP..**50.00**

Doll, cloth, Knickerbocker, 26", NM..**65.00**

Doll, cloth, Knickerbocker, 9", EX..**25.00**

Doll, Dream Along Heather, cloth, Knickerbocker, 9", MIB.....**60.00**

Doll, porcelain, musical, Gorham Anniversary Edition, 1983..**65.00**

Doll, vinyl, Knickerbocker, 11", NM..**15.00**

Doll, vinyl, Knickerbocker, 16", NM..**35.00**

Doll pattern, Simplicity #6006, ca 1973, uncut, EX.................**20.00**

Easy Bake Oven, Coleco #7360, missing mixes & cookbooks, 1976, EXIB........................**45.00**

Figurine, A Day To Enjoy, HH Classic Series 3, 1981, 8¼", NM.......**35.00**

Figurine, Gentle Hearts, Holly w/lamb, HH Classics, 1979, 8½".....**40.00**

Figurine, Good Friends & Fun, Sweet Rememberance Collection III, NM .....................................**32.50**

Figurine, Grandparent's Keepsake, 2 kids in rowboat, 1981, NM..**35.00**

Figurine, Holly w/2 lambs, porcelain, China, 1977, 5½", EX .............**50.00**

Figurine, Something, ballet dancer in chair, 1983, 3", NM ................................**30.00**

Figurine, True Friends, American Greetings, 1971, 6" ............**20.00**

Figurine, Water Pump Girl w/Cat, HH Creation, 1974, 8"......**35.00**

Mug, Happiness Is Having..., ceramic, footed ...............................**8.00**

Mug, milk glass w/red fired-on figure .....................................**10.00**

Plate, Mother's Day, 1979, image w/verse, American Greetings, NM .....................................**25.00**

Play set, Amy w/baby & carriage, Knickerbocker #9871, MIP..**40.00**

Quilt kit, crib size, American Greetings, 1972, MIP..................**40.00**

Trinket box, Gather a Bouquet..., ceramic heart shape, 1970s, 3" ......................................**14.00**

Vase, spill; white w/Holly w/cat, gold rim, Spode, 1972, NM...........**35.00**

**Figurine, I Love a Parade, 1976, rare, from $900.00 to $1,200.00.** (Photo courtesy Helen

Figurine, Months of Joy, December, American Greeting, '83, 5½", NM .....................................**50.00**

# Holt Howard

Ceramic novelty items marked Holt Howard are hot! From the late 1950s, collectors search for the pixie kitchenware items such as cruets, condiments, etc., all with flat, disk-like pixie heads for stoppers. In the '60s the company designed and distributed a line of roosters — egg cups, napkin holders, salt and pepper shakers, etc. Items with a Christmas theme featuring Santa or angels, for instance, were sold from the '50s through the '70s, and you'll also find a line of white cats collectors call Kozy Kitten. These are only a sampling of the wonderful novelties imported by this company. Most are not only marked but dated as well.

Bluebird, candle ring, 1958, 1¾"...**35.00**
Butler (Jeeves), ashtray...........**40.00**
Butler (Jeeves), martini shaker, 9", from $175 to.....................**200.00**
Christmas, ashtray, starry-eyed Santa...................................**35.00**
Christmas, bell, winking Santa, 1958, 4", from $12 to.........**15.00**
Christmas, bracelet, 4 charms w/Santa faces, 1959, 8" .....**70.00**
Christmas, candleholder, Santa in convertible, 1959, 3½", ea...........**35.00**
Christmas, candleholder, Santa w/wreath (O from Noel), '59, 4½", 4 in series, ea.............**35.00**
Christmas, candleholders, Santa on SS Noel boat, 1959, 2¾", pr..**30.00**
Christmas, candleholders, Santa w/gift bag, 3½", pr .............**30.00**
Christmas, candleholders, Santa seated, 4", pr from $20 to...........**25.00**
Christmas, candleholders/bells, 3 Wise Men, 3½", set from $65 to........................................**85.00**
Christmas, chip & cheese dish, starry-eyed Santa, w/gold, 1960, 12" .....................................**40.00**
Christmas, face dish, starry-eyed Santa, 6¼x6½"..................**20.00**
Christmas, head vase, Christmas decor, 1959, 4"....................**60.00**
Christmas, mug, starry-eyed Santa, straight handle, stackable, from $10 to..................................**15.00**
Christmas, ornament, Santa sits on edge w/mirror behind, 1959, 5½" .....................................**45.00**

Christmas, planter, Santa Express, Santa riding train, 6x7½".**45.00**
Christmas, salt & pepper shakers, Holly Girls, 4", pr .............**20.00**
Christmas, salt & pepper shakers, Santa inside tree, 4¼", pr .....**18.00**

**Christmas, salt and pepper shakers, Santa and presents, from $15.00 for the set.**

Christmas, salt & pepper shakers, starry-eyed Santa, pr ........**20.00**
Cowboys, salt & pepper shakers, 6½", pr................................**70.00**
Dandy-Lion, bank, nodder, 6", from $100 to.............................**150.00**
Ear of corn, salt & pepper shakers, 4½", pr...............................**30.00**
Figurines, pheasants, wings spread, 1958, 10x8", 7x5½" & 5½x4"..**80.00**
Jolly Girls, salt & pepper shakers, flat-head finials, EX, pr.....**55.00**
Kissing Kids, salt & pepper shakers, 2 seated kids, 3¼", pr ...............**55.00**
Kozy Kitten, butter dish, 2 kittens peek from under lid, 7", from $100 to.............................**125.00**
Kozy Kitten, coffee jar, Instant Coffee, attached spoon, from $300 to........................................**400.00**

Kozy Kitten, cookie jar, head form, from $40 to..........................**50.00**

Kozy Kitten, cottage cheese jar, 2 cats on lid, 4¼x4¼", from $45 to......................................**60.00**

Kozy Kitten, memo minder, 7", from $60 to..................................**75.00**

Kozy Kitten, salt & pepper shakers, heads only, male in hat, pr.................................**45.00**

Kozy Kitten, tape measure, cat on cushion...............................**75.00**

Kozy Kitten, vase, full-body cat, male or female, 6½", ea ...**100.00**

Kozy Kitten, wall pocket, full bodied cat w/hook tail, 7¾"...........**60.00**

Mermaid on sea horse, wall pocket, missing chain, 1959, 6¾" .**70.00**

Pixie Ware, bottle hanger, Scotch, head only, 2⅛x2½" ..........**300.00**

Pixie Ware, candlesticks, pr, from $50 to..................................**65.00**

Pixie Ware, Cherries, head finials, from $145 to......................**185.00**

Pixie Ware, chili sauce, rare, minimum value........................**350.00**

Pixie Ware, cocktail onions, onion-head finial..........................**185.00**

Pixie Ware, decanter, Devil Brew, striped base, rare, 10½", minimum................................**225.00**

Pixie Ware, honey jar, very rare, from $400 to......................**500.00**

Pixie Ware, Italian dressing bottle, from $125 to......................**270.00**

Pixie Ware, ketchup jar, orange tomato-like head finial, from $75 to..................................**90.00**

Pixie Ware, mayonnaise jar, winking head finial, 5x4¼" dia, $225 to......................................**265.00**

**Pixie ware, mustard jar, yellow head finial, from $80.00 to $110.00.**

Pixie Ware, nut dish, 5" W.....**140.00**

Pixie Ware, olives jar, green-faced finial, 1958, 5½"..............**150.00**

Pixie Ware, relish jar, male pixie head finial, 1959, from $265 to ....................................**295.00**

Pixie Ware, Russian dressing bottle, from $175 to.....................**200.00**

Ponytail Princess, double tray, from $50 to..................................**65.00**

Ponytail Princess, lipstick holder, from $50 to..........................**65.00**

Ponytail Princess, salt & pepper shakers, 3½-4", pr from $35 to ........................................**45.00**

Rooster, bowl, cereal; 6" .............**9.00**

Rooster, bud vase, figural rooster, from $35 to..........................**45.00**

Rooster, butter dish, stick style, 1961, from $35 to...............**45.00**

Rooster, candleholders, figural, 1960, 5x4", pr from $25 to...........**40.00**

Rooster, coffeepot, electric, from $50 to.........................................**60.00**

Rooster, condiment set, white w/3-D rooster on lid, 4x4".............**35.00**

Rooster, cookie jar, embossed, from $75 to...............................**100.00**

Rooster, dish, figural rooster w/open-body receptacle .....**15.00**

Rooster, jam & jelly jar, embossed, from $30 to..........................**40.00**

Rooster, mug, embossed (3 sizes), ea from $5 to............................**10.00**

**Rooster, napkin holder, $40.00.**

Rooster, pincushion, 3¼x4", from $50 to...................................**60.00**

Rooster, pitcher, milk; tail handle, 1964, 8½" ...........................**50.00**

Rooster, plate, embossed rooster, 8½", from $15 to .................**22.00**

Rooster, platter, embossed rooster, oval, from $28 to ................**35.00**

Rooster, recipe box, wood w/painted-on rooster .........................**75.00**

Rooster, spoon rest, figural, 1961, 4x3½" ................................**20.00**

Starry-eyed birds, salt & pepper shakers, 4", pr...................**45.00**

# Homer Laughlin

The Homer Laughlin China Company has produced millions of pieces of dinnerware, toiletry items, art china, children's dishes, and hotel ware since its inception in 1874. On most pieces the backstamp includes company name, date, and plant where the piece was produced, and nearly always the shape name is included. We have listed samples from many of the decaled lines; some of the more desirable patterns will go considerably higher. Refer to *The Collector's Encyclopedia of Homer Laughlin China* by Joanne Jasper; *Homer Laughlin China Company, A Giant Among Dishes,* by Jo Cunningham; and *The Collector's Encyclopedia of Fiesta* by Sharon and Bob Huxford. See Clubs and Newsletters for information concerning *The Laughlin Eagle,* a newsletter for collectors of Homer Laughlin dinnerware. See also Fiesta.

## Century

Baker, oval, 8", from $20 to......**25.00**

Bowl, onion soup; lug handles, from $18 to.................................**25.00**

Casserole, w/lid, from $65 to....**85.00**

Cup, coffee; from $10 to............**15.00**

Jug, w/lid, 2½-pt, from $85 to...**100.00**

Plate, deep (rim soup); from $10 to.........................................**13.00**

Sugar bowl, w/lid, from $20 to ..**25.00**

Teacup, from $6 to.....................**8.00**

## Debutante

Bowl, nappy, 10", from $16 to.....**18.00**

Chop plate, 15", from $16 to......**20.00**

Creamer, from $9 to .................**12.00**

Plate, 10", from $8 to..................**9.00**

Tea saucer, from $3 to...............**5.00**

## Eggshell Georgian

Baker, 10", from $16 to ............**18.00**

Casserole, w/lid, from $60 to ......**85.00**
Creamer, from $12 to ...............**15.00**
Plate, rim soup; deep; from $15 to .**18.00**
Plate, sq, 8", from $16 to ..........**22.00**
Plate, 7", from $6 to..................**10.00**
Salt & pepper shakers, pr from $25
    to.........................................**35.00**

## Empress

Bowl, fruit; 6", from $6 to...........**8.00**
Cake plate, 10", from $15 to.....**20.00**

**Creamer, gold trim, from $14.00 to $16.00; Casserole with lid, 9", from $35.00 to $45.00.** (Photo courtesy Joanne Jasper)

Jug, 24s, 27-oz, from $26 to .....**28.00**
Platter, 8", from $12 to.............**16.00**
Sauce boat, from $18 to............**22.00**
Tureen, oyster; 8", from $45 to......**50.00**

## Marigold

Bowl, oatmeal; from $6 to ..........**8.00**
Casserole, w/lid, from $60 to .....**80.00**
Creamer, from $12 to ...............**15.00**
Pitcher, milk; from $25 to ........**35.00**
Plate, 10", from $8 to................**11.00**

## Nautilus

Bowl, coupe soup; from $6 to......**8.00**

Mug, Baltimore coffee; from $15 to ..**20.00**
Plate, 10", from $7 to................**10.00**
Sauce boat, from $12 to............**14.00**
Teacup, from $4 to.....................**6.00**

## Rhythm

Bowl, coupe soup; from $7 to.......**9.00**
Cup & saucer, coffee AD; from $14
    to.........................................**20.00**
Salt & pepper shakers, Swing, pr
    from $10 to.........................**15.00**
Sauce boat, from $12 to............**14.00**
Tea saucer, from $3 to...............**5.00**

## Swing

Butter dish, Jade, from $40 to......**50.00**
Egg cup, double; from $12 to .....**18.00**
Sauce boat, from $15 to............**20.00**
Sugar bowl, w/lid, from $14 to......**18.00**
Teapot, from $65 to..................**75.00**

## Virginia Rose

Values are for Moss Rose (JJ59) and Fluffy Rose (VR128); for other patterns, deduct 65%.

**Baker, pattern known as Tulips in a Basket, 8", from $18.00 to $24.00; Matching sugar bowl with lid, from $25.00 to $35.00.** (Photo courtesy Joanne Jasper)

Baker, 9", from $18 to ..............**26.00**

Bowl, nappy, 10".............................**30.00**
Bread plate, rare, from $20 to......**25.00**
Jug, 5" ......................................**150.00**
Salt & pepper shakers, Debutante,
    pr from $125 to..................**150.00**
Sauce boat, from $23 to............**38.00**

## Wells

Bowl, bouillon; from $10 to ......**12.00**
Bowl, cream soup; from $20 to......**25.00**
Chop plate, from $18 to............**24.00**
Coffee cup, AD; from $22 to .....**30.00**
Plate, 9", from $9 to.................**12.00**
Teacup & saucer, from $9 to......**14.00**
Teapot, from $85 to ................**100.00**

# Hot Wheels

An instant success in 1968, Hot Wheels are known for their racy style and custom paint jobs. Kids loved them simply because they were the fastest model cars on the market. Keeping up with new trends in the big car industry, Hot Wheels also included futuristic vehicles, muscle cars, trucks, hot rods, racers, and some military vehicles. A lot of these can still be found for very little, but if you want to buy the older models (collectors call them 'Red Lines' because of their red sidewall tires), it's going to cost you a little more, though many can still be found under $25.00. By 1971, earlier on some models, black-wall tires had become standard.

Though recent re-releases have dampened the collector market somewhat, cars mint in the original packages are holding their values and still moving well. Near-mint examples (no package) are worth about 50% to 60% less than those mint and still in their original package, excellent condition about 65% to 75% less. For further information we recommend *Hot Wheels, The Ultimate Redline Guide, Volumes 1 and 2,* by Jack Clark and Robert P. Wicker (Collector Books).

'31 Doozie, 1986, white walls, maroon w/red-brown fenders, MIP.....................................**12.00**
'57 Ford Delivery, 1989, black walls, turquoise, MOC ...................**5.00**
Alive '55, 1973, red line, plum, EX+ .................................**120.00**
American Tipper, 1976, red line, red, M................................**55.00**
AW Shoot, 1976, red line, olive, NM+ ....................................**40.00**
Baja Bruiser, 1974, red line, orange, metal base, NM...................**50.00**

**Beatnik Bandit, 1968, red line, lime-green, based on an Ed 'Big Daddy' Roth design, M, $40.00 (M in blister package, $100.00).**

Blown Camaro, 1980s, black walls, turquoise, MOC .................**20.00**
Boss Hoss, 1971, red line, olive w/black roof, NM .............**160.00**

Bye Focal, 1971, red line, light green, M .....................................**265.00**

Captain America, 1970, black walls, red, white & blue, NM..........**20.00**

Carabo, 1970, red line, yellow, NM+..**400.00**

CAT Dump Truck, 1990, black walls, yellow, MOC..............**5.00**

Chapparal 2G, 1969, red line, yellow, NM+............................**45.00**

Chief's Special, 1976, red line, red w/red bar, NM....................**35.00**

Classic '31 Woody, 1969, red line, orange, M ...........................**50.00**

Classic Cobra, 1990s, black walls, red, MOC.............................**5.00**

Classic Nomad, 1970, red line, blue, M .......................................**85.00**

Corvette Stingray, 1988, black walls, yellow w/multicolored tampo, MOC.........................**5.00**

Custom AMX, 1969, red line, blue, NM+ ...................................**85.00**

Custom Charger, 1969, red line, gold, M .............................**175.00**

Custom Continental Mark III, 1969, red line, gold, NM+ ..............**50.00**

Custom Cougar, 1968, red line, metallic orange, MIP.........**25.00**

Custom Eldorado, 1968, red line, yellow w/white interior, NM+..**70.00**

Custom Firebird, 1968, red line, red w/brown interior, M...........**100.00**

Custom Mustang, 1968, red line, ice blue, NM ..........................**100.00**

Demon, 1970, red line, olive w/white interior, NM+....................**75.00**

Double Vision, 1973, red line, light green, NM+.......................**150.00**

Dumpin' A, 1983, black walls, gray, M .......................................**27.00**

El Ray Special, 1974, red line, dark blue, NM+ ........................**400.00**

Ferarri 512P, 1973, red line, pink, NM+ .................................**250.00**

Ferarri 512S, 1972, red line, gold, NM+ .................................**140.00**

Fire Eater, 1977, red line, red, M..**25.00**

Ford J-Car, 1968, red line, white, NM+ ...................................**55.00**

Formula Fever, 1983, black walls, yellow, MIP........................**12.50**

Funny Money, 1974, red line, plum, M..**80.00**

Gremlin Grinder, 1975, red line, green, NM+ .........................**50.00**

Gulch Stepper, 1987, black walls, red, MIP...............................**7.00**

Hairy Hauler, 1971, red line, magenta, NM+...................**40.00**

Heavy Chevy, 1974, red line, yellow, NM+ .................................**110.00**

Heavyweight Scooper, 1971, red line, blue, NM+................**100.00**

Highway Robber, 1973, red line, red, NM+ .................................**120.00**

Hot Heap, 1968, red line, orange, NM+ ...................................**40.00**

Hummer, 1990s, black walls, beige camouflage, MOC ................**5.00**

Ice T, 1971, red line, light yellow, M..**75.00**

Inferno, 1976, red line, yellow, M..**55.00**

Lola GT-70, 1969, red line, metallic brown, EX ...........................**25.00**

Lotus Turbine, 1969, red line, orange, NM+ ......................**30.00**

**Mantis, 1970, red line, green, open canopy, NM, $40.00.** (Photo courtesy June Moon)

Mercedes SL, 1991, black walls, M (NM International card).....**10.00**

Minitrek, 1983, black walls, white, NM+ ...................................**40.00**

Mongoose Funny Car, 1970, red line, red, NM+..................**100.00**

Mutt Mobile, 1971, red line, magenta, NM+............................**160.00**

Nitty Gritty Kitty, 1970, red line, metallic brown, NM.........**100.00**

Old Number 5, 1982, black walls, red, NM+............................**10.00**

Omni 024, 1981, black walls, gray, MIP......................................**8.00**

Paramedic, 1975, red line, yellow w/red tampo, MOC .............**65.00**

Peeping Bomb, 1970, red line, metallic orange, M.............**65.00**

Porsche 911, 1976, red line, Super Chromes, M.........................**40.00**

Porsche 971, 1970, red line, yellow, NM+ ..................................**50.00**

Python, 1968, red line, yellow w/white interior, NM+.......**38.00**

Road King, 1974, red line, yellow, w/original trailer, rare, EX+ ................................**330.00**

**Rock Buster, 1976, red line, chrome, NM, $50.00. (Photo courtesy Jack Clark and Robert P. Wicker)**

Rocket Bye Baby, 1971, red line, aqua, NM+ .........................**85.00**

Sand Crab, 1970, red line, yellow, NM+ ...................................**30.00**

Sheriff Patrol, 1988, black walls, black, MIP..........................**10.00**

Short Order, 1973, red line, dark blue, NM+ ..........................**80.00**

Side Kick, 1972, red line, magenta, NM+ .................................**165.00**

Silhouette, 1968, red line, light green, M ...........................**120.00**

Snake, 1970, red line, yellow, NM+ ..**30.00**

Special Delivery, 1971, red line, light blue, M ......................**80.00**

Street Beast, 1988, black walls, red, MIP.....................................**10.00**

Street Snorter, 1973, red line, fluorescent pink, EX................**50.00**

SWAT Van Scene, 1979, black walls, dark blue, VG ...................**15.00**

Sweet 16, 1973, red line, fluorescent lime green, M...................**125.00**

T-4-2, 1971, red line, magenta, EX.......................................**50.00**

Thor Van, 1979, black walls, yellow, M .........................................**10.00**

TNT Bird, 1970, red line, metallic blue w/#3 tampo, NM ........**25.00**

Turbo Mustang, 1982, black walls, red, MIP.............................**10.00**

Waste Wagon, 1971, red line, metallic aqua, NM ......................**60.00**

Winnipeg, 1974, red line, yellow w/ blue & orange tampo, M....**130.00**

# Hull

Established in Zanesville, Ohio, in 1905, Hull manufactured stoneware, florist ware, art pottery, and tile until about 1935, when they began to produce the lines of pastel matt-glazed artware which are today very collectible. The pottery was destroyed by flood and fire in 1950. The factory was rebuilt and equipped with the most modern machinery which they soon discovered was not geared to duplicate the matt glazes. As a result, new lines — Parchment and Pine and Ebb Tide, for example — were introduced in a glossy finish. During the '40s and into the '50s, their kitchenware and novelty lines were very successful. Refer to *Robert's Ultimate Encyclopedia of Hull Pottery* and *The Companion Guide,* both by Brenda Roberts (Walsworth Publishing) for more information. Brenda also has authored *The Collector's Encyclopedia of Hull Pottery* and *The Collector's Ultimate Encyclopedia of Hull Pottery,* which are published by Collector Books.

Blossom Flite, basket, #T-9, 10"..**235.00**
Blossom Flite, console bowl, #T-10, 16½" ................................**165.00**

**Bow-Knot, vase, 10½", from $550.00 to $700.00.**

Butterfly, ewer, #B-11, 8¾"....**215.00**

Calla Lily, bowl, #500/32, 10"...**265.00**
Calla Lily, ewer, #506, 10" .....**480.00**
Calla Lily, vase, cornucopia; #570/33, 6" .....................................**160.00**
Camellia, ewer, #115, 8½"......**315.00**
Camellia, vase, #123, 6½" ......**175.00**
Capri, swan, #23, 8½"..............**60.00**
Capri, vase, #58, 13¾"..............**75.00**
Continental, basket, #55, 12¾"..**215.00**
Continental, candleholder, unmarked, 4" .....................................**35.00**
Continental, planter, #41, 15½".**40.00**
Dogwood, cornucopia, #522, 3¾"..**135.00**
Dogwood, jardiniere, #514, 4"...**155.00**
Ebb Tide, basket, unmarked, 6¼"..**195.00**
Ebb Tide, ewer, #E-10, 14".....**295.00**
Floral, bowl, #40, 5"..................**18.00**
Floral, grease jar, #43, 5¾" ......**55.00**
Heritageware, mug, #A-8, 3¼" ..**10.00**
Heritageware, pitcher, #A-7, 4½" ..**25.00**
Imperial, bowl, #117, 9" ...........**10.00**
Imperial, swan, #80, 6".............**45.00**
Iris, basket, #408, 7"...............**365.00**
Iris, rose bowl, #412, 7" ..........**210.00**
Lusterware, bud vase, unmarked, 8" .....................................**120.00**
Lusterware, pitcher, unmarked, 4"......................................**85.00**
Magnolia, gloss; candleholder, #H-24, 4" ................................**65.00**
Magnolia, gloss; teapot, #H-20, 6½" ...................................**225.00**
Magnolia, matt; creamer, #24, 3¾" ...................................**80.00**
Magnolia, matt; teapot, #23, 6½" ...................................**275.00**
Magnolia, matt; vase, double cornucopia; #6, 12"....................**255.00**
Mardi Gras/Granada, vase, #47, 9"....................................**110.00**
Novelty, basket girl, #954, 8"......**45.00**
Novelty, flowerpot, #95, 4½"......**20.00**

Novelty, Old Spice Shaving Mug, 3" .......................................**30.00**

**Novelty, piggy bank, brown with cork in nose, 5x6½", from $140.00 to $175.00.**

Novelty, shrimp planter, #201, 5" ..**40.00**
Orchid, bookends, #316, 7"...**1,400.00**
Orchid, jardiniere, #317, 4¾" ..**200.00**
Parchment & Pine, ashtray, #S-14, 14" ....................................**185.00**
Parchment & Pine, candleholder, unmarked, 5", ea ...............**35.00**
Parchment & Pine, teapot, unmarked, 6" ......................................**325.00**
Poppy, basket, #601, 12" .....**1,600.00**
Poppy, vase, #607, 6½"...........**180.00**
Rosella, creamer, #R-3, 5½" .....**65.00**
Rosella, sugar bowl (open), #R-4, 5½" .....................................**65.00**
Rosella, vase, cornucopia; #R-13, 8½" ....................................**165.00**
Serenade, basket, #S-14, 12x11½" ..**500.00**
Serenade, ewer, #S-2, 6½"......**125.00**
Serenade, vase, #S-1, 6½" ........**70.00**
Sueno Tulip, ewer, #109, 8" ...**325.00**
Sueno Tulip, jardiniere, #115-33, 7" ......................................**345.00**
Sunglow, bowl, #50, 9½"...........**45.00**
Sunglow, flowerpot, #97, 5½" ...**55.00**
Sunglow, pitcher, #52, 24-oz ....**65.00**
Utility, flowerpot, 4" .................**50.00**
Water Lily, cornucopia, #L-7, 6½" .**150.00**

Water Lily, jardiniere, #L-23, 5½"..**170.00**
Wildflower, ewer, #W-2, 5½" ...**140.00**

**Wildflower, pitcher, 8½", from $190.00 to $245.00.**

Wildflower, vase, #W-1, 5½" ....**90.00**
Wildflower (# series), console bowl, #70, 12" .............................**495.00**
Wildflower (# series), vase, #78, 8½"..**440.00**
Woodland, matt, jardiniere, #W-7, 5½" ...................................**230.00**
Woodland, matt, window box, #W-14, 10" ..............................**235.00**

### Dinnerware

Avocado, bean pot, w/lid, 2-qt, from $22 to.................................**28.00**
Avocado, bowl, fruit; 5¼"............**5.00**
Avocado, plate, salad; 6½"..........**5.00**
Centennial Brown, casserole, 4½x11", from $90 to ........**110.00**
Centennial Brown, pitcher, milk; unmarked, 7½", from $90 to ..**110.00**
Centennial Brown, stein, 32-oz, from $45 to.................................**55.00**
Heartland, cup, coffee; from $6 to ..**7.00**
Heartland, quiche dish, from $18 to.........................................**28.00**
Mirror Brown, bowl, mixing; 8", from $10 to.........................**12.00**

Mirror Brown, coffee cup, 7-oz, from
$3 to......................................**5.00**

**Mirror Brown, creamer and
sugar bowl with lid, $10.00 each;
Teapot, $30.00.**

Mirror Brown, custard cup, 8-oz,
from $5 to............................**7.00**
Mirror Brown, gravy boat & saucer,
from $17 to.........................**22.00**
Mirror Brown, plate, luncheon; 8½",
from $7 to............................**9.00**
Mirror Brown, platter, w/chicken
lid, from $90 to ................**110.00**
Mirror Brown, tidbit, 2-tiered, from
$22 to..................................**28.00**
Provincial, bowl, mixing; 8¼", from
$19 to..................................**23.00**
Provincial, creamer, 8-oz, from $12
to.........................................**16.00**
Provincial, plate, dinner; 10¼", from
$12 to..................................**15.00**
Ring, creamer, from $10 to.......**15.00**
Ring, plate, salad; from $5 to.....**7.00**
Tangerine, bowl, soup/salad; 6½",
from $5 to............................**9.00**
Tangerine, ice jug, 2-qt, from $25
to.........................................**28.00**
Tangerine, tray (for snack set) .....**5.00**

# Indiana Carnival Glass

Though this glass looks old, it

really isn't. It's very reminiscent of
old Northwood carnival glass with
its grape clusters and detailed leaves
and vines, but this line was actually
introduced in 1972! Made by the
Indiana Glass Company, Harvest
(the pattern name assigned by the
company) was produced in blue, lime
green, and marigold. Although they
made a few other carnival patterns
in addition to this one, none are as
collectible or as easy to recognize.

This glassware is a little difficult to evaluate as there seems to be
a wide range of 'asking' prices simply because some dealers are unsure
of its age and therefore its value. If
you like it, now is the time to buy it!

For further information we recommend *Garage Sale & Flea Market
Annual* (Collector Books).

### Iridescent Amethyst (Heritage)

Basket, footed, 9x5x7"..............**40.00**
Butter dish, 5x7½" dia, from $40
to .......................................**50.00**
Center bowl, 4¾x8½", from $30
to .......................................**40.00**
Goblet, 8-oz, from $12 to ..........**18.00**
Pitcher, 8¼", from $40 to .........**60.00**
Punch set, 10" bowl & pedestal+8
cups+ladle (11 pcs), from $150
to .......................................**200.00**
Swung vase, slender & footed
w/irregular rim, 11x3", from $30
to .......................................**40.00**

### Iridescent Blue

Butter dish, Harvest, embossed grapes,
¼-lb, 8" L, from $25 to ......**35.00**

Candy box, Harvest, embossed grapes w/lace edge, w/lid, 6½", from $35 to.........................**45.00**

**Canister/candy jar, Harvest, embossed grapes, 7", from $30.00 to $45.00.**

Canister/Candy jar, Harvest, embossed grapes, 9", from $125 to ......**175.00**
Canister/Snack jar, Harvest, embossed grapes, 8", from $120 to..**150.00**
Garland bowl (comport), paneled, 7½x8½" dia, from $15 to ...**20.00**
Goblet, Harvest, embossed grapes, 9-oz, from $10 to.................**15.00**
Hen on nest, from $18 to..........**25.00**
Pitcher, Harvest, embossed grapes, 10½", common, from $25 to..**35.00**
Plate, Bicentennial; American Eagle, from $15 to .............**18.00**
Punch set, Princess, complete w/ladle & hooks, 26-pc, from $95 to..**115.00**
Wedding bowl (sm compote), Thumbprint, footed, 5x5", from $10 to ................................**12.00**

**Iridescent Gold**

Basket, Monticello, lg faceted allover diamonds, sq, 7x6", $25 to..**30.00**

Canister/Snack jar, Harvest, embossed grapes, 8", from $40 to .......................................**50.00**
Cooler (iced-tea tumbler), Harvest, 14-oz, from $8 to................**12.00**
Egg relish plate, 11", from $18 to .......................................**25.00**
Goblet, Harvest, embossed grapes, 9-oz, from $10 to................**14.00**
Hen on nest, 5½", from $18 to......**25.00**
Pitcher, Harvest, embossed grapes, 10", from $30 to .................**35.00**

**Pitcher, Harvest, embosssed grapes, 10", from $30.00 to $35.00; Cooler, 14 ounce, 5½", from $8.00 to $12.00.**

Relish tray, Vintage, 6 sections, 9x12¾", from $15 to .........**18.00**
Wedding bowl (sm compote), 5x5", from $9 to..........................**12.00**

**Iridescent Lime**

Canister/Snack set, Harvest, embossed grapes, 8", from $40 to .......................................**55.00**
Compote, Harvest, embossed grapes, 7x6", from $15 to..................**20.00**
Egg/relish tray, 12¾", from $18 to .......................................**25.00**
Goblet, Harvest, embossed grapes, 9-oz, from $10 to................**12.00**
Hen on nest, from $15 to..........**22.00**

Pitcher, Harvest, embossed grapes, 10½", from $35 to ...............**45.00**

Punch set, Princess, complete w/ladle & hooks, 26-pc, from $85 to ..............................**110.00**

**Iridescent Sunset (Amberina)**

Basket, footed, 9x5x7", from $30 to ........................................**45.00**

Basket, sq, 9½x7½", from $40 to ..**55.00**

Bowl, crimped, 3¾x10", from $32 to ........................................**40.00**

Butter dish, 5x7½" dia, from $32 to ........................................**38.00**

Creamer & sugar bowl, $30 to .**40.00**

Goblet, 8-oz, from $10 to ..........**15.00**

Pitcher, 8¼", from $45 to .........**50.00**

Rose bowl, 6½x6½", from $25 to .....**35.00**

Tumbler, 3½", from $15 to .......**18.00**

# Japan Ceramics

Though Japanese ceramics marked Nippon, Noritake, and Occupied Japan have long been collected, some of the newest fun-type collectibles on today's market are the figural ashtrays, pincushions, wall pockets, toothbrush holders, etc., that are marked 'Made in Japan' or simply 'Japan.' In *Collector's Encyclopedia of Made in Japan Ceramics*, Carole Bess White explains the pitfalls you will encounter when you try to determine production dates. Collectors refer to anything produced before WWII as 'old' and anything made after 1952 as 'new.' You'll find all you need to know to be a wise shopper in her book.

See also Black Cats; Blue Willow; Egg Timers; Enesco; Fishbowl Ornaments; Flower Frogs; Geisha Girl; Head Vases; Holt Howard; Lefton; Moss Rose; Nippon; Noritake; Occupied Japan; Rooster and Roses; Sewing Items; Toothbrush Holders; Wall Pockets.

Ashtray, calico dog at side of blue lustre base, black mark, 3¼" ...**45.00**

Ashtray, camel figural, multicolor w/lustre, black mark, 4¼".**25.00**

Ashtray, elephants (3) along side, multicolor, Maruyama, 2¼" .......**35.00**

Ashtray, peasant lady at side, w/snuffers, blue mark, 5½", $40 to ........................................**50.00**

Bank, 2 Mexicans beside lg green cactus, black mark, 3¾", from $25 to ................................**35.00**

Basket, floral bowl form w/reed handle, multicolor, 7¾" dia .....**20.00**

Basket, majolica-style floral on blue, black mark, 4½", from $30 to ..**45.00**

Bell, geometric band, yellow & black on orange, marked, 3", from $18 to ........................................**28.00**

**Bonbon/sandwich server, flowers on white with green rim, center handle with gold trim, red mark, 7¼", from $15.00 to $25.00.** (Photo courtesy Carole Bess White)

Bookends, Art Deco cat, green gloss, black mark, 7¾", from $85 to .......................................**125.00**

Bookends, Colonial man (lady) seated against book, black mark, 4¼" .....................................**40.00**

Bookends, orange anchor on white base, red mark, 4¾", from $35 to ..........................................**45.00**

Bookends, owl beside books, avocado green, black mark, 1970s, 5¼"..**15.00**

Bowl, floral band, multicolor & glossy, footed, green mark, 6½"....**45.00**

Bowl, river scenic, free-form rim, Meito, 5½", from $12 to.....**18.00**

Bowl, tulips, multicolor lustre, red Noritake mark, 8¾", from $65 to ..........................................**85.00**

Cache pot, frog playing cello by pot, multicolor, black mark, 4"...........**25.00**

Cache pot, lady w/loaf of bread beside lg basket, black mark, 4" ........................................**20.00**

Cache pot, man w/2 horses pulling covered wagon w/open top, green, 10"...........................**16.00**

Candle climber, angel child, multicolor, black mark, 3", from $12 to .......................................**18.00**

Candy box, Art Deco Revival bellhop by multicolor box, 1981, 5¼" ..**35.00**

Candy jar, floral on blue & white, flower finial, red mark, 5", from $25 to ...............................**40.00**

Celery tray, celery stalk on leaf shape, red mark, 12", from $50 to .........................................**65.00**

Child's feeding dish, blue lustre, children w/balloon inside, 5".......**50.00**

Cigarette box, flapper on lid, multicolor & shiny, red mark, 5" up to .......................................**125.00**

Cigarette holder & 4 ashtrays, palms on white, gold mark, from $20 to.......................**35.00**

Condiment set, Dutch people (3 of various sizes), multicolor, from $60 to .................................**90.00**

Condiment set, majolica-like roses on green leafy base, 6" W, from $20 to .................................**35.00**

Condiment set, 3 chicks in boat, multicolor lustre, black mark, from $60 to.........................**90.00**

Creamer & sugar bowl, lobster figural, red & yellow, 1930s, 4" .....**55.00**

Creamer & sugar bowl, owl figural, multicolor, black mark, from $55 to .................................**75.00**

Creamer & sugar bowl on tray, Deco fruit, multicolor lustre, 4½" W .......................................**85.00**

Egg cup, bulldog figural, tan lustre w/multicolor details, red mark..............................**35.00**

Egg cup, truck figural, multicolor, red mark, 2¼", from $18 to..**28.00**

Figurine, cat sleeping, white w/gold & multicolor details, Kutani, 8" L .........................................**90.00**

Figurine, comical fireman w/hose, multicolor, 3", from $12 to..**18.00**

**Figurine, lady in boat, multicolored shiny glazes, from $22.00 to $32.00.** (Photo courtesy Carole Bess White)

Figurine, pixie on tummy in blue polka-dot outfit, marked, 4½" L.......**12.50**

Figurine, pixie seated, green outfit & hat, unmarked, 2¾", from $10 to .......................................**15.00**

Flower frog, bird on stump, multicolor lustre, black mark, 4½".....**25.00**

Flower frog, bird w/long plume, majolica style, multicolor, 8", from $45 to........................**60.00**

Humidor, river scenic at sunset, green Noritake mark, 5½", from $125 to .............................**250.00**

Incense burner, hookah smoker, multicolor, red mark, 3¾", from $20 to .................................**30.00**

Jardiniere, Nouveau flowers on brown & green, Awaji, 6¼", from $40 to........................**60.00**

Lamp base, bird on stump figural, multicolor & blue lustre, 6", from $75 to ......................**100.00**

Lemon server, green fronds on white, red mark, 6¼", from $10 to .......................................**15.00**

Lemon server, Niagara Falls scene (souvenir), red mark, 6", from $25 to .................................**35.00**

Mayonnaise set, floral, multicolor, red mark, bowl+ladle+6" plate..**45.00**

Perfume bottle, Spanish lady figural, multicolor, black mark, 4"..**135.00**

Pincushion, calico rabbit beside cushion, red mark, 2¾", from $18 to .................................**28.00**

Pincushion, girl in oversize boots by seat (cushion), black mark, 5" .......................................**22.50**

Pitcher, fish w/lg open mouth figural, multicolor, marked, 6½" ...**45.00**

Powder box, lady figural, multicolor w/blue skirt, red mark, 5¼" ..**125.00**

Relish, lobster amid 3 lg yellow leaves, red mark, 8¾", from $65 to .......................................**85.00**

Shaker, frogs (2 stacking), multicolor lustre, green mark, 2¾", pr ..**30.00**

Shelf sitters, Asian boy & girl, multi-color, 5¼", pr from $15 to....**25.00**

**Shelf sitters, courting Asian couple, multicolored, marked, 4¾", 5 ", from $18.00 to $20.00 for the pair. (Photo courtesy Carole Bess White)**

Shoe, Deco flowers on Dutch shape, multicolor, marked, 8¼" ...**30.00**

Teapot, clovers on white basketweave, Belleek type, Mahuron, 6¼"....................**40.00**

Toothpick holder, Dutch girl by lg tulip, multicolor, red mark, 3½" .....................................**30.00**

Vase, airbrushed floral on black, Arts & Crafts style, 5", from $275 to .............................**325.00**

Vase, bird on stump branch, flowers along side, multicolor, 8½"..**35.00**

Vase, dark green gloss, integral handles, marked Japan, 9", from $50 to .................................**85.00**

Vase, Deco butterflies on black & red, bulbous body, red mark, 7" ......................................**70.00**

Vase, Deco flowers on black to orange, waisted, Noritake, 9", up to ................................**125.00**
Vase, fish scene, multicolor, Goldcastle, 7¼", from $50 to .....**75.00**
Vase, Mexican man standing beside white tree trunk, red mark, 6" ........................................**20.00**
Vase, orange 'clouds' on green, upturned handles, Awaji, 5½" ......................................**50.00**
Vase, yellow, wrapped in woven cane, handles, Awaji, 9½", from $65 to ................................**85.00**

# Jewelry

Anyone interested in buying jewelry will soon find out that antique gems are the best values. Not only are prices from one-third to one-half less than on comparable new jewelry, but the older pieces display a degree of craftsmanship and styling seldom seen in modern-day jewelry. Costume jewelry from all periods is popular, especially Art Nouveau and Art Deco examples. Signed pieces are particularly good, such as those by Miriam Haskell, Eisenberg, Trifari, Hollycraft, and Weiss, among others.

There are some excellent reference books available if you'd like more information. Marcia 'Sparkles' Brown has written *Unsigned Beauties of Costume Jewelry; Signed Beauties of Costume Jewelry, Volume I* and *Volume II;* and *Coro Jewelry*. Lillian Baker has written several: *Plastic Jewelry of the Twentieth Century; 50 Years of Collectible Fashion Jewelry;* and *100 Years of Collectible Jewelry*. Books by other authors include *Costume Jewelry* and *Collectible Silver Jewelry* by Fred Rezazadeh; *Collectible Costume Jewelry* by Cherri Simonds; *Christmas Pins, Past & Present* by Jill Gallina; *Costume Jewelry 101* by Julia C. Carroll; *Inside the Jewelry Box* by Ann Mitchell Pitman; *Vintage Jewelry for Investment & Casual Wear* by Karen Edeen; and *Brilliant Rhinestones* and *20th Century Costume Jewelry*, both by Ronna Lee Aikins. All are published by Collector Books. See Clubs and Newsletters for information on the Vintage Fashion & Costume Jewelry newsletter and club.

Belt buckle, celluloid, HP Nouveau design, French, 1930 .........**95.00**
Bracelet & earrings, M Boucher, gold-plated w/blood red rhinestones ...............................**170.00**
Bracelet, 5 rows of pink rhinestones, 2" W................................**110.00**
Bracelet, Bakelite, reverse-carved amber & black links, 1935.......**250.00**
Bracelet, Bakelite, reverse-carved apple juice w/paint decor, 1930 ..**350.00**
Bracelet, bangle, Lucite, teal blue pearlized, 1950 ..................**45.00**
Bracelet, bangle; DVF, Bakelite, yellow carved to black saucer shapes ..............................**100.00**
Bracelet, bangle; Lea Stein, cellulose, snake form, 1960-80 ........**125.00**
Bracelet, bangle; Lea Stein, laminate cellulose w/carving, 1960-80 .....................................**350.00**

Bracelet, Charel, green thermoset plastic links, 1960-70 ........**55.00**

Bracelet, chunky metalwork sqs w/red glass stones, 1940s..**55.00**

Bracelet, Ciner, Bakelite & gilt brass links, 1950 .............**150.00**

Bracelet, clear hand-set rhinestones in single strand .................**18.00**

Bracelet, cuff; KJL, Bakelite & wood on gilded brass cuff .........**195.00**

Bracelet, Florenza, lavender faceted glass stones w/seed pearls..**55.00**

Bracelet, Joseff of Hollywood, silver w/fuchsia glass stones.....**280.00**

Bracelet, pearls & topaz rhinestones in single row ......................**30.00**

**Bracelet, unsigned, elastic, featuring black plastic diamond-studded segments with metal strip dividers, 1950s, $75.00.** (Photo courtesy Marcia Brown)

Brooch, Austria (unsigned), multicolor rhinestone floral nosegay..**85.00**

Brooch, Bakelite, black & chrome sword, 1935......................**100.00**

Brooch, Cadoro, 4 rectangular crystals (multicolor) form sq.........**320.00**

Brooch, chaton rhinestone snowflake, very lg ...............................**55.00**

Brooch, gold-plated 5-leaf clover w/green chatons.................**48.00**

Brooch, H Carnegie, gold-plated cameo ...............................**110.00**

Brooch, H Carnegie, gold-plated trembler bug w/clear rhinestone trim ....................................**95.00**

Brooch, Hollycraft, silver-plated bow w/blue rhinestones ............**48.00**

Brooch, KJ Lane, silver & gold dinosaur w/green rhinestone eyes ....................................**135.00**

Brooch, KJL, thermoset scarab, Egyptian Revival, 1970...**175.00**

Brooch, Lea Stein, plastic, vintage limosine, 1960 .................**175.00**

Brooch, plastic, sailor w/movable limbs, 1930s repro, French, 1980s................................**150.00**

Brooch, Robert Originals, ocean turtle, enameled .....................**80.00**

Brooch, Schiaparelli, gold & brown rhinestones w/3 drops .....**180.00**

Brooch, silver bug w/rhinestone center.......................................**85.00**

Brooch, Trifari, butterfly w/red & clear rhinestones.............**125.00**

Brooch, Trifari, gold-plated leaf w/clear rhinestones ...........**60.00**

Brooch, Trifari, spider w/clear 'jelly belly'...............................**575.00**

Brooch, Weiss, owl, multicolor enameling ..........................**55.00**

Brooch, Weiss, pink & clear rhinestones ...............................**125.00**

Brooch, wooden bird w/carved Lucite & brass beading, 1930 ....**125.00**

Brooch & earrings, Kramer, pink/fuchsia/aurora borealis rhinestones ......................**280.00**

Brooch & earrings, Trifari, faux pearls & gold leaves ..........**80.00**

Brooch & earrings, Weiss, dark blue rhinestones in clusters....**165.00**

Buckle, Bakelite, green/butter-scotch/orange/brown circle, 1935 ..................................**125.00**
Clip, Catalin, carved ivory & black comb style, 1936-41 ..........**75.00**
Dress clip, Bakelite, 3-color Deco design, 1925......................**95.00**
Dress clip, carved Bakelite banjo w/gold-plated center..........**95.00**
Dress clip, pink & clear rhinestone mushrooms (2)..................**110.00**
Earrings, aurora borealis rhinestone cluster ...............................**38.00**
Earrings, Bakelite, butterscotch, carved-button type, 1935 ..**45.00**
Earrings, Bakelite, carved cherries, 1930s...............................**175.00**
Earrings, M Haskell, turquoise bed w/5 diamanté rhinestone points ...............................**60.00**
Earrings, orange rhinestones dangle from 3 lime green navettes..**24.00**
Earrings, thermoset plastic set in rhodium ..............................**15.00**

**Earrings, unsigned, button type rimmed with clear rhinestones, from $12.00 to $18.00 for each pair. (Photo courtesy Marcia Brown)**

Earrings, yellow plastic flower held by rhinestone center .........**14.00**
Hat ornament, plastic, brown w/rhinestones, Deco design, 1930....**45.00**

Necklace & earrings, Hollycraft, clear & yellow rhinestones.......**110.00**

**Necklace and earrings, Schiaparelli, triple strand of blue and green beads, $190.00 for the set. (Photo courtesy Marcia Brown)**

Necklace & earrings, Trifari, silver flowers................................**90.00**
Necklace & earrings, Trifari, 6 strands of green beads & crystals .....**80.00**
Necklace & earrings, 3-strand aurora borealis beads ...............**95.00**
Necklace, Bakelite, black rigid segments, 1935 .....................**125.00**
Necklace, bracelet & earrings, Kramer, pink & clear rhinestones...............................**225.00**
Necklace, brooch & earrings, Hollycraft, gold plated w/red rhinestones..............................**340.00**
Necklace, dark green hand-set chaton rhinestones..................**58.00**
Necklace, H Carnegie, 10 strands of crystal beads...................**110.00**
Necklace, KJL, Angel Skin floral design, 1960-90 ...............**325.00**
Necklace, KJL, thermoset faux jade pendant on chain, 1965.....**65.00**
Necklace, Kramer, diamond-look double rhinestone chain..**310.00**

Necklace, linked dark green hand-set chaton rhinestones ......**58.00**

Necklace, pink & fuchsia beads w/cranberry rhinestones ...**35.00**

Necklace, sterling silver & abalone shells, 1950s ......................**85.00**

Necklace, 2 strands of pearls w/pavé rhinestone clasp ................**48.00**

Necklace, Weiss, lavender beads & clear rhinestones ................**90.00**

Ring, gold-plated dome w/red rhinestones ...................................**28.00**

Ring, gold-plated sq filled w/opalene chatons................................**38.00**

Ring, gold-plated twin diamond rhinestone navettes...........**20.00**

Ring, Silver Cloud, silver w/lg faux turquoise stone...................**35.00**

Ring, tiger-eye cabochon w/in clear rhinestone circle................**45.00**

Ring, topaz chatons form chrysanthemum.............................**55.00**

# Johnson Brothers

Dinnerware marked Johnson Brothers, Staffordshire, is bought and sold with considerable fervor on today's market, and for good reason. They made many lovely patterns, some scenic and some florals. Most are decorated with multicolor transfer designs, though you'll see blue or red transferware as well. Some, such as Friendly Village (one of their most popular lines), are still being produced, but the lines are much less extensive now, so the secondary market is being tapped to replace broken items that are no longer available anywhere else.

Some lines are more valuable than others. Unless a pattern is included in the following two categories, use the base values below as a guide. (Some of the most popular base-value lines are Bird of Paradise, Mount Vernon, Castle on the Lake, Old Bradury, Day in June, Nordic, Devon Sprays, Old Mill, Empire Grape, Pastorale, Haddon Hall, Pomona, Harvest Time, Road Home, Indian Tree, Vintage (older version), Melody, and Windsor Fruit.) One-Star patterns are basically 10% to 20% higher and include Autumn's Delight, Coaching Scenes, Devonshire, Fish, Friendly Village, Gamebirds, Garden Bouquet, Hearts and Flowers, Heritage Hall, Indies, Millstream, Olde English Countryside, Rose Bouquet, Sheraton, Tulip Time, and Winchester. Two-Star lines include Barnyard King, Century of Progress, Chintz — Victorian, Dorchester, English Chippendale, Harvest Fruit, His Majesty, Historical America, Merry Christmas, Old Britain Castles, Persian Tulip, Rose Chintz, Strawberry Fair, Tally Ho, Twelve Days of Christmas, and Wild Turkeys. These patterns are from 25% to 35% higher than our base values.

For more information refer to *Johnson Brothers Dinnerware* by Mary J. Finegan. She is listed in the Directory under North Carolina.

Bowl, cereal/soup; round, sq or lug, ea........................................**14.00**

Bowl, soup, round or sq, 7" ......**16.00**

Bowl, vegetable; oval ................**35.00**
Chop/cake plate ........................**55.00**
Coffee mug ................................**16.00**
Coffeepot ...................................**70.00**
Covered butter dish .................**55.00**
Demitasse set, 2-pc ..................**20.00**
Egg cup .....................................**20.00**
Pitcher/jug ...............................**38.00**
Plate, dinner .............................**20.00**
Plate, salad; round or sq .........**12.00**
Platter, med, 12-14", ea ...........**38.00**

**Salt and pepper shakers, Mayflower, 3", $30.00 for the pair.**

Salt & pepper shakers, pr ........**32.00**
Sauce boat/gravy ......................**32.00**
Sugar bowl, open ......................**28.00**
Teacup & saucer ........................**20.00**
Teapot .......................................**70.00**
Turkey platter, 20½" ..............**175.00**

# Kentucky Derby Glasses

Kentucky Derby glasses are the official souvenir glasses that are filled with mint juleps and sold on Derby Day. The first glass (1938), picturing a black horse within a black and white rose garland and the Churchill Downs stadium in the background, is said to have either been given away as a souvenir or used for drinks among the elite at the Downs. This glass, the 1939, and two glasses said to have been used in 1940 are worth thousands and are nearly impossible to find at any price.

1940, aluminum ...................**1,000.00**
1941-44, plastic Beetleware, ea, from
    $2,500 to ........................**4,000.00**
1945, jigger ..........................**1,000.00**
1945, regular .......................**1,600.00**
1945, tall ................................**450.00**
1946-47, ea .............................**100.00**
1948, clear bottom .................**225.00**

**1948, frosted bottom, $250.00.**

1949 .......................................**225.00**
1950 .......................................**450.00**
1951 .......................................**650.00**
1952 .......................................**225.00**
1953 .......................................**200.00**
1954 .......................................**225.00**
1955 .......................................**200.00**
1956, 1 star, 2 tails ................**275.00**
1956, 1 star, 3 tails ................**400.00**
1956, 2 stars, 2 tails ..............**200.00**
1956, 2 stars, 3 tails ..............**250.00**
1957, gold & black on front ....**125.00**
1958, Gold Bar .......................**175.00**
1958, Iron Leige .....................**225.00**
1959-60, ea .............................**100.00**
1961 .......................................**110.00**

1962, Churchill Downs, red, gold & black
  on clear..............................**190.00**
1963 ...........................................**70.00**
1964 ...........................................**55.00**
1965 ...........................................**85.00**
1966 ...........................................**65.00**
1967-68, ea ...............................**60.00**
1969 ...........................................**65.00**

1970, $70.00.

1971 ...........................................**55.00**
1972 ...........................................**55.00**
1973 ...........................................**60.00**
1974, Federal, regular or mistake,
  ea .......................................**200.00**
1974, mistake (Canonero in 1971
  listing on back) ..................**18.00**
1974, regular (Canonero II in 1971
  listing on back) ..................**16.00**
1975 ...........................................**16.00**
1976 ...........................................**16.00**
1976, plastic ............................**16.00**
1977 ...........................................**14.00**
1978-79, ea ...............................**16.00**
1980 ...........................................**22.00**
1981-82, ea ...............................**15.00**
1983-85 .......................................**12.00**
1986 ...........................................**14.00**
1986 ('85 copy) .........................**20.00**
1987-89, ea ...............................**12.00**
1990-92, ea ...............................**10.00**
1993-95, ea ................................**9.00**

1996-97 ........................................**8.00**
1998-99 ........................................**6.00**
2000-02, ea .................................**5.00**
2003 mistake, 1932 incorrectly listed
  Derby Triple Crown Winner..**6.00**
2003-2004, ea .............................**4.00**
2004 .............................................**3.50**
2005 .............................................**3.00**

# Kitchen Collectibles

From the early patented apple peelers, cherry pitters, and food hoppers to the gadgets of the '20s through the '40s, many collectors find special appeal in kitchen tools. Refer to *Kitchen Antiques, 1790 – 1940,* by Kathryn McNerney; and *Kitchen Glassware of the Depression Years* by Gene and Cathy Florence for more information. Both are published by Collector Books.

See also Aluminum; Clothes Sprinkler Bottles; Cookie Cutters; Egg Timers; Enesco; Graniteware; Griswold.

Apple peeler, Goodell White Mountain, cast iron, clamps to table, 12" .....................................**65.00**
Apple peeler, Penn H Co, cast iron w/wooden handle, 8x9"......**50.00**
Apple peeler, Sinclair Scott Co, black-painted cast iron......**40.00**
Bean/crock pot, marked USA on bottom, brown stoneware ............**18.00**
Blender, Osterizer Model 403, chrome base w/black rubber lid, 15¼" .....................................**50.00**
Bottle warmer, Sunbeam Model B2, chrome, 1940s-50s, MIB....**38.00**

Bowl, mixing; fired-on color, Pyrex, set of 4, from $28 to...........**36.00**

Bowl, mixing; glass, Jade-ite, 2-qt, 7⅝", from $60 to ...............**65.00**

Bowl, mixing; Granite Ware, blue, 8⅜", from $35 to ................**40.00**

Bowl, mixing; Red Dots on ivory glass, 3-qt, 8½", from $25 to...........**27.50**

Butter dish, pink glass, bow finial, rectangular, from $65 to ...**75.00**

Cake plate, Fry, glass, round, 9", from $30 to........................**38.00**

Can opener, Dazey, red-painted metal w/wooden handle.....**15.00**

Can opener, Edlund Jr No 5, hand type, 6½" L........................**22.50**

Can opener, Sunbeam, yellow, 1960s .................................**37.00**

Can opener/ice crusher, General Electric, olive green...........**20.00**

Canister, caramel glass, black lettering, tin lid, 48-oz, from $100 to........................................**125.00**

Canister, Hazel-Atlas, transparent green glass, from $60 to ....**65.00**

Carving set, Landers Frary & Clark, carved ivory handles, 3-pc..**125.00**

Casserole, McKee, clear glass, heart-shaped, from $25 to...........**30.00**

Casserole, Red Dot on clear crystal glass, McKee, from $10 to.**12.50**

Cruet, pink glass, ribbed & beaded, Imperial, from $45 to ........**55.00**

Egg beater, Androck, rotary, green Bakelite handles................**20.00**

Egg beater, Holt's, flared dashers, 10½" ..................................**50.00**

Egg beater, Ladd Beater No 1 United Royalties...1908...1915, 11" ......................................**35.00**

Egg beater, T&S Made in USA Pat Applied for, crank type, 9".....**35.00**

Egg beater, Turbine...Pat Aug 20 191...Chicago USA, gear wheel ..................................**30.00**

Egg cooker, Oster Model #581, dark chocolate brown, 4-7 eggs..**20.00**

Egg cup, solid black glass, from $20 to........................................**25.00**

Food mill, Foley, crank handle..**15.00**

Food warmer, alumnium, 4-pc set, 1950s, 17x7"......................**22.00**

Fork, A&J, 3-tine, green wooden handle ...............................**10.00**

Grater, cheese; aluminum, drum type, mounts to table.........**15.00**

Grater, tin, cylindrical, 1940s, 9½x4" dia ..........................**18.00**

Grater, wooden frame, pull-out drawer w/porcelain knob...**20.00**

Heater, Barber 'Health Master,' 1960s ..................................**22.00**

Ice pick, red wooden handle w/metal end to protect hand, 8¼"...**16.00**

Ice pick, wooden handle, 1920s, EX........................................**10.00**

**Juice bottle, Hazel Atlas, fired-on oranges, Concentric Ring neck, green lid, marked HA-K-4, 7⅛", from $15.00 to $18.00.** (Photo courtesy Gene and Cathy Florence)

Juicer, fruit; Kitchen Aid K5-A, all metal, complete ................**68.00**

Juicer, Juice-O-Mat, metal w/white base, pre-1950s, EX...........**30.00**

Juicer, Wear-Ever, aluminum, ca 1930s, 9x9".........................**45.00**

Ladle, Fostoria, crystal, from $12 to........................................**15.00**

Loaf pan, McKee, clear glass, 3x5x10", from $6 to..............**8.00**

**Mayonnaise maker, J. Hutchinson, trademark S&S Long Island, from $125.00 to $150.00.** (Photo courtesy Gene and Cathy Florence)

Measuring cup, US Glass, pink, 2-cup, from $200 to.............**225.00**

Measuring pitcher, fired-on green glass, from $25 to ..............**30.00**

Measuring pitcher, US Glass, green, slick handle, from $45 to...**50.00**

Melon baller, green wooden handle, EX........................................**10.00**

Mixer, Hobart #404305, red, 3-speed, 10-qt, 1931, NM ...**110.00**

Mixer/juicer, General Electric Model M12, all white, 12-speed, NM..**55.00**

Mug, Fire-King, sapphire blue, from $22 to.................................**25.00**

Nut cracker, Ideal, nickel-plated cast iron, ca 1915, 5" .........**22.00**

Pie plate, Pyrex, blue, 10", from $30 to........................................**35.00**

Popcorn popper, Fostoria, aluminum w/glass lid, 3-qt, EXIB .........**20.00**

Pot scrubber, metal rings on wire handle, early 1900s ...........**37.50**

Potato masher/ricer, red pliers type w/3⅛x3¼" strainer cup.......**15.00**

Potato peeler, pierced metal blade, wooden handle...................**30.00**

**Range shakers, Jade-ite, red and white screw-on lids, from $80.00 to $90.00 for the pair.** (Photo courtesy Gene and Cathy Florence)

Rolling pin, clear glass, Roll-Rite, end cap, 14".......................**35.00**

Rolling pin, Coke bottle blue, molded glass, from $85 to ............**100.00**

Rolling pin, clear glass, cork end..**25.00**

Rolling pin, tiger maple w/cherry handles, 16¾" ....................**60.00**

Rolling pin, turned wood, made in 1 pc, extra-lg, 24".................**40.00**

Rolling pin, white w/green handles, Imperial Glass, EX............**65.00**

Salad fork & spoon, glass, crystal w/red teardrop handle, from $85 to........................................**95.00**

Salt & pepper shakers, glass, black lettering on white, pr from $15 to........................................**18.00**

Salt & pepper shakers, glass, Chalaine blue, pr from $125 to..**135.00**

Salt & pepper shakers, glass, Dots, red on white, pr from $25 to .......**35.00**

Sifter, Androck Handi-Sift, tin, pies & cakes on red ..................**27.50**

Skillet, Sunbeam, Atomic Turquoise, detachable cord, 1955 ........**43.00**

Skimmer, cast iron, slotted bowl, Taiwan, 11x2½" dia...........**50.00**

Spatula/spreader, Cutco #28, lamb handle ................................**15.00**

Sugar shaker, crystal, Paden City, 2-part dispenser, from $20 to ..**25.00**

Teakettle, white, Glasbake, ribbed, black handle, from $45 to..**50.00**

Timer, hen figural, red & white, 3½x2½" .............................**18.00**

Timer, Lux, pink w/white knob, 1950s ..................................**45.00**

Timer, Lux/Ekco, black letters on white, 3½x3" ......................**25.00**

Timer, Mirro, aluminum, Bakelite dial, ca 1950s .....................**28.00**

Timer, Mirro Matic, white w/red numbers, 1950s, MIB........**30.00**

Toaster, chrome & red plastic, 2-slice, 1950s, EX...............**112.00**

Toaster, Sunbeam AT-W, chrome, 1950s ................................**67.00**

Waffle iron, Aladdin, aluminum w/cast-iron base, EX..........**45.00**

Water bottle, clear glass w/lattice design, w/lid, from $45 to..**50.00**

Whip, red handle, Archimedes type, 8¾", EX .............................**15.00**

# Kliban

B. Kliban, artist and satirist, was extremely fond of cats and usually had more than one as companion to him in his California home. This led to his first book (published in 1975), simply titled *Cat*. The popularity of the Kliban cat led to sales of various types of merchandising featuring his likeness. Among the items you may encounter are calendars, mugs, note pads, Christmas cards, stuffed toys, and many other items, the majority of which are of recent production.

Bank, w/red sneakers, from $50 to........................................**60.00**

Beach towel, Momcat, baby in pouch, from $32 to.............**40.00**

Candlestick, climbing tree, 8", from $35 to.................................**45.00**

Cat watering dish, self-feeding, 9" H........................................**17.50**

Cookie jar, climbing out of top hat, 8½", from $120 to ...........**130.00**

Cookie jar, playing guitar, atop red stool, from $150 to...........**165.00**

Cookie jar, upright w/baby & cookies, from $165 to.....................**180.00**

Doll, in hula skirt w/pink lei, plush, 8" ......................................**32.50**

Grocery bag caddy, cloth tube, printed cotton, 21" L..................**18.00**

Ice bucket, flying over skyline w/red cape on back, 8¼".............**40.00**

Kleenex holder, pictured in red sneakers, 5½x10½"...........**12.50**

Mug, dressed as chef cooking mice, white, Kiln Craft .............**15.00**

Mug, playing guitar on stool w/ Love To Eat Those Mice verse, 3½" .....................................**30.00**

Mug, white w/2 cats w/Bad in between, 3¾", MIB ...........**30.00**

Picture frame, clinging to side, 9¼x7¼" ...........................**110.00**

Picture frame, Love a Cat, seated bottom right corner, 5x7", from $40 to..................................**50.00**

Pitcher, cream; mouth as spout, 4½x7½".............................**40.00**

Salt & pepper shakers, rare, pr from $500 to.............................**525.00**

Sleeping bag, many cats in red sneakers, 77", EX..............**15.00**

Soap dish, lying on back, tail in air, 4⅛x4¾x8½", from $110 to..**125.00**

T-shirt, Sumo cat on blue, adult size .....................................**22.50**

Teapot, in rocket ship, rare, from $425 to.............................**450.00**

Teapot, in tuxedo & top hat, 12", from $210 to....................**225.00**

Teapot, upright, wearing Santa hat, 7½", from $180 to ............**200.00**

Trinket box, in bathtub (lid) w/swimming mouse, 4x7", from $465 to.............................**480.00**

Wall clock, in red sneakers atop clock, 15" ............................**40.00**

**Wall plaque, from $70.00 to $90.00.**

Wastebasket, flying over skyline w/red cape on back, white, metal, EX...........................**20.00**

# Knives

Knife collecting as a hobby began in earnest during the 1960s when government regulations required that knife companies mark their product with the country of origin. The few collectors and dealers cognizant of this change at once began stockpiling the older knives made before this law was enacted. Another impetus to the growing interest in this area came with the Gun Control Act of 1968, which severely restricted gun trading. Frustrated gun dealers transferred their attention to knives. Today there are collectors' clubs in many of the states.

The most sought-after pocketknives are those made before WWII. However, Case, Schrade, and Primble knives of a more recent manufacture are also collected. Most collectors prefer knives 'as found.' Do not attempt to clean, sharpen, or in any way 'improve' on an old knife.

The prices quoted here are for knives in used, excellent condition. For further information refer to *The Standard Knife Collector's Guide; Cattaragus Cutlery Co.; Big Book of Pocket Knives*; and *Remington Knives, Past & Present,* by Ron Stewart and Roy Ritchie (all published by Collector Books); and *Sargent's American Premium Guide to Knives and Razors, Identification and Values, 3rd Edition,* by Jim Sargent.

Aerial Cutlery Co, 2-blade jackknife, bone handle, 3⅜".............**60.00**

Boker, Henrich (German), 1-blade, bone handle, 4½".............**65.00**

Boker (USA), 3-blade stockman, imitation pearl handle, 4" ......**40.00**

Boker (USA), 4-blade congress, bone handle, 3¾".......................**65.00**

Case, Tested XX, 6203 1½, 2-blade, green bone handle, 3¾"...**150.00**

**Case, XX, 5165, 1976 Bicentennial folding hunter, The American Spirit etched in blue and red on blade, genuine stag handle, M in display case, from $160.00 to**

Case, XX, 5254, 2-blade, genuine stag handle, trapper pattern, 4⅛" ...................................**300.00**

Case, XX, 623 1½, 2-blade, bone handle, 3¾".......................**75.00**

Case, XX, 6308, 3-blade, bone handle, whittler pattern, 3¼" ......**100.00**

Case Bros, Little Valley NY, 2-blade, wood handle, 3¼" .**125.00**

Cattaraugus, 22346, 2-blade, wood handle, jackknife pattern, 3⅜"..**85.00**

Diamond Edge, 2-blade, bone handle, jackknife, 3⅜" .............**75.00**

Hammer Brand, NY Knife Co, 2-blade, bone handle, 3⅜" ....**85.00**

Hammer Brand, 1-blade, tin shell handle, powder-horn pattern, 4¾" .....................................**25.00**

Hammer Brand, 2-blade, wood handle, jackknife, 3¾" .............**85.00**

Henckels, JA; 4-blade, bone handle, congress pattern, 4".........**150.00**

Holley Mfg Co, 1-blade, wood handle, 5" .....................................**140.00**

Honk Falls Knife Co, 1-blade, bone handle, 3".........................**125.00**

Imperial Knife Co, 2-blade, multicolored handle, 3¼"...............**35.00**

John Primble, Belknap Hardware Co, 3-blade, bone handle, 4" ......**75.00**

Ka-Bar, 2-blade, genuine stag handle, Old Time Trapper, 4⅛" .......**85.00**

Ka-Bar, 3-blade, bone handle, cattle pattern, 3⅜" .....................**100.00**

Keen Kutter, bone handle, Barlow, 3⅜" .....................................**75.00**

Keen Kutter, EC Simmons, 1-blade, bone handle, 3¼" ...............**50.00**

Keen Kutter, 1-blade, bone handle, TX toothpick, 5"...............**125.00**

LF&C, 3-blade, genuine pearl handle, whittler, 3½".............**125.00**

Miller Bros, 2-blade, bone handle, jackknife, 3½" ..................**100.00**

Morley, WH & Sons; 3-blade, bone handle, whittler, 3¼".........**65.00**

Napanoch Knife Co, 4-blade, bone handle, 3¼" ......................**150.00**

Pal, 2-blade, bone handle, easy-open, 3¾"...........................**85.00**

Remington, R1153, 2-blade, bone handle, jackknife, 4½".....**250.00**

Remington, R1225, 2-blade, white composition handle, 4¼" .**125.00**

Remington, R775, 2-blade, red, white & blue handle, 3½"..**185.00**

Russell, 2-blade, bone handle, Barlow, 3⅜"...........................**125.00**

Russell, 2-blade, bone handle, Barlow, 5"...............................**200.00**

Schrade Walden, 3-blade, peach-seed bone handle, 3⅜".......**75.00**

Ulster Knife Co, 4-blade, imitation bone handle, Scout/campers..**30.00**

Wards, 4-blade, bone handle, cattle pattern, 3⅝".......................**85.00**

# Kreiss

These novelties were imported from Japan during the 1950s. There are several lines. One is a totally off-the-wall group of caricatures called Psycho Ceramics. There's a Beatnik series, Bums, and Cave People (all of which are strange little creatures), as well as some that are very well done and tasteful. Others you find will be inset with colored 'jewels.' Many are marked either with an ink stamp or an in-mold trademark (some are dated).

Values are lower than we reported in the last edition; this is only one of many collectibles that have been affected by the Internet.

Ashtray, white w/pink poodles, rests on ea end, 4⅛x12¼" ............**25.00**
Bank, Christmas pig, standing, 2 verses on sides, 4x4x6"......**30.00**
Bank, Christmas pig on back w/slot in belly, red gloves, from $20 to..**25.00**
Bank, creature looks up, Money Hungry on tummy, Psycho Ceramics, 6"........................**15.00**
Bank, pig, Our New Car...........**25.00**
Bank, poodle, black & white cold paint, pink details, 8¾".....**35.00**
Candleholders, angels kneeling, 1 black dress/1 red, 5½", pr..**32.50**
Clothes brush, figural kitten handle, 5" ......................................**27.50**
Dresser valet, Bucky Beaver, coin slot in tummy, 6½x3½x5¼"........**20.00**
Figurine, choir boy, red robe & book, 5" ......................................**20.00**
Figurine, creature, blue, Looking for...w/Authority, Psycho Ceramics ...........................**40.00**

Figurine, creature, purple w/rhinestone eyes, fuzzy hair, 5½"..**35.00**
Figurine, creature w/4 bulging eyes, sm hat on head ..................**40.00**
Figurine, devil boy, in red w/pipe-cleaner pointed tail, 1955, 5"..............**30.00**
Figurine, dinosaur w/little caveman on head, 7" ........................**25.00**
Figurine, Frankenstein-like creature w/candle atop head .............**50.00**
Figurine, horse running, brown & white legs, 6¼"..................**30.00**
Figurine, hula girl in red dress w/shell at feet, 6¼" ............**75.00**
Figurine, poodle, pink w/much 'spaghetti,' 7" ....................**75.00**
Figurine, Santa waving, drunken, Psycho Ceramics, 6½" .......**25.00**

**Figurine, Santa, Yes But What Did You Get for Santa?, $25.00.**

Figurine, schoolboy, Elegant Heirs, 6" ........................................**30.00**
Figurines, boy & girl dressed in red, white & blue, stars on base, 9", pr ......................................**45.00**
Figurines, caveman family, mom & dad (5") & 2 kids (2¼"), from $35 to...............................**45.00**
Figurines, cocker spaniel w/2 puppies attached by chain.......**17.50**

Flower holder, girl in pink, blue rhinestones eyes, hugs vase, 4⅜" .....................................**25.00**

Mug, pink guy w/sm blue hat on shoulder, plaque on back, 5" ..........**30.00**

Mug, purple creature w/plugs in ears, Psycho Ceramics.......**35.00**

Napkin holder, lady in pink w/gold trim, slotted skirt, 9", from $45 to........................................**55.00**

Perfume bottle, figural skunk w/flower bouquet on head, 5"...............**40.00**

Salt & pepper shakers, Christmas reindeer, pr .......................**25.00**

Salt & pepper shakers, ducklings, yellow w/multicolor, 3½", pr.......**15.00**

Salt & pepper shakers, Jose Carioca Bird (3 Caballeros), 3", pr .**20.00**

Salt & pepper shakers, monks, pepper is sneezing, pr .............**20.00**

## Lefton China

Since 1940 the Lefton China Co. has been importing and producing ceramic giftware which may be found in shops throughout the world. Because of the quality of the workmanship and the beauty of these items, they are eagerly sought by collectors of today. Lefton pieces are usually marked with a fired-on trademark or a paper label.

See Clubs and Newsletters for information concerning the National Society of Lefton Collectors.

Ashtray, Blue Paisley, shell shape, #2357, 3½" .........................**10.00**

Ashtray, milk china w/applied roses, 2 rests, #844, 3½"...................**12.00**

Baby set, Mr Toodles, #3293, 2-pc ..**60.00**

Basket, Green Holly, #5186, 4¾"..**18.00**

Bell, figures in relief, bisque w/brown wash, #295, 5½", from $14 to................................**18.00**

Bell, Green Holly, 3½".............**15.00**

Bone dish, Lilac Chintz, #669, from $12 to.................................**15.00**

Butter dish, Mr Toodles, #3294, 6¾" ...................................**125.00**

Candleholder, Green Holly, #717, pr from $25 to........................**30.00**

Candleholder, Green Holly votive, #6027, 2" .............................**8.00**

Candy box, egg form w/roses decals, #2209, 5½" .........................**25.00**

Candy box, Floral Mood, leaf form, #4669.................................**15.00**

Candy dish, Violet Heirloom, footed, #1377, 5" .............................**40.00**

Canister set, Sweet Violets, #2879, 4-pc....................................**95.00**

Cheese dish, Miss Priss, #1505, 5½" ...................................**175.00**

Coffeepot, Brown Heritage Floral, #062...................................**150.00**

Cookie jar, Dainty Miss, #040, 7½" ...................................**150.00**

**Creamer and sugar bowl, Miss Priss, 1950s, from $70.00 to $90.00.**

Creamer & sugar bowl, Mr Toodles, #3292..................................**45.00**

Cup & saucer, Blue Paisley, #2339 ..**18.00**

Cup & saucer, demitasse; floral reserves on green w/gold, #801........**50.00**

Cup & saucer, Green Holly ......**15.00**

Egg cup, Miss Priss, #1510 ......**40.00**

Figurine, angel climber, #389, 4" ........................................**25.00**

Figurine, Chinese lady, white w/heavy gold, #0600, 8".....**85.00**

Figurine, cockatoo, floral base, #1542, 7" ............................**75.00**

Figurine, girl in bonnet & apron, #5153, 5½" ........................**15.00**

Figurine, heron on leafy base, #1532, 5½" ........................**45.00**

Figurine, kissing couple, #10530, 4¼", pr..............................**45.00**

Figurine, panda bear, bisque, #4910, 5¼" ....................................**35.00**

Figurine, rooster w/long tail on stump, #1507, 10"............**100.00**

Frame, oval w/2 cherubs at base, #7221, 6¼" ........................**60.00**

Jam jar, Dutch Girl, #2597 ......**65.00**

Jam jar, grapes, #4852, 5"........**25.00**

Lamp, Elegant Rose, #931, 13½"................................**110.00**

**Lamp, miniature; Green Holly, $50.00.**

Mug, Abraham Lincoln, #2364, 5½" ....................................**40.00**

Planter, hobo clown's head, #4498, 4" ........................................**35.00**

Planter, Santa w/bag, #3656, 8"...**20.00**

Plaque, To Mother, roses & reticulated hearts, #508, 7¾" .....**18.00**

Plate, Festival, #2621, 9" ........**22.00**

Platter, Green Holly, #2369, 18"....................................**75.00**

Salt & pepper shakers, Green Holly, #1353, pr from $22 to ........**25.00**

Salt & pepper shakers, pig in overalls, #3079, 3", pr..............**22.00**

Soap dish, Pink Clover, #2504, 7¼", from $8 to..........................**12.00**

Tea bag holder, Miss Priss, #1506, 4" ........................................**40.00**

Teapot, Cuddles, #1448 ............**85.00**

Teapot, Dainty Miss, #321 .....**150.00**

Teapot, Miss Priss, #1516 ......**145.00**

Toothbrush holder, French Rose, holds 4, #2646, 3¾", from $15 to..............................................**20.00**

Tray, Violet Chintz, #651, from $30 to........................................**35.00**

Vase, pitcher form w/applied flowers, #4209, 7", from $22 to..........**24.00**

Wall plaque, angel w/lamb, #3206, 5½" ....................................**80.00**

Wall pocket, Miss Priss, #1509..**100.00**

Wall pocket, violin w/rose, #369..**28.00**

## Letter Openers

Here's a chance to get into a hobby that offers more than enough diversification to be both interesting and challenging, yet requires very little room for display. Whether you prefer the advertising letter openers or the more imaginative models with handles sculpted as a dimensional figure or incorporating a gadget such as a penknife or a cigarette lighter, you should be able to locate enough for a nice collection. Materials are varied as well, ranging from silver plate to wood. Some are inlaid with semiprecious stones.

Advertising, First Bank of Monticello, steel .................................**6.00**
Advertising, Lincoln Center New York, plastic.......................**3.00**
Advertising, Mobile Asphalt Co...Ala, white metal...........**6.00**
Advertising, WN Clark Canned Foods, stamped Metal Arts Co...NY...............................**25.00**
Aluminum, Arts & Crafts style w/cut-out dogwood on handle........**15.00**

**Bakelite, brass and aluminum with Bakelite and aluminum wire inlay, $35.00. (Photo courtesy Everett Grist)**

Brass, anchor forms handle .....**12.00**
Brass, lizard figural, tail forms blade, marked China.........**10.00**
Brass, nude woman 3-D handle, Great Smoky Mountains souvenir ...................................**18.00**
Brass, whale figural handle, slim blade...................................**12.00**
Brass & pewter, griffin over lion head....................................**12.00**
Brass w/enameled flowers on white, red tassel............................**30.00**
Bronze, sea-horse handle, Province Town MA souvenir ............**18.00**
Butterscotch Bakelite, hand-painted flowers, Ocean City MD souvenir ...................................**25.00**

Chromed steel, President By Peerless, Japan ..........................**5.00**
Copper, Arts & Crafts style......**10.00**
Green onyx & sterling, Latin American motif ...........................**35.00**
Lucite, encapsulated gold leaf, Victoria BC souvenir ..............**12.00**
Plastic (green) w/magnifier, marked SP, made in USA..................**3.00**
Plastic & gold plate, University of Alabama in Appreciation, w/sheath...............................**3.00**
Plastic & steel, cigarette-lighter handle, ruler blade, Japan.........**40.00**
Plastic blade (blue) w/leather handle ...................................**3.00**
Porcelain, hand-painted roses, signed R Riddle.................**45.00**
Stainless steel, embossed floral, Japan.....................................**7.00**
Steel blade w/French ivory handle, Kentucky Lithographing Co... KY........................................**14.00**
Steel blade w/stag handle ........**10.00**
White metal, End of the Trail (cowboy on horse) handle .................**10.00**
White metal & brass, Blowing Rock NC souvenir .........................**8.00**
White metal & steel dagger form, serrated edge on blade ......**10.00**
Wooden, carved duck handle, slim tapered wooden blade........**20.00**

# Liberty Blue

'Take home a piece of American history!,' stated an ad from the 1970s for this dinnerware made in Staffordshire, England. Blue and white depictions of George Washington at Valley Forge, Paul Revere, Independence Hall — fourteen historic scenes in all — were offered on different pieces. The ad goes on to describe this 'unique...truly unusual..museum-quality...future family heirloom.'

For every five dollars spent on groceries you could purchase a basic piece (dinner plate, bread and butter plate, cup, saucer, or dessert dish) for fifty-nine cents on alternate weeks of the promotion. During the promotion, completer pieces could also be purchased. The soup tureen was the most expensive item, originally selling for $24.99. Nineteen completer pieces in all were offered along with a five-year open stock guarantee. For more information we recommend Jo Cunningham's book, *The Best of Collectible Dinnerware.*

**Bowl, cereal; $12.50; Cup and saucer, $4.50.**

| | |
|---|---|
| Bowl, flat soup; 8¾" | **20.00** |
| Bowl, fruit; 5" | **4.00** |
| Bowl, vegetable; oval | **35.00** |
| Bowl, vegetable; round | **30.00** |
| Butter dish, w/lid, ¼-lb | **55.00** |
| Casserole, w/lid | **125.00** |
| Coaster | **12.50** |
| Creamer, from $18 to | **22.00** |
| Creamer & sugar bowl, w/lid, original box | **80.00** |

| | |
|---|---|
| Gravy boat | **45.00** |
| Gravy boat liner | **25.00** |
| Mug | **14.00** |
| Pitcher, 7½" | **95.00** |
| Plate, bread & butter; 6" | **2.50** |
| Plate, dinner; 10" | **5.00** |
| Plate, luncheon; scarce, 8¾" | **24.00** |
| Plate, scarce, 7", from $9 to | **12.00** |
| Platter, 12", from $35 to | **45.00** |
| Platter, 14" | **75.00** |
| Salt & pepper shakers, pr | **35.00** |
| Soup ladle, plain white, no decal | **35.00** |
| Soup tureen, w/lid | **350.00** |
| Sugar bowl, no lid | **10.00** |
| Sugar bowl, w/lid | **28.00** |
| Teapot, w/lid | **100.00** |

# License Plates

Early porcelain license plates are treasured by collectors and often sell for more than $500.00 per pair when found in excellent condition. The best examples are first-year plates from each state, but some of the more modern plates with special graphics are collectible too. Prices given below are for plates in good or better condition.

| | |
|---|---|
| Alabama, 1942 | **30.00** |
| Alaska, 1962 | **12.50** |
| Arizona, 1939 | **55.00** |
| Arkansas, 1986-89 | **3.50** |
| California, 1991-94, ea | **2.50** |
| Colorado, 1938 | **20.00** |
| Connecticut, 1990-2003, ea | **12.50** |
| Delaware, 1972-99, ea | **5.50** |
| Florida, 1996, orange map | **4.50** |
| Georgia, 1998-99, lg peach, ea | **4.50** |

Hawaii, 1975 .............................**8.50**
Idaho, 1941 ...........................**40.00**
Illinois, 1940 .............................**9.50**
Indiana, 1976, Bicentennial.......**2.50**
Iowa, 1948..................................**9.50**
Kansas, 1959-61, ea...................**4.00**
Kentucky, 1989-90, tan wheat, ea..........................................**4.50**
Louisiana, 2001-2003, ea .........**10.50**
Maine, 1941 .............................**25.00**
Massachusetts, 1941 ...............**15.50**
Michigan, 1970 ..........................**2.50**
Minnesota, 1954 ........................**7.50**
Mississippi, 1977 .......................**3.50**
Missouri, 1967 ...........................**7.00**
Montana, 1992-98, ea.................**3.50**
Nebraska, 1952...........................**6.00**
Nevada, 1933 ...........................**30.00**
New Hampshire, 1980-84, blue, ea..........................................**5.50**
New Jersey, 1948........................**9.50**
New Mexico, 1982-83, ea............**4.50**
New York, 1936 ........................**15.50**

**New York World's Fair, 1939, $40.00 each.**

North Carolina, 1981, First in Freedom.....................................**10.50**
North Dakota, 1941..................**20.00**
Ohio, 1958-59, ea ......................**7.50**
Oklahoma, 1977..........................**4.50**
Oregon, 1988, orange.................**5.50**

Pennsylvania, 1970 ...................**4.00**
Rhode Island, 1947..................**10.00**
South Carolina, 1983-85, ea.......**4.50**
South Dakota, 1962.................**10.50**
Tennessee, 1972-73, ea..............**5.50**
Texas, 1956 .............................**12.50**
Utah, 1973..................................**3.00**
Vermont, 1999 .........................**10.50**
Virginia, 1951 ..........................**15.50**
Washington, 1941....................**40.00**
Washington DC, 1977, Inaugural..**7.50**
West Virginia, 1996...................**7.50**
Wisconsin, 1955 ......................**12.50**
Wyoming, 1947 ........................**20.00**

# Little Red Riding Hood

This line of novelties and kitchenware has always commanded good prices on the collectibles market. In fact, it became valuable enough to make it attractive to counterfeiters, and now you'll see reproductions everywhere. They're easy to spot, though, watch for one-color eyes. Though there are other differences, you should be able to identify the imposters armed with this information alone.

Little Red Riding Hood was produced from 1943 to 1957. The Regal China Company was by far the major manufacturer of this line, though a rather insignificant number of items were made by the Hull Pottery of Crooksville, Ohio, who sent their whiteware to the Royal China and Novelty Company (a division of Regal China) of Chicago, Illinois, to be decorated. For further information we recommend *The*

*Ultimate Collector's Encyclopedia of Cookie Jars* by Joyce and Fred Roerig (Collector Books).

Bank, standing, 7", from $900 to ....................................**1,350.00**
Butter dish, from $350 to.......**400.00**
Canister, cereal....................**1,375.00**
Canister, coffee, sugar or flour; ea from $600 to.....................**700.00**
Canister, salt .......................**1,100.00**
Canister, tea ...........................**700.00**
Cookie jar, closed basket, from $450 to....................................**650.00**
Cookie jar, full skirt, from $750 to....................................**850.00**

**Cookie jar, open basket, from $400.00 to $500.00.**

Cracker jar, unmarked, from $600 to.......................................**750.00**
Creamer, top pour, no tab handle, from $400 to.....................**425.00**
Creamer, top pour, tab handle, from $350 to.............................**375.00**
Dresser jar, 8¾", from $450 to.......................................**575.00**
Lamp, from $2,000 to ..........**2,650.00**

Match holder, wall hanging, from $800 to.............................**850.00**
Mustard jar, w/original spoon, from $375 to.............................**460.00**
Pitcher, 7", from $450 to ........**675.00**
Pitcher, 8", from $550 to .......**850.00**
Planter, wall hanging, from $400 to.......................................**500.00**
Salt & pepper shakers, lg, 5", pr from $125 to.....................**150.00**
Salt & pepper shakers, Pat design 135889, med size, pr (+), from $800 to.............................**900.00**
Salt & pepper shakers, 3¼", pr from $95 to...............................**140.00**
Salt & pepper shakers, 5½", pr from $180 to.............................**235.00**
Spice jar, from $650 to ...........**750.00**
String holder, from $1,800 to..**2,500.00**
Sugar bowl, crawling, no lid, from $300 to.............................**450.00**
Sugar bowl, standing, no lid, from $175 to.............................**225.00**
Sugar bowl, w/lid, from $350 to.......................................**425.00**
Sugar bowl lid, minimum value..**175.00**
Teapot, from $400 to .............**450.00**
Wolf jar, red base, from $925 to ...................................**1,000.00**
Wolf jar, yellow base, from $750 to .....................................**850.00**

# Lu-Ray Pastels

Introduced in 1938 by Taylor, Smith, and Taylor of East Liverpool, Ohio, Lu-Ray Pastels is today a very sought-after line of collectible American dinnerware. It was first made in these solid colors: Windsor Blue, Surf Green, Persian Cream, and

Sharon Pink. Chatham Gray was introduced in 1948 and is today priced higher than the other colors.

| | |
|---|---|
| Bowl, cream soup | **70.00** |
| Bowl, fruit; Chatham Gray, 5" | **16.00** |
| Bowl, fruit; 5" | **6.00** |
| Bowl, lug soup; tab handle | **24.00** |
| Bowl, mixing; 7" | **125.00** |
| Bowl, mixing; 10¼" | **150.00** |
| Bowl, salad; yellow | **55.00** |
| Butter dish, any color other than Chatham Gray, w/lid | **50.00** |
| Butter dish, Chatham Gray, rare color, w/lid | **90.00** |
| Cake plate | **70.00** |
| Casserole | **140.00** |
| Chop plate, 15" | **38.00** |
| Coffee cup, AD | **20.00** |
| Creamer | **8.00** |
| Egg cup, double | **30.00** |
| Jug, water; footed | **150.00** |

**Juice set: Tumblers, $50.00 each; Pitcher, $200.00; coaster/nut dish, $65.00; pitcher, bulbous with flat bottom, yellow, $95.00.**

| | |
|---|---|
| Muffin cover, w/8" underplate | **165.00** |
| Pitcher, juice | **200.00** |
| Plate, 6" | **3.00** |
| Plate, 8" | **25.00** |
| Plate, 10" | **25.00** |
| Platter, oval, 13" | **24.00** |

| | |
|---|---|
| Sauce boat | **28.00** |
| Saucer, coffee; AD | **8.50** |
| Saucer, tea | **2.00** |
| Sugar bowl, AD; w/lid, individual | **40.00** |
| Teacup | **8.00** |
| Teapot, curved spout, w/lid | **125.00** |
| Teapot, flat spout, w/lid | **160.00** |
| Tumbler, water | **80.00** |

# Lunch Boxes

In the early years of this century, tobacco companies often packaged their products in tins that could later be used for lunch boxes. By the 1930s oval lunch boxes designed to appeal to school children were being produced. The rectangular shape that is now popular was preferred in the 1950s. Character lunch boxes decorated with the faces of TV personalities, super heroes, Disney, and cartoon characters are especially sought after by collectors today. Our values are for lunch boxes only (without the Thermos, unless one is mentioned in the line).

Refer to *Pictorial Price Guide to Vinyl and Plastic Lunch Boxes and Thermoses* and *Pictorial Price Guide to Metal Lunch Boxes and Thermoses* by Larry Aikens (L-W Book Sales) for more information. For an expanded listing, see *Schroeder's Collectible Toys, Antique to Modern* (Collector Books).

| | |
|---|---|
| A-Team, metal, 1980s, EX/M, from $25 to | **40.00** |
| Annie, metal, 1980s, EX/M, from $30 to | **40.00** |

Annie, vinyl, 1980s, EX/M, from $50 to..........................................**75.00**

Barbie, plastic, 1990s, EX/M, from $10 to....................................**15.00**

Battle of the Planets, metal, 1970, EX/M, from $50 to .............**75.00**

Betsy Clark, metal, 1970s, from $35 to..........................................**55.00**

Black Hole, metal, 1970s, plastic bottle, EX/NM, from $10 to ......**20.00**

Bozo the Clown, metal, 1960s, dome top, EX/M, from $175 to ..**225.00**

Buck Rogers, metal, 1970s, EX/M, from $25 to..........................**50.00**

Cabbage Patch Kids, plastic, EX/M, from $15 to..........................**20.00**

Carnival, metal, 1950s, EX/M, from $350 to..............................**450.00**

Chuck E Cheese, plastic, 1990s, EX/M, from $25 to .............**35.00**

Cracker Jack, metal, 1970s, EX/M, from $30 to..........................**60.00**

Denim, vinyl, 1970s, EX/M, from $45 to....................................**65.00**

**Disney Express, metal, 1970s, EX/M, from $30.00 to $60.00.**

Disneyland, 1950s-60s, EX/M, from $150 to..............................**200.00**

Dr Seuss, plastic, 1990s, EX/M, from $20 to....................................**25.00**

Dynomutt, metal, 1970s, EX/M, from $35 to..........................**55.00**

Fire Engine Co #1, vinyl, 1970s, EX/M, from $115 to .........**135.00**

Flintstones, plastic, Denny's logo, 1989, EX/M, from $20 to .....**30.00**

Flipper, metal, 1960s, EX/M, from $100 to..............................**150.00**

Garfield, plastic, 1980s, EX/M, from $15 to................................**20.00**

Get Smart, metal, 1960s, EX/M, from $125 to.....................**175.00**

Green Hornet, metal, 1960s, metal bottle, EX/M, from $50 to..**100.00**

Gremlins, metal, 1980s, metal bottle, EX/M, from $5 to .........**10.00**

**Gunsmoke, metal, 1959, EX/M, from $100.00 to $200.00.**

Guns of Will Sonnet, metal, 1960s, EX/M, from $100 to .........**150.00**

Hansel & Gretel, metal, 1980s, EX/M, from $40 to .............**60.00**

Hee Haw, metal, 1970, EX/M, from $50 to................................**70.00**

Hogan's Heroes, metal, 1960s, metal bottle, EX/M, from $20 to..**40.00**

Incredible Hulk, metal, 1970s, EX/M, from $50 to ..........**100.00**

Jabberjaw, plastic, 1970s, EX/M, from $30 to..........................**40.00**

Jet Patrol, metal, 1950s, EX/M, from $200 to..............................**300.00**

Jr Miss, metal, 1973, attic scene, EX/M, from $15 to .............**30.00**

Keebler Cookies, plastic, 1980s, EX/M, from $30 to .............**50.00**

Korg, metal, 1970s, EX/M, from $35 to.......................................**65.00**

Lassie, metal, 1970s, EX/M, from $35 to................................**55.00**

Li'l Jodie, vinyl, 1980s, EX/M, from $50 to................................**75.00**

Lone Ranger, metal, 1980s, EX/M, from $25 to.........................**50.00**

Lucy Luncheonette, plastic, 1980s, dome top, EX/M, from $25 to..**35.00**

Mardi Gras, vinyl, 1970s, EX/M, from $100 to.....................**150.00**

Mickey Mouse Club, metal, 1960s, EX/M, from $65 to ...........**100.00**

Mighty Mouse, plastic, 1970s, EX/M, from $25 to.........................**35.00**

Monroes, metal, 1960s, EX/M, from $75 to................................**150.00**

Muppets, metal, 1970s, EX/M, from $25 to................................**50.00**

Nestlé's Quik, plastic, 1980s, EX/M, from $25 to.........................**30.00**

Orbit, metal, 1950s, EX/M, from $175 to..............................**250.00**

Pac Man, vinyl, 1980s, EX/M, from $40 to................................**60.00**

Pathfinder, metal, 1959, EX/M, from $300 to..............................**400.00**

Peanuts, metal, 1980, EX/M, from $15 to................................**30.00**

Pigs in Space, metal, 1970s, dome top, EX/M, from $35 to......**50.00**

Pink Panther, vinyl, 1980s, EX/M, from $75 to.......................**100.00**

Popeye, metal, 1980, plastic bottle, EX/M, from $10 to .............**20.00**

Popeye, plastic, 1979, dome top, EX/M, from $30 to .............**40.00**

Psychedelic Blue, vinyl, 1970s, EX/M, from $40 to .............**60.00**

**Rat Patrol, metal, 1960s, EX/M, from $75.00 to $125.00.**

Return of the Jedi, metal, 1980s, plastic bottle, EX/M, from $10 to.......................................**20.00**

Rocky Roughneck, plastic, 1970s, EX/M, from $25 to .............**35.00**

Rose Petal Place, metal, 1980s, EX/M, plastic bottle, EX/M, from $5 to...........................**15.00**

School Days, metal, 1980s, from $350 to..............................**450.00**

Secret Agent T, metal, 1960s, EX/M, from $50 to.......................**100.00**

Snoopy & Woodstock, plastic, 1970, dome top, EX/M, from $20 to..**30.00**

Snoopy at Mailbox, vinyl, 1960s, red, EX/M, from $65 to......**85.00**

Space: 1999, metal, 1970s, plastic bottle, EX/M, from $15 to..**25.00**

Speedy Turtle, vinyl, 1970s, drawstring bag, EX/M, from $50 to.......................................**75.00**

Star Trek The Motion Picture, metal, 1980, EX/M, from $100 to....................................**200.00**

Submarine, metal, 1960, EX/M, from $50 to......................**100.00**

Super Powers, metal, 1980s, EX/M, from $45 to........................**85.00**

Superman, plastic, 1980s, phone booth scene, EX/M, from $30 to........................................**40.00**

Three Little Pigs, metal, 1980s, EX/M, from $40 to.............**80.00**

Tic-Tac-Toe, vinyl, 1970s, EX/M, from $50 to........................**75.00**

Tom & Jerry, plastic, 1990s, EX/M, from $10 to........................**20.00**

Transformers, metal, 1980s, EX/M, from $25 to........................**50.00**

Underdog, metal, 1970s, EX/M, from $350 to.............................**750.00**

Wagon Train, metal, 1960s, metal bottle, EX/M, from $25 to..**50.00**

Walton's, metal, 1970s, plastic bottle, EX/M, from $15 to.......**30.00**

Young Astronauts, plastic, 1980s, EX/M, from $20 to.............**30.00**

Ziggy, vinyl, 1979, EX/M, from $50 to........................................**75.00**

# Magazines

Some of the most collectible magazines are *Life* (because of the celebrities and important events they feature on their covers), *Saturday Evening Post* and *Ladies' Home Journal* (especially those featuring the work of famous illustrators such as Parrish, Rockwell, and Wyeth), and *National Geographics* (with particularly newsworthy features). As is true with any type of ephemera, condition and value are closely related.

Unless they're in fine condition (clean, no missing or clipped pages, and very little other damage), they're worth very little; and cover interest and content are far more important than age.

American Shetland Pony Journal, 1954, September, VG+......**17.50**

Audubon, 1942, July/August, Bald Eagle, EX...........................**45.00**

Boys' Life, 1944, February, Scout saluting (Norman Rockwell), VG+.................................**32.50**

Car Life, 1965, May, Testing the Supercars, EX....................**25.00**

Collier's, 1934, May 19, Elephant & Clown (Louis Fancher), VG+..**30.00**

Collier's, 1937, November 6, Goofy, Mickey & Donald (Walt Disney), EX .................................**60.00**

Collier's, 1942, December 26, Buy War Bonds (Floyd Munson), EX .................................**30.00**

Collier's, 1948, December 11, Charlie Justice (football player), EX .................................**95.00**

Cosmopolitan, 1901, November, Theodore Roosevelt, VG.....**25.00**

Cosmopolitan, 1944, November, Bradshaw Crandall illustration, VG+.................................**15.00**

Cosmopolitan, 1947, January, Coby Whitmore illustration, VG..**45.00**

Cosmopolitan, 1953, May, Marilyn Monroe, EX........................**50.00**

Cosmopolitan, 1958, February, Sophia Loren, EX..............**30.00**

Cosmopolitan, 1959, March, Marilyn Monroe, EX........................**35.00**

Cosmopolitan, 1972, April, Burt Reynolds centerfold, VG......**20.00**

Cosmopolitan, 1972, January, Astrid Heeren, EX.............**25.00**

**Cosmopolitan, 1980, July, Gia Carangi cover by Scavullo, NM, $48.00.**

Cosmopolitan, 1980, March, Michelle Stevens, NM.......**10.00**

Cosmopolitan, 1981, July, Kelly LeBrock, EX.......................**17.50**

Dogs Today, 1998, November, EX..**25.00**

Drag Racing, 1965, November, EX .....................................**45.00**

Dune Buggies, 1969, December, VG+ ....................................**35.00**

Esquire, 1951, August, Marilyn Monroe fold-out poster, EX....**15.00**

Esquire, 1952, April, Elizabeth Taylor, VG+ .............................**25.00**

Esquire, 1953, January, Esquire Calendar Girls pull-out, EX ....**25.00**

Esquire, 1955, May, Gina Lollobridgida, EX+ ...................**12.50**

Esquire, 1975, February, Cher, EX..**25.00**

Esquire, 1979, January, Burt Reynolds/Dolly Parton, NM..**13.50**

Esquire, 1983, December, 100th Anniverary, EX .................**10.00**

Family Circle, 1950, July, youthful woman on horse, NM........**12.00**

Family Circle, 1953, September, Lucille Ball, EX+ ...............**17.50**

Family Circle, 1957, March, Doris Day, EX...............................**12.00**

Family Circle, 1967, December, Santa Claus (Norman Rockwell), NM ...........................**15.00**

Films in Review, 1972, August/September, Alfred Hitchcock, NM..**15.00**

Fortune, 1943, March, Glass: Now & Tomorrow, EX ....................**17.50**

Fortune, 1948, March, diesel trains, G+.......................................**25.00**

Fossils Magazine, 1976, May, 1st issue, EX............................**20.00**

Good Housekeeping, 1951, April, girl w/umbrella (Alex Ross), VG .....................................**17.50**

Good Housekeeping, 1972, May, Sonny & Cher, EX.............**17.50**

High-Tech Performance, 1997, January, Camaro Pace Car, NM..**25.00**

Hot Rod, 1950, December, NM......**35.00**

Hot Rod, 1965, January, World Record Jets, EX .................**80.00**

Hot Rod, 1968, February, GTO vs Firebird, EX.......................**25.00**

Life, 1943, July 12, Roy Rogers on Trigger, EX........................**30.00**

Life, 1945, April 9, Battle of Iwo Jima, EX ............................**30.00**

**Life, 1945, July 16, Audie Murphy Most Decorated Soldier, VG+, $30.00.**

Life, 1948, November 22, President Truman, EX.......................**25.00**

Life, 1949, August 1, Joe DiMaggio, EX ......................................**22.50**

Life, 1949, January 5, Jinnah of Pakistan, EX .....................**22.00**

Life, 1950, May 8, Jackie Robinson, EX ......................................**25.00**

Life, 1952, September 1, Ernest Hemmingway, EX+, from $70 to ..........................................**90.00**

Life, 1953, December 7, Audrey Hepburn, NM ....................**62.50**

Life, 1954, March 1, Rita Moreno, VG ......................................**27.50**

Life, 1955, August 8, Ben Hogan, EX..**25.00**

Life, 1955, March 14, 50th Anniversary, EX+ ...........................**22.00**

Life, 1961, August 18, Mantle & Maris, EX+ .......................**55.00**

Life, 1961, October 23, Elizabeth Taylor as Cleopatra, NM..**55.00**

Life, 1961, September 1, First Lady Jacqueline Kennedy, EX+.**32.50**

Life, 1964, August, Beatles, NM..**75.00**

Life, 1964, January, Charlie Chaplin's Daughter, VG+ .........**22.00**

Life, 1965, July 30, Mickey Mantle, NM ......................................**23.50**

Life, 1966, November, Did Oswald Act Alone?, EX..................**25.00**

Life, 1969, December 19, Charles Manson, EX ......................**30.00**

Look, 1941, November 18, US Navy Has a New Plan To Fight Japan, EX ......................................**12.50**

Look, 1944, July 11, General Eisenhower, EX ..........................**12.50**

Look, 1946, October 29, 10th Anniversary, EX................**12.50**

Look, 1951, September 25, Jeanne Crain/Roy Campanella, EX..**42.50**

Look, 1952, April 22, Martin & Lewis, EX............................**22.00**

Look, 1954, February 9, Howard Hughes, Oscar Tribute, EX..**35.00**

Look, 1955, March 22, Bing Crosby & Judy Garland, EX+ ......**20.00**

Look, 1960, August 2, John Wayne, EX ......................................**15.00**

Look, 1963, December 3, John F Kennedy w/John Jr, EX....**13.50**

Look, 1966, May 3, Ku Klux Klan, EX+ ......................................**15.00**

Look, 1967, December 26, Dean Martin, EX+.......................**15.00**

Look, 1971, June 1, Howard Hughes, EX ......................................**13.50**

Look, 1971, May, Elvis Presley, EX.**17.50**

Look, 1971, September 7, Lucille Ball, EX................................**18.00**

Look, 1973, July, David Bowie, EX+ ......................................**15.00**

Look, 1979, May 14, Johnny Carson's Mid-Life Crisis, EX+**15.00**

Mad Magazine, 1972, June, #151, EX+ ......................................**17.50**

McCall's, 1967, July, Twiggy, EX..**35.00**

McCall's, 1967, June, Jean Shrimpton, EX ..............................**15.00**

Motocross Action, 1974, December, Adolf Weil, EX+ ....**110.00**

Motor Life, 1959, January, Road Test Comparison, EX ........**23.50**

Movie Fan, 1952, December, Marilyn Monroe, NM ................**80.00**

Movie Life, 1944, March, Lucille Ball, EX+ ...........................**45.00**

Movie Life, 1959, September, Mardy Kruger, EX.......................**25.00**

Movie Spotlight, 1954, August, Jane Powell, NM .......................**18.50**

Movie Star Parade, 1948, October, Rita Haywood, NM...........**37.50**

Movies, 1950, October, Doris Day, NM .....................................**35.00**

National Lampoon, 1970, April, 1st edition, EX..........................**35.00**

National Lampoon, 1975, January, #58, NM+ ...........................**25.00**

Newsweek, 1942, June 8, Nazi War Machines Goes Into Action Again, EX...........................**35.00**

Newsweek, 1955, June 20, Henry Ford II, EX+ ......................**20.00**

Newsweek, 1961, March, Shah of Iran, NM+..........................**90.00**

Newsweek, 1965, June 21, Gemini 4 in Space, NM .....................**20.00**

Newsweek, 1967, April 10, Twiggy, NM+ ..................................**35.00**

**Newsweek, 1969, May 26, Janis Joplin, EX, $25.00.**

Newsweek, 1970, February 23, The (Black) Panthers & the Law, EX ......................................**12.00**

Newsweek, 1973, December 17, Bette Midler, EX ...............**12.50**

Newsweek, 1979, January 1, Superman, NM............................**20.00**

Outdoor Life, 1918, November, flying duck, EX....................**120.00**

Outdoor Life, 1940, June, man fishing from boat, NM+...........**30.00**

Outdoor Life, 1941, April, fisherman smoking pipe (Edgar Whittack), EX .....................................**22.00**

Outdoor Life, 1947, August, man in boat w/very sm fish, VG+..**22.50**

Playboy, 1954, October, College Issue, NM ..........................**95.00**

Playboy, 1955, February, Jane Mansfield, EX...................**95.00**

Playboy, 1955, November, Barbara Cameron, EX .....................**40.00**

Playboy, 1955, September, Marilyn Monroe, EX.......................**65.00**

Playboy, 1957, January, June Blair, Playmate Review, EX.......**25.00**

Playboy, 1958, October, Mara Corday & Pat Sheehan, EX..**35.00**

Playboy, 1960, February, Best of Jayne Mansfield, EX.........**37.50**

Playboy, 1961, June, Heidi Becker, NM .....................................**32.50**

Playboy, 1964, March, Nancy Scott, VG+ ....................................**40.00**

Playboy, 1973, April, Linda Lovelace, NM...................**105.00**

Playboy, 1973, September, Geri Glass, NM+........................**35.00**

Playboy, 1974, January, 20th Anniversary, Nancy Cameron, EX+ ....................................**35.00**

Playboy, 1974, November, Hunter S Thompson, EX ...................**60.00**

Playboy, 1979, May, Secret Life of Marilyn Monroe, NM ........**30.00**

Playboy, 1979, October, Burt Reynolds on cover, NM .....**30.00**

Playboy, 1989, January, 35th Anniversary, NM..............**25.00**

Redbook, 1946, March, Rita Daigle, EX .....................................**17.50**

Rolling Stone, 1976, August 12, Bob Marley, #219, NM .............**60.00**

Rolling Stone, 1977, September 22, #248, Passing of Elvis Presley, EX+ ....................................**60.00**

Sports Illustrated, 1954, August 16, baseball, NM+ .................**165.00**

Sports Illustrated, 1956, June 18, Mickey Mantle, NM+ ......**205.00**

Sports Illustrated, 1960, December 26, John & Jackie Kennedy, NM ....................................**40.00**

Sports Illustrated, 1960, January 20, Joe Namath, EX+ ........**55.00**

Sports Illustrated, 1966, October 31, Bart Starr, EX...................**37.50**

Sports Illustrated, 1973, June 11, Secretariat, EX.................**25.00**

Sports Illustrated, 1974, September 2, Evel Knievel, EX ............**35.00**

Sports Illustrated, 1977, November 28, Larry Bird w/IN State, EX....................................**20.00**

The New Mad Magazine, 1955, September, VG ......................**65.00**

Time, 1941, April 14, Hitler, VG+ ...................................**35.00**

Time, 1954, December 13, Ernest Hemingway, EX+ ..............**60.00**

Time, 1959, January 26, Fidel Castro, VG ...............................**25.00**

Time, 1969, August 8, John Wayne, EX+ ....................................**42.50**

TV & Movie Screen, 1959, July, Debbie Reynolds, EX+.......**25.00**

Wrestling Life, 1955, October, Len Rossi, VG+ ........................**23.50**

# Marilyn Monroe

Her life was full of tumult, her career short, and the end tragic, but in less than a decade she managed to establish herself as the ultimate Hollywood sex goddess; and though there have been many try, none has ever came close to evoking the same devotion movie goers have always felt for Marilyn Monroe. Her sexuality was innocent, almost unintentional. She was one of the last from the era when stars wore designer fashions, perfectly arranged hair styles, and flawless makeup. Her relationships with the men in her life, though all were unfortunate, only added to the legend. Fans today look for the dolls, photographs, and various other collectibles that have been produced over the years.

**Bank, Funtime Savings, when coin is inserted fan blows dress up, 1980s, 7", MIB, $85.00.** (Photo courtesy David Spurgeon)

Book, Life & Curious Death of Marilyn Monroe, R Slatzer, 1975, NM ....................................**30.00**

Book, The Last Sitting, Bert Stern, 1st edition, 1982, NM w/dust cover...................................**35.00**

Calendar, 1953, A New Wrinkle, complete, 12 x 9", EX+..............**105.00**

Calendar, 1955, Lure of Lace, complete, NM..........................**45.00**

Calendar, 1974 Marilyn Monroe Datebook, Norman Mailer, complete, EX.............................**15.00**

Cookie jar, bust from Seven Year Itch, Clay Art, 1996, MIB, $35 to.........................................**45.00**

Datebook, Earl Moran image, Schroeder Hotels, 1949, 3½x6", NM.....................................**30.00**

Doll, Forever Marilyn, on stomach w/feet in air, Franklin Mint, MIP.....................................**200.00**

Doll, Happy Birthday Mr President, Mattel Timeless Treasures, NMIB.................................**60.00**

Doll, How To Marry a Millionaire, Royal Orleans, 9", MIB.....**75.00**

Doll, Seven Year Itch, Mattel's Hollywood Legends #17155, MIB..**55.00**

Doll, Unforgettable Marilyn, Franklin Mint, complete, MIB......**150.00**

Figurine, red dress, plays Diamonds Are a Girls Best Friend, PSC, MIB..................................**35.00**

Music box, PSC International, limited edition, 9", MIB............**40.00**

Ornament, in pink satin gown, Hallmark, MIB.........................**35.00**

Outfit, Gentlemen Prefer Blondes, Franklin Mint, MIB..........**35.00**

Pinback, Fan Club, black dress on blue, 1956, 3", NM..........**15.00**

Plate, Bus Stop, Bradex, 8½", MIB ..**25.00**

Plate, Gentlemen Prefer Blondes, 3-D, oval, Bradford Exchange, MIB..................................**40.00**

Plate, Golden Glow, Bradford Exchange, 1998, 8"............**27.50**

Plate, Seven Year Itch, in white dress on red, Bradex, 8½", NM....................................**25.00**

Playing cards, nude, double deck, photo by Tom Kelley, MIB (sealed)...............................**35.00**

Pocketknife, nude photo on side, 1 blade, USA, 1960s, 4"........**30.00**

Statuette, caricature, Continental Studios, 1970s, 20¾".......**145.00**

Statuette, Memories of Marilyn Monroe, Franklin Mint, porcelain, 10½"..........................**50.00**

Stein, Seven Year Itch, Cinema Sweethearts.......................**35.00**

Stereoview card, Marilyn looking at 3-D Movie Magazine, early 1960s, EX..........................**30.00**

Trading card, Barber's Tea Card #24, 1955, EX+..................**30.00**

Tray, nude on red w/wooden frame, tin litho, 1950s, 4" dia, NM, $60 to.........................................**70.00**

Wall hanging, face only, Clay Art of San Francisco, 1980s, 10¼", EX.....................................**30.00**

# Matchbox Cars

Introduced in 1953, the Matchbox Miniatures series has always been the mainstay of the company. There were seventy-five models in all but with enough variations to make collecting them a real challenge. Larger, more detailed models were introduced in 1957. This series, called Major Pack, was replaced a few years later by a similar line called King Size. To compete with Hot Wheels, Matchbox converted most models over to a line called SuperFast that sported thinner, low-friction axles and wheels. (These are much more readily available from the original 'regular wheels,' the last of which was made in 1959.) At about the same time, the King size series became known as Speed Kings; in 1977 the line was reintroduced under the name Super Kings.

Another line that's become very popular is their Models of Yesteryear. These are slightly larger replicas of antique and vintage vehicles. Values of $20.00 to $60.00 for mint-in-box examples are average, though a few sell for even more.

Sky Busters, introduced in 1973, are small-scale aircraft measuring an average of 3½" in length. Models currently being produced sell for about $4.00 each.

To learn more we recommend *Matchbox Toys, 1947 to 2003; The Other Matchbox Toys, 1947 to 2004;* and *Toy Car Collector's Guide,* all by Dana Johnson; and a series of books by Charlie Mack: *Lesney's Matchbox Toys* (there are three: *Regular Wheels, SuperFast Years,* and *Universal Years*).

To determine values of examples in conditions other than given in our listings, based on MIB or MOC prices, deduct a minimum of 10% if the original container is missing, 30% if the condition is excellent, and as much as 70% for a toy graded very good.

## King Size, Speed Kings, and Super Kings

K-2-B, Dart Dump Truck, 1964, MIP, from $25 to ...............**50.00**

K-5-B, Racing Car Transport, 1967, MIP ....................................**45.00**

K-6-A, Allis-Chalmers Earth Scraper, 1961, MIP ...........**50.00**

K-7-B, Refuse Truck, 1967, black wheels, MIP.......................**40.00**

K-10-B, Pipe Truck, 1967, w/4 original pipes, EX .....................**30.00**

K-11-C, Breakdown Tow Truck, 1976, red, MIP...................**60.00**

K-15-A, Merryweather Fire Engine, 1964, MIP, from $65 to .....**75.00**

**K-15-B, Londoner Bus, The Royal Wedding, 1981, MIB, $35.00.** (Photo courtesy Dana Johnson)

K-16-B, Petrol Tanker, 1974, Total decal, MIP.........................**35.00**

K-19-A, Scammel Tipper Truck, 1967, MIP .........................**45.00**

K-22-A, Dodge Charger, 1969, MIP ....................................**25.00**

K-24-B, Michelin Scammel Container Truck, 1977, MIP..**30.00**

K-29-A, Muira Seaburst Set, 1971, MIP ....................................**45.00**

K-34-A, Thunderclap Racer, 1972, MIP .................................**20.00**

K-40-B, Pepsi Delivery Truck, 1980, white, MIP ............................**30.00**

K-45-A, Marauder Racer, 1973, MIP ..**20.00**

K-60-A, Ford Mustang, 1976, MIP..**20.00**

K-90-A, Mastro Rancho, 1982, MIP..**20.00**

## Models of Yesteryears

Y-1-B, 1911 Ford Model T, 1965, cream, MIP ..........................**25.00**

Y-2-B, 1911 Renault 2-Seater, 1963, silver-plated, MIP .................**75.00**

Y-2-C, 1914 Prince Henry Vauxhall, 1970, blue w/white seats, MIP ......................................**30.00**

Y-5-A, 1929 Lemans Bentley, 1958, green tonneau, MIP.........**95.00**

Y-6-C, 1913 Cadillac, 1967, gold-plated, MIP.....................**250.00**

Y-8-D, 1945 MG TC, 1978, cream w/tan top, MIP...................**15.00**

Y-11-B, 1012 Packard Landaulet, 1964, beige & tan, MIP .....**30.00**

Y-11-D, 1932 Bugatti Type 35, 1987, MIP ....................................**25.00**

Y-16-C, 1957 Ferrari Dino 246/V12, 1986, MIP ..........................**25.00**

Y-16-D, 1922 Scania Vabis Postbus, MIP ....................................**35.00**

Y-23-B, 1930 Mack Tanker, 1989, MIP ....................................**20.00**

**Y-26-A, 1918 Crossley Beer Lorry, 1984, MIB, $20.00.** (Photo courtesy Dana Johnson)

Y-43-A, 1943 Busch Steam Fire Engine, 1991, MIP ............**75.00**

## Skybusters

SB-3-A, NASA Space Shuttle, 1980, white & gray, MIP ...............**10.00**

SB-8-A, Spitfire, 1973, dark brown & gold, MIP .......................**20.00**

SB-15-A, Marine Phantom F4E, 1975, pink, MIP..................**8.00**

SB-19-A, Piper Comanche, 1977, beige & dark blue, Macau cast, MIP ......................................**8.00**

SB-22-A, Toronado, 1978, light purple & white, MIP .................**8.00**

SB-24-A, F-16, 1979, any, MIP.....**10.00**

SB-31-A, Boeing 747-400, 1990, any, MIP ......................................**8.00**

SB-36-A, Lockheed F-117A Stealth, 1991, white w/no markings, MIP ......................................**8.00**

## 1 – 75 Series

1-A, Diesel Road Roller, 1953, dark green, MIP, from $100 to.....................................**130.00**

1-A, Road Roller, 1953, light green, MIP, from $180 to............................**220.00**

1-J, Toyman Dodge Challenger, 1983, MIP, from $3 to ........**5.00**

2-A, Dumper, 1953, unpainted metal wheels, MIP, from $65 to ......................................**80.00**

3-A, Cement Mixer, 1953, blue w/orange metal wheels, MIP, from $60 to.........................**80.00**

3-C, Mercedes Benz Ambulance, 1968, opening rear hatch, MIP........**20.00**

4-A, Massey-Harris Tractor, 1954, w/fenders, MIP, from $75 to..**95.00**

4-E, Dodge Stake Truck, 1970, Super-Fast, MIP, from $20 to......**25.00**

4-F, Gruesome Twosome, 1971, gold w/amber windows, MIP, from $10 to .................................**15.00**

4-H, '57 Chevy Bel Air, 1979, metallic magenta, MIP, from $5 to....**10.00**

4-K, '97 Corvette, 1997, metallic blue, MIB, from $2 to..........**4.00**

5-A, London Bus, 1954, red, MIP, from $75 to.........................**95.00**

6-A, 6-Wheel Quarry Truck, 1964, yellow, MIP, from $20 to..**25.00**

6-C, Euclid Quarry Truck, 1964, yellow, MIP, from $20 to..**25.00**

7-D, Ford Refuse Truck, 1970, Super-Fast, MIP, from $30 to ....**40.00**

8-E, Ford Mustang Fastback, 1966, orange, MIP, from $360 to..**400.00**

8-G, Ford Mustang Wildcat Dragster, 1970, MIP, from $20 to .....**30.00**

11-A, Road Tanker, 1955, yellow w/metal wheels, MIP, from $110 to .......................................**130.00**

11-F, Flying Bug, 1972, MIP, from $15 to .................................**20.00**

12-E, Setra Coach, 1970, metallic gold w/tan roof, MIP, from $20 to .......................................**25.00**

12-F, Big Bull Bulldozer, 1975, orange rollers, MIP, from $5 to.....**10.00**

13-C, Ford Thames Trader Wreck Truck, 1961, gray wheels, from $100 to .............................**120.00**

13-F, Dodge BP Wreck Truck, 1970, SF, MIP, from $55 to.......**70.00**

14-A, Daimler Ambulance, 1956, MIP, from $65 to ...............**85.00**

14-F, Ralleu Royale, 1973, MIP, from $8 to.........................**12.00**

15-J, Saab 9000, 1988, Laser Wheels, metallic blue, MIP, from $8 to..........................**12.00**

16-D, Case Bulldozer, 1969, black treads, MIP, from $35 to..**50.00**

17-E, AEC Ergomatic Horse Box, 1970, SuperFast, MIP, from $25 to ........................................**40.00**

18-E, Field Car, 1969, green plastic hubs, MIP, from $800 to..**1,000.00**

19-F, Road Dragster, 1970, red, MIP, from $16 to ...............**20.00**

21-E, Foden Concrete Truck, 1970, SuperFast, MIP, from $25 to..**40.00**

23-F, Mustang GT350, 1979, MIP, from $10 to.........................**15.00**

23-H, Honda ATC, 1985, red, MIP, from $9 to...........................**12.00**

26-A, Racing Mini, 1970, orange, MIP, from $10 to ...............**15.00**

30-E, Beach Buggy, 1970, SF, lavender, EX+, from $16 to......**20.00**

31-D, Lincoln Continental, 1970, Superfast, green-gold, NM+, from $50 to.........................**65.00**

40-C, Hay Trailer, 1967, beige (rare color), from $160 to........**220.00**

42-C, Iron Fairy Crane, 1969, MIP, from $12 to.........................**16.00**

42-G, 1957 T-Bird, 1982, red, MIP, from $4 to...........................**8.00**

45-C, Ford Group 6, 1970, Super-Fast, dark green, MIP, from $900 to .........................**1,200.00**

47-F, Pannier Tank Locomotive, 1979, MIP, from $5 to .......**10.00**

48-C, Dodge Dump Truck, 1966, MIP, from $10 to ...............**15.00**

49-E, Crane Truck, 1976, red, MIP, from $60 to.........................**80.00**

49-E, Crane Truck, 1976, yellow, MIP, from $6 to .................**12.00**

49-G, Dune Man Volkswagen Beetle, 1984, from $4 to...................**5.00**

54-D, Ford Capri, 1971, MIP, from $10 to ................................**15.00**

58-C, DAF Girder Truck, 1968, MIP, from $10 to.........................**16.00**

71-E, Jumbo Jet Motorcycle, 1973, MIP, from $15 to ...............**20.00**

72-B, Standard Jeep CJ5, 1966, red interior, MIP, from $15 to..**20.00**

72-B, Standard Jeep CJ5, 1966, white interior, MIP, from $900 to ....................................**1,200.00**

72-C, Standard Jeep CJ5, 1970, SuperFast, MIP, from $30 to......................................**40.00**

**75-B, Ferrari Berlinetta, green, 1965, 3", MIB, from $160.00 to $240.00 (M, from $140.00 to $190.00).**

# McCoy

A popular collectible with flea market goers, McCoy pottery was made in Roseville, Ohio, from 1910 until the late 1980s. They are most famous for their extensive line of figural cookie jars, more than two hundred in all. They also made amusing figural planters as well as dinnerware, and vases and pots for the florist trade. Though some pieces are unmarked, most bear one of several McCoy trademarks. Beware of reproductions made by a company in Tennessee who at one time used a very close facsimile of the old McCoy mark. They made several cookie jars once produced by McCoy as well as other now-defunct potteries. Some of these (but by no means all) were dated with the number '93' below the mark.

For more information refer to *McCoy Pottery, Volumes I, II*, and *III*, by Margaret Hanson, Craig Nissen, and Bob Hanson, and *McCoy Pottery Wall Pockets & Decorations* by Craig Nissen (Collector Books). See also Cookie Jars. See Clubs and Newsletters for information concerning the newsletter *NM (Nelson McCoy) Xpress*.

Ashtray, space capsule form, brown w/Feb - 20, from $40 to....**50.00**

Ashtray, top-hat form, yellow, from $20 to ................................**25.00**

Bell, various decals on white, 1970s, ea from $20 to....................**40.00**

Bowl, red roses decal on white, late 1950s, 10", from $30 to.......**35.00**

Canisters, Bamboo, 1974, set of 3, from $75 to .....................**100.00**

Canisters, Blue Windmill, 1974, 4-pc set, from $75 to................**100.00**

Casserole, Brown Antique Rose, stick handle, w/lid, individual.....**25.00**

Chip & dip, 2 green shells, Morano Line, #911, 1966, from $35 to ......................................**40.00**

Creamer, Mediterranean Line, 1980, from $12 to.........................**15.00**

Creamer & sugar bowl, Elsie & Elmer on white, from $30 to ................................**50.00**

Deviled-egg plate, chicken shape, yellow, 1973, from $20 to..**30.00**

**Flower holder, angelfish, white or green, unmarked, 1940s, 6", from $300.00 to $400.00. (Photo courtesy Margaret Hanson, Craig Nissen, and Bob Hanson)**

Flowerpot, wavy lines on green, w/saucer, 1960s, 6", from $25 to .......**40.00**

Goblet, Classic Line, marked, 1962, 6½", from $20 to ................**30.00**

Jardiniere, brown onyx, embossed rim, 1920s – 1930s, 7", from $50 to ..............................**60.00**

Jardiniere, Holly, brown onyx, unmarked, 1930s, 10½", from $85 to ..............................**100.00**

Jug, children decal, Happytime Line, 1974, from $20 to .....**25.00**

Lamp, hyacinth form, pink w/green leaves, 1950, 8", from $800 to ...................................**1,000.00**

Matchbox holder, white w/blue speckles, 1970s, 5¾x3¼"................**40.00**

Mug, coffee; Mr Do Bee advertising, from $10 to.........................**20.00**

Mug, coffee; Sandstone, brown & white, 1978, from $8 to .....**12.00**

Mug, coffee; Spirit of '76, from $10 to ....................................**20.00**

Napkin holder, yellow pineapple Islander Collection, 1979, from $15 to ................................**20.00**

Pitcher, cobalt ball form, 7", from $85 to ...............................**125.00**

Pitcher, donkey figural, green or yellow, 1940s, 7", from $250 to..**300.00**

Pitcher, Western Wear, brown w/embossed belt at base, 1979, 9"........................................**70.00**

Planter, alligator, green w/gold trim, 1950, 10" L, $100 to ...........**150.00**

Planter, Artisan Line, white, 1965, 7½", from $35 to ...............**45.00**

Planter, auto, green, Floraline #532L, 3½x8", from $10 to .................**20.00**

Planter, baby rattle, EX cold paint on white, unmarked, 1954, 3x5½" ..............................**100.00**

**Planter, bird dog, 1954, 12½" long, from $200.00 to $250.00. (Photo courtesy Margaret Hanson, Craig Nissen, and Bob Hanson)**

Planter, caterpillar, white, Floraline #416L, 13½", from $30 to..**45.00**

Planter, gondola, white, Floraline #508, 4½x14½", from $25 to..**35.00**

Planter, goose w/cart, green or blue, 1940s, 4¾x8", from $35 to..**45.00**

Planter, grapes on leaf base, 1953, 5x6½", from $200 to ........**300.00**

Planter, Happy Face, 1970s-80s, from $25 to..........................**35.00**

Planter, lamb, white w/gold trim, 1954, 8½", from $90 to ....**110.00**

Planter, Madonna, white, Floraline, 6x7", from $200 to ...........**250.00**

Planter, Sunburst Gold, footed, marked, 9¼", $30 to ........**35.00**

Planter, Swirl, white, Floraline #410L, 4¼", from $15 to ....**20.00**

Planter, wheelbarrow w/rooster, yellow & black, 7x10½", $100 to ......................................**125.00**

Planter, yellow w/pedestal foot, Floraline #473, 6x5", from $12 to..**15.00**

Planting dish, Capri, white w/pink interior, 14½", $40 to........**50.00**

Plate, dinner; Stonecraft, colored bands, 10", from $10 to....**15.00**

Plate, fondue; Gourmet Parisianne Line, #1055, 10½", from $15 to ..**25.00**

Salt & pepper shakers, Bluefield Line, blue on speckled tan, 1977, pr..............................**25.00**

Spoon rest, penguin form, 2-tone green, 1953, 7", from $100 to .....**150.00**

Stein, Oktoberfest, Model 6395, 1973, from $15 to...............**25.00**

Sugar bowl, yellow w/white lid, yellow finial, 1962, 12-oz, from $20 to ......................................**25.00**

Tea set, Pine Cone, blue (unusual), 1940s – 1950s, pot, creamer, sugar bowl, 3-pc .................**125.00**

Tray, silver w/embossed ribs, Floraline #498, 3x15", from $20 to ......................................**25.00**

Tumbler, green, embossed rings, flared, stoneware, 5", from $40 to ......................................**50.00**

Vase, Antique Rose, waisted cone form, 10", from $40 to .......**45.00**

Vase, cat figural, black, gray or white, ca 1960, 14", from $200 to ......................................**225.00**

**Vase, fish embossed on blue pastel, USA mark, 1940s, 10", from $60.00 to $75.00.** (Photo courtesy Margaret Hanson, Craig Nissen, and Bob Hanson)

Vase, fan; flower form w/leaves at base, white, 1954, 14½" ..**275.00**

Vase, Floraline Fineform, peach, 12x4", from $50 to............**75.00**

Vase, hand, white w/cold-painted fingernails, 1940s, 6½" ...**175.00**

Vase, Ivy, hand decorated, 1955, 9", from $200 to ...................**300.00**

Vase, peacock embossed on standard glaze, handles, 1948, 8", from $50 to ................................**60.00**

Vase, Ribbed Pedestal, dark green, #407, 6½x3¾", from $15 to..**20.00**

Vase, square top, green, Floraline #446, 9", from $20 to .........**25.00**

Wall pocket, clown, red cold paint, 1940s, 8", from $100 to....**150.00**

Wall pocket, leaves & berries embossed on aqua, unmarked, 1940s, 7" .........................**250.00**

Wall pocket, violin, 1950s, 10¼", from $150 to .................**200.00**

# Melmac Dinnerware

Melmac was a product of the postwar era, a thermoplastic material formed by the interaction of melamine and formaldehyde. It was popular because of its attractive colors and patterns, and it was practically indestructible. But eventually it faded, became scratched or burned, and housewives tired of it. By the late '60s and early '70s, it fell from favor.

Collectors, however, are finding its mid-century colors and shapes appealing again, and they're beginning to reassemble melmac table services when pristine, well designed items can be found.

For more information we recommend *Melmac Dinnerware* by Alvin Daigle Jr. and Gregg Zimmer (see the Directory under Minnesota).

Ashtray, red, center rests .......... **5.00**
Bowl, black w/red Oriental motif w/bamboo handles, K LaMoyne, 13½" ..................................... **28.00**
Bowl, blue w/multicolored spatter, #118, 4½x10" ..................... **50.00**
Bowl, fruit; lime green, 5", set of 5 ..**22.00**
Bowl, multicolored marbleized pattern, 2½x9" .......................... **45.00**
Bowl, orange w/multicolored spatter, Texas Ware #111, 3¾x8" ................................. **70.00**
Bowl, pea green w/multicolored spatter, #511A-2Q, 4½x7" .. **24.00**
Bowl, pink w/multicolored spatter, 3¼" ..................................... **17.00**
Bowl, pumpkin w/multicolor spatter, Texas Ware #125, 5¼x11¼" ..**80.00**

Bowl, red, #A118, 10" dia ......... **60.00**

**Bowl, yellow with multicolored spatter, Texas Ware, marked B-118 USA, 10" diameter.**

Bowls, black w/white spatter, Texas Ware, 5½" dia, set of 6 ..................................... **38.00**
Creamer w/covered sugar bowl, lime green ................................. **18.00**
Ice bucket, white w/incased burlap weave, w/lid handle, 9" .... **30.00**
Pitcher, beverage; tan over white, Raffiaware, 9" .................... **25.00**
Pitcher, light green, #322-1, 2-cup, 6¼" ..................................... **18.00**
Plate, dinner; Golden Dawn, 9½" dia, set of 8 ........................ **30.00**
Plate, Jellystone Park gang, #8202-8, 8" .................................. **24.00**
Plate, red, Texas Ware, 10¼" ..... **10.00**
Plate & bowl set, Magilla Gorilla, child's, #8209-12, 1960s .... **28.00**
Platter, light green, Boonton #606, 14¼" dia ............................ **20.00**
Salt & pepper shakers, chartreuse, rectangular, 2½", pr .......... **25.00**
Tray, cafeteria; red, #915CW, 14⅞x8¾", set of 12 ............ **35.00**

# Metlox

Since the 1940s, the Metlox company of California has been producing dinnerware, cookie jars, novelties, and decorative items, and their earlier wares have become very collectible. Some of their best-known dinnerware patterns are California Provincial (the dark green and burgundy rooster), Red Rooster (in red, orange, and brown), Homestead Provincial (dark green and burgundy farm scenes), and Colonial Homestead (farm scenes done in red, orange, and brown). See also Cookie Jars.

Carl Gibbs is listed in the Directory under Texas; he is the author of *Collector's Encyclopedia of Metlox Potteries* (Collector Books), highly recommended if you'd like to learn more about this company.

California Apple, bowl, salad; 11¼", from $65 to..........................**70.00**
California Apple, cup, 6-oz, from $10 to .......................................**11.00**
California Apple, platter, oval, 13", from $40 to..........................**45.00**
California Golden Blossom, butter dish, from $70 to ...............**75.00**
California Golden Blossom, jam & jelly, from $60 to ...............**65.00**
California Golden Blossom, plate, salad; from $12 to..............**14.00**
California Ivy, egg cup, from $35 to .......................................**38.00**
California Ivy, jam & jelly, from $40 to .......................................**45.00**
California Ivy, pepper mill, from $45 to .......................................**50.00**
California Ivy, plate, dinner; 10¼", from $16 to..........................**18.00**
California Ivy, tray, 3-tier, from $65 to .......................................**70.00**

California Peach Blossom, coaster, from $25 to..........................**28.00**
California Peach Blossom, plate, dinner; from $16 to............**18.00**
California Peach Blossom, teapot, from $115 to .....................**125.00**
California Provincial, bowl, vegetable; basket design, 8⅛", $55 to ........................................**60.00**
California Provincial, gravy, 1-pt, from $45 to..........................**50.00**
California Provincial, soup server (aka lug soup); 5", from $32 to .......................................**35.00**
California Strawberry, bowl, fruit; 5⅜", from $12 to ................**14.00**
California Strawberry, cup & saucer, 7-oz, 6", from $12 to...........**14.00**
California Strawberry, plate, salad; 8", from $9 to .....................**10.00**
Camellia, bowl, fruit; 6⅛", from $12 to .......................................**15.00**
Camellia, cup & saucer, from $12 to .......................................**14.00**
Camellia, plate, dinner; 10", from $12 to .................................**15.00**
Camellia, salt & pepper shakers, pr from $24 to..........................**28.00**
Colonial Heritage, buffet server, round, from $65 to.............**70.00**
Colonial Heritage, canister, tea; w/lid, from $45 to ..............**50.00**

**Colonial Heritage, coaster, from $18.00 to $20.00; Fruit bowl, from $12.00 to $14.00.** (Photo courtesy Carl Gibbs, Jr.)

Colonial Heritage, pitcher, lg, from $75 to ...............................**80.00**

Colonial Heritage, platter, oval, lg, from $45 to.........................**50.00**

Delphinium, coffeepot, from $70 to ......................................**75.00**

Delphinium, plate, luncheon; 9", from $10 to.........................**12.00**

Golden Fruit, coaster, 3¾", from $16 to .......................................**18.00**

Golden Fruit, pitcher, 1½-pt, from $35 to ...............................**40.00**

Golden Fruit, saucer, 6¼", from $3 to ..........................................**4.00**

Homestead Provincial, bowl, lug soup; 5", from $32 to .........**35.00**

Homestead Provincial, bowl, vegetable; divided rectangle, 12", from $65 to.........................**60.00**

Homestead Provincial, coffeepot, 42-oz, 7-cup, from $125 to ..**135.00**

Homestead Provincial, oil cruet, 7-oz, from $42 to ...................**45.00**

Homestead Provincial, salt & pepper shakers, pr from $30 to....**32.00**

Homestead Provincial, sugar bowl, w/lid, 8-oz, from $35 to......**38.00**

Jamestown, bowl, soup; from $14 to .......................................**16.00**

Jamestown, sauce boat, from $45 to .......................................**50.00**

Lotus, banana leaf, 11", from $40 to .......................................**45.00**

Lotus, cup & saucer, demitasse; from $26 to.........................**30.00**

Navajo, gravy ladle, from $20 to .................................**22.00**

Navajo, plate, dinner; 10½", from $14 to .................................**15.00**

Provincial Whitestone, cruet set, 5-pc complete, from $135 to .................................**150.00**

Provincial Whitestone, plate, dinner; 10½", from $11 to.......**12.00**

Red Rooster, ashtray, 10", from $30 to .......................................**35.00**

Red Rooster, butter dish, from $50 to .......................................**55.00**

Red Rooster, cookie jar, from $100 to .....................................**110.00**

Red Rooster, creamer, 6-oz, from $25 to ...............................**28.00**

Red Rooster, cup & saucer, 7-oz, 6⅛", from $14 to ................**16.00**

**Red Rooster (Decorated), two-tier tray with metal divider, $60.00.** (Photo courtesy Carl Gibbs, Jr.)

Red Rooster, egg cup, from $32 to.....................................**35.00**

Red Rooster, plate, salad; 7½", from $10 to ...............................**12.00**

Rooster Bleu, cup & saucer, from $12 to ...............................**14.00**

Rooster Bleu, sugar bowl, w/lid, 8-oz, from $22 to ...................**25.00**

Sculptured Daisy, bowl, vegetable; divided, med, from $45 to..**50.00**

Sculptured Daisy, casserole, w/lid, 1½-qt, from $85 to .............**90.00**

Sculptured Daisy, plate, salad; 7½", from $9 to...........................**10.00**

Sculptured Daisy, salt & pepper shakers, pr from $24 to.....**26.00**

Sculptured Grape, butter dish, from
$60 to ...................................**65.00**
Sculptured Grape, creamer, 10-oz,
from $28 to.........................**30.00**
Sculptured Grape, pitcher, 2¼-qt,
from $75 to.........................**80.00**
Sculptured Zinnia, mug, 8-oz, from
$22 to ...............................**25.00**
Sculptured Zinnia, sugar bowl,
w/lid, 10-oz, from $30 to....**32.00**
Vineyard, gravy server stand, from
$10 to .................................**12.00**
Vineyard, mug, 8-oz, from $22
to .....................................**25.00**
Vineyard, pitcher, 1-qt, from $50
to ......................................**55.00**
Vineyard, plate, dinner; 10¾", from
$12 to .................................**13.00**
Woodland Gold, baker, oval, 12",
from $45 to.........................**50.00**
Woodland Gold, bowl, salad; 11",
from $65 to.........................**70.00**

**Woodland Gold, individual soup
server, from $12.00 to $13.00; Buffet server, 13¼", from $55.00 to
$60.00; Cheese server, from
$60.00 to $65.00. (Photo courtesy
Carl Gibbs, Jr.)**

Woodland Gold, pitcher, 1½-pt, from
$40 to .................................**45.00**
Woodland Gold, plate, dinner; 10¼",
from $12 to.........................**13.00**
Woodland Gold, teapot, 6-cup, from
$100 to ...............................**110.00**

Woodland Gold, tumbler, 12-oz,
from $28 to........................**30.00**
Yorkshire, cup & saucer, from $13
to ......................................**16.00**
Yorkshire, pitcher, 2-qt, from $60
to ......................................**65.00**
Yorkshire, plate, luncheon; 9", from
$12 to ...............................**15.00**

## Miller Studio

Brightly painted chalkware
plaques, bookends, thermometers,
and hot pad holders modeled with
subjects that range from Raggedy
Ann and angels to bluebirds and
sunfish were the rage during 1950s
and 1960s, and even into the early
1970s you could buy them from the
five-&-dime store to decorate your
kitchen and bathroom walls with
style and flair. Collectors who like
this 'kitschy' ambience are snapping
them up and using them in the vintage rooms they're re-creating with
period appliances, furniture, and
accessories. They're especially fond
of the items marked Miller Studio, a
manufacturing firm located in New
Philadelphia, Pennsylvania. Most
but not all of their pieces are
marked and carry a copyright date.
If you find an unmarked item with
small holes on the back where sta-
pled-on cardboard packaging has
been torn away, chances are very
good it's Miller Studio as well.
Miller Studio is still in business and
is today the only U.S.A. firm that
continues to produce hand-finished
wall plaques. (Mr. Miller tells us

that although they had over three hundred employees back in the 1960s and 1970s, they presently have approximately seventy-five.)

Anthropomorphic apple & pear, hot pad holders, 1970, pr..........**25.00**

Anthropomorphic corn, yellow, note pad & pen holder, 1964, 12x5"..**22.00**

Anthropomorphic tomato, red w/green, hot pad holder, 1959 .........**15.00**

Bird in bonnet on twig, 2 hot pad hooks, 1952........................**15.00**

Bluebird couple in hats, bright colors, 1973, 5½", 6", pr.........**20.00**

Bo Peep & 2 sheep, pink & blue, 1965, 3-pc...........................**15.00**

Boy toddler praying in blue pajamas, 1984...........................**15.00**

Campbell Soup Kid boy & girl, yellow, 1964, pr from $20 to .............**25.00**

Cardinal, red on green leaves, 1972, 7x5", 6½", pr ......................**25.00**

Cat mother w/2 kittens, 1970, 3-pc set.......................................**20.00**

Cockatoos, bright colors, 1957, 14½x5", facing pr...............**25.00**

Dog's head, brown w/dark ears, 1961, 3x4¼" ........................**10.00**

Dutch girl, blond in blue dress, toothbrush holder, 1964, from $50 to ...............................**60.00**

Fish, gaping mouths, pink, pr w/bubbles, 7", 4-pc set, from $27.50 to ...........................**30.00**

Fish, male w/top hat & female w/umbrella, 1969, 6x4½", pr.....**20.00**

Fish family, pink, 1960s, 6½" mom +3 smaller (smallest 5x5"), 4-pc.......................................**30.00**

Fish w/lg eyes & lips, iridescent, 1964, 10x6¼", 8¾x6¼", pr..**40.00**

Frog mama w/parasol, bathometer in tummy, +2 babies, 1970, 3-pc..**25.00**

Gnome in green beside mushrooms, 1979, 6x5", pr from $20 to..**25.00**

Horse head, palomino, 1977, 6"..**15.00**

Mammy w/broom (pencil handle), note pad (apron) holder, 1954..**75.00**

Monkey, brown, bank, 11x9x8".....**40.00**

Mushroom groups, 1974, 13x15" & 2 12x7", 3-pc set ...................**45.00**

Mushrooms, orange tops, hot pad holder, 1981, 5⅜".............**15.00**

Owl, white w/gold trim, 1978, 11x5½" ...............................**20.00**

Owl mother & baby, hot pad holder, orange w/red & green trim, 5"..**15.00**

Owl w/glasses beside book, orange tones, note pad holder, 1970..**15.00**

Parrot, bright colors, 1963, 10x9"..**25.00**

Poodle, white on black oval back, 1970s, 8x5", pr...................**45.00**

Recipe box w/vegetables & spoon, hot pad holder, 1981, 6x6½"..**12.00**

Rooster, copper colored, thermometer, 1969..............................**30.00**

Sailing ship, black & gold, 1964, 10¼x8" ...............................**26.00**

Skunk w/flowers, thermometer in tail, 1954............................**35.00**

Swans, white, 1968, 7x6½", pr.....**25.00**

Swans, white on pink circles, 1958, pr.......................................**35.00**

**Wishing well, brown, thermometer, 1966, 7x6", $15.00.**

Wood stove w/verse, hot pad holder, 1974, 6½x7" ..................**15.00**

Worm in top hat on apple w/window & thermometer, hot pad holder, 1976..................................**15.00**

# Model Kits

The best-known producer of model kits today is Aurora. Collectors often pay astronomical prices for some of the character kits from the 1960s. Made popular by all the monster movies of that decade, ghouls like Vampirella, Frankenstein, and the Wolfman were eagerly built up by kids everywhere. But the majority of all model kits were vehicles, ranging from 3" up to 24" long. Some of the larger model vehicle makers were AMT, MPC, and IMC. Condition is very important in assessing the value of a kit, with built-ups priced at about 50% lower than one still in the box. Other things factor into pricing as well — who is selling, who is buying and how badly they want it, locality, supply, and demand. For more information, we recommend *Schroeder's Collectible Toys, Antique to Modern* (Collector Books).

Addar, Evel Knievel's Wheelie, 1974, MIB ........................**125.00**

Airfix, Sam-2 Missile, 1973, MIB.**40.00**

AMT, My Mother the Car, 1965, MIB ..................................**75.00**

AMT, Star Trek, Spock, 1967, MIB ..................................**150.00**

AMT/Ertl, Monkeemobile, 1990, MIB (sealed) ....................**100.00**

AMT/Ertl, Star Trek: TNG, USS Enterprise, 1988, MIB ......**30.00**

Arii, Regult Missile Carrier, MIB..**25.00**

Aurora, Batman, 1964, MIB (sealed)............................**375.00**

Aurora, Castle Creatures, Vampire, 1966, MIB ........................**175.00**

Aurora, Dick Tracy Space Coupe, 1967, MIB ........................**125.00**

Aurora, Famous Fighters, Gold Knight of Nice, 1957, MIB..........**225.00**

Aurora, Forgotten Prisoner, 1966, MIB (sealed) ....................**450.00**

Aurora, Green Beret, MIB .....**225.00**

Aurora, Hunchback of Notre Dame (Anthony Quinn), 1964, MIB................................**350.00**

Aurora, King Kong, 1964, MIB ..............................**500.00**

Aurora, Lone Ranger, 1967, MIB (sealed)............................**325.00**

Aurora, Mummy's Chariot, 1965, MIB ................................**450.00**

**Aurora, Prehistoric Scenes, Cro-Magnon Woman, 1971, MIB, $75.00.**

Aurora, Rat Patrol, 1967, partially assembled, EXIB ...............**85.00**

Aurora, Superboy, 1964, MIB..**300.00**

Aurora, USB Sealab III, 1969, MIB ...................................**300.00**

Aurora, Witch, 1969, glow-in-the-dark, MIB (sealed) ...........**300.00**

Aurora, Wonder Woman, 1965, MIB ...................................**450.00**

Bachmann, Dogs of the World, Bassett Hound, 1960s, MIB ..**30.00**

Bandai, Pegila, 1990, MIB .......**15.00**

Billiken, Mummy, vinyl, MIB ..**225.00**

Dark Horse, Predator II, 1994, MIB ...................................**175.00**

Geometric Design, Boris Karloff as The Mummy, MIB.............**50.00**

Hawk, Cobra II, 1950s, MIB .....**75.00**

Horizon, Bride of Frankenstein, MIB ....................................**75.00**

Horizon, Invisible Man, MIB .....**50.00**

Horizon, Robocop, ED-209, 1989, MIB ....................................**70.00**

Imai, Orguss, Cable, 1994, MIB ..**40.00**

KGB, Space Ghost (TV), MIB ..**35.00**

Lindberg, Flying Saucer, 1952, MIB ...................................**200.00**

Lindberg, US Space Station, 1958, MIB ...................................**200.00**

Monogram, Boss a Bone, 1969, assembled, EX ...................**25.00**

Monogram, Godzilla, 1978, glow-in-the-dark, MIB...................**100.00**

Monogram, Space Buggy, 1969, MIB ...................................**100.00**

Monogram, Wolfman, 1983, MIB (sealed)..............................**60.00**

MPC, Batman, MIB (sealed) ....**35.00**

MPC, Hulk, 1978, MIB (sealed)..**75.00**

MPC, Mannix Roadster, 1968, MIB ...................................**150.00**

MPC, Star Wars, Darth Vadar TIE Fighter, 1978, MIB............**35.00**

MPC, Strange Changing Vampire, 1974, MIB .........................**55.00**

Palmer, US Navy Vanguard Missile, 1958, MIB ........................**225.00**

Pyro, Gladiator Sho Cycle, 1970, MIB ....................................**50.00**

Pyro, Surf's Up!, 1970, MIB.....**50.00**

Revell, Baja Humbug, 1971, MIB ................................**85.00**

**Revell, Cat in the Hat, 1958, MIB, $100.00.**

Revell, Disney's Love Bug Rides Again, 1974, MIB ............**100.00**

Revell, Endangered Animals, Gorilla, 1991, MIB .....................**30.00**

Revell, History Makers, Jupitor C, 1983, MIB (sealed) ............**60.00**

Revell, Love Bug, 1970s, MIB...**50.00**

Revell, Peter Pan Pirate Ship, 1960s, MIB ......................**125.00**

Screamin', Friday the 13th's Jason, MIB ...................................**125.00**

Strombecker, Interplanetary Vehicle, 1959, MIB .................**175.00**

Toy Biz, Storm, 1996, MIB (sealed) ..............................**30.00**

Tsukuda, Frankenstein, 1985, MIB..**100.00**

Tsukuda, Mummy, MIB.........**100.00**

Tsukuda, Wolfman, MIB........**100.00**

# Mood Indigo

Quite an extensive line, this ware was imported from Japan during the 1960s. It was evidently quite successful, judging from the amount of it still around today. It's inexpensive, and if you're into blue, this is for you! It's a deep, very electric shade, and each piece is modeled to represent stacks of various fruits, with handles and spouts sometimes turned out as vines. All pieces carry a stamped number on the bottom which identifies the shape. There are more than thirty known items to look for, more than likely others will surface.

Ashtray, rest in ea corner, E-4283, 9".........................................**20.00**
Bell, 5".....................................**10.00**
Candleholder, goblet shape, 4½", pr.......................................**28.00**
Cigarette lighter, E-3100, 3¾".....**22.00**
Cookie jar/canister, E-2374, 8".....**18.00**
Creamer & sugar bowl, w/lid, from $10 to.................................**12.00**
Cruet.......................................**25.00**

**Ginger jar, E-5241, 10¼", $35.00.**

Gravy boat, 6½".......................**15.00**
Jar, cylindrical, w/lid, 6½".......**15.00**
Ladle, 9¾"................................**25.00**
Mug, coffee; 4⅛", from $5 to........**7.00**
Pitcher, footed, E-2429, 6½"....**18.00**
Salt & papper shakers, E-2371, 3½", pr.......................................**12.00**
Teapot, 8"................................**15.00**
Tray, 8½x5¾"...........................**28.00**
Trivet, 6" dia............................**10.00**
Tureen/covered dish, E-3379.....**30.00**

# Moon and Star

A reissue of Palace, an early pattern glass line, Moon and Star was developed for the market in the 1960s by Joseph Weishar of Island Mould and Machine Company (Wheeling, West Virginia). It was made by several companies. One of the largest producers was L.E. Smith of Mt. Pleasant, Pennsylvania, and L.G. Wright (who had their glassware made by Fostoria and Fenton, perhaps others as well) carried a wide assortment in their catalogs for many years. It is still being made on a very limited basis, but the most collectible pieces are those in red, blue, amber, and green — colors that are no longer in production. The values listed here are for pieces in red or blue. Amber, green, and crystal prices should be 30% lower.

Ashtray, moons at rim, star in base, 6-sided, 5½".......................**18.00**
Ashtray, moons at rim, star in base, 6-sided, 8½".......................**25.00**
Bell, pattern along sides, plain rim & handle...........................**35.00**

Bowl, allover pattern, footed, crimped rim, 7½".............**25.00**

Butter/cheese dish, patterned lid, plain base, 7" dia, ..........................**65.00**

Cake plate, allover pattern, low collared base, 13" dia, from $50 to ......................................**60.00**

Candle bowl, allover pattern, footed, 8", from $25 to ...................**30.00**

Candle lamp, patterned shade, clear base, 2-pc, 7½", from $20 to ..**25.00**

Candleholders, allover pattern, flared base, 4½", pr from $20 to ......................................**25.00**

Canister, allover pattern, 1-lb or 2-lb, from $15 to ...................**20.00**

Canister, allover pattern, 3½-lb or 5-lb, from $18 to ...................**28.00**

Cheese dish, patterned base, clear plain lid, 9½" .....................**60.00**

Compote, allover pattern, footed, flared crimped rim, 5".......**15.00**

Compote, allover pattern, scalloped rim, footed, 5½x8"...............**28.00**

Compote, allover pattern, scalloped rim, footed, 7x10" ..............**35.00**

Creamer, allover pattern, raised foot w/scalloped edge, 5¾x3"..............................**30.00**

Cruet, vinegar; 6¾", from $60 to ...................................**65.00**

Epergne, allover pattern, 2-pc, 9"....................................**65.00**

Fairy lamp, from $18.00 to $25.00.

Goblet, water; plain rim & foot, 5¾" .....................................**12.00**

Goblet, wine; plain rim & foot, 4½" .......................................**9.00**

Lamp, miniature; amber, from $115 to ......................................**125.00**

Lamp, miniature; blue, from $165 to ......................................**190.00**

Lamp, miniature; green .........**135.00**

Lamp, miniature; milk glass, from $200 to ............................**225.00**

Lamp, miniature; red, from $175 to ......................................**200.00**

Lighter, allover patterned body, metal fittings, from $40 to .................................**50.00**

Nappy, allover pattern, crimped rim, 2¾x6", from $12 to ....**15.00**

Plate, patterned body & center, smooth rim, 8", up to.........**45.00**

Relish bowl, 6 lg scallops form allover pattern, 1½x8" ......**30.00**

Relish dish, allover pattern, 1 plain handle, 2x8" dia, from $35 to ......................................**35.00**

Salt cellar, allover pattern, scalloped rim, sm flat foot..................**6.00**

Soap dish, allover pattern, oval, 2x6" .....................................**9.00**

Sugar shaker, allover pattern, metal top, 4½x3½" .......................**45.00**

Toothpick holder, allover pattern, scalloped rim, sm flat foot..**9.00**

Tumbler, no pattern at rim or on disc foot, 7-oz, 4¼", from $10 to ......................................**12.00**

## Mortens Studios

Animal models sold by Mortens Studios of Arizona during the 1940s are some of today's most interesting collectibles, especially among animal lovers. Hundreds of breeds of dogs, cats, and horses were produced from a plaster-type composition material constructed over a wire framework. They range in size from 2" up to about 7", and most are marked. Crazing and flaking are nearly always present to some degree. Our values are for animals in excellent to near-mint condition, allowing for only minor crazing. Heavily crazed examples will be worth much less.

Airedale terrier, w/sticker, I Am an Airedale, 4¾x6" .................**80.00**
Arabian horse, plaque............**125.00**
Beagle, standing, #872, 4½x5½"..**55.00**
Boston bull terrier, black & white, 3½x7", from $75 to ..........**100.00**
Boxer (male) dog, standing, 5½".............................**140.00**
Boxer pup, recumbent, unclipped ears, 5½" L........................**65.00**

**Cat, #395, 4¼x4", $50.00.**

Chihuahua, standing, 5½x6½"...**95.00**
Chow Chow, red, standing, 5½"..**110.00**
Collie, recumbent, 5¼x5¼" .....**135.00**
Dachshund, red, 4¼x9¼", from $65 to ........................................**80.00**

Doberman pinscher, #783, 7¼" ..**135.00**
English setter, w/label, 6¼x10¾"..**95.00**
German shepherd pup, 3½".....**40.00**
Horse, gray, mane erect, #704, 8x8½" ................................**95.00**
Irish setter, Show Dog series......**90.00**
Kerry blue terrier, decal, 4¾x6"..**165.00**
Poodle, standing, 3½x3½", from $50 to ......................................**60.00**
Saddlebred horse, black, walking, w/sticker ...........................**80.00**
Spaniel, begging, 5¼"..............**70.00**
St Bernard, 6½".......................**75.00**

# Moss Rose

Though the Moss Rose pattern has been produced by Staffordshire and American pottery companies alike since the mid-1800s, the lines we're dealing with here are all from the twentieth century. Much was made from the late 1950s into the 1970s by Japanese manufacturers. Even today you'll occasionally see a tea set or a small candy dish for sale in some of the chain stores. (The collectors who are already picking this line up refer to it as Moss Rose, but we've seen it advertised as Victorian Rose, and some companies called their lines Chintz Rose or French Rose; but for now, Moss Rose seems to be the accepted terminology.

Rosenthal made an identical pattern, and prices are generally higher for examples that carry the mark of that company. The pattern consists of a briar rose with dark green mossy leaves on stark white glaze. Occasionally, an item is trimmed in gold. In addition to dinnerware, many accessories and novelties were made as well.

For further listings, refer to *Garage Sale & Flea Market Annual* (Collector Books).

Atomizer, original bulb, Japan, 4x2" dia .......................................**25.00**
Bell, heart handle, Golden Crown, Made in England, sm........**16.00**
Bowl, Japan, 7½".........................**5.00**
Butter dish, rectangular, unmarked Japan, ¼-lb ..........................**25.00**
Candleholder, gold trim, 1½x3¼" dia ......................................**25.00**
Canister, Instant Coffee, gold trim, unmarked Japan................**34.00**
Cigarette box, Japan ................**15.00**
Creamer & sugar bowl w/lid, Sango Japan ................................**20.00**
Cup & saucer, pearlized, gold trim, 1960, 2½x3¾" ......................**9.00**
Cup & saucer, Sango Japan, 2x4", 6", from $15 to ..................**20.00**
Egg cup, footed, Japan, 2½", from $15 to ...............................**17.50**
Gravy boat, attached undertray, Japan, 9x6" ........................**37.50**
Incense burner, gold handles & finial, 1940s, 3¼x3½"........**65.00**
Pin dish, rectangular, Fujiyama Japan ................................**20.00**
Plate, dinner; pearlized, gold trim, Japan label, 1960, 10½"....**12.50**
Platter, Japan, 12¼x8⅞" .........**45.00**
Platter, Ucagco, 14¼x10¼" ......**50.00**
Snack set, cup & plate w/indent, Ucagco..............................**25.00**
Sugar bowl, ornate handles, w/lid, unmarked Japan, 4x5¾"....**25.00**

Sugar bowl, pearlized w/gold trim, w/lid, Japan label, 1960s, 3½".....................................**15.00**
Teapot, bulbous, Japan, 3½"......**25.00**

**Teapot, creamer and sugar bowl with lid, Japan, $35.00.**

Teapot, electric, Japan label, 8" ..**35.00**
Teapot, music box in base, 6¼"......**25.00**
Teapot, w/warmer & stand, Japan sticker ...............................**115.00**

## Music Boxes

So many of the music boxes you'll find at flea markets today are related to well-known characters or special holidays. These have a crossover collectible appeal, and often are priced in the $75.00 to $100.00 range — some even higher. Many are animated as well as musical.

Most modern music boxes are figural, but some have been made by children's toy companies to look like grandfather clocks or radios, for instance.

Unless noted otherwise our values are for mint-condition examples.

Anri, boy & girl w/Christmas tree, Lara's Theme, 5" ..............**60.00**

Anri, Lucy & Charlie Brown, Try To Remember, 1960s, 8¾" .....**95.00**

**Anri, Lucy of Peanuts gang, plays tune from Love Story, UFS 1972, 5½", $95.00.**

Anri/Reuge, Charlie Brown w/baseball bat & hat, 1968, 6½"..**60.00**

Anri/Reuge, girl playing cello w/pet friends, 8" .........................**65.00**

Anri/Reuge, Linus & Snoopy, 1968..**120.00**

Anri/Reuge, Snoopy playing hockey, 5½" ....................................**210.00**

Anri/Thorens, boy & girl back-to-back w/woodland friends....**45.00**

Anri/Thorens, children playing cowboys & Indians w/teepee & pets....................................**90.00**

Disney's Musical Memories, Sleeping Beauty, limited edition .....**50.00**

Disney/Elliot, Cinderella & Prince Charming dancing, 6x4", MIB..................................**60.00**

Disney/Elliot, Jasmine & Aladdin dancing, limited edition, 6x4", MIB.................................**115.00**

Disney/Grolier, Peter Pan w/Wendy & Peter, limited edition, MIB..**40.00**

Disney/Schmid, Jiminy Cricket, 7x4" dia base............................**70.00**

Disney/Schmid, Mickey as Sorcerer's Apprentice, 1980s, 12"....**100.00**

Disney/Schmid, Mickey Mouse in top hat & tails, 1970s, 8"..........**80.00**

Disney/Schmid, Snow White & Happy, 6½" ........................**30.00**

Disney/Schmid, Snow White w/ Prince Charming & the 7 Dwarfs, 8"........................................**45.00**

Enesco, Musicola coin-op juke box, plays Hey Jude, 5½"..........**85.00**

Enesco, Scooter & Polly at the Toy Shop, Country Cousins .....**45.00**

Enesco, 1965 Corvette Convertible, blue ...................................**35.00**

Fisher-Price, Ferris Wheel, #969, 1966...................................**45.00**

Japan, Hummel-like children on (wooden) seesaw, ceramic...**50.00**

Japan, owls cuddling, ceramic, Love Makes the World Go Round, 1950s.................................**40.00**

Japan/Maruho, boy & girl embrace, ceramic, Lara's Theme, 7"..**20.00**

Japan/Otagiri, birds on red bow among greenery, Silver Bells, 1970s.................................**30.00**

Japan/Sanyo, bluebird on branch, Send In the Clowns, 8"......**65.00**

Lefton, older couple dressed for walk, Love Is a Many Splendored... .**35.00**

Rockwell, Prom Dress, painted porcelain, 1981, 7"...........**110.00**

Rockwell, Toy Maker (w/2 children), bisque, It's a Small world, 1985...................................**55.00**

San Francisco Music Box Co, Jewels of the Empire, carousel, 13", MIB .....................................**45.00**

San Francisco Music Box Co, Phantom of the Opera monkey w/cymbals, MIB.................**70.00**

Schmid, Beatrix Potter's Appley Dapply, w/tag, 6" ............**100.00**
Schmid, Beatrix Potter's Cecily Parsley, 1982 .....................**85.00**
Schmid, Bozo the Clown, plastic, Yankee Doodle Dandy, 5¾" ...**25.00**
Schmid, Raggedy Ann & Andy by wood house, Theme from Love Story, 1975 ......................**175.00**
Schmid, Snoopy & Woodstock, spinning umbrella, 7¼" ............**170.00**
Schmid, Snoopy as Joe Cool, green shirt w/shamrock, 7¾" ......**75.00**
Schmid, Snoopy as Red Baron on doghouse, 1969, 9x5x4¼", MIB..**150.00**
Schmid, teddy bear revolves, This Old Man, 1983 ...................**40.00**
Topper, Dawn doll on stand, purple platform, 1972, MIB......**135.00**
Warner Brothers, Michigan J Frog dancing, 1993, MIB ...........**60.00**
Westland, 3 Stooges at dinner table, MIB .....................................**90.00**

# Niloak

Produced in Arkansas by Charles Dean Hyten from the early 1900s until the mid-1940s, Niloak (the backward spelling of kaolin, a type of clay) takes many forms — figural planters, vases in both matt and glossy glazes, and novelty items of various types. The company's most famous product and the most collectible is their Swirl or Mission Ware line. Clay in colors of brown, blue, cream, red, and buff are swirled within the mold, the finished product left unglazed on the outside to preserve the natural hues. Small vases are common; large pieces or unusual shapes and those with exceptional coloration are the most valuable. Refer to *Collector's Encyclopedia of Niloak* by David Edwin Gifford (Collector Books) for more information.

Note: The terms '1st' and '2nd art mark' used in the listings refer to specific die-stamped trademarks. The earlier mark was used from 1910 to 1924, followed by the second, very similar mark used from then until the end of Mission Ware production. Letters with curving raised outlines were characteristic of both; the most obvious difference between the two was that on the first, the final upright line of the 'N' was thin with a solid club-like terminal.

Ashtray, Mission Ware, 5" dia..**215.00**
Basket, blue & tan matt, Hywood mark, 6½", from $75 to .....**95.00**
Basket, vertical handle, woven appearance, 3½" .................**42.00**
Bowl, Peacock Blue II, Hywood mark, 3¾", from $35 to .....**55.00**
Creamer, cow figural, tail handle, glossy, unmarked, 4½"......**55.00**
Creamer, Ozark Dawn II, 1st Hywood mark by Niloak, 4¼", $35 to .................................**50.00**
Cup & saucer, Ozark Blue, Peterson petal design, from $75 to..**100.00**
Ewer, green-brown tobacco spit, unmarked, 5¾" .................**18.00**
Ewer, Mission Ware, w/stopper ..**1,000.00**
Figurine, cannon, Ozark Dawn, 3½" ....................................**58.00**
Figurine, razor-back hog on base, maroon, unmarked, 3¾"..................................**250.00**

Figurine, Trojan horse, white matt, 8¼"....................................**230.00**

Flower frog, duck on wing, Ozark Dawn, unmarked, 6".........**70.00**

Head vase, w/hat, burgundy matt, 7¾"....................................**95.00**

Pitcher, bull's-eye decor, 1st Hywood mark by Niloak, 6".........**67.00**

Pitcher, deep maroon matt, melon ribs, 8¼"...........................**155.00**

Pitcher, Delft Blue, unmarked, miniature, 2½"...................**42.50**

Pitcher, Mission Ware, Pat Pend, 10½"...........................**1,200.00**

Pitcher, Ozark Dawn, bowling ball shape, ice lip spout, 7"......**55.00**

Planter, camel resting, glossy, attached bowl, 3½x6".......**16.00**

Planter, cradle, Ozark Dawn, 6½" L............................................**44.00**

Planter, parrot perched on side of dish, 4½", from $40 to.......**55.00**

Planter, polar bear, hand-painted features, attached bowl, 6½"..**58.00**

Planter, pouter pigeon, ivory, 9"..**185.00**

Planter, rocking horse, Ozark Blue, 6½"....................................**100.00**

Planter, rooster crowing, yellow gloss, 9"..........................................**65.00**

Planter, seal resting on bowl, flippers extended, hand-painted details...............................**48.00**

Planter, southern belle kneeling, skirt extended, holds basket, 4½"....................................**150.00**

Planter, squirrel w/upright extended bushy tail, 6"......................**20.00**

Planter, wishing well w/detailed shingles, matt, 7½".......**42.50**

Plate, dinner; Ozark Blue, 10", from $75 to ..................**100.00**

Strawberry jar, Ozark Blue, 5".....**26.00**

Sugar bowl, green & tan matt, 1st Hywood mark by Niloak, 4", from $50 to........................**75.00**

Teapot, Fox Red, Aladdin style, 6½"....................................**20.00**

Vase, cornucopia; feather-like detail, 7½x7"...............................**48.00**

Vase, Deco style w/accordion pleats, Ozark Dawn, Hywood mark, 7½"....................................**55.00**

Vase, Mission Ware, 9"..........**300.00**

Vase, Ozark Blue, tulip shape, miniature, 3"......................**16.00**

Vase, Ozark Dawn II, sq rim, Potteries sticker, 5½", from $20 to ........................................**48.00**

Vase, Sea Green, Hywood Art Pottery mark, 9", from $450 to ......**550.00**

Vase, tulip; 7 openings, marked, 8"..**27.00**

Vase, wing-like handles, matt, Hywood mark, 7¼"............**36.00**

Wall pocket, pitcher form, green-brown tobacco spit, marked, 5½"....................................**55.00**

**Water bottle, Ozark Blue, clay stopper, Potteries sticker, 7¾", $125.00.**
(Photo courtesy David Edwin Gifford)

# Nippon

In complying with American

importation regulations, from 1891 to 1921 Japanese manufacturers marked their wares 'Nippon,' meaning Japan, to indicate country of origin. The term is today used to refer to the highly decorated porcelain vases, bowls, chocolate pots, etc., that bear this term within their trademark. Many variations were used. Refer to *Van Patten's ABC's of Collecting Nippon Porcelain* by Joan Van Patten (Collector Books) for more information. See Clubs and Newsletters for information concerning the International Nippon Collectors Club.

Ashtray, pipe & matches painted inside, 3 rests, marked, 5¼" H .....................................**175.00**

Bowl, floral reserves, 8 scallops, maple-leaf mark, 7½".......**160.00**

Bowl, floral w/ornate gold rim, 3-legged, 6-sided, 7¼" ....**145.00**

Bowl, grapes, simple gold handles, M-in-wreath mark, 8½" .........**175.00**

Box, powder; floral band on white w/gold, M-in-wreath mark, 5½" .....................................**70.00**

Cake plate, floral band w/gold, crown mark, 10½" ...........**100.00**

Candlestick, floral w/moriage trim, flared foot, M-in-wreath mark, 6" .....................................**300.00**

Chocolate set, floral band on white, green mark, 9" pot+6 cups/saucers ............................**315.00**

Coffeepot, river scenic, earth tones, stick handle, 6".................**150.00**

Creamer & sugar bowl, landscape scenic, w/lid, M-in-wreath mark.................................**125.00**

Egg cup, sampan in sunset scene, Rising Sun mark, 2½".......**65.00**

Ewer, purple flowers, inverted cone form, Royal Kinran mark, 9½" ...................................**225.00**

Ferner, floral w/gold, lion-head handles, green mark, 5¾"...**465.00**

Figurine, bird on stump, black mark, 4" ...........................**350.00**

Hatpin holder, floral w/gold, hanging, Maple Leaf mark, 7" ......**500.00**

Humidor, playing cards on brown, M-in-wreath mark, 7" .....**800.00**

Inkwell, Deco flowers on blue, M-in-wreath mark, 4" ..............**275.00**

Pitcher, roses on white w/gold, 6-sided, RC mark, 7" .........**275.00**

Pitcher, roses w/gold, footed, unmarked, 8"...................**425.00**

Plaque, cat looks from window, hand-painted mark, 9½" ........**650.00**

Plaque, owl in woodland scene, M-in-wreath mark, 8¾".......**385.00**

Plaque, still life of fruit, M-in-wreath mark, 12" ...........**600.00**

Plaque, windmill scenic, green M-in-wreath mark, 10" ............**275.00**

Potpourri jar, swallows, blue on white, 5½".......................**235.00**

Sugar bowl, floral band on cream, w/lid, M-in-wreath mark, 6½" dia .....................................**80.00**

Tea set, Oriental decor w/gold, Pat mark, 5" pot, creamer & sugar bowl, 4 cups & saucers...**400.00**

Toast rack, floral on white, 2-slice, Rising Sun mark, 5"........**175.00**

Trivet, Black man stands w/camel, 8-sided, M-in-wreath mark, 7" .....................................**250.00**

Vase, bird on branch w/flowers, ring handles, 12" ............**350.00**

Vase, floral on black, angle handles, green M-in-wreath mark, 13"..**400.00**

Vase, floral on blue, bottle neck, M-in-wreath mark, 9½".....**850.00**

Vase, floral w/gold, integral handles, bulbous, Maple Leaf mark, 5"..**300.00**

Vase, lady & flowers reserve on cobalt w/gold, M-in-wreath mark, 8".......................**1,700.00**

Vase, lady w/stick & geese, integral handles, M-in-wreath mark, 6"......................................**625.00**

Vase, lilies on brown, gold handles, M-in-wreath mark, 9¾".**350.00**

Vase, roses on brown w/gold, M-in-wreath mark, 12"............**600.00**

Vase, swan scenic, earth tones, sm neck, M-in-wreath mark, 9"..**325.00**

**Vase, winter scenic, gold handles, blue Imperial Nippon mark, 6½", from $200.00 to $260.00.**
(Photo courtesy Joan Van

Vase, woodland scene, white w/ moriage, shouldered, 9"..**500.00**

# Noritake

Since the early 1900s, the Noritake China Company has been pro-ducing fine dinnerware, occasional pieces, and figural items decorated by hand in delicate florals, scenics, and wildlife studies. Azalea and Tree in the Meadow are two very collectible lines of dinnerware. We've listed several examples. Note: Tree in the Meadow is only one variant of the Scenic pattern. It depicts a thatched-roof cottage with a tree growing behind it, surrounded by a meadow and some water. Other variants that include features such as swans, bridges, dogs, windmills, etc., are not Tree in the Meadow.

## Azalea

Bowl, #12, 10"...........................**42.50**

Bowl, fruit; #9, 5¼"....................**8.00**

Bowl, vegetable; divided, #439, 9½"...................................**295.00**

Butter chip, #312, 3¼".............**90.00**

Candy jar, w/lid, #313............**625.00**

**Coffeepot, AD; #182, $695.00.**

Compote, #170..........................**98.00**

Creamer & sugar bowl, gold finial, #410................................**155.00**

Egg cup, #120...........................**45.00**

Mustard jar, #191, 3-pc............**35.00**

Olive dish, #194........................**25.00**

Plate, breakfast/luncheon; #98..**22.00**

Plate, dinner; #13, 9¾"............**22.00**
Platter, #17, 14"......................**60.00**
Relish, oval, #18, 8½"..............**20.00**
Spoon holder, #189, 8"............**120.00**
Teapot, #15 ...........................**125.00**

## Tree in the Meadow

Bowl, cream soup; 2-handle.....**75.00**
Bowl, vegetable; 9" ..................**35.00**

Cake plate, $35.00.

Celery dish................................**35.00**
Cheese dish..............................**95.00**
Compote ...................................**95.00**
Creamer & sugar bowl, berry..**125.00**
Gravy boat ...............................**40.00**
Lemon dish ..............................**15.00**
Platter, 10"..............................**125.00**
Tea tile .....................................**75.00**
Teapot ......................................**95.00**
Vase, fan form..........................**95.00**

## Miscellaneous

Ashtray, flowers on shaded cream, 4
    rests, 4¼" sq ......................**90.00**
Basket vase, red w/floral interior,
    gold handle, 5½"..............**140.00**
Bowl, irises on white, blue rim
    w/gold handles, 10½" ........**85.00**
Cake plate, exotic birds, pink border
    w/gold, 8¼" ......................**70.00**

Candy jar, river reserve & band on
    gold lustre, 6½" ..............**225.00**
Cheese dish, yellow band w/Deco
    flowers on white, slant lid, 8"
    L......................................**125.00**
Compote, floral on cream w/gold
    handles, footed, 9¾".........**80.00**
Condensed milk container, Deco
    floral w/gold, 5¼", +tray..**160.00**

**Cruet set, floral on white
with gold trim, red M-in-
wreath mark, from $60.00 to
$80.00.** (Photo courtesy Joan
Van Patten)

Egg cup, windmill & river scenic,
    earth tones, 3½" ...............**40.00**
Humidor, geometric floral on blue,
    pipe finial, 3¾" ...............**200.00**
Napkin ring, multicolored roses, 2¼"
    W.......................................**45.00**
Nappy, roses, pastels on cream, sin-
    gle handle, 5"....................**40.00**
Salt & pepper shakers, river scenic,
    earth tones, 2½", pr ..........**16.00**
Sugar shaker, floral band on white,
    gold top, 6½".....................**30.00**
Tea caddy, red mark, 3¾", from
    $235 to ............................**275.00**
Tea set, floral on black w/gold, 6" pot+,
    creamer & sugar bowl....**165.00**
Trinket dish, desert scene, earth
    tones, center handle, 2¼"..**25.00**

Vase, roses on long stems on white, handles, 8½" .....................**165.00**
Wall pocket, butterflies on tan lustre, red mark, 9" .............**125.00**

# Novelty Telephones

Novelty telephones representing well-known advertising or cartoon characters are proving to be the focus of lots of collector activity — the more recognizable the character, the better. Telephones modeled after product containers are collectible as well. For more information refer to *Schroeder's Collectible Toys, Antique to Modern* (Collector Books).

Alvin (Alvin & the Chipmunks), 1984, MIB ..........................**50.00**
Batmobile, Columbia, 1990, MIB, from $25 to.........................**35.00**
Bugs Bunny, Warner Exclusive, MIB, from $60 to ...............**70.00**
Darth Vader, 1983, MIB ........**200.00**
Garfield, MIB...........................**50.00**
Ghostbusters, Remco, 1987, MIB ...................................**30.00**
Mickey Mouse, Western Electric, 1976, MIB .......................**200.00**
Poppin' Fresh, Pillsbury, 1984, MIB .................................**100.00**
Power Rangers, MIP ................**30.00**
Raggedy Ann & Andy, Pay Phone, 1983, MIB ..........................**75.00**
Roy Rogers, 1950s, plastic wall type, MIB .................................**100.00**
R2-D2 (Star Wars), head spins, 12", MIB .................................**100.00**
Snoopy as Joe Cool, 1980s, MIB ..**50.00**
Star Trek Enterprise, 1993, MIB...**50.00**

Strawberry Shortcake, MIB.....**75.00**
Superman, early rotary type, MIB ...........................**500.00**
Ziggy, 1989, MIB .....................**75.00**

# Occupied Japan

Items with the 'Occupied Japan' mark were made during the period from the end of World War II until April 1952. Porcelains, novelties, paper items, lamps, silver plate, lacquer ware, and dolls are some of the areas of exported goods that may bear this stamp. Because the Japanese were naturally resentful of the occupation, it is felt that only a small percentage of their wares were thus marked. Although you may find identical items marked simply 'Japan,' only those with the 'Occupied Japan' stamp command values such as we have suggested below. For more information we recommend *Occupied Japan Collectibles* by Gene and Cathy Florence, published by Collector Books. Items in our listings are ceramic unless another material is noted, and figurines are of average, small size. See Clubs and Newsletters for information concerning The Occupied Japan Club.

Ashtray, baseball glove, metal......**15.00**
Ashtray, Georgia, shape of state, from $12.50 to....................**20.00**
Bell, Dutch girl figure in orange lustre skirt, sm ......................**20.00**
Butter dish, basketweave, holds stick butter .......................**20.00**

Candy dish, metal, 3-part, center handle, from $12.50 to ......**15.00**

Cigarette box, pagoda scene ....**30.00**

Cigarette lighter, metal knight figural, from $10 to................**25.00**

Coasters, papier-maché, floral decor, 8-pc set, w/box ...................**25.00**

Cookie jar, cottage shape .........**75.00**

Creamer, demitasse; floral w/lustre..................................**10.00**

Cup & saucer, pink chintz, marked Merit, from $10 to .............**25.00**

Cup & saucer, white w/vining floral decor, Merit .......................**20.00**

Dinnerware, complete set for 4 w/3 sizes of plates+various serving pcs ....................................**200.00**

Doll, celluloid, football player, 6", from $12 to.........................**20.00**

Egg cup, plain white w/gold middle & rim band .........................**12.50**

Figurine, bird on stump, multicolor, 7⅞", from $30 to ................**35.00**

Figurine, black musicians, 2¾", from any set of 5, ea..........**20.00**

Figurine, bride & groom on base, bisque, 6⅛" ........................**50.00**

Figurine, clown in striped suit, 5¼", from $35 to.........................**40.00**

**Figurine, couple at harpsicord, marked Mariyama, 4", $30.00.**

Figurine, dog, spaniel type, seated, 4⅜", from $20 to ...............**25.00**

Figurine, dog beside lamp, 2" ....**8.00**

Figurine, girl holding basket, 5½" ..................................**20.00**

Figurine, horse on base, white, 2¼", from $4 to.............................**5.00**

Figurine, Indian maiden standing, 4¼" ..................................**15.00**

Figurine, man in turban, 6".....**20.00**

Figurine, man w/cape, bisque, pastels, 6", from $25 to ...........**30.00**

Figurine, Oriental lady w/basket on head, 7⅞", from $20 to.....**25.00**

Figurine, Pacific island girl in grass skirt, 4" ..............................**20.00**

Ice bucket, lacquerware, 7⅝", from $50 to .................................**60.00**

Incense burner, elephant, white w/gold trim, 2½" ................**20.00**

Mug, elephant w/trunk forming handle, brown, 4¾"..................**20.00**

Pitcher, chicken form, white w/multicolor accents...................**25.00**

Planter, donkey w/green cart.....**15.00**

Planter, duck in bonnet, white w/floral decor .............................**15.00**

Planter, duck w/cart, 3x5", from $6 to ..........................................**7.50**

Planter, stuffed dog form, white w/roses & pink bow at neck, 5¾" ........**12.50**

Plate, roses, multicolor on shaded ground, 7", from $25 to .....**35.00**

Salt & pepper shakers, penguin form, metal, pr...................**20.00**

Tea set, floral, pot, creamer & sugar bowl, 2 cups/saucers, child's ..**45.00**

Teapot, windmill form..............**50.00**

Wall pocket, peacock on branch decor..................................**30.00**

Wall pocket, teapot w/flower decor, 6x8" ..................................**25.00**

# Paper Dolls

Though the history of paper dolls can be traced even farther back, by the late 1700s they were being mass produced. A century later, paper dolls were being used as an advertising medium by retail companies wishing to promote sales. But today the type most often encountered are in book form — the dolls on the cardboard covers, their wardrobe on the inside pages. These have been published since the 1920s. Celebrity and character-related dolls are the most popular with collectors, and condition is very important. If they have been cut out, even if they are still in fine condition and have all their original accessories, they're worth only about half as much as an uncut doll. In our listings, if no condition is given, values are for mint, uncut paper dolls. For more information, we recommend *Price Guide to Lowe and Whitman Paper Dolls* and *20th Century Paper Dolls*, both by Mary Young (see the Directory under Ohio) and *Paper Dolls of the 1960s, 1970s, and 1980s*, by Carol Nichols (Collector Books). For an expanded listings of values, see *Schroeder's Collectible Toys, Antique to Modern* (Collector Books). See Clubs and Newsletters for information concerning the *Paper Doll News*.

**Baby Dreams, Whitman #1982, 1976, from $8.00 to $15.00.** (Photo courtesy Carol Nichols)

Annette Cut-Outs, Disney, Whitman #1958, 1961, from $30 to...**50.00**

Ava Gardner, Whitman #965, 1949 ...............................**175.00**

Baby Go Bye Bye, Whitman/Western/Mattel #1988, 1971, from $10 to ..............................**20.00**

Baby PeeWee, Whitman/Western/Uneeda #4607, 1968, from $12 to ..............................**25.00**

Ballet Paper Doll, Saalfield/Artcraft #4233, 1972, from $15 to...**25.00**

Barbara Britton, Saalfield #4318, 1954, from $85 to ...........**150.00**

Barbie, Whitman/Mattel #1961, 1963, from $95 to ...........**125.00**

Big Jim & Big Jack,Whitman/Western/Mattel #1988, 1976, from $8 to ......................................**15.00**

Blondie, Saalfield #4434, 1968..**40.00**

Bride & Groom, Whitman #2070, 1963, from $20 to..............**30.00**

Bride Doll, Lowe #1043, 1946..**60.00**

Buffy, Whitman/Western #1995, 1968, from $35 to..............**45.00**

Carmen Miranda, Dover/Tim Tierney #24285-4, 1982, from $4 to..**10.00**

Cheerful Tearful, Whitman/Mattel #4740, 1966, from $15 to...**25.00**

Chitty-Chitty Bang-Bang, Whitman #1982, 1968........................**40.00**

Country Music Star Dottie West, Estelle Ansley Worrell, 1973, $8 to..**16.00**

Crissy & Velvet, Whitman/Western/Ideal #1996, 1971, from $20 to .........................................**35.00**

Cute Quintuplets, Watkins Strathmore/Western #1818-5, 1964, $15 to ...............................**30.00**

Dodie, Artcraft/Columbia Pictures #5115, 1971, from $25 to...**45.00**

Finger Ding, Whitman/Western/Remco #1993, 1971, from $10 to .........................................**18.00**

Gilda Radner, Avon #75217, 1979, from $9 to..........................**18.00**

Goldilocks & the Three Bears, Saalfield/ArtCraft #4211, 1970, from $20 to ...............................**30.00**

Grace Kelly, Dover/Tom Tierney #25180-2, 1986, from $5 to..**12.00**

Jack & Jill, 6 dolls, Merrill #1561, 1962, from $25 to...............**35.00**

Jackie & Caroline, Magic Wand Corp #107, 1960s, from $25 to....**40.00**

Joan Crawford, Dover/Tom Tierney #2456-9, 1983, from $4 to .**10.00**

Joanne Woodward, Saalfield #4436, 1958......................................**90.00**

Kewpie Dolls, Saalfield/Artcraft #6088, 1963, from $50 to...**80.00**

Magic Mary Ann, Milton Bradley #4010-2, 1972, from $10 to ..**25.00**

Marilyn Monroe, Dover Publications #23769-9, 1979, from $5 to..**12.00**

Mod Fashions Featuring Jane Fonda, Saalfield #4469, 1966, from $45 to..........................**65.00**

Mother & Daughter, Saalfield #4243, 1970, from $20 to...**30.00**

Oklahoma!, Whitman #1954, 1956..**100.00**

Paper Doll Playmates, Saalfield #1971, 1968, from $15 to...**25.00**

Petticoat Junction, Whitman #1954, 1964 ...............................**100.00**

**Pretty Belles, Whitman/Western, from $15.00 to $25.00.**
(Photo courtesy Carol Nichols)

Ricky Nelson, Whitman #2081, 1959 ...............................**100.00**

Sandra Dee, Saalfield #4417, 1959..**65.00**

Shirley Temple, Whitman/Western/Shirley T Black #1986, 1976, from $10 to...............**20.00**

Snow White, Peck-Gandre, 1987, from $5 to...........................**10.00**

Sugar 'n Spice, Saalfield #3644A, 1969, from $12 to...............**20.00**

Tabatha, Magic Wand #115, 1966..**100.00**

That Girl, Saalfield #1379, 1967..**55.00**

The Mods, Milton Bradley #4727, 1967, from $55 to...............**75.00**

Tiny Tots, Whitman/Western #1983, 1967, from $50 to...............**65.00**

Trixie, Lowe #3920, 1961.........**35.00**

Vera Miles, Whitman #2986, 1957, from $80 to ......................**125.00**

Wishnik, Whitman/Uneeda Doll Co #6503, 1965, from $15 to...**25.00**

Wonder Woman, Whitman #1398, 1979....................................**25.00**

Ziegfeld Girls, Merrill #3466, 1941 ...............................**400.00**

# Peanuts Collectibles

First introduced in 1950, the *Peanuts* comic strip soon became the world's most widely read cartoon, ultimately appearing in about 2,200 daily newspapers. From that funny cartoon about kids (that seemed to relate to readers of any age) sprung an entertainment arsenal featuring movies, books, Broadway shows, toys, theme parks, etc. At any flea market you'll always spot several *Peanuts* collectibles. United Media, the company that syndicates and licenses the *Peanuts* comic strip, estimates there are approximately 20,000 new products produced each year. If you want to collect, you should know that authenticity is important. The United Features Syndicate logo and copyright dates must appear somewhere on the item. In most cases the copyright date simply indicates the date that the character and his pose as depicted on the item first appeared in the comic strip.

For more information we recommend *Peanuts Collectibles* by Andrea Podley with Derrick Bang (Collector Books).

Banner, Love Is Walking Hand in Hand, Linus & Sally, 1967, 33x15" ...............................**22.50**
Banner, Snoopy in mailbox, I've Become Allergic to People, 34x14" ...............................**25.00**
Bell, Lucy & Snoopy, porcelain, Japan, 1958, 1½" ...............**20.00**

**Bell, Snoopy on doghouse, Willits Christmas Signature Series, 1987, 5", from $20.00 to $30.00.**

Book, The World According to Lucy, Schultz/Hallmark, 1969, NM ..**12.00**
Book, You're Supposed To Lead Charlie Brown, softcover, 1988, EX .....................................**12.50**
Bowl, ice cream; white w/Snoopy images, Fire-King, 2x4" .....**35.00**
Box, Peanuts Beauties, Marcie/Peppermint Patty, tin, 7x13" ..**17.50**
Crewel stitchery kit, Charlie Brown & Snoopy, UFS, 1958, MIP .....**12.00**
Doll, Linus, plastic, Boucher Assoc, 7½x4x3", EX .....................**20.00**
Doll, Linus, rubber, UFS, 8½", EX .....................................**40.00**
Doll, Sally, plush, Irwin Toy USA #2600, 7", MIB..................**17.50**
Earrings, Snoopy figural, marked 14k gold/UFS, ½", pr.........**35.00**
Figurine, Charlie Brown, w/bat & ball cap, painted wood, Anri, 1972 ................................**140.00**
Figurine, Charlie Brown w/Snoopy as Easter Bunny, resin, UFS, 4" .......................................**18.00**
Figurine, Lucy, Hungerford Plastics, 1958, 8½", MIP .................**250.00**

Figurine, Sally, ...Warms the Heart, Hallmark #LE14573, 2002..**10.00**

Game, Lucy's Tea Party, Milton Bradley, 1971, complete, EXIB..........**8.00**

Jack-in-the-box, Snoopy, Mattel, 1966, EX ............................**15.00**

**Mug, Put Snoopy in the White House, milk glass, Anchor Hocking, 1980, $25.00.**

Nodder, Charlie Brown, Ledo, 1960s................................**135.00**

Ornament, Linus playing sax, UFS 1952, Made in Japan.............**30.00**

Ornament, Linus w/Snoopy & Woodstock, w/verse, Hallmark, 2¾", MIB ....................................**35.00**

Plaque, Linus, sucking thumb/holding blanket, UFS, 1966, 10½x8"..**140.00**

Plate, Linus & Snoopy, Mother's Day 1976, Schmid, M (EX box)..**20.00**

Plate, Mother's Day 1976, Linus & Snoopy, Made in Japan, 7½"..**20.00**

Playset, Great Pumpkin Halloween, MIB ....................................**35.00**

Playset, Marcie/Peppermint Patty ...Baseball Dugout, Memory Lane, MIB..........................**40.00**

Puzzle, frame-tray; Linus w/blanket, Playskool #230-25, 7-pc, 1952, EX ......................................**12.00**

Puzzle, frame-tray; Lucy skipping rope, Playskool, 11-pc, 1952, EX ......................................**17.50**

Recipe box, white & orange w/graphics, Hallmark, 1965, 3x5", EX..**27.50**

Rug kit (latch hook), Charlie Brown, JP Coats, 13x13", MIB ........**15.00**

Salt & pepper shakers, Charlie Brown & Snoopy, china, 2⅜", pr......................................**25.00**

Snow Cone Machine, Snoopy atop doghouse, Hasbro, 1999, MIB....**18.00**

Snow globe, The Doctor Is In, musical, 50th Anniversary, M (EX box)....................................**25.00**

Tea set, white w/the Gang's images, pot w/2 cups, Choco Emmy, MIB ....................................**20.00**

Toy, Snoopy's Wind-Up Train, International Trading Technology, MIB ....................................**30.00**

Trash can, metal w/painted scene, Cheinco, 1966, 13", NM ....**22.50**

Tray, white w/Peanuts gang, tin litho, 1961, 7⅝x5⅝", NM ..**22.50**

TV tray, Peanuts Gang, litho tin, 1960s-70s, 12¾x17½", NM ....................................**30.00**

## Pennsbury Pottery

From the 1950s through the 1970s, dinnerware and novelty ware produced by the Pennsbury company was sold through tourist gift shops along the Pennsylvania turnpike. Much of their ware was decorated in an Amish theme. A group of barbershop singers was another popular design, and they made a line of bird figures that were very similar to Stangl's, though today much harder to find.

Ashtray, It's Making Down......**18.00**
Ashtray, Pennsbury Inn, 8".....**45.00**
Bowl, Hex, 9"...........................**40.00**
Bowl, pretzel; Amish, 12x8".....**100.00**
Butter dish, 3 Tulips................**45.00**
Candlesticks, Bird Over Heart, 2x5",
    pr.......................................**90.00**
Candlesticks, hummingbirds, #117,
    5", pr ...............................**250.00**
Canister, Folkart, Tea, 6½"......**100.00**
Cigarette box, Eagle, w/lid, 2½x4¼"...**50.00**
Coaster, Luigi...........................**20.00**

**Coaster, $20.00; Pitcher, 7", $50.00; Mug, beer, $25.00.**

Coffee mug, Amish, 3¼"..........**30.00**
Coffee mug, Gay Ninety, 3¼".....**40.00**
Coffee mug, Hex.......................**22.00**
Cookie jar, Red Barn, w/lid .....**250.00**
Cup & saucer, Penna Hex........**30.00**
Egg cup, Red Rooster, 4".........**20.00**
Figurine, Cardinal, #120, 6½".....**175.00**
Figurine, Crested Chickadee, #101,
    4".....................................**150.00**
Figurine, Slick-Chick, bluebird, 5½"..**45.00**
Figurine, Wood Duck, #114, facing
    right, 10"..........................**375.00**
Pie pan, Hex Star.....................**60.00**
Pitcher, Amish, Amish lady depict-
    ed, 2½"...............................**30.00**
Plaque, Eagle, 13"..................**110.00**
Plaque, Toleware, brown, 5x7".....**40.00**

Plate, Blue Dowery, 10"...........**35.00**
Plate, Red Barn, 8"..................**75.00**
Platter, Folkart, 14x11"...........**30.00**
Powder jar, Hex, w/lid, 6½".....**65.00**
Tile, Harvest, sq, 6"................**12.00**
Wall pocket, Red Rooster, sq,
    6½"...................................**65.00**

## Pez Dispensers

Originally a breath mint target-ed for smokers, by the '50s Pez had been diverted toward the kid's candy market, and to make sure the kids found them appealing, the company designed dispensers they'd be sure to like — many of them characters the kids could easily recognize. On today's collectible market, some of those dispensers bring astonishing prices!

Though early on collectors pre-ferred the dispensers with no feet, today they concentrate primarily on the character heads. Feet were added in 1987, so if you want your collection to be complete, you'll need to buy both styles. For further infor-mation and more listings, see *Schroeder's Collectible Toys, Antique to Modern* (Collector Books). Our values are for mint dispensers. Very few are worth collecting if they are damaged or have missing parts. See Clubs and Newsletters for informa-tion concerning *Pez Collector News*.

Angel, no feet...........................**75.00**
Bambi, no feet...........................**50.00**
Batman, no feet.......................**10.00**
Bozo, no feet, diecut...............**175.00**

| | |
|---|---|
| Bullwinkle, no feet ................**200.00** | Spike, w/feet ..............................**6.00** |
| Casper, no feet........................**175.00** | Thor, no feet...........................**300.00** |
| Chip, w/feet..............................**45.00** | Tom, no feet .............................**35.00** |
| Cool Cat, w/feet .......................**75.00** | Tweety Bird, no feet................**15.00** |
| Daffy Duck, no feet..................**15.00** | Tyke, w/feet .............................**15.00** |
| Doctor, no feet........................**200.00** | Wile E Coyote, w/feet ..............**60.00** |
| | Wolfman, no feet ...................**275.00** |
| | Woodstock, w/feet, from $1 to ....**3.00** |
| | Zorro.......................................**65.00** |

**Donald Duck and Mickey Mouse, no feet, from $10.00 to $15.00 each.** (Photo courtesy Michael Stern)

Donald Duck's Nephew, no feet..**30.00**
Dumbo, w/feet, blue head.........**25.00**
Fireman, no feet ......................**80.00**
Football Player .......................**175.00**
Frog, w/feet, whistle head........**40.00**
Girl, w/feet, yellow hair..............**3.00**
Hulk, no feet, light green, remake..**3.00**
Inspector Clouseau, w/feet.........**5.00**
Koala, w/feet, whistle head......**40.00**
Lucy, w/feet, from $1 to..............**3.00**
Mowgli, w/feet...........................**15.00**
Odie, w/feet ................................**5.00**
Papa Smurf, w/feet, red .............**6.00**
Pilgrim, no feet .......................**150.00**
Pluto, no feet............................**15.00**
Ringmaster, no feet................**250.00**
Road Runner, w/feet................**15.00**
Sheik, no feet............................**55.00**
Spaceman, no feet ..................**150.00**

## Pfaltzgraff Pottery

Since early in the seventeenth century, pottery has been produced in York County, Pennsylvania. The Pfaltzgraff Company that operates there today is the outgrowth of several of these small potteries. A changeover made in 1940 redirected their efforts toward making the dinnerware lines for which they are now best known. Their earliest line, a glossy brown with a white frothy drip glaze around the rim, was called Gourmet Royale. Today collectors find an abundance of good examples and are working toward reassembling sets of their own. Village, another very successful line, is tan with a stencilled Pennsylvania Dutch-type floral design in brown. It was all but discontinued a few years ago (they do make a few pieces for collectors now), and already Village fans are turning to secondary market sources to replace and replenish their services. The line is very extensive and offers an interesting array of items.

Giftware consisting of ashtrays, mugs, bottle stoppers, a cookie jar, etc., all with comic character faces were made in the 1940s. This line was called Muggsy, and it is also very collectible, with the more common mugs starting at about $35.00 each. For more information refer to *The Collector's Encyclopedia of American Dinnerware* by Jo Cunningham (Collector Books) and *Pfaltzgraff, America's Potter*, by David A. Walsh and Polly Stetler, published in conjunction with the Historical Society of York County, York, Pennsylvania.

Christmas Heritage, bowl, soup/cereal; #009, 5½", from $4 to ..**7.00**
Christmas Heritage, pedestal mug, #290, 10-oz............................**5.00**
Gourmet Royale, ashtray, #321, 7¾", from $9 to ..................**12.00**

**Gourmet Royale, au gratin, #7633, 11" long, $9.00.**

Gourmet Royale, baker, #321, oval, 7½", from $8 to ..................**10.00**
Gourmet Royale, bean pot, #11-1, 1-qt, from $10 to ....................**12.00**
Gourmet Royale, bean pot, #11-3, 3-qt ......................................**25.00**
Gourmet Royale, bean pot, #30, w/lid, lg, from $30 to .........**40.00**
Gourmet Royale, bowl, #241, oval, 7x10", from $10 to .............**12.00**
Gourmet Royale, bowl, mixing; 6", from $8 to............................**12.00**

Gourmet Royale, bowl, soup; 2¼x7¼", from $6 to..............................**9.00**
Gourmet Royale, bowl, vegetable; #341, divided .....................**14.00**
Gourmet Royale, canister set, 4-pc, from $50 to................**60.00**
Gourmet Royale, casserole, stick handle, 1-qt, from $9 to.....**12.00**
Gourmet Royale, casserole, stick handle, 4-qt, from $25 to............**35.00**
Gourmet Royale, cheese shaker, bulbous, 5¾", from $12 to.........**15.00**
Gourmet Royale, creamer, #382, from $3 to............................**5.00**
Gourmet Royale, cup & saucer, from $4 to ....................................**5.00**
Gourmet Royale, egg/relish tray, 15" L, from $16 to ....................**20.00**
Gourmet Royale, gravy boat, w/stick handle, 2-spout, from $8 to..**12.00**
Gourmet Royale, jug, #386, ice lip, from $25 to.........................**30.00**
Gourmet Royale, ladle, 3½" dia bowl w/11" handle, from $12 to.**15.00**
Gourmet Royale, mug, #391, 12-oz, from $5 to............................**7.00**
Gourmet Royale, pie plate, #7016, 9½", from $10 to ................**15.00**
Gourmet Royale, plate, grill; #87, 3-section, 11", from $9..........**12.00**
Gourmet Royale, plate, steak; 12", from $10 to.........................**15.00**
Gourmet Royale, platter, #337, 16", from $18 to.........................**20.00**
Gourmet Royale, relish dish, #265, 5x10", $12 to .....................**15.00**
Gourmet Royale, roaster, #326, oval, 16", from $25 to .................**32.00**
Gourmet Royale, salt & pepper shakers, bell shape, pr ......**18.00**
Gourmet Royale, shirred egg dish, #360, 6", from $7 to ...........**10.00**

Gourmet Royale, sugar bowl, from
$4 to .....................................**6.00**

Gourmet Royale, tray, 3-part, 15½"
L ...........................................**25.00**

Heritage, cup & saucer, #002-002, 9-
oz ...........................................**3.00**

Muggsy, ashtray.....................**125.00**

Muggsy, cigarette server..........**95.00**

Muggsy, clothes sprinkler bottle,
Myrtle, white...................**275.00**

Muggsy, mug, Black action figure ..**125.00**

Muggsy, shot mug, character face,
ea, from $40 to...................**50.00**

Planter, donkey, brown drip, common, 10", from $15 to........**20.00**

Village, baker, #240, oval, 10¼",
from $6 to..........................**8.00**

**Village, batter bowl, 8", from
$32.00 to $40.00.**

Village, bean pot, 2½-qt, from $22
to ........................................**28.00**

Village, beverage server, #490, from
$18 to ................................**22.00**

Village, bowl, rim soup; #012, 8½"..**6.00**

Village, bowl, soup/cereal; #009, 6",
from.....................................**4.50**

Village, bread tray, 12", from $14
to ........................................**16.00**

Village, canisters, #520, 4-pc set,
from $45 to.........................**55.00**

Village, coffee mug, #89F, 10-oz,
from $5 to............................**8.00**

Village, creamer & sugar bowl,
#020, from $9 to.................**12.00**

Village, flowerpot, 4½", from $12
to .......................................**15.00**

Village, pedestal mug, #90F,
10-oz..................................**10.00**

Village, plate, dinner; #004, 10¼",
from $3 to............................**4.00**

Village, spoon rest, #515, 9" L, from
$6 to ...................................**7.50**

# Pie Birds

What is a pie bird? It is a functional and decorative kitchen tool
most commonly found in the shape of
a bird, designed to vent steam
through the top crust of a pie to prevent the juices from spilling over into
the oven. Other popular designs were
elephants and black-faced bakers.
The original vents that were used in
England and Wales in the 1800s
were simply shaped like funnels.

From the 1980s to the present,
many novelty pie vents have been
added to the market for the baker
and the collector. Some of these
could be obtained from Far East
Imports; others have been made in
England and the US (by commercial
and/or local enterprises). Examples
can be found in the shapes of animals (dogs, frogs, elephants, cats,
goats, and dragons), people (police-
men, chefs with and without pies,
pilgrims, and carolers), or whimsical
figurals (clowns, leprechauns, and
teddy bears). A line of holiday-related pie vents was made in the 1990s.

Consequently a collector must
be on guard and aware that these
new pie vents are being sold by deal-

ers (knowingly in many instances) as old or rare, often at double or triple the original cost (which is usually under $10.00). Though most of the new ones can't really be called reproductions since they never existed before, there's a black bird that is a remake, and you'll see them everywhere. Here's how you can spot them: they'll have yellow beaks and protruding white-dotted eyes. If they're on a white base and have an orange beak, they are the older ones. Another basic tip that should help you distinguish old from new: older pie vents are air-brushed versus being hand painted. Please note that incense burners, one-hole pepper shakers, dated brass toy bird whistles, and ring holders (for instance, the elephant with a clover on his tummy) should not be mistaken for pie vents. See Clubs and Newsletters for information concerning *Pie Birds Unlimited Newsletter.*

Apple, red on white base, paper label: Our Own Import Japan, EX ..................................... **300.00**

Bear in green jacket, w/hat & shoes, England, 4½" ..................... **55.00**

Benny the Baker, w/2 utensils, 5½" ................................... **150.00**

Bird, cream w/floral decor, gold beak, porcelain, 4½" .................... **200.00**

Bird, multicolored, Morton, from $45 to ............................... **65.00**

Bird, white w/blue, Royal Worchester, 1960s, 4¼", MIB ... **90.00**

Bird, white w/pink eyes & wings, green base & beak, EX ...... **30.00**

Blackbird, blue w/beige beak, 4" .. **30.00**

Blackbird, yellow beak, 2½", NM ................................... **110.00**

Blackbird, yellow beak & eyes, 4" ........................................ **35.00**

Cherries, paper label reads Our Own Import Japan, on white base ................................... **300.00**

Chicken in chef's hat, Made in England, 3¾" ........................... **50.00**

Crow, black, Made in England, 1950s-60s, 4¼" ................... **55.00**

Dalmatian, seated, 1980s ........ **40.00**

**Duck, bright rose with black and yellow, unmarked, 5", $75.00.**

Eagle, golden color, marked Sunglow, from $75 to ............... **85.00**

Funnel, marked Grimwade Perfection, 1909, from $90 to ............ **110.00**

Funnel, wheat stalk, brown, from $150 to ............................. **175.00**

Humpty Dumpty, trimmed in gold, 1999, 5" ............................. **50.00**

Pie Duckling, blue or pink, American Pottery Co, 5", from $55 to.. **65.00**

Rooster, multicolored tail feathers, Cleminson, 4¼", EX .......... **50.00**

Rooster on chimney peak, 6" .....**50.00**

Welch lady, marked Cyrmu, from $75 to ................................**95.00**

Whites of Guilford, black letters on white, 2½" ..........................**35.00**

3-fruits series, peach, apple & cherries, Japan, 2½", ea from $350 to ......................................**400.00**

# Pin-Back Buttons

Because most of the pin-backs prior to the 1920s were made of celluloid, collectors refer to them as 'cellos.' Many were issued in sets on related topics. Some advertising buttons had paper inserts on the back that identified the company or the product they were advertising. After the 1920s lithographed metal buttons were produced; they're now called 'lithos.'

See also The Beatles; Elvis Presley; Political.

Aerial Bloodline Program, American Red Cross, TN Valley Region, EX ......................................**40.00**

Bozo the Clown, 2¼", EX .........**55.00**

Buttermilk, Dale Evan's horse, 1953 Post Grapenuts, EX............**27.50**

Dick Tracy Detective, Read Dick Tracy Everyday in Chicago Tribune, VG+ ..........................**45.00**

Hooters Superwoman/Server, NM ......................................**55.00**

Hyde Park Milk & Ice Cream, Hoppy's Favorite, Hopalong Cassidy, EX .......................**70.00**

I've Seen the 1953 Chevrolet It's Great, logo center, EX.......**45.00**

International Balloon Fiesta, hot-air balloon shape, 1976, EX.....**100.00**

Jordan (MN) Winter Sports, I Belong, 1940, 1¾", EX.......**25.00**

Member Babe Ruth Baseball Club, black on white, 1930s, 1", EX ..**35.00**

Member Dick Tracy Secret Service Patrol, Parisian Novelty, 1½", EX ......................................**25.00**

Merrill Lynch, New Mexico, hot-air balloon, 1¼", EX................**40.00**

Merry Christmas, American Baptist Publication Society on back, 1", EX ......................................**25.00**

MN Vikings 1974 National Conference Champs, team image, 6" dia, EX ..............................**32.50**

New York Giants 1951 World Series, Press, ball shape, NM........**375.00**

Peter Max Clan Fub, lg toothy smile, Peter Max style, 2½", EX ......................................**27.50**

Rough Rider, Teddy Roosevelt in uniform, celluloid, 2¼" dia, EX ................................**1,150.00**

Snow White & the Seven Dwarfs, marked 1938 WD Ent, 3½" dia, EX+ ................................**580.00**

Souvenir of Beech-Nut Gum Autogiro 1931, 1¾", EX.............**32.50**

Stan the Man Musial, stained, 2", VG ......................................**65.00**

The In Crowd, Charlie Brown & friends, celluloid, 1966, 3", NM ............**35.00**

**To Hell With Hitler, white on blue, 1940s era, 1¼", NM, $20.00.**

Trixy, Old Style Cooking Molasses,
DB Scully, Black Americana,
EX ......................................**30.00**
Workmen's Circle Camp, Swan Lake
NY, men in boats, 1¼", EX..**25.00**

## Pep Pins

In the late '40s and into the '50s, some cereal companies packed a pin-back button in each box of their product. Quaker Puffed Oats offered a series of movie star pin-backs, but Kellogg's Pep Pins are probably the best known of all. There were eighty-six different Pep pins. They came in five sets — the first in 1945, three more in 1946, and the last in 1947. They were printed with full-color lithographs of comic characters licensed by King Features and Famous Artists — Maggie and Jiggs, the Winkles, and Dagwood and Blondie, for instance. Superman, the only D.C. Comics character, was included in each set. Most Pep pins range in value from $10.00 to $15.00 in NM/M condition; for a complete listing we recommend *Garage Sale & Flea Market Annual* (Collector Books).

Barney Google, EX+ .................**55.00**
BO Plenty, EX .........................**20.00**
Brenda Star, EX......................**20.00**
Chester Gump, MIP .................**32.00**
Cindy, EX..................................**15.00**
Corky, 1946, EX.......................**15.00**
Daddy Warbucks, EX...............**12.00**
Denny, EX.................................**40.00**
Dick Tracy, EX .........................**20.00**
Felix the Cat, 1946, EX............**40.00**

**Fire Chief, EX, $14.00.**

Flash Gordon, EX....................**20.00**
Flat Top, EX .............................**55.00**
Fritz, EX ...................................**12.00**
Kayo, NM...................................**12.00**
Little Joe, EX.............................**12.50**
Little King, NM .........................**15.00**
Maggie, EX ................................**15.00**
Moon Mullins, NM ...................**10.00**
Navy Torpedo Squadron, NM.....**15.00**
Olive Oyl, NM............................**18.00**
Orphan Annie, EX....................**18.00**
Pat Patton, EX............................**9.00**
Perry Winkle, NM ....................**15.00**
Popeye, EX................................**18.00**
Punjab, EX.................................**15.00**
Superman, EX ...........................**20.00**
Tess Trueheart, EX..................**14.00**
The Captain, EX........................**14.00**
Toots, EX...................................**10.00**
Uncle Avery, EX .......................**15.00**
Wimpy, M (in cello wrapper)......**55.00**
Yellow Kid, #10, I'm Jist As Irish
As You If Me Dress Is Taller,
EX ......................................**35.00**
Yellow Kid, #6, w/hat & cane, Say I
Won't Do a Ting Ter Broadway,
EX ......................................**35.00**

# Pinup Art

Collectors of pinup art look for blotters, calendars, prints, playing cards, etc., with illustrations of sexy girls by artists who are famous for their work in this venue: Vargas, Petty, DeVorss, Elvgren, Moran, Mozert, Ballantyne, Armstrong, and Davis among them. Though not all items will be signed, most of these artists have a distinctive style that is easy to recognize.

**Calendar, Elvgren girl on scale, thermometer insert, 1947, 10x8", EX, $125.00.** (Photo courtesy Dunbar Gallery)

Calendar page, April, 1970, Willis, Brown & Bigelow, 12x9", EX...**22.50**

Calendar page, March, 1947, Esquire, Vargas, 12x8½", EX ...............**22.50**

Calendar page, November, 1950, Al Moore, Esquire, 12x8½", EX ..**25.00**

Calendar page, October, 1947, Esquire, Vargas, 8x12", EX..**22.50**

Calendar print, Esquire, Vargas, June, 1947, 12x8½", EX......**40.00**

Calendar print, fishing lady in overalls, 1955, Petty, 11x8", EX ......**45.00**

Calendar print, girl fishing off rock w/dog, Miller, 24x20", EX .....**35.00**

Calendar print, girl w/dress pulled up hitchhiking, Elvgren, 9x7", EX ......................................**12.00**

Calendar print, Is My Face Red, bowler, Elvgren, 1940s, 9x7", EX .....................................**16.50**

Calendar print, lady in white & pink, Armstrong, 1940s, 16x19½", EX....................**110.00**

Calendar print, Lovely To Look At, Frahm, 1947, 30x14", EX.....**20.00**

Calendar print, Nightie in a Cape, DeVorss, 1930s, 7x5", EX.....**15.00**

Calendar print, nude w/black shawl, Elvgren, 1940s, 16x19½", EX..**85.00**

Calendar print, Reflection, Oval & Koster, 1944, 30x16", EX.....**45.00**

Calendar print, Remember Me, Esquire, Petty, 1940s, 19¾x14½", EX .......................................**22.50**

Calendar print, Reverie, Moran, 1940s, 15x19", EX .............**85.00**

Calendar print, She Knows the Ropes, lady on swing, Best, 1940s, EX...........................**18.50**

Calendar print, Sit Down Stripes, Frahm, 1940s, 9½x7½", EX..**16.50**

Pocket mirror, nude on crescent moon, 1940s, 3x2", EX ......**30.00**

Print, girl on beach w/dog pulling off top, Layne, 1960s, 9x7", EX..**30.00**

Print, nude blonde on phone, Petty, 19¾x14½", EX ...................**50.00**

Print, nude in sheer nightie, phone hangs from hand, Petty, 18x12", EX .......................................**45.00**

Print, Over Exposed, Elvgren, 1940s, 9½x7½", EX ...........**35.00**

Print, Study in Blue, J Erbit, Oval & Koster #1632, 1944, 30x16", NM .................................**125.00**

Print, The Pink Lady, DeVorss, 1940s, 9¼x7½", EX ...........**30.00**

Punch board, lady w/dog & shopping boxes, Elvgren, 9¾x8⅞", EX..**30.00**

Puzzle, jigsaw; blond, Vargas, 500 pcs, 1940s, unopened, MIP (tube)..................................**17.50**

# Playing Cards

Here is another collectible that is inexpensive, easy to display (especially single cards), and very diversified. Variations are endless. Some backs are printed with reproductions of famous paintings or pinup art. Others carry advertising messages, picture tourist attractions, or commemorate a world's fair. Early decks are scarce, but those from the 1940s on are usually more attractive anyway, so pick an area that interests you most and have fun! Though they're usually not dated, you may find some clues that will help you to determine an approximate date. Telephone numbers, zip codes, advertising slogans, and patriotic messages are always helpful.

Bicycle #808 Ivory Finish, red Cupid backs, EXIB ......................**125.00**
Caterpillar, 25 Years of Service, 1952, double deck, MIB.....**65.00**
Chessie & Peake, C&O RR, double deck, plastic case, M (sealed)................................**45.00**
Chicago & North Western RW, scene w/train passing, sealed deck, EX box ......................**40.00**
Dogs (3), SR Huntley, 1932, 52+2 Jokers, EX+ ......................**40.00**
Flamingos on turquoise, plastic, Kem, 1947, double deck, M in case ..................................**110.00**

Fox Hunt, mounted hunter w/foxes, linen finish, 52 no Joker, EX ......................................**15.00**
Golden Nugget Gambling Hall, MIB (sealed)..............................**65.00**
Great Lakes, Indian maiden on blanket, 52+Joker+2 extra cards, 1910, M .................**110.00**
Great Northern RR, Indian image on ea, double deck, MIB (sealed)..............................**55.00**
Hamm's Beer, Hamm's Bear on face, 1950s, EXIB......................**30.00**
Hooters, different girls on back, 2000, MIP (sealed) ............**15.00**
Hummingbirds, double deck, KEM #356, EXIB ........................**40.00**
Hummingbirds, plastic, Kem, 1947, double deck, M in case ......**90.00**
IL Central RR, piggyback yard scene, double deck, M (sealed case) ....................................**38.50**
Kennedy Kards, caricatures of family, Humor House, 1963, NMIB ..**38.50**
Kerrang Magazine, black & white pictures of Rock Stars, 1990s, MIB ....................................**55.00**
Knights of the Sea, Elco PT's, Brown & Bigelow, 1940s, MIP (sealed)..............................**45.00**
Lady w/Scottie dog, double deck, 52+ Joker (Buy War ...Bonds), EXIB ..................................**50.00**
Lockheed Military Airplanes, 52+Joker, EXIB.................**40.00**
Louis Vuitton, Heron Company (France), 1970s, MIP (sealed)...................**60.00**
Minneapolis Moline, machinery on face, 52 no Joker, EXIB ....**35.00**
Nixon Presidential Yacht, w/Presidential Seal, 52+2 Jokers, EXIB ..................................**80.00**

Olympic Games Melbourne, 1956,
double deck, plastic case,
EX .....................................**40.00**
Pabst Blue Ribbon, white w/logo,
MIB ...................................**30.00**

**Peacock backs, US Playing
Card Co., double deck, 1950s,
MIB, $20.00.**

Pepsi-Cola, white w/logo, 1963,
EXIB ..................................**45.00**
Pete Rose, Pepsi-Cola 1976 Super-
stars of Baseball #643, MIP
(sealed)..............................**40.00**
Playboy, Bicycle back version, ca
1973, MIB (sealed) ............**65.00**
Red Cross, dated 7/7/48, US Playing
Cards, EXIB ......................**35.00**
Sailor Jerry, various tattoos by Jerry
Collins, MIB (sealed).........**45.00**
Tennent's Pilsner, crooked cards (die-
cut Z-shape), 1980s, MIB ....**17.50**
Wabash RR, train scene, felt case,
MIP (sealed) .....................**35.00**

# Plush Toys

Always popular with the children, soft and cuddly plush toys are
gaining the interest of adult collectors
as well. Character-related plush toys
seem to be most popular, especially
characters that are movie or Disney
related. Condition is everything. Look
for items that are in the finest and
cleanest condition possible. There is
little or no interest in plush items
that are soiled, damaged, or faded.

**Bear in the Big Blue House,
Disney, 18", M, $40.00.**

Big Bird, 60" .............................**50.00**
Bugs Bunny, Warner Bros Studio,
40" .....................................**45.00**
Count Von Count, Sesame Street,
Gund, 13" ...........................**35.00**
Curious George, Knickerbocker,
13½" ...................................**65.00**
Dash, The Incredibles, talking,
13½" ...................................**60.00**
Donkey, Shrek, 17x18".............**30.00**
Elmo, w/car on T-shirt, Sesame Steet,
Gund #75890, 13" ...............**30.00**
Flower, Bambi, Disney, 9" .......**35.00**
Geoffrey the Giraffe, Toys-R-Us,
talking, 18" ........................**40.00**
Kermit the Frog, Sesame Street,
60" .....................................**70.00**
Lilo, Lilo & Stitch, 10¼" ..........**35.00**
Mickey Mouse, Disney, 45"......**60.00**
Paploo the Ewok, Star Wars, 1984,
16" .....................................**35.00**
Rabbit, Winnie the Pooh, Disney,
20" .....................................**37.50**

Ren & Stimpy, Nickleodeon, pr .**40.00**
Roadrunner, Looney Tunes, 53"..**130.00**
Scooby Doo, 24"..........................**55.00**
Scrat, Ice Age, w/tag, 14".........**70.00**
Sid the Sloth, Ice Age, 10"........**50.00**
Sponge Bob Square Pants, 42x27"..**50.00**
Tazmanian Devil, Looney Tunes,
    48".....................................**40.00**
Teddy Ruxpin, JC Penney mail-
    order, 1992, w/storybook & cas-
    sette, MIB..........................**65.00**
Tickle Me Elmo, Sesame Street,
    Tyco, MIB ..........................**40.00**
Tigger, Winnie the Pooh, back-pack,
    15⅜".................................**40.00**
White Rabbit, Alice in Wonderland,
    Silvestri, 1985, 27"............**90.00**
White Snuffles, Snap-On Tools, 13",
    M (w/tags).......................**105.00**
Winnie the Pooh, 27"...............**55.00**

# Political Collectibles

Pennants, posters, badges, pamphlets — in general, anything related to a presidential campaign or politicians — are being sought by collectors who have an interest in the political history of our country. Most valued are items from a particularly eventful period or those things having to do with an especially colorful personality.

Celluloid pin-back buttons ('cellos') were first widely used in the 1896 presidential campaign; before that time medals, ribbons, and badges of various kinds predominated. Prices for political pin-backs have increased considerably in the last few years, more due to specula-tive buying and selling rather than inherent scarcity or unusual demand. It is still possible, however, to find quality collectible items at reasonable prices. In flea markets, recent buttons tend to be overpriced; the goal, as always, is to look for less familiar items that may be priced more reasonably. Most buttons issued since the 1964 campaign, with a few notable exceptions, should be in the range of $2.00 to $10.00. Condition is critical: cracks, scratches, spots, and brown stains ('foxing') seriously reduce the value of a button.

Prices are for items in excellent condition. Reproductions are common; many are marked as such, but it takes some experience to tell the difference. The best reference book for political collectors is Edmund Sullivan's *Collecting Political Americana, 2nd Edition*.

See Clubs and Newsletters for information concerning Political Collectors of Indiana.

Book, One Brief Shining...Kennedy,
    Manchester, 1983 1st edition ..**16.00**
Book, Quotations From Our Presi-
    dents, Peter Pauper Press,
    1969, M ............................**18.00**
Bookends, JFK w/quote on
    top, bronze, 1960s, 8x5¾x3",
    EX .....................................**95.00**
Booklet, Barry Goldwater Speaks
    Out on Issues, 1964, 24 pages,
    EX .....................................**20.00**
Bracelet, blue enamel w/gold-tone
    PT boat, gold-plated chain, JFK,
    EX .....................................**45.00**

Brochure, Welcome Aboard, Air Force One, 1970s, 12 pages, 5x7", NM ............................**65.00**

Brochure, 1968 Democratic Convention, Chicago, Yippie, 8 pages, EX ....................................**170.00**

Bust, Reagan, painted resin on wooden base, J Randell, 8", M ....**55.00**

Candy, M&M's served on Air Force One, seal & Bill Clinton on box, NM ....................................**20.00**

Candy holder, boot, porcelain, 5½", M (sealed w/jelly beans)....**20.00**

Christmas card, green w/embossed wreath & White House, 1970, EX ....................................**50.00**

Christmas card, The President's House Washington, Hallmark, 1974, EX ...........................**22.50**

**Cigarette pack, Eisenhower portrait, I Like Ike, red, white, and blue, 1950s, unopened, EX, $75.00.** (Photo courtesy B.J. Summers)

Coffee cup, Socks the cat (Clinton's), white w/black, 2", NM.......**20.00**

Coin, Clinocchio, Clinton caricature w/long nose, 1-oz silver, 1½"....................................**17.50**

Cuff links, presidential seal, George W Bush engraved on back, MIB..**85.00**

Cuff links, presidential seal, Gerald Ford engraved on back, MIB............**75.00**

Dashboard ornament, Barry Goldwater, Emco, 1964, 3", M (VG box)......................................**35.00**

Easter egg, for White House Staff, white w/black letters, 1997, NM ....................................**35.00**

Easter egg, White House for Children 1994 on green, NM ...**17.50**

Hat, white floppy beach style w/Nixon Now in circles, cotton, 1972, EX ...........................**15.00**

Invitation, Inauguration, Clinton, 1997, M ...........................**50.00**

Invitation, Inauguration, George HW Bush, 1989, 11x8½", M.......**20.00**

Invitation, Inauguration, Reagan/ Bush, 1981, 11½x8⅜", NM..**40.00**

Invitation, White House Coffee, from Mrs Bush, 1989, NM ..........**25.00**

Invitation, White House Holiday Tour, 2000, 5½x6", NM.....**12.00**

License plate, Happy Birthday President Reagan, 1989, IL, NM..**45.00**

Magnet set, Slick Willy, Clinton in underwear, complete, MIP..**15.00**

Matchbook, presidential seal, Ronald William Reagan on back, unused, M ................**30.00**

Medallion, embossed Reagan image w/Capitol Building on back, bronze, M ...........................**60.00**

Menu, Amtrak's Peanut Special, Jimmy Carter's Inaugural train, 1977, M ...........................**110.00**

Money clip, gold w/presidential seal, Bill Clinton on box, 2x1", MIB ....................................**25.00**

Necktie, Kennedy for President & donkey head, white on blue, EX ....................................**50.00**

Paperweight, 1964 Republican National Convention, elephant on base, EX .........................**45.00**

Pennant, Kennedy/Johnson Inauguration, 1961, 27", EX......**35.00**

Pin, gold donkey w/Carter, 2", NM+ ..................................**25.00**

**Pin-back button, Nixon/Agnew flasher, 2½", M, $15.00.**

Pin-back, Don't Settle for Peanuts, Elect Ford, elephant w/peanut, EX ......................................**27.50**

Pin-back, Dukakis for President, portrait & flag, sq, 1988, 2", M .........................................**12.00**

Pin-back, Ford/Dole 1976, red, white & blue, 1½", EX.................**10.00**

Pin-back, Ford/Rockefeller, Dec 19 1974, 3½", EX....................**40.00**

Pin-back, Fox Valley IL, McGovern '72, celluloid, 2¼", NM ......**90.00**

Pin-back, I Go-Fer Clinton/Gore '96/Univerity of MN, football shape, M ...........................**30.00**

Pin-back, Jewish Americans for Ford, blue on white, 1976, 1½", EX ......................................**20.00**

Pin-back, Keep Dick on the Job, celluloid, 1960, 3½", NM.........**55.00**

Pin-back, Kennedy For President in red w/image, 1960, 1", NM ....................................**35.00**

Pin-back, Kennedy For Senator (Robert), 1964, celluloid, 3½", NM ....................................**35.00**

Pin-back, PT Boat shape, gold-tone metal, 1960 (JFK), 1¾", NM ..**80.00**

Pin-back, Robert F Kennedy w/red RFK & stars, celluloid, 1968, 2¼" .....................................**45.00**

Pin-back, Support ERA Now, celluloid, 1970s, 1¾", EX, .........**35.00**

Pocketknife, Vote 1992 Bill Clinton, blue on white, 1 blade, 2", EX .....................................**15.00**

Poster, Barry Goldwater/Bill Miller, ...Choice, Not an Echo, 1964, EX .....................................**40.00**

Poster, Clinton Governor, 1990, 14" dia, NM .............................**22.50**

Poster, Gerald Ford, He's Making Us Proud Again, 1970s, 25x15", EX .....................................**15.00**

Poster, Nixon & Agnew as cartoon bikers, black & white, 22x34", EX ....................................**100.00**

Poster, President Ford '76, 50x38", EX .....................................**22.50**

Poster, Reagan for President, ...America Great Again, 1980, 24x17", NM .......................**35.00**

Poster, Reagan/Bush, Bringing America Back, 1984, 24x16", NM ..................................**20.00**

Poster, Vice President Spiro Agnew dressed as hippie, 30x21", VG ....................................**30.00**

Poster, Vote for JFK & LBJ, blue & red on white, 1960, 44x28", EX .....................................**75.00**

Program, Easter at the White House, 1995, 8 pages, NM...............**22.50**

Program, Inauguration, Reagan, 1981, 22 pages, NM+.........**25.00**

Program, JFK Inauguration, Limited Deluxe Edition, 1961, EX ......................................**85.00**

Publication, Jimmy Carter & How He Won, Peterson Publishing, 1976, EX .............................**28.00**

Publication, Meet LBJ, Tatler Publishing, 1964, EX...............**24.00**

Statue, Reagan w/jelly bean bag & axe, plaster, Esco, 1981, EX .......................................**40.00**

Stick-pin, presidential seal, Ronald Reagan on box lid, MIB.....**17.50**

Ticket, beverage; Reagan, 1981 Inaguration, unused, NM .**12.50**

Ticket, Nixon Inauguration Ceremonies, 1969, EX...............**35.00**

Tickets, Clinton Presidential Library Dedication Ceremony, 2004, M, pr .......................**35.00**

Tie tac, gold bar w/presidential seal, Reagan's embossed signature, NM ......................................**45.00**

Wristwatch, Ford in convertible, Win w/Ford, Trying Times, 1974, EX ..........................**140.00**

Wristwatch, Hillary Clinton caricature, 1993, NM .................**75.00**

ples. For further information we recommend *The Official Precious Moments Collector's Guide to Figurines* by John & Malinda Bomm (Collector Books).

Figurine, Believe the Impossible, #109487, 1987 .................**105.00**

Figurine, Easter's On Its Way, #521892, 1989....................**84.00**

Figurine, Eggs Over Easy, #E3118, 1981 ................................**115.00**

Figurine, Especially for Ewe, #E-9282, dove symbol, 1982, 3", M .......................................**12.00**

Figurine, Fall Festival, #732494, set of 7, 2000 .........................**150.00**

Figurine, Forgiving Is Forgetting, #E9252, 1982....................**45.00**

Figurine, Fork Over Those Blessings to Others, #307033, 1998.................................**50.00**

Figurine, God Sent His Love, #15881, 1985.....................**46.00**

Figurine, Happy Birdie, #527343, 1993.................................**30.00**

Figurine, Hay Good Lookin', #649732, 1999....................**45.00**

# Precious Moments

Precious Moments, little figurines with inspirational captions, were created by Samuel J. Butcher and are produced by Enesco Inc. in the Orient. They're sold through almost every gift store in the country, and the earlier, discontinued models are becoming very collectible. Uness noted otherwise, our prices are for mint in the box exam-

**Figurine, He Careth, #E1378, 1974, retired, $395.00.**

Figurine, He Walks With Me, #107999, 1987....................**52.00**

Figurine, I'll Never Tire of You, #307068, 1998....................**51.00**

Figurine, Let's Be Friends, #527270, 1992....................................**35.00**

Figurine, Love Is the Best Gift of All, #110930, 1987.............**50.00**

Figurine, Make a Joyful Noise, #272450, 1997...................**30.00**

**Figurine, Nobody's Perfect, #E9268, 1987, $40.00.**

Figurine, Oh Holy Night, #522546, 1989....................................**50.00**

Figurine, Oinky Birthday, #524506, 1996....................................**16.00**

Figurine, Puppy Love, #520764, 1988, 2¾x2¼", M...............**20.00**

Figurine, Rejoice O Earth, #E5636, 1981....................................**77.00**

Figurine, Showers of Blessings, 1988....................................**50.00**

Figurine, Tubby's First Christmas, #E0511, 1984...................**240.00**

Figurine, Wishing Well, #292753, 1998....................................**30.00**

Figurine, Wishing You a Merry Christmas, #E5383, 1984 ..............**46.00**

Figurine, World's Grestest Student, #491586, 1999....................**20.00**

Figurine/night light, Praying Girl, #427594, 1990, 8", M.........**15.00**

Ornament, Cheers to the Leader, #113999, 1989....................**33.00**

Ornament, I'll Play My Drum for Him, #E2359, 1982............**95.00**

Ornament, Love Is the Best Gift of All, #109770, 1987.............**47.00**

Ornament, The First Noel, #E2367, 1983....................................**70.00**

Picture frame, Jesus Loves Me, #E7170, 1982.....................**66.00**

## Princess House Glassware

The home party plan of Princess House was started in Massachusetts in 1963 by Charlie Collis. His idea was to give women an opportunity to have their own business by being a princess in their house, thus the name for this company. Though many changes have been made since the 1960s, the main goal of this company is to better focus on the home party plan.

Most Princess House pieces are not marked in the glass — they carry a paper label. Heritage is a crystal cut floral pattern, introduced not long after the company started in business. Fantasia is a crystal pressed floral pattern, introduced about 1980. Both lines continue today; new pieces are being added, and old items are continually discontinued.

Bowl, trifle, Heritage; #021, crystal, MIB....................................**40.00**

Bowl, vegetable; Fantasia, #521, crystal, 8¼".......................**24.00**

Butter dish, Heritage, #461, crystal, domed lid, 4½" L, MIB........**20.00**

**Baker, Fantasia, #588, crystal, 3¼x12¾x8¾", MIB, $35.00.**

Casserole, Fantasia, #529, crystal, w/lid, +#317 metal frame, both MIB .......................................**45.00**

Champagne flute, Heritage, #436, crystal, 10" ...........................**12.00**

Coffeepot, Heritage, #210, crystal ...**38.00**

Compote, dessert; Fantasia, #575, crystal, footed, 10-oz.............**7.00**

Figurine, bull, #770, Wonders of the Wild, crystal, MIB..............**45.00**

Figurine, bunny, #814, crystal, 3x4¼" .................................**18.00**

Figurine, kitten, #811, crystal, 3¾"..**16.00**

Figurine, lion, #881, crystal, Wonders of the Wild, 4½x7" ..**35.00**

Figurine, teddy bear, #813, crystal, 3" ........................................**15.00**

Glass, soda fountain; Heritage, #497, crystal, 16-oz..............**8.00**

Goblet, water; Fantasia, #519, crystal, 10½-oz, 7" ......................**8.00**

Pie plate, Fantasia, #539, crystal, 9" ........................................**18.00**

Plate, dinner; Fantasia, #513, crystal, 10"...............................**12.00**

Plate, luncheon; Fantasia, #639, ruby red, 8", MIB.................**8.00**

Salt & pepper shakers, Fantasia, #542, crystal, 3¼", pr ........**14.00**

Salt & pepper shakers, Heritage, #471, crystal/chrome, 4¾", pr .....**14.00**

Straw dispenser, Heritage, #091, crystal w/brass lid, 10½", MIB ...................................**35.00**

Tumbler, cooler; Heritage, #462, crystal, 23-oz, 6¼" .............**10.00**

Tumbler, Heritage, #497, crystal, 16-oz, MIB ........................**10.00**

Tumbler, iced tea; Fantasia, #5230, green ...................................**8.00**

Vase, trumpet; Heritage; #380, crystal, w/flower arranger, 10⅜" ...................................**40.00**

**Wonders of the World, Bull, #770, $40.00.**

# Purinton

Popular among collectors due to its 'country' look, Purinton Pottery's dinnerware and kitchen items are easy to learn to recognize due to their bold yet simple designs, many of them of fruit and flowers, created with basic hand-applied colors on a creamy white gloss.

Ashtray, Apple, divided, wire handle, 5½" .............................**40.00**

Baker, Maywood, 7" .................**15.00**

Baker, Pennsylvania Dutch, 7"..**45.00**

Baker, Turquoise, 7" ................**30.00**

Bean pot, Mountain Rose, 6¼" ......**50.00**

Beer mug, Brown Intaglio, Palm Trees .................................**150.00**

Bowl, fruit; Sunflower, 12".......**85.00**

Bowl, range; Fruit, cobalt trim, w/lid, labeled Fats, 5½".....**45.00**

Bowl, range; Saraband, w/lid, 5½"..**20.00**
Bowl, salad; Apple, 11" ............**50.00**
Bowl, vegetable; Chartreuse, open, 8½" ....................................**30.00**
Bowl, vegetable; Intaglio, divided, 10½" ..................................**30.00**
Bowl, vegetable; Normandy Plaid, open, 8½" ..........................**20.00**
Candleholder, Pennsylvania Dutch, star..................................**100.00**
Candleholder, Saraband, 8-sided, 2x6", ea ..............................**20.00**
Canister, Chartreuse, oval, tall..**60.00**
Canister, Daisy, cobalt trim, 9"..**75.00**
Cocktail dish, Fruit, sea-horse handle, 11¾" ............................**55.00**
Coffee mug, Apple, 4"..............**40.00**
Coffeepot, Apple, 8-cup, 8" .......**90.00**
Coffeepot, Ivy, Red; 8-cup ........**25.00**
Cookie jar, Pennsylvania Dutch, slant top, wooden lid, 7x7"..**125.00**
Creamer, Fruit, 3" ....................**15.00**
Creamer, Heather Plaid, 3" .....**20.00**

**Creamer and sugar bowl with lid, Apple, 5½", 3½", $25.00. (Photo courtesy Susan Morris-Snyder)**

Creamer & sugar bowl, Brown Intaglio, w/lid ....................**20.00**
Creamer & sugar bowl, Heather Plaid, w/lid........................**25.00**
Cup & saucer, Ming Tree.........**30.00**
Honey jug, Morning Glory, 6¼"...**50.00**
Jug, Dutch; Apple, 2-pt, 5¾"......**35.00**
Jug, Dutch; Crescent, 2-pt .......**50.00**

Jug, Dutch; Petals, 5-pt ...........**50.00**
Jug, honey; Ivy, Yellow; 6¼"....**18.00**
Jug, honey; Palm Tree, 6¼" .....**75.00**
Jug, Kent; Peasant Garden .....**125.00**
Jug, Oasis; Fruit, rare, minimum value ...............................**750.00**
Mug, beer; Palm Tree.............**150.00**
Pitcher, Apple, Rubel mold, 5".....**75.00**
Plate, breakfast; Apple, 8½" ....**20.00**
Plate, breakfast; Cactus, Desert Scene, 8½" .........................**95.00**
Plate, breakfast; Peasant Garden, 8½" ..................................**100.00**
Plate, chop; Intaglio, 12" ..........**25.00**

**Plate, chop; Mountain Rose, $85.00. (Photo courtesy Susan Morris-Snyder)**

Plate, dinner; Maywood, 9½" ...**30.00**
Plate, dinner; Sunflower, 9¾"..**25.00**
Plate, lap; & cup, Chartreuse ..**35.00**
Plate, salad; Maywood, 9¾" .....**10.00**
Plate, salad; Pennsylvania Dutch, 6¼" ....................................**18.00**
Platter, meat; Apple, 12"..........**40.00**
Platter, meat; Intaglio, 12" ......**30.00**
Platter, meat; Pennsylvania Dutch, 12" ....................................**50.00**
Platter, Saraband, 12" .............**20.00**
Platter, Turquoise Intaglio, 12"..**45.00**
Relish, Apple, 2 round sections ..**25.00**
Relish, Provincial Fruit, 3-part..**75.00**
Salt & pepper shakers, Fruit, jug style, miniature, 2½", pr......**20.00**

Salt & pepper shakers, Ivy - Red Blossom, jug style, 2½", pr......................................**20.00**

Salt & pepper shakers, Turquoise, jug style, 2¼", pr ...............**30.00**

Sprinkler can, Ming Tree, 7" ...**50.00**

Sugar bowl, Fruit, w/lid, 4"......**25.00**

Sugar bowl, Heather Plaid, w/lid, 4"......................................**30.00**

Teapot, Intaglio, 6-cup, 6½".....**65.00**

Teapot, Mountain Rose, 2-cup....................................**20.00**

Teapot, Normandy Plaid, 6-cup....................................**65.00**

Vase, cornucopia; Ivy-Red Blossom, 6" ......................................**25.00**

# Puzzles

Of most interest to collectors of vintage puzzles are those made of wood or plywood, especially the early hand-cut examples. Character-related examples and those representing a well-known personality or show from the early days of television are coming on strong right now, and values are steadily climbing in these areas. For an expanded listing, see *Schroeder's Collectible Toys, Antique to Modern* (Collector Books).

Aquaman, jigsaw, Whitman, 1968, Aquaman & Mera, 100 pcs, EXIB.................................**30.00**

Archie, jigsaw, Jaymar, 1960s, malt shop scene, 60 pcs, NMIB ................................**75.00**

Babes in Toyland, jigsaw, WDP, 1061, 70 pcs, EXIB............**28.00**

Captain Kangaroo, jigsaw, Fairchild #1560, 1960s, EXIB...........**18.00**

Captain Kangaroo, jigsaw, Fairchild #4430, 1971, EXIB ............**18.00**

Charlie's Angels, jigsaw, Pro Arts/1977, Farrah w/flower, 11x17", EXIB.....................**18.00**

Cheyenne, jigsaw, Milton Bradley #47405-52, 1950s, set of 3, EXIB ................................**50.00**

Chip 'N Dale Rescue Rangers, frame-tray, Golden #4464C-14, 11x14", NM..........................**6.00**

Dukes of Hazzard, frame-tray, 1980s, plastic, 4x4", EX ......**6.00**

Dukes of Hazzard, jigsaw, American Publishing #1600, 1981, NMIB ................................**15.00**

Gulliver's Travels, jigsaw, Saafield, 1930s, set of 2, EXIB.......**100.00**

Gulliver's Travels, jigsaw, Saafield /Paramount, 1939, set of 3, EXIB ...............................**125.00**

Hopalong Cassidy, jigsaw, Milton Bradley, 1950, 12x9", set of 3, NMIB ................................**75.00**

Jungle Book, frame-tray, Golden, 8x11", EX .............................**5.00**

Katzenjammer Kids, jigsaw, Featured Funnies, 1930s, 14x10", EXIB ................................**80.00**

Lady & the Tramp, frame-tray, Whitman, 1954, EX+.........**25.00**

Lamb Chop, frame-tray, Golden #8206, 8x11", EX ................**6.00**

Lindy Looneys Picture Puzzle, Lindberg, 1965, w/Big Wheeler, EXIB ................................**65.00**

Marvel Superheros, jigsaw, Milton Bradley, 1967, 100 pcs, EXIB..**50.00**

Mary Poppins, frame-tray, Jaymar, 1964, NM+ ......................**25.00**

Our Gang, jigsaw, Saafield #912, set of 3, EX (G+ window box)..**100.00**

**Patty Duke, Jr. Jigsaw Puzzle, Whitman, 100 pieces, 1963, from $35.00 to $45.00.** (Photo courtesy Greg Davis and Bill Morgan)

Pink Panther, jigsaw, Whitman, 100 pcs, EXIB ............................**25.00**

Pinocchio Picture Puzzles, Whitman, 1939, set of 2, 10x8½", NMIB ................................**50.00**

Rescuers, jigsaw, Golden, 200 pcs, NMIB ................................**6.00**

Smokey Bear, jigsaw, Whitman #4610, 1971, 100 pcs, EXIB..............**15.00**

Smurfs, jigsaw, Milton Bradley, 1983, toboggan scene, NMIB..........**8.50**

Smurfs, jigsaw, Milton Bradley #4278-2, beach scene, NMIB...........**10.00**

Smurfs, jigsaw, Peyo, 1988, camping scene, EXIB ........................**8.00**

Superman, frame-tray, Whitman, 1966, various scenes, EX+, ea......................................**30.00**

Superman Saves a Life, jigsaw, Saalfield, 1940s, 500 pcs, NMIB .............................**300.00**

Superman the Man of Tomorrow, jigsaw, Saafield, 1940s, 300 pcs, NMIB .............................**200.00**

Wizard of Oz, frame-tray, Jaymar, 1960s, NM+ .......................**25.00**

Wizard of Oz, frame-tray, Whitman, 1976, NM+ ..........................**10.00**

# Radios

Novelty radios are those that carry an advertising message or are shaped like a product bottle, can or carton; others may be modeled after the likeness of a well-known cartoon character or disguised as anything but a radio — a shoe or a car, for instance. It's sometimes hard to recognize the fact that they're actually radios. To learn more, we recommend *Collector's Guide to Antique Radios,* by John Slusser and the Staff of Radio Daze (Collector Books).

Transistor radios are collectible as well. First introduced in 1954, many feature space-age names and futuristic designs. Prices here are for complete, undamaged examples in at least very good condition.

### Novelty Radios

Archie, jukebox form, Vanity Fair/Archie Co, 1977, 6", M ......................................**50.00**

Ballentine's Scotch, bottle shape, made in Hong Kong, 9", EX....................................**25.00**

Big Bird, head only, yellow plastic, AM, EX...............................**15.00**

Bullwinkle, 1969, 12", NM.....**150.00**

Bumper car, Playtime Concepts, 14", NM, from $100 to ............**125.00**

Charlie the Tuna, clamp for handle-bar, AM, 1973, EX..............**65.00**

Dukes of Hazzard, plastic w/paper label, Warner Bros, AM, 1981, EX......................................**65.00**

Evel Kneivel, tire shape, Mont-gomery Wards, 1974, battery-operated, EX......................**35.00**

Fonzie, plastic figure, Sutton, 1974, M........................................**65.00**

Heileman's Old Style Beer, can shape, NM...........................**65.00**

Helping Hand, lg white glove w/face, 6½", NM............................**75.00**

Hershey's Syrup, bottle shape, battery-operated, 8", MIB.**40.00**

Kendall Dual Action Heavy Duty Motor Oil, sm profile can, NM ....................................**35.00**

Kodak Copy Machine, AM, 6¼x3½", EX....................................**170.00**

Mr T, figure flexing muscles, belt clip on back, battery, 1983, 5", NM ....................................**30.00**

NASA Space Shuttle Columbia, AM, Made in Hong Kong, 11", MIB ....................................**60.00**

Nestlé Nesquik Milk Shake Mix, NM, from $35 to ................**50.00**

Old Spice Can, Isis Model 105, 7", NM, from $75 to ..............**100.00**

Pepsi, shirt-pocket style...........**25.00**

Pig in overalls, blinking eyes, AM, 1970s-80s, MIB..................**25.00**

Pink Panther, stuffed cloth, 12", NM, from $25 to ................**35.00**

Polaroid 600 Plus Film Pack, AM/FM, built-in antenna, 1980s, NM..........................**40.00**

Radio Shack, round battery shape, AM, 4½x2½" dia, NM........**20.00**

R2D2 robot, AM, Kenner, MIB..**140.00**

**Sears Best Easy Living Paint, Hong Kong, from $35.00 to $40.00.** (Photo courtesy Bunis and Breed)

Smurf, stereo series, w/speakers, Peyo, 1964, NM, from $50 to..........**75.00**

Smurf's head, hand carried, 1982, EX.......................................**47.50**

Sunkist Orange Soda, AM/FM, NM ....................................**40.00**

Tune-A-Fish, shower radio, AM/FM, Spectra, MIP......................**20.00**

Watkins Baking Powder, can shape, battery, 5½", NMIB.............**35.00**

Wilson NFL Football, w/kick-off stand, 6½", MIB.................**60.00**

### Transistor Radios

Admiral, Y2023, Super 7, horizontal, 7 transistors, AM, 1960.....**25.00**

Airline, GEN-1202B, horizontal, M/W logo, 1962 .................**35.00**

Ambassador, A-1064, horizontal, 10 transistors, AM, 1965.........**15.00**

Bulavo, #278, horizontal, 4 transis-tors, AM, 1958 ..................**45.00**

Bulova, 685, vertical, swing handle, 4 transistors, AM, 1962.........**65.00**

Cameo, 64N06-03, 1964, vertical, 6 transistors, AM.................**15.00**

Commadore, YTR-601, vertical, 6 transistors, Japan, AM .....**45.00**

Crosley, JM-8BK, Enchantment, book shape, 2 transistors, 1956..**150.00**

Delmonico, TR-7C, horizontal/watch radio, 7 transistors, AM, 1963..**65.00**

GE, P815A, horizontal, 7 transistors, AM, 1961 ..................**25.00**

General Electric, CT455A, horizontal, clock, 6 transistors, AM, 1960..................................**20.00**

Golden Shield, #7186, vertical, 6 transistors, AM..................**20.00**

Hitachi, KH-915, horizontal, 9 transistors, FM, 1963 ..............**25.00**

Holiday, ST-600, horizontal, 6 transistors, AM, Japan.............**45.00**

ITT, #600, 6 transistors, AM, 1963..**55.00**

Lincoln, L640, vertical, 6 transistors, AM, 1963 .................**125.00**

**Magnavox, AM-60, vertical, six transistors, upper round dial, thumbwheel tuning, metal perforated grill, AM, 1961, Japan, 4⅛x2⅝x1", $25.00. (Photo courtesy Marty and Sue Bunis)**

Magnovox, AM-81, vertical, 8 transistors, Japan, AM.............**20.00**

Motorola, #7X25W, Power 9, vertical, 7 transistors, AM, 1959...........**40.00**

Motorola, X48E, horizontal, leather, 7 transistors, AM, 1962.....**15.00**

NEC, NT-6B, horizontal, AM.....**30.00**

Panasonic, #T-745, horizontal/table, 12 transistors, AM/FM, 1964 ..**30.00**

Philips, L1X75T, Fanette, horizontal, 7 transistors, Germany, AM, 1958...........................**45.00**

Raytheon, T-100 Series, AM, USA, 1956................................**250.00**

Realtone, TR-1859, vertical, 8 transistors, AM, 1964...............**15.00**

Realtone, TR-870, 6 transistors, AM, Japan, 1959 ....................**125.00**

Seminole, #1205, horizontal, 12 transistors, AM/FM, 1964........**20.00**

Sony, TFM-96, horizontal, 9 transistors, 2-band dial, AM/FM, 1964..................................**35.00**

Standard, SR-F25, horizontal, 6 transistors, AM..................**95.00**

Tempest, HT-8041, Deluxe, vertical, 8 transistors, Japan, AM........**25.00**

Truetone, DC3270, horizontal, 9 transistors, USA, AM........**40.00**

Valiant, 655, Hi-Fi, vertical, 6 transistors, AM..........................**10.00**

Zenith, Royal 130, vertical, AM.....**35.00**

Zenith, TR-122, vertical, 12 transistors, dial knob, AM, 1965.............**15.00**

# Ramp Walkers

Ramp walkers date back to at least 1873 when Ives produced a cast-iron elephant walker. Wood and composite ramp walkers were made in Czechoslovakia and the USA from the 1920s through the 1940s. The most common were made by John Wilson of Watsontown, Pennsylvania. These sold worldwide and became known as 'Wilson Walkies.' Most are two-legged and stand approximately 4½" tall.

Plastic ramp walkers were manufactured primarily by the Louis Marx Co. from the 1950s through the early 1960s. The majority were produced in Hong Kong, but some were made in the USA and sold under the Marx logo or by the Charmore Co., a subsidiary of Marx.

The three common sizes are 1) small premiums about 1½" x 2"; 2) the more common medium size, 2¾" x 3"; and 3) large, approximately 4" x 5". Most of the smaller walkers were unpainted, while the medium and large sizes were hand or spray painted. Several of the walking types were sold with wooden or colorful tin lithographed ramps. For more extensive listings and further information, see *Schroeder's Collectible Toys, Antique to Modern* (Collector Books).

Astro & George Jetson, Hanna Barbera ....................................**75.00**
Brontosaurus w/monkey, Marx ....**40.00**
Chilly Willy, penguin on sled pulled by parent, Hanna-Barbera.**25.00**
Clown, Wilson ...........................**30.00**
Donald Duck, pulling nephews in wagon, Disney....................**35.00**
Donald Duck, Wilson..............**175.00**
Elephant, Wilson ......................**30.00**
Eskimo, Wilson........................**100.00**
Figaro the Cat, w/ball, Disney.....**30.00**
Fred Flintstone on Dino, Hanna-Barbera ..............................**75.00**
Jiminy Cricket, w/cello, Disney.....**30.00**

Lion w/clown, Marx ..................**40.00**
Little Red Riding Hood, Wilson..**40.00**
Mad Hatter w/March Hare, Disney ................................**50.00**
Mammy, Wilson........................**40.00**
Mickey Mouse & Pluto, hunting, Disney ................................**40.00**
Minnie Mouse, pushing baby stroller, Disney .................**35.00**
Olive Oyl, Wilson....................**175.00**
Pebbles on Dino, Hanna-Barbera..**75.00**
Popeye, pushing spinach-can wheelbarrow, Hanna-Barbera....**30.00**
Popeye, Wilson........................**200.00**
Popeye & Wimpy, heads on springs, Hanna-Barbera, MIB ........**85.00**
Sailor, Wilson............................**30.00**
Santa, w/yellow or white sack, Hanna-Barbera, ea............**40.00**
Santa & Mrs Claus, faces on both sides, Hanna-Barbera .......**50.00**
Soldier, Wilson..........................**30.00**
Top Cat & Benny, Hanna-Barbera..**65.00**
Wimpy, Wilson........................**175.00**
Zebra w/native, Marx ...............**40.00**

# Records

Records that made it to the 'Top Ten' in their day are not always the records that are prized most highly by today's collectors, though they treasure those which best represent specific types of music: jazz, rhythm and blues, country and western, rock 'n roll, etc. Many search for those cut very early in the career of artists who later became superstars, records cut on rare or interesting labels, or those aimed at ethnic groups. A fast-growing area of related interest is picture sleeves for 45s. These are often worth more than the record itself, especially if they feature superstars from the '50s or early '60s.

Condition is very important. Record collectors tend to be very critical, so learn to watch for loss of gloss; holes, labels, or writing on the label; warping; and scratches. Unless otherwise noted, values are for records in like-new condition — showing little sign of wear, with a playing surface that retains much of its original shine, and having only a minimal amount of surface noise. EP (extended play 45s) and LPs (long-playing 33⅓ rpm 'albums') must have their jackets (cardboard sleeves) in nice condition free of tape, stickers, tears, or obvious damage. *The American Premium Record Guide* by Les Docks is a great source for more information.

### Children's Records

All in the Family, 1971, 33⅓ rpm, w/book, EX (w/sleeve)........**25.00**
Aristocats, 1970, 33⅓ rpm, w/book, VG+ ....................................**10.00**
Benji, 1976, 33⅓ rpm, EX (w/sleeve)..**15.00**
Daffy Duck Meets Yosemite Sam, Capitol, 1940s, 78 rpm, EX+ (w/sleeve) ...........................**15.00**
Flintstones Time Machine, 1966, 33⅓ rpm, EX (w/sleeve).....**20.00**
Hansel & Gretel, Disney, 1964, 33⅓ rpm, NM...........................**20.00**
Hey It's Yogi Bear, Columbia Pictures, LP, EX+, from $15 to ...........**20.00**
Jumbo's Lullaby, 1950s, red, 45 rpm, EX (w/sleeve).............**10.00**

Lone Ranger Authentic Story & Song, 1980, 33⅓ rpm, EX (w/sleeve) ...........................**45.00**
Meet the Brady Bunch, Paramount, 1972, LP, EX, from $5 to...**10.00**
Paddington Bear & Friends, 1982, 33½ rpm, NM.....................**20.00**
Pinocchio, RCA-Victor #349, 1940, 78 rpm, VG (w/sleeve).......**65.00**

**Raiders of the Lost Ark, book and record set, #452, 33⅓ rpm, Buena Vista Records, copyright 1981, EX, $10.00.**

Ruff & Reddy, Golden, 1959, 78 rpm, EX+ (w/sleeve) ..........**15.00**
Scooby Doo Christmas Stories, 1978, 33⅓ rpm, EX.....................**25.00**
War of the Worlds, 1978, 45 rpm, EX (w/sleeve) .....................**10.00**

### LP Albums

American Breed, The; Bend Me, Shape Me, EX, from $5 to ...**8.00**
Beach Boys, Surfer Girl, Pickwick, common reissue, EX, from $5 to...........................................**8.00**
Beatles, Rock 'N Roll Music, Capitol SKBO-1137, set of 2, EX ...**35.00**

Bilk, Mr Archer; Strangers at the Shore, EX, from $5 to ..........**8.00**

Campbell, Glen; Rhinestone Cowboy, Capitol SW-11430, EX, from $5 to .............................**8.00**

Cannon, Freddie; Palisades Park, Swan 507, EX ...................**50.00**

**Chubby's Folk Album, Loddy Lo, Paramount Records, ca 1963, from $20.00 to $30.00.** (Photo courtesy P.J. Gibbs)

Cline, Patsy; Patsy Cline, Coral 8611, EX.............................**30.00**

Coasters, One By One, Atco 123, EX......................................**35.00**

Darren, James; Sing the Movies, Colpix 418, EX...................**20.00**

Domino, Fats; Rockin' & Rollin' With Fats Domino, Imperial 9004, EX.............................**40.00**

Durante, Jimmy; in Person, MGM, 1950s, 12 humorous songs, VG+ ....................................**15.00**

Ellington Jazz Party in Stereo, Columbia CS8127, EX, from $5 to...........................................**8.00**

Five Satins, Five Satins Encore, Ember 401, EX ................**125.00**

Francis, Connie; More Greatest Hits, MGM E-3893, VG, from $5 to...........................................**8.00**

Horton, Johnny; Johnny Horton, Dot 3221, EX......................**40.00**

Jones, George; Salutes Hank Williams, Mercury 20596, EX......................................**30.00**

Little Richard, Here's Little Richard, Specialty, EX....**100.00**

Meet the Monkees, Colgems 101, EX, from $5 to......................**8.00**

Nelson, Rick; Sings for You, EX, from $7 to...........................**10.00**

Nelson, Ricky; Ricky Nelson, Imperial 9050, EX .......................**40.00**

Oliver, Good Morning Starshine, Crewe Records, EX..............**8.00**

Redding, Otis; Dictionary of Soul, EX, from $10 to...................**15.00**

Rogers, Kenny; Liberty/United Records LWAK979, 1979, EX..**4.00**

Rogers, Roy; Souvenir Album, RCA Victor 3041, EX.................**20.00**

Vee, Bobby; Just Today, Liberty LST-7554, EX, from $5 to ...**8.00**

Who, Happy Jack, Decca, VG+ ..**6.00**

Young, Neil; Harvest, Reprise 2032, NM, from $5 to....................**8.00**

77 Sunset Strip Soundtrack, WB 1289, EX.............................**15.00**

## 45 rpms

Adventurers, Rock & Roll Uprising, Columbia 42227, EX..........**10.00**

Archies, Jingle Jangle, Kirshner 5002, M ...............................**5.00**

Bachelors, Delores, Earl 101, EX..**30.00**

Ball, Earl; Party of One, Pathenon 101, EX..............................**10.00**

Beatles, I Want To Hold Your Hand, VG+ .....................................**45.00**

Bee Gees, You Should Be Dancing (1-sided), RSO 853, NM.....**10.00**

Benton, Brook; The Ties That Bind, Mercury 71566, NM ............**20.00**

Blondie, Private Stock 45141, 1977, EX.......................................**10.00**

Buckinghams, Mercy Mercy Mercy, Columbia 44182, NM ........**10.00**

Burke, Eddie; Rock Mop, D 1063, EX.........................................**10.00**

Cadillacs, Speedo, Josie 785, EX..**8.00**

Capitols, Day By Day, Getaway 721, EX.........................................**20.00**

Coasters, Searchin', Atco 6087, EX..**20.00**

Cupids, The Answer to Your Prayer, Decca 30279, EX.................**12.00**

Dixon, Floyd; Time & Peace, Aladdin 3101, EX ..............**30.00**

Domino, Fats; Little School Girl, Imperial 5272, EX ..............**15.00**

Duprees, You Belong to Me, Coed 569, EX.................................**8.00**

Five Chords, Red Wine, Cuca 1031, EX.........................................**20.00**

Five Satins, Our Love Is Forever, Ember 1014, EX ................**10.00**

Gallahads, Keeper of Dreams, Starla 15, EX.............................**12.00**

Guitar Frank, Wild Track, Bridges 2203/2204, EX....................**20.00**

Hooker, John Lee; Blue Monday, De Luxe 6004, EX ...................**30.00**

Isley Brothers, The Drag, Gone 5048, NM, from $10 to ......**15.00**

Jan & Dean, There's a Girl, Dore 531, EX...............................**12.00**

Jive Bombers, Bad Boy, Savoy 1508, EX...........................................**8.00**

Lillie, Lonnie; Truck Driver's Special, Marathon 5003, EX ...**75.00**

Little Jr., Jessie; Funky Stuff, Metro-Dome 1003, NM....**150.00**

McKown, Gene; Rock-A-Billy Rhythm, Aggie 101, EX.....**50.00**

Motley Crue, Smokin' in the Boys Room, Elektra 69625, NM ..**2.00**

Neville, Aaron; Show Me the Way, Minit 618, EX ....................**10.00**

Parton, Dolly; Here You Come Again, RCA 11123, NM.......**5.00**

Peter & Gordon, Nobody I Know, Capitol 5211, NM ..............**15.00**

Pratt, Lynn; Tom Cat Boogie, Hornet 1000, EX ......................**30.00**

Presley, Elvis; Money Honey, RCA Victor 6641, EX..................**20.00**

Rascals, People Got To Be Free, Atlantic 2537, NM ...............**5.00**

Rodgers, Buck; Little Rock Rock, Starday 245, EX ................**20.00**

Snappers, The; If There Were, 20th Fox 148, EX........................**15.00**

Turner, Ike & Tina; I Wanna Jump, Minit 32077, NM ..............**25.00**

**Vinton, Bobby; Just As Much As Ever/Another Memory, Epic 5-10266, VG, $4.50.**

Vinton, Bobby; Roses Are Red, Epic 9509, NM..............................**8.00**

Wayne, Scott; Roobie Doobie, Talent 1011, EX.............................**12.00**

## 78 rpms

Andrews, Mose; Ten Pound Hammer, Decca 7388, EX...................**25.00**

Astaire, Fred; Cheek to Cheek, Brunswick 7486, EX..........**10.00**

Baker, Buddy; Box Car Blues, Victor 21549, EX............................**15.00**

Baldwin, Luke; Travelin' Blues, Champion 16343, EX ........**25.00**

Big Sister, Pig Meat Mama, Varsity 6063, EX..............................**15.00**

Billy & Lilly; La Dee Dah, Swan 4002, EX..............................**20.00**

Boots & His Buddies, Ain't Misbehavin', Bluebird 7241, EX.**10.00**

Cadillac, Bobby; Carbolic Acid Blues, Columbia 14413-D, EX.......**100.00**

Cash, Johnny; Luther Played the Boogie, Sun 316, EX..........**60.00**

Clifford, Bob; Hobo Jack's Last Ride, Vocalion 5499, EX................**20.00**

Dells, Time Makes You Change, Vee-Jay 258, EX .................**30.00**

Duncan Sisters, Dusty Roads, Columbia 15745-D, EX......**10.00**

Garland, Judy; Stompin' at the Savoy, Decca 848, EX..........**8.00**

Garland, Judy; You Can't Have Everything, Decca 1463, EX..**10.00**

Hall Brothers, Hitch-Hike Blues, Bluebird 7801, EX ..............**10.00**

Holiday, Billie; & Her Orchestra, Solitude, Okeh 6270,EX ..**10.00**

Jenkins, Robert; Steelin' Boogie, Parkway 103, EX................**75.00**

Jolson, Al; April Showers, Brunswick 6502, EX..........**30.00**

Justice, Dick; Cocaine, Brunswick 336, EX..............................**20.00**

Martin, Dean; One Foot in Heaven, Embassy 124, EX................**35.00**

Meyers, Hazel; Plug Ugly, Banner 1358, EX..............................**15.00**

Newman, Fred; San Antonio, Paramount 3267, EX..................**15.00**

Porter's Blue Devils, Steamboat Sal, Gennett 5249, EX..............**15.00**

Powell, Lewis; Mushmouth Blues, Vocalion 0404, EX .............**15.00**

Presley, Elvis; Blue Moon, RCA Victor 20-6640, EX..................**50.00**

Rodgers, Jessie; Rattlesnake Daddy, Bluebird 5839, EX...............**10.00**

Rounders, Broadway Melody, Regal 8744, EX..............................**8.00**

St Louis Jimmy, Florida Hurricane, Aristocrat 7001, EX...........**80.00**

Sykes, Roosevelt; Drivin' Wheel, Regal 3286, EX ..................**15.00**

Tampa Blue Jazz Band, Get Hot, Okeh 4397, EX...................**10.00**

Uncle Jim Hawkins, Arkansas Traveler, Challenge 301, EX.........................................**8.00**

Varsity Eight, Fallin' Down, Cameo 782, EX..............................**10.00**

Wanderers, Tiger Rag, Bluebird 5887, EX............................**15.00**

Weaver, Sylvester; Polecat Blues, Okeh 8608, EX...................**60.00**

# Red Glass

Ever popular with collectors, red glass has been used to create decorative items such as one might find in gift shops, utilitarian bottles and kitchenware, figurines and dinnerware lines such as were popular during the Depression era. For further information and study, we recommend *Ruby Glass of the 20th Century* by Naomi Over.

Basket, Inverted Thistle, crystal handle, Mosser, 1980, 5½"..**30.00**

**Basket, ruffled rim, clear twist handle, Morgantown Glass, 12x10", $100.00.** (Photo courtesy Naomi Over)

Bell, gold band, crystal handle, Italy, 6¼" ..........................**25.00**

Bottle, Benjamin Franklin portrait, Wheaton, 1980s, 7¾"..........**40.00**

Bowl, Daisy & Button, 4-footed, oval, American Glassworks, 6¼"..**20.00**

Bowl, Hobnail, fluted, Viking...**22.00**

Bowl, ruffled rim, Blenko, 1980, 9½"..**28.00**

Butter dish, Imperial, late 1960s, 3¼" ....................................**15.00**

Cake salver, plain, Viking, 1982, 11¾" ...................................**75.00**

Candleholder, Ring Stem, 1-light, Cambridge, 1949-53, 5", ea ..**65.00**

Candlestick, Diamond Thumbprint, flared bowl on pedestal, Viking, 11" ......................................**35.00**

Candlesticks, Iris & Herringbone, ruby flashed, Jeannette, 5½", pr ......................................**85.00**

Candy dish, Optic Rib, Blenko, 1930-53, 3½" dia .................**6.00**

Cordial, in Farberware holder, 3-oz .**20.00**

Cornucopia candleholders, silver overlay, Paden City, 1¼", pr ..**100.00**

Cornucopia nut dish, unknown manufacturer, 3¾" L ................**25.00**

Creamer, Argus, Fostoria, 1967, 6-oz...**30.00**

Decanter, clear lid, Blenko, 1980-85, 4½" dia ..............................**20.00**

Muddler/stir stick, twist design, Cambridge, 1930s, 4½" .....**40.00**

Paperweight, round, England, ca 1950, 3" ............................**15.00**

Plate, ABC type, plain rim, AA Imports, 1980, 8" ..............**15.00**

Plate, Epic, Viking, 17" ............**55.00**

Plate, Forget-Me-Not border, Mary Gregory Winter girl, 1983, 8"..**75.00**

Plate, Holly & Berry, Fostoria, ca 1980, 12½" ........................**60.00**

Plate, Pineapple, flashed florals, Indiana, 1970, 8" ...............**15.00**

Plate, plain, Dalzell-Viking, ca 1986, 12" ....................................**60.00**

Salt & pepper shakers, LG Wright, 1970s, 3½", pr ...................**40.00**

Sherbet, crystal stem w/knop, Cambridge, ca 1949-53, 7-oz.....**20.00**

Slipper, Daisy & Button, made for LG Wright, 1950, sm .........**12.00**

Sugar bowl, Popeye & Olive, handles, #994, Paden City, 1932, 3"..**20.00**

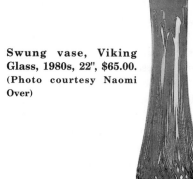

**Swung vase, Viking Glass, 1980s, 22", $65.00.** (Photo courtesy Naomi Over)

Tray, Regina, Paden City, 1936, 13¼x7¾" ............................**45.00**

Tumbler, footed, crystal stem, Cambridge, 1949-53, 11-oz .......**25.00**

Tumbler, juice; Standard Glass, 1940s, 6-oz .........................**10.00**

Tumbler, Swirl, Cambridge, ca 1949-53, 12-oz....................**35.00**

Tumbler, water; Standard Glass, 1940s, 8-oz ...........................**7.00**

Wine, crystal stem, Paden City, 1932, 2-oz ...........................**25.00**

Wine, flared rim, unknown manufacturer .............................**12.00**

# Red Wing

Taking their name from the location in Minnesota where they located in the late 1870s, the Red Wing Company produced a variety of wares, all of which are today considered noteworthy by pottery and dinnerware collectors. Their early stoneware lines, Cherry Band and Sponge Band (Gray Line), are especially valuable and often fetch prices of several hundred dollars per piece on today's market. Production of dinnerware began in the '30s and continued until the pottery closed in 1967. Some of their more popular lines — all of which were hand painted — were Bob White, Lexington, Tampico, Normandie, Capistrano, and Random Harvest. Commercial artware was also produced. Perhaps the ware most easily associated with Red Wing is their Brushware line, unique in its appearance and decoration. Cattails, rushes, florals, and similar nature subjects are 'carved' in relief on a stoneware-type body with a matt green wash its only finish.

For more information, we recommend *Collector's Encyclopedia of Red Wing Art Pottery* by B.L. Dollen. To learn about the conmapny's stoneware production, refer to *Red Wing Stoneware* and *Red Wing Collectibles*, both by Dan DePasquale, Gail Peck, and Larry Peterson. All are published by Collector Books.

## Art Ware

Ashtray, gold/brown, sq w/sm cigarette rest in center, #M3005, 11" .....................................**35.00**

Bowl, brown w/orange interior, flat, #414, 7" ..............................**38.00**

Bowl, centerpiece; Renaissance, ivory/brown wipe, #526, 12", $45 to..................................**60.00**

Bowl, hat shape, Hyacinth semimatt, #670, 1960s, 5x6", from $20 to..................................**26.00**

Bowl, Magnolia, ivory/brown wipe, wing handles, #1016, 10½", $38 to.........................................**46.00**

Bowl, shell; flecked Nile Blue, #M1567, 9" .........................**50.00**

Bowl, Zephyr Pink Fleck, curled edge, #M1463, 12" .............**45.00**

Candleholder, English Garden, ivory/brown wipe, #1190, 6", ea $22 to..................................**28.00**

Candleholder, Hyacinth, tapered, #678, 6", ea..........................**30.00**

Compote, white, pedestal, brass handles, #M1598, 8"..........**55.00**

Compote, white semimatt, med pedestal, #M1597, 50s-60s, 7", $22 to..................................**28.00**

Dish, marmalade; aqua, pear shaped, 4½" ....................................**18.00**

Figurine, bird on perch, forest green gloss, 1950s-60s, 10", from $125 to.........................................**22.00**

Jardiniere, flecked pink, scalloped top, #M1610, 6"..................**22.00**

Juicer, yellow, pedestal, #256..**150.00**

Pitcher urn, Vintage, semi-matt ivory/brown wipe, #616, 11", from $75 to................................**110.00**

Pitcher vase, Magnolia, ivory/brown wipe, #1012, 7", from $28 to..**40.00**

Pitcher vase, Zephyr Pink Fleck, #1559, 1950s-60s, 9½", from $32 to.........................................**40.00**

Planter, gray w/coral interior, sq, #1378, 5½" ..........................**40.00**

Planter, violin shape, black semi-matt, #1484, 1950s-60s, 13", from $48 to.................................**58.00**

Teapot, yellow, chicken figural, #257..................................**125.00**

Vase, Brushware, walnut green, embossed cattails, cylindrical, 10"...**130.00**

Vase, gloss gray w/coral interior, #B1397, 7"..........................**35.00**

Vase, gloss yellow, swirled mold, #1590, 10" ..........................**50.00**

Vase, Mandarin type, white w/green interior, #1553, 1950s-60s, 6½"..**29.00**

Wall pocket, Cypress Green, funnel shaped, #M1630, 10" .........**90.00**

### Dinnerware

Blossom Time, plate, 10½".......**10.00**
Blossom Time, supper tray ......**14.00**
Bob White, bowl, salad; 12"......**52.50**
Bob White, plate, 6½"................**8.00**
Bob White, tray, 24" ................**65.00**
Brittany, plate, chop; 12" .........**50.00**

Capistrano, bowl, cereal...........**14.00**
Capistrano, bread tray .............**28.00**
Capistrano, nappy ....................**18.00**
Capistrano, platter, 13"............**20.00**
Capistrano, teacup & saucer....**12.00**
Capistrano, teapot ....................**70.00**
Desert Sun, bean pot, w/lid, 1½-qt...**40.00**
Desert Sun, bowl, fruit.............**40.00**
Desert Sun, cup & saucer, AD......**18.00**
Desert Sun, pitcher, water; 1½-qt........**55.00**
Desert Sun, platter, 13" ...........**18.00**
Frontenac, platter, 13" ............**22.50**
Iris, celery dish ........................**18.00**
Lexington, beverage server, w/lid ....**50.00**
Lexington, coffee cup ................**10.00**
Lexington, creamer....................**9.00**
Lexington, relish dish...............**16.00**
Lexington Rose, sugar bowl .....**14.00**
Lotus, bowl, rim soup ...............**10.00**
Lotus, cup, coffee ......................**10.00**
Lotus, gravy boat, w/tray .........**20.00**
Lotus, teacup & saucer.............**10.00**
Lute Song, bread tray...............**28.00**
Lute Song, creamer ..................**12.00**
Lute Song, salt & pepper shakers, pr ........................................**16.00**
Magnolia, casserole, w/lid ........**30.00**
Magnolia, gravy boat, w/tray......**22.00**
Magnolia, salt & pepper shakers, pr..**12.00**
Normandy, plate, 10" ...............**17.50**
Pepe, beverage server, w/lid.....**70.00**

**Pepe, bread tray, from $30.00 to $38.00; Bean pot with lid, from $32.00 to $40.00. (Photo courtesy Brenda Dollen)**

Pepe, plate, 10" .........................**10.00**
Plum Blossom, bowl, cereal......**12.00**
Random Harvest, dish, vegetable; divided...............................**24.00**

**Random Harvest: relish tray, $30.00; pitcher, $45.00; casserole, $40.00; gravy boat, $30.00; sugar bowl, $25.00; creamer, $20.00.** (Photo courtesy Brenda Dollen)

Round-Up, cocktail tray ...........**50.00**
Round-Up, creamer & sugar bowl, w/lid....................................**75.00**
Round-Up, platter, 13" ..............**95.00**
Round-Up, salt & pepper shakers, pr .........................................**80.00**
Smart Set, cup & saucer ..........**15.00**
Tampico, creamer ......................**18.00**
Tampico, mug, coffee ................**22.00**
Tampico, pitcher, water; 2-qt.....**80.00**
Tampico, plate, 8½" ..................**16.00**
Tampico, teapot .........................**65.00**
Town & Country, bowl, mixing; 9".....**80.00**
Town & Country, plate, 8" .......**20.00**
Town & Country, syrup jug......**50.00**
Village Green, dish, vegetable .......**30.00**
Village Green, syrup jug ..........**30.00**

# Restaurant China

Restaurant china is specifically designed for use in commercial food service. Not limited to restaurants, this dinnerware is used on planes, ships, and trains as well as hotel, railroad, and airport dining rooms. Churches, clubs, and department and drug stores also put it to good use.

The popularity of good quality American-made heavy gauge vitrified china with traditional styling is very popular today. Some collectors look for transportation system top-marked pieces, others may prefer those with military logos. It is currently considered fashionable to serve home-cooked meals on mismatched top-marked hotel ware, adding a touch of nostalgia and remembrances of elegant times past. For a more thorough study of the subject, we recommend *Restaurant China, Identification & Value Guide for Restaurant, Airline, Ship & Railroad Dinnerware, Volume 1* and *Volume 2,* by Barbara Conroy (Collector Books). She is listed in the Directory under California.

Ashtray, Conti-Hansa Hotel, Hutschenreuther, 1950s-60s ..................**10.00**
Ashtray, Erawan Hotel, Noritake, ca 1960s ..................................**12.50**
Ashtray, President Hotel, Noritake, 1970s ..................................**10.00**
Bowl, fruit; Humbolt County Fairgrounds, Wallace, 1950s, 5"..**18.00**
Bowl, rice; NYK Line, Nitta Maru pattern, Mino & NYK backstamp ................................**30.00**
Butter pat, Iberia Airlines, Spanish Globe pattern, Alvarez, 1970s..**25.00**
Cup, American Hotels, footed, Caribe mark, 1963 date code ............**24.00**

**Cup and saucer, United Airlines 'Red Carpet Club III,' backstamped, 1996, from $15.00 to $20.00.** (Photo courtesy Barbara Conroy)

Cup, Star Clippers Inc, Star Flyer pattern, Victoria, mid-1990s ..**20.00**

Cup & saucer, AD; Silver's, Trenton, 1920s .................................**40.00**

Cup & saucer, Highlands Inn, Jackson, 1977 & 1978 date codes.....**20.00**

Match stand, Commodore Hotel, Lenox, 1930s.....................**42.00**

Match stand, Washington Hotel, Mayer, 1930s .....................**30.00**

Mug, Dunkin Donuts, Rego, 1980s..**25.00**

Mug, Moustache Cafe, Inter American, late 1980s-early 1990s ......**18.00**

Mug, Qwikee Donut Shop, Shenango, 1969 date code ..................**80.00**

Mug, Sears Restaurant, Syracuse, 1973 date code ..................**20.00**

Mug, Tony's Restaurant, Jackson, 1981 date code ..................**18.00**

Mug, Treasure Island Naval Station, Crestor Inc, 1970s.....**20.00**

Mug, Walgreens, Shenango, 1975 date code ..........................**25.00**

Mug, White Tower, Sterling, ca 1936-50s............................**45.00**

Plate, Blue Willow, Jackson, 1940s, 8" .........................................**18.00**

Plate, Carriage House, Tepco, 1950s-60s, 10½"............................**22.00**

Plate, Hotel Stewart, Maddock, dated 1930 ........................**28.00**

Plate, Maxim's Restaurant, Rego, 1980s, 12"...........................**25.00**

Plate, Miramar (hotel), Mayer, 1940s, 7¼".........................**22.00**

Plate, Neptune's Palace, Jackson, 1980 date code, 6½"...........**15.00**

Plate, service; Surfside Hotel, Iroquois, 1930s, 10¾".............**35.00**

Plate, Sun Line, Stella Solaris pattern, Richard-Ginori, 1980s, 6"..**25.00**

Platter, Colonial Line, Lexington pattern, Warwick, 1930s, 12½"..**90.00**

Platter, Scobee Little Neck, Homer Laughlin, 1991 date code, 11¼" .................................**24.00**

Sauce boat, Marilyn pattern, Mayer, 1930s .................................**18.00**

Sugar bowl, Blue Willow, Buffalo, 1980s .................................**20.00**

Teapot, Amtrak National pattern, blue, Hall ...........................**24.00**

Teapot, Chefsware, aqua blue, HF Coors, 1960s.......................**24.00**

Teapot, CP Air, metallic gold logo, ca 1968-88, 4½"..................**70.00**

Teapot, Wardman Park Inn™, Warwick, 1920s ........................**50.00**

Tray, Trans World Airlines, green plastic, Plastics Inc, 1960s..**15.00**

# Rock 'n Roll

Concert posters, tour books, magazines, sheet music, and other items featuring rock 'n roll stars from the '50s up to the present are today being sought out by collectors who appreciate this type of music and like having these mementos of their favorite performers around to enjoy.

See also Elvis Presley; Records.

Aerosmith, poster, promotional for Bootleg album, 1970s, 42x44", EX......................................**85.00**

Alice Cooper, belt buckle, enameled face, 1978, 3x2¼"...............**30.00**

Alice Cooper, pillow, Billion Dollar Babies, 1973, 13x13", NM......**200.00**

Andy Gibb, beach towel, Stigwood Group, 1979, M..................**50.00**

Beach Boys, concert poster, Santa Barbara Campus, 1975, 17x16", EX....................................**110.00**

Bee Gees, book, The Legend, Illustrated Story of the Bee Gees, 1979, M .............................**45.00**

Bee Gees, notebook, spiral-bound, Rock On, 1979, M, from $35 to.......................................**40.00**

Bobby Sherman, sheet music, La La La (If I Had You), EX..........**12.00**

Bobby Vinton, concert program, 1970s, 16 pages, VG+ ........**40.00**

Brenda Lee, magazine, The Journal, April 1999, on cover, 16 pages, NM ...................................**15.00**

Brenda Lee, promotional ad, Billboard 9/11/71, 11x14", EX...............**10.00**

Dave Clark 5, sheet music, Glad All Over, 1963, EX...................**15.00**

Dave Clark 5, tour program, 1966, 24 pages, VG......................**25.00**

David Cassidy, poster, Artko, 1972, 11x17", EX ..........................**18.00**

David Cassidy, puzzle, jigsaw; Whitman #7492, 224 pcs, EXIB..**42.00**

David Cassidy, sheet music, Lyin' to Myself, 8 pages, 1990, M.....**20.00**

Doors, stationery, 1960s, NM.....**100.00**

**Elton John, tour program, Rock of the Westies, 1975, from $20.00 to $30.00.** (Photo courtesy Joe Hilton and Greg Moore)

Grateful Dead, belt buckle, Space Your Face, #3133, 2½x3", M..**30.00**

Grateful Dead, concert ticket, Summer Jam 1973, unused, EX ......**40.00**

Grateful Dead, doll, Jerry Garcia, Gund, Liquid Blue, w/guitar, MIB ....................................**20.00**

Grateful Dead, gunnysack, featuring Electric Sam, EX ...............**15.00**

Grateful Dead, plate, Jerry Garcia images, Gartlan, 1997, 3" dia, MIB ....................................**35.00**

Grateful Dead, poster, Grass Valley CA, 9/18/89, 14x18", M .......**35.00**

Grateful Dead, tour poster, sunflower w/dragonfly, 1995, M............**35.00**

Jimi Hendrix, concert poster, Waikiki Shell Concert, 1969, 11x8½", M ........................................**35.00**

Jimi Hendrix, doll, w/stage, guitar & amp, McFarlane, MIP.........**20.00**

Jimi Hendrix, magazine, Rolling Stones 10/15/70, on cover, EX...............**50.00**

Jimi Hendrix, movie poster, Jimi Hendrix documentary, 1973, 37x57", EX..**50.00**

KISS, Army Kit, complete, 1st edition, 1975, NM ................**200.00**

KISS, belt buckle, brass w/logo, 1976, M ............................**35.00**

KISS, doll, Gene Simmons, Mego, 1978, 14", EX+ ...................**95.00**

KISS, ink pen, Peter, 1970s, MOC ..**200.00**

KISS, key chains, faces, 1 of ea member, set of 4, M .........**800.00**

KISS, pool cue, logo & faux signatures, 1997, MIP ..............**150.00**

KISS, poster calendar, 1975, 18x36", NM ...................................**150.00**

KISS, tour book, Destroyer Tour, 1976, EX...........................**120.00**

KISS, tour program, 10th Anniversary, EX ...........................**140.00**

KISS, Your Face Makeup Kit, missing 1 brush, 1970s, VG+..............**275.00**

Madonna, program, Who's That Girl Tour, 1987, 28 pages, NM .....**70.00**

**Monkees, musical toy guitar, paper face, about 15", EX, from $110.00 to $135.00.** (Photo courtesy Bob Gottuso)

Pink Floyd, belt buckle, Wish You Were Here, 1970s, NM......**45.00**

Pink Floyd, concert program, The Wall, 1980, 20 pages, EX.....**50.00**

Pink Floyd, concert tickets, The Division Bell, 4/14/94, NM, pr ....................................**25.00**

Pink Floyd, T-shirt, The Wall, 1982, EX+................................**35.00**

Pink Floyd, tour program, Animals, 1977, EX............................**30.00**

Rolling Stones, banner, red w/blue print, 1975 tour, 68x42", VG+ ...................................**50.00**

Rolling Stones, guest pass, No Security Tour, 1999, laminated, M......**50.00**

Rolling Stones, movie flyer, Gimme Shelter, 1970, 5½x7½", EX..**80.00**

Rolling Stones, program, 1965, 20 pages, 11x11", EX..............**55.00**

Rolling Stones, tour program, 1978, EX........................................**20.00**

Rolling Stones, 9" balloons, 1983, MIP....................................**55.00**

# Rooster and Roses

Rooster and Roses is a quaint and provincial line of dinnerware made in Japan from the '40s and '50s. The rooster has a yellow breast with black crosshatching, a brown head, and a red crest and waddle. There are full-blown roses, and the borders are yellow with groups of brown diagonals. Several companies seem to have made the line, which is very extensive — more than seventy-five shapes are known. For a complete listing of the line, see *Garage Sale & Flea Market Annual* (Collector Books).

Ashtray, rectangular, 3x2".........**9.50**

Ashtray, sq, lg, from $30 to......**35.00**

Biscuit jar, w/wicker handle, from $55 to................................**70.00**

Bowl, cereal; from $14 to..........**25.00**

Bowl, 8", from $45 to ................**55.00**
Butter dish, ¼-lb, from $20 to ......**25.00**
Candy dish, w/3-dimensional leaf
    handle, from $25 to ...........**45.00**
Canister set, sq, 4-pc, from $100 to..**150.00**
Carafe, no handle, w/stopper lid, 8",
    from $65 to .........................**85.00**
Casserole dish, w/lid, from $65 to.....**85.00**
Chamberstick, saucer base, ring
    handle, from $25 to ...........**35.00**
Cigarette box w/2 trays, hard to
    find, from $55 to ................**65.00**
Condiment jar, w/lid, 2x2½"......**15.00**
Cookie jar, ceramic handles, from
    $85 to................................**100.00**
Creamer & sugar bowl on rectangu-
    lar tray, from $65 to ..........**75.00**
Cruets, oil & vinegar; sq, lg, pr from
    $30 to.................................**35.00**
Cup & saucer, from $15 to .......**20.00**
Deviled egg dish, 9¾" ...............**40.00**
Egg cup on tray, from $35 to ......**45.00**
Flowerpot, buttress handles, 5",
    from $35 to .........................**45.00**
Instant coffee jar, spoon-holder tube
    on side, rare ......................**45.00**
Jam jar, attached underplate, from
    $35 to.................................**45.00**
Match holder, wall mount, from $65
    to........................................**85.00**
Mug, round bottom, med, from $20
    to........................................**25.00**
Napkin holder, from $30 to ......**40.00**
Pitcher, 3½", from $15 to..........**20.00**
Plate, dinner; from $25 to ........**35.00**
Relish tray, 3 wells w/center handle,
    from $55 to .........................**65.00**
Salt & pepper shakers, w/handle, pr
    from $15 to .........................**20.00**
Salt box, wooden lid, from $50 to .**60.00**
Snack tray w/cup, oval, 2-pc, mini-
    mum value .........................**45.00**

Teapot, 6x9", from $50 to .........**60.00**

**Wall pocket, lavabo,
two-piece, mounted
on board, from $85.00
to $125.00. (Photo cour-
tesy Jackie Elliott)**

Wall pocket, scalloped top, bulbous
    bottom, from $55 to ..........**65.00**
Watering can, 8x6", from $45 to .....**60.00**

# Roselane Sparklers

A line of small figures with a
soft shaded finish and luminous
jewel eyes was produced during the
late 1950s by the Roselane Pottery
Company who operated in Pasadena, California, from the late 1930s
until possibly the 1970s. The line
was a huge success. Twenty-nine
different models were made, including elephants, burros, raccoons,
fawns, dogs, cats, and fish. Not all
pieces are marked, but some carry
an incised 'Roselane Pasadena,
Calif.,' or 'Calif. U.S.A'; others may
have a paper label.

Angelfish, 4½", from $20 to......**25.00**
Bassett hound pup, 2", from $12 to..**15.00**

Bassett hound sitting, 4", from $15 to.........................................**18.00**

Bulldog, fierce expression, looking right, 2", from $12 to.........**15.00**

Bulldog sitting, slender body, looking right, 6"........................**25.00**

**Cat and kittens, 5",
from $40.00 to $45.00.**

Cat, Siamese, sitting, facing forward, jeweled collar, 7", from $40 to ..**50.00**

Cat, sitting, head turned right, tail out behind, from $25 to.....**28.00**

Chihuahua sitting, left paw raised, looking straight ahead, 6½" ..**28.00**

Cocker spaniel, 4½" ..................**20.00**

Deer standing, head turned right, looking downward, 5½" .....**25.00**

Deer w/antlers, standing, jewelled collar, 4½", from $22 to .....**28.00**

Elephant, trunk raised, striding, jeweled headpiece, 6", from $35 to.........................................**40.00**

Elephant sitting on hind quarters, 6", from $35 to ...................**40.00**

Fawn, legs folded under body, 4x3½" ..**25.00**

Fawn, upturned head, 4x3½".....**20.00**

Fawn, 4½x1½" ...........................**20.00**

Kangaroo mama w/babies, 4½", from $40 to...................................**45.00**

Kitten sitting, 1¾" ....................**12.00**

Owl, very stylized, lg round eyes, teardrop-shaped body, lg.....**25.00**

Owl, 3½"...................................**15.00**

Owl, 5¼"...................................**25.00**

Owl, 7".....................................**30.00**

Owl baby, 2¼", from $12 to......**15.00**

Pig, lg .....................................**25.00**

Pouter pigeon, 3½"....................**20.00**

Raccoon standing, 4½", from $20 to.........................................**25.00**

Whippet sitting, 7½", from $25 to ..**28.00**

# Rosemeade

Novelty items made by the Wapheton Pottery Company of North Dakota from 1941 to 1960 are beginning to attract collectors of American pottery. Though smaller items (salt and pepper shakers, figurines, trays, etc.) are readily found, the larger examples are scarce and can be very expensive. The name of the novelty ware, 'Rosemeade,' is indicated on the paper labels (many of which are still intact) or by the ink stamp.

Ashtray, black w/toy spaniel head, 7", minimum value..........**350.00**

Ashtray, fish, 6¼", from $100 to......................................**125.00**

**Bank, buffalo, World's Largest – Jamestown, ND, 3½", $400.00. (Photo courtesy Jim and Beverly Mangus)**

Bank, fish, green, 3x4½", from $300 to............................................**350.00**

Creamer & sugar bowl, blue tulips, 2"............................................**90.00**

Cup, man w/mustache on side of cup, black, 3½"....................**80.00**

Figurine, alligator, 1½x7¾", rare, minimum value............**1,000.00**

Figurine, circus horse, solid, 4¼x4¾", from $350 to.....**400.00**

Figurine, cock pheasant, 9x14½", from $250 to....................**300.00**

Figurine, hen pheasant, 4x11½", from $350 to....................**400.00**

Figurine, kitty, tail in air, white, w/sticker, 2x2"...................**45.00**

Figurine, walrus, 4¼x6½"......**500.00**

Figurines, Russian wolfhounds, w/Prairie Rose sticker, 6½x7", pr......................................**210.00**

Figurines, tiger kittens, 1x2¾", 1¼x2", pr, minimum value..........**500.00**

Hen on a basket, 5½x5½", from $350 to........................................**400.00**

Novelty, brussel sprout, 1¾x1¼", from $50 to........................**75.00**

Pin, mallard drake, 4", minimum value..............................**1,000.00**

Planter, cock pheasant, 3¾x9¼", minimum value...............**500.00**

Planter, swan, 4¾x5", from $35 to......................................**65.00**

Plaque, walleye decal, 6" dia, from $75 to...............................**125.00**

Salt & pepper shakers, beaver, brown, 3", pr.....................**50.00**

Salt & pepper shakers, buffalo, brown, w/sticker, pr.........**135.00**

Salt & pepper shakers, bull head, 2¼", pr from $75 to..........**100.00**

Salt & pepper shakers, chihuahua head, pr............................**420.00**

Salt & pepper shakers, deer leaping, pr........................................**70.00**

Salt & pepper shakers, elephant, gray, w/stickers, 2½x2½", pr......**60.00**

Salt & pepper shakers, kitten, white, 2¼", pr from $50 to..**75.00**

Salt & pepper shakers, parrot, w/stickers, 3", pr..............**100.00**

Salt & pepper shakers, pelican, pink, 3¼", pr from $85 to..**100.00**

Salt & pepper shakers, pointer dog, rare, 2¼", pr, minimum value .**800.00**

Salt & pepper shakers, puppy begging, 3", pr from $75 to......**85.00**

Salt & pepper shakers, Siamese cat, 3", pr..................................**60.00**

Serving dish, mallard hen, w/lid, 4½x6½", from $300 to .....**350.00**

**Shakers, pheasant cock and hen, with sticker, 3", $45.00 for the pair.**

Spoon rest, Prairie Rose, 4¼", from $75 to................................**100.00**

Tea bell, flamingo on mud nest, 3¼", from $250 to....................**300.00**

Tile, pheasant decal, 6x6" sq, from $75 to................................**100.00**

Toothpick holder, cock pheasant, w/sticker, 4".......................**75.00**

Toothpick holder, cock strutting, 3¾x2¾", from $100 to .....**125.00**

Toothpick holder, ear of corn, 1½" ..**75.00**

Vase, peacock figural, green, 7¾",
from $250 to......................**300.00**
Vase, yellow, 5½x4¼" dia.........**40.00**
Vase, Yellow Fleck, w/sticker, 6"..**80.00**
Wall pocket, deer lying in leaves,
off-white to pink, 5"...........**45.00**

# Roseville

This company took its name
from the city in Ohio where they
operated for a few years before moving to Zanesville in the late 1890s.
They're recognized as one of the
giants in the industry, having produced many lines in art pottery from
the beginning to the end of their
production. Even when machinery
took over many of the procedures
once carefully done by hand, the pottery they produced continued the
fine artistry and standards of quality
the company had always insisted
upon.

Several marks were used along
with paper labels. The very early art
lines often carried an applied ceramic seal with the name of the line
under a circle containing the words
Rozane Ware. From 1910 until 1928
an Rv mark was used. Paper labels
were common from 1914 until 1937.
From 1932 until closure in 1952, the
mark was Roseville in script or R
USA, Pieces marked RRP Co
Roseville, Ohio, were not made by
Roseville Pottery but by Robinson
Ransbottom of Roseville, Ohio. Don't
be confused. There are many jar-
dinieres and pedestals in a brown
and green blended glaze that are
being sold at flea markets and
antique malls as Roseville that were
actually made by Robinson Ransbottom as late as the 1970s and 1980s.
That isn't to say they don't have
some worth of their own, but don't
buy them for old Roseville.

If you'd like to learn more about
the subject, we recommend *The Collector's Encyclopedia of Roseville
Pottery, Vols. 1* and *2,* by Sharon
and Bob Huxford and Mike Nickel.
Mr. Nickel is listed in the Directory
under Michigan. Note: Watch for
reproductions! They're flooding the
market right now; be especially
wary at flea markets and auctions.
These pieces are usually marked
only Roseville (no USA), though
there are exceptions. These have a
'paint by number' style of decoration
with little if any attempt at blending.

See Clubs and Newsletters for
information concerning *Rosevilles of
the Past* newsletter.

Apple Blossom, bowl, #326-6, pink
or green, 2½x6½", from $150
to.......................................**175.00**
Apple Blossom, vase, #390-12, green or
pink, 12½", from $400 to ....**450.00**
Apple Blossom, vase, #392-15, blue, handles, 15½", from $900 to ..**1,000.00**
Apple Blossom, window box, #368-8,
blue, 2½x10½", from $200
to.......................................**225.00**
Baneda, center bowl, #233, pink, han-
dles, 3½x10", from $375 to..**425.00**
Baneda, vase, #594, green, 9", from
$1,000 to .......................**1,100.00**
Baneda, vase, #594, pink, 9", from
$750 to.............................**800.00**

Baneda, vase, #596, green, handles, 9", from $1,500 to................**1,750.00**

Baneda, vase, #596, pink, handles, 9", from $1,000 to...............**1,250.00**

Baneda, vase, #603, green, 4½", from $625 to..............................**675.00**

Baneda, vase, #603, pink, 4½", from $400 to..............................**450.00**

Bittersweet, basket, #809-8, 8½", from $200 to.....................**250.00**

Bittersweet, cornucopia, #857-4, 4½", from $100 to ............**125.00**

Bittersweet, double vase, #858, 4", from $150 to.....................**175.00**

Bittersweet, planter, #827-8, 11½", from $150 to.....................**175.00**

Bittersweet, vase, #888-16, 15½", from $450 to.....................**500.00**

Bleeding Heart, candlesticks, #1139-4½", blue, 5", pr from $275 to..**325.00**

Bleeding Heart, plate, #381-10, blue, 10½", from $200 to.............**225.00**

Bleeding Heart, plate, #381-10, green or pink, 10½", from $150 to..**175.00**

Bleeding Heart, vase, #968-9, blue, 8½", from $375 to.............**425.00**

Bleeding Heart, vase, #968-9, green or pink, 8½", from $375 to...**350.00**

Bushberry, double cornucopia, #155-8, blue, 6", from $200 to ..**225.00**

Bushberry, hanging basket, green, 7", from $400 to ...............**425.00**

Bushberry, hanging basket, orange, 7", from $375 to.................**425.00**

Bushberry, vase, #39-14, blue, 14½", from $550 to.....................**650.00**

Bushberry, window box, #383-6, green, 6½", from $125 to...............**150.00**

Capri, bowl, #527-7, 7", from $20 to.........................................**30.00**

Capri, leaf dish, #532-16, 16", from $35 to.................................**45.00**

Capri, planter, #558, 7", from $85 to.........................................**95.00**

Capri, window box, #569-10, 3x10", from $45 to.........................**55.00**

Cherry Blossom, hanging basket, #350, brown, 8", from $400 to...**500.00**

Clemana, bowl, #281, blue, 4½x6½", from $250 to.....................**275.00**

Clemana, bowl, #281, green, 4½x6½", from $225 to .....**250.00**

Clemana, vase, #112, blue, 7½", from $450 to.....................**500.00**

Clemana, vase, #112, green, 7½", from $350 to.....................**400.00**

Clemana, vase, #112, tan, 7½", from $300 to..............................**350.00**

Clematis, center bowl, #456-6, brown or green, 9", from $125 to..**150.00**

Clematis, flower arranger vase, #192-5, blue, 5½", from $100 to..**125.00**

Columbine, bookend planter, #8, blue or tan, 5", pr from $350 to..**400.00**

Columbine, cornucopia, #149-6, pink, 5½", from $175 to..............**200.00**

Columbine, hanging basket, pink, 8½", from $375 to ............**425.00**

Columbine, vase, #17-7, pink, handles, 7½", from $225 to ......**275.00**

**Florentine II, vase, #233, ca 1940, 10", from $200.00 to $250.00.**

Foxglove, flower frog, #46, blue or pink, 4", from $125 to......**150.00**

Foxglove, hanging basket, #466, pink, 6½", from $300 to.............**350.00**

Foxglove, tray, #424, 15" W, green or pink, from $350 to.......**400.00**

Foxglove, vase, #47-8, blue, handles, 8½", from $250 to.............**300.00**

Foxglove, vase, #53-14, blue, 14", from $450 to.....................**500.00**

Freesia, basket, #390-7, tangerine, 7", from $225 to ..............**250.00**

Freesia, bowl, #465-8, green, handles, 11", from $175 to.....**200.00**

Freesia, center bowl, #464-6, blue, 8½", from $125 to ............**150.00**

Freesia, flowerpot & saucer, #670-5, tangerine, 5½", from $185 to.......**210.00**

Freesia, vase, #463-5, green, from $225 to............................**250.00**

Freesia, window box, #1392-8, green, 10½", from $200 to.............**225.00**

Fuchsia, candlesticks, #1132, blue, 2", pr from $175 to...........**200.00**

Fuchsia, center bowl, #351-10, green, 3½x12½", from $225 to.......**250.00**

Fuchsia, vase, #893-6, blue, handles, 6", from $250 to ..............**300.00**

**Fuchsia, vase, #903-12, tan, 12", from $550.00 to $650.00.**

Gardenia, basket, #610-12, 12", from $350 to.............................**400.00**

Gardenia, bowl, #641-5, 5", from $125 to.............................**150.00**

Gardenia, hanging basket, #661, 6", from $300 to.....................**350.00**

Gardenia, tray, #631-14, 15", from $200 to.............................**250.00**

Gardenia, vase, #689-14, handles, 14", from $375 to .............**425.00**

Gardenia, window box, #658-8, 3x8½", from $100 to ........**125.00**

Iris, basket, #355-10, blue, 9½", from $475 to.....................**550.00**

Iris, basket, #355-10, pink or tan, 9½", from $425 to ............**475.00**

Iris, center bowl, #361-8, blue, handles, 3x10", from $200 to .........**225.00**

Iris, pillow vase, #922-8, blue, 8½", from $325 to.....................**375.00**

Iris, pillow vase, #922-8, pink or tan, 8½", from $175 to ...........**200.00**

Iris, vase, #928-12, blue, 12½", from $550 to.............................**650.00**

Iris, vase, #928-12, pink or tan, 12½", from $300 to ..........**350.00**

Ixia, basket, #346, 10", from $300 to.........................................**350.00**

Ixia, bowl, #327, 6", from $150 to......**175.00**

Ixia, center bowl, #330-7, 3½x10½", from $150 to.....................**175.00**

Jonquil, bowl, #523, 3", from $200 to...**225.00**

Jonquil, candlesticks, #1082, 4", pr from $450 to.....................**550.00**

Jonquil, center bowl, #219, 3½x9", from $325 to.....................**375.00**

Jonquil, vase, #529, handles, 8", from $500 to.....................**600.00**

Luffa, candlesticks, #1097, brown or green, 5", pr from $500 to.....**600.00**

Luffa, jardiniere, #631, 7" H, from $350 to.............................**400.00**

Luffa, lamp, blue/rose or blue/green, 9½", from $1,200 to ......**1,400.00**

Luffa, vase, #683, handles, 6", from $350 to..............................**400.00**

Luffa, vase, handles, footed, 15½", from $2,000 to...............**2,500.00**

Magnolia, ashtray, #28, brown or green, 7", from $100 to ....**125.00**

Magnolia, conch shell, #453-6, 6½", from $95 to.......................**110.00**

Magnolia, ewer, #14-10, 10", from $175 to..............................**200.00**

Magnolia, planter, #388-6, brown or green, 8½", from $85 to.........**95.00**

Magnolia, vase, #91-8, brown or green, handles, 8", from $125 to......................................**150.00**

Ming Tree, ashtray, #599, 6", from $75 to.................................**85.00**

Ming Tree, basket, #509-12, 13", from $275 to....................**300.00**

Ming Tree, bookends, #559, 5½", from $200 to....................**235.00**

Ming Tree, bowl, #526-9, 4x11½", from $95 to.......................**110.00**

Ming Tree, vase, #585-14, 14½", from $400 to....................**450.00**

Ming Tree, window box, #569-10, 4x11", from $125 to .........**150.00**

Moss, bowl vase, #290, blue, from $300 to..............................**350.00**

Moss, candlesticks, #1109, orange/green or pink/green, 2", pr, from $200 to..............................**225.00**

Moss, candlesticks, #1109, 2", pr from $150 to....................**175.00**

Moss, pillow vase, #781, blue, 8", from $300 to....................**350.00**

Peony, basket, #379-12, 11", from $250 to..............................**275.00**

Peony, bookends, #11, 5½", from $200 to..............................**250.00**

Peony, conch shell, #436, 9½", from $110 to..............................**135.00**

Peony, mug, #2-3½, 3½", from $100 to......................................**125.00**

Peony, planter, #387-8, 10", from $85 to.................................**95.00**

Pine Cone, ashtray, #499, brown, 4½", from $175 to ............**200.00**

Pine Cone, ashtray, #499, green, 4½", from $100 to ............**125.00**

Pine Cone, basket, #353-11, brown, from $500 to.....................**550.00**

Pine Cone, bowl, #320-5, green, 4½", from $150 to....................**175.00**

**Pine Cone, pitcher, #708-9, blue, 9½", from $1,250.00 to $1,500.00.**

Pine Cone, pitcher, #708-9, green, from $400 to.....................**450.00**

Pine Cone, planter, #124, blue, 5", from $250 to....................**300.00**

Raymor, butter dish, #181, 7½", from $75 to.......................**100.00**

Raymor, divided vegetable bowl, #165, 13", from $55 to .......**65.00**

Raymor, gravy boat, #190, 9½", from $30 to.................................**35.00**

Raymor, shirred egg, #200, 10", from $40 to.................................**45.00**

Silhouette, box, #740, w/lid, 4½", from $150 to..............................**175.00**

Silhouette, double planter, #757-9, 5½", from $125 to ............**150.00**

Silhouette, vase, #780-6, 6", from $90 to................................**110.00**

Silhouette, vase, #789-14, 14", from $350 to............................**400.00**

Snowberry, basket, #1BK-12, green, 12½", from $275 to............**325.00**

Snowberry, tray, #1BL-12, blue or pink, 14", from $250 to......**275.00**

Snowberry, tray, #1Bl-12, green, 14", from $200 to ............**225.00**

Thorn Apple, bowl vase, #305-6, 6½", from $200 to ............**250.00**

Thorn Apple, hanging basket, 7" dia, from $300 to.....................**350.00**

Thorn Apple, vase, #816-8, handles, 8½", from $250 to.............**300.00**

Thorn Apple, vase, #820-9, handles, 9½", from $275 to.............**325.00**

Thorn Apple, vase, #822-10, handles, 10½", from $300 to............**350.00**

Water Lily, candlesticks, #1155-4½, rose w/green, 5", pr, $225 to ..**250.00**

Water Lily, frog, #48, brown w/green, 4½", from $140 to...............**165.00**

Water Lily, hanging basket, #468, blue, 9", from $350 to......**375.00**

Water Lily, hanging basket, #468, rose w/green, 9", from $375 to..**425.00**

Water Lily, vase, #78-9, brown, 9", from $300 to.....................**325.00**

White Rose, double candlesticks, #1143, 4", pr from $200 to..**250.00**

White Rose, vase, #992-15, 15½", from $300 to.....................**400.00**

Wincraft, basket, #210-12, 12", from $500 to............................**600.00**

Wincraft, bookends, #259, 6½", pr from $175 to.....................**225.00**

Wincraft, cornucopia, #221-8, 9x5", from $150 to.....................**175.00**

Wincraft, ewer, #218-18, 19", from $650 to..............................**750.00**

Zephyr Lily, fan vase, #205-6, brown, 6½", from $150 to...............**175.00**

Zephyr Lily, hanging basket, blue, 7½", from $350 to ............**400.00**

Zephyr Lily, pillow vase, #206-7, blue, 7", from $225 to......**275.00**

Zephyr Lily, tray, brown, 14½", from $225 to..............................**250.00**

**Zephyr Lily, tray, #477, 12", from $150.00 to $200.00.**

## Royal China

Several lines of the dinnerware made by Royal China (Sebring, Ohio) are very collectible. Their Currier and Ives pattern (decorated with scenes of early American life in blue on a white background) and the Blue Willow line are well known, but many of their others are starting to take off as well. Since the same blanks were used for all patterns, shapes and sizes will all be the same from line to line. Both Currier and Ives and Willow were made in pink as well as the more familiar blue, but pink is hard to find and not especially collectible in either pattern. See Club and Newsletters for information on Currier & Ives Dinnerware Collectors Club.

## Blue Willow

Ashtray, 5½" ...............................**12.00**
Bowl, fruit nappy; 5½"................**6.50**
Bowl, soup; 8½".........................**15.00**
Bowl, vegetable; 10" .................**22.00**
Butter dish, ¼-lb.......................**45.00**
Cake plate, tab handles............**20.00**
Chop plate, 12"...........................**18.00**
Creamer, from $9 to .................**12.00**
Cup & saucer .............................**7.00**
Gravy boat.................................**22.00**
Mug, 2⅞" ...................................**10.00**
Pie plate, 10"..............................**30.00**
Plate, dinner; 10".........................**8.00**
Platter, oval, 13" .......................**32.00**
Salt & pepper shakers, pr ........**25.00**
Sugar bowl, w/lid, from $15 to.....**20.00**
Teapot, unmarked, from $80 to.....**90.00**

## Colonial Homestead

Bowl, cereal; 6¼" ......................**15.00**
Bowl, soup; 8¼".........................**12.00**
Casserole, angle handles, w/lid.**75.00**
Cup & saucer .............................**5.00**
Pie plate .....................................**25.00**
Plate, chop; 12" .........................**18.00**
Plate, salad; rare, 7¼" ................**7.00**
Platter, serving; tab handles, 11".**15.00**
Sugar bowl, w/lid ......................**15.00**

## Currier and Ives

Ashtray, 5½" ...............................**15.00**
Bowl, fruit nappy; 5½".................**6.00**
Bowl, salad/cereal; tab handles, 6¼" ....................................**48.00**
Bowl, vegetable; deep, 10"........**30.00**

Butter dish, Fashionable decal, ¼-lb, from $35 to....................**45.00**
Casserole, tab handles, w/lid.......**200.00**
Clock plate, blue numbers, 2 decals..**225.00**
Creamer, angle handle...............**8.00**
Gravy boat, pour spout.............**20.00**
Gravy ladle.................................**50.00**
Pie baker, 9 decals, 10", ea $25 to ..**35.00**
Plate, calendar; ca 1969-86, ea .....**20.00**
Plate, chop; Rocky Mountains, 11½"..**300.00**
Plate, luncheon; 9"....................**20.00**

**Plate, snack; 9", $125.00.**
(Photo courtesy Jack and Treva Hamlin)

Platter, oval, 13" .......................**35.00**
Salt & pepper shakers, pr ........**30.00**
Sugar bowl, no handles, straight sides, w/lid .........................**35.00**
Tumbler, juice; glass, 5-oz, 3½", from $8 to...........................**12.00**
Tumbler, water; glass, 4¾" ......**12.00**

## Memory Lane

Bowl, cereal; 6¼" ......................**15.00**
Bowl, soup; 8½"..........................**12.00**
Butter dish, ¼-lb.......................**35.00**
Gravy boat.................................**18.00**
Gravy ladle, plain, white for all sets, from $45 to.........................**65.00**
Plate, chop; 12" .......................**25.00**
Plate, dinner ..............................**8.00**

Plate, salad; rare, 7" .................**10.00**
Platter, tab handles, 10½" .......**15.00**
Sugar bowl, w/lid ......................**15.00**
Tumbler, juice; glass..................**9.00**

## Old Curiosity Shop

Bowl, fruit nappy; 5½"................**5.00**
Bowl, vegetable; 9" ..................**22.00**

**Casserole, w/lid, $90.00.**

Cup & saucer ..............................**5.00**
Plate, bread & butter; 6⅜".........**3.00**
Platter, tab handles, 10½" .......**15.00**
Sugar bowl, w/lid ......................**12.00**
Teapot ....................................**115.00**

# Royal Copley

Produced by the Spaulding China Company of Sebring, Ohio, Royal Copley is a line of novelty planters, vases, ashtrays, and wall pockets modeled after appealing puppy dogs, lovely birds, innocent-eyed children, etc. The decoration is airbrushed and underglazed; the line is of good quality and is well received by today's pottery collectors.

See Clubs and Newsletters for information concerning *The Copley Currier*.

Ashtray, buterfly shape, USA on bottom, paper label, 5x9" ...........**25.00**

Ashtray, leaf shape, green stamp on bottom, 5" ...........................**18.00**
Bank, Farmer Pig, paper label, flat unglazed bottom w/2 holes, 5½" ....................................**80.00**
Bank, rooster, paper label, 8" .......**95.00**

**Bank, teddy bear, 7½", $65.00.**

Candy dish, leaf shape, impressed USA on bottom ..................**25.00**
Coaster, Dutch painting w/man & woman in garden, 4⅝".......**40.00**
Coaster, paintings of antique automobiles, unmarked, ea......**40.00**
Figurine, dog w/raised right foot, paper label, 7½" .................**95.00**
Figurine, kitten w/yellow ball of yarn, gold trim, paper label, 8¼" ....................................**70.00**
Figurine, lark, paper label, 6½".....**24.00**
Figurine, nuthatch, paper label, hand-painted mask, 4½" ...**18.00**
Figurine, sea gull, white w/gold trim, 8" ..............................**55.00**
Figurine, swallow w/extended wings, paper label, 7" ........**90.00**
Figurine, wren, paper label, 3½", from $20 to ..........................**24.00**
Lamp, Oriental boy or girl, 7½", ea..**85.00**
Lamp, pig, flat unglazed bottom, 6½" ...................................**100.00**
Pitcher, Floral Beauty, green stamp, 8" .......................................**60.00**

Pitcher, Pome Fruit, green stamp on bottom, 8".............................**50.00**

Planter, barefooted boy, tan hat, paper label, 7½"..................**45.00**

Planter, big apple & finch, paper label, 6½" .............................**45.00**

Planter, Big Blossoms, green stamp, 3" ..........................................**12.00**

Planter, cat w/cello, 8", from $100 to.........................................**125.00**

Planter, clown, 2 runners, paper label, 8¼" .............................**85.00**

Planter, deer & fawn, 2 runners, paper label, 8¼".................**35.00**

Planter, dog at mailbox, paper label, 8½", from $35 to ................**45.00**

Planter, dog in picnic basket, paper label, 7¾" .............................**75.00**

Planter, fish decoration, oval, paper label, 3¾" .............................**30.00**

Planter, gloved lady, raised letters on back of planter, 6".........**75.00**

Planter, Joyce decal, gold stamp, 4" ..........................................**15.00**

Planter, kitten in cradle, paper label, 7½" ..........................**125.00**

Planter, Linley decal, gold stamp on bottom, 4"............................**15.00**

Planter, Peter Rabbit, paper label, 6½" .....................................**65.00**

Planter, poodle, white, sitting beside planter, 7⅛x5½" ................**50.00**

Planter, teddy bear w/mandolin, paper label, 6¾".................**75.00**

Planter, Water Lily, pink w/gray background, 6¼".................**75.00**

Planter/wall pocket, Chinese girl w/big hat, 7½"....................**45.00**

Vase, bamboo, cylindrical, paper label, 8" ..............................**20.00**

Vase, fish, yellow & black w/brown stripe, paper label, 6" ........**60.00**

Vase, floral decal w/2 handles, gold stamp on bottom, 6¼" .......**14.00**

Vase, Floral Elegance, cobalt blue, 8" ........................................**32.00**

Vase, Lord's Prayer, cylindrical, decal, #339, 8"....................**45.00**

Vase, trailing leaf & vine, paper label, 8½" ..........................**30.00**

Window box, Harmony, paper label, 4¼" .....................................**15.00**

# Royal Haeger, Haeger

Manufactured in Dundee, Illinois, Haeger produced some very interesting lines of artware, figural pieces, and planters. They're animal figures designed by Royal Hickman are well known. These were produced from 1938 through the 1950s and are recognized by their strong lines and distinctive glazes. For more information we recommend *Haeger Potteries Through the Years* by David Dilley (L-W Books); he is listed in the Directory under Indiana.

Ashtray, boomerang shape, orange, #R-1718 USA, 13½x8".......**15.00**

Ashtray, leaf form, Mandarin Orange, #177, ca 1950s, 5x4".............**8.00**

Ashtray, palette shape, Pearl Grey Drip, #R-811, 9½x6¼" .......**10.00**

Ashtray, rectangular, Briar Agate, #R-125, 8X4½" .....................**8.00**

Ashtray, sq leaf w/applied acorns, green, #2145, 1976, 10".....**10.00**

Bookend/planter, stallion head, Chartreuse, #R-641, unmarked, 9x5x3"................................**50.00**

Bowl, centerpiece; palm leaf form, Pearl Shell, #R-1824, 4¾x26" .....**30.00**

Bowl, curving rim, light blue & white, #R-466, 3½x14¾x6"...........**20.00**

Bowl/planter, oval, brown w/dark purple, #106, unmarked, 1930, 8x3" ......................................**30.00**

Candleholder, Brown Earth Graphic Wrap, #3142, 5½x3¾" dia, ea.........................................**20.00**

Candleholder, triple plum, Mauve Agate, #R-433, unmarked, 5x11", ea............................**25.00**

Candleholders, cornucopia, Green Briar, #R-312, unmarked, 5", pr .........................................**35.00**

Candy dish, triple leaf w/bird finial, Mauve Agate, #R-457, 3x8"..**50.00**

Cigarette lighter, ball form, blue w/black streaks, #8167, 3x3½" .......**15.00**

Cigarette lighter, fish form, Jade Crackle, #812-H, 1960s, 10x4"..**15.00**

Compote, hexagonal, Lilac, #342, 6x7" ......................................**15.00**

Dish, shell form, Chartreuse & Silver Spray, #R-97, 2¾x14x7½" ..**30.00**

Figurine, brown w/white drip glaze, #R-1762, ca 1973, 20"......**150.00**

Figurine, duck, head up w/open mouth, white, #F-3, unmarked, 1941, 5" ..............................**10.00**

Figurine, elephant, Chartreuse & Honey, #R-784, 6x8¼x3¾"..**40.00**

Figurine, gypsy girl w/2 baskets, brown & green, #R-1224, 16½" ..................................**75.00**

Figurine, hen pheasant, Mauve Agate, #R-424, 15x5¼" ......**50.00**

Figurine, Peasant Woman, Green Agate, #R-383, 17x5" .........**75.00**

Figurine, recumbent panther, Oxblood, #R-649, 2⅝x7½x2½"..........**45.00**

Flower frog, mermaid w/child, green matt, #86, unmarked, 7x3¾" ..**200.00**

Flower frog, nude sitting, Mauve Agate, #R-1189, unmarked, 6x4" ..................................**200.00**

Flower frog, 2 birds, Cloudy Blue, #R-359, unmarked, 1940s, 8¾x5" ..............................**150.00**

Lamp, petal louvre reflector, Walnut & Ebony, #5353, 1954, 11¼"..**50.00**

Lamp, wall; horse head, glossy Ebony, #5240, crown label, 1947, 9x5" .......................**150.00**

Lamp base, fish riding wave, yellow, unmarked, 10½" ..............**125.00**

Lamp base, lady's head, green w/ brown accents, #3003, 14x3½" ..**250.00**

Lamp base, mermaid, gray on Green Agate base, #5398, 16x8½x7" .........................**200.00**

Pitcher, rooster handle, Persian Blue, #H-608, 9x6¾x4"......**40.00**

Pitcher/vase, Bennington Brown Foam, brown textured, #8183 ......**20.00**

Planter, donkey cart, blue, #3296, unmarked, ca 1943, 3x5"...**15.00**

Planter, fish w/open mouth, yellow, #14, unmarked, 1936, 3x3x3½"..**15.00**

Planter, panther, Ebony & Chartreuse, #3511, 5x13½x6" ...**45.00**

Planter, prospector w/2 mules, 11x6", from $200 to .........**300.00**

Planter, trout, blue, white & green, #R-248, 1942, 6¾x9x4½"...**60.00**

Planter, turtle, Green Agate, #R-540, 4x13½x9½"..................**45.00**

Planter, violin-shaped bowl, Mallow, #R-293, 1⅝x16x5¾"...........**60.00**

Vase, bottle style, off-white w/blue, yellow & brown, #2-H, 14x3¼"..**100.00**

Vase, goblet, metallic gold w/white interior, #928, ca 1962-69, 9⅜".....**15.00**

**Vase, matt blue-green, #34, 13x18", from $85.00 to $100.00.**

Vase, onion jug, Cloudy Blue, #R-251, 20½x4⅛" .................**100.00**

# Russel Wright Dinnerware

Dinnerware with a mid-century flair was designed by Russel Wright, who was at one time one of America's top industrial engineers. His most successful lines are American Modern, manufactured by the Steubenville Pottery Company (1939 – 1959), and Casual by Iroquois, introduced in 1944. He also introduced several patterns of melmac dinnerware and an interesting assortment of spun aluminum serving and decorative items such as candleholders, ice buckets, vases, and bowls.

To calculate values for items in American Modern, use the high end for Cedar, Black Chutney, and Seafoam; add 50% for Bean Brown, White, Glacier Blue, and Cantaloupe. For patterned lines, deduct 25%. In Casual, Brick Red, Cantaloupe, and Aqua items go for about 200% more than any other color, while those in Avocado Yellow are priced at the low end of our range of suggested values. Other colors are in between, with Oyster, White, and Charcoal at the higher end of the scale. Glassware prices are given for Flair in Crystal and Pink; other colors are higher. Add 100% for Imperial Pinch in Cantaloupe. Ruby is very rare, and market value has not yet been established. For more information refer to *Collector's Encyclopedia of Russel Wright* by Ann Kerr (Collector Books).

Bowl, baker; American Modern, from $40 to .........................**50.00**
Bowl, bouillon; Sterling, 7-oz, from $18 to .................................**20.00**
Bowl, cereal; Iroquois Casual, 5", from $12 to .........................**15.00**
Bowl, lug soup; #706, plastic, from $10 to .................................**12.00**
Bowl, soup; Iroquois Casual, 11½-oz, from $20 to .........................**25.00**
Bowl, Spun Aluminum, from $75 to .......................................**95.00**
Bowl, vegetable; #709, plastic, oval, deep, from $15 to ...............**18.00**
Bowl, vegetable; American Modern, divided, from $135 to ........**150.00**
Bowl, vegetable; White Clover, 7½", from $65 to .........................**75.00**
Bun warmer, Spun Aluminum, from $75 to .................................**85.00**
Casserole, American Modern, stick handled, from $35 to .........**40.00**
Clock, White Clover, General Elecric, from $75 to .................**85.00**
Coffee bottle, Sterling, scarce, from $125 to .............................**150.00**

Coffeepot, Iroquois Casual, from $150 to..............................**175.00**

**Creamer and sugar bowl, stacking; American Modern, from $30.00 to $38.00.**

Creamer, Highlight, from $40 to........................................**55.00**

Creamer, Knowles Esquire, from $35 to..................................**45.00**

Cup, #701, plastic, from $6 to ....**8.00**

Cup, Highlight, from $40 to .....**55.00**

Cup, White Clover, from $12 to........................................**15.00**

Gravy stand, Iroquois Casual, from $15 to..................................**20.00**

Ice box jar, American Modern, from $250 to..............................**275.00**

Ice bucket, Spun Aluminum, from $75 to................................**100.00**

Muddler, Spun Aluminum, from $75 to........................................**100.00**

Pitcher, water; Sterling, 2-qt, from $125 to..............................**150.00**

Plate, bread & butter; Knowles Esquire, 6", from $6 to.........**8.00**

Plate, chop; White Clover, Clover decoration, 11", from $40 to........................................**50.00**

Plate, dinner; Highlight, from $35 to........................................**40.00**

Plate, salad; Sterling, 7½", from $19 to........................................**24.00**

Platter, Highlight, oval, sm, from $50 to..................................**75.00**

Platter, Iroquois Casual, oval, 14½", from $45 to.........................**55.00**

Salt & pepper shakers, Knowles Esquire, pr from $30 to .....**40.00**

Salt & pepper shakers, White Clover, either size, pr from $30 to........................................**35.00**

Sauce boat, Sterling, 9-oz, from $25 to........................................**27.00**

Sugar bowl, American Modern, redesigned, from $25 to.....**30.00**

Sugar bowl, Knowles Esquire, w/lid, from $40 to.........................**45.00**

Teapot, Knowles Esquire, from $250 to........................................**300.00**

Tumbler, #715, plastic, from $15 to........................................**18.00**

Wastebasket, Spun Aluminum, from $125 to..............................**150.00**

# Salt Shakers

You'll probably see more salt and pepper shakers during your flea market forays than T-shirts and tube socks! Since the 1920s they've been popular souvenir items, and a considerable number has been issued by companies to advertise their products. These advertising shakers are always good, and along with miniature shakers (1½" or under) are some of the more valuable. Of course, those that have a crossover interest into other categories of collecting — Black Americana, Disney, Rosemeade, Shawnee, Ceramic Arts Studios, etc. — are often expensive as well. There are many good books on the market;

among them are *Florences' Big Book of Salt & Pepper Shakers* and *Florences' Glass Kitchen Shakers* by Gene and Cathy Florence, and *Salt and Pepper Shakers* by Helene Guarnaccia. All are published by Collector Books. See also Advertising Collectibles; Ceramic Arts Studio; Character Collectibles; Disney; Shawnee; Rosemeade.

Alligator, ceramic, realistic, Japan, 4" L, pr from $8 to ..............**10.00**

Amish couple, ceramic, multicolored, 4", pr from $15 to ..............**18.00**

Apple, ceramic, red to cream, 2½", pr..........................................**8.00**

Baseball player mice, ceramic, multicolored, Japan, 1950s, 3¼", pr........................................**75.00**

Bible & lamp, ceramic, multicolored, 1½", pr from $15 to............**18.00**

**Black couple, St. Anne de Beaupre label on aprons, ceramic, 4", 3¾", $50.00 for the pair.**

Boy & girl kissing, Goebel Germany, #899, 3½", pr .....................**49.00**

Boy in space suit, ceramic, multicolored, Japan, 1950s, 3¾", pr........................................**39.00**

Carrot, ceramic, orange & green, c HH Japan, 3⅝", pr from $5 to ...**6.00**

Cat & fishbowl, ceramic, multicolored, Japan, 2½", pr..........**15.00**

Cat ice skater, ceramic, multicolored, 4½", pr from $8 to..............**10.00**

Choir boy, ceramic, multicolored, red Japan mark, 1950s, 4¾", pr......................................**22.00**

Churn, rough wood, Japan, 3⅞", pr from $6 to............................**8.00**

Clock, Lexington KY, plastic, 4¼", pr from $10 to....................**12.00**

Cow, pottery, multicolored, B542, 1-pc, 10" L.............................**26.00**

Cucumber, ceramic, green, 3⅝", pr from $6 to ......................................**8.00**

David the Gnome, ceramic, c 1979 Uleboek BV, 5", pr.............**60.00**

Dinosaur, pottery, various colors, spiny back, 1950s, 2⅜", pr..**55.00**

Dish & spoon, ceramic, multicolored, Japan, 4¾", pr ...................**25.00**

Dog musician, ceramic, multicolored, Japan, 2⅛", pr..........**15.00**

Dutch boy & girl, ceramic, Delft blue, Holland, 4", pr from $15 to .....................................**20.00**

Dutch girl & windmill, ceramic, multicolored, Japan, 4¼", pr....**35.00**

Elephant & drum, ceramic, brown, 5¼", pr ..............................**12.00**

Flying saucer, ceramic, multicolored, 1950s, 2¼x3¼", pr....**28.00**

Golf bag & ball, ceramic, Japan, #H-151, bag, 3¼", pr................**20.00**

Horse head, ceramic, multicolored, Japan, 2⅜", pr from $8 to .**10.00**

Hula girl, ceramic, multicolored, Miko BES Co, 1966, 6", pr..........**135.00**

Ice cream soda, plastic, multicolored, 1950s, 3½", pr...........**17.00**

Indian seated, ceramic, multicolored, Japan label, 2⅝", pr, $10 to ........................................**12.00**

Lion tamer & lion, ceramic, multicolored, Japan mark, 1950s, 4", pr......................................**26.00**

Mary & lamb, ceramic, multicolored, Japan, 3⅝", pr from $15 to..**18.00**

**Mermaids, either pair, $15.00.**

Metal boot, Kansas, Japan, Pat Pend, 2", pr from $6 to........**8.00**

Moon Mullins, glass w/plastic hat lid, cold paint, Japan, 3", pr.......**55.00**

Paul Bunyan & Babe the Blue Ox, ceramic, multicolored, pr from $35 to ................................**42.00**

Peacock, ceramic, multicolored, c MK, 3¾", pr ......................**18.00**

Pear, ceramic, realistic, Japan, 2½", pr from $5 to........................**7.00**

Pepper, plastic, red & green, 3¾", pr from $6 to......................**8.00**

Pheasant, ceramic, realistic, 1½", pr from $8 to...........................**10.00**

Phonograph, metal, 2" L, pr from $10 to .................................**12.00**

Praying hands, plastic, bronze colored, Japan mark, 3¾", pr .........**12.00**

Rose, plastic, pink w/green leaves, Jay Don #5, 2¼", pr from $4 to.....**5.00**

Salmon, ceramic, pink & red, 4½" L, pr from $10 to....................**12.00**

Seal, ceramic, realistic, 2⅞", pr from $12 to ................................**15.00**

Skillet, plastic, tan & black, marked Pat Pend, 4⅝", pr from $3 to..**4.00**

St Lawrence Seaway ship, ceramic, stacks are shakers, 1950s, 2x6½"...............................**29.00**

Statue of Liberty, ceramic, green, copyright 1992, 5⅜", pr.....**28.00**

Stove, ceramic, black w/red details, pr from $8 to......................**10.00**

Suitcase, ceramic, black, Japan label, 2", pr from $6 to ........**8.00**

Sunbonnet Sue, ceramic, blue & white, pr from $12 to.........**15.00**

Toy soldier, ceramic, multicolored, 4⅝", pr from $12 to............**15.00**

Trophy cup, Hills of Kentucky, plastic, 3", pr from $4 to ............**5.00**

TX Alamo building, metal replica, Japan, 2¾x2½", pr ............**50.00**

Umbrella stand, ceramic, yellow, 3¾", pr ...............................**18.00**

Violin, cobalt glass w/plastic cap, 4", pr from $15 to....................**18.00**

Walnut, ceramic, realistic, Arcadia Ceramics, 1½", pr from $15 to .......................................**18.00**

Wooden pitcher, MS Gulf Coast, 2½", pr from $6 to................**8.00**

Zodiac girl, ceramic, multicolored, Japan ink stamp, 4½", pr..**45.00**

# Scottie Dogs

An amazing array of Scottie dog collectibles can be found in a wide range of prices. Collectors might choose to specialize in a particular area, or they may enjoy looking for everything from bridge tallies to original portraits or paintings. Most of the items are from the 1930s and 1940s.

Many were used for advertising purposes; others are simply novelties. For further information we recommend *A Treasury of Scottie Dog Collectibles* by Candace Sten Davis and Patricia Baugh (Collector Books).

Bowl, w/5 red dogs, Hazel Atlas, 2¼x5" dia ...........................**55.00**
Button, embossed metal, ¾" ....**12.00**
Cigarette box, metal, back opens, FBS Made in Japan, 7¼" L, EX ......................................**52.50**
Cookie jar, ceramic, unmarked, Japan, 8¾x11" ...................**85.00**
Doorstop, cast iron, old dark paint, 5½x6", EX .......................**150.00**

**Figurine, bronze, Asprey, ca 1950, 2⅞x2x2⅞", from $300.00 to $350.00. (Photo courtesy Candace Sten Davis and Patricia Baugh)**

Figurine, porcelain, black glossy paint, 1¾" ...........................**10.00**
Napkin holder, cvd wooden front, glass eye, 1930s, 4½x4⅛"..**55.00**
Paperweight, cast iron, black w/red collar, Hubley, 1½x1¾" ......**75.00**
Pin, gold-tone w/rhinestone collar, 1¼" L....................................**7.00**
Pin/brooch, black Bakelite, deeply carved, painted eye, 2x3".....**75.00**

Pitcher, white & red pyro on clear glass, Bartlett-Collins, 2-qt .......................................**35.00**
Planter, pulling cart, ceramic w/metallic gold finish, Japan, 5½" L................................**15.00**
Planter, white, opening in back, unmarked American, 1940s, 7".........................................**25.00**
Postcard, lining, Waiting for my Pal, EX .......................................**8.00**
Tablecloth, dogs/card suits, printed purple & orange on white, 30" sq........................................**25.00**

**Tumbler, black and red on clear glass, Federal Glass Co., 1950s, 3½", from $12.00 to $18.00.**

Tumbler, dog above fence, Hazel Atlas Glass Co, ca 1940s, from $12 to .................................**18.00**

# Scouting Collectibles

Founded in England in 1907 by Major General Lord Baden-Powell, scouting remains an important institution in the life of young boys and girls everywhere. Recently scouting-related memorabilia has attracted a following, and values of many items have escalated dramatically in the last few years. Early first edition handbooks often bring prices of $100.00 and more. Vintage uniforms are scarce and highly valued, and one of the rarer medals, the Life Saving Honor Medal, is worth several hundred dollars to collectors.

Rolland J. Sayers is the author of *A Complete Guide to Scouting Collectibles*; he is listed in the Directory under North Carolina.

## Boy Scouts

Belt buckle, Santa Fe Trail Council, 30th Anniversary, only 100 issued ................................**50.00**

Book, Camp Fire Leader's; Hazelwood & Thurman, 111 pages, 1964, EX ...........................**22.00**

Book, Nautical Scouting, Charles Longstreth, 1915, G+ ......**525.00**

Bookends, Be Prepared w/emblem, metal, EX...........................**50.00**

Catalog, Uniforms & Equipment, 16 pages, 1963-64, 11x9", EX ...................................**12.00**

Handbook, Handbook for Boys, 1930s, scout profile on cover, EX ....................................**50.00**

Lunch pail, scouts in camping scenes, tin litho, 1930s-40s, VG .....................................**55.00**

Neckerchief, Daniel Boone Council, 1960s, NM..........................**20.00**

Patch, Air Explorer, red & white on blue, M ..............................**85.00**

Patch, 1937 World Jamboree, in Netherlands, VG .............**915.00**

Poster, 1950 World Jamboree, Valley Forge PA, 20x13", EX .........**50.00**

Sleeping bag, regulation, 1950s, EX ....................................**40.00**

## Girl Scouts

Badge, Golden Eaglet, 10k, 1920-30 ...................................**550.00**

Bank, elf's head, emblem on hat, Brush-McCoy, 7x5", NMIB........**70.00**

Camera, box; Jem Jr 120, JE Mergott Co, Official GSA, EX ......**50.00**

Catalog, Brownie Scout Equipment, 1957, 23 pages, EX............**45.00**

Doll, Uneeda, hard plastic, ca 1961-63, 8", MIB......................**125.00**

Earrings, emblem shape, gold-tone, EX, pr................................**27.50**

Marbles, Girl Scout Premium, 10¢, 20 in original bag, MIP .....**27.50**

**Patch, Be Prepared, green, yellow, and red, unused, M, $27.50.**

Pin, Community Service, enameled, Be Prepared on ribbon, ¾", EX..**135.00**

Ring, spoon; embossed emblem on silver, Wm A Rogers, EX ........**60.00**

# Sears Kitchen Ceramics

During the 1970s the Sears Company sold several lines of novelty kitchen ware, including Country Kitchen, Merry Mushrooms, and Neil the Frog. These lines, espcially Merry Mushrooms, are coming on strong as the collectibles of tomorrow. There's lots of it around and unless you're buying it from someone who's already aware of its potential value, you can get it at very low prices. It was made in Japan. Besides the ceramic items, you'll find woodenware, enamelware, linens, and plastics.

## Country Kitchen

Butter dish.................................**15.00**
Canisters, set of 4.....................**40.00**
Creamer, 4¼"............................**9.00**
Napkin holder, 4½x5¾" ...........**15.00**

**Salt and pepper shakers, 4¾", $15.00 for the pair.**

Spoon rest, rectangular, 2 rests..**10.00**

## Merry Mushrooms

Ashtray, 2 rests, 5x6"...............**20.00**
Birdhouse, mushroom shape, w/chain for hanging...........................**28.00**

Bowl, salad; w/original wooden fork & spoon, rare .....................**60.00**
Bread box, enamel ware w/mushroom with decal, drop-down front, 2-shelf.................................**30.00**
Butter dish................................**15.00**
Canister set, basketweave background, 4-pc.......................**65.00**
Canister set, mushroom shape, 4-pc....................................**50.00**
Canister set, plastic, brown lids, 4-pc.........................................**32.00**
Canister set, smooth background, cylindrical, w/wooden lids, 4-pc.....................................**50.00**
Cheese tray, wood, compartment for crackers, glass dome & knife ..**60.00**
Clock, wall mount, battery operated...**25.00**
Coffee grinder, wood w/ceramic insert.................................**25.00**
Coffee mug, textured background, 10-oz.....................................**9.00**
Coffee mug, thermo-plastic......**16.00**
Coffee mugs, smooth background, cylindrical, 4 on wooden tree .....**45.00**
Coffee mugs, textured background, 4 on scrolling metal tree ......**45.00**
Coffeepot, tall & slim, 8¾".......**40.00**
Coffeepot, yellow enamelware, clear glass lid, black handle .........**35.00**
Contact paper, 3-yard roll........**15.00**

**Cookie jar/large canister, $18.00.**

Cookie jar, mushroom shape ....**18.00**

Creamer & sugar bowl w/lid ....**30.00**

Dinner bell .................................**32.00**

Gravy boat, 5½" L, w/7" L under-tray .....................................**30.00**

Jell-O mold/wall plaque, oval ......**70.00**

Miniature: napkin holder, salt & pepper shakers, flowerpot, etc, ea .............................................**8.00**

Napkin holder ...........................**18.00**

Pillow kit, to embroider, makes 14" pillow, MIB .........................**25.00**

Pitchers, graduated in size from 4" to 3", set of 4 ......................**45.00**

Planter, textured background, on brown undertray ...............**35.00**

Salt & pepper shakers, 5", pr ......**16.00**

Salt shaker & pepper mill, wood w/clear laminate over mush-room insert .........................**25.00**

Soup mug, hard to find, 3x4¾" ......**25.00**

Spice jar, paper label identifies con-tents, sm ..............................**5.00**

Spice rack, walnut, 5 drawers over 3 for coffee, tea & miscellaneous ..**50.00**

Spice rack, 2-tier, 2 drawers in base, w/12 spice jars, minimum value ...................................**65.00**

Spoon rest, 2 indents at bottom, 7½x5" ...................................**25.00**

Teapot, yellow lid & handle, squat, 32-oz .....................................**25.00**

Timer, windup ...........................**40.00**

Toaster cover, printed cloth .....**15.00**

Tray, plastic w/6 repeats of mush-room clusters, 13" ..............**28.00**

Trivet, sq tile in ornate cast-iron frame, 12x8" ......................**15.00**

Tureen, w/underplate & ladle, 2½ qt .........................................**58.00**

Wall pocket, pitcher & bowl shape ...............................**35.00**

## Neil the Frog

Bowl, water lily leaves on sides, 2 3-D frogs play on rim, 3¾x7" .......**60.00**

Canister set, plastic w/green lids, 4-pc .........................................**16.00**

Canisters, 4-pc set, from $50 to ......**60.00**

Clock, lotus leaf shape, wall mount, 7½x7" .................................**18.00**

Coffee mug .................................**6.00**

Cookie jar, frog final, 10½" ......**35.00**

Creamer & sugar bowl .............**20.00**

Cruets, oil & vinegar, 5", pr .....**30.00**

Cutting board, sq paddle shape w/handle, 15x8" .................**50.00**

Kitchen towel, frogs playing among mushrooms, 11½x11½" .......**5.00**

Kitchen towel, frogs playing among mushrooms, 15½x24" ...........**9.00**

Mustard jar, slot in lid for spoon (present) ..............................**20.00**

Napkin holder, frog on lotus on lily pad background .................**14.00**

Salt & pepper shakers, frog on lotus, lily pad background, 3¼", pr..**22.00**

**Salt and pepper shakers, frog on lotus blossom, 4½", $14.00 for the pair.**

Salt & pepper shakers, 1 is lotus blossom, 2nd is frog...........**22.00**

Skillet, enamelware, 10" ..........**20.00**

# Shawnee

The novelty planters, vases, cookie jars, salt and pepper shakers, and 'Corn' dinnerware made by the Shawnee Pottery of Ohio are attractive, fun to collect, and still available at reasonable prices. The company operated from 1937 until 1961, marking their wares with 'Shawnee, U.S.A.,' and a number series, or 'Kenwood.'

Refer to *Shawnee Pottery, An Identification and Value Guide,* by Jim and Bev Mangus (Collector Books) for more information. See also Cookie Jars. See Clubs and Newsletters for information concerning the Shawnee Pottery Collectors' Club.

Ashtray, Valencia, from $16 to .....**18.00**
Baker, Lobster Ware, open, #915, 5", from $35 to.........................**40.00**
Bowl, fruit; Corn Ware, King, #92, 6", from $45 to ..................**48.00**
Butter dish, Lobster Ware, Kenwood USA #927, from $95 to....**110.00**
Carafe, Valencia, no lid, from $35 to .......................................**45.00**

**Casserole, Corn line, #74 large, from $50.00 to $60.00.**

Cookie jar, Corn Ware, King or Queen, Shawnee #66, ea from $175 to .............................**225.00**

Creamer, Corn Ware, Queen, Shawnee #70, from $24 to.................**26.00**
Creamer, elephant, allover gold, Pat USA, from $350 to...........**400.00**
Egg cup, Valencia, from $15 to ..**18.00**
Figurine, gazelle, gold, USA #614, 5", from $75 to.........................**85.00**
Flower frog, snail, USA, 4x5", from $35 to .................................**45.00**
Grease jar, cottage, USA #8, from $325 to ............................**350.00**
Hors d'oeuvres holder, Lobster Ware, USA, 7¼", from $250 to ..**275.00**
Mug, Lobster Ware, Kenwood USA #911, 8-oz, from $75 to......**85.00**
Pie plate, Valencia, 10½", from $22 to .........................................**24.00**
Planter, baby skunk, Shawnee #512, from $30 to .........................**35.00**
Planter, bicycle built for 2, Shawnee USA #735, from $55 to......**65.00**
Planter, canopy bed, Shawnee #734, from $70 to.........................**80.00**
Planter, cat & sax, USA #729, from $30 to .................................**35.00**
Planter, fawn, 9", from $8 to......**10.00**
Planter, girl w/umbrella, USA #560, from $25 to.........................**28.00**
Planter, hobby horse, Shawnee #660, from $15 to...........................**20.00**
Planter, lovebirds, USA, from $10 to ..**12.00**
Planter, pony, Kenwood #1509, from $55 to .................................**65.00**
Planter, rabbit & stump, USA #606, from $12 to.........................**16.00**
Planter, top hat, USA, from $10 to ..**12.00**
Planter, tractor & trailer, #680 & #681, pr from $60 to..........**70.00**
Planter, train engine, Shawnee USA, from $55 to...........**65.00**
Planting dish, Shawnee USA #2002, 14½", from $15 to ..............**20.00**

Plate, salad; Corn Ware, King, Shawnee #93, 8", from $40 to ...........**50.00**

Popcorn set, Corn Ware, Queen, from $175 to .....................**200.00**

Refrigerator set, Valencia, from $65 to ........................................**75.00**

**Salt and pepper shakers, fruit, $50.00 for the pair.**

Salt & pepper shakers, Lobster Ware, claw, USA, pr from $35 to ........................................**40.00**

Salt & pepper shakers, Lobster Ware, full body, USA, pr $200 to ........................................**225.00**

Salt & pepper shakers, Muggsy, pr from $160 to .....................**175.00**

Salt & pepper shakers, Smiley, blue bib, pr from $125 to.........**135.00**

Salt & pepper shakers, Winnie & Smiley, hearts, lg, pr from $170 to ........................................**180.00**

Spoon holder, double; Lobster Ware, USA #935, 8½", $225 to ..**250.00**

Teapot, blue & red flowers w/gold, USA, from $65 to...............**75.00**

Teapot, embossed rose, gold gilded, USA, from $125 to...........**150.00**

Utility tray, Valencia, from $15 to......................................**18.00**

Vase, bud; Valencia, from $15 to .......................................**17.00**

Vase, burlap, USA #885, 5", from $10 to ...............................**12.00**

Vase, wheat, USA #1266, 6", from $18 to ...............................**22.00**

Wall pocket, Little Bo Peep, USA #586, from $35 to...............**40.00**

# Sheet Music

The most valuable examples of sheet music are those related to early transportation, ethnic themes, Disney characters, a particularly popular actor, singer, or composer, or with a cover illustration done by a well-known artist. Production of sheet music peaked during the 'Tin Pan Alley Days,' from the 1880s until the 1930s. Covers were made as attractive as possible to lure potential buyers, and today's collectors sometimes frame and hang them as they would a print. Flea markets are a good source for sheet music, and prices are usually very reasonable. Most are available for under $5.00. Some of the better examples are listed here. Refer to *The Sheet Music Reference and Price Guide* by Anna Marie Guiheen and Marie-Reine A. Pafik (Collector Books).

After All Is Said & Done, Dave Ringle, 1931.........................**6.00**

Autumn Serenade, Sammy Gallop & Peter DeRose, 1945.............**5.00**

Blue Skirt Waltz, Mitchell Parish & Vaclav Blaha, 1944 .............**5.00**

Careless Hands, Hillard & Sigman, photo cover: John Laurenz, 1949.....................................**3.00**

Carlotta, Cole Porter, movie: Can Can, 1943............................**5.00**

Cherries, Marois & Dartmouth, photo cover: Doris Day, 1952............**3.00**

Cold Cold Heart, Hank Williams, 1951......................................**4.00**

Dashing Cavaliers, ET Paull, cover artist: ET Paull, 1938.........**35.00**

Down in the Glens, Harry Gordon & Tommie Connor, 1947.........**3.00**

Enchanted Sea, Frank Metis & Randy Starr, 1959...............**5.00**

Every Time You Touch Me, Charlie Rich & Billy Sherril, 1975...**2.00**

First Time I Saw Your Face, Ewan MacColl, 1972......................**3.00**

Five Minutes With Mr Thornhill, Claude Thornhill, 1942.......**5.00**

Going Out of My Head, Teddy Randazzo & Bobby Weinstein, 1964....................................**5.00**

Guitar Boogie, Arthur Smith, photo cover: Arthur Smith, 1946..**5.00**

He's in Love, Robert Wright & Chet Forest, musical: Kismet, 1953.....................................**6.00**

Hello, It's Me; Todd Rundgren, 1968.....................................**4.00**

Holiday for Strings, David Rose, 1943.....................................**5.00**

I Beg of You, Elvis Presley, 1957..**20.00**

I'm Not Your Stepping Stone, Monkees, 1966 ...........................**5.00**

Ike for Four More Years, Irving Berlin, 1956 ......................**25.00**

In My Arms, Frank Loesser & Ted Grouya, 1943 ......................**3.00**

In the Middle of an Island, Nick Aquaviva & Ted Varneck, 1957......**3.00**

It Was Written in the Stars, Robin & Arlen, movie: Casbah, 1948....................................**6.00**

Keep It a Secret, Jessie Mae Robinson, 1952.............................**3.00**

Lady Bird, Cha Cha Cha, cover artist: Norman Rockwell, 1968....**25.00**

Little Toot, Allie Wrubel, movie: Melody Time, Disney, 1948..**10.00**

Love Star, Al Lewis, Larry Stock & Vincent Rose, 1945..............**3.00**

Make It With You, David Gates, 1970.....................................**3.00**

Misty, Johnny Burke & Erroll Garner, 1955 .............................**3.00**

**Moon River, Johnny Mercer and Henry Mancini, 1961, from the movie Breakfast at Tiffany's, Audrey Hepburn cover, $5.00.** (Photo courtesy Guiheen and Pafik)

My Ten Ton Baby & Me, Wilson, Transportation, 1942 ..........**5.00**

Only One, Anne Croswell & Lee Pochriss, musical: Tovarich, 1963....................................**3.00**

Rainbow, Russ Hamilton, 1957..**5.00**

Right Into Your Arms, Charles Lynes, 1945..........................**3.00**

Rose With a Broken Stem, Tolchard Evans, 1937 ..........................**4.00**

Silver in the Moon, HA Pooley, 1945..**3.00**

Sky Anchors, Waring, Transportation, 1942....................................**10.00**

Strip Polka, Johnny Mercer, photo cover: Andrew Sisters, 1942.......**3.00**

Take Care When You Say Te Quiero, Henry Prichard, 1946......................................**5.00**

There Is a Tavern in Town, Harry Henneman, 1942..................**5.00**

This Is the First Time, Wally Peterson, 1949.............................**2.00**

Tom Dooley, El Jackson, 1958...**3.00**

Tulips & Heather, Milton Carson, photo cover: Perry Como, 1950......................................**3.00**

Under the Bridges of Paris, Dorcas Cochran & Vincent Scotto, 1953......................................**3.00**

Warm All Over, Frank Loesser, musical: Most Happy Fella, 1956......................................**6.00**

Windshield Wiper, Joseph J Lilley & Dick Peterson, 1948............**5.00**

Woody Woodpecker, George Tibbles & Ramsey Idriss, 1947........**5.00**

# Shot Glasses

Shot glasses, old and new, are whetting the interest of today's collectors, and they're relatively easy to find. Basic values are given for various categories of shot glasses in mint condition. These are general prices only. Glasses that are in less-than-mint condition will obviously be worth less than the price given here. Very rare and unique items will be worth more. Sample glasses and other individual one-of-a-kind oddities are a bit harder to classify and really need to be evaluated on an individual basis.

Mark Pickvet is the author of *Shot Glasses: An American Tradition*. He is listed in the Directory under Michigan. See Clubs and Newsletters for information concerning the Shot Glass Club of America.

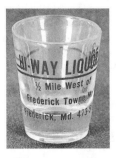

**Advertising, Hi-Way Liquors, Frederick, MD, red pyro on clear, 2¼", from $4.00 to $5.00.**

Barrel shape, from $5 to.............**7.50**

Black porcelain replica, from $3.50 to...........................................**5.00**

Carnival colors, plain or fluted, from $100 to.............................**150.00**

Carnival colors, w/patterns, from $125 to.............................**175.00**

Colored glass tourist, from $4 to..**6.00**

Culver 22k gold, from $6 to........**8.00**

Depression, colors, from $10 to.....**12.50**

Depression, colors w/patterns or etching, from $17.50 to......**25.00**

Depression, tall, general designs, from $10 to.........................**12.50**

Depression, tall, tourist, from $5 to...........................................**7.50**

Frosted w/gold designs, from $6 to...........................................**8.00**

General, advertising, from $4 to...........................................**6.00**

General, enameled design, from $3 to...........................................**4.00**

General, frosted designs, from $3.50 to...........................................**5.00**

General, gold designs, from $6
to ............................................**8.00**

General, porcelain, from $4 to......**6.00**

General tourist, from $3 to ........**4.00**

Inside eyes, from $5 to ...............**7.50**

Iridized silver, from $5 to...........**7.50**

Mary Gregory or Anchor Hocking
Ships, from $150 to .........**200.00**

Nudes, from $25 to ...................**35.00**

Plain, w/ or w/out flutes, from 50¢
to ............................................**75**

Pop or soda advertising, from $12.50
to .......................................**15.00**

Porcelain tourist, from $3.50
to ..........................................**5.00**

Rounded European designs w/gold
rims, from $4 to ...................**6.00**

Ruby flashed, from $35 to........**50.00**

Sayings & toasts, 1940s-50s, from
$5 to .....................................**7.50**

Sports, professional teams, from $5
to ..........................................**7.50**

Square, general, from $6 to........**8.00**

Square, w/etching, from $10 to .....**12.50**

Square, w/pewter, from $12.50 to .....**15.00**

Square, w/2-tone bronze & pewter,
from $15 to..........................**17.50**

Standard glass w/pewter, from
$12.50 to ............................**15.00**

Steuben crystal, from $150 to .....**200.00**

Taiwan tourist, from $2 to .........**3.00**

Tiffany, Galle or fancy art, from
$600 to .............................**800.00**

Turquoise & gold tourist, from $6
to ..........................................**8.00**

Whiskey or beer advertising, mod-
ern, from $5 to .....................**7.50**

Whiskey sample glasses, from $75
to ......................................**350.00**

19th-century cut patterns, from $35
to .......................................**50.00**

# Silhouette Pictures

Silhouettes and reverse paintings on glass were commercially produced in the US from the 1920s
through the 1950s. Some were hand
painted, but most were silkscreened.
Artists and companies used either
flat or convex glass. Common subjects include romantic couples, children, horses, dogs, and cats. Many
different styles, sizes, colors, and
materials were used for frames.
Backgrounds also vary from textured paper to foils, colorful lithographs, wildflowers, or butterfly
wings. Sometimes the backgrounds
were painted on the back of the
glass in gold or cream color. These
inexpensive pictures were usually
sold in pairs, except for the advertising kind, which were given by mer-
chants as gifts.

For more information we recommend *The Encyclopedia of Silhouette
Collectibles on Glass* by Shirley Mace
(Shadow Enterprises); she is listed in
the Directory under New Mexico.

Art Publishing Co, boy & girl feeding ducks, flat....................**40.00**

Benton, boy on rocking horse followed by
girl w/flag, convex.................**35.00**

Benton, boys stands beside girl in
pumpkin, convex ...............**50.00**

Benton, child plays w/cat while
mother watches, convex....**60.00**

Benton, couple at piano, convex..**35.00**

Benton, couple kissing at fence, pastel
floral background, convex..**35.00**

Benton, couple sitting having drinks, convex....................**40.00**

Benton, couple taking ride in 1-horse sleigh, convex ..........**45.00**

Benton, courting couple dancing outdoors, convex .....................**35.00**

Benton, fence & tree, courting couple airbrushed background, convex......................................**30.00**

Benton, Indian maiden & wagon trail scene, convex.............**65.00**

Benton, lady looks upon well on hill, convex ................................**30.00**

Benton, man sits blowing bubbles from pipe while boy watches, convex ................................**35.00**

Benton, sailing ship scene, convex ..**35.00**

**Benton, Scottie dog among flowers and butterfly on convex glass, 1940s, 5x4", from $40.00 to $50.00. (Photo courtesy Candace Sten Davis and Patricia J. Baugh)**

Benton, Scottie dog barks at bird on fence, convex......................**30.00**

Buckbee-Brehm, Happy Bride, lady adjusts veil for bride, flat ..**40.00**

Buckbee-Brehm, Little Jack Horner sat in a corner, boy w/pie, flat..**40.00**

C&A Richards, elfin music, flat ..**140.00**

C&A Richards, sprite-like figure on flower, rainbow background, flat....................................**240.00**

Harry Henrikson, girl feeding swans, flat .........................**25.00**

Lee Mero, nude about to dive into water, flat ...........................**50.00**

PF Volland, children dance around maypole, Gleam o' Gold label, flat....................................**50.00**

Reliance Products, courtship, flat...**22.00**

**RF-7, wood frame, convex glass, 5" diameter, $25.00. (Photo courtesy Shirley and Ray Mace)**

Unknown maker, child says prayers at bedtime w/dog watching, flat....................................**50.00**

# Snow Domes

Snow domes are water-filled paperweights. The earliest type was made in two pieces with a glass globe on a separate base. First made in the mid-nineteenth century, they were revived during the 1930s and 1940s. The most common snow domes on today's market are the plastic half-moon shapes made as souvenirs or Christmas toys, a style that originated in West Germany during the 1950s. Other shapes such as round and square bottles, tall and short rectangles, cubes, and other simple shapes are found as well.

Advertising, Corona Beer, tropical theme w/palm tree through dome, NM ..........................38.00

Advertising, Pepsi, St Bernard w/Pepsi can around neck, 1980s, EX ......................................45.00

Character, Aunt Jemima, Atlas Crystal Works, 1940s, EX........................................40.00

Character, Beauty & the Beast, Disney, musical, 1990s, MIB ....................................60.00

Character, Eeyore Asleep, 4", NM ....................................25.00

Character, Freddy Kreuger w/girl on globe, NECA, MIB.............60.00

Character, gnome petting rabbit beside pine tree, Unieboak, 1980, EX ...........................25.00

Character, Rudolph the Red-Nosed Reindeer, EX decal on red base, 1950s..................................40.00

Character, Santa in sleigh pulled by reindeer, dome in sleigh, EX ......................................30.00

Character, Superman w/His Fortress of Solitude, 2000, MIB ......35.00

Character, Unicorn w/overall floral decor, musical, Westland, NM .....................................25.00

Character/souvenir, Camp Snoopy, Mall of America, Snoopy & friends, NM........................25.00

Figural, sailing ship, Atlas Crystal Works, 1940s, EX..............25.00

Souvenir, Chicago Water Tower, musical, EX ......................35.00

Souvenir, Crown Royal, Millennium Collection, NM...................30.00

Souvenir, Darien Lake, roller coaster, EX ................................40.00

Souvenir, Disney Millennium, musical, NM+ ...........................50.00

Souvenir, Disneyland, Pirates of the Caribbean, 1960s, EX .......45.00

Souvenir, Mickey Mouse As The Sorcerer, musical, NM ......45.00

Souvenir, Mission Inn CA, 1903-2003, MIB .........................35.00

Souvenir, New York City w/famous landmarks, 6¾", EX..........40.00

Souvenir, Paris, Eiffel Tower, 1950s, EX ......................................22.00

Souvenir, Statue of Liberty, musical, Hallmark, EX ....................25.00

Souvenir, Tel-Aviv, sailboat w/skyline background, EX..........40.00

Souvenir, 1964-65 New York World's Fair, calendar in base, EX.25.00

# Soda Pop

Now that vintage Coca-Cola items have become rather expensive, interest is expanding to include some of the less widely known flavors of soda — Dr. Pepper, Nehi, and Orange Crush, for instance. For more information, we recommend *Collectible Soda Pop Memorabilia* by B.J. Summers (Collector Books).

### Dr. Pepper

A young pharmacist, Charles C. Alderton, was hired by W.B. Morrison, owner of Morrison's Old Corner Drug Store in Waco, Texas, around

1884. Alderton, an observant sort, noticed that the drugstore's patrons could never quite make up their minds as to which flavor of extract to order. He concocted a formula that combined many flavors, and Dr. Pepper was born. The name was chosen by Morrison in honor of a beautiful young girl with whom he had once been in love. The girl's father, a Virginia doctor by the name of Pepper, had discouraged the relationship due to their youth, but Morrison had never forgotten her. On December 1, 1885, a U.S. patent was issued to the creators of Dr. Pepper.

Ashtray, clear glass w/chevron logo in center, EX......................**35.00**

Beverage heater, for drinking hot, electric, 7", NM...................**75.00**

Bottle, glass, Desert Storm commemorative, 10-oz, EX......**10.00**

Bottle, glass, San Diego America's Finest City, sealed, 1978, 11", NM.....................................**10.00**

Bottle, plastic blow-up, Dr Pepper in script, 27", EX....................**25.00**

Bottle topper, Cindy Gardner, EX+..**165.00**

Can, metal, old pull tab, opened, EX......................................**45.00**

Carrier, bottle; cardboard, holds 6 16-oz bottles, 1950s, EX..........**15.00**

Clock, metal & glass, 2/4/10 in red, name banner, 1950s, 15" dia, NM.....................................**850.00**

Clock, neon, 8-sided, reverse-painted glass, EX+................**1,350.00**

Clock, octagonal, neon, reverse-painted glass, EX+.......**1,200.00**

Fan, cardboard w/wooden handle, pretty girl, Earl Morgan art, EX......................................**75.00**

License plate, metal, oval name panel, 6x12", NM.................**8.00**

Menu board, metal over cardboard, plaid logo at top, 23x17", VG..**155.00**

Menu board, tin chalkboard, bottle/clock/grid logo on yellow, 23x17", VG......................**200.00**

**Menu, tin over cardboard, 23x17", EX, $195.00.** (Photo courtesy B.J. Summers)

Pencil/opener, bullet form, logo, 1930s-40s, 4½", G..............**75.00**

Shirt, striped cotton w/Dr Pepper patch on sleeve, Pepsi on front, NM.....................................**20.00**

Sign, cardboard, Join Me!, girl in car, 1940s, 32x40", NM...**500.00**

Sign, plastic, woodgrain look w/oval name, 1960s, 10x26", EX..**25.00**

Sign, porcelain, Drink..Good for Life red, white, green, 10½x26½"........**125.00**

Sign, porcelain, self-framed, Drink..., red & white, 9¼x24", G`.....................................**65.00**

Sign, porcelain, triangular, white letters on red, 18x23", EX....**875.00**

Sign, porcelain, 10-2-4/Drink DP, red-on-white circle, 10" dia, NM.....................................**150.00**

Sign, tin, Dr Pepper, 7x20", EX.**30.00**

Sign, tin, 2-sided flange, bottle cap, 1959, 18x22", EX..........**1,000.00**

Thermometer, dial, Hot or Cold, Pam, 1950s-60s, 12" dia, NM .....**125.00**

Thermometer, tin, Frosty Cold beside scale, 23¾x9¾", G..**90.00**

Thermometer, tin, Hot or Cold, red & white, 26x7", NM.........**150.00**

Toy truck, 1931 Kenworth delivery, Ertl, 1996, 1/34 scale, MIB..**30.00**

Tray, You'll Like It Too!, w/graphics, 1930s-40s, VG+ ...............**280.00**

## Hires

Did you know that Hires Root Beer was first served to fairgoers at the Philadelphia Centennial in 1876? It was developed by Charles E. Hires, a druggist who experimented with roots and herbs to come up with the final recipe. The company originally chose the Hires boy as their logo, and if you'll study his attire, you can sometimes approximate a guess as to when an item he appears on was manufactured. Very early on he appeared in a dress, and from 1906 until 1914 it was a bathrobe. He sported a dinner jacket from 1915 until 1926.

Banner, Enjoy a Hires Float/Only 50¢..., canvas, 32x42", EX..**125.00**

Bottle, syrup; reverse-painted label, original metal lid, 12", EX ...................................**225.00**

Bottle carrier, cardboard, cold frosty mugs, NM ..........................**15.00**

Bottle carrier, wood w/dovetail corners, Quarter Case, VG+ ..**30.00**

Bottle topper/bottle, die-cut cardboard, 10¢ Off/Try a Real Black Cow ....................................**15.00**

Box, ...Improved Root Beer Liquid, dovetail wood, 5½x7¼x5¼"..**100.00**

Clock, glass face, light-up, Drink Hires, 15" dia, EX............**385.00**

Clock, metal & glass, Drink Hires Root Beer, EX...................**275.00**

**Clock, metal and glass, electric light-up, tilted bottle in center, 1956, VG, $1,050.00.** (Photo courtesy B.J. Summers)

Dispenser, hourglass shape, w/spigot & pump, 13", EX ..........**1,550.00**

**Door push, tin, Finer Flavor Because..., EX, $150.00.** (Photo courtesy B.J. Summers)

Drinking glass, curved top, etched, Enjoy Hires..., NM+ ........**160.00**

Mug, German made, 5", EX .....**210.00**

Mug, Ugly Kid, by Mettlach, 4¼", EX ...................................**220.00**

Recipe folder, boy looking at Hires sign, VG .............................**20.00**

Sign, cardboard, Enjoy...above lady's head on red frame, 12x9", EX+ .................................**660.00**

Sign, cardboard, girl & paper label bottle, 22x12", EX ..........**200.00**

Sign, tin, bottle shape, 1950s, 22", M ....................................**200.00**

Sign, tin, boy w/mug pointing, 28½x20½", EX..............**2,900.00**

Sign, tin, diecut, embossed, bottle, 15½x57", VG....................**325.00**

Sign, tin, embossed, In Bottles - Ice Cold, 27¼x19⅜", G-...........**60.00**

Sign, tin, oval diecut, Drink Hires, bottle, white, blue stripes, 20x29" ..............................**175.00**

Sign, tin, R-J logo on disc, light blue border, 12" dia, NM+ ....**75.00**

Sign, tin litho, Hires...w/Real Root Juices, 4-color, 7x12", NM.....**75.00**

Thermometer, bottle diecut, 1950s, 28", EX.............................**165.00**

Thermometer, dial, Drink...on wood-grain, 12" dia, EX+ ..............**80.00**

Thermometer, tin bottle form, blue dot logo, 18", EX..............**120.00**

## Nehi

Clock, glass & metal, Drink...& other Nehi flavors, 15" dia, EX..**325.00**

Sign, painted tin, Drink, bottle in spotlight, 45x18", EX ......**125.00**

Sign, paper, Drink...Nehi flavors, 7¼x12", EX ........................**40.00**

Sign, paper lithograph, pretty lady w/hat holding bottle ..........**75.00**

Sign, tin, diecut, double-sided flange, Drink...Ice Cold, 18x13½" ...........................**525.00**

Sign, tin, embossed, Curb Service...Sold Here Ice Cold, 19⅝x27¾".......**95.00**

Tray, metal, woman in ocean wave, VG ....................................**195.00**

## Nesbitt's

Clock, glass front, light-up, bottle on dial, round, 1956, EX+..**1,000.00**

Poster, cardboard lithographed, family outgoing, 36x25", EX...**155.00**

Sign, porcelain, black disc, die-cut corners, sq, 1950s, 33", NM+ .................................**400.00**

Thermometer, Nesbitt's Made From Real Oranges, 27", EX.....**115.00**

## Orange-Crush

Blotter, cardboard, Compliments of..., 1940s, VG .................**35.00**

Clock, plastic, light-up, Taste, sq, 15", EX.............................**135.00**

Glass, Bakelite & frosted glass, Art Deco style, rare, EX.........**450.00**

Glass, flared top & etched syrup line, NM...........................**195.00**

Sign, cardboard, lady & her dog, 14x19", EX.......................**190.00**

Sign, cardboard diecut, Krinkle bottle w/Crushy, 14x30", EX ....................................**175.00**

Sign, metal, embossed, self-framing, bottle in center, 17x53¼", EX ...................................**460.00**

Sign, metal, single-sided, bottle, 31½x11¾", VG.................**125.00**

Sign, paper on cardboard, woman & dog, 13½x19½", EX .........**150.00**

Sign, tin, clear ribbed bottle, Come In..., 1940s, 3x10", EX.....**500.00**

Thermometer, painted metal, Thirsty...Crush That Thirst, EX ....................................**165.00**

## Pepsi-Cola

Pepsi-Cola has been around about as long as Coca-Cola, but since collectors are just now beginning to discover how fascinating this line of advertising memorabilia can be, it's generally much less expensive. You'll be able to determine the approximate date your items were made by the style of logo they carry. The familiar oval was used in the early 1940s, about the time the two 'dots' (indicated in our listings with '=') between the words were changed to one. But the double dots are used nowadays as well, especially on items designed to be reminiscent of the old ones - beware! The bottle cap logo was used from about 1943 until the early to mid-1960s with variations. For more information refer to *Pepsi-Cola Collectibles* by Bill Vehling and Michael Hunt and *Introduction to Pepsi Collecting* by Bob Stoddard.

**Bottle cap sign, metal flange, double-sided, 1950s, 15x14", VG, $475.00.** (Photo courtesy B.J. Summers)

Bottle, clear glass, P=C paper label/shoulder ribbon, 12-oz, VG .....................................**65.00**

Bottle, clear glass, paint P=C label, 12-oz, EX............................**45.00**

Bottle, green glass, P=C paper label, 1930s-40s, 12-oz, EX .........**75.00**

Bottle cap, light-up, 16" dia, EX ..**575.00**

Bottle carrier, wood, Buy Pepsi-Cola, 1940s, EX ...............**100.00**

Bottle carrier, wood, 6-pack, triangular w/cut-out handle, 1930s, EX+ ....................................**150.00**

Box, tin, Gibson girl on lid w/glass, 1989, 5x3½x4", EX ............**12.00**

Calendar holder, celluloid on tin, bottle cap & ribbon, 1940s, 8x6" ...**725.00**

Can, cone top, P=C bottle cap/2 Full Glasses, 1940s, VG+........**425.00**

Can, metal, cap on side, diagonal stripes, Seattle WA, 1950s, EX .....................................**65.00**

Carrier, bottle; embossed tin, holds 6 pack, Enjoy..., Union Products...**45.00**

Clock, double bubble, 1950s, EX..**875.00**

Clock, light-up, Think Young, Say Pepsi Please, 15" dia, M .......**400.00**

**Clock, metal and glass, electric light-up, tilted bottle in center, 1956, VG, $1,050.00.** (Photo courtesy B.J. Summers)

Clock, metal/glass, Say Pepsi Please & later cap, 16" sq, EX ...**190.00**

Clock, metal/plastic w/neon tube, battery, single dot, 15" dia, EX .....................................**85.00**

Coaster, double-dot label in center, 1940s, 4", VG ...................**8.00**

Game, cardboard, Vest Pocket Baseball, 1941, EX ...................**145.00**

Glass, syrup line & double dot, NM .......................................**45.00**

Legos, plastic, Happy Holidays from..., 1985, 27-pc set, EX ..........................................**25.00**

License plate adapter, metal, P=C logo, Lose a Minute..., 1940s, EX .........................................**95.00**

Menu board, tin, Have a Pepsi, yellow stripes, 30", NM ........**135.00**

Mirror, glass, cap logo, hangs from chain, 1950s, 9½" dia, EX ..............**295.00**

Pull toy, puppy w/hot-dog wagon, wood, 10", EX ...................**250.00**

Radio, plastic bottle form, P=C oval logo, 23", EX .....................**400.00**

Sign, cardboard lithograph, hostess/festive table, metal frame, 29" L ........................**90.00**

Sign, glass, light-up, convex cover, Light...1950s, 16" dia, NM..**1,350.00**

Sign, metal, embossed bottle, More Bounce..., 1950s, 48x18", EX..**525.00**

Sign, metal/glass/cardboard/mirror, Enjoy...Now, cap, 1950s, 12" sq......................................**500.00**

Sign, paper, Listen to Country-Spy, 8x19", NM+ ........................**85.00**

Sign, paper lithograph, Bigger & Better, bottle at left, 6¼x19⅝" ..**275.00**

Sign, plywood arrow, Beverage Dept, 1940s, 15½x15", NM .........**950.00**

Sign, porcelain, bottle cap diecut, Canada, 1950s, EX..........**230.00**

Sign, porcelain, double-sided, Hit the Spot, 56x23", G .........**700.00**

Sign, porcelain, Enjoy a Pepsi/bottle cap, 12¼x29¼", VG ..........**230.00**

Sign, tin, bottle cap, P=C logo, 37" dia, EX ..............................**275.00**

Sign, tin, double-sided, flange, Buy...Here, 16x12", EX ...**695.00**

Sign, tin, embossed bottle cap, 19¼" dia, NM ...........................**200.00**

Sign, tin, for bottle rack, 5x18¾", EX ......................................**95.00**

Sign, tin bottle diecut, P=C logo, 29½x8", VG.....................**525.00**

Standup figure, grocer w/carton, cardboard, 1930s, 68x24", VG ..**675.00**

Straw box, cardboard, bottle cap above clear window, 1950s, 10½" ................................**150.00**

Straws, in original unopened box w/5¢ bottle, NM...............**540.00**

String holder, Join the Swing..., double-dot name, 1940s, 16x12", EX ....................................**650.00**

Thermometer, metal, convex glass cover, dial type, 20½" dia, EX .....................................**180.00**

Thermometer, metal & glass, cap at top of scale, 27x8", VG ....**250.00**

Thermometer, self-framed tin w/ center scale tube, logos at top, 28x7" .................................**45.00**

Thermometer, tin, Bigger, Better, 6¼x15¾", G ......................**175.00**

Thermometer, tin, Pepsi Please, 1969, 28x7¼", NM...........**185.00**

Thermometer, tin w/embossed cap on yellow, 27x7¼", EX ....**150.00**

Tray, Enjoy P=C/Hits the Spot, 10x14", EX .........................**90.00**

Tray, storybook scene, 1930s, 13¾x10¼", NM ..................**45.00**

Vending machine, metal, Vendolater, #3D-33, 1950s, G..**750.00**

Whistle, plastic twin bottles, 3x1½", EX .....................................**20.00**

## Royal Crown Cola

Can, metal, flat top, large RC letter-
ing, EX .............................**40.00**
Clock, light-up, Pam Clock Co, 14½"
dia, EX ............................**235.00**
Poster, cardboard, Shirley Temple,
29½x12¼", VG.................**300.00**
Poster, cardboard, 1-sided, girl on
phone, 28x11", EX...........**115.00**
Sign, metal, embossed, self-framing,
31½x12", EX ......................**95.00**
Sign, metal, heavily embossed bot-
tle, 15½x58½", NM..........**225.00**
Thermometer, red, white & blue metal,
Fresher Refresher, 10x26", G ..**130.00**

## Seven-Up

Though it was originally touted
to have medicinal qualities, by 1930
7-Up had been reformulated and
was simply sold as a refreshing
drink. The company who first made
it was the Howdy Company, who by
1940 had changed its name to 7-Up
to correspond with the name of the
soft drink. Collectors search for the
signs, thermometers, point-of-sale
items, etc., that carry the 7-Up slogans.

Clock, metal & plastic, neon tube
on face, battery, 15" dia,
NM .....................................**75.00**
Clock, plastic & wood, light-up, You
Like It..., sq, 15", G.............**95.00**
Cooler, metal w/embossed logo,
drain plug, swing handles,
1950s, VG .........................**35.00**
Pencil, mechanical; metal & plastic,
w/long-term calendar, G ..**12.00**

Sign, cardboard, You Stand-By, man
w/bottle, easel back, 18", EX ..**295.00**
Sign, plastic, 2-sided, revolves,
lights up, 1940s, 30x20x8",
NM ...................................**375.00**
Sign, sidewalk; tin, 2-sided, bubble
design on wire frame, 50x28",
VG ....................................**150.00**
Sign, tin, First Against Thirst,
Canada, 1960s, 20x28",
VG......................................**40.00**
Sign, tin, Fresh Up..., bottle on
white, 17⅜x6⅜", NM.......**225.00**
Sign, tin, 2-sided flange, bubble
logo, 1940s, 10x12½", EX .**250.00**
Sign, tin litho, Your Fresh Up, 30½"
L, VG...............................**180.00**

**Thermometer, alu-
minum dial type, 10",
NM, $225.00. (Photo
courtesy B.J. Summers)**

Thermometer, Fresh Up..., bottle at
right, 15x6", VG ..............**160.00**
Thermometer, logo on face, Fresh Clean
Taste, dial type, 10", VG.......**225.00**
Thermometer, 7-Up Likes You, dial
type, 10", NM...................**230.00**

## Miscellaneous

Moxie, glass, straight sides, frosted
logo, NM+ ........................**165.00**

Moxie, sign, tin, Try Our Soda Syrups, lists flavors, 19" ......**665.00**

Moxie, tip tray, tin lithograph, blond w/glass, gray rim, 6", EX..**135.00**

Nu Icy, sign, porcelain, You Can't..., bottle, 1930s-40s, 12x24", EX+ ..**350.00**

NuGrape, sign, tin, Drink...A Flavor..., bottle, 1940s, 12x16", EX .....................................**500.00**

Palmer's Root Beer, porcelain sign, curved oval, Drink..., 14x21", EX+ .................................**550.00**

Ski, sign, metal disc w/skiing bottle, self-frame, 1950s, 30" dia, NM ...........................**375.00**

Sprite, doll, Lucky Lymon, vinyl talker, 1990s, 7½", M ........**25.00**

Squirt, clock, light-up, boy/bottle, Telechron, 1946, 15" dia, NM ...................................**625.00**

Squirt, flange sign, Drink..., flag on yellow, 1941, 14x18", EX..**350.00**

Squirt, sign, paper, $5.95 value, Squirt doll, 6-pack, 1962, 10x21", M ..........................**50.00**

**Squirt, sign, tin, flange, 1942, 14x8", VG, $400.00.**
(Photo courtesy B.J. Summers)

Squirt, tin sign, drink..., boy on panel, framed, sq, 36", VG..**350.00**

Whistle, sign, tin, Just Thirsty?, hand-held bottle, 7x10", NM ....**750.00**

Whistle, tin sign, embossed, elf, bottle, cart, 30x26", EX ..........**400.00**

# Souvenir Spoons

Originating with the Salem Witch spoons designed by Daniel Low, souvenir spoons are generally reasonably priced, easily displayed, and often exhibit fine artwork and craftsmanship. Spoons are found with a wide range of subject matter including advertising, commemorative, historic sites, American Indians, famed personalities, and more. Souvenir spoons continue to capture the imaginations of thousands of collectors with their timeless appeal. For further information we recommend *Collectible Souvenir Spoons, Books I* and *II,* by Wayne Bednersh (Collector Books).

Alaska, transfer print enamel finial, sterling, demitasse, from $5 to.**15.00**

Black boy w/watermelon in bowl, squirrel finial, Watson, from $95 to ...............................**125.00**

Buffalo NY on handle, buffalo finial, plain bowl, Durgin, from $30 to ........................................**50.00**

CA state handle w/Mt Lowe Incline Railroad embossed, from $40 to ........................................**75.00**

California on handle, bear finial, plain bowl, Shiebler, from $75 to .....................................**125.00**

Chimney Rock Wisconsin Dells on handle, plain bowl, from $10 to ........................................**20.00**

Denver Capitol embossed in bowl, Pike's Peak on handle, from $25 to ........................................**40.00**

Ft Sumter Charleston SC engraved in bowl, gold washed, Towle, from $25 to ...................................**50.00**

Hastings MN, Spiral Bridge engraved in bowl, Gorham, from $50 to ..................................**70.00**

Hotel Colorado Glenwood Springs Co engraved in bowl, from $25 to ........................................**40.00**

Indianapolis 500 on handle, plain bowl, demitasse, from $15 to ........................................**25.00**

**Louisiana Purchase, wagon train and railroad handle, US Government building in bowl, from $30.00 to $45.00.**

Madison WI, scenes in bowl, various handles, ea from $15 to.....**50.00**

Mardi Gras New Orleans painted in bowl, simple handle, from $45 to ........................................**70.00**

Masonic Temple Chicago engraved in bowl (EX detail), from $30 to ........................................**50.00**

New York stacked skyline figural handle, Shepard, from $75 to ......................................**150.00**

NY Flatiron Building embossed in bowl, various handles, from $20 to ........................................**75.00**

Philadelphia PA & House of Betsy Ross on handle, Robbins, from $20 to ..................................**40.00**

Pike's Peak CO engraved in bowl, wavy handle, Shepard, from $30 to ........................................**50.00**

Pine tree figural handle, plain bowl, Watson, from $75 to........**150.00**

Pinocchio finial, enameled stainless steel, from $5 to.................**10.00**

Pontiac IL State Reformatory engraved in bowl, Towle, from $30 to ..................................**50.00**

San Diego Mission ruins in bowl, silver plate, from $10 to .........**15.00**

San Francisco Bay embossed in bowl, orange finial, from $15 to ........................................**25.00**

Steer rider figural handle, plain bowl, Meyer Bros, from $75 to ......................................**100.00**

Train engraved in bowl, flowered handle, Shepard, from $25 to ..................................**45.00**

WC Fields figural handle, stainless w/red jeweled eyes, from $25 to ........................................**50.00**

Whale in bowl, whaling ship finial, Gorham, from $75 to.......**125.00**

Woman in bathing suit (risque) figural handle, Paye & Baker, $75 to ......................................**100.00**

# Sporting Collectibles

When sports cards became so widely collectible several years, other types of related memorabilia started to interest sports fans. Now they search for baseball uniforms, autographed baseballs, game-used bats and gloves, and all sorts of ephemera. Although baseball is America's all-time favorite, other sports have their own groups of interested collectors.

Banner, Minnesota Twins 1987 World Champions, EX ......**12.00**

Banner, The Pirates Welcome You to Three Rivers Stadium, lg, NM ...................................**265.00**

Baseball bat, miniature; H&B Model 40 Tony Lazzeri, 16", EX ..**50.00**

Baseball bat, Tony Kubek Store Model, 1960s, 34", NM ......**20.00**

Book, Golden Stamp Book of the Brooklyn Dodgers, 1955, complete, NM .........................**295.00**

Comic book, 500 Miles, Indianapolis Race, 1949, 12-pg, VG+ .....**60.00**

Decal, Boston Patriots, Fleer Football, 1960, M .....................**17.50**

**Doll, Joe Montana, stuffed printed cloth in San Francisco 49ers #16 uniform, Ace Novelty, NM, $30.00.** (Photo courtesy Patricia Smith)

Magazine, Pro Football 5th Annual Editon, 1960, 132 pgs, EX ..**15.00**

Media guide, 1984 Boston Red Sox, Wade Boggs & Jim Rice on cover, EX ..........................**10.00**

Patch, NCAA Football, 1990s, 3x2¾", NM .........................**6.00**

Patch, Philadelphia Phillies 100 Years, 1883-1983, 4" dia, EX ........**60.00**

Patch, Rose Bowl, Pasadena Tournament of Roses, 1998, NM ...**15.00**

Pennant, Ali vs Liston, blue & yellow felt, 1965, w/ticket, EX ................................**1,630.00**

**Pennant, Motorama, Boston, Mass., felt, 12x28¼", G, $50.00.** (Photo courtesy B.J. Summers)

Pennant, Washington Redskins, Super Bowl VII, 1973, felt, 30", EX ..**310.00**

Pennant, 1983 Chicago White Sox, American League West Champions, EX .............................**8.00**

Pin-back, Ernie Banks, black image & letters on yellow, 1950s, EX ..................................**240.00**

Plate, Spirit of Victory, Notre Dame Football, 1999, Bradford, 8", NM ...................................**22.50**

Press pin, 1957 All Star; St Louis Cardinals, cardinal on bat, EX ..................................**210.00**

Program, All-Star Game, Chicago, 1990, M ............................**12.00**

Program, Cotton Bowl Classic, Dallas TX, 1946, 80 pages, EX ..**175.00**

Program, Denver vs Raiders, 1st AFL Game, 1960, EX+ .............**470.00**

Program, Orange Bowl Classic, 49th Annual, Nebraska vs LSU, 1983, NM ...................................**27.50**

Program, Purdue vs Indiana, 1970, EX ......................................**15.00**

Program, Yale vs Cornell, football, 1950, 48 pages, EX ............**12.00**

Program, 30th 500 Mile Race, May 30, 1946 on red cover, EX .**45.00**

Record, 500 Miles to Glory, Mercury SR-60024, 33 rpm, 1947, NM ..**45.00**

Schedule, San Francisco Giants, magnetic, 4x7", NM ............**6.00**

Statue, Cleveland Indians mascot, w/ball & bat, Mazzolini Artcraft, 8" ..........................**775.00**

Stein, NY Yankees World Champions, Danbury Mint, 2000, 9½" ....................................**85.00**

Ticket stub, 1956 World Series Game 5, NM ....................**825.00**

Ticket stub, 1969 All-Star Game, Washington DC, EX..........**35.00**

Yearbook, 1951 Boston Red Sox, NM+ ................................**265.00**

Yearbook, 1963 NY Mets, NM.....**325.00**

# Stangl

The Stangl Company of Trenton, New Jersey, produced many striking lines of dinnerware from the 1920s until they closed in the late 1970s. Though white clay was used earlier, the red-clay patterns made from 1942 on are most often encountered and are preferred by collectors. Decorated with both hand painting and sgraffito work (hand carving), Stangl's lines are very distinctive and easily recognized. Virtually all is marked, and most pieces carry the pattern name as well. For more information, we recommend *Collector's Encyclopedia of Stangl Artware, Lamps, and Birds*, by Robert C. Runge, Jr. (Collector Books).

Bowl, cereal; Cranberry, 1973 .....**25.00**

Bowl, cereal; Tiger Lily, 1957......**25.00**

Bowl, coupe soup; Americana #2000, 7½", from $10 to ................**12.00**

Bowl, divided vegetable; Blueberry #3770, oval.........................**30.00**

Bowl, divided vegetable; Yellow Tulip #3637, oval, from $35 to .......................................**45.00**

Bowl, fruit; Town & Country #5287, brown, straight sides, 10", from $30 to .................................**40.00**

Bowl, lug soup; Mediterranean, 1966....................................**20.00**

Bowl, rim soup; Tulip #3365, from $15 to .................................**20.00**

Bowl, salad; Country Garden #3942, 12", from $80 to ................**100.00**

Bowl, salad; Sunflower #3340, extra deep, 10", from $75 to..........**80.00**

Bowl, soup/cereal; Olde Glory, blue, 1975, 6" ..............................**20.00**

Bread tray, Tiger Lily #3965, from $35 to .................................**40.00**

Butter chip, Colonial #1388.....**10.00**

Butter dish, Fruit #3697, from $50 to ........................................**60.00**

Butter dish, Garland, 1959......**65.00**

Butter dish, Wild Rose #3929, from $35 to .................................**40.00**

Candleholder, Sun Flower #3340, ea from $10 to..........................**15.00**

Candy dish, Sculptured Fruit #5179, w/lid, from $50 to ................**60.00**

Casserole, Bittersweet #5111, skillet shape, 8", from $15 to..........**20.00**

Cigarette box, Thistle #3847, from $35 to .................................**45.00**

Coaster/ashtray, Magnolia #3870, from $12 to..........................**15.00**

Coffeepot, Blue Tulip #3637, 8-cup, from $100 to ....................**125.00**

Coffeepot, Star Flower #3864, individual, from $75 to............**85.00**

Creamer, Antique Gold #1902, from $10 to ..................................**15.00**

Creamer, Fruits & Flowers, 1958..**25.00**

Cruet, Country Garden, 1956.....**40.00**

Cup, Town & Country, blue, 1974..**25.00**

**Dinner plate, Tulip, 9",
from $25.00 to $30.00.**
(Photo courtesy Robert C.
Runge, Jr.)

Gravy boat, Blueberry #3770, from
$20 to .................................**25.00**

Gravy boat, Colonial, 1931 ......**35.00**

Lamp, Town & Country #5287, blue,
sq, lg, from $125 to.............**175.00**

Mug, coffee; Magnolia; from $20
to ........................................**25.00**

Mug, Festival, 2-cup, 1961.......**50.00**

Mug, Wild Rose, 2-cup, 1955......**45.00**

Napkin ring, Town & Country, blue,
1974...................................**20.00**

Pickle dish, Florette, 1961 .......**15.00**

Pickle dish, Star Flower #3864, from
$10 to .................................**15.00**

Pitcher, Americana #2000, 1½-pt,
from $15 to.........................**20.00**

Pitcher, Yellow Tulip #3637, 2-qt,
from $70 to.........................**80.00**

Plate, Harvest #3341, 9" ..........**20.00**

Plate, Pink Lily, 1953, 11" .......**20.00**

Plate, Sculptured Fruit #5179, 10",
from $10 to.........................**12.00**

Plate, Tulip #3365, 9", from $15 to...**20.00**

Relish dish, Festival, 1961.......**30.00**

Salt & pepper shakers, Golden Blossom #5155, pr ....................**10.00**

Salt shaker, Cranberry, 1973 .....**10.00**

Sauce boat, Country Garden #3942,
from $35 to........................**40.00**

Shaving mug, Town & Country,
blue, from $45 to ...............**50.00**

Soup tureen, Town & Country, blue,
w/lid, 1974 ......................**245.00**

Sugar bowl, Colonial #1388, bird
finial, from $45 to..............**50.00**

Teapot, Antique Gold #1902, from
$75 to ..............................**100.00**

Teapot, Cosmos #3339, from $75 to.**100.00**

Teapot, Thistle #3847, from $75 to..**85.00**

Teapot, Wild Rose #3929, from $85
to ......................................**95.00**

Tidbit, Garland, 1959, 10" .......**15.00**

Tidbit, Yellow Tulip, 1942 .......**15.00**

Tray, Caughley, blue, oval, 1964,
8¼" ...................................**35.00**

Warmer, Fruit #3697, from $35
to ......................................**40.00**

Warmer, Provincial, 1957........**25.00**

**Warming dish, Rabbit,
1961, from $350.00 to
$400.00.** (Photo courtesy
Robert C. Runge, Jr.)

## Star Wars

Capitalizing on the ever-popu-
lar space travel theme, the movie
*Star Wars* with its fantastic special

effects was a mega box office hit of the late 1970s. A sequel called *Empire Strikes Back* (1980) and a third adventure called Return of the Jedi (1983) did just as well, and as a result, licensed merchandise flooded the market, much of it produced by the Kenner company. The last two films were *Star Wars Episode I* and, of course, *Episode II* soon followed. *Episode III* was released in 2004.

Original packaging is very important in assessing a toy's worth. As each movie was released, packaging was updated, making approximate dating relatively simple. A figure on an original *Star Wars* card is worth more than the same character on an *Empire Strikes Back* card, etc.; and the same *Star Wars* figure valued at $50.00 in mint-on-card condition might be worth as little as $5.00 'loose.' Especially prized are the original 12-back *Star Wars* cards (meaning twelve figures were shown on the back). Second issue cards showed eight more, and so on. For more information we recommend *Star Wars Super Collector's Wish Book* by Geoffery T. Carlton, and *Schroeder's Collectible Toys, Antique to Modern*. Both are published by Collector Books.

Note: Because space was limited, SW was used in our descriptions for Star Wars; ROTJ was used for Return of the Jedi, ESB for Empire Strikes Back, and POTF for Power of the Force.

Bank, C3-PO, Roman Ceramics ....... **75.00**
Bank, Yoda, SW, Sigma ........... **90.00**

Bop Bag, Jawa, Kenner, MIB ..... **225.00**
Figure, A-Wing Pilot, Droids, MOC ... **150.00**
Figure, A-Wing Pilot, POTF, MOC .. **175.00**
Figure, Amanaman, POTF, MOC .. **325.00**
Figure, AT-AT Driver, ESB, MOC .. **90.00**
Figure, AT-ST Driver, ROTJ, MOC .. **45.00**
Figure, Ben (Obi-Wan) Kenobi, ESB, gray hair, MOC ................ **225.00**
Figure, Bespin Security Guard, ESB, Black, MOC .............. **70.00**
Figure, Bib Fortuna, loose, M ..... **10.00**
Figure, Boba Fett, ROTJ, MOC (desert scene) ................... **365.00**
Figure, Bossk, ROTJ, MOC ..... **90.00**
Figure, C-3PO, ROTJ, removable limbs, MOC ....................... **50.00**

**Figure, Chewbacca, molded plastic, jointed at hips and shoulders, marked GMFGI 1978, complete, M, from $50.00 to $60.00. (Photo courtesy Linda Baker)**

Figure, Chewbacca, POTF, MOC .. **225.00**
Figure, Chief Chirpa, ROTJ, MOC .. **50.00**
Figure, Darth Vader, loose, M ....... **12.00**
Figure, Darth Vader, SW, MOC (21-back) ................................ **335.00**
Figure, Death Star Droid, RTOJ, MOC ................................. **125.00**

Figure, Emperor, loose, M .......**10.00**
Figure, Emperor, ROTJ, MOC .....**50.00**
Figure, EV-909, POTF, MOC .....**225.00**
Figure, FX-7, ROTJ, MOC .......**75.00**
Figure, Greedo, loose, M .........**10.00**
Figure, Hammerhead, ROTJ, MOC..**100.00**
Figure, Han Solo, ESB, Bespin outfit, loose, M .........................**15.00**
Figure, Han Solo, ROTJ, Hoth gear, MOC..................................**90.00**
Figure, Han Solo, ROTJ, trench coat, MOC ..........................**60.00**
Figure, Imperial Gunner, loose, M....................................**95.00**
Figure, Jann Tosh, Droids, loose, M ........................................**25.00**
Figure, Jawa, ESB, MOC.......**125.00**
Figure, Jord Dusat, Droids, loose, M ........................................**22.00**
Figure, Kez-Iban, Droids, loose, M..**16.00**
Figure, Lando Calrissian, ROTJ, MOC....................................**45.00**
Figure, Lobot, loose, M...............**9.00**
Figure, Logray, ROTJ, MOC......**50.00**
Figure, Luke Skywalker, ESB, Hoth battle gear, MOC..............**200.00**
Figure, Luke Skywalker, POTF, X-Wing Pilot, MOC .............**145.00**
Figure, Luke Skywalker, ROTJ, blue light saber, loose, M.............**65.00**
Figure, Luke Skywalker, ROTJ, brown hair, loose, M..........**26.00**
Figure, Luke Skywalker, ROTJ, Hoth battle gear, MOC .....**50.00**
Figure, Lumat, POTF, MOC.....**125.00**
Figure, Nien Nunb, loose, M .....**10.00**
Figure, Nikto, POTF, loose, M .....**15.00**
Figure, Paploo, POTF, MOC .....**125.00**
Figure, Power Droid, ROTJ, MOC..**95.00**
Figure, Princess Leia, ESB, MOC ...**375.00**
Figure, Princess Leia, ROTJ, Boushh outfit, loose, M .....**26.00**

Figure, Princess Leia, ROTJ, combat poncho, MOC...............**70.00**
Figure, Pruneface, ROTJ, MOC..**75.00**
Figure, Rebel Commando, loose, M .......................................**10.00**
Figure, Ree-Yees, ROTJ, loose, M .....**10.00**
Figure, R2-D2, Droids, loose, M.....**55.00**
Figure, R5-D4, loose, M............**10.00**
Figure, Sise Fromm, Droids, MOC..................................**175.00**
Figure, Snaggletooth, ROTJ, MOC ..**65.00**
Figure, Stormtrooper, ESB, MOC..**185.00**
Figure, Teebo, loose, M ............**15.00**

**Figure, Tie Fighter Pilot, Empire Strikes Back, Kenner, MIP, $60.00.**

Figure, TIE Fighter Pilot, loose, M.**18.00**
Figure, Tig Fromm, Droids, loose, M .......................................**60.00**
Figure, Ugnaught, ROTJ, MOC..**50.00**
Figure, Wicket, Ewoks, loose, M .......................................**28.00**
Figure, Wicket Warrick, ROTJ, MOC....................................**75.00**
Figure, Yoda, POTF, brown snake, MOC..................................**365.00**
Game, Adventures of R2-D2, Parker Bros, MIB ..........................**25.00**

Game, Destroy Death Star, VG.....**20.00**

Game, Laser Battle, SW, MIB.....**75.00**

Keychain, Boba Fett, flat vinyl, Applause..............................**4.00**

Pencils, ROTJ, C-3PO, 4-pack, M on blister card...........................**6.00**

Playset, Cloud City, ESB, MIB.....**475.00**

Playset, Creature Catina, SW, loose, M.........................................**75.00**

Playset, Dagobah, Darth Vader & Luke Battle, ESB, MIB.....**150.00**

Playset, Droid Factory, SW, MIB..**145.00**

Playset, Ewok Village, ROTJ, loose, complete, EX....................**225.00**

Playset, Imperial Attack Base, ESB, MIB.................................**145.00**

Playset, Jabba the Hutt Dungeon w/Amanaman, ROTJ, MIB...................**335.00**

Scissors, ROTJ safety, Butterfly Originals, M.......................**12.00**

Statue, Clash of the Jedi diarama, Applause, M.......................**42.00**

Vehicle, A-Wing Fighter, Droids, M.........................................**175.00**

Vehicle, B-Wing Fighter, ROTJ, M..**65.00**

Vehicle, Desert Sail Skiff, ROTJ, Minirig, MIB......................**45.00**

Vehicle, Ewok Battle Wagon, POTF, M.........................................**60.00**

Vehicle, Imperial Shuttle, ROTJ, M.........................................**100.00**

Vehicle, Interceptor (INT-4), ESB, Minirig, MIB......................**30.00**

Vehicle, Landspeeder, SW, MIB.....**85.00**

Vehicle, Multi-Terrain Vehicle (MTV-7), ESB, Minirig, MIB...............**35.00**

Vehicle, One-Man Sand Skimmer, POTF, MIB.......................**100.00**

Vehicle, Rebel Transport, ESB, yellow background, MIB......**175.00**

Vehicle, Scout Walker (AT-ST), M.........................................**35.00**

Vehicle, TIE Fighter, ESB, MIB..**265.00**

Vehicle, X-Wing Fighter, M.....**65.00**

# Strawberry Shortcake Collectibles

Strawberry Shortcake came onto the market around 1980, and immediately captured the imagination of little girls everywhere. A line of related merchandise soon hit the market, including swimsuits, bed linens, blankets, anklets, underclothing, coats, shoes, sleeping bags, dolls and accessories, games, toys, and delightful items to decorate the rooms of Strawberry Shortcake fans. It was short lived, though, lasting only until near the middle of the decade.

### Dolls

Almond Tea w/Marza Panda, 1982, MIB.................................**135.00**

Angel Cake w/Souffle, 1981, MIB, from $40 to........................**50.00**

Apple Dumplin w/Tea Time Turtle, MIB, from $50 to................**60.00**

**Apricot with Hopsalot, 1980, MIB, from $45.00 to $55.00.**

Banana Twirl w/Berrykin, complete, NRFB ..............................**245.00**

Banana Twirl w/out Berrykin, M ......................................**150.00**

Blueberry Muffin w/Cheesecake, 1981, MIB, from $50 to .....**60.00**

Café Olé w/Burrito, no cards, 1982, MIB, from $70 to ...............**85.00**

Cherry Cuddler w/Goosenberry, 1981, MIB, from $60 to .....**70.00**

Crepe Suzette w/Eclair, 1982, MIB, from $45 to.........................**60.00**

Hucklebrry Pie w/Pupcake, 1981, MIB, from $60 to ...............**75.00**

Lemon Meringue w/Frappe, 1981, MIB, from $50 to ...............**75.00**

Lime Chiffon w/Parfait Parrot, 1981, MIB, from $50 to ...............**60.00**

Mint Tulip w/Marsh Mallard, 1982, NRFB ..............................**115.00**

Orange Blossom w/Marmalade, 1981, MIB, from $50 to .....**60.00**

Plum Pudding w/Elderberry Owl, NRFB ..............................**245.00**

Purple Pieman w/Berry Bird, 1980, MIB, from $60 to ...............**75.00**

Raspberry Tart w/Rhubarb, 1981, MIB, from $60 to ...............**70.00**

Sour Grapes w/Dregs, 1981, MIB, from $25 to.........................**35.00**

Strawberry Shortcake w/Strawberrykin, MIB, from $50 to........**65.00**

## Strawberryland Miniatures

Figure, Almond Tea w/Marza Panda, 1984, M, from $30 to............**40.00**

Figure, Café Olé w/Burrito, EX.....**25.00**

Figure, Peach Blush w/mirror, 1984, M ......................................**70.00**

Figure, Plum Pudding w/Elderberry Owl, M ..............................**50.00**

Figure, Plum Pudding w/pencil, 1984, M ..............................**75.00**

Figure, Strawberry Shortcake on tricyle w/Custard, 1984, NM..**60.00**

Figure, Strawberry Shortcake reading book w/Custard in rocker, 1984, M ..............................**50.00**

Playset, Apricot & Hopsalot Play at the Vanity, 1983, MIB ......**40.00**

Playset, Raspberry Tart w/Rhubarb in her car, 1983, EX+ ........**30.00**

Playset, Shortcake House, MIB.....**75.00**

Playset, Strawberry Shortcake on Rocking Chair, MIB ..........**40.00**

Playset, Strawberry Shortcake w/ Custard on a Sailboat, MIB ..**30.00**

## Miscellaneous

Berry Bake Shop, complete, M (EX box)....................................**35.00**

**Big Berry Trolley, 1982, M, $30.00 ($45.00 if MIB).**

Charm bracelet, gold-tone w/5 charms, American Greetings, EX ......................................**65.00**

Dollhouse furniture, attic, 6-pc, NM..**165.00**

Dollhouse furniture, Berry Happy Home bathroom furniture, 6-pc, NM ......................................**60.00**

Dollhouse furniture, flower-shaped table & 2 chairs, Kidkraft, MIB.**80.00**

Dollhouse furniture, rocking chair w/base & lamp, 1984, EX ...............**325.00**

Dollhouse furniture, sq table & chairs (2), Kidkraft #12210, MIB ....................................**95.00**

Lunchbox w/thermos, American Greetings, 1980, NM.........**45.00**

Mug, Raspberry Tart, Anchor Hocking ......................................**20.00**

Plaque, Enjoy Each Day in a Berry Sweet Way, 12x10", EX.....**85.00**

# Swanky Swigs

Swanky Swigs are little decorated glass tumblers that once contained Kraft Cheese Spread. The company has used them since the Depression years of the 1930s up to the present time, and all along, because of their small size, they've been happily recycled as drinking glasses for the kids and juice glasses for adults. Their designs range from brightly colored flowers to animals, sailboats, bands, dots, stars, checkers, etc. There is a combination of 223 verified colors and patterns. In 1933 the original Swanky Swigs came in the Band pattern, and at the present time they can still be found on the grocery shelf, now a clear plain glass with an indented waffle design around the bottom.

They vary in size and fall into one of three groups: the small size sold in Canada, ranging from 3¹⁄₁₆" to 3¼"; the regular size sold in the United States, ranging from 3⅜" to 3⅞"; and the large size also sold in Canada, ranging from 4³⁄₁₆" to 5⅝".

A few of the rare patterns to look for in the three different groups are small group: Band No. 5 (two red and two black bands with the red first); Galleon (two ships on each glass in black, blue, green, red, or yellow); Checkers (in black and red, black and yellow, black and orange or black and white, with black checkers on the top row); and Fleur-de-lis (black with a bright red filigree design).

In the regular group: Dots Forming Diamonds; Lattice and Vine (white lattice with colored flowers); Texas Centennial (cowboy and horse); Special Issues with dates (1936, 1938, and 1942); and Tulip No. 2 (black, blue, green, or red).

Rare glasses in the larger group are Circles and Dots (black, blue, green, or red); Star No. 1 (small stars scattered over the glass in black, blue, green, or red); Cornflower No. 2 (dark blue, light blue, red, or yellow); Provincial Crest (red and burgundy with maple leaves); and Antique No. 2 (assorted antiques on each glass in lime green, deep red, orange, blue, and black).

Band #1, red & black, 1933, 3⅜"..**3.00**

Band #2, black & red, Canadian, 1933, 4¾" ............................**20.00**

Band #2, black & red, 1933, 3⅜"..**3.00**

Band #3, white & blue, 1933, 3⅜"..**3.00**

Band #4, blue, 1933, 3⅜" ...........**3.00**

Bicentennial Tulip, green, red or yellow, 1975, 3¾", ea.........**15.00**

Blue Tulips, 1937, 4¼" .............**20.00**

Carnival, blue, green, red or yellow, 1939, 3½", ea .......................**9.00**

Checkerboard, white w/blue, green or red, 1936, 3½", ea ........**20.00**

Circles & Dot, any color, 1934, 3½", ea.........................................**7.00**

Cornflower #1, light blue & green, Canadian, 1941, 4⅝", ea.....**20.00**

Cornflower #1, light blue & green, Canadian, 3¼", ea ...............**8.00**

Crystal Petal, clear & plain w/fluted base, 1951, 3½", ea..............**2.00**

Dots Forming Diamonds, any color, 1935, 3½", ea .....................**50.00**

Forget-Me-Not, dark blue, light blue, red or yellow, 1948, 3½", ea...**4.00**

Galleon, black, blue, green, red or yellow, Canadian, 1936, 3⅛", ea.**30.00**

Hostess, clear & plain w/indented groove base, 1960, 3¾", ea.....**1.00**

Jonquil (Posy Pattern), yellow & green, Canadian, 1941, 3¼"..**8.00**

Jonquil (Posy Pattern), yellow & green, 1941, 3½", ea............**4.00**

**Kiddie Kup, pig, Canadian, 1956, 4¾", $20.00; Bustlin' Betty, Canadian, 1953, $20.00; Kiddie Kup, deer, Canadian, 1956, 4¾", $20.00.**

Lattice & Vine, white w/blue, green or red, 1936, 3½", ea.............**100.00**

Petal Star, clear w/indented star base, Canadian, 1978, 3¼", ea.........**2.00**

Plain, clear, like Tulip #1 w/out design, 1940, 3½", ea...........**4.00**

Provincial Crest, red & burgundy, Canadian, 1974, 4⅝", ea ...**25.00**

Sailboat #1, blue, 1936, 3½", ea.**12.00**

Sailboat #2, blue, green, light green or red, 1936, 3½", ea .........**12.00**

Stars #1, black, blue, green or red, 1935, 3½", ea .......................**7.00**

Stars #1, yellow, 1935, 3½", ea..**25.00**

Stars #2, clear w/orange stars, Canadian, 1971, 4⅝", ea .....**5.00**

Tulip (Posy Pattern), red & green, Canadian, 1941, 3¼", ea .....**8.00**

Tulip (Posy Pattern), red & green, 1941, 3½", ea .......................**4.00**

Tulip #1, black, blue, green, red or yellow, 1937, 3½", ea...........**4.00**

Tulip #2, black, blue, green or red, 1938, 3½", ea .....................**25.00**

Tulip #3, dark blue, light blue, red or yellow, 1950, 3⅞", ea ......**4.00**

Violet (Posy Pattern), blue & green, 1941, 3½", ea .......................**4.00**

## Syroco

From the early 1940s until 1962, Syroco items were replicas of wood carvings cast from wood fibre, but most of what you'll find today are made of resin. They're not at all hard to find; and because they were made in so many shapes and designs, it's easy and inexpensive to build an interesting collection. Some are hand painted, and others are trimmed in gold. You may also find similar products stamped 'Orna-wood,' 'Decor-A-Wood,' and 'Swank.' These items ar collectible as well.

Ashtray, Yellowstone National Park, w/pipe stand, 1940s, 10x6¼" ..............................**35.00**

Bookends, Girl Scout insignia, 1940s, 5¾x5"......................**70.00**

Bookends, maple leaf design, 5½x4½"..............................**22.50**

Bottle opener, horse-head handle, 6"......................................**50.00**

Bottle opener, rooster head, 5¾"..**25.00**

Brush holder, 3 Scottie dogs on front, brush holder in back, 5x6"..**20.00**

Clock, gold starburst design, 32" dia....................................**110.00**

**Corkscrew, bartender, Syroco label, 8½", from $45.00 to $60.00.**

Corkscrew, German shepherd head, 8⅛"....................................**155.00**

Corkscrew, Job Trotter in top hat, 5"......................................**125.00**

Corkscrew top, bald-headed laughing man w/lg grin, 6", EX..**265.00**

Figurine, bulldog, seated, glass eyes, green painted collar, 7".....**60.00**

Figurine, Fritz (Katzenjammer Kids), KFS 1944, 3"...........**20.00**

Figurine, matador fighting bull, 1968, 35½"..........................**25.00**

Figurine, Scottish terrier, green collar, 3¼x4x1¼".....................**25.00**

Figurine, The Capt (Katzenjammer Kids), KFS 1944, 4½".........**22.50**

Figurines, skinny horse w/big grin & Indian w/potbelly, pr.........**40.00**

Frame, Estes Park CO, Indian, cabin, deer, pine cones, etc, 7x4½"................................**25.00**

Frame, oval w/floral & vine border, 14x12"..............................**35.00**

Mirror, oval w/eagle atop, #4007, 20x14½"............................**45.00**

Pen holder, cannon, 4x3".........**25.00**

Pipe holder, horseshoe shape w/ embossed jocky's cap & crop, 1940s, 4"............................**20.00**

Plaque, pink roses w/green leaves, 15x11"................................**20.00**

Plaques, bird on branch, gold, 14½x9", 13½x8", pr...........**25.00**

Sconce/candle holder, floral & vines w/scrolls, glass globe, 13¼"......................................**25.00**

Smoker set, tobacco holder w/ashtray on ea side, Multi Producing, 1955..**25.00**

Thermometer, sea captain on boat deck....................................**20.00**

Towel bar, puppies across top, 4½x12"..............................**35.00**

Tray, Adirondack Mountains w/Indian at teepee, acorns on border, 11x7"................................**25.00**

Tray, horse head over tray w/arrows along side, 9½x4½"............**60.00**

Wall hanging, Boy Scouts Oath w/insignia, 5x3¼", EX (original box)....................................**40.00**

Wall hanging, tree branch w/2 shelves, 11¼x9½"..............**40.00**

# Tea Bag Holders

These are fun and inexpensive to collect. They were made, of course, to hold used tea bags, but aside from being functional, many are whimsical and amusing. Though teapots are the most commonly found shape, you can find fruit, bird, and vegetable shapes as well.

Lady seated on chair drinking tea, holder in lap, JSNY Taiwan, 5½".**12.00**
Miss Cutie Pie, teapot shape w/2 birds atop, Napco, 1950s ...**35.00**
Moss Rose, flower shape w/drain basin, gold trim, T-103, Japan, 2½" .........................................**25.00**
Rooster, multicolor, Holt Howard, 1960, 5½" ...........................**15.00**
Swan, white, marked Lenox w/gold 'L,' 2x2½".............................**15.00**
Teapot shape, white roses, Lefton #6672, 4½" ...........................**10.00**
Teapot shape, white w/African Gray parrot, English China, 5⅛" .....................................**25.00**

**Teapot shape with smiling face, Japan, $8.50.**

Violets on white china, strainer top w/cup bottom, 2-pc.............**15.00**

# Teapots

The popularity of teatime and tea-related items continues, and vin-tage and finer quality teapots have become harder to find. Those from the 1890s and 1920s reflect their age with three and four digit prices. Examples from the 1700s and 1800s are most often found in museums or large auction houses. Teapots listed here represent examples still available at the flea market level.

Most collectors begin with a general collection of varied teapots until they decide upon the specific category that appeals to them. Collecting categories include miniatures, doll or toy sets, those made by a certain manufacturer, figurals, or a particular style (such as Art Deco or English floral). Some of the latest trends in collecting are Chinese Yixing (pronounced yee-shing, teapots from an unglazed earthenware in forms taken from nature), 1950s pink or black teapots, Cottageware teapots, and figural teapots (those shaped like people, animals, or other objects). While teapots made in Japan have waned in collectibility, collectors have begun to realize many detailed or delicate examples are available. Of special interest are Dragonware teapots or sets. Some of these sets have the highly desired lithophane cups — where a Geisha girl is molded in transparent relief in the bottom of the cup. When the cup is held up to the light, the image becomes visible.

For more information we recommend *Teapots, The Collector's Guide,* by Tina Carter. Two quarterly publications are also available; see Clubs and Newsletters for information on *Tea Talk* and *TeaTime Gazette.*

China, violet chintz, scalloped edge, Enesco, Japan..................**140.00**

China, violets w/gold, Japan Fine China mark, late 1950s, sm...............**30.00**

Figural, cabbage leaf (majolica-like), unmarked Japan, 5"............**35.00**

Figural, elephant w/howdah, multicolor lustre, Japan, lg........**75.00**

**Figural, lady with gray hair, pottery, English, 8½", $50.00.**

Figural, old lady w/umbrella, multicolor, Made in England.........**110.00**

Figural, orange, leaf at finial, green handle, Maruhan, 5½"........**35.00**

Figural, rabbit w/vegetables, head forms lid, Fitz & Floyd, 8½"...............**50.00**

Figural, watermelon slice, flower finial, Taiwan, modern......**30.00**

Figural, windmill, hand painted under glaze, Japan mark, 1940s-50s..**45.00**

Glass, round w/blown handle, Pyrex USA, 1930s-40s, from $110 to.**125.00**

Ironstone, floral on white, Wood & Sons, 1950s, lg..................**40.00**

Miniature, blue lustre w/applied flowers, Made in Germany..........**25.00**

Miniature, flowers & trellis on white, Japan, 1960s, 2½"...............**20.00**

Porcelain, floral chintz w/gold, bamboo-wrapped handles, Hong Kong, 7"..............................**75.00**

Porcelain, Moss Rose, musical base (Tea for Two), Japan, 1960..**65.00**

Pottery, apples & leaves on white, cylindrical, Japan, 7".........**25.00**

Pottery, blue jasper putti scene, black & orange lustre, Gibson, 1930s...................................**70.00**

Pottery, Castlewood pattern (floral), angle handle, Blue Ridge..**195.00**

Pottery, dainty floral on brown gloss, Japan, 3x6".............**20.00**

Pottery, Deco flowers & orange lustre, Japan mark, 5"..........**25.00**

Pottery, floral w/gold & cobalt, orange lustre trim, Japan................**45.00**

**Pottery, floral on white with gold trim, Ellgreave, marked Div of Wood and Sons England, four cup, $35.00; two cup, $30.00.** (Photo courtesy Tina Carter)

Pottery, Green Arbor pattern (floral) on white, Continental Kilns, 7".......................................**45.00**

Pottery, leaves & swirl enamel on brown gloss, Gibson, ca 1912, 4½".....................................**60.00**

Pottery, Quimper-like Breton decor, 6-sided, Japan, 5½"..........**55.00**

Pottery, roses decal on white w/gold, #10095, 5½x8"...................**30.00**

Pottery, roses painted on white, loop handle, Hand-Painted Japan mark..................................**95.00**

Pottery, Tree in Meadow-like pattern, unmarked Japan, 5".**28.00**

Pottery, wildflowers on white, 6-sided, Saddler, 6".............**75.00**

# Tiara Exclusives

Collectors are just beginning to take notice of the glassware sold through Tiara in-home parties, their Sandwich line in particular. Several companies were involved in producing the lovely items they've marketed over the years, among them Indiana Glass, Fenton, Dalzell Viking, and L.E. Smith. In the late 1960s Tiara contracted with Indiana to produce their famous line of Sandwich dinnerware (a staple at Indiana Glass since the late 1920s). Their catalogs continue to carry this pattern, and over the years, it has been offered in many colors: ruby, teal, crystal, amber, green, pink, blue, and others in limited amounts. We've listed a few pieces of Tiara's Sandwich below, and though the market is unstable, our values will serve to offer an indication of current values. Unless you're sure of what you're buying, though, don't make the mistake of paying 'old' Sandwich prices for Tiara. To learn more about the two lines, we recommend *Collectible Glassware from the '40s, '50s, and '60s,* by Gene and Cathy Florence (Collector Books). Also refer to *Collecting Tiara Amber Sandwich Glass* by Mandi Birkinbine; she is listed in the Directory under Idaho.

Basket, amber, tall & slender, 10¾x4¾", from $40 to........**50.00**

Basket, Sandwich, amber, 10¾", from $40.00 to $50.00. (Photo courtesy Mandi Birkinbine)

Bowl, amber, 6-sided, 1¼x6¼".....**12.00**

Bowl, salad; amber, slant-sided, 3x8⅜" ................................**20.00**

Butter dish, Bicentennial Blue, from $25 to.................................**35.00**

Cake plate, Chantilly Green, footed, 4x10", from $55 to .............**70.00**

Candleholders, Chantilly Green, 8½", pr................................**45.00**

Canister, amber, 26-oz, 5⅝", from $12 to.................................**20.00**

Canister, amber, 52-oz, 8⅞", from $18 to.................................**26.00**

Clock, amber, wall hanging, 12" dia, from $20 to.........................**25.00**

Compote, amber, 8" .................**25.00**

Cup, coffee; amber, 9-oz.............**4.00**

Cup, snack; amber......................**4.00**

Dish, club, heart, diamond or spade shape, clear, 4", ea................**3.00**

Egg tray, Chantilly Green, from $15 to........................................**22.00**

Fairy lamp, Chantilly Green, from $18 to.................................**26.00**

Goblet, table wine; amber, 8½-oz, 5½" ......................................**7.50**

Goblet, water; Bicentennial Blue, 8-oz, 5¼", from $8 to.............**12.00**

Goblet, water; Spruce Green, 8-oz, 5¼", from $4 to .................**5.50**

Mug, amber, footed, 5½".............**8.00**

**Napkin holder, amber, 4x7½", from $15.00 to $20.00. (Photo courtesy Mandi Birkinbine)**

Plate, dinner; amber, 10", from $9.50 to..............................**12.50**

Plate, salad; amber, 8" ...............**7.00**

Platter, amber, sawtooth rim, 12", from $8.50 to.....................**12.00**

Salt & pepper shakers, amber, 4¾", pr, from $18 to ...................**25.00**

Tray, amber, footed, 1¾x12¾".**35.00**

Tray, divided relish; amber, 4-compartment, 10", from $25 to........................................**30.00**

Tumbler, juice; amber, 8-oz, 4", from $12 to.................................**14.00**

Vase, amber, ruffled, footed, 3¼x6½" .............................**16.00**

Wine set, amber, decanter, tray & 8 goblets ...............................**55.00**

# Toothbrush Holders

Children's ceramic toothbrush holders represent one of today's popular collecting fields, with some of the character-related examples bringing $150.00 and up. Many were made in Japan before WWII.

For more information we recommend *A Pictorial Guide to Toothbrush Holders* by Marilyn Cooper; she is listed in the Directory under Texas. Plate numbers in the following listings correspond with her book.

Andy Gump & Min, bisque, plate #221, 4", from $85 to .......**110.00**

Annie Oakley, Japan, plate #11, 5¾", from $125 to ............**165.00**

Baby Bunting, Germany, plate #1, 6¾" ...................................**400.00**

Betty Boop w/toothbrush & cup, KFS, 5", from $85 to........**100.00**

Big Bird, Taiwan (RCC), plate #263, 4¼", from $85 to ..............**110.00**

Candlestick Maker, Japan (Goldcastle), plate, #150, 5", from $70 to........................................**85.00**

Cat (Calico), Japan, 5½", from $90 to........................................**120.00**

Cat w/Bass Fiddle, Japan, plate #38, 6", from $115 to ...............**140.00**

Clown head w/bug on nose, Japan, 5", from $170 to ...............**190.00**

Clown Juggling, Japan, plate #60, from $80 to........................**90.00**

Dalmatian, Germany, 4", from $170 to........................................**210.00**

Ducky Dandy, Japan, 4", from $150 to........................................**175.00**

Flapper, plate, #230, 4¼", from $120 to........................................**160.00**

Indian chief, 2 holes, hangs, tray holds toothpaste, 4½", from $250 to ...........................**300.00**

Kayo, Japan, plate #116, 5", from $100 to..............................**125.00**

Lone Ranger on Silver, Lone Ranger Inc, chalk, plate #249, 4", from $80 to.................................**95.00**

**Man in derby hat, tube tray, blue and tan lustre with black shiny glaze, Japan mark, 5", from $95.00 to $135.00; Man in top hat, tube tray, multicolor with lustre, inscribed Tacoma (souvenir), Japan mark, 5½", from $95.00 to $135.00.** (Photo courtesy Carole Bess White)

Mary Poppins, Japan, plate #119, 6", from $100 to ...............**150.00**

Old King Cole, Japan, plate #125, 5¼", from $85 to ..............**100.00**

Old Mother Hubbard, plate #3, from $350 to..............................**425.00**

Penguin, Japan, 5½", from $85 to ......................................**115.00**

Peter Rabbit, Germany, plate #4, 6¼", from $350 to ............**400.00**

Popeye, Japan, bisque, plate #244, 5", from $475 to ...............**575.00**

Sailor boy beside sq holder, unmarked Japan, 3½", from $45 to ....**65.00**

Snow White, plate #246, 6", from $225 to..............................**270.00**

Tom, Tom the Piper's Son, Japan, plate #154, 5¾", from $95 to..........**150.00**

Toonerville Trolley, Japan (Fountain Fox), plate #155, 5½".......**550.00**

Traffic cop, Germany, Don't Forget the Teeth, plate #243, 5", from $350 to..............................**375.00**

Uncle Willie, 2 holes, hangs, feet form tray, Japan, 5⅛", from $85 to......................................**115.00**

# Toys

Toy collecting remains a very popular hobby, and though some areas of the market may have softened to some extent over the past two years, classic toys remain a good investment. Especially strong are the tin windups made by such renowned companies as Strauss, Marx, Lehmann, Chein, etc., and the battery-operated toys made from the '40s through the '60s in Japan. Because of their complex mechanisms, few survive.

Toys from the 1800s are rarely if ever found in mint condition but should at least be working and have all their original parts. Toys manufactured in the twentieth century are evaluated more critically. Compared to one in mint condition, original box intact, even a slightly worn toy with no box may be worth only about half as much. Character-related toys, space toys, toy trains, and toys from the '60s are very desirable.

Several good books are available, if you want more information: *Collector's Guide to Tootsietoys,* by David E. Richter; *Matchbox Toys, 1947 – 2003,* by Dana Johnson; *Hot Wheels: The Ultimate Redline Guide Volumes I and II,* by Jack Clark and Robert Wicker; *Star Wars Super Collector's Wish Book,* by Geoffrey T. Carlton;

*Big Book of Toy Airplanes,* by W. Tom Miller; *Toy Car Collector's Guide,* by Dana Johnson; and *Schroeder's Collectible Toys, Antique to Modern.* All are published by Collector Books. See also Action Figures; Breyer Horses; Hartland; Character Collectibles; Star Wars; Western Heroes; Club and Newsletters.

**Battery-Operated**

Ace, Xylophone, 1950s, 6" L, NM ....................................**60.00**

Alps, Antique Gooney Car, 1960s, 9", EX ...............................**120.00**

Alps, Cable Car, 1950s, 7x6", EXIB...................................**125.00**

Alps, Charlie the Funny Clown, 9", NMIB, from $300 to ........**350.00**

Alps, Clown the Magician, 1950s, 12", MIB............................**375.00**

Alps, Ducky Duckling, 1960s, 8", M ........................................**75.00**

Alps, Mary's Little Lamb, 1950s, 10½", EX ...........................**150.00**

Alps, Musical Comic Jumping Jeep, 12", M..............................**175.00**

Alps, Pipie the Whale, 1950s, 12", NM ...................................**325.00**

Alps, Talking Trixie, 1950s, 6½", EX.......................................**65.00**

B-C Toy, Jungle Jumbo, 1950s, rare, 10", M................................**650.00**

Bandai, Dune Buggy, 1970s, 10", M .........................................**75.00**

Bandai, Sea Bear #7, 1950s, 10", EX...................................**100.00**

Bandai, Swimming Duck, 1950s, rare, 8", NM.....................**150.00**

CK, Clucking Clara, 1950s, NM ..................................**130.00**

Cragstan, Chimp & Pup Rail Car, rare, 9", EX ......................**140.00**

Cragstan, Dilly Dalmatian, 1950s, 10", EX ............................**130.00**

Cragstan, Radar Jeep, 11", NMIB..**100.00**

Gakken, Playland Train, 1970s, 7½" dia, NM .............................**40.00**

Hasbro, Mentor Wizard, MIB, from $120 to..............................**150.00**

Hubley, Mr Magoo, 1961, 8", NMIB ...............................**275.00**

K, Zoom Boat F-570, 1950s, 10", EXIB................................**170.00**

Linemar, Army Radio Jeep, 1950s, 7", EX ...............................**150.00**

Linemar, Linemar Hauler, 1950s, 14", MIB..........................**250.00**

Linemar, Rocky, 1950s, 3" dia, MIB .................................**200.00**

**Linemar, Sleeping Baby Bear, 1950s, 9", MIB, $525.00.** (Photo courtesy Don Hultzman)

Linemar, Switchboard Operator, 1950s, rare, 7½", NM ......**525.00**

Linemar, Walking Donkey, 1950s, 9", MIB............................**250.00**

Linemar, Walking Gorilla, 1950s, 8", MIB .................................**475.00**

Marx, Barking Boxer Dog, 1950s, 7", EX....................................**100.00**

Marx, Barking Spaniel Dog, 1950s, 7", EX ...............................**25.00**

Marx, Big Parade, 1963, 15" L, NMIB ...............................**200.00**

Marx, Colonel Hap Hazard, 1968, 11", EX ..............................**700.00**

Marx, Hootin' Hollow Haunted House, 1960s, 11", NM+.....**750.00**

Marx, Marx-A-Copter, 1961, NMIB..**250.00**

Marx, Penny the Poodle, 1960s, NM (EX box) ...........................**125.00**

Marx, Yeti the Abominable Snowman, 1950s, 11", NMIB ............**975.00**

Masudaya, Overland Express Locomotive, EXIB ...................**140.00**

MT, Airport Saucer, 1960s, 8" dia, NM ...................................**140.00**

MT, Big Ring Circus, NM.......**175.00**

MT, Electric School Bus, 1950s, 10", NM ...................................**100.00**

MT, Lucky Cement Mixer, 1960s, 12", from $265 to .............**325.00**

MT, Puzzled Puppy, 1950s, 5", EX....................................**150.00**

MT, Radicon Bus, 14", NMIB .....**250.00**

MT, Rambling Ladybug, 1960s, 8", EX....................................**100.00**

Remco, Barney's Auto Factory, 1964, unused, NMIB .......**300.00**

Remco, Batman's Flying Batplane, 1966, 12", EXIB ...............**125.00**

S&E, Cragston Telly Bear, 1950s, 8", MIB...........................**475.00**

S&E, Dentist Bear, 1950s, 9", NM, from $400 to.....................**475.00**

S&E, Teddy the Manager, 1950s, 8", MIB .................................**350.00**

SAN, Cragston Tugboat, 1950s, 13", NM ...................................**125.00**

Taito, Musical Melody Mixer, 1970s, 11", M.................................**100.00**

Technofix, Big Dipper, 1960s, 21" L, EX....................................**150.00**

TN, Bartender, 1960s, 11½", MIB..**65.00**

TN, Drinking Licking Cat, 1950s, 10", MIB ...........................**275.00**

TN, Fire Command Car, 1950s, EX....................................**260.00**

TN, Marvelous Locomotive, 1950s, TN, 10", M........................**100.00**

TN, Pee Pee Puppy, 1960s, 9", NMIB ...............................**150.00**

TN, Police Car With Stick Shift, 1960s, 12", NMIB ............**175.00**

TN, Slalom Game, 11" base, EXIB................................**150.00**

TN, Tunnel Train, 1950s, 18", M .....................................**125.00**

Tomiyama, Winston the Barking Bulldog, 1950s, 10", NM............**120.00**

Y, Captain Blushwell, 1960s, 11", VG .....................................**65.00**

Y, Mr Fox the Magician, 1960s, EXIB................................**500.00**

Y, Pat the Elephant, 1950s, 9", EX....................................**285.00**

### Diecast Vehicles

Corgi, Adams Bros Dragster, #165, MIP, from $35 to................**50.00**

Corgi, Bentley Mulliner, #274, MIP, from $80 to........................**100.00**

Corgi, Chevrolet Astro 1, w/ whizwheels, #347, MIP, from $40 to..................................**60.00**

Corgi, Ferrari Daytona, #300, MIP, from $25 to.........................**40.00**

Corgi, Fiat 2100, #232, MIP, from $75 to.................................**90.00**

Corgi, Jaguar E Type, #312, MIP, from $100 to.....................**125.00**

Corgi, Lotus Elan, red or blue, #319, MIP, from $75 to..............**100.00**

Corgi, Lotus Elite, #382, MIP, from $30 to.................................**45.00**

Corgi, Massey-Ferguson 165 Tractor, #66, MIP, from $75 to.**95.00**

Corgi, Rover 2000, metallic blue, #252, MIP, from $80 to......**95.00**

Corgi, Superman Van, #435, MIP, from $50 to.........................**75.00**

Corgi, Touring Caravan, #490, MIP, from $30 to.........................**45.00**

Ertl, Buick, 1912, red & black, 1985, from $20 to.........................**25.00**

Ertl, Dodge Ram Truck, 1995, red or black, ea from $30 to .........**35.00**

Ertl, 1967 Corvette L-71 Roadster, Sunfire yellow, from $35 to .**40.00**

Ertl, Pontiac Trans Am Coupe (1996), metallic red, from $30 to .......................................**35.00**

Gama, Ford Taunus 17M, #901, 1959, from $45 to................**55.00**

Gama, Henschel Wrecker, #31, 1969, from $25 to................**35.00**

Goodee, Lincoln Capri Hardtop (1953), 3", from $16 to........**20.00**

Goodee, Moving Van...................**15.00**

Johnny Lightning, Custom El Camino, 1969, MIP........**1,250.00**

Johnny Lightning, Custom Eldorado, 1969, standard finish, doors open, MIP...........................**400.00**

Johnny Lightning, Custom XKE, doors open, 1969...............**125.00**

Johnny Lightning , Indy 500 Racing set, w/original container, MIP................................**1,000.00**

Johnny Lightning, Sand Stormer, 1970, roof same color as body ...**150.00**

Lledo, Fire Engine, 1983, from $15 to .........................................**20.00**

Lledo, Ford Model I Tanker, 1983 from $15 to...........................**20.00**

Lledo, Packard Town Van, 1986, from $15 to...........................**20.00**

Manoil, Bus, 1945 – 55, from $35 to .........................................**50.00**

Manoil, wrecker, 1935 – 41, from $85 to ...............................**100.00**

Mebetoys, 1966 Fiat 850, from $28 to .........................................**35.00**

## Wind-Ups, Friction, and Other Mechanicals

AAA, Pinky Racer, litho tin, 5½", EXIB.................................**125.00**

Alps, Happy Life, tin & celluloid, 9½", NMIB ......................**475.00**

Alps, Proud Peacock, litho tin, 7", EX..**150.00**

Alps, Reading Bunny, tin & plush w/cloth outfit, 7", MIB.....**175.00**

Alps, Twirly Whirly Rocket Ride, litho tin, NMIB................**850.00**

Arnold, Bee & Flower Sparkler, litho tin, 4½", NM............**175.00**

Asahi, Jumpy Rudolph, cable action, 1950s, 6", EX....................**150.00**

Borgfeldt, Pinocchio, composition, 10½", NM ..........................**450.00**

Chein, Fish, litho tin, advances as tail fin moves, 1940s, NM.........**125.00**

CK, King Merry, celluloid, 12", EXIB...............................**200.00**

Courtland, Rocking R Ranch, litho tin, 18", G+.......................**150.00**

**Distler, BMW roadster, friction, forward and reverse action, 9½", EX, $200.00.**

G&K, Clown on Cart, litho tin, 4½", VG .....................................**400.00**

Haiji, Animal Scooter w/Rabbit, litho tin, NM (VG box).....**125.00**

Irwin, C Race Car, 1950s, red & yellow plastic, scarce, 12½", MIB ..................................**200.00**

Irwin, Dancing Cinderella & Prince, plastic, 1950s, 5", M (EX box)....................................**200.00**

Irwin, Racing Car, plastic, 1950s, scarce, 12½", MIB............**200.00**

Japan, Circling Helicopter H-2, litho tin, 1950s, 6", EXIB.........**100.00**

Japan, Mr Tortoise, litho tin, 1960s, NMIB ..................................**75.00**

Japan, Pirate w/Peg Leg & Spy Glass, litho tin, 1960s, 7", NM+ ..................................**175.00**

KO, Lucky Scooter Bumper Car, litho tin, 1950s, 5½", NMIB.....**200.00**

KO, Mystery Police Car, litho tin, friction, 6", NMIB............**450.00**

Kohler, Duck, litho tin, quacks & flaps wings, 1950s, NM .....**75.00**

**Kohler Western Germany, duck, tin litho, quacks and flaps wings as it walks, 1950s, MIB, from $75.00 to $85.00**

Linemar, Banjo Player, litho tin, 5", NM ..................................**200.00**

Linemar, Clarabelle the Clown, litho tin, 5", EX ........................**300.00**

Linemar, Clown Juggler, 8½", NM, from $450 to....................**550.00**

Linemar, Fifer Pig (Three Little Pigs), litho tin, 4½", NM .**175.00**

Linemar, Flintstone Turnover Truck, litho tin, 1960s, 4", MIB ..................................**800.00**

Linemar, Mickey's Delivery Cycle, litho tin & celluloid, friction, NM ..................................**600.00**

Linemar, Olive Oyl on Bell Trike, litho tin, 4", EX................**500.00**

Linemar, Pluto Pulling Cart, litho tin, friction, 1960s, NM ...........**450.00**

Linemar, Superman Turnover Truck, litho tin, 4", NM ................**350.00**

Linemar/WDP, Babes in Toyland Soldier, litho tin, 6", EXIB ..**425.00**

Marx, Big Aerial Acrobats, EXIB ..**300.00**

Marx, Careful Johnny, tin w/plastic bobbing head, 6½", NMIB.**250.00**

Marx, Cowboy Rider, 1941, NMIB ...**375.00**

Marx, Dick Tracy Police Car, litho light on roof, 1950s, 7", EX+ ..................................**200.00**

Marx, Flintstone Car (Fred), 1960s, 11", EXIB ........................**450.00**

Marx, Flintstone Log Car, plastic, friction, 1959, 4", EXIB ...**225.00**

Marx, Mickey Mouse Express, 1950s, 9" dia, NMIB ........**900.00**

Marx, Thor on Tricycle, 1960s, litho tin, NM............................**200.00**

Mattel, Music Box Carousel, litho tin & plastic, 1953, 9", NMIB..**150.00**

MT, Miss Automatic Ironer, 1950s, litho tin, 4", NMIB.............**50.00**

Ny-Lint, Howdy Doody Cart, litho tin, 9" L, VG, from $325 to......................................**425.00**

Occupied Japan, Donkey w/Rider, celluloid, 5", NMIB..........**200.00**

Occupied Japan, Monkey Playing Banjo, celluloid, 7½", VG.....**175.00**

Schuco, Flippo the Frog, tin w/felt covering, 3", NMIB..........**100.00**

Schuco, Motorcycle w/Driver, litho tin, 5", VG........................**200.00**

STE, Bear in Rowboat, 1950s, 10", NMIB..............................**275.00**

TPS, Bozo the Clown, litho tin, 6", EX (VG box).....................**400.00**

TPS, Magic Circus, litho tin & plastic, 6", EXIB, from $150 to ....**180.00**

TPS, Monkey Golfer, litho tin, 1950s, NMIB, from $200 to ........**275.00**

Unique Art, Hobo Train, litho tin, 8", EX..............................**350.00**

Unique Art, Kiddie Fireman, 8½", G+.....................................**175.00**

Unique Art, Sky Rangers, litho tin, 10", EXIB........................**400.00**

Wolverine, Action Jumper, litho tin, 26" ramp, MIB.................**350.00**

Wolverine, Dandy Andy Rooster, litho tin, 10", NMIB.........**600.00**

Wolverine, Native on Alligator, litho tin, 15", EX......................**400.00**

**Wyandotte, Acrobatic Monkeys, 10" diameter, EX, $285.00.**

Wyandotte, Easter Bunny on Motorcycle, litho tin, 9½", G.....**200.00**

Wyandotte, Hoky & Poky, litho tin, 6", NM (EX box)...............**400.00**

Yonezawa, Monkey Banana Vendor, litho tin, 8½", MIB...........**100.00**

# Trolls

The first trolls to come to the United States were molded after a 1952 design by Marti and Helena Kuuskoski of Tampere, Finland. The first to be mass produced in America were molded from wood carvings made by Thomas Dam of Denmark. They were made of vinyl, and the orignal issue carried the mark 'Dam Things Originals copyright 1964 – 1965 Dam Things Est.; m.f.g. by Royalty Designs of Fla. Inc.' (Other marks were used as well; look on the troll's back or the bottom of his feet for Dam trademarks.) As the demand for these trolls increased, several US manufacturers became licensed to produce them. The most noteworthy of these were Uneeda doll company's Wishnik line and Inga Dykin's Scandia House True Trolls. Thomas Dam continued to import his Dam Things line.

The troll craze from the '60s spawned many items other than dolls such as wall plaques, salt and pepper shakers, pins, squirt guns, rings, clay trolls, lamps, Halloween costumes, animals, lawn ornaments, coat racks, notebooks, folders, and even a car.

In the '70s, '80s, and '90s, more new trolls were produced. While these trolls are collectible to some, the avid troll collector still prefers those produced in the '60s. Condition is a very important worth-assessing factor; our values are for examples in EX/NM condition. To evaluate trolls in only G/VG condition, decrease these numbers by half or more.

Astronaut pencil topper, Scandia House, 1967, MIP ..............**65.00**

Bank, girl w/pink hair, Dam, 1960s, 7", VG ................................**50.00**

Beatle, blue jumpsuit, w/guitar, JN Reisler, 3", VG ..................**70.00**

Belle of the ball in green lace, long blond mohair, Dam, 1960s, 2½" ......................................**35.00**

Bo Peep, Storybook Collection, Norfin, 1977, 9", M ............**35.00**

Born To Ski, Russ, 3½"..............**12.00**

Boy, green vest, orange pants, Dam, 1960s, 12"........................**120.00**

Boy, long yellow hair, felt outfit, Dam, 1960s, 2½"................**30.00**

Boy, nude, Dam, 1964, 2¾"......**18.00**

Boy in patched burlap pants, striped sweater, Dam, #604, 1977, 8"..**50.00**

Bride & Groom, Uneeda Wishnik, 1970s, 6", pr ......................**35.00**

Caveman, nude, Dam, 1960s, 3"..**135.00**

Cow, Dam (no mark), Dam tag around neck, 7"..................**80.00**

Cow, white hair & brown eyes, Dam, 3½" ......................................**55.00**

Donkey, head swivels, Dam Things, 1964, 8½", VG..................**110.00**

Elvis, white satin outfit w/gold trim, guitar, Norfin, 1977, 9", M..**25.00**

Eskimo boy, unmarked (Scandia House), 6", VG ..................**90.00**

Eskimo girl, white hair & shirt, red attire, Dam Things, 1960s, 6" ........................................**80.00**

Fire Chief, Treasure Trolls, blue hair & eyes, 4", NM ...........**12.00**

Fox, fuzzy mohair on head & chest, Lephrechaun LTD, 1970s, 6½" ......................................**30.00**

Giraffe, seated, Dam (European), 11" ......................................**95.00**

Girl, seated, Dam, 1979, 18", NM .**65.00**

Girl in long-sleeved pink shirt, checked bibbed pants, Uneeda, 17" ......................................**50.00**

Girl in red dress, lace cap & apron, Dam, 1960s, 7"..................**50.00**

Girl Scout, Dam Things, 1960s, 12", VG ......................................**55.00**

Goo-Goo Baby, Russ Trolls, 1990s, 9", NM ................................**13.00**

Green monster, pink hair, white robe, L Khem, 1964, 3½"...**60.00**

Henry in bib overalls, shaggy hair, TH Dam, Made in Denmark, 1979, 18" ............................**60.00**

Hobo clown, Russ #18716, 6" ......**70.00**

Hula dancer, unmarked (Scandia House), 8", VG ..................**75.00**

Hunt-Nik, Totsy Wishnik, w/rifle, from $20 to........................**25.00**

**Ice Skater, white jacket and skates, red scarf and skirt, Dam, 1960s, 3", $145.00.** (Photo courtesy Miss Kitty at the Cat's Pajamas Vintage)

Iggy Normous in 'leopard skin,' Dam Things, 1960s, 13" .............**65.00**

Lady, extremely long yellow mohair, Dam/Made in Denmark, 2½" ..........................**25.00**

Lion, Dam, 1968-72, 6¾x8¼"......**60.00**

Lion keychain, rare, sm............**15.00**

Little Red Riding Hood, Russ Story-book, 4½".............................**14.00**

Mermaid, iridescent hair & outfit, Russ, 5"..............................**25.00**

Mouse, allover orange hair, on blue hang cord, 1968, 3½".........**35.00**

Old man in green longjohns, toothy smile, Nyrform, 26"...........**90.00**

Owl, allover red animal fur, on hang cord, Gonk, #953577 England, sm........................................**20.00**

Petal People, Wishnik, 1964, 7"..**10.00**

Piggy bank, blue felt necktie, Dam, 1984, 6½" L......................**30.00**

Redhead in lime shirt & green jumper, Dam Things, 1960s, 12"....................................**95.00**

**Santa, Dam Things, pre-1975, EX, $50.00.** (Photo courtesy Cathie Tomlinson; Seattle, Washington)

Santa, Wishnik, 7"....................**35.00**

Seal, Norfin Pets/Dam, 1984, 6½"....................................**50.00**

Seal bank, Dam, Made in Denmark, 1984, 6"..............................**18.00**

Snorkler, w/googles & swim fins, Russ, 4"..............................**15.00**

Sock-It-To-Me, Uneeda Wishnik, 6", NM....................................**50.00**

Squeek Mouse, troll in mouse costume, Norfin/Dam, 1985, 3½"....................................**15.00**

St Louis Cardinals troll nodder, Russ, 1992.........................**14.00**

Tailed troll, Dam Things, 1960s, VG, 6½"..............................**150.00**

Tailed troll, lg pointed ears, black mohair, burlap vest, Dam, 1960s, 6"............................**135.00**

Teenage Mutant Ninja Turtle, 1992, 7", MIB...............................**8.00**

Troll House, carrying case, ca 1960s, 12x10x6"............................**60.00**

Troll lying on log, Nyform, 5x5"..**75.00**

Turtle, Norfin/Dam, 1984, amber eyes, 4"..............................**50.00**

Turtle, smiling face, long hair, unmarked (Dam?), 1960s, 7", L.......................................**110.00**

Two-headed troll, nude, Uneeda, 1965, 3"..............................**35.00**

Viking, Dam Things, 1960s, 5½"....................................**90.00**

# Universal

Located in Cambridge, Ohio, Universal Potteries Incorporated produced various lines of dinnerware from 1934 to the late 1950s, several of which are very attractive, readily available, and therefore quite collectible. Refer to *The Collector's Encyclopedia of American Dinnerware* by Jo Cunningham (Collector Books) for more information. See also Cattail.

Baby's Breath, plate, bread & butter; from $3 to.....................**6.00**

Baby's Breath, sugar bowl, w/lid, from $12 to..........................**15.00**
Ballerina, egg cup, from $20 to ..........................................**22.00**
Ballerina (Dove Gray), sugar bowl, w/lid....................................**15.00**
Ballerina (Mist), bowl, serving; 7½" ......................................**14.00**
Ballerina (Mist), creamer, open..**12.00**
Ballerina (Mist), plate chop; tab handles...............................**18.00**
Ballerina (Mist), platter, round, from $10 to..........................**14.00**
Ballerina (Mist), sauce boat.....**15.00**
Bittersweet, covered jar, 2"......**32.50**
Bittersweet, pepper shaker, range style....................................**28.50**
Blue & White, plate, chop; 11½" dia......................................**25.00**
Calico Fruit, cup & saucer.......**32.50**
Calico Fruit, custard cup, 5-oz, from $6 to....................................**7.50**
Calico Fruit, pitcher, flip-top lid, 7" ........................................**35.00**
Calico Fruit, plate, bread & butter, from $5 to.............................**6.00**
Calico Fruit, plate, 9" ..............**17.50**
Camwood, salt & pepper skakers, gold trim, 2¾", pr.................**8.50**
Cherry Blossom, sauce boat.....**15.00**
Circus, batter jug, metal lid w/red Bakelite handle, 9½".........**70.00**
Circus, bowl, design on 2 sides, 2¾x9¾x6⅜"........................**70.00**
Cottage Garden, plate, dinner, 9⅛"..**32.50**
Harvest, pie plate, gold trim......**20.00**
Highland, gravy boat, no underplate..**20.00**
Iris, bowl, mixing; 4x9".............**32.00**
Moss Rose, butter dish, w/lid, 8½" L ........................................**25.00**
Moss Rose, pitcher, 8½" .........**115.00**
Moss Rose, teapot, w/lid, 7"......**55.00**

Oriental Flower, platter, lug handles, 13", from $12 to.........**14.00**
Rambler Rose, creamer, open, from $18 to................................**22.00**
Red & White, casserole, w/lid......**20.00**
Woodvine, cup & saucer, from $8 to........................................**10.00**

**Woodvine, gravy liner/relish dish, from $12.00 to $15.00; Creamer and sugar bowl, from $20.00 to $25.00.**

Woodvine, pitcher, 7¼"............**40.00**
Woodvine, relish dish, from $12 to........................................**15.00**

# Valentines

Valentine's day is every day of the year for valentine collectors who are always on the endless search for that special piece to add to their collection. Advertising, party favors, paper dolls, comic characters, transportation, and postcards cover just a few of the valentine categories.

All valentines are collectible. Remember the cards you gave to fellow students, and the boxes you used to put them in? The new baby boomers are now starting to search for their childhood memories and, yes, that includes valentines. How about trolls? Disney? and 'for the teacher' valentines? All of them are special in their own way.

Whatever you collect, chances are good there will be one valentine that fits right in, i.e., lamps, African American, record players, dolls, track and field, dogs, cats, sewing machines, etc.

Please keep in mind the seven factors before purchasing a card: condition, size, manufacturer, category, scarcity, artist signature, and age. For more information we recommend *Valentines With Values, One Hundred Years of Valentines,* and *Valentines for the Eclectic Collector* by Katherine Kreider.

Key:
D — dimensional
PIG — Printed in Germany
HCCP — honeycomb paper puff

D, carousel, 3-D, American Greetings, printed in Italy, 8x10x4", EX......................................**15.00**
D, carriage filled w/fairies, Buzza Cardza, 1950s, 7x9x3", EX.....**25.00**
D, Cinderella coach, Hallmark, 1950s, 9¾x7½x4½", EX.....**25.00**
D, Cupid's Theater, Campbell Soup Kids, USA, late '30s, 6x6x1½", EX......................................**15.00**
D, Loveland Valentine Train Station, no maker, 1940s, 4x7x10", EX......................................**15.00**
D, punch-out card, Dutch children series, 1940s, USA, 3½x3x½", EX..**2.00**
Flat, boy on tricycle, 1950s, 5x2½", EX........................................**2.00**
Flat, canaries in cage, 1950s, 4½x2", EX........................................**2.00**
Flat, letter series, B-e Yourself, Carrington, '40s, 3¾x2½", EX...**6.00**

**Flat, long-stemmed rose, unmarked, 1930s, 6½x4", EX, $10.00.** (Photo courtesy Katherine Kreider)

Flat, magic rabbit in hat, 1960s, 4x1", EX ..............................**2.00**
Flat, Piglet, Pig of Myself, 1950s, 4x1", EX ..............................**1.00**
Flat, poppy children, 1920s, 4½x2", EX........................................**3.00**
Folded-flat, Big Bad Wolf, USA, 1940s, 8½x3", EX..............**15.00**
Folded-flat, Dick Tracy, 1940s, 6x5½", EX ..........................**25.00**
Folded-flat, Moon Mullins, 1920s, 4x5", EX ............................**15.00**
Folded-flat, Wonder Woman, USA, 1940s, rare, 6x6", EX.........**50.00**
Greeting card, cowboy & guitar, Hallmark, 1950s, 4½x2½"...**2.00**
Greeting card, Cupid sledding, Whitney, 1920s, 4x4"..........**2.00**
Greeting card, Dear Wife, Rust Craft Artist Guild, 1940s, 6x4½" ..**5.00**
Greeting card, miniature flower, hidden children, Whitney, 1930s, EX ............................**8.00**
Greeting card, roller skater, Americard, 1940s, 4½x3½"............**2.00**
Greeting card pop-up, Lov-O-Gram, Twelvetrees, 1940s, 5x4"...**15.00**
HCPP, Beistle basket, USA, 1920s, 10x7x6", EX ......................**15.00**

HCPP, big-eyed children w/teapot, airbrushed, '20s, 8x8x3½", EX......................................**25.00**

HCPP, hanging heart decoration, no maker, 1920s, 8x8x3½", EX......................................**15.00**

Mechanical-flat, dressed animals, USA, 1950s, 9½x6", EX.......**8.00**

Mechanical-flat, elephant w/moving neck, PIG, 1920s, 4x2" ........**3.00**

Mechanical-flat, fortune teller, USA, 1920s, 4½x4¼"......................**3.00**

Mechanical-flat, garbage can, HCPP accent, no maker, 1940s, 6x4½"..................................**3.00**

**Mechanical-flat, Geppetto on raft, Walt Disney Productions, 1939, 7½x6", VG, $20.00.** (Photo courtesy Katherine Kreider)

Mechanical-flat, nurse, PIG, easel back, Trademark G, 1940s, 7x5", EX .............................**10.00**

Mechanical-flat, Snow White, USA, 1930s, 5¾x3", EX...............**75.00**

Novelty, Disney Fun Time Valentines, Fuld & Co, 1970s, EXIB...................................**25.00**

Novelty, Love Boat w/original lollipop, USA, 1950s, 5½x6x1¼", EX...................................**150.00**

Novelty, punch-out, Crush Soda, Pink Panther, 12 per 5x3½" sheet...................................**25.00**

Novelty, punch-out Pillsbury Dough Boy, 9 per sheet, 12¼x9¾", EX......................................**25.00**

Novelty, 28 Assorted Valentines, USA, 1950s, various sizes, MIB.....**25.00**

Novelty booklet, dog w/plastic eyes, '30s, 4 pages, 6x3½", EX......**8.00**

Novelty lollipop card, Farmer, Rosen, USA, 1920s, 5½x6", EX ........**8.00**

# Van Briggle

The Van Briggle Pottery of Colorado Springs, Colorado, was established in 1901 by Artus Van Briggle upon the completion of his quest to perfect a complete flat matt glaze. His wife, Ann, worked with him and they, along with George Young, were responsible for the modeling of the wares. Known for their flowing Art Nouveau shapes, much of the ware was eventually made from molds with each piece carefully trimmed and refined before the glaze was sprayed on. Their most popular colors were Persian Rose, Ming Blue, and Mustard Yellow.

Van Briggle died in 1904, but the work was continued by his wife. With new facilities built in 1908, tiles, gardenware, and commercial lines were added to the earlier artware lines. Reproductions of some early designs continue to be made, The Double A mark has always been in use, but after 1920 the dates and/or shape numbers were dropped.

The Anna Van Briggle glaze was developed for a later line that was made between 1956 and 1968.

Bowl, arrowfoot motif, green, #698, ca 1920, 6½"......................**250.00**

Bowl, dragonflies (4) at rim, mulberry, USA, 1920s, 2¾x8¾" .**345.00**

Bowl, leaves, maroon multicolor, ca 1920, 4"...........................**200.00**

Bowl, leaves on comma-like stems, turquoise blue, ca 1925, 3¾" H.......................................**150.00**

Bowl vase, spade leaves, maroon w/blue overspray, ca 1920, 6½" dia ...............**145.00**

**Vase, Anna Van Briggle, 1955 – 58, from $25.00 to $35.00.** (Photo courtesy Richard Sasicki and Josie Fania)

Vase, bears at rim (2, 3-dimensional), Persian Rose, 1920s, 15x4½"...........................**1,900.00**

Vase, blue to maroon, handles, post-1930s, 2¼"........................**100.00**

Vase, buds on stems, Persian Rose, bulbous w/handles, 1930s, 6½"...................................**200.00**

Vase, butterflies under blue & maroon, post-1930s, 4"....**100.00**

Vase, Despondency, blue & green, post-1930s, 13½"..............**550.00**

Vase, dragonfly, brown/green, ca 1920-30, 7¼"....................**350.00**

Vase, floral, blue-gray w/turquoise overspray, slender ovoid, 1920, 6"......................................**375.00**

Vase, floral, blue/turquoise, ca 1920, 7⅜"....................................**350.00**

Vase, floral, brown w/green overspray, #833, ca 1920, 5½"..**230.00**

Vase, floral, dark purple on maroon, 1921, 2¾x2¾"...................**165.00**

Vase, floral, maroon w/blue overspray, #645, ca 1920, 4"..**115.00**

Vase, Indian heads (3), maroon & blue, pre-1930s, 12".........**375.00**

Vase, irises, Persian Rose, low handles, ca 1920s, 13¼"........**375.00**

Vase, leaves, blue to maroon, post-1930s, 4½".........................**100.00**

Vase, leaves, Mountain Craig Brown, squat, 1930s, 4¼x5"..........**150.00**

Vase, leaves form body, blue & aqua mottled, post-1930s, 3½".**100.00**

Vase, Lorelei, blue shaded to turquoise, AA Van Briggle, ca 1970+, 11"........................**325.00**

Vase, poppies, brown & green, 1920s-30s, 8¼", NM........**250.00**

Vase, shell form, green gloss, post-1930s, 13" L......................**50.00**

Vase, swirled leaves, Persian Rose, ca 1940s, 4¾x7½"............**400.00**

# Vernon Kilns

From 1931 until 1958, Vernon Kilns produced hundreds of patterns of fine dinnerware that today's collectors enjoy reassembling. They retained the services of famous artists and designers such as Rockwell Kent and Walt Disney, who designed both dinnerware lines and novelty items. Examples of their work are at a premium. (Nearly all artist-designed lines utilized the Ultra Shape. To evaluate the work of Blanding, use 200% of our high range; for Disney lines, 700% to 800%; Kent — Moby Dick and Our America, 250%; for Salamina, 500% to 700%.)

For more informtion, we recommend *Collectible Vernon Kilns* by Maxine Nelson (Collector Books). See Clubs and Newsletters for information concerning *Vernon Views* newsletter. Our values are average. The more elaborate the pattern, the higher the value.

Chatelaine, bowl, chowder; Topaz or Bronze, 6", from $12 to......**15.00**
Chatelaine, creamer, decorated Platinum or Jade, from $35 to.........................................**45.00**
Chatelaine, plate, chop; Platinum or Jade, decor, 14", from $50 to.........................................**65.00**
Chatelaine, platter, Topaz or Bronze, 16", from $50 to....**65.00**
Fantasia, figurine, Baby Weems (from Reluctant Dragon), #37, from $250 to.....................**350.00**
Fantasia, figurine, donkey unicorn, #16, from $600 to.............**700.00**
Fantasia, figurine, hippo, any #, from $350 to.....................**400.00**
Fantasia, vase, Cameo Goddess, #126, from $1,500 to.....**2,000.00**
Melinda, bowl, rim soup; 8", from $12 to...................................**18.00**
Melinda, coffeepot, AD; 2-cup, from $65 to.................................**75.00**
Melinda, egg cup, from $18 to..**25.00**

**Melinda in Hawaii pattern (same as Lei Lani), pitcher, two quart, $100.00; Chop plate, 12½", $30.00.**

Melinda, plate, luncheon; sq, 8½", from $15 to..........................**20.00**
Melinda, platter, 12", from $20 to...**30.00**
Melinda, sauce boat, from $20 to..**30.00**
Montecito, ashtray, 5½" dia, from $12 to.................................**20.00**
Montecito, bowl, mixing; 7", from $22 to.................................**30.00**
Montecito, coaster, 4½", from $18 to..**25.00**
Montecito, plate, grill; 11", from $20 to.........................................**25.00**
San Clemente (Anytime), bowl, fruit; 5½", from $5 to...........**8.00**
San Clemente (Anytime), bowl, vegetable; divided, 9", from $15 to.........................................**22.00**
San Clemente (Anytime), platter, 11", from $14 to .................**20.00**
San Clemente (Anytime), teapot, from $35 to........................**65.00**
San Fernando, bowl, fruit; 5½", from $6 to...................................**10.00**
San Fernando, bowl, lug chowder; 6", from $12 to ...................**18.00**
San Fernando, coaster, ridged, 3¾", from $15 to........................**20.00**
San Fernando, mug, 9-oz, from $20 to.........................................**25.00**

San Fernando, olive dish, oval, 10",
from $20 to.........................**35.00**
San Fernando, teacup, from $12
to.........................................**20.00**
San Marino, coffee server, w/stopper,
10-cup, from $35 to.............**45.00**
San Marino, creamer, from $10
to .......................................**12.00**
San Marino, cup, jumbo; from $25
to.........................................**35.00**
San Marino, sugar bowl, w/lid, from
$12 to..................................**18.00**
Transitional (Year 'Round), bowl,
soup/cereal; from $8 to......**10.00**
Transitional (Year 'Round), cof-
feepot, 6-cup, from $25 to..**45.00**
Transitional (Year 'Round), platter,
11", from $12 to .................**20.00**
Transitional (Year 'Round), platter,
13½", from $15 to ..............**25.00**
Ultra, bowl, serving; round, 9", from
$18 to...................................**30.00**
Ultra, egg cup, from $18 to ......**25.00**
Ultra, teapot, 6-cup, from $45
to .......................................**100.00**

# Vietnam War Collectibles

There was confict in Vietnam
for many years before the United
States was drawn into it during the
Eisenhower years. Fighting raged
until well into 1975 when commu-
nist forces invaded Saigon and
crushed the South Vietnamese government there. Today items from
the 1960s and early 1970s are
becoming collectible. Pins, booklets,
uniforms, patches, and the like
reflect these troubled times when
anti-war demonstrations raged and

unsound political policies cost the
lives of many brave young men.

Book, Vietnam, Images from Combat
Photographers, Andrews &
Elliot, EX ..........................**15.00**
Brassard, Security Police, blue &
yellow, wool w/elastic fasteners,
EX...................................**40.00**

**Flag, (translated): Armed Forces
for the Liberation of South Vietnam, with North Vietnamese
Army Unit 271, 1968, red and
blue cotton with yellow star,
27x36", VG, from $45.00 to $55.00.**
(Photo courtesy kingcobra 1969)

Hand grenade, US M-26, inert,
EX....................................**210.00**
LAW rocker tube, M72A2 Light Anti-
Tank Weapon, EX .............**285.00**
Patch, Fire; Prevention & Protection,
Chu Lai, US Marine Corps,
EX.........................................**8.00**
Pin, Nurse/Army/Navy/Air Force, center
red cross w/Vietnam, 1", EX...**12.00**
Pin-back, How Many More?, black crosses
on blue, 2½" dia, EX..........**14.00**
Pin-back, Oct 15-16 International
Days of Protest Vietnam, 1½",
EX.......................................**35.00**
Pin-back, Out Now Nov 6th, Demon-
strate Against the War, NPAC,
1¾", M ..............................**20.00**

Pin-back, Superman Get Out of Viet Nam, LBJ caricature, 1¾", EX......................................15.00

Pin-back, Tell It to Hanoi, blue letters on white, 1⅝" dia, EX......................................10.00

Pin-back, Vote Against the War, Mel Dublin for Congress, 4", NM ....................................22.00

Poster, I Want Out, Uncle Sam bleeding w/bandages, 1971, 44x31", EX ........................60.00

Poster, War Is Hell, Ask the Man Who Fought One, 22x19", EX......................................50.00

Stick grenade, steel body w/wooden handle, inert, w/capture papers, EX....................................360.00

Survival ax tool, Type 4 #8642C, 1967, M w/EX canvas sheath ......265.00

T-shirt, Agent Orange Keeps on Killing, 1970s, EX..............30.00

# Wall Pockets

Here's a collectible that is easily found, relatively inexpensive, and very diversified. They were made in Japan, Czechoslovakia, and by many companies in the United States. Those made by companies best known for their art pottery (Weller, Roseville, etc.) are in a class of their own, but the novelty, just-for-fun wall pockets stand on their own merits. Examples with large, colorful birds or those with unusual modeling are usually the more desirable. For more information we recommend *Collector's Encyclopedia of Made in Japan Ceramics* by Carole Bess White, who is listed in the Directory under Oregon (Collector Books). See also California Pottery, Cleminson; McCoy; Shawnee; other specific manufacturers.

**Art Deco flowers, multicolor on red, incised Japan mark, from $65.00 to $85.00. (Photo courtesy Carole Bess White)**

Baby w/swan, white lustre, Bradley Exclusives, Japan................22.00

Bird on flowerpot, multicolor lustre, Made in Japan, 6½".............40.00

Bird on paradise, multicolor on orange lustre, Noritake, 8".....................................100.00

Boy at stone well, multicolor, Made in Japan, 5½" ....................15.00

Carrots (3), glossy orange w/green tops, 5½"............................35.00

Cat on creel, multicolor, 5½"......20.00

Conical form w/swirl design, dark green, European, 10" ........12.00

Cowboy boot, side view, plain glossy brown, Japan, 3½"................7.00

Cuckoo clock, w/weights, blue & white, 6½" ....................................20.00

Daffodils, yellow w/green stems, Japan, #994, 4"..................12.00

Dutch girl stands before basket, multicolor, Made in Japan, 6" ...18.00

Elf in leaves, multicolor, 5½"...14.00

Fish, round body w/brown airbrushing, glossy finish, Japan, 4" .....15.00

Floral on orange lustre, Made in
Japan, 5"............................**30.00**
Girl on cornucopia, multicolor,
Japan, 6"............................**14.00**
Girl w/wide-brimmed hat, green lus-
tre, Stanford, 7".................**22.00**
Goat amid palm trees, multicolor,
Made in Japan, 5½x7"......**20.00**
Horse head in horseshoe, glossy
brown, Made in Japan, 8½"..**25.00**
Horsehead & horseshoe, brown,
Made in Japan, 8½"..........**25.00**
Indian's chief's head, multicolor,
Made in Japan, 6".............**20.00**
Lovebirds & heart w/flower decor on
white, 5"............................**12.00**

**Majolica-style moon
with geisha girl, multi-
color, Japan mark, 7¾",
from $65.00 to $85.00.**
(Photo courtesy Carole Bess

Mums (3) in relief, red on black cone
shape, Made in Japan, 6"..**10.00**
Parakeets (2) on perch, multicolor,
7¼".....................................**15.00**
Rose & bud on stem, pink & green,
Czechoslovakia, 10½"........**35.00**
Sailboat, metallic gold & blue lustre,
Brown China, 5¾".............**20.00**
Squirrel w/nut, brown tones, Japan,
4⅜".....................................**12.00**
Thistle in relief, brown tones, Made
in Japan, 6¼" ....................**15.00**

Tulip, pink w/green leaves, Made in
Japan, 5½".........................**12.00**
Vase, cream w/brown handles,
Brown China, 5½".............**15.00**
Windmill scene, multicolor lustre,
Made in Japan, 6¼"..........**45.00**

# Western Heroes

Interest is very strong right
now in western memorabilia — not
only that, but the kids that listened
so intently to those after-school
radio episodes featuring one of the
many cowboy stars that sparked the
air-waves in the '50s are now some
of today's more affluent collectors,
able and wanting to search out and
buy toys they had in their youth.
Put those two factors together, and
it's easy to see why these items are
so popular. For more information,
we recommend *The W.F. Cody Buffalo Bill Collector's Guide* by James
W. Wojtowicz.

See also Coloring Books; Comic
Books; Games; Puzzles.

### Davy Crockett

Davy Crockett had long been a
favorite in fact and folklore. Then
with the opening of Disney's Frontier-
land and his continuing adventures
on 1950s television came a surge of
interest in all sorts of items featuring
the likeness of Fess Parker in a coon-
skin cap. Millions were drawn to the
mystic excitement surrounding the
settlement of our great country. Due
to demand, there were many types of

items produced for eager fans ready to role play their favorite adventures.

Binoculars, plastic, Harrison, MIB..**175.00**
Dart Gun Set, MIB....................**50.00**
Fix-It Stagecoach, plastic, Ideal, 14",
    NMIB...............................**85.00**
Lamp, ceramic figure w/bear by tree
    stump, lithoed shade, 12",
    NM...................................**200.00**
Lamp, rotating cylinder, Econolite,
    11", NM............................**275.00**
Marionette, talker, Hazelle's, 15",
    MIB.................................**350.00**
Moccasin kit, Old Town Crafts, com-
    plete & unused, NMIB........**75.00**
Napkins, Beach Prod, 1950s, 30
    in unopened package, 5" sq,
    MIP...................................**40.00**
Soap, detailed figure holding gun,
    1950s, unused, EXIB ........**75.00**
Stamp book, 1955, EX+............**55.00**
T-shirt, w/graphics & fringe, Shir-
    tees, 1950s, EX+................**55.00**
Towels, Kiddie Towel Set, Cannon,
    MIB.................................**100.00**
Tray, litho tin, image of Davy fighting
    Indians, WDP, 1955, 13x17",
    VG....................................**75.00**
Wallet, brown vinyl w/imitation
    fur & color graphics, 1955,
    EXIB ................................**75.00**
Western Rodeo, plastic figures, Ajaz,
    unused, NMIB...................**85.00**

### Gene Autry

First breaking into show business as a recording star with Columbia Records, Gene went on to become
one of Hollywood's most famous
singing cowboys. From the late

1930s until the mid-1950s, he rode
his wonder horse 'Champion'
through almost ninety feature films.
He did radio and TV as well, and
naturally his fame spawned a wealth
of memorabilia originally aimed at
his young audiences, now grabbed
up just as quickly by collectors.

Flashlight, Cowboy Lariat, EXIB .**100.00**
Guitar, plastic, Emenee, 32", NMIB..**230.00**

**Official Cowboy Spurs,
MIB, $185.00.** (Photo
courtesy Phil Helley)

Pistol Horn, Metal Products, 6½",
    NMIB...............................**175.00**
Record player, plastic w/Flying A
    decal, electric, Columbia, 13" L,
    VG..................................**250.00**
Wallet, plastic, image of Autry &
    Champion, NMIB..............**85.00**

### Hopalong Cassidy

One of the most popular western
heroes of all time, Hoppy was the
epitome of the highly moral, role-
model cowboys of radio and the silver
screen that many of us grew up with
in the '40s and '50s. He was por-
trayed by William Boyd who personally endorsed more than 2,200 items
targeting Hoppy's loyal followers.

Camera, Wm Boyd/Galter, 1940, unused, NMIB.................**200.00**

Crayon & Stencil Set, Transogram, 1950s, complete, some use, EXIB.........**50.00**

Doll, rubber head, cloth clothes, gun & holster, 1950, 21", NM ....**300.00**

Figure, chalk, 1950s, 14", NM+..**350.00**

Figure & Paint Set, Laurel Ann, complete, used, EXIB......**265.00**

**Hair Trainer, eight ounce, 6½", $90.00.**

Hand puppet, cloth body w/vinyl head, 1950s, scarce, NM..**200.00**

Hat, felt w/longhorn logo, VG.....**125.00**

Stationary folio, w/paper & envelopes, complete, VG+ ...................**50.00**

Woodburning set, American Toy, 1950s, unused, EXIB ......**100.00**

## The Lone Ranger

Recalling 'those thrilling days of yesteryear,' we can't help but remember the adventures of our hero, The Lone Ranger. He's been admired since that first radio show in 1933, and today's collectors seek a wide variety of his memorabilia; premiums, cereal boxes, and even carnival chalkware prizes are a few examples. See Clubs and Newsletters for information on *The Silver Bullet*.

Flashlight, tin, USA Lite, MIB.....**200.00**

Flicker ring, Lone Ranger/Captain Action, 1960s, NM.............**20.00**

Guitar, heavy cardboard w/wooden neck, Jefferson, 1950s, 28½" L, EX.**100.00**

Hi-Yo Silver the Lone Ranger Target Game, Marx, EXIB..**65.00**

Horseshoe set, rubber, Gardner, NMIB................................**85.00**

Oil Painting by Numbers, Hasbro, 1958, complete, partially used, EXIB .................................**75.00**

Ring-Toss, cardboard diecut, Rosebud Art, complete, MIB .............**300.00**

School bag, canvas w/plastic handle, image on side pocket, 1950s, EX.**100.00**

Soap figure, Tonto, Kerk Guild, unopened, 1939, 4", EXIB......**50.00**

Soap figure set, Lone Ranger, Tonto & Silver, Kerk, 1939, 4", VG...**50.00**

Target, litho tin w/metal support, Marx, TLR Inc, 1930s, 9½" sq, EX.**50.00**

## Roy Rogers

Growing up during the Great Depression, Leonard Frank Sly was determined to make his mark in the entertainment industry. In 1938 after landing small roles in films featuring Gene Autry and others, Republic Studios (recognizing his talents) renamed their singing cowboy Roy Rogers and placed him in his first leading role in *Under Western Stars*. By 1943 he had become America's 'King of the Cowboys.' And his beloved wife Dale Evans and his horse Trigger were at the top with him. See Clubs and Newsletters for information on the Roy Rogers— Dale Evans Collectors Association.

Archery set, Ben Pearson, scarce, 37", unused, NMOC ........**185.00**

Bank, boot shape, bronzed metal, Almar, 6", EX ....................**75.00**

Bolo tie, Bustin' Bull, Putnam Prod, EX (on photo card)...................**125.00**

Branding set/ink pad, tin container, 1950s, ½x2" dia, unused, EX........**65.00**

Crayon set, Standard Toykraft #940, 1950s, VGIB ......................**75.00**

Fountain pen, name on black plastic barrel, gold trim, 1950s, 5", VG.....................................**50.00**

Gloves, Sears, unused, MIP .....**150.00**

Hand puppet, cloth w/vinyl head & hat, 1950s, 7", EX+ ...........**75.00**

Lucky Horseshoe Game, Ohio Art, 1950s, EX...........................**75.00**

Pony Contest entry form, Hudson's Bay Co, 1950s, 12x9", unused, NM ....................................**50.00**

School tablet, w/Dale Evans, Frontiers Inc, 1950s, 10x8", unused, EX .....................................**25.00**

Trick Lasso, Classy Products, 1950s, complete, EXIP.................**75.00**

**Miscellaneous**

Bat Masterson, outfit, shirt/pants/tie, Gene Barry labels, Kaynee, MIB....**160.00**

**Bonanza, Ponderosa Ranch litho tin cup, Hoss, Ben, and Joe Cartright portraits, EX, $12.50.**

Gunsmoke, hat, felt w/photo image of Marshall Dillon, 1960s, EX..**20.00**

Maverick, Eras-O-Picture Book, Hasbro, 1958, complete, EX ...........**40.00**

Tom Mix, luminous arrowhead w/compass & magnifying glass, EX .....................................**35.00**

Wild Bill Hickok, toothbrush holder, double metal holsters, Tek, NMOC ..**80.00**

Wild Bill Hickok, wallet, fastens w/western buckle, NM+ ....**75.00**

Zorro, bowl & plate, Sun-Valley Melmac, 1950s-60s, 5", 7¼", EX, set ..**40.00**

Zorro, hand puppet, vinyl head/ cloth body, Gund/WDP, 1950s, EX+ ....................................**75.00**

Zorro, Magic Slate, Watkins-Stratmore/WDP, 1950s-60s, EX ..**75.00**

# Westmoreland

Originally an Ohio company, Westmoreland relocated in Grapesville, Pennsylvania, where by the 1920s they had became known as one of the country's largest manufacturers of carnival glass. They are best known today for the high quality milk glass which accounted for 90% of their production. For further information we recommend contacting the Westmoreland Glass Society, Inc., listed in Clubs and Newsletters. See also Glass Animals and Birds.

We also suggest reading *Westmoreland Glass, The Popular Years*, by Lorraine Kovar, published by Collector Books.

Ashtray, English Hobnail, amber or crystal, 4½" sq ....................**7.50**

Basket, Paneled Grape, milk glass w/decor, ruffled, 8" ............**70.00**

Bonbon, Wakefield, crystal w/red stain, crimped, metal handle, 6" ........................................**35.00**

Bowl, Lotus/#1921, black, round, lg..**50.00**

Bowl, nappy, amber or crystal, 4½" sq ..........................................**7.00**

Bowl, Paneled Grape, milk glass w/decor, bell shape, footed, 9½" ....................................**110.00**

Bowl, pickle; English Hobnail, amber or crystal, 8" ...........**15.00**

Bowl, Wakefield, crystal w/red stain, crimped, flat, 12" ...............**75.00**

Box, heart shape, Chocolate ....**55.00**

Candleholder, Paneled Grape, milk glass w/decor, Colonial handle, 5" .........................................**37.50**

Candlestick, English Hobnail, amber or crystal, round base, 9" ........................................**25.00**

**Candy dish, Della Robbia, milk glass with bows decoration, DR-17, $75.00.** (Photo courtesy Lorraine Kovar)

Celery/spooner, Paneled Grape, milk glass w/decor, 6" ................**40.00**

Cheese dish, English Hobnail, amber or crystal, 8¾" ........**60.00**

Compote, mint; Wakefield, crystal w/red stain, high foot, 5½" ..........**30.00**

Covered animal dish, cat on rectangular lacy base, purple slag......**250.00**

Covered animal dish, chick on pile of eggs, milk glass, no details..**35.00**

Covered animal dish, fox on diamond base, chocolate ......**200.00**

Covered animal dish, hen on diamond base, purple slag, 5½" .......**85.00**

Covered animal dish, lion on lacy base, milk glass, 8" .........**175.00**

Covered animal dish, rabbit w/eggs on diamond base, milk glass, 8"..**150.00**

Covered animal dish, rooster on diamond base, chocolate, 7½".**175.00**

Creamer, English Hobnail, sq, footed..........................................**8.50**

Creamer, Wakefield, crystal, footed..**25.00**

Cup, coffee; Paneled Grape, milk glass w/decor, flared..........**15.00**

Egg cup, English Hobnail, amber or crystal ................................**14.00**

Figurine, butterfly, any Mist color, lg, ea..................................**40.00**

Figurine, cardinal, ruby carnival, solid....................................**30.00**

Figurine, owl on 2 stacked books, milk glass, 3½" ..................**20.00**

Figurine, penguin on ice floe, blue ..................................**100.00**

Figurine, Porky Pig, cobalt carnival, 3" ........................................**40.00**

Lamp, candle; Cameo, Crystal Mist w/Roses & Bows, w/shade, mini...**55.00**

Lamp, fairy; Thousand Eye, crystal, footed ................................**20.00**

Lamp, fairy; Thousand Eye, ruby, flat or footed, ea ................**50.00**

Mayonnaise, English Hobnail, amber or crystal, 6"...........**10.00**

Mayonnaise set, Paneled Grape, milk glass w/decor, 3-pc..............**35.00**

Pin tray, Heart/#1820, Blue Mist .**30.00**

Pitcher, English Hobnail, amber or crystal, straight sides, 32-oz ..........**55.00**

Pitcher, Paneled Grape, milk glass w/decor, 16-oz ....................**45.00**

Plate, Bicentennial, Paneled Grape/#1881, limited edition, 14½" ................................**225.00**

Plate, English Hobnail, amber or crystal, plain rim, 8½" ........**8.00**

Plate, English Hobnail, amber or crystal, sq, 12" ....................**22.00**

Plate, luncheon; Wakefield, crystal w/red stain, 8½" ................**22.50**

Plate, Wicket border, milk glass w/Revolutionary War scenes, 9" ........................................**60.00**

Punch bowl stand, English Hobnail, amber or crystal ..................**70.00**

Relish, Paneled Grape, milk glass w/decor, 3-part, 9" .............**40.00**

**Rose and Lattice, vase, Golden Sunset, plain top, RL-10, $40.00.** (Photo courtesy Lorraine Kovar)

Shakers, English Hobnail, amber or crystal, round, footed, pr.......**20.00**

Stem, water goblet; English Hobnail, amber or crystal, footed, 8-oz......................................**10.00**

Stem, wine; Wakefield, crystal w/red stain, 2-oz ..........................**30.00**

Sugar bowl, English Hobnail, amber or crystal, low, flat................**7.50**

Sweetmeat, Wakefield, crystal w/red stain, crimped....................**35.00**

Toothpick holder, Paneled Grape, milk glass w/decor.............**25.00**

Trinket box, egg, any Mist color, w/white daisy, w/lid ..........**25.00**

Tumbler, juice; English Hobnail, amber or crystal, footed, 7-oz......................................**9.00**

Vase, English Hobnail, amber or crystal, flared top, 8½"......**40.00**

# World's Fairs and Expositions

Souvenir items have been issued since the mid-1800s for every world's fair and exposition. Few fairgoers have left the grounds without purchasing at least one. Some of the older items were often manufactured right on the fairgrounds by glass or pottery companies who erected working kilns and furnaces just for the duration of the fair. Of course, the older items are usually more valuable, but even souvenirs from the past fifty years are worth hanging on to.

See Clubs and Newsletters for information concerning the World's Fair Collectors' Society, Inc.

### 1939 New York

Ashtray, logo w/blue marbles in hammered rim, brass, Fisher, 3⅜" ....................................**65.00**

Badge, NYWF Safety Team, enameled logo in gold horseshoe, 1½" ..**70.00**

Bank, clear glass w/etched fair logo, Esso, 6x6x4" ......................**65.00**

Cup & saucer, Trylon & Perisphere w/rainbow-colored ground, Japan ..**75.00**

Dish, lemon yellow w/white Trylon & Perisphere, Lenox, 3¾" ......**150.00**

Dresser carpet, Trylon & Perisphere scene, w/fringe, Italy, 18x8", NM .....................................**75.00**

Drink stirrers, colored glass w/white lettering & logo, set of 4....**55.00**

**Oval dish, Trylon and Perisphere scene, red Japan mark, from $35.00 to $50.00.** (Photo courtesy Carole Bess White)

Paint book, Bag Full...Pictures, suitcase shape, Whitman, 32 pages, EX ....................................**120.00**

Pencil sharpener, Trylon & Perisphere, amber w/dark blue base, 3¾" ....................................**50.00**

Pin-back, G Washington Bridge w/skyline, metal, ¾x1¾" .....**35.00**

Plate, blue & white w/orange Trylon & Perisphere, #2960, 7¼"..**100.00**

Pocketwatch and stand w/multicolored enameled fair scene, Ingraham, EX...........................**375.00**

Salt & pepper shakers, Trylon & Perisphere in tray, ceramic, Japan, EX.........................**45.00**

Spoon set, fair buildings, Rogers Mfg Co, 6", set of 12, M (EX boxes).**90.00**

Thermometer, Trylon & Perisphere, orange Bakelite w/black base, 3½" ....................................**85.00**

Toy, trolley, Greyhound Lines NY World's Fair, Arcade Toy, CI, EX ....................................**210.00**

Vase, cobalt w/raised Trylon & Perisphere in white, Lenox/Ovington, 5"..............................**365.00**

## 1939 San Francisco

Belt, beaded, World's Fair 1962, 34", NM .....................................**17.50**

Booklet, World's Fair Pictorial Panorama, 24 page, 11x8½", EX .....**12.00**

Bracelet, logo & Space Needle on 1⅛" dia medallion, copper, EX .....................................**30.00**

Cigarette snuffer, Space Needle shape, Vica Novelty, 3⅛", EXIB .................................**30.00**

Coloring book, Trans-Canada, 30 pages, 16x11½", EX ..........**13.50**

Dish, Monorail, glass, 4x4¾", EX..**20.00**

Lighter, floor; Space Needle shape, goldtone w/silver wash, 10½" ..**60.00**

Paperweight, Space Needle shape, CI w/silver finish, 6½" ......**35.00**

Pennant, fair scenes on red w/yellow fringe, 8x25", EX ..............**25.00**

Pillow, San Francisco scenes, fringe, 10½x10½", EX...................**17.50**

Social Security card, brass, stamped at fair, NM........................**40.00**

## 1964 New York

Badge, Ford Motors Pavillion, New York, plastic .....................**15.00**

Bank, dime register; orange & blue scene, ¾x2½x2½", NMOC ..**30.00**

Bank, mechanical; rocket shoots coin into globe, silvered metal, 9"..**45.00**

Bank, Sinclair Dinosaur, molded plastic, 3¾x8" .....................**35.00**

Book, Persistence of Vision, Disney's involvement, 144 pages, NM..**30.00**

Booklet, Vatican Pavilion at the World's Fair, M .................**12.50**

Cooler, Pepsi Cola, Disneyland Fun, red, white & blue w/strap, EX..**85.00**

Counter sign, Kodak, Going to the World's Fair, 14x11", NM ....**190.00**

Cup, folding; swirled pink plastic, gold logo on lid, EX ...........**20.00**

Decanter, Jim Beam, 11½" ......**60.00**

Flash cards, NYWF Pictures, fair exhibits, 28 cards, EXIB .....**35.00**

Glide-A-Ride, Greyhound, tram vehicle, friction, Lowell, 1963, NMIB ...............................**295.00**

Hat, Adam Bermuda, NMIB (fair logo on lid) .........................**25.00**

License plate, orange & blue, 5x12", M .......................................**50.00**

Lighter, copper w/raised fair scenes, chrome top, Japan, EX .......**25.00**

Map, Official Souvenir, NM.....**25.00**

Menu, Theatre Bar in Spain Pavilion, folded, 13½x8¼", EX.............**40.00**

Model kit, Santa Maria - Ship in a Bottle, Multistate Toy, EXIB ...............................**100.00**

Paperweight, Unisphere, base metal, US Steel, 2½x5½" ....**6.00**

Paperweight, Unisphere, silvered metal, 3" dia on base, EX..**140.00**

Poster, Denmark Pavilion, soldier w/cannon, 36x24", EX .......**85.00**

Slide set, 64 color scenes, 2" sq, EXIB .................................**40.00**

Spoon, demitasse; Unisphere, silver plated, w/sleeve .................**12.50**

Toy, Karosel Kitchen, Marx for Sears, 12", EXIB ...............**50.00**

Viewmaster reel set, Industrial Area, 21 reels, EXIB .........**45.00**

## 1982 Knoxville

Coin, commemorative; logo/aerial view, gold-tone, ½" dia......**10.00**

Creamer, brown glaze w/cream speckled rim, Hull, 4½", EX.........**15.00**

Guide book, official; 200+ pages w/fair map, EX ....................**8.00**

Pen, floating; fair scene, Denmark on pocket clip, EX..............**15.00**

Pin-back, We're Going to...w/ Greyhound, NM..........................**6.50**

Plate, collector's; The 1982 World's Fair, Knoxville Tennesee, MIB .....................................**10.00**

Plate, 1982 World's Fair..., pewter, Superb Heritage Series, 5½"..**3.50**

Pocket knife, white Bakelite w/ red Coca-Cola logo, 2-blade, NM .....................................**10.00**

Postcard, US Pavilion ................**2.50**

Spoon, Sunsphere finial, engraved bowl, 5" ..............................**10.00**

# Wrestling Collectibles

The World Wrestling Federation boasts such popular members as the Iron Sheik, Hulk Hogan, the colorful Sycho Sid, and The Undertaker. Recent tag-team wrestlers include the Legion of Doom and Cactus Jack and Chainsaw Charlie. With these colorful names and (to put it mildly) assertive personalities, one can only imagine the vast merchandising possiblities. Posters, videos, trade cards, calendars, lighters and magazines are all popular collectibles, but the variety of items available is limitless.

Doll, Hulk Hogan, stuffed cloth, Ace Novelty, 1991, 42", EX........**50.00**
Doll, Hulk Hogan, vinyl in cloth outfit & cape, 1980s, 18", MIB.....**100.00**
Figure, Andre the Great, Hasbro, MOC..................................**60.00**

**Figure, Andre the Giant in blue, LJN, EX, $20.00.**

Figure, Big John Stud, LJN/Titan, 1985, MOC..........................**18.50**
Figure, Dusty Rhodes, Hasbro, 1991, EX+..........................**45.00**
Figure, Eugene, WWE Ruthless Aggression 11, Jakks, MIP..**20.00**
Figure, Giant Gonzalez, Hasbro, NM+...................................**25.00**
Figure, Greg 'The Hammer' Valentine, Hasbro, MOC.............**15.00**
Figure, Hulk Hogan (mail-in), Hasbro, MIP..............................**55.00**

Figure, Jeese 'The Body' Ventura, Titan, 1985, MOC .............**35.00**
Figure, Jim 'The Anvil' Neidhart, Hasbro, MOC.....................**10.00**
Figure, Junkyard Dog, w/red chain, LJN, NM............................**22.50**
Figure, Kamala, Hasbro, NM..**22.50**
Figure, Luscious Johnny Valiant, LJN, NM............................**20.00**
Figure, Macho Man, Hasbro, MOC..**20.00**
Figure, Miss Elizabeth, LJN, MOC....................................**35.00**
Figure, New Age Outlaws (2-Tuff #2), Jakks, MOC ...............**15.00**
Figure, Rick Rude, LJN, 1989, MOC....................................**95.00**
Figure, Ricky 'The Dragon' Steamboat, LJN/Titan, 1985, MOC ........**25.00**
Figure, Roddy Piper, LJN, MOC..**45.00**
Figure, The Warlord, Hasbro, MOC .**18.00**
Figure, Ultimate Warrior, LJN, 1989, NM+..........................**90.00**
Figure, Undertaker, Jakks Classic Superstar Series 1, MOC..**70.00**
Figure, 1-2-3 Kid, Hasbro, MOC..**40.00**
Figure, 123 Kid, w/Real Wrestling Action, Hasbro, MOC........**85.00**
Figure set, Evolution of Sting, set of 6, Toybiz, NMIB................**65.00**
Figures, Killer Bees, LJN, 1986, NM, pr ...............................**30.00**
Pillow, Hulk Hogan, Wrestling Buddies Pillow, Tonka, 1990, EXIB ....................................**35.00**
Pillow, Sting, Wrestling Buddies Pillow, Tonka, 1991, EX........**27.50**
Real Sounds Arena, Jakks Pacific, MIB....................................**50.00**
Sling 'Em-Fling 'Em Wrestling Ring Cage Accessory, NM (EX box) ....................................**50.00**

# Directory

The editors and staff take this opportunity to express our sincere gratitude and appreciation to each person who has contributed to the preparation of this guide. We believe the credibility of our book is greatly enhanced through their participation. Check these listings for information concerning their specific areas of expertise.

If you care to correspond with anyone listed here in our Directory, you must send a SASE with your letter.

If you are among those listed, please advise us of any changes in your address, phone number, or e-mail.

## Alabama
Cataldo, C.E.
4726 Panorama Dr. SE
Huntsville, 35801
256-536-6893

## California
Ales, Beverly L.
4046 Graham St.
Pleasanton, 94566-5619
925-846-5297
Beverlyales@hotmail.com
Specializing in knife rests; editor of *Knife Rests of Yesterday and Today*

Conroy, Barbara J.
P.O. Box 2369
Santa Clara, 95055-2369
http://restaurantchina@ attbi.com
Author of *Restaurant China, Restaurant, Airline, Ship & Railroad Dinnerware, Vol I* and *II* (Collector Books)

Elliott, Jacki
9790 Twin Cities Rd.
Galt, 95632
209-745-3860
Specializing in Rooster and Roses

Harrison, Gwynne
P.O. Box 1
Mira Loma, 91752-0001
951-685-5434
morgan99@pe.net
Buys and appraises Autumn Leaf; edits newsletter

Hibbard, Suzi
849 Vintage Ave.
Fairfield, 94585-3332
Specializing in Dragonware

Lewis, Kathy and Don
187 N Marcello Ave.
Thousand Oaks, 91360
805-499-8101
chatty@ix.netcom.com
Authors of *Chatty Cathy Dolls, An Identification and Value Guide,* and *Talking Toys of the 20th Century*

Needham, Leonard
*MacAdam's Antiques*
www.tias.com/stores/macadams
Specializing in automobilia, advertising

Thoerner, Sharon
15549 Ryon Ave.
Bellflower, 90706
562-866-1555
Specializing in covered animal dishes, powder jars with animal and human figures, slag glass

Utley, Bill; Editor
*Flashlight Collectors of America*
P.O. Box 40945
Tustin, 92781
714-730-1252, fax 714-505-4067
Specializing in flashlights

## Colorado
Diehl, Richard
5965 W Colgate Pl.
Denver, 80227
303-985-7481
Specializing in license plates

Stifter, Craig
225 Redstone, Blvd.
Redstone, 81623
mcstifter@gsb.uchicago.edu
Specializing in soda memorabilia such as Coca-Cola, Hires, Pepsi, 7-Up, etc.

## Connecticut
Sabulis, Cindy
P.O. Box 642
Shelton, 06484
203-926-0176
www.dollsntoys.com
Specializing in dolls from the '60s – '70s (Liddle Kiddles, Barbie, Tammy, Tressy, etc.); co-author of *The Collector's Guide to Tammy, The Ideal Teen*, and author of *Collector's Guide to Dolls of the 1960s & 1970s*

## Florida
Kuritzky, Lewis
4510 NW 17th Pl.
Gainesville, 32605
352-377-3193
Author of *Collector's Guide to Bookends*

Poe, Bill and Pat
220 Dominica Cir. E
Niceville, 32578-4085
850-897-4163 or fax 850-897-2606
BPoe@cox.net
Buy, sell, trade fast-food collectibles, cartoon character glasses, PEZ, Smurfs, California Raisins, M&M items

Posner, Judy
PO Box 2194 SC
Englewood, 34295
judyandjef@yahoo.com
Specializing in figural pottery, cookie jars, salt and pepper shakers, Black memorabilia, and Disneyana; sale lists available; fee charged for appraisals

Snyder-Haug, Diane
1415 7th Ave N.
St. Petersburg, 33705
Collector Book author specializing in clothing

## Idaho
Birkinbine, Mandi
P.O. Box 121
Meridian, 83680-0121
tiara@shop4antiques.com
www.shop4antiques.com
Author of *Collecting Tiara Amber Sandwich Glass*, available from the author for $18.45 ppd. Please allow 4 to 6 weeks for delivery.

McVey, Jeff
1810 W State St. #427
Boise, 83702-3955
Author of *Tire Ashtray Collector's Guide,* available from the author

## Illinois
Garmon, Lee
1529 Whittier St.
Springfield, 62704
217-789-9574
Specializing in Borden's Elsie, Reddy Kilowatt, Elvis Presley, and Marilyn Monroe

Jungnickel, Eric
P.O. Box 4674
Naperville, 60567-4674
630-983-8339
Specializing in Indy 500 memorabilia

Kadet, Jeff
TV Guide Specialists
P.O. Box 20
Macomb, 61455
Buying and selling of *TV Guide* from 1948 through the 1990s

Karman, Lori and Rich
815 S. Douglas
Springfield, 62704
217-787-8166
Specializing in Fenton glass

Klompus, Eugene R.
Just Cuff Links
P.O. Box 5970
Vernon Hills, 60061
847-816-0035
genek@cufflinksrus.com
Specializing in cuff links and men's accessories

## Indiana
Dilley, David
Indianapolis
317-251-0575
glazebears@aol.com or
bearpots@aol.com
Author of book on Royal Haeger; available from the author

McQuillen, Michael and Polly
P.O. Box 50022
Indianapolis, 46250-0022
317-845-1721
michael@politicalparade.com
www.politicalparade.com
Specializing in political memorabilia

## Iowa
Devine, Joe
D&D Antique Mall
1411 3rd St.
Council Bluffs, 51503
712-232-5233 or 712-328-7305
Author of *Collector's Guide to Royal Copley With Royal Winton and Spaulding, Books I* and *II*

## Kentucky
Hornback, Betty
707 Sunrise Ln.
Elizabethtown, 42701
bettysantiques@KVNET.org
Specializing in Kentucky Derby and horse racing memorabilia; send for informative booklet, $15 ppd.

## Louisiana
Langford, Paris
415 Dodge Ave.
Jefferson, 70121
504-733-0676
Author of *Liddle Kiddles*; specializing in dolls of the 1960s – 1970s

## Maine
Hathaway, John
*Hathaway's Antiques*
3 Mills Rd.
Bryant's Pond, 04219
207-665-2214
Specializing in fruit jars, mail order a specialty

## Maryland
Losonsky, Joyce and Terry
7506 Summer Leave Ln.
Columbia, 21046-2455
Authors of *The Illustrated Collector's Guide to McDonald's® Happy Meal® Boxes, Premiums, and Promotions* ($11 postpaid); *McDonald's Happy Meal Toys in the USA* in full color ($27.95 postpaid); *McDonald's® Happy Meal® Toys Around the World,* full color ($27.95 postpaid); and *Illustrated Collector's Guide to McDonald's® McCAPS®* ($6 postpaid); autographed copies available from the authors

Welch, Randy
Raven'tiques
27965 Peach Orchard Rd.
Easton, 21601-8203
410-822-5441
Specializing in walking figures and tin wind-up toys

Yalom, Libby
The Shoe Lady
3200 NLW Blvd. #615
Silver Spring, 20906
301-598-0290
Specializing in glass and china shoes and boots, author of *Shoes of Glass* (with updated values), available from the author by sending $15.95 plus $2 to above address

## Massachusetts
Porter, Richard T.
*Porter Thermometer Museum*
Box 944
Onset 02558
thermometerman@aol.com
Specializing in thermometers

Wellman, BA
P.O. Box 673
Westminster, 01473-0673
BA@dishinitout.com
Specializing in all areas of American ceramics; researches Royal China

White, Larry
108 Central St.
Rowley, 01969-1317
978-948-8187;
larrydw@erols.com
Specializing in Cracker Jack; author of books; has newsletter

## Michigan
Nickel, Mike; and Cindy Horvath
P.O. Box 456
Portland, 48875
517-647-7646
mandc@voyager.net
Specializing in Ohio art pottery, Kay Finch, author of *Kay Finch Ceramics,*

*Her Enchanted World,* available from the authors; co-author of *Collector's Encyclopedia of Roseville Pottery Revised Edition, Vol I* and *Vol II*

Pickvet, Mark
5071 Watson Dr.
Flint, 48506
Author of *Shot Glasses: An American Tradition,* available for $12.95 plus $2.50 postage and handling from Antique Publications, P.O. Box 553, Marietta, OH 45750

Ross, Michele
P.O. Box 94
Berrien Center, 49102
616-925-1604
peartime1@cs.com
Specializing in Van Briggle and other American pottery

Whitmyer, Margaret and Kenn
P.O. Box 80806
Gahana, 432230-2704

## Missouri
Allen, Col. Bob
P.O. Box 56
St. James, 65559
Author of *A Guide to Collecting Cookbooks;* specializing in cookbooks, leaflets, and Jell-O memorabilia

## Nebraska
Johnson, Donald-Brian
3329 S 56th St. #611
Omaha, 68106
donaldbrian@webtv/net
Specializing in Ceramic Arts Studio

## Nevada
Hunter, Tim
4301 W Hidden Valley Dr.
Reno, NV 89502
702-856-4357
thunter885@aol.com
Author of *The Bobbing Head Collector and Price Guide*

## New Hampshire
Holt, Jane
P.O. Box 115

Derry, 03038
Specializing in Annalee dolls

## New Jersey
Litts, Elyce
P.O. Box 394
Morris Plains, 07950
973-361-4087
happy.memories@worldnet.att.net
Specializing in Geisha Girl (author of book); also ladies' compacts

Palmieri, Jo Ann
27 Pepper Rd.
Towaco, 07082-1357
201-334-5829
Specializing in Skookum Indian dolls

Sparacio, George
P.O. Box 791
Malaga, 08328
609-694-4167; fax 609-694-4536
mrvesta@aol.com
Specializing in match safes

Visakay, Stephen
P.O. Box 1517
W Caldwell, 07007-1517
SVisakay@aol.com
Specializing in vintage cocktail shakers (by mail and appointment only); author of *Vintage Bar Ware*

## New Mexico
Mace, Shirley
Shadow Enterprises
P.O. Box 1602
Mesilla Park, 88047
505-524-6717; fax 505-523-0940
shadow-ent@zianet.com
www.geocities.com/MadisonAv
enue/Boardroom/1631
Author of *Encyclopedia of Silhouette Collectibles on Glass* (available from the author)

## New York
Beegle, Gary
92 River St.
Montgomery, 12549
914-457-3623
Liberty Blue dinnerware, also most lines of collectible modern American dinnerware as well as character glasses

Dinner, Craig
39-74 45th St.
Sunnyside, 11104 or
P.O. Box 184
Townend, VT 05353 (summer)
718-729-3850
ferrouswheel123@aol.com
Specializing in figural cast-iron items (door knockers, lawn sprinklers, doorstops, windmill weights, etc.)

Schleifman, Roselle
16 Vincent Rd.
Spring Valley, 10977-3829
Specializing in Duncan & Miller, New Martinsville glass

Weitman, Stan and Arlene
P.O. Box 1186
Massapequa Park, 11758
scrackled@earthlink.net
www.crackleglass.com
Authors of *Crackle Glass, Identification and Value Guide, Volumes I* and *II* (Collector Books)

## North Carolina
Brooks, Ken and Barbara
4121 Gladstone Ln.
Charlotte, 28205
Specializing in Cat-Tail Dinnerware

Finegan, Mary
Marfine Antiques
P.O. Box 3618
Boone, 28607
828-262-3441
Author of book on Johnson Brothers dinnerware; available from the author

Sayers, Rolland J.
Southwestern Antiques and Appraisals
P.O. Box 629
Brevard, 28712
Researches Pisgah Forest pottery; Author of *Guide to Scouting Collectibles,* available from the author for $32.95 pp.

## North Dakota
Farnsworth, Bryce L.
1334 14½ St.
S Fargo, 58103
701-237-3597
Specializing in Rosemeade

## Ohio
Benjamin, Scott
P.O. Box 556
LaGrange, 44050-0556
www.oilcollectibles.com
Specializing in automobilia, gas globes

Graff, Shirley
4515 Grafton Rd.
Brunswick, 44212-2005
Specializing in Pennsbury

Mangus, Beverly and Jim
5147 Broadway NE
Louisvile, 44641-8869
Authors (Collector Books) specializing in Shawnee Pottery

Young, Mary
P.O. Box 9244
Wright Bros. Branch
Dayton, 45409
937-298-4838
Author of books; specializing in paper dolls

## Oklahoma
Phyllis Boone
14535 E 13th St.
Tulsa, 74108-4527
Specializing in Frankoma pottery

Ivers, Terri
Terri's Toys and Nostalgia
206 E. Grand
Ponca City, 74601
580-762-8697 or 580-762-5174
toylady@cableone.net
Specializing in character collectibles, lunch boxes, advertising items, Breyer and Hartland figures, etc.

Moore, Shirley and Art
4423 E. 31st St.
Tulsa, 74135
918-747-4164
Specializing in Lu-Ray Pastels and Depression glass

## Oregon
Brown, Marcia
Sparkles
P.O. Box 2314
White City, 97503

541-830-8385
Collector Books author specializing in jewelry

Coe, Debbie and Randy
Coes Mercantile
2459 SE TV Hwy. #321
Hillsboro, 97123
Specializing in Elegant and Depression glass, art pottery, Cape Cod by Avon, Golden Foliage by Libbey Glass Company, Gurley candles, and Liberty Blue dinnerware

Morris, Tom
Prize Publishers
P.O. Box 8307
Medford, 97504
chalkman@cdsnet.net
Author of *The Carnival Chalk Prize*

White, Carole Bess
PO Box 819
Portland, 97207
Specializing in Japan ceramics; author of books

## Pennsylvania
BOJO/Bob Gottuso
P.O. Box 1403
Cranberry Twp., 16066-0403
Phone or fax 724-776-0621
www.bojoonline.com
Specializing in the Beatles and rock'n roll memorabilia

Cerebro
P.O. Box 327
East Prospect, 37317-0327
www.cerebro.com
Specializing in advertising labels

Greenfield, Jeannie
310 Parker Rd.
Stoneboro, 16153-2810
724-376-2584
Specializing in cake toppers and egg timers

Kreider, Katherine
Kingsbury Antiques
P.O. Box 7957
Lancaster, 19604-7957
Kingsbry@aol.com
Specializing in valentines

McManus, Joe
P.O. Box 153
Connellsville, 15425
jmcmanus@hhs.net
Specializing in Blair and Purinton pottery

Turner, Art and Judy
Homestead Collectibles
P.O. Box 173
Mill Hall, 17751
570-726-3597
jturner@cub.kcnet.org
Specializing in Jim Beam decanters and Ertl diecast metal banks

## South Carolina
Belyski, Richard
P.O. Box 14956
Surfside Beach, 29587
Specializing in Pez

Cassity, Brad
2391 Hunter's Trail
Myrtle Beach, 29574
843-236-8697
Specializing in Fisher-Price pull toys and playsets up to 1986 (author of book)

Greguire, Helen
79 Lake Lyman Heights
Lyman, 29365
864-848-0409
Author (Collector Books) specializing in Graniteware

## Tennessee
Chase, Mick and Lorna
Fiesta Plus
380 Hawking Crawford Rd.
Cookeville, 38501-6658
Specializing in Franciscian, Fiesta, and other fine china

Fields, Linda
158 Bagsby Hill Lane
Dover, 37058
931-232-5099 after 6 pm
Fpiebird@compu.net.
Specializing in pie birds

## Texas
Cooper, Marilyn M.
8408 Lofland Dr.
Houston, 77055-4811

or summer address:
PO Box 755
Douglas, MI 49406
Author of *The Pictorial Guide to Tooth-brush Holders* ($22.95 postpaid)

Docks, L.R. 'Les'
Shellac Shack; Discollector
Box 691035
San Antonio, 78269-1035
docks@texas.net
Author of *American Premium Record Guide;* specializing in vintage records

Gibbs, Carl, Jr.
P.O. Box 4691035
San Antonio, , 78269-1035
Author of *Collector's Encyclopedia of Metlox Potteries* (Collector Books); specializing in American dinnerware

Jackson, Joyce
900 Jenkins Rd.
Aledo, 76008-2410
817-441-8864
jjpick@firstworld.net
Specializing in Swanky Swigs

Nossaman, Darlene
5419 Lake Charles
Waco, 76710
Specializing in Homer Laughlin China information and Horton Ceramics

Woodard, Dannie
P.O. Box 1346
Weatherford, 76086
371-594-4680
Author of *Hammered Aluminum, Hand Wrought Collectibles*

Pogue, Larry
L and J Antiques & Collectibles
8142 Ivan Ct.
Terrell, 75161-6921
www.landjantiques.com
Specializing in head vases, string holders, general line

Woodard, Dannie
P.O. Box 1346
Weatherford, 76086
371-594-4680
Author of *Hammered Aluminum, Hand Wrought Collectibles*

## Utah

Spencer, Rick
Salt Lake City
801-973-0805
Specializing in Shawnee, Roseville, Weller, Van Tellingen, Regal, Bendel, Coors, Rookwood, Watt; also salt and pepper shakers, cookie jars, cut glass, radios, and silver flatware

## Washington

Morris, Susan
P.O. Box 1231
Gig Harbor 98335-3231
Co-Author of *Watt Pottery — An Identification and Value Guide,* and *Purinton Pottery — An Identification and Value Guide*

## Wisconsin

Helley, Phil
Old Kilbourn Antiques
629 Indiana Ave.
Wisconsin Dells, 53965
608-254-8770
Specializing in Cracker Jack items, radio premiums, dexterity games, toys (especially Japanese wind-up toys), banks, and old Dells souvenir items marked Kilbourn

Wanvig, Nancy
Nancy's Collectibles
P.O. Box 12
Thiensville, 53092
Author of book; specializing in ashtrays

## West Virginia

Apkarian-Russell, Pamela
Halloween Queen Antiques
577 Boggs Run Rd.
Benwood, 26031-1001
Specializing in Halloween collectibles, postcards of all kinds, and Joe Camel

# Clubs and Newsletters

Akro Agate Collectors Club
*Clarksburg Crow*
Roger Hardy
10 Bailey St.
Clarksburg, WV 26301-2524
304-624-4523
www.akro-agate.com
Annual membership fee: $25

American Bell Assn. International, Inc.
P.O. Box 19443
Indianapolis, IN 46219
bobbam@bellsouth.net
www.americanbell.org

*Antique and Collector Reproduction News*
Mark Chervenka, Editor
P.O. Box 12130
Des Moines, IA 50312-9403
800-227-5531 (subscriptions only) or 515-274-5886
acrn@repronews.com
Monthly newsletter showing differences between old originals and new reproductions; subscription: $32 per year

*The Antique Trader Weekly*
P.O. Box 1050
Dubuque, IA 52004-1050
collect@krause.com
www.collect.com
Subscription: $38 (52 issues) per year; sample: $1

Autographs of America
Tim Anderson
P.O. Box 461
Provo, UT 84603
801-226-1787 (afternoons, please)
www.AutographsOfAmerica.com
Free sample catalog of hundreds of autographs for sale

*Autumn Leaf*
Bill Swanson, Editor
807 Roaring Springs Dr.
Allen, TX 75002-2112
972-727-5527
www.nalc.org

*Avon Times*
c/o Dwight or Vera Young
P.O. Box 9868, Dept. P.
Kansas City, MO 64134
AvonTimes@aol.com
Send SASE for information

Bookend Collector Club
Louis Kuritzky, M.D.
4510 NW 17th Place
Gainsville, FL 32650
352-377-3193
lkuritzky@aol.com
Membership (includes newsletter): $25 per year

Candy Container Collectors of America
*The Candy Gram* Newsletter
c/o Jim Olean
115 Mac Beth Dr.
Lower Burrel, PA 15068-2628
www.candycontainer.org

Cat Collectors Club
*Cat Talk* Newsletter
Karen Shank
P.O. Box 150784
Nashville, TN 37215-0784
615-297-7403
musiccitykitty@yahoo.com
www.CatCollectors.com

Ceramic Arts Studio Collector's Association
PO Box 46
Madison, WI 53701
800-241-9138
Annual membership: $15; Inventory record and price guide available
China Specialties, Inc.

*Collectibles Flea Market Finds* Magazine
Magazines of America
13400 Madison Ave.
New York, NY 44107
800-528-9648
Subscription: $18.97 for 4 issues per year

*Cookie Crumbs*
Cookie Cutter Collectors Club
CCC
Box 245
Cannon Falls, MN 55009
Subscription: $20 per year, payable to club

Currier & Ives Dinnerware Collector Club
E.R. Aupperle, Treasurer
29470 Saxon Rd.
Toulton, IL 61483
309-896-3331 or fax 309-856-6005

Czechoslovakian Collectors Guild
  International
Alan Bodia, Membership
15006 Meadowlake St.
Odessa, FL 33556-3126
www.czechartglass.com/ccgi

*Doll News* Magazine
United Federation of Doll Clubs
10900 N. Pomona Ave.
Kansas City, MO 64153
816-891-7040

Doorstop Collectors of America
Jeanie Bertoia
2413 Madison Ave.
Vineland, NJ 08630
609-692-4092
Membership: $20 per year, includes 2
newsletters and convention; send 2-
stamp SASE for sample

Dragonware Club
c/o Suzi Hibbard
849 Vintage Ave.
Fairfield, CA 94585
Dragon_Ware@hotmail.com

*FBOC* (Figural Bottle Opener
  Collectors)
Mary Link
1774 N. 675 E.
Kewanna, IN 46939
www.fbocclub.com

Fenton Art Glass Collectors of
  America, Inc.
*Butterfly Net* newsletter
P.O. Box 384
702 W. 5th St.
Williamstown, WV 26187
fkagcainc@wildfire.com
Membership: $20; Associate member: $5

*Fiesta Collector's Quarterly*
P.O. Box 471
Valley City, OH 44280
www.chinaspecialties.com/fiesta.html
Subscription: $12 per year

Fisher-Price Collector's Club
Jeanne Kennedy
1442 N Ogden
Mesa, AZ 85205
fpclub@aol.com
www.fpclub.org
Monthly newsletter with information and
ads; send SASE for more information

*Flashlight Collectors of America
  Newsletter*
Bill Utley
P.O. Box 4095
Tustin, CA 92781
714-730-1252
flashlight@worldnet.att.net
*Flashlights, Early Flashlight Makers of the
1st 100 Years of Eveready,* full color, 320
pages, now available; quarterly flashlight
newsletter, $12 per year.

Frankoma Family Collectors
  Association
c/o Nancy Littrell
P.O. Box 32571
Oklahoma City, OK 72123-0771
www.frankoma.org
Membership dues: $35 (includes quarter-
ly newsletter and annual convention)

*The Front Striker Bulletin*
Bill Retskin
P.O. Box 18481
Asheville, NC 28814-0481
704-254-4487 or fax 704-254-1066
bill@matchcovers.com
www.matchcovers.com
Membership: $10 per year

Griswold & Cast Iron Cookware
  Association
G&CICA Secretary
P.O. Box 552
Saegertown, PA 16433
Membership: $20 per individual or $25
per family (2 members per address)
payable to club

*Hall China Collectors' Club*
  Newsletter
Virginia Lee
P.O. Box 360488
Cleveland, OH 44136

*Head Hunters Newsletter*
c/o Maddy Gordon
P.O. Box 83 H
Scarsdale, NY 10583
For collectors of head vases; subscrip-
tion: $24 yearly for 4 quarterly issues.
Ads free to subscribers

International Nippon Collectors
  Club (INCC)
Jennifer Cavedo, Membership
  Chairperson
8363 Dusty Lane

**407**

Mechanicsville, VA 23116
www.nipponcollectorsclub.com
Membership: $30 per year includes
newsletter (published 6 times per year)

International Perfume and Scent
  Bottle Collectors Association
c/o Randall B. Monsen
P.O. Box 529
Vienna, VA 22183
Fax 703-242-1357
www.perfumebottles.org

*Knife Rests of Yesterday and Today*
Beverly L. Ales
4046 Graham St.
Pleasanton, CA 94566-5619
Subscription: $20 per year for 6 issues

Marble Collectors' Society of
  America
51 Johnson St.
Trumbull, CT 06611
blockschip@aol.com
www.blocksite.com

McDonald's ® Collector Club
PMB 200
1153 S. Lee St.
Des Plains, Il 60016-6503
www.mcdclub.com
Membership: $25 individual per year;
$30 family

National Association of Avon Collectors
Department AT
6100 Walnut
Kansas City, MO 64113
Send large SASE for information

*National Blue Ridge Newsletter*
Norma Lilly
144 Highland Dr.
Bloutville, TN 37617
Subscription: $15 per year (6 issues)

The National Cuff Link Society
Eugene R. Klompus, President
  Emeritus
P.O. 5970
Vernon Hills, IL 60061
847-816-0035
genek@cufflinksrus.com
Membership: $30 per year

National Depression Glass Assoc.
P.O. Box 48624
Wichita, KS 67208-0264
www.ndga.net
Membership: $20 per year

National Fenton Glass Society
P.O. Box 4008
Marietta, OH 45750
Membership: $20; includes *The Fenton
Flyer* newsletter

National Graniteware Society
P.O. Box 9248
Cedar Rapids, IA 52409-9248
www.graniteware.org
Membership: $20 per year

National Imperial Glass Collectors'
  Society, Inc.
P.O. Box 534
Bellaire, OH 43906
www.imperialglass.org
Membership: $15 per year (+$1 for each
associate member), quarterly newsletter

National Milk Glass Collectors' Society
  and *Opaque News*, quarterly
  newsletter
Barb Pinkston, Membership Chariman
9238 E. Kenosha Ct.
Floral City, FL 34436-2438
membership@nmgsc.org
www.nmgsc.org
Membership: $20

National Reamer Association
c/o Debbie Gilham
47 Midline Ct.
Gaithersburg, MD 20878
reamers@erols.com
www.reamers.org

National Society of Lefton Collectors
*The Lefton Collector* Newsletter
Loretta DeLozier
P.O. Box 50201
Knocksville, TN 3795-0201
leftonlady@aol.com

National Valentine Collectors
  Association
Nancy Rosen
P.O. Box 1404

Santa Ana, CA 92702
714-547-1355
Membership: $16

*NM (Nelson McCoy) Xpress*
Carol Seman, Editor
8934 Brecksville Rd., Suite 406
Brecksville, OH 44141-2318
McCjs@aol.com
www.members.aol.com/nmXpress
Subscription: $26 per year

The Occupied Japan Club
c/o Florence Archambault
29 Freeborn St.
Newport, RI 02840-1821
florence@aiconnect.com
Publishes *The Upside Down World of an O.J. Collector,* a bimonthly newsletter.
Information requires SASE.

*On the LIGHTER Side*
International Lighter Collectors
Judith Sanders, Editor
136 Circle Dr.
Quitman, TX 75783
903-763-2795 or fax 703-763-4953
Annual convention held in different cities in the US; send SASE when requesting information

Paden City Glass Collectors Guild
Paul Torsiello, Editor
42 Aldine Road
Parsippany, NJ, 07054
pcguild@yahoo.com

*Paper Collectors' Marketplace*
P.O. Box 128
Scandinavia, WI 54977-0128
715-467-2379 or fax 715-467-2243 (8 am to 8 pm)
pcmpaper@gglbbs.com
www.pcmpaper.com
Subscription: $19.95 for 12 issues per year

*Paper Doll News*
Emma Terry
P.O. Box 807
Vivian, LA 71082
Subscription: $13 per year

Peanut Pals
Judith Walthall, Founder
P.O. Box 4465

Huntsville, AL 35815
205-881-9198
Associated collectors of Planters Peanuts memorabilia, bimonthly newsletter *Peanut Papers;* annual directory sent to members; annual convention and regional conventions. Dues: $20 per year (+$3 for each additional household member); membership information: P.O. Box 652, St. Clairsville, OH, 43950. Sample newsletter: $2

*Pez Collector's News*
Richard Belyski, Editor
P.O. Box 14956
Surfside Beach, SC 29587
peznews@juno.com
www.pezcollectorsnews.com

*Pie Birds Unlimited Newsletter*
Rita Reedy
1039 NW Hwy. 101
Lincoln City, OR 97367
ritazart@lycol.com

Political Collectors of Indiana
Michael McQuillen
P.O. Box 50022
Indianapolis, IN 46250-0022
317-845-1721
michael@politicalparade.com
www.politicalparade.com
Official APIC (American Political Items Collectors) Chapter comprised of over 100 collectors of presidential and local political items

*The Prize Insider*
Newsletter for Cracker Jack Collectors
Larry White
108 Central St.
Rowley, MA 01969
978-948-8187
larrydw@erols.com

*Rosevilles of the Past* Newsletter
Nancy Bomm, Editor
P.O. Box 656
Clarcona, FL 32710-0656
407-294-3980
rosepast@worldnet.att.net
Send $19.95 per year for 6 to 12 newsletters

Roy Rogers — Dale Evans
   Collectors Association
Nancy Horsley, Exec. Secretary

P.O. Box 1166
Portsmouth, OH 45662-1166
www.royrogers.commm

Shawnee Pottery Collectors' Club
c/o Pamela Curran
P.O. Box 713
New Smyrna Beach, FL 32170-0713
Send $3 for sample copy

The Shot Glass Club of America
Mark Pickvet, Editor
P.O. Box 90404
Flint, MI 48509

*The Silver Bullet*
Lone Ranger Fan Club
P.O. Box 1493
Longmont, CO 80502
www.lonerangerfanclub.com
Membership: $36

Stretch Glass Society
P.O. Box 3305 Society
Quartz Hill, CA 93586
http://stretchglasssociety.org
Membership: $22 (US); $24 (International-al); holds annual convention

Tea Talk
P.O. Box 860
Sausalito, CA 94966
415-331-1557
teatalk@aol.com

*The TeaTime Gazette*
P.O. Box 40276
St. Paul, MN 55104
612-227-7415
info@teatimegazette.com

Toy Shop
700 E. State St.
Iola, WI 54990-0001
715-445-2214
www.toyshopmag.com
Subscription (3rd class) $33.98 (US) for 26 issues

*The Trick or Treat Trader*
Pamela E. Apkarian-Russell
  The Halloween Queen and
  C.J. Russel
4 Lawrence St. & Rt. 10
Winchester, NH 03470
603-239-8875
halloweenqueen@cheshire.net;
subcription: $15 per year for 4 issues or $4 for sample copy

*Vintage Fashion & Costume
  Jewelry* Newsletter/Club
P.O. Box 265
Glen Oaks, NY 11004
718-969-2320 or 718-939-3095
www.lizjewels.com/VF
Yearly subscription: $20 (US) for 4 issues; sample copy available by sending $5

*The Wade Watch, Ltd.*
8199 Pierson Ct.
Arvada, CO 80005
303-421-9655 or 303-424-4401
fax 303-421-0317
wadewatch@wadewatch.com
Subscription: $8 per year (4 issues)

Westmoreland Glass Society
Steve Jensen
P.O. Box 2883
Iowa City, IA 52240-2883
www.glassshow.com/clubs/wgsi/wgsi.html
Membership: $15

*The Willow Review*
P.O. Box 41312
Nashville, TN 37204
Send SASE for information

World's Fair Collectors' Society
  *Fair News* newsletter
Michael R. Pender, Editor
P.O. Box 20806
Sarasota, FL 34276-3806
941-923-2590
Dues: $20 per year in US and Canada, $30 overseas

# Index